CADOGANguides

LANGUEDOC-ROUSSILLON

'The resulting aqueduct...was like a giant needle hemming the landscape, piercing tunnels through hills and looping its arches over the open spaces of the garrigue, and all measured precisely to allow a slope of 0.07 centimetres per metre.'

Dana Facaros & Michael Pauls

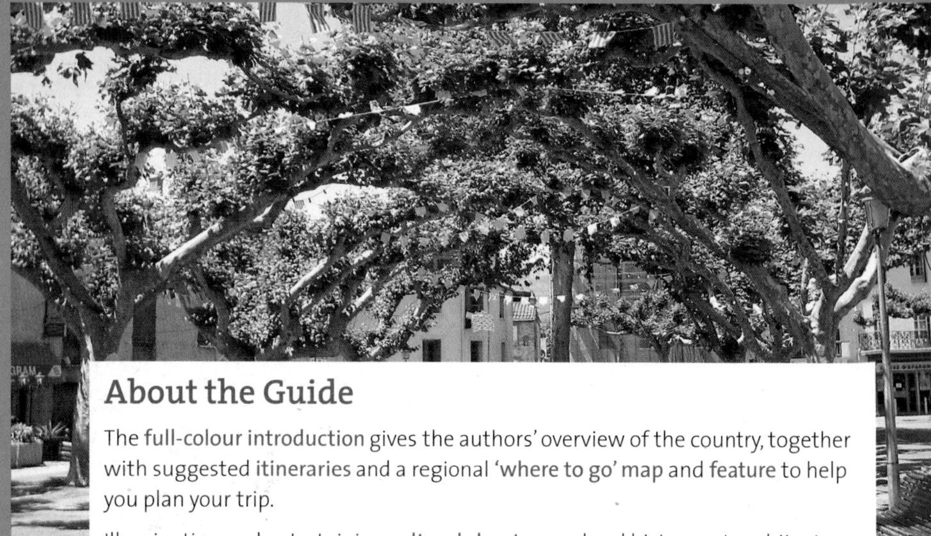

About the Guide

The **full-colour introduction** gives the authors' overview of the country, together with suggested **itineraries** and a regional **'where to go' map and feature** to help you plan your trip.

Illuminating and entertaining **cultural chapters** on local history, art, architecture, food, wine and everyday life give you a rich flavour of the country.

Planning Your Trip starts with the basics of when to go, getting there and getting around, coupled with other useful information, including a section for disabled travellers. The **Practical A–Z** deals with all the **essential information** and **contact details** that you may need while you are away.

The **regional chapters** are arranged in a loose touring order, with plenty of public transport and driving information. The authors' top **'Don't Miss'** sights are highlighted at the start of each chapter.

A **language and pronunciation guide**, a **glossary** of cultural terms, ideas for **further reading** and a comprehensive **index** can be found at the end of the book.

Although everything we list in this guide is **personally recommended**, our authors inevitably have their own favourite places to eat and stay. Whenever you see this **Authors' Choice** icon beside a listing, you will know that it is a little bit out of the ordinary.

Hotel Price Guide (*see also* p.70)

Luxury	€€€€€	over €230
Very expensive	€€€€	€150–230
Expensive	€€€	€100–150
Moderate	€€	€60–100
Inexpensive	€	under €60

Restaurant Price Guide (*see also* p.77)

Very expensive	€€€€	over €60
Expensive	€€€	€30–60
Moderate	€€	€15–30
Inexpensive	€	under €15

About the Authors

Dana Facaros and Michael Pauls have written over 30 books for Cadogan Guides. They have lived all over Europe with their son and daughter, and are currently ensconced in an old *presbytère* in southwest France.

3rd Edition published 2011

01 INTRODUCING LANGUEDOC-ROUSSILLON

Previous page: Pont du Gard, pp.93–5

Opposite page: Plane trees on Place de la République, Prades, pp.272–3

Above, from top: Eus, pp.273–4; Antigone, Montpellier, pp.141–2

You can sail halfway around the Mediterranean coast, from Gibraltar as far as Tuscany, and you'll only find one little slice of coastline that doesn't advertise itself as a 'Costa' or a 'Riviera'. Why such humility? There's certainly no lack of beaches; Languedoc-Roussillon is lined with sand from the Rhône to the Pyrenees, and behind the sand you'll find as many bustling resorts as in any region of France.

Languedoc has had something of an identity crisis. Provence, the region's pampered sister across the Rhône, conjures up images of mimosa and lavender, rich *bouillabaisse* and dramatic seafront *corniches*. France's southwest is the land of *foie gras* and truffles and strong red wine. Poor Languedoc in the middle has its share of fatted ducks and mimosas and good fish soup and everything else; it even has a couple of modest *corniches*, and enough wine to sozzle visitors by the billion. What it lacks, to the despair of the regional tourism authorities, is something unique, something it can call its very own.

Promotion is their job, fortunately, not ours. If we can't boil down this region into a single image or a handful of clichés, let's take it as a sweet invitation to look at the place a little more closely and find out what's really there. If you do that, you'll find it a real grab-bag, with a little bit of everything and plenty of surprises – Gothic cathedrals and space-age beach resorts, bullfights and nautical jousts. Within the space of a day you can visit one town founded by the ancient Greeks, another with the refined air of a little Paris from the days of Louis XIV, and its lively neighbour, a brash workaday port famous for sardines.

The landscapes, too, conspire to surprise. In an area roughly the size of Wales or New Jersey, they've managed to squeeze in the best

Above: Arènes, Nîmes, p.86

Opposite page: The Cirque de Navacelles, p.152

part of the Pyrenees, a swampy Rhône delta populated by cowboys and flamingos, chestnut forests and olive groves, not to mention a lost plateau where the French army does its desert training. Rolling hills covered in vines seem to stretch on forever, but when they finally run out they leave you in a dry *garrigue* country studded with ancient monasteries that could be a stage set from the Crusades.

History hasn't always been kind here. Languedoc seems to blossom only every thousand years. Once this was the richest part of Gaul; the Romans left their calling card in neatly squared masonry at the famous Pont du Gard and the great amphitheatre and temple at Nîmes. A thousand years later, after rude interruptions by Goths, Franks, Arabs and other troublemakers, it resurfaced as the land of the troubadours, one of the morning stars of early medieval civilization. Once again though, outsiders would come to spoil things. Languedoc had to be dragged kicking and screaming into what is now called France, and for centuries the French weren't very nice to it. Though the region languished culturally and economically, however, it kept up its habit of providing the unexpected – these sunny Mediterranean shores gave Protestantism a warm welcome, and later on they would fill up with textile mills and help France along with its Industrial Revolution.

If that big historical clock runs right, Languedoc should be set to bloom again soon. Long one of the poorest corners of France, it has been making great strides over the last few decades. You'll sense the air of a young region, an up-and-coming one. Its buzzing modern capital, Montpellier, has not only been making up for lost time – it's doing more than its share in pulling France into the 21st century. Tourism, and government planning, have transformed the once-lonely coasts; some of the biggest resorts here didn't exist 60 years ago. And the land once called France's 'culinary desert', famous for its oceans of plonk and dismal restaurants, has now smartened itself up considerably in both. Let Provence keep the clichés. This side of the Rhône is a land for discovering.

Where to Go

With its complex history, just what constitutes 'Languedoc' has always been a matter for debate. Back in the 1980s, when the government in Paris decided to decentralize some of its functions by creating new regions, they went about it in a thoroughly French way, chopping up the country more or less arbitrarily into similar-sized bits, and throwing some of historical Languedoc into a region with Catalan Roussillon. Our book covers, from east to west, the *départements* of the Gard, Hérault, Aude and Pyrénées-Orientales (Roussillon).

The **Gard** shares the Rhône valley with Provence, and our side is a delightful garden of olives and vines, with only a fraction of the tourists that Provence gets – except perhaps at the magnificent Pont du Gard, one of the five most visited sights in France. This is near **Nîmes**, the 'Rome of France', and the delicious art town of Uzès. Languedoc's share of the Cévennes is a lovely deeply forested area famous for the Camisards' guerrilla warfare against the Protestants who hid there in the early 18th century. The Gard also has the Petite Camargue, part of the mighty Rhône delta. Here you can visit two exceptional relics of the Middle Ages: St-Gilles, with its famous statuary, and Aigues-Mortes, the port Saint Louis built to ship him and his armies off to the Crusades.

Eastern Languedoc's two big cities, Nîmes and Montpellier, are eternal rivals, only 40km apart. They make an interesting pair of bookends – Nîmes with its famous Roman monuments, full of atmosphere and tradition, and dynamic, up-and-coming **Montpellier**, the region's capital and a university city with a thousand years' of history behind it, but quickly making up for lost time as the fastest-growing city in France.

The **Hérault** is the biggest wine-producing *département* of France, with rural delights equal to those of Provence, including wine regions like the Minervois, Pézenas (Languedoc's 'little Paris'), and the Mediterranean end of the serendipitous tree-lined Canal du Midi – the most beautiful canal in the world, and a lovely spot for spending some lazy time on the water. North of Montpellier lies the haunted, austere *garrigue* country, with medieval St-Martin-de-Londres and St-Guilhem-le-Désert, as well as the small, green mountain chain of the Espinouse, now a regional park. The Hérault's coast offers long miles of open beaches, coastal lagoons full of oysters, and resorts ranging from the pretty town of Agde, founded by the Greeks, to futuristic La Grande Motte; Cap d'Agde, Europe's capital of naturism, is probably the most fashionable of the region's resorts.

The **Aude** *département* offers the surprising city of Narbonne, with its magnificent cathedral, and **Carcassonne**, the biggest and

Above, from top: Marina at Cap d'Agde, p.171; Béziers cathedral, pp.178–9

Opposite page: Collioure, pp.262–4

best-preserved medieval fortress city in Europe. There's the vortex of *Da Vinci Code* madness at Rennes-le-Château, on the way to scores of spectacular Cathar castles hanging over the strange and rugged landscapes of the Corbières.

Beyond these lies **Roussillon**. The Catalan corner of France is another world, one that increasingly looks more towards Barcelona than Paris. Perpignan, the 'centre of the universe' according to Salvador Dalí, has a wealth of medieval art, and nearby is Collioure, inspiration of the Fauvist painters, on the pretty Côte Vermeille. Up in the Pyrenees, two valleys flank the Catalan holy mountain, Canigou, each with its exceptional treasures of Romanesque architecture and sculpture, skiing and scenery.

Chapter Divisions

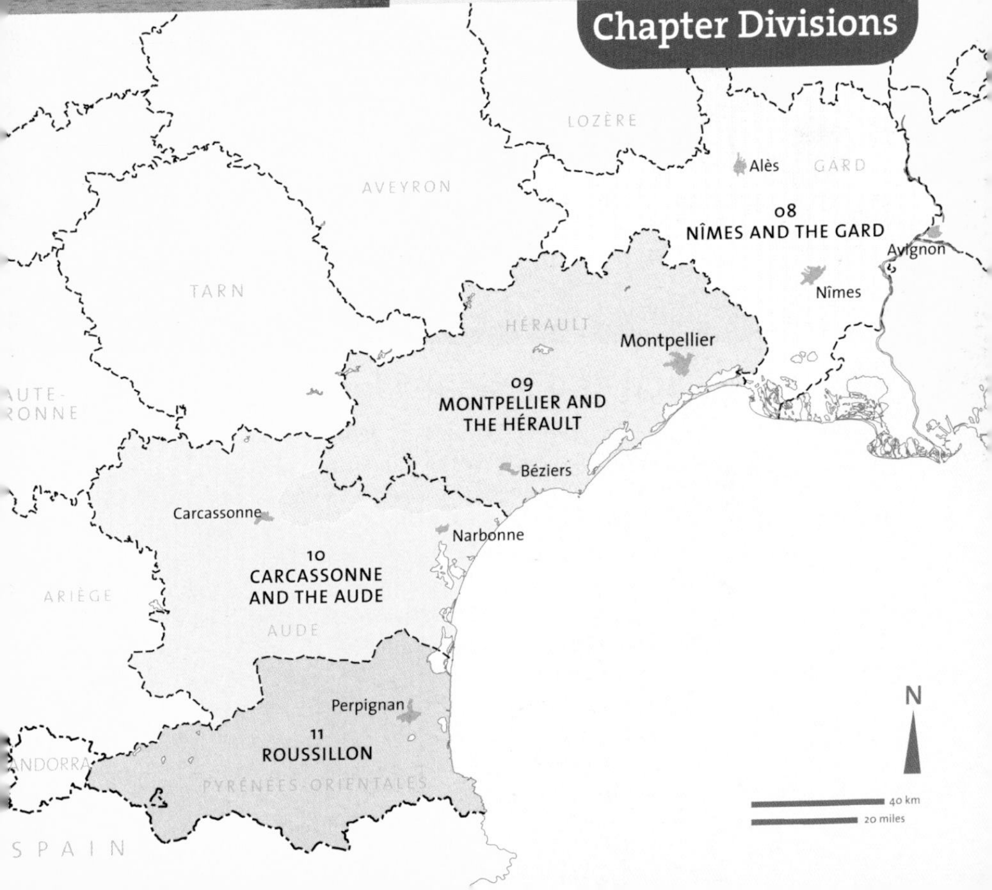

LOZÈRE
Alès
GARD
AVEYRON
08
NÎMES AND THE GARD
Avignon
Nîmes
TARN
HÉRAULT
Montpellier
09
MONTPELLIER AND THE HÉRAULT
Béziers
Carcassonne
Narbonne
10
CARCASSONNE AND THE AUDE
ARIÈGE
AUDE
Perpignan
11
ROUSSILLON
ANDORRA
PYRÉNÉES-ORIENTALES
SPAIN
N
40 km
20 miles

Above: Château de Peyrepertouse, pp.222–3

Opposite page: Cathédrale St-Just, Narbonne, pp.231–3

Land of the Troubadours

Don't ever make the mistake of thinking you're in just another part of France. Languedoc, like the rest of the south, was once a world of its own, and in the early Middle Ages this was the place to be, amid a brilliant, tolerant Occitan culture far ahead of its time.

Wherever you go, relics of this lost world lie at hand, from the delicate springtime sculpture of the 'Master of Cabestany' to the astonishing architecture of Catalan Perpignan. Landscapes of sparse *garrigue* and sandy coastline conspire to add a touch of the Mediterranean and exotic. When the French came, they added northern ideas and styles to the mix, including the matchless citadel of Carcassonne, and Gothic cathedrals in Narbonne and Béziers that would look entirely at home in the Île-de-France.

What's Roussillon?

The little corner that gives this book (and the region) its hyphenated title hasn't much to do at all with Languedoc – or even France, for that matter. Historically and culturally, Roussillon is Catalan. The French grabbed it away four hundred years ago to gain a more defensible border on the Pyrenees, but they've never really won over the Roussillonais' hearts and minds. Behind a coast lined with beaches there's an impressive little capital, Perpignan, and behind that three valleys leading up into the hills. Fortune gave the Catalans (and the French) some of the best of the Pyrenees, in fact: skiing and hiking, rugged mountain villages, unique, robust medieval art and spectacular scenery, all tugging at the skirts of the Catalans' holy mountain of Canigou.

Above: Colourful houses in Perpignan, pp.249–58

Right: The 14th-century bridge over the Tech, Céret, p.286

Above: Ripening vines, Tavel, p.111

Wines of a Southern Sun

Not too long ago, the *vignerons* of France's biggest wine-growing region spent their free time rioting against governments that wouldn't guarantee a market for all the plonk they made. Finally, they decided instead to try and improve it. Against all odds, they did – enough so that many of the exciting new wine regions of France are right here in Languedoc. There are 24 official denominations, and, while we wouldn't recommend such velocity, you could speed through the region and sample a new AOC variety every hour or so (or, at a slightly slower pace, follow the suggested itinerary on p.15). It is Languedoc's wide range of soils and microclimates that make all this variety possible.

Under the southern sun, the best wines are red, though you'll find some surprising whites and rosés too, not to mention a strong tradition of fortified dessert wines in Roussillon.

Above: clockwise from top left: A wine shop in Limoux advertising the Limoux carnival, pp.210–11; Céret cherries; local olives

Bon Appétit!

Provence has its *bouillabaisse*, known around the world. But so what? Across the Rhône in the Languedoc they simmer up their fish in a spicy *bourride* that is every bit as tasty. For centuries a poor and out-of-the-way place, Languedoc never was one of France's culinary stars, but, as with the wine, that's changing fast. You'll see the region's main advantage as soon as you tour one of its wonderful city markets – the basic ingredients are terrific. And it's not just about seafood; in fact Languedoc-Roussillon shows a very gratifying split personality when it comes to cooking. Look towards the sea and there are fish stews, Sète's stuffed cuttlefish, Collioure's anchovies and everything else, done up with plenty of tomatoes, garlic and olive oil. Look the other way, however, and you'll see the fine traditional country cooking of the southwest, the land of duck, *cèpes* and *foie gras*.

This page: Market produce, including 'petits pâtés de Pézenas' and the famous Bouzigues oysters

Water Everywhere

Sum up the Languedoc coast in a sentence? Don't even try. Instead, imagine a sort of geographer's catalogue of shorelines, where the scenery changes by the hour. It starts in the Rhône delta, with the flamingos and white horses of the glistening green Camargue. After that, the coast goes into high gear at the space-age resort of La Grande Motte, bringing in landscapes of coastal lagoons full of oysters and mussels. Next comes Sète, a major port with its thousands of sardines, and Cap d'Agde with its thousands of naturists. Sixty miles of open sandy beaches later, it all finishes with the delicious *corniche* coast around Collioure, the Côte Vermeille.

Languedoc offers plenty of fresh water too, in the mountain streams of the Pyrenees and the Corbières, and the delightful tree-lined Canal du Midi, the perfect spot for a lazy holiday on a slow barge.

Above, from top: The Canal du Midi, pp.181–5; Sète harbour, pp.165–8; St-Cyprien beach, p.259

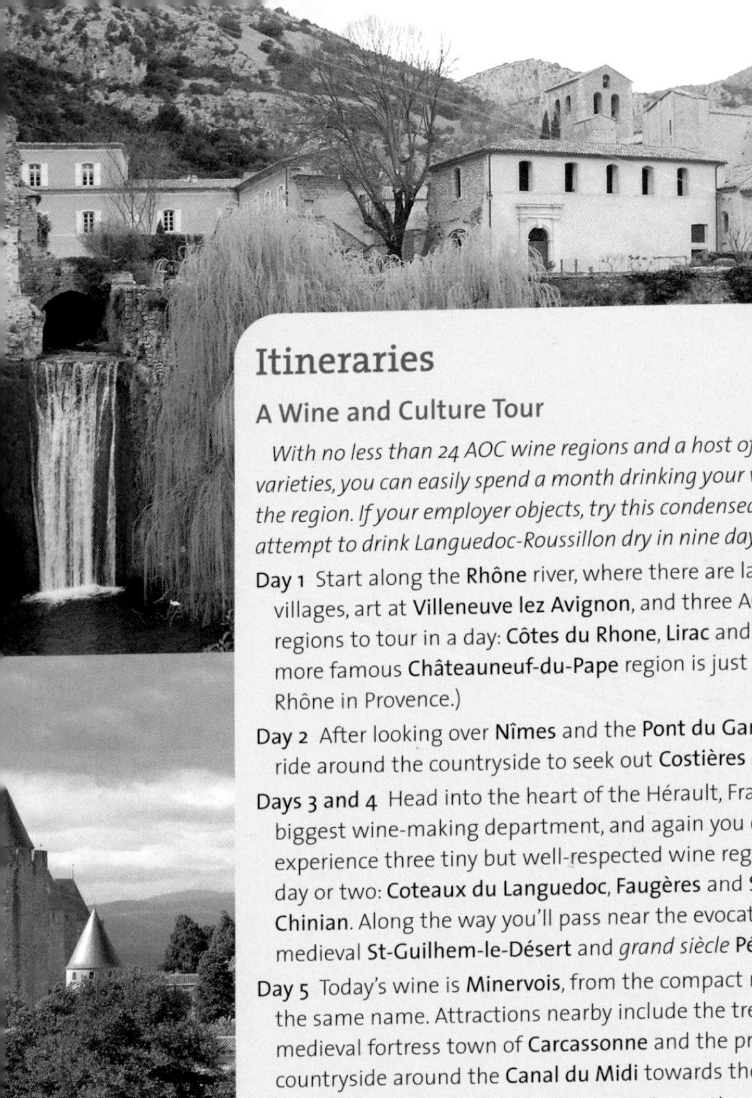

Above, from top: St-Guilhem-le-Désert, p.154; Carcassonne and vines, pp.194–204

Itineraries

A Wine and Culture Tour

With no less than 24 AOC wine regions and a host of lesser varieties, you can easily spend a month drinking your way across the region. If your employer objects, try this condensed version and attempt to drink Languedoc-Roussillon dry in nine days.

Day 1 Start along the **Rhône** river, where there are laid-back villages, art at **Villeneuve lez Avignon**, and three AOC wine regions to tour in a day: **Côtes du Rhone**, **Lirac** and **Tavel**. (The more famous **Châteauneuf-du-Pape** region is just across the Rhône in Provence.)

Day 2 After looking over **Nîmes** and the **Pont du Gard**, take a ride around the countryside to seek out **Costières de Nîmes**.

Days 3 and 4 Head into the heart of the Hérault, France's biggest wine-making department, and again you can experience three tiny but well-respected wine regions in a day or two: **Coteaux du Languedoc**, **Faugères** and **Saint-Chinian**. Along the way you'll pass near the evocatively medieval **St-Guilhem-le-Désert** and *grand siècle* **Pézenas**.

Day 5 Today's wine is **Minervois**, from the compact region of the same name. Attractions nearby include the tremendous medieval fortress town of **Carcassonne** and the pretty countryside around the **Canal du Midi** towards the coast.

Day 6 Spend most of this day getting to know the elegant and historic city of **Narbonne**, with a trip to the coast to sample some of the vintage from the tiny mountain area of **La Clape**.

Days 7 and 8 The **Corbières** will be good for two days of wine-tasting and touring. The areas between the villages of **Fitou** and **Tuchan** have some of the most interesting wine estates, and the great medieval castles of the Corbières – **Peyrepertuse**, **Quéribus** and **Aguilar** – are conveniently nearby.

Day 9 The last day of this gastronomical-cultural feast will be dessert, so to speak, among the sweet wines of Roussillon: a taste of **Maury**, and a ride through the scenic **Fenouillèdes**, and then to the coast for some **Banyuls**, and maybe an afternoon on the beach at **Collioure** or **Banyuls-sur-Mer**.

Above: Detail from the façade of the abbey of St-Gilles-du-Gard, pp.119–21

Below: Llo church in the Cerdagne, p.283

A Ten-day Medieval Mystery Tour

Day 1 Start on the Languedoc side of the **Camargue**, the Rhône delta, a romantic setting for the famous sculpture of **St-Gilles-du-Gard**, and **Aigues-Mortes**, the port Saint Louis built to send his armies off to the Crusades.

Day 2 Skirt around **Montpellier** and head for the lonely *garrigue* north of the city, to visit the evocative villages and churches of **St-Martin-de-Londres** and **St-Guilhem-le-Desert**.

Day 3 Head back towards the coast, making a stop at the great **abbey of Valmagne** on your way to two of the greatest Gothic cathedrals of southern France, conveniently located near each other at **Béziers** and **Narbonne**.

Day 4 Head north, and then west, following the route of the **Canal du Midi**; the route goes through pretty **Colombiers** and then takes in medieval relics at **Capestang**, **Quarante** and **Trèbes**, and then the mystical seven-sided church at **Rieux-Minervois** before arriving at Carcassonne.

Day 5 The full tour of **Carcassonne**'s walls and towers, as well as its medieval Cité, museums and cathedral, is good for a whole day.

Day 6 From here, the D118 south takes you into the old Cathar heartland, where you can explore the mysteries of **Rennes-le-Château**, and perhaps make a side trip to the Cathars' last redoubt, the castle of Montségur.

Day 7 Continue on south, into the Pyrenees, where the micro-region of the **Cerdagne** offers not only gorgeous scenery, but a number of unique and peculiar Romanesque village churches.

Day 8 Find your way out of the mountains down the valley of the **Conflent**, with some masterpieces of medieval Catalan architecture and sculpture at **St-Michel-de-Cuxa**, **St-Martin-du-Canigou** and **Serrabonne**, on the slopes of holy Canigou.

Day 9 Spend another day with the Catalans in **Perpignan**, home to a fine cathedral and the 13th-century Palace of the Kings of Majorca. If there's time, drive out to **Elne**, for a cloister that contains some of the finest medieval sculpture in the region.

Day 10 North of Perpignan, have a look at a strange, almost barren vortex of occult mysteries, the **Plateau d'Opoul**. From here, head into the Corbières. The most impressive collection of castles in southern France waits here, including cloudtop **Peyrepertuse** and the Cathar redoubt of **Quéribus**.

CONTENTS

The Guide

Reference

Maps and Plans

History

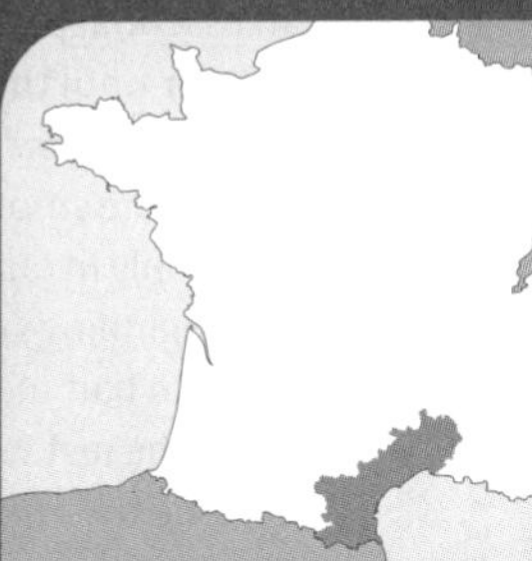

02

First, we'll try to set the terminology straight. When the Romans ruled here, they called all of southern Gaul 'Provence' at first, then 'Gallia Narbonensis'. Finally, the region between the Rhône and the Pyrenees was sorted out as 'Septimania', a name that survived up to medieval times. In the days of the troubadours almost all the south was poetically 'Provence', but the political split continued, between lands subject to the Holy Roman Emperors (Provence) and those claimed by France (Languedoc). Today, southern regionalists call the entire south of France 'Occitania' (a word only invented in the 17th century).

Roussillon, the modern *département* of Pyrénées-Orientales, followed an entirely different course of history: part of the Catalan nation since the 10th century, it was an essential part of the County of Barcelona and later the Catalan Kingdom of Aragon, until the French annexed it in 1559.

Under the *ancien régime*, the Revolution and all the regimes that followed it these areas were smothered, politically and culturally, by France. The turning of the tide came only in our own time, with the election of the 1981 socialist government and the beginnings of regional autonomy. The old Languedoc was cut in two: the western half, including its traditional capital Toulouse, became the Midi-Pyrénées, while the rest was combined with the *département* of Pyrénées-Orientales to become the region covered in this book: Languedoc-Roussillon.

Just Another of Prehistory's Backwaters

Tools and traces of habitation in southern France go back as far as 1,000,000 BC. The first identifiable personality on the stage, however, is 'Tautavel Man': a remarkable recent find in the small Roussillon village of that name has unearthed hundreds of thousands of bones of a people who rate among the very first Europeans yet discovered – from at least 450,000 BC, and perhaps as far back as 680,000 BC. Someone may have been around through all the millennia that followed, but evidence is rare; Neanderthal Man turns up about 60,000 BC (at Ganges, in the Hérault, and other places). The first evidence of the Neanderthals' nemesis, that quarrelsome and unlovable species *Homo sapiens*, comes some 20,000 years later.

Neolithic civilization arrived as early as 3500 BC, and endured throughout the region for the next 2,000 years. People knew agriculture and raised sheep, traded for scarce goods (obsidian from the islands around Sicily, for example), and built dry-stone houses; one of these has been reconstructed by archaeologists at Cambous, in the Hérault. Unlike Provence, Languedoc has few important Neolithic monuments, just a few large dolmens in the Minervois in the southern Hérault, and the exotic 'statue-menhirs' you can see in the museum at St-Pons-de-Thomières. Of succeeding ages we know more about the technology than the culture and changes in population: the use of copper began about 2000 BC, iron *c.* 800 BC. In both cases the region was one of the last parts of the Mediterranean basin to catch on.

The first settled villages appear about 800 BC. Who built them is a matter of conjecture; later Roman and Greek writers would call the people along the coast 'Iberians', though just about this time Languedoc was feeling the great invasion of the Celts, who were then spreading their control over most of continental Europe.

The Celts by nature didn't much care for towns, but you will find traces of their settlements today, called by the Latin name *oppida*. An *oppidum* is a small, fortified village, usually on a hilltop, built around a religious sanctuary or trading centre. Already, more advanced outsiders were coming to make deals with the natives: the Phoenicians, the Etruscans and, most importantly, the Greeks.

In the 7th century BC, Greek merchant activity around the Mediterranean turned into full-scale colonization. The Ionian city-states of Asia Minor had become over-populated, agriculturally exhausted and politically precarious, and their citizens sought to reproduce them in new lands. The first was Massalia – Marseille – *c.* 600 BC. Soon Massalia was founding colonies of its own, including Agde in Languedoc. Greek influence over the indigenous peoples was strong from the start; as everywhere else they went, they brought the vine (wild stocks were already present, but the Celts hadn't worked out what to do with them) and the olive, and also their art. The Celts loved Greek vases, and had metals and other raw materials to offer in return. Increased trade turned some of the native *oppida* into genuine cities, such as Ensérune, near Béziers.

The Romans Arrive to Wake It Up

From the start, the Greeks were natural allies of the young city of Rome – if only because they had common enemies. Besides the strong Etruscan federation, occupying the lands in between the two, there were their trade rivals, the Phoenicians (later Carthaginians) and occasionally the Celts and Ligurians. As Rome gobbled up Etruria and the rest of Italy, the area became of increasing importance, a fact Hannibal demonstrated when he marched his armies through Languedoc towards Italy in 218 BC, with the full support of the Celts (historians still argue over how and where he got the elephants across the Rhône).

When the Romans took Spain in the Second Punic War (206 BC), the coasts of what they called Gaul became a logical next step. In 125 BC, Roman troops saved Marseille from another Celtic attack. This time, though, they had come to stay. The reorganization of the new province – Provincia – was quick and methodical. Domitius Ahenobarbus, the vanquisher of the Celts, began the great Italy–Spain highway that bears his name, the Via Domitia, in 121 BC. New cities were founded, most importantly Narbo Martius (Narbonne, 118 BC), which became the capital of the quickly developing western half, reorganized into a new province called Gallia Narbonensis. Dozens of other new foundations, including Perpignan and Carcassonne, followed over the next century, many of them planned colonies with land grants for veterans of the legions. The Celts were not through yet, though. Two northern tribes, the Cimbri and Teutones, mounted a serious invasion of Gaul and Italy in 115 BC. They raided those areas continuously until 102 BC, when they were destroyed by a Roman army under Marius in Provence.

The last Celtic invasions came at a time when the Roman Republic was in disarray at home. Marius, leader of the populist faction, was only one of the generals who won political power in the capital. After his death, the new military boss of Rome was Sulla, a bloody reactionary whose tyranny inspired resistance in many corners of the empire. A general named Quintus Sertorius, who had fought under Marius, seized Spain and parts of Gaul and defeated five armies sent against him from

Rome. Sertorius held out until he was poisoned at a banquet in the Pyrenees by a subordinate named Perpenna (he must have been well rewarded; Perpignan is named for him).

Rome's internal struggles continued to be reflected in the fortunes of Mediterranean Gaul. Marseille's downfall came in 49 BC. Always famed for its careful diplomacy, the city made the fatal mistake of supporting Pompey over Julius Caesar in the civil wars. A vengeful Caesar crippled its trade and stripped it of nearly all its colonies and dependencies. Thereafter, the influence of Marseille gave way to newer, more Romanized towns, including Narbo Martius and Nemausus (Nîmes).

Throughout all this, the region had been easily assimilated into the Roman economy, supplying food and raw materials for the insatiable metropolis. With Caesar's conquest of the rest of Gaul, the Rhône trade route (which had always managed to bring down a little Baltic amber and tin from Cornwall) became a busy river highway and military route. Under the good government and peace bestowed by Augustus (27 BC–AD 14) and his successors, Gaul blossomed with an opulence never before seen. The cities, especially those of the Rhône valley, acquired theatres, amphitheatres for games, aqueducts, bridges and temples. Gallia Narbonensis participated in the political and cultural life of the empire, even contributing one of the better emperors, Antoninus Pius (from Nîmes, AD 138–61), only obscure because his reign was so peaceful and prosperous.

Archaeological digs throughout France turn up a preponderance of wealthy villas. This is the dark side of Roman Gaul: from the beginning of their rule, wealthy Romans were able to grab up much of the land, forming large estates and exploiting the indigenous population. This trend was magnified in the decadent, totalitarian and economically chaotic late Empire, when, throughout Roman territory, the few remaining free farmers were forced to sell themselves into virtual serfdom to escape crushing taxation. After AD 200, in fact, everything was going wrong; trade and the cities stagnated while art and culture decayed. The first of the barbarian raids brought Germans into the south in the 250s, when they raided Provence.

Constantine, while yet emperor of only the western half of the empire (AD 312–23), often resided at Arles in Provence. His pro-Christian policy gave the cult its first real influence in Gaul, at least in the cities; under his auspices, the first state-sponsored Church council was held at Arles in 314.

600 Years of Unwanted Guests

French historians always blame the barbarian invaders of the 5th century for destroying the cities of Gaul – as if Teutonic warriors enjoyed pulling down temple colonnades on their days off. Alans, Suevi and Vandals passed through the region, but they were in a hurry to get to Spain; the Visigoths, in the early 400s, came to stay. Though government collapsed in chaos, business went on much as usual, with the Roman landowners (and their new German colleagues) gradually making their transition to feudal nobles. The weakness of central power brought some long-due upheavals in the countryside, with guerrilla bands and vigilante justice against the landlords. The old and new rulers soon found common cause. For a while, a clique of a hundred of the biggest landowners took over administration in Gaul, even declaring one of their own as 'emperor' in Arles (455), with the support of the Visigoths.

The Visigoths soon tired of such games, and assumed total control in 476, the year the Western Empire formally expired. They had to share it, however, with the Ostrogoths, who had established a strong kingdom in Italy and seized all of Provence east of the Rhône – the beginnings of a political boundary that would last in various forms for a thousand years. When the Eastern Empire under Justinian tried to recapture Italy, the Franks took the opportunity to snatch the Ostrogoths' domain in Gaul (535). They were never able to hold it effectively and the area gradually slipped into quiet anarchy.

By now, the region west of the Rhône had come to be known as 'Septimania', for its seven important towns: Narbonne, Béziers, Agde, Elne, Maguelone, Lodève and Nîmes. Most of these, unfortunately, were only shadows of what they had been in Roman times. The Visigoths kept most of this land, the northernmost province of their Spanish kingdom, until the Arab invasion of the early 700s rolled over the Pyrenees. In 711 the Arabs conquered the Visigothic kingdom in Spain. Eight years later they came over the Pyrenees and took Narbonne.

The next two centuries are as wonderfully confused as anything in prehistory. There is the legend of the great Spanish Caliph Abd ar-Rahman campaigning here, and a document survives in which the bishops of Agde are rebuked by the pope for minting coins with the image of Muhammad. Charles Martel, the celebrated Frankish generalissimo who stopped the Arab wave at Poitiers, made an expedition to the southern coast in 737–9, brutally sacking Agde. His mission was hardly a religious crusade – rather taking advantage of the Visigothic defeat to increase Frankish hegemony in the south. The Arabs still held many fortified towns, and they are recorded as petitioning Córdoba, unsuccessfully, to help them keep the half-barbarous Franks out.

Córdoba couldn't help; the climate was too eccentric and the pickings too slim for the Arabs to mount a serious effort in Gaul. The nascent Franks gained control everywhere, and the entire coast was briefly absorbed by Charlemagne's father, Pépin the Short, in 759. Under Charlemagne (768–814), Toulouse regained some of its old prominence under his cousin Guilhem de Gellone, the Count of Toulouse, a great warrior, and later a saint (*see* p.155); one of his many titles was 'Prince of Gothia' in recognition of the strong Visigothic element remaining in Languedoc. Monastic reformers such as Benedict of Aniane (a Visigothic), helped start a huge expansion of Church institutions. Hard-working monks reclaimed land from forests and swamps, and later they sat back and enjoyed the rents, while always keeping up the holy work of education and copying books.

The Beginnings of the Middle Ages

The Treaty of Verdun in 843 (*see* **Topics**, p.40) confirmed the Rhône as a boundary, and politically Provence and Languedoc went their separate ways. By 849, all of modern Languedoc was part of the County of Toulouse. In the beginning their hold was nominal at best, but under a capable dynasty of counts, all named Raymond, Toulouse gradually extended its control over towns and fiefs throughout the region. Pilgrimages became an important activity, as at St-Gilles-du-Gard and St-Guilhem (near Aniane), getting a sleepy and locally bound society moving again and providing an impetus to trade.

Another result of the Carolingian decline was the birth of a new nation in the eastern Pyrenees – Catalonia. The Catalans, who spoke a language closely related to Occitan, coalesced around the County of the Cerdagne, deep in the Pyrenees, under the legendary Wilfred the Hairy, who became count in 874. In the 10th century his dynasty gained control of Barcelona, and expanded its control throughout what is now Roussillon. The Franks, their nominal overlords, offered the Catalans no help in their constant battles with the Arabs of Spain, and in 985 Count Borrell II declared Catalonia an independent and sovereign state; the Franks could do nothing about it. By then the Counts of Toulouse were nearly as autonomous, while owing allegiance on paper to the Carolingians. They became even more independent when a whole new dynasty – the Capets – took over in Paris at the death of Louis V in 987.

Occitan and Catalan Medieval Civilization

All over Europe, the year 1000 can be taken as the rough milestone for the sudden and spectacular development of the medieval world, including Occitania. Towns and villages found the money and energy to build impressive new churches. The end of foreign raids made the seas safe for merchants. New cities were founded, notably Montpellier, in 985. In 1002 the first written document in Occitan appeared, highlighting the linguistic faultline that had grown up between the '*langue d'oïl*' of the north and the '*langue d'oc*' of the south (so called from the two words, *oïl* and *oc*, that they used for 'yes'). The pilgrimage to Compostela, in Spain, made what was left of the old Roman roads into busy highways once more, and along the main southern route the first of the medieval trade fairs appeared, at the new town of St-Gilles-du-Gard.

Populations and economies boomed throughout the 11th century, and the trend was given another boost by the Crusades, which began in 1095. With increased prosperity and contact with a wider world, better manners and the rudiments of personal hygiene were not slow to follow. Feudal anarchy began to look quite genteel, maintaining a delicate balance of power, with feudal ties and blood relations keeping the political appetites of rulers from ever really getting out of hand. From the more civilized East, and from nearby Muslim Spain, came new ideas, new technologies and a taste for luxury and art. As an indication of how far Occitania had come, there were the troubadours (*see* **Topics**, p.43), creating modern Europe's first lyric poetry. Almost every court of the south was refined enough to welcome and patronize them.

The growing cities began to assert themselves in the 12th century, often achieving a substantial independence in *communes* governed by consuls: Perpignan and Nîmes both won these rights in 1198. In the countryside, successive waves of monastic reform spawned a huge number of new institutions: first the movement led from Cluny, in the 11th century, and in the 12th the Cistercians, who set up a score of important monasteries. Efficiently exploiting the lands bequeathed by noblemen made them rich, and also did much to improve the agricultural economy all round. Probably the richest corner of the south was the Catalan Pyrenees; substantial iron deposits, and the most advanced methods of smelting them, provided the capital for a Catalan trading empire based in Barcelona and Perpignan. From then on, Catalonia's rise was dramatic. For a brief time the Catalans attempted to expand northwards; under Ramon Berenguer I (d. 1076) their domains stretched as far as Carcassonne and Montpellier. By 1125 the counts of Barcelona controlled much of Provence south of the Durance; in 1137 they became kings of Aragon, which included much of western Spain. Besides its wealth, Catalonia was characterized by its unique constitution, recognizing the interests of the new middle class as well as nobles, and writing down elaborate codes of rights called *fueros* as a check on royal absolutism.

The other leading power in the region, the 'Raymonds' of Toulouse, eventually took back the Catalan conquests in Languedoc, while contending with them for control of Provence. The strong state they built controlled everything from the Rhône to the Lot valley and the central Pyrenees – except for Carcassonne and Béziers, ruled by their allies the Trencavel family, Montpellier, a Catalan possession, and Narbonne, ruled by its independent viscounts.

The Cathars and the Rape of Languedoc

It was a great age for culture, producing not only the troubadours but also an impressive display of Romanesque architecture, and an original school of sculpture in Roussillon. Perhaps the most remarkable phenomenon of the times was a widespread religious tolerance, shared by rulers, the common people and even many among the clergy. A long and fruitful exposure to the culture of Muslim Spain, as well as the presence of a large Jewish community, an important element in the towns since Roman times, must have helped. Still, such goodwill is hard to account for in medieval Europe. Like the troubadour poetry, it is an indication of just how advanced Occitan society was at its height in the 12th century.

Unfortunately, this tolerance was also to bring about the fall of the Occitan nation. Religious dissenters of various persuasions sprang up everywhere. Most of the new sects soon died out and are little known today, like the extremist 'Petrobrusians' of St-Gilles, who didn't fancy sacraments or relics; some of them favoured burning down churches and killing all priests and monks.

One sect, however, made startling inroads into every sector of society in 11th- and 12th-century Languedoc – the Cathars, or Albigensians. This Manichaean doctrine (*see* **Topics**, pp.41–3), obsessed with Good and Evil, had in its upright simplicity a powerful attraction for both industrious townspeople and peasants. In many ways it was the very picture of 17th-century English Puritanism, though without any of the Puritans' noxious belligerence towards the less perfect; this kept it in good standing with the worldly nobility, and also allowed Cathar and Catholic villagers to live peacefully side by side.

The Cathars were never a majority in any part of the south; in most places they never made up more than 10 per cent of the population. They might have passed on as only a curious footnote to history, had they not provided the excuse for the biggest and most flagrant land-grab of the Middle Ages. The 'Albigensian Crusade', arranged after the 1208 murder of a papal legate, was a cynical marriage of convenience between two old piratical enemies, the papacy and the crown of France. One wanted the religious competition stifled; the other sought to assert its old Carolingian claim to the lands of the counts of Toulouse. Diplomacy forced King Philip Augustus to disclaim any part in the affair, but nevertheless a big army of knights from the Ile-de-France went south in 1209 to burn some heretics and snatch what they could. Their leader made the difference: too smart, too brutal and too lucky, the sort of devil who changes history – Simon de Montfort. His vicious massacres at Béziers, where the Catholic population tried to defend the heretics and were incinerated along with them inside the churches, and his taking of the impregnable fortress town of Carcassonne by trickery, put the fear of God into the southerners; Montfort won battle after battle and took every town he attacked, save only Beaucaire.

In a last attempt to save their fortunes, Count Raymond VI of Toulouse and King Peter II of Aragon combined to meet the northerners. With an overwhelmingly superior force, they blundered their way to crushing defeat at the Battle of Muret in 1213. Montfort soon claimed the titles of Count of Toulouse and Viscount of Carcassonne and Béziers for himself. The Languedociens continued to resist until after his death in 1218; six years later, again under the pretence of a 'crusade', Louis VIII took the matter in his own hands. Coming south with another army, he forced the annexation of all eastern Languedoc and Carcassonne, the fortress key to the Midi, in 1229. The remainder of the century saw the inexorable consolidation of French power: the building or rebuilding of great fortifications, as at Carcassonne and Peyrepertuse, begun by Saint Louis (King Louis IX, 1226–70), and the new port of Aigues-Mortes, used by Louis as base for his two Crusades (1249 and 1270).

Four centuries after the fall of the Carolingian Empire, the French once again had their foothold in the south. Languedoc was finished, its distinctive culture quickly snuffed out. If Montfort's men had been shock troops from France, the occupying force was made up of French bureaucrats and monks. The monks took charge of many village churches, replacing parish priests to keep an eye on the population. The Inquisition arrived to take care of the heretics – and of course anyone the northerners found politically suspect, or whose property they coveted. The last Cathar stronghold, the Château de Quéribus, surrendered in 1255. The troubadours found less and less around them worthy of song. One of the most famous, Folquet de Marseille, had already gone over to the side of France and bigotry. As a zealous convert and, later, Bishop of Toulouse, he became an extremely ferocious oppressor of the few surviving Cathars.

French Oppression and Religious Wars

Under French rule, the region languished both culturally and economically. For the next few centuries there is little news to report, and most of it bad. The strong hand from Paris had at least the virtue of maintaining peace. Roussillon wasn't so lucky, enduring occasional French invasions, and Languedoc suffered again in the early campaigns of the Hundred Years' War. Edward the Black Prince marched through the region, pillaging and burning, in the 1340s. Along with the disruptions of war came peasant rebellions, while crop failures brought some parts close to famine.

The Black Death topped it off in 1348, taking a third of the population as it did almost everywhere else it struck.

One exception to the sorry state of Languedoc was Montpellier. Under the Catalan Kingdom of Majorca, this relatively young town became fat and wealthy from cloth and other manufacturing, while its famous medical school attracted students from across Europe. Doubting their ability to hold it much longer, the Catalans sold the city to France in 1349, though its prosperity continued.

More troubles came in the 16th century. The cultural effacement of Occitania became complete with the 1539 Edict of Villers-Cotterêts, which decreed French as the official language throughout the kingdom. The language of the troubadours was now derided by the northerners as nothing more than a '*patois*', a rustic dialect. Worse, at the same time a big dose of the new Protestant heresy was floating down the Rhône from Calvin's Geneva. The Occitans received it warmly, and soon there were large Protestant communities in all the towns. Although this seems like a repeat of the Cathar story, the geographical distribution is fascinating – the old Cathar areas (like the Aude) were now loyally Catholic, while the orthodox regions of the 13th century now came out strongly for the dissenters. In eastern Languedoc (the Hérault and Gard) they attracted about half the population. Tolerance was still out of fashion, and the opening round of a pointless half-century of religious wars came with the 1542 massacres in the Lubéron mountains of Provence.

The open warfare that followed across the south saw massacres and atrocities enough on both sides. Protestants distinguished themselves by the wholesale destruction of churches and their art (as at St-Gilles); churches were often converted into fortresses, as can be seen throughout Languedoc. Henry IV's 1598 Edict of Nantes put an end to the wars, and acknowledged Protestant control of certain areas (Nîmes, Montpellier, Uzès, Gignac, Clermont-l'Hérault, Aigues-Mortes, Sommières, Castres).

The French monarchy had been weakened by the conflict, but, as soon as it recovered, new measures were introduced to keep the provinces in line. Under Cardinal Richelieu, in the 1630s, the laws and traditions of local autonomy were swept away. As insurance, scores of feudal castles (such as Beaucaire) were demolished to eliminate possible points of resistance. Richelieu and Louis XIII warred against the increasing independence of the Protestant (or 'Huguenot') enclaves; in 1622 they besieged and captured Montpellier, and knocked down its walls. After that, Protestant resistance survived only in the Cévennes, where the Duc de Rohan carried out desultory campaigns until 1629. Royal control over Languedoc became total with the failed rebellion of the Duc de Montmorency, 'First Duke of France' and royal governor of Languedoc. Richelieu beat him in battle near Castelnaudary, in 1632, and beheaded him in the main square of Toulouse.

Louis XIV's revocation of the Edict of Nantes in 1685 reawakened the religious troubles. Vicious repression saw many Protestants killed, exiled to the colonies or sentenced to the galleys. Bands of armed missionaries called '*dragons*' travelled through Languedoc enforcing conversions. When Louis killed or imprisoned the best of the Protestant ministers, their places were often filled by wild-eyed millenarian fanatics. These 'prophets' led many of their followers into the '*Desert*', the difficult terrain of the Cévennes, where they hid from the missionaries and royal troops and made a living as best they could. The king determined to root them out completely, occasioning the Camisard Wars that began in 1702. The 'Camisards' (so called because they had no uniforms, only plain shirts) waged guerrilla battles for years through the Cévennes and the plains of the Gard, with a little aid from the British and the Dutch; a British force briefly occupied Sète in 1710. The king's generals pursued a scorched-earth policy, while the Camisards themselves were not above the occasional pillage or massacre. One by one the Camisard leaders died in battle, or escaped to safety in Switzerland. Some of the 'prophets' made it to London, where they would have an influence on the thinking of Rousseau and of Ann Lee, founder of the Shakers.

By 1715 it was all over. In that year Louis XIV finally had the decency to expire; the repression slackened off, and such Protestants as survived were tolerated, if only just. Most of them, some of the south's most productive citizens, had already left. Louis' long and oppressive reign continued the impoverishment of the south, despite well-intentioned economic measures by his brilliant minister Colbert, who started new manufactories (Villeneuvette, near Clermont-l'Hérault), founded the port of Sète, and helped Paul Riquet build the Canal du Midi (*see* **Topics**, pp.44–6). That great work, completed in 1681, would help more than anything else in slowly bringing trade and industry back to the region. In the 18th century, things picked up considerably, with the beginnings of an important textile industry, largely fostered by the remaining Protestants. Silk was made around Nîmes and parts of Provence (where farmers gave up their bedrooms to raise the delicate silkworms in them), while Montpellier and Carcassonne made names for themselves in linen and cotton goods. It was a good start, though unfortunately the English and their new mechanized production would ruin much of Languedoc's cloth trade after 1800.

Apropos of nothing at all, to close out the *ancien régime* we'll mention a little historical sidebar – Languedoc's invasion of America. This occurred during the Seven Years' War, known in the USA as the 'French and Indian War', when the king sent the Régiment de Languedoc into what is now New York State, in 1755. They made a brave start, ambushing a British column with the help of their Native American allies, but then lost an important battle at Lake George. Later they would fight at Ticonderoga and Québec, finally surrendering at the siege of Montréal.

The Misfortunes of Catalonia

Roussillon had followed a quite different history, though the result was the same. Under Jaume I the Conqueror (1213–76), Aragon reached the height of its merchant empire, while keeping the French at bay along the castle-strewn Roussillon–Languedoc border. Before his death, Jaume decided to divide the kingdom between his two sons, leading to the brief but exotic interlude of the 'Kingdom of Majorca' and an equally brief golden age for Perpignan, its capital. The French tried to take advantage of the split, again shamelessly proclaiming a 'crusade' against the piously orthodox Catalans (the pope, who wanted the Aragonese out of Italy, had given his approval), but they were thrown back across the border in 1285.

Aragon was reunited in 1344, but its troubles were just beginning. After the Black Death in 1348, recessions and political strife led to a long and disastrous decline in Catalan commerce. The union of Aragon and Castile to form the Kingdom of Spain in 1492 was a disaster for the Catalans, meaning the introduction of the Inquisition, the gradual destruction of the *fueros* (*see* p.25) and a total ruin of their commerce. The long series of wars between France and Spain resulted in the ceding of Roussillon to France in 1659. Immediately, the province suffered systematic and heavy-handed Frenchification, leading to revolts in the mountain valleys that were violently suppressed. The southern angle of France's hexagon was now substantially complete; Roussillon would be treated as a conquered province for centuries.

Revolution, and Other Disappointments

The French Revolution was largely a Parisian affair, though southerners often played important roles (such as the Abbé Sieyès and Mirabeau), while bourgeois delegates from the manufacturing towns fought along with the Girondins in the National Assembly for a liberal republic. Unfortunately, the winning Jacobin ideology was more centralist and more dedicated to destroying any taint of regional difference than the *ancien régime* had ever dreamed of being. Whatever was left of local rights and privileges was soon decreed out of existence, and, when the Revolution divided France into homogenous *départements* in 1790, terms like 'Languedoc' ceased to have any real political meaning.

In the beginning, southerners greeted the Revolution with wild enthusiasm. Volunteers from Marseille brought the 'Marseillaise' to Paris, while local mobs wrecked and looted hundreds of churches and châteaux. Soon, however, the betrayed south became violently counter-revolutionary. The Catalans raised regiments of volunteers against the Revolution. The royalists and the English occupied Toulon after a popular revolt and were only dislodged by the brilliant tactics of a young commander named Bonaparte in 1793.

After Waterloo, the restored monarchy started off with a grisly White Terror in Nîmes and elsewhere. After the revolution of 1830, the 'July Monarchy' of King Louis-Philippe brought significant changes. The old industrious Protestant strain of the south finally got its chance with a Protestant prime minister from Nîmes, François Guizot (1840–48); his liberal policies and his slogan – '*Enrichissez-vous!*' – opened an age where there would be a little Protestant in every Frenchman. Guizot's countrymen were rapidly demanding more; radicalism and anti-clericalism increased throughout the century.

Southerners supported the revolution of 1848 and the Second Republic, and many areas put up armed resistance to Louis-Napoléon's 1851 coup. In Béziers, a rebellion led by the mayor himself had to be put down by French troops.

The second half of the 19th century saw the beginnings of a nationalist revival in Occitania. In Provence it was all cultural and apolitical: a linguistic and literary revival bound up with Nobel Prize-winning poet Frédéric Mistral and the cultural group called the Félibrige, founded in 1854. In Languedoc it was all political and unconcerned with culture, focusing on the first of modern France's agricultural movements. Markets since the 1800s had encouraged Languedoc to become one vast vineyard. Monoculture had its dangers, however: a fungus called oïdium threatened to destroy the vines in 1850 before farmers learned to control it with copper sulphate. A graver disease, phylloxera, hit in 1875, and ruined tens of thousands of vintners; the quick recovery favoured the biggest producers, who could afford the new, phylloxera-resistant American vine stocks. A huge wine boom in the 1880s was followed by an even huger bust, with competition from Algeria and Italy and changes in the laws that permitted the sale of cheap adulterated wines (made of the distilled *marc* from the wine residues, mixed with water and sugar and called *piquette*). By 1904 prices had dropped to one-third of 1890 levels.

All over the Midi, you'll see streets named for Marcellin Albert. In a time when many country districts had been brought perilously close to famine, this charismatic *vigneron* and café-keeper from the Aude began the first of modern France's agricultural movements, to stamp out *la piquette* and give growers an honest living for their labour. In 1907 the farmers went on the warpath. Albert spoke at monster meetings in towns across Languedoc, each time raising a bigger crowd; the last, in Montpellier, attracted some 600,000. Paris sent troops to occupy the region with guns blazing; scores were killed or injured, and some local officials got thrown into prison. This only inflamed the situation further. The leftist prime minister Georges Clemenceau made the mistake of including some local regiments among the force sent to put down the movement, and one of them mutinied at Béziers. Albert threatened to call a general strike, but Clemenceau invited him to Paris and tricked him into calling it off. Albert was nearly lynched when he got home, and the movement dwindled, but the farmers devoted their attention to building a strong co-operative system and keeping the political pressure up by more orthodox means; French politics would never be quite the same.

Southerners had other reasons to grumble. The post-1870 Third Republic pursued French cultural oppression to its wildest extremes. History was rewritten to make Occitania and Roussillon seem eternal parts of the 'French nation'. Parisians derided the Occitan languages as mere bastard 'dialects' of French, and children were punished for speaking their own language in the schoolyard, a practice that lasted until the 1970s. Catalan Roussillon was not even permitted political participation – the government and parties arranged to have outsiders stand for its seats in the National Assembly.

After 1910, economic factors conspired to defeat both the political and cultural aspirations of the Midi; rural depopulation, caused by the break-up of the pre-industrial agricultural society, drained the life out of the villages, and decreased the percentage of people who spoke the native languages. The First World War decimated a generation – visit any village church or war memorial in the south and look at the plaques; from a total population of a few hundred, you'll see maybe 30 names of villagers who died for the 'Glory of France'. By 1950, most villages had lost at least half their population; some died out altogether.

After the French débâcle of 1940, the south found itself under the Vichy government. German occupation came in November 1942, following the American landings in North Africa. After 1942, the Résistance in Languedoc was active and effective, most of all in the mountains: in Haut Languedoc, the Cévennes and the Pyrenees. Two months after D-Day, in August 1944, American and French troops hit the beaches around St-Tropez, and in a successful (and little-noticed) operation they had most of Provence liberated in two weeks. This inspired the Résistance to come out into the open in Languedoc, where the partisans of the upper Hérault defeated a German column sent against them, just weeks before liberation.

A Long-delayed Rebirth

The postwar decades brought many changes. The population got a good shaking. First came refugees from the Spanish Civil War in 1939; you'll find them and their descendants everywhere, especially in Roussillon. A bigger wave of refugees hit in 1962: the *pieds-noirs*, French settlers forced to flee Algeria after its independence. Languedoc took in 100,000 of them, a quarter in Montpellier. More recently, the new arrivals have been North Africans, concentrated in the cities.

Agriculture has been transformed. Languedoc vintners have learned their lesson; they make less wine, and much better. Their region, which only stopped losing population in about 1955, is on an upward swing once more. According to INSEE, the national statistics office, the number of inhabitants in Languedoc-Roussillon at 1 January 2006 was 2,520,000 – it was the only region in France, along with the Midi-Pyrénées next door, where the population increased more than one per cent between 1999 and 2006. So far, much of the economy is based on tourism. A typically French national planning effort of 1968 made its coastline into a growing resort region, with new holiday towns at Cap d'Agde and La Grande Motte. Now, much of the energy comes from the cities. Montpellier, inspired by its dynamic mayor Georges Frêche (1977–2004), strives to become the futuristic metropolis of the Midi; jealous Nîmes bestirs itself to keep pace, looking to Toulouse for inspiration.

An important political event was the election of the Socialist Mitterrand government in 1981, followed by the creation of regional governments across France. Though their powers and budgets are extremely limited, this represented a major turning point, the first reversal of a thousand years of increasing Parisian centralism. Its lasting effects will not be known for decades, perhaps centuries. Already a small revival of Occitan language and culture is resuming; indicators include such things as new school courses in the language, and some towns and villages changing the street signs to Languedocien or Catalan. Roussillon is just beginning to feel the great upsurge of Catalan culture that began after the restoration of democracy in Spain. Political and cultural movements such as the Bloc Català (which in 2006 became the Convergència Démocràtica de Catalonia) have sprung up to reinforce ties with the rest of Catalonia; Occitan and Catalan festivals and events are held throughout the year.

Ironically, Roussillon became something of a stronghold for the Front National. Due mostly to concerns over immigrants, the far-right party grew steadily in southern regions like Languedoc. Many of its voters are former socialists, disgusted by the massive corruption that socialist politicians enjoyed during the Mitterrand years. In France's tightly controlled political system, where the established parties collaborate closely to monopolize power and exclude grass-roots challenges, a vote for Le Pen seemed like the only kind of protest vote available. In 2007, new president

Nicolas Sarkozy, with his centre-right appeal, temporarily drew many of Le Pen's supporters back into the mainstream.

Within the region, the political scene was long dominated by the imposing figure of Georges Frêche, who led his Socialists to control of the regional council in 2004. Frêche's policies of high taxes to promote development schemes showed mixed results, while his flamboyant behaviour and bitter grudge matches with opponents – not to mention a total disdain for political correctness – provided the kind of piquant political theatre Languedociens have always appreciated (*see* **Topics**, pp.46–8).

One of the biggest issues in this region has been the region itself: not only the matter of finding an economic future for it, but discussions over the size and shape, and even the name of it. Paris's bureaucrats made the current 'Languedoc-Roussillon' the queer, artificial two-headed creature it is, and they're content to leave it that way. People on the ground, and many of the politicians, are inclined to tinker. Some grumble that all the money and effort currently goes to aggrandizing Montpellier. They would like to see the region merge with the Midi-Pyrénées, thus restoring the old County of Toulouse with its natural capital. The gentlemen in Paris, who all know their medieval history well, aren't likely to let that happen. The Catalans in Roussillon have been agitating for a one-department region of their own, which would be called 'Catalonia Nord'. Paris doesn't like that one, either.

Georges Frêche had an opinion on this subject too. He liked the region as it is, but wanted to change the name to 'Septimanie', recalling the old Roman province that roughly corresponded to the current one. After a long battle, Frêche had to give up that idea; polls showed that 95 per cent of the prospective Septimanians were dead against it. Twice thrown out of the Socialist Party for making provocative comments about Jews and Muslims in the press, Frêche enjoyed a final triumph by leading his own list of candidates to victory in the elections of 2010. Six months later he died, leaving an enormous vacuum in Languedoc that no one right now looks able to fill. There's a lot to be done. A weak economy, based on little more than tourism, agriculture and the public sector, keeps incomes low and unemployment high by French standards. Social pressures and immigrant problems are on the rise in the big cities. The post-Frêche era is only beginning, and which way it will go is anyone's guess.

Art and Architecture

03

Despite a number of promising starts over the centuries, this has seldom been one of the great regions for art, and a difficult history has ensured that many of its best works were lost. As in so many other things, Languedoc seems doomed always to be overshadowed by its flashier sister across the Rhône, Provence. Nevertheless, there are plenty of monuments and fine museums to see. Great art and architecture native to the region neatly coincides with its two periods of prosperity: the Roman era and the Middle Ages. Real prosperity is coming back once more, and already there are signs that the region may have some surprises for us in the future.

Prehistoric, Celto-Ligurian and Roman

France as a nation is full of Neolithic monuments from the period 5000–1500 BC, but Neolithic Languedociens left few traces of their passing: just dolmens and a few menhirs in the Hérault and Gard. **Cambous**, north of Montpellier, has made a unique attempt to reconstruct life in this era, including a communal Neolithic house, with low walls and a thatched roof that resembles the traditional cowboy dwellings (*cabanes de gardians*) in the Camargue. The Bronze Age peoples who followed left fascinating 'statue-steles' – menhirs with faces – all around the coasts from Languedoc to Tuscany, as well as Corsica. You can see some around **Nîmes** (in the Musée de la Préhistoire) and at **St-Pons** in the Espinouse mountains of Hérault.

The arrival of the Celts around 800 BC coincided with an increase in trade; Greek, Etruscan and Celtic influences can be seen in the artefacts of this age (as at the **Oppidum d'Ensérune** near Béziers). The local Celts had a talent for jewellery, ironwork and sculpture – and the habit of decapitating enemies and carving stone images of warriors clutching their heads. Look for them in the archaeology museum in **Nîmes**.

The Romans brought wealth and urbanization to the region for the first time, with public works such as the great **Pont du Gard**, and a smaller, little-known arcade of an aqueduct at **Ansignan**, west of Perpignan. Nothing but fragments is left of the great capital of 'Gallia Narbonensis', Narbonne, but **Nîmes** retains two of the most spectacular Roman relics outside Italy: the 1st-century BC Maison Carrée, the best-preserved of all ancient temples, and the Arènes, best-preserved of all Roman amphitheatres.

The Dark Ages, and the Romanesque Reawakening

Very few places in France had the resources to create any art at all during this period. The meagre attempts at churches were nearly always rebuilt later; the only things you're likely to see from Merovingian or Carolingian times are crudely carved reliefs and capitals. Many crypts are really the foundations of original Dark Age churches, and sculptural fragments will often be found set in a later church's wall.

When good times returned in the 11th century (in some places a little earlier), people began to build again, inspired by the ancient buildings they saw around them. There is a great stylistic continuity not only from Roman to Romanesque architecture (rounded arches, barrel vaults, rounded apses), but also a wealth of new forms and styles, as well as a rebirth of sculpture.

This region shows several distinct varieties of Romanesque – Provençal, Languedocien and Catalan, along with some imported styles – although the terms must be applied loosely; the enduring charm of Romanesque is in its very lack of restrictions and codes, giving architects the freedom to improvize and solve problems in original, sophisticated ways. Although parish and monastic churches were usually in the basilican form (invented for Roman law courts and used in Rome's first churches), the masons also created extremely esoteric works, often built as funeral chapels in pre-Christian holy sites (see the unique seven-sided church at **Rieux-Minervois** or the triangular one at **Planès** in the Pyrenees). Churches that could double as fortresses were built along the pirate-plagued coast in the 11th and 12th centuries; the basalt parish church at **Agde** is a striking example.

In general, churches in the Rhône valley are more ornate, thanks to a talented group of sculptors known as the **School of Arles**. The wealth of ruins around inspired them to adapt Roman forms and decorations to the new religion, complete with triumphal arches, gabled pediments and Corinthian columns. Some time in the 12th century (exactly when is a matter of dispute), Arlésien artists also created the remarkable façade of **St-Gilles-du-Gard**, portraying the New Testament – the true dogma in stone for all to see, perhaps meant as a refutation of the Cathar and other current heresies.

As you move west through Languedoc, Romanesque becomes more decorative and fanciful, befitting the land of troubadours (**St-Martin-de-Londres** and the frescoed **Chapelle de Centeilles** in the Minervois). Even when the austere Cistercians built here, as at the **Abbaye de Fontfroide** near Narbonne, the mood is much less sombre. Itinerant Lombard masons in the 12th century introduced their own form of Romanesque, characterized by blind arcading and bands of decorative stonework, especially around the apse (as at **St-Guilhem-le-Désert** and **Maguelone**). The Lombard campanile, pierced with patterns of windows, was adapted by the Catalans, especially in the Pyrenees (**Elne**). But **Uzès** has something even rarer in its Tour Fenestrelle: a round, arcaded six-storey campanile, typical of Byzantine Italy.

The **Catalans** produced many fine Romanesque buildings, as well as the finest medieval sculpture in the south. They got a head start on the French with the school of sculptors at the magnificent 11th-century abbey of **St-Michel-de-Cuxa**. Their work is characterized by precise and fanciful detail, arabesques and floral patterns, supremely elegant without the classicizing of the Arles school; more of their best sculpture may be seen at **Serrabonne** and **Elne**, the most beautiful cloister in the Midi. St-Michel itself is one of the great Catalan monuments, with an architecture that shows an intriguing mix of influences that includes the Lombards, Cluny and Muslim Spain. The Pyrenean valley of the **Cerdagne**, the heartland of Catalunya, contains a dozen interesting Romanesque churches in out-of-the-way villages, more than any other region, reflecting its early prosperity.

Catalunya also produced the vigorous and original, sometimes surreal **Master of Cabestany**. Even though his real name is unknown, he is one of the very first medieval artists with a personal style so unique that it can be recognized anywhere. In the early 12th century he even went to Tuscany to teach the Italians how to sculpt (some experts believe he really was an Italian, though others speculate he was a French Cathar). His best works in France are the tympanum at **Cabestany**, at **St-Papoul** (near Castelnaudary), **St-Hilaire-de-l'Aude** and a pair of capitals at **Rieux-Minervois**. Catalans could paint, too, though you will see little of it in Roussillon; there are rare medieval frescoes at **St-Martin-de-Fenollar**, south of Perpignan.

Although examples of medieval palaces still stand in **St-Gilles**, and **Villemagne** in the Hérault, the greatest secular architecture of the period is military, often displaying surprising originality. The vertiginous castle of **Peyrepertuse** is only the most enormous example of the scores of imposing works around the Languedoc and Roussillon border. Saint Louis built the walls and towers of Carcassonne in a romantic fairytale style that has few equals, while the king's other project, **Aigues-Mortes** (1270s), is a grid-planned, square and functional modern town encased in a perfect set of walls.

Gothic, Renaissance and Neoclassical

Though Gothic elements first appeared in Languedoc as early as 1250 (**Abbaye St-Martin-du-Vignogoul**), the ogival vaulting and pointy arches belonged to a foreign, northern style that failed to touch southern hearts. Builders stuck to their Romanesque guns longer than anywhere else in France, and when Gothic made its final triumph it was usually a pale reflection of the soaring cathedrals of the Ile-de-France. There are notable exceptions, all built by northerners: the huge **Abbaye de Valmagne** near Montpellier, or the cathedrals of **Béziers**, **Carcassonne** and especially **Narbonne**, an unfinished, spectacular work that is the third-tallest Gothic church in France.

The Catalans, as ever marching to a different drum, developed their own brand of Gothic, where width and strength counted more than height. The best examples are in **Perpignan**. They also produced one of the greatest architects of the 15th century, **Guillem Sagrera** (d. 1454). Sagrera, born in Majorca, is a one-off, the Frank Lloyd Wright of his day, employing great technical skill in forms and shapes never seen before or since. His greatest works are in Naples and Palma de Mallorca, but he also designed Perpignan's cathedral and the vaulting in its Salle Capitulaire.

Subjugation by the French and in the Wars of Religion made the Renaissance a non-event in Occitania outside Provence. Of painting there is very little, though the Gard shows influences from nearby Avignon and its school of painters; there is a great work of Enguerrand Quarton, the *Couronnement de la Vierge*, in the museum at **Villeneuve lez Avignon.** Architecture largely reflected styles in the north, and the best place to see it is **Pézenas**. From its golden age, when it was home to the Estates-General of Languedoc, this little town made itself a museum of the era's architecture – film directors often use its streets as a set for old Paris.

The French call this, the age of Louis XIV and all the Louis that followed, their *époque classique*, and admittedly even in the poor benighted south many fine things were done. Towns laid out elegant squares, fountains and promenades; trees were planted on a grand scale on market squares, along the Canal du Midi and on the roads, especially in the western Aude, which is crossed with 18th-century avenues of plane trees. **Montpellier** has collections from their thriving faïence industries of the day (as does **Narbonne**'s art museum). Southerners went ape for organs, gargantuan works sheathed in ornate carved wood. The mother of them all is in **Narbonne cathedral**; others adorn the churches in **Béziers** and **Uzès**. Equally elaborate are the retables of many Catalan churches, lofty carved altarpieces that show the influence of the fevered, intricate Churrigueresque style of Spain (**Perpignan** cathedral, **Collioures, Prades**). Some of the best are by the sculptor Joseph Sunyer.

But nearly everything else is all wrong. People took the lovely churches left to them by their ancestors and tinkered so much with the architecture that it's often difficult to tell the real age of anything. New churches tend to be austere and unimpressive, though there are exceptions (the truly florid Baroque of St-Sauveur at **Aniane**). The 17th- and 18th-century *hôtels particuliers* of **Pézenas**, **Uzès** and **Montpellier**, and public buildings such as the 1683 *hôtel de ville* in **Beaucaire**, while lending a distinctive urbanity and ostentation to these cities, are rarely first-rate works of architecture in their own right, but rather eclectic jumbles with touches from Gothic, Renaissance and Baroque style-books. One provincial boy from Roussillon made it big at the court of Versailles in this tepid period: **Hyacinthe Rigaud** (1659–1743). Born in Perpignan, this painter of royal portraits was in great demand for his ability to make his subjects look lofty yet amiable, as well as for his accurate depiction of their clothes (museums in **Perpignan** and **Narbonne**). The most sincere paintings of the age are probably the naïve *ex votos* in many churches (some of the best are from sailors, as at Notre-Dame-des-Auzils, near **Gruissan**).

One architect who never lacked for work was Louis XIV's maréchal **Sébastien Vauban**, whose forts and fortress-towns crop up everywhere; his fortress-town of **Villefranche-de-Conflent** is a perfectly preserved example of 17th-century urban design. Vauban also worked on the Canal du Midi after the death of Paul Riquet, and nearly wrecked Collioure, demolishing much of the town to perfect its fortifications.

The 19th and 20th Centuries

The French Revolution destroyed far more than it built; the wanton devastation of the region's greatest Romanesque art (begun in the Wars of Religion) was a loss matched only by the mania for selling it off in the early 20th century to the Americans – that is what happened to the sculptural work of the abbey of St-Michel-de-Cuxa, now in the Cloisters Museum in New York.

The 19th century, however, would bring a renewal of appreciation of medieval art, as well as the first reaction against the purposeful destruction of the past. The great champion of the Middle Ages, **Viollet-le-Duc** (1814–79), came to Languedoc to restore the walled Cité of **Carcassonne**, and the archbishop's palace of **Narbonne**.

In a great century for French painting, Languedoc and Roussillon contributed only a little. It seemed as if the Rhône had somehow become a barrier to inspiration. While new revolutions in art grew up one after another in the hothouse atmosphere of Provence, very little of it trickled into Languedoc. This, despite the fact that the man who started it all, **Gustave Courbet**, had a wealthy banker of **Montpellier** for a patron. One of the best collections of his works can be seen in that city's Musée Fabre. Courbet's journey to the region in 1854 contributed to the luminosity of his later work. His new style came to be called Realism – almost as if it took the invention of photography by Louis Daguerre (1837) to make the eye see what was 'really' there. 'Do what you see, what you want, what you feel,' was Courbet's proto-hippy advice to his pupils. The lesser-known **Frédéric Bazille** was a native of Montpellier. He met Monet in Paris in 1862 and, with him, was the first to paint the human figure (even nudes) out of doors, inspired by the spontaneity of photography. His career was cut short in the Franco-Prussian war of 1870 (Musée Fabre, **Montpellier**).

Impressionists, like the artists of the movements that followed, came south by the score to paint in the bright skies and dramatic landscapes of Provence. Only one movement, however, had any ties with this region: the group of painters nicknamed the **Fauves** ('wild beasts') for the violence of their colours. The Fauves used colour to interpret, rather than describe, moods and rhythms, to the detriment of perspective and detail and even recognizable subject matter. As a movement the Fauves lasted only from 1904 until 1908, but in those few years they revolutionized centuries of European art. Fauvism came to Roussillon in 1905, when Henri Matisse and André Derain settled at **Collioure** on the Côte Vermeille. None of their works can be seen there today, though Matisse lived for a while in the Roussillon mountain town of **Céret**; so, briefly, did Chagall, Picasso and Salvador Dalí, and works by all of these artists can be seen in the town's small art museum.

Roussillon itself produced a decidedly non-revolutionary sculptor, though he was one of the best-known figures of the early 20th century: **Aristide Maillol**, from Banyuls. Maillol spent much of his career in Paris, though he never forgot his home town, returning each summer to model endless female nudes on the pulchritude of local nymphets (Hôtel de Ville, **Perpignan**; war memorials and museum in **Banyuls**).

Since the Second World War, big government projects promoting tourism and urban renewal have brought a new impetus to architecture in the region. In the 1960s, the national government ordained the creation of two entirely new cities. One, **Cap d'Agde**, was a disappointment, a pastiche of a traditional town centre, surrounded by zones of tired academic planning (though today it is a very popular holiday resort). The other, though sniffed at by highbrow critics, may be one of the real triumphs of French postwar architecture. Work on the resort of **La Grande Motte** began in 1968. The Paris planners entrusted the job to an obscure but very well-connected architect, **Jean Balladur** (his cousin Edouard would later be prime minister). He gave them something startling: a town of glass pyramids by the sea complete with futuristic bridges and public spaces. None of the individual buildings stands out, but the ensemble is a lively, very real community, popular with residents and tourists alike.

Since the 1970s, ambitious mayors in many southern cities have embarked on more grand projects. None has been more ambitious than the late Georges Frêche, the human dynamo who ran **Montpellier** between 1977 and 2004 (*see* **Topics**, pp.46–8). Most of the city's showcase works are middle-of-the-road at best, with the exception of its huge residential quarter called Antigone, designed by the Catalan neoclassicist (some say neo-Stalinist) Ricardo Bofill, begun in 1979. In **Nîmes**, Sir Norman Foster's glass and steel Carré d'Art was also beset by criticism when it opened in May 1993, but his influence has led to a heightened taste for architectural expansion in the region – notably in Montpellier, which has now stretched from Antigone all the way to the river Lez with new projects by the likes of Jean Nouvel and Zaha Hadid to rival Paris in the race as France's most dynamic metropolis of the 21st century.

Topics

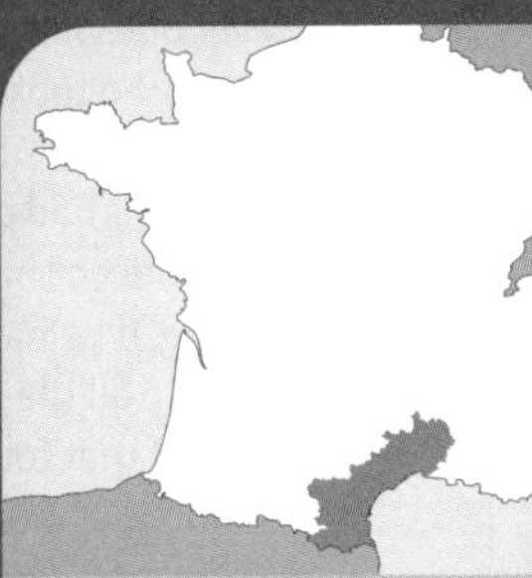

04

Occitans, Catalans and Related Species

The place is Verdun, the date AD 843, and a fellow named Lothair is about to mess up European history for good. The three contentious grandsons of Charlemagne, unable to manage the Carolingian Empire peaceably, were deciding how to carve it up between them. The resulting Treaty of Verdun would be a linguistic landmark – one of the first documents issued in two new-fangled languages later called French and German. It would also determine the future map of Europe. Lothair's brothers were sensible: Louis took the east, the future Germany, and Charles the Bald got the western half, most of what is now France. Lothair must have thought he was the clever one. Besides the imperial title (of dubious value) and the imperial capital, Aachen, he took away the richest lands of the Empire: northern Italy, Provence, Lorraine and Burgundy, along with Switzerland and the Low Countries.

If Lothair had considered what he would be leaving to his descendants, he might have noticed that this random collection of territories could never be held together for long. If he had had any sense of historical necessity, he might have said: 'You two can keep all the northern bits; just let me have what we Franks know as Aquitania, the land that folks in a thousand years are going to call southern France and Catalonia.' It would have made sense even then, a more coherent possession both culturally and politically. In the later Middle Ages, it would have seemed the obvious choice. This is western Europe's nation that never was. It would have been called Languedoc, most likely, as that was the name in the later Middle Ages for the Occitan-speaking lands that stretched from the Atlantic to the Alps. Its capital would probably have been Toulouse. Instead, after the collapse of Lothair's and his brothers' kingdoms, the Occitan-speaking peoples south of the Loire got centuries of balanced feudal anarchy with no real overlord. Real power became fatally divided between two main centres, the County of Toulouse and the Catalan County of Barcelona, later the Kingdom of Aragon.

The Occitans didn't mind; the relative freedom gave them the chance to create their open, advanced civilization of poetry and tolerance, a March crocus heralding the blossoming of medieval Europe. The Catalans learned to sail and trade, and built themselves a maritime empire in the Mediterranean. When they finally combined forces against the invading northerners at the Battle of Muret in 1213, their failure to prevail against a much smaller army doomed the former to a brutal French military conquest followed by the near-extinction of their language and culture. The Catalans, at least those south of the Pyrenees, would later suffer the same fate at the hands of Spain.

The great castles of Languedoc and Roussillon – Quéribus, Carcassonne, Salses and the rest – are the gravestones of the Lost Nation, the sites of defeats that marked its gradual, inexorable assimilation by the power of Paris and the north. Today, if you visit them in the off season, the only other car in the car park will be likely to have a white Spanish tag with a 'B' for Barcelona. You may see the inscrutable Catalans – picnicking in the snow at Peyrepertuse in December, or at Salses furtively taking voluminous notes on the guided tour. Catalans abroad, even when encumbered by children and small dogs, often have the raffish air of spies or infiltrating *provocateurs*; it's part of their charm. Here, they're on a real mission, piecing together the memorials and cultural survivals of a forgotten world – forgotten by everyone else, maybe, but a dream that the Catalans and France's Occitanian malcontents will never let die.

The Cathars

...because we are not of this world, and this world is nought of ours, give us to understand that which Thou understandest, and to love that which Thou lovest.

Cathar prayer

Dualism, as the philosophers call it, has always been with us. The Greek Gnostics saw Good and Evil as contending, independent forces that existed forever. Good resided somewhere beyond the stars; Evil was here and now – in fact creation itself was evil, the work not of God but of a fallen spirit, identifiable with Satan. Our duty on earth was to seek purity by refusing to have anything to do with creation. In the 3rd century AD, a Persian holy man named Mani took up the same theme and made quite a splash, and his teachings spread gradually back into the West, where the earliest Church councils strongly condemned them as the 'Manichaean Heresy'. Among other places, the Manichaeans were active in southern Gaul.

Always present in the Byzantine Empire, Manichaean ideas hit the Balkans in the 9th century; the 'Bogomil' or 'Bulgar' dualists reached a wide following, leaving hundreds of oddly carved crosses as monuments. From there, the idea spread rapidly throughout Europe. The new sect appears in chronicles of the 11th century, variously called Bulgars or Patarenes, Albigensians or Cathars (from a Greek word meaning 'pure'). The Church was not slow to respond. In Italy and northern France the heretics were massacred and burned; in England, apparently, they were only branded with hot irons. In worldly and open Occitania, however, they gained a foothold and kept it. The new faith was popular among peasants, townspeople and even many nobles. Occitan Catharism was organized into a church at a council at St-Félix-de-Caraman in 1167, presided over by a prelate named Nicetas, or Nikita, from Dragovici in the Balkans.

The Cathars probably believed that their faith was a return to the virtue and simplicity of the early Church. Their teaching encouraged complete separation from the Devil's world; feudal oaths, for example, were forbidden, and believers solved differences between themselves by arbitration rather than going to law. Some features were quite modern: Cathars promoted vegetarianism and non-violence, and marriage was by simple agreement, not a sacrament, enhancing the freedom and status of women by doing away with the old Roman paternalist tradition and laws. Two other points made Catharism especially attractive to an increasingly modern society: it had a much more mature attitude towards money and capitalism than the Roman church – no condemnation of loans as usury, and no church tithes. This earned it support in the growing cities; like the later Protestants, many Cathars were involved in the textile trades.

Cathar simplicity and its lack of a big church organization also made a very favourable contrast with the bloated, bullying and thoroughly corrupt machinery of the Church of Rome. Cathars referred to themselves as 'the Good Christians' and believed in the universal salvation of all people. Then there was the rather strange but beguiling belief in an 'ethereal substance' called *partatge*, that included chivalry, honour, joy, the balance of nature, and cosmic order.

Best of all, Catharism had a very forgiving attitude towards sinners. If creation itself was the Devil's work, how could we not err? Cathars were divided into two levels: the mass of simple believers, upon whom the religion was a light yoke indeed – no Mass and few ceremonies, no money-grubbing, easy absolution – and the few *perfecti*, those who had received the sacrament called the *consolament*, and were thenceforth required to lead a totally ascetic life devoted to faith and prayer. Most Cathars conveniently took the *consolament* on their deathbeds.

Catharism was a strong and growing force when the Albigensian Crusade began in 1209; the papacy, the behaviour of which had always been a strong argument for the basic tenet of dualism, saw enough of a threat to its power to require a policy of eradication by death. The terror, enforced by French arms and overseen by the Dominicans and Cistercians, was vicious and successful, a blueprint for all subsequent police states. The climax came in 1244, with the fall of the Cathar holy-of-holies, the temple-fortress at Montségur in the Pyrenees (*département* of Ariège). Cathars who survived the mass exterminations were hunted down ruthlessly by the new Inquisition; Guillaume Bélibaste, the last of the *perfecti*, was burned at Villerouge-Termenès in the Aude in 1321. Nevertheless, doctrines are always more difficult to kill than human beings, and Catharism survived its persecutors in a number of forms, especially in its influence on the later southern Protestants and on the Catholic Jansenists of the 17th century.

There are practising Cathars today, although there are probably fewer actual Cathars than books about them. Catharism did have a strong esoteric tinge to it, reserved for the *perfecti*. In the past few decades, this angle has been explored in every sort of work, from the serious to the inane, speculating on various 'treasures', real or metaphysical, that the last *perfecti* may have hidden, or connecting the sect with other favourite occult themes: the Templars (who in fact were their enemies), the Holy Grail (said to have been kept at Montségur, or perhaps in the holy Catalan mountain of Canigou), the Illuminati and Rosicrucians of the 15th century and onwards, or somehow with the curious doings in Rennes-le-Château (*see* p.214).

Modern-day sympathiser René Nelli and other authors have some provocative things to say about the greatest and most mysterious of all the Arthurian epics, Wolfram von Eschenbach's *Parzifal* – they see the poem as a sweeping Cathar allegory, confirming Montségur as the Grail castle and identifying Parzifal with the Cathars' protector, Raymond Trencavel of Carcassonne. Trencavel's chroniclers also have an uncanny habit of comparing the viscount to Christ, especially after his betrayal and death at the hands of Simon de Montfort; his dynasty, like that of the counts of Toulouse, was quite a vortex for this sort of weirdness. The weirdest of all modern Europe's occultist sects, the Nazis, were obsessed with the Cathars and the legends that have grown up around them. After their occupation of the south in 1942, they sealed off all the important Cathar sites and cave refuges in the Pyrenees, and Nazi high-priest Alfred Rosenberg sent teams of archaeologists to dig them up amidst the utmost secrecy. In 1944, not long before liberation, a group of local Cathars sneaked up to Montségur for an observance to commemorate the

700th anniversary of their forebears' last stand. A small German plane, with a pilot and one passenger, appeared and circled the castle. The Cathars, expecting the police, watched in amazement as the plane, by means of skywriting equipment, traced a strange, eight-branched cross over their heads, and then disappeared beyond the horizon.

Troubadours

Lyric poetry in the modern Western world was born around the year 1095 with the rhymes of Count William (1071–1127), grandfather of Eleanor of Aquitaine. William wrote in the courtly language of Old Provençal (or Occitan), although his subject matter was hardly courtly ('Do you know how many times I screwed them? / One hundred and eighty-eight to be precise; / So much so that I almost broke my girth and harness...'). A descendant of the royal house of Aragon, William had Spanish-Arab blood in his lusty veins and had battled against the Moors in Spain on several occasions, but at the same time he found inspiration (for his form, if not his content) in a civilization that was centuries ahead of Christian Europe in culture.

The word *troubadour* may be derived from the Arabic root for lutenist (*trb*), and the ideal of courtly love makes its first appearance in the writings of the spiritual Islamic Sufis. The Sufis believed that true understanding could not be expressed in doctrines, but could be suggested obliquely in poetry and fables. Much of what they wrote was love poetry addressed to an ideal if unkind and irrational muse, whom the poet hopes will reward his devotion with enlightenment and inspiration. Christians who encountered this poetry in the Crusades converted this ideal muse into the Virgin, giving birth to the great 12th-century cult of Mary. But in Occitania this mystic strain was reinterpreted in a more worldly fashion by troubadours, whose muses became flesh and blood women, although these darlings were equally unattainable in the literary conventions of courtly love. The lady in question could only be addressed by a pseudonym. She had to be married to someone else. The poet's hopeless suit to her hinged not on his rank, but on his virtue and worthiness. The greatest novelty of all was that this love had to go unrequited.

Art songs of courtly love were known as *cansos*, and rarely translate well, as their merit was in the poet's skill in inventing new forms in his rhyming schemes, metres, melodies and images. The troubadours wrote other songs as well, called *sirventes*, which followed established forms but took for their subjects politics, war, miserly patrons and even satires on courtly love itself. The golden age of the troubadours began in the 1150s, when the feudal lords of Occitania warred among each other with so little success that behind the sound and fury the land enjoyed a rare political stability. Courts indulged in new luxuries and the arts flourished, and troubadours found ready audiences, travelling from castle to castle.

Today there is a rival of Occitan song across the south of France that began in the 1980s. Look out for Gérard Zuchetto, who interprets 12th- and 13th-century troubadour songs and founded CREMM Trobar Na Loba de Pennautier, a music research centre near Carcassonne; or for modern troubadour Claude Sicre, traditional singer Renat Jurié and bands such as Eydolon, Peyraguda, Nadau and the neo-traditional Familha Artus.

A Man, a Plan, a Canal

Il faut finir l'ouvrage, ou mourir à la peine.
(Better to die in the process, than to leave this great work unfinished.)
Plaque on the lock-keeper's house, Ecluse de la Criminelle

Languedoc owns its share of the great works of man, enough to delight any engineer on holiday. There's the great Pont du Gard, of course (and another sturdy Roman aqueduct that no one ever sees at the region's opposite end, at Ansignan). In between is something the French, back in the days of Louis XIV, trumpeted as the 'Eighth Wonder of the World'. Today, the Canal du Midi seems more of a decoration than a practical economic asset. Avenues of plane and poplar trees still shade much of its extent, just as they once did along all the great highways of France. Cyclists cruise the old towpaths in summer, stopping to admire the graceful stone bridges and the hand-operated locks of the pre-industrial age. You can hire a boat for a lazy canal tour, and stop for a memorable lunch of *confits de canard* at any of the sweet and drowsy villages that grew up along its landings. There are few better places to be in all of France; time spent on the canal charms the soul. For our enjoyment today, it required only that 12,000 men work for 15 years, and remove 12 million cubic feet of earth and cart it away by hand. And develop a technique for ordering the flow of waters, uphill and down, that no one had ever dreamed possible.

Pierre Paul Riquet, a man of infinite stubbornness, was born in Béziers in 1604. Well connected and wealthy from the start, he managed to land one of the jammiest jobs *ancien régime* France had to offer – tax farmer for Languedoc's salt pans. Taxation in those days was privatized; a tax farmer guaranteed the government an agreed amount of revenue, and was allowed to keep whatever else he could wring out of people and businesses. Forty years of this allowed Riquet to build up quite a fortune, and we can imagine he had plenty of time on his hands. Apparently, he spent much of it dreaming about canals. A presentation he had seen at court as a child left a lasting impression. People had dreamt of cutting through the 'French Isthmus' since Roman times, but no one had ever figured out a way to do it. Gated locks (a medieval contribution, invented independently by the Chinese and the Dutch) would help, but the problem would be keeping the entire system filled with water. Riquet liked to go on long walks up in the wild Montagne Noire, an unusual pastime for a Frenchman of that era. He was probably thinking about his canal all the while. Eventually the idea came to him – build a huge reservoir up here in the mountains, near the watershed, and dig down channels east and west from it to keep the entire waterway full.

Riquet took his plan to Versailles, where it was warmly received by Jean-Baptiste Colbert, Louis XIV's mercantile-minded chief minister. The king was interested too. Connecting the Atlantic and the Mediterranean would save French traders the perils of sailing around hostile Spain, not to mention the Barbary pirates and the pesky English. Even so, it took four years of navigating the treacherous, intrigue-filled waters of the court at Versailles before the king finally gave his assent. The argument was about money. The canal was going to gobble up a lot of it, and Riquet could only seal the bargain by putting up his own great fortune, even his daughters' dowries, for the works. Riquet wasn't entirely mad; in return for his two million *livres* his family would have the right to collect canal tolls in perpetuity.

Work began on the 'Canal Royal des Deux Mers' in 1667. Riquet oversaw the works himself, and his men rewrote the engineering textbooks along the way. The great reservoir, in its day the largest ever built, came first, along with its supply channels. You can visit it today; the Bassin de St-Ferréol now also serves as a popular recreation area, north of Castelnaudary near the town of Revel. That worked fine, but digging the actual canal provided some novel problems too. Beside the little matter of building 130 bridges, 64 locks and an entire town, the canal's Mediterranean terminus of Sète, they had to find a way of keeping the water level on a constant slope over 240km. When it became apparent that the canal would cause flooding in its surrounding villages after heavy rains, just as a river does, they had to design a system of channels to carry off excess water.

That was only one of their firsts. Riquet couldn't find a way around the great hill at Ensérune, near Béziers, so he dug 173m through it, creating the world's first canal tunnel. A canal of any length has to cross streams and even rivers. Usually, the problem could be solved by turning it into the natural waterway by means of a lock, following its course for a while, and then using another lock to get it out again. One little river, near the village of Paraza, could not be crossed in this way, and here Riquet produced his greatest trick, the first canal bridge, the Pont-canal de Répudre. Running one waterway over another one so astonished the French that, for some years after the opening of the canal, passenger boats would stop and let everyone off to admire it. Riquet's children installed a plaque over the central arch, weathered though still readable today, to remind people that it was their father's invention.

Riquet was equally ahead of his time in the way he treated his labourers. Like Henry Ford, he startled his contemporaries by paying them twice the going wage – 20 *livres* a month. Furious protests from the region's landowners reached the ear of King Louis, claiming that now their men wanted higher wages too, and Riquet was soon forced to cut his down to 12 *livres*. Still, he didn't deduct for holidays or rainy days. He also provided subsidized housing and other benefits. French historians sometimes give him credit for inventing the welfare state, 200 years ahead of its time.

But social welfare and engineering advances were only the means to an end. All Riquet cared about was building his canal. He didn't live to see it, dying in October 1680, with slightly over a mile left to go. The part he almost completed was in truth only half of the original plan, between Toulouse and the Mediterranean. But it gave a big economic boost to that city, which erected a statue in his honour, and later on it made possible the textile and other industries in the Haut-Languedoc. His family didn't fare so well. Riquet ran up such enormous personal debts to speed along the construction that his descendants didn't get to keep a penny of the tolls for themselves until 1724.

Without Riquet to push things through, the rest of the original plan, the Canal Latéral de la Garonne that linked Toulouse to the Atlantic, wasn't completed until 1830. For a while, the canal would be the great highway of the southwest, the centre of its economic life. The landings that Riquet placed along its length for rest stops grew into villages. 1856 proved to be its record year, when it carried 110 million tons of goods and 100,000 passengers. But it would soon suffer the fate that awaited all the old canals. The very next year, the railroad men completed the Chemin de Fer du Midi from Bordeaux to Sète. When the Riquets lowered the tolls to compete, the railroad simply bought the canal from them to avoid the threat. Some commercial traffic continued to use the canal, though it had become a relic – motor transport didn't replace mule teams until the 1930s. The last commercial boat finally retired in 1979.

Paul Riquet never dreamed his great work would end up as nothing more than a tourist attraction. But his canal survives also to remind us of a truth about real building. Almost everything along its length is both functional and beautiful, built on a human scale. Utility and aesthetics combine in endless ways – the 45,000 mostly plane trees that line the canal were planted not for decoration, but to hold the soil along its banks. A modern engineer would probably just line them with concrete. Behind it all is a way of thinking we have lost, a natural instinct for fitness and rightness. Imagine if we could bring back Riquet and his men today to design a motorway, with all its interchanges, overpasses and rest stops.

Beyond that, while you are lazing down the canal on your *péniche*, you might also reflect that something rather important happened here. Paul Riquet, this provincial contemporary of Newton and Descartes, pulled off an impressive job. The very scale of it, along with the technical precision and capacity for innovation, the can-do spirit and the vast mobilization of men and machines, were all something new in his day. Like the first printing presses, or the voyages of discovery to distant lands, or the beginnings of the Industrial Revolution, Paul Riquet's canal was a major step towards a new world, the world we know today.

The Best Political Show in France

He was an enormous man, both in height and girth, a man full of life. You wouldn't have missed him in a crowd, with his owlish glasses and electrified shock of hair, and crowds were exactly where Georges Frêche liked to be. The socialist mayor of Montpellier from 1977 to 2004, Frêche presided over its remarkable transformation into one of the most vibrant and fastest-growing cities in France, while still finding time to teach a full schedule of courses on the history of law at the university. No mayor in France ever presided over such a gargantuan building programme: shopping malls, convention halls and cultural institutions, governmental palaces and a middle-income housing project called 'Antigone' that looks like Versailles on steroids.

To accompany it, Frêche created an equally gargantuan public relations machine that embarrassed many of the French. In truth, it would have embarrassed P.T. Barnum. New slogans were churned out on an annual basis, most memorably *Montpellier le surdoué* (the 'specially gifted'). Frêche was big on mascots, too. All his projects seem to have one; the new tramway's was a sort of pink panther. Meanwhile the government painted giant blue Ms all over town to remind citizens of their imperial destiny.

With all the hoopla, it would be understandable that a fellow like Frêche might arouse some controversy. In fact, for decades the flamboyant Frêche put on the most uproarious political theatre in France, and nothing on the agenda was ever a bigger issue than the man himself. Frêche often compared himself to the Medici of Florence or (with an eye to the local Muslim vote) the Caliphs of Córdoba. Opponents called him 'Ramses II', among other things; one of them likened him to a 'tyrannosaurus' who gobbled up first Montpellier, and then all of Languedoc.

Frêche started out as a Maoist, and anyone who ever crossed him would tell you he carried over some old totalitarian attitudes into his later career. Anyone who disagreed with him, whether intellectuals or associations of cyclists, got covered in vituperation and then methodically squashed. Unlike most high-profile French mayors, Frêche was never given a seat in the cabinet. He was far too outspoken for that, and perhaps too contemptuous of what he called the 'Caviar Left'. François Mitterrand himself put the kibosh on his national aspirations. He once publicly called Frêche a 'traitor to his party' – it isn't clear whether the old scoundrel couldn't tolerate an uncorrupted politician, or just couldn't stand Georges Frêche.

While the fur was flying, all was not necessarily rosy in the Specially Gifted City. The rates of crime and taxes ballooned to become among the highest in France. Frêche's economic promotion efforts attracted some big firms, such as IBM, though unemployment remained significantly higher than the national average. Montpellier has made a big gamble on its incubator for new technology businesses, the Centre Européen d'Entreprises et d'Innovation. Scores of small start-up firms have already appeared from its research, but it's still too early to tell whether many will really grow.

In the long run, though, the worst of the city's problems may be Ramses' monumental works. France, to put it charitably, is not a country where urban design flourishes; other ambitious cities such as Toulouse and Grenoble have already built futuristic grand developments they now heartily regret. In a time when planners around the world have finally come to realize that mixing land uses is the right way to create lively, successful neighbourhoods, Montpellier planners still file everything into separate pigeonholes: one zone for residences, another for government offices, another for green space, another for shopping and entertainment. If they have a vision at all, it would be something like Milton Keynes.

There was a strange American streak in the works of the former Maoist. One of Frêche's biggest projects was France's answer to Minnesota's Mall of America: 'Odysseum', a giant suburban shopping mall and retail power centre with cinemas, a skating rink, planetarium, bowling alley and spa, surrounded by a sea of car parks. Many people in Montpellier fought it for a decade, and now they worry it is sucking all the life out of the rest of the city.

In his later years, Frêche moved on to even bigger things. In 2004 he led the socialists in capturing the Languedoc-Roussillon regional council, for the first time in 18 years. As president of the Regional Council of Languedoc-Roussillon and the Community of the Agglomeration of Montpellier, he immediately proposed raising taxes by 52 per cent. The then interior minister Nicolas Sarkozy acerbically awarded him the 'National Grand Prize for Taxation' (for his part, Frêche once called Sarkozy a 'pansy in platform shoes').

Frêche's presence in the grandiose new Hôtel de Région in Montpellier made the regional political circus more fun than ever. He called the Harkis, Algerians who fought to support French rule in the 1950s, 'sub-humans', and earned a big fine in court for it. Most recently, in 2007 he was booted out of his own Socialist Party for complaining that the national soccer team had too many black players. (On the other hand, he once mystified reporters by lecturing them on how the Senegalese were 'more French' than the Bretons.)

Frêche wasn't the only bad cat in the ring. His conservative nemesis, who ran the region all those years with the help of the Front National, was the Union pour un Mouvement Populaire (UMP)'s MP Jacques Blanc, a neuropsychologist who enjoyed psychoanalyzing Frêche before the cameras. He called him the most difficult pathological case history he had ever encountered. Blanc claims he only played footsie with the FN for so long because he 'couldn't let such a brute have so much power'.

Another political enemy was Jean-Paul Fournier, the mayor of Montpellier's arch-rival Nîmes. In 2001 Fournier took over the city from Jean Bousquet, CEO of Cacharel, who had run the city deep into debt trying to keep up with Frêche. In 1950, Nîmes was bigger than Montpellier; now it has slipped far behind. Fournier credits the problem to its not being the regional capital, to the lack of an important university, and to the city's old habit of electing Communist mayors. Nîmes realizes now that it doesn't need to build megaprojects. Montpellier can have the temporary fizz, and the debt; Nîmes has charm and a sense of place. In truth, the cities' destinies are too close together to fight; underneath the gaudy headlines, they have to work closely together on such issues as economic strategy, a common airport and a common TGV terminal.

In his last years, Frêche may have met his match in the Catalans – specifically in the nationalist party in Roussillon, the Convergència Démocràtica de Catalunya (formerly called Bloc Català). What riled the Catalans most was Frêche's ill-fated plan to change the name of the region to 'Septimanie', thus erasing Roussillon's identity. They put up posters screaming 'No to Septicemia!', and referred to Frêche and his allies as 'Septimaniacs'. To make it worse, Frêche made the unforgivable gaffe of suggesting that the Catalan language was only a *patois*. The then Bloc Català's activists cornered him soon after, at the opening of a new school in Perpignan, and forced him to admit Catalan was really a language after all. 'Now can you say a few words in Catalan for us?' they asked politely. Frêche replied '*Bon dia!*', and went home to Montpellier.

Frêche went out with a bang. After he made a tasteless crack about political rival Laurent Fabius's nose (he's Jewish), the party tried to run a substitute list against him in Languedoc for the 2010 elections. The old fox enjoyed going completely over the top, accusing the Socialists of being an 'anti-bigot, anti-alcoholic, anti-smoking, anti-racist, pro-homosexual, pro-black, pro-white, pro-yellow, pro-Jewish, pro-Muslim, pro-garden gnome, anti-pitbull, anti-unhappiness, anti-vulgar' party drowning in political correctness. His rebel slate romped home to victory, and he died six months later, still on top. Now that he's gone, Languedoc's political sphere is going to be a sadder and duller place.

Food and Drink

05

Twenty cooks could make a living here, but a bookseller would starve to death.
Jean Racine, in a letter from Uzès in the 1670s

With sea on one side and mountains on the other, Languedoc-Roussillon is rich in quality local ingredients: seafood and shellfish, lamb and duck, mushrooms, truffles and herbs, fruit and vegetables, often within plucking distance of the table: even if you aren't self-catering, don't miss the chance to visit a market to get a sense of all the region has to offer – the groaning stalls of asparagus, tomatoes, cherries, apricots, peaches, figs, onions (the region is famous for sweet ones), olives and all kinds of honey. Wedged between Provence, southwest France and Catalonia, its traditional cuisine shows influences from all three, although centuries of poverty made it something of a culinary backwater filled with mediocre restaurants. Now Michelin stars twinkle over the land, as Languedoc-Roussillon finds a new role as a gourmet destination, with food to match the growing reputation of its wines.

Restaurant Basics

Restaurants generally serve between 12 noon and 2pm and in the evening from 7 to 10pm, with later summer hours; *brasseries* in the cities generally stay open continuously. Most offer a choice of set-price menus, with good-value weekday lunch menus, which are an economical way to experience some of the finer gourmet temples. Some of these also offer a set-price gourmet *menu dégustation* – a selection of chef's specialities, which can be a great treat. At the humbler end of the scale, bars and brasseries often serve a simple *plat du jour* (daily special) and the no-choice *formule*, which is more often than not steak and *frites*. Eating *à la carte* anywhere will always be more expensive.

Menus sometimes include the house wine (*vin compris*), which is usually very acceptable. If you choose a better wine, expect a big mark-up; the French wouldn't dream of a meal without wine, and the arrangement is a simple device to make food prices seem lower. Service is nearly always included in the final tab; if not it will say *service non compris* or *s.n.c.*

Vegetarians usually have a hard time in France, especially if they don't eat fish or eggs, but most establishments will try to accommodate them. Don't overlook hotel restaurants, some of which are absolutely top notch. To avoid disappointment, always book a table, especially in the evening.

The Cuisine of Languedoc and Roussillon

They have an expression here, *manjar fòrça estofat* (to eat lots of stew), which describes a masochist or someone who suffers martyrdom without complaint. Only 20 years ago, a food critic could refer to this region as France's 'culinary desert'. It was unkind at the time, though not *entirely* unkind; we remember that stew all too well. They used to say the same things about Spain. But, as in Spain, increasing prosperity and tourism, and a renewed pride in the country and its traditions, has brought about a revolution here.

There have always been several gustatory divides ambling irregularly through this region. In the Gard close to the Rhône, you'll find dishes similar to those in neighbouring Provence. From upper Languedoc around Carcassonne and Castelnaudary, it's the good hearty food of the southwest: duck and beans, roast and grilled meats, *foie gras*, *cèpes*, occasionally truffles, and everything else that makes one walk away from the table slowly. In Roussillon, it's Catalan, another world altogether. There's a trend towards the mashing together of all styles of Mediterranean cooking these days, and in restaurants you'll often be treated to something that seems a creative *mélange* of all three, both in the cities and in the hotel restaurants in villages, taken over by talented young chefs.

In the east, fish soups such as *bouillabaisse* are popular, although here they may call it a *bourride*, and throw in tomatoes, ham and leeks. Along with it goes the familiar Provençal *aïoli* (or *aïllade*), garlic mayonnaise, often flavoured with cayenne pepper, to make *rouille* – which is even better. There's also *bourboulhade*, a kind of poor man's *bouillabaisse* made of salt cod and garlic, or yet another 'B' soup, *boullinade*, a thicker fish soup made with Banyuls wine. Ever since the Middle Ages, Nîmes has been known for *brandade de morue*, salt cod puréed with garlic, olive oil and milk, and for its olives and *tapenades* (olive and garlic pastes, served on toast or as a dip) from the olives grown around Uzès. In winter, the same area is famous for its black truffles; you can also find them in the northern Aude and Hérault. The Cévennes (and the Cerdagne in Roussillon) are reputed for their *charcuterie*.

Sète, France's biggest Mediterranean fishing port, is famous for seafood (notably sea bass, tuna and sardines), while shellfish is cultivated in the Etang de Thau (where oyster lovers can feast on the famous *huitres de Bouzigues*). The area also specializes in *seiches farcies*, cuttlefish stuffed with the meat of its tentacles mixed with sausage, and *langouste à la Sètoise*, crayfish with cognac, tomatoes and garlic, not to mention the *tielle Sètoise*, the little seafood pie that has become a favourite across much of France.

Land dishes you may encounter include beef from the Camargue, often in a rich stew called a *gardiane de taureau* with olives, garlic, red wine and vegetables. Lamb is one of the most popular staples, especially in the mountains, along with wild boar and venison in winter and spring; there'll always be plenty of *cèpes* and other wild mushrooms in the autumn. *Escargots*, or snails, come at you in all directions, with anchovies, as in Nîmes, or grilled (*cargolade*); Catalans are particularly fond of them. Some special dishes to look out for are *mourtayrol*, a delicious chicken *pot-au-feu* flavoured with saffron, and *rouzoles*, crêpes filled with ham and bacon. When the cheese platter comes around, it may have *pelardons*, the favourite goat's cheese from the Cévennes. There's a fondness for such exotic aromas as saffron, cinnamon and almond paste, which may well date back to the long-ago times when the Arabs ruled here (they also introduced oranges and lemons). In Pézenas, the special dish is called *petits pâtés de Pézenas*, little spool-shaped pies stuffed with lamb and raisins. This speciality comes from India, courtesy of Lord Clive, a former royal governor who spent time here in the 18th century with his cook.

Throughout this rustic region, there's also a rich tradition of what the Italians call *cucina povera*: up in the mountains, this includes *soupe de châtaignes* (chestnut soup), or a *potée cévenole* with pork, bacon and cabbage, or *aligot*, a big hot, fragrant mess of cheese, cream, garlic and mashed potatoes. A *rousole* is the traditional omelette of the Aude, an area that also makes cornbread (*millas*).

Towards Castelnaudary, that eternal baked bean dish *cassoulet* (*see* pp.207–8), with sausage, garlic and duck or goose, remains the king of the Languedocien table, along with regional variations like the *fricassée* of Limoux. In western Languedoc there's plenty of duck – fatted duck, the ones from which *foie gras* is made. Usually it comes in the form of a *confit* (cooked and preserved in its own fat – much better than it sounds), or a *magret*, a grilled duck breast which can be better than a steak.

In Catalan Roussillon, the totem fish is the little anchovy of Collioure, which hardy souls from Spain to Marseille pulverize with garlic, onion, basil and oil to make *anchoïade*, a favourite *apéritif* spread on toast. You'll also find them served with strips of red pepper. A popular starter is *gambas à la planxa*, prawns grilled and served on a 'plank', or *ollada*, a hearty soup made with pork. Main courses include *roussillonnade*, a dish of *bolet* mushrooms and sausages grilled over a pine-cone fire, and *boles de Picolat*, Catalan meatballs with mushrooms cooked in sauce. The classic dessert is *crème catalane*, a caramel-covered baked cream flavoured with anise and cinnamon.

Drink

You can order any kind of drink at any bar or café – except cocktails, unless it has a certain cosmopolitan *savoir-faire* or stays open into the night. Cafés are also a home from home, a place to read the papers, meet friends and watch the world go by. You can spend hours over a coffee and no one will hurry you. Prices are listed on the *tarif des consommations*: note they are more expensive depending on whether you're served at the bar (*comptoir*), at a table (*la salle*) or outside (*la terrasse*).

French **coffee** is strong and black, but lacklustre next to the aromatic brews of Italy or Spain. If you order *un café* you'll get a small black *express* (espresso); if you want milk, order *un crème*. If you want more than a few drops of caffeine, ask them to make it *grand*. For decaffeinated, the word is *déca*. Some bars offer cappuccinos; in the summer try a *frappé* (iced coffee). The French only order *café au lait* (a small coffee topped off with lots of hot milk) when they stop in for breakfast, and if what your hotel offers is expensive or boring, consider joining them; many bars also have croissants in the morning. *Chocolat chaud* (**hot chocolate**) is usually good; if you order *thé* (**tea**), you'll get an ordinary bag and the water will be hot rather than boiling. An *infusion* is a **herbal tea**, good for the digestion – *camomille*, *menthe* (mint), *tilleul* (linden blossom), or *verveine* (verbena).

Mineral water (*eau minérale*) comes either sparkling (*gazeuse* or *pétillante*), as the region's Perrier, or still (*non-gazeuse*). The usual international corporate **soft drinks** are available, and all kinds of bottled fruit juices (*jus de fruits*). Some bars also do fresh lemon and orange juices (*citron pressé* or *orange pressée*, served with a separate *carafe d'eau* to dilute to taste). The French are also fond of fruit syrups – red *grenadine* and ghastly green *menthe*. If you like mint but not so sweet, try a refreshing sparkling Riqlès.

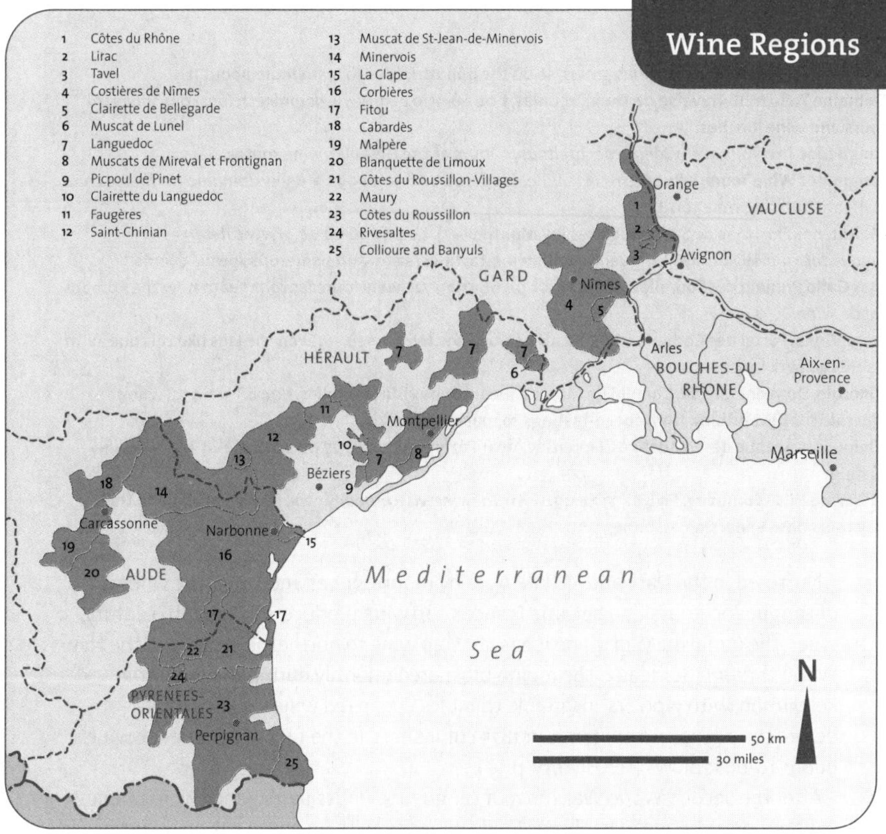

Beer (*bière*) in most bars and cafés is run-of-the-mill big brands from Alsace, Germany and Belgium. Draft (*à la pression*) is cheaper than bottled beer.

The strong spirit of the Midi comes in a liquid form called ***pastis***, first made popular in Marseille as a plague remedy; its name comes from the Latin *passe-sitis*, or thirst-quencher. A pale yellow 90 per cent nectar flavoured with anise, vanilla and cinnamon, *pastis* is drunk as an *apéritif* before lunch and in rounds after work; most people drink their '*pastaga*' with lots of water and ice (*glaçons*), which makes it almost palatable. Popular ***apéritifs*** from Languedoc-Roussillon include Noilly Prat vermouth for your martini and Byrrh 'from the world's largest barrel', a sweet wine mixed with quinine and orange peel, similar to Dubonnet.

Wine

The south holds a special place in the saga of French wines, with a tradition dating back to the Greeks, who first introduced grapes to their coastal colonies. Later, amphorae full of wine sent back to Rome met with such fervent demands for more that the wine-makers back in Italy went to court to curtail the competition – history's first round of the great French–Italian wine battle. The Gauls won this one, perhaps because they hired the oratory of Cicero.

Wine Tourism

As interest in the region's wines grows, so do the opportunities to learn more about it.

Domaine Treloar, 16 Traverse de Thuir, Trouillas, **t** 04 68 95 02 29, *www.domainetreloar.com*. Vineyard tours and wine lunches.

Languedoc Taxi Tour, *www.languedoctaxitour.fr*. Tours of the Hérault's wine routes.

Languedoc Wine Tours, 8 Rue Derrière la Ville, Faugères, **t** 06 50 61 99 03, *www.domaine-de-fraisse.com*. Half- and full-day wine tours.

Maison des Fins, Mas de Saporta, Lattes (by Montpellier), **t** 04 67 06 04 44, *www.coteaux-languedoc.com*. HQ of AOC Languedoc, with wine-tastings, sales, and numerous special events.

Mas Gallo Romain des Tourelles, Beaucaire, **t** 04 66 59 19 72, *www.tourelles.com*. Learn how the Romans made wine.

Terra Vinea, Portel des Corbières, **t** 04 68 48 64 90, *www.terra-vinea.eu*. Even the kids like this one, with its theme park touches.

Vinécole, Domaine Gayda, Chemin de Moscou (near Limoux), Brugairolles, **t** 04 68 31 64 14, *www.vinecole.com*. Everything from speed-tastings to masterclasses.

Vinipolis, 5 Avenue des Vendanges, Florensac (near Pézenas), **t** 04 67 77 00 20. State-of-the-art wine-tasting.

The Wine Wise Company, **t** 06 42 33 34 09, *www.thewinewisecompany.com*. Day, weekend and three-day tours based near Carcassonne.

Nurtured in the Dark and Middle Ages by monks, popes and kings, the vineyards of Languedoc-Roussillon became France's top wine producers in the 18th century, when the Canal du Midi made it easy to ship wine to northern Europe and the New World through Bordeaux. The region prospered mightily during the Industrial Revolution, with workers' insatiable thirst for cheap red wine – *le gros rouge* – before the phylloxera epidemic in 1875 cut it short, in the first of Languedoc wine's boom-to-bust blows (*see* **History**, p.30).

After the Second World War, most of Languedoc-Roussillon's wines were tannic, fruitless, and vinified in badly equipped wineries, with an emphasis on quantity. Old wine-makers believed that they hadn't quite the right soil and climate to compete with Bordeaux and Burgundy, and the region's poverty left small growers unable to keep up with advancing techniques. So Languedoc, the most productive wine region in France, got to be France's land of plonk.

Beginning in the 1970s, however, things began to change. New faces have appeared on the scene, convinced that the region, with its extraordinary patchwork quilt of soils, exposures, sun, heat and wind, ranging from lush valleys to arid rocky *garrigue*, can make great wines after all, and they've backed up that belief by producing countless new, distinctive estate-bottled wines; even once-stodgy wine co-operatives, long the backbone of the region, have become dynamos of innovation and started to win awards. The critics are impressed; some have called Languedoc the 'most exciting new wine district in France'. The reds in particular, blended mainly from grenache noir, cinsault and syrah, are extraordinary, powerful, fruity and packed full of character or *terroir* well able to rival Bordeaux, but costing a fraction of Bordeaux prices.

Today the region produces some 7.7 million hectolitres, in 24 AOC denominations, many overlapping and confusing, even to the French. In order to help simplify matters, the Conseil Interprofessional des Vins du Languedoc (CIVL) has divided the wines into four main groupings covering 61 different areas, all marketed under the new pan-Languedoc-Roussillon label **Sud de France**: **AOC Languedoc** (*www.languedoc-wines.com*), **AOC Roussillon** (*www.vinsduroussillon.com*), **Vin de Pays d'Oc IGP** (*www.vindepaysdoc. com*), and **Vin de Pays Languedoc-Roussillon**. Don't make the mistake of thinking that the *vin de pays* designation in Languedoc means the wines are in any way inferior: because it allows innovative winemakers to experiment, it yields some of the finest wines of all – the *vin de pays de* **Daumas Gassac has** become a legend (*see* p.157). The Gard, home to Tavel (the first rosé), shares the **Côtes du Rhône** *appellation* with other regions along the big river (*www.vins-rhone.com*).

Information on the different wines can be found throughout this book. The Hérault still makes more wine than any other department in France, much of it **AOC Languedoc** (formerly Coteaux du Languedoc) along with the *vins de pays* that have generated so much excitement of late. The same is true for the smaller varieties up in the hills, including **Pic Saint-Loup**, **Faugères**, **St-Chinian**, **Cabardès** (one of the newest) and **Fitou**, Languedoc's oldest AOC wine in the region (and a favourite of Louis XIV). The Aude, the land of Corbières, is also famous for the world's first 'champagne', **Blaquette de Limoux**, and its **chardonnays**. Roussillon, always known for naturally sweet dessert wines (*vins doux naturels*, or VDNs) such as **Banyuls, Maury** and **Rivesaltes**, has been turning heads with its newly improved non-sweet wines.

French Menu Reader

Poissons et Coquillages (Crustacés) (Fish and Shellfish)

aiglefin little haddock
anchois anchovies
anguille eel
bar sea bass
barbue brill
bulot whelk
cabillaud cod
calamar squid
carrelet plaice
colin hake
congre conger eel
coques cockles
coquillages shellfish
coquilles St-Jacques scallops
crabe crab
crevettes grises shrimps
crevettes roses prawns
cuisses de grenouilles frogs' legs
darne slice or steak of fish
daurade sea bream
écrevisse freshwater crayfish
escargots snails
espadon swordfish
fruits de mer seafood
gambas giant prawns
hareng herring
homard lobster
huîtres oysters
langouste spiny Mediterranean lobster
langoustines Dublin Bay prawns (scampi)
limande lemon sole
lotte monkfish
loup (de mer) sea bass
maquereau mackerel
merlan whiting
morue salt cod
moules mussels
oursin sea urchin
palourdes clams
poulpe octopus
praires small clams
raie skate
rascasse scorpion fish
rouget red mullet
St-Pierre John Dory
saumon salmon
sole sole
telline tiny clam
thon tuna
truite trout

Viandes et Volailles (Meat and Poultry)

agneau lamb
ailerons chicken wings
andouillette chitterling (tripe) sausage
biftek beefsteak

blanc breast or white meat
bœuf beef
boudin black pudding
brochette meat (or fish) on a skewer
caille quail
canard, caneton duck, duckling
carré crown roast
cassoulet haricot bean stew with sausage, duck, goose, etc.
cervelle brains
chair flesh, meat
cheval horsemeat
civet meat (usually game) stew, in wine and blood sauce
cœur heart
confit meat cooked and preserved in its own fat
côte, côtelette chop, cutlet
cuisse thigh or leg
dinde, dindon turkey
entrecôte ribsteak
épaule shoulder
faux-filet sirloin
foie liver
gésier gizzard
gibier game
gigot leg of lamb
graisse, gras fat
grillade grilled meat, often a mixed grill
jambon ham
jarret knuckle
langue tongue
lapereau young rabbit
lapin rabbit
lard, lardons bacon, diced bacon
lièvre hare
magret breast of duck
manchons duck or goose wings
marcassin young wild boar
merguez spicy red sausage
moelle bone marrow
noix de veau topside of veal
oie goose
os bone
perdreau, perdrix partridge
petit salé salt pork
pieds trotters
pintade guinea fowl
plat-de-côtes short ribs or rib chops
porc pork
poulet chicken
queue de bœuf oxtail
ris (de veau) sweetbreads (veal)
rognons kidneys
rosbif roast beef
rôti roast
sanglier wild boar
saucisses sausages
selle (d'agneau) saddle (of lamb)
taureau bull meat
tête (de veau) calf's head, fatty and usually served in vinaigrette
tournedos thick round slices of beef fillet
veau veal
venaison venison

Légumes, Herbes, etc. (Vegetables, Herbs, etc.)

ail garlic
aïoli garlic mayonnaise
aneth dill
artichaut artichoke
asperges asparagus
aubergine aubergine (eggplant)
avocat avocado
basilic basil
betterave beetroot (beet)
blette Swiss chard
céleri celery
céleri-rave celeriac
cèpes ceps, wild boletus mushrooms
champignons mushrooms
chanterelles wild yellow mushrooms
chicorée curly endive (US chicory)
chou cabbage
choucroute sauerkraut
chou-fleur cauliflower
choux de bruxelles Brussels sprouts
ciboulette chives
citrouille pumpkin
clou de girofle clove
concombre cucumber
cornichons gherkins
courgettes courgettes (zucchini)
cresson watercress
échalote shallot
endive chicory (endive)
épinards spinach
estragon tarragon
fenouil fennel
fèves broad (fava) beans
flageolets white beans
fleurs de courgette courgette blossoms
frites chips (French fries)
genièvre juniper
gingembre ginger
haricots blancs white beans
haricots rouges kidney beans
haricots verts green (French) beans
laitue lettuce
lentilles lentils
marjolaine marjoram
menthe mint
mesclun salad of various leaves
morilles morel mushrooms
moutarde mustard
navet turnip
oignons onions

oseille sorrel
panais parsnip
persil parsley
petits pois peas
piment chilli peppers
poireaux leeks
pois chiches chickpeas (garbanzo beans)
poivron sweet pepper
pomme de terre potato
potiron pumpkin
radis radishes
riz rice
romarin rosemary
roquette rocket
safran saffron
sauge sage
thym thyme
truffes truffles

Fruits et Noix (Fruit and Nuts)

abricot apricot
amandes almonds
ananas pineapple
banane banana
cassis blackcurrant
cerise cherry
citron lemon
citron vert lime
fraises (des bois) strawberries (wild)
framboises raspberries
fruit de la passion passion fruit
grenade pomegranate
groseilles redcurrants
mandarine tangerine
mangue mango
marrons chestnuts
mirabelles mirabelle plums
mûre (sauvage) mulberry, blackberry
myrtilles bilberries
noisette hazelnut
noix walnuts
noix de cajou cashews
noix de coco coconut
pamplemousse grapefruit
pastèque watermelon
pêche, pêche blanche peach, white peach
pignons pine nuts
pistache pistachio
poire pear
pomme apple
prune plum
pruneau prune
raisins, raisins secs grapes, raisins
reine-claude greengage plums

Desserts

Bavarois mousse or custard in a mould
charlotte sponge fingers and custard cream dessert
clafoutis fruit baked in batter
coulis thick fruit sauce
coupe ice cream: a scoop or in cup
crème anglaise egg custard
crème caramel vanilla custard with caramel sauce
crème Chantilly sweet whipped cream
crème fraîche slightly sour cream
gâteau cake
gaufre waffle
génoise rich sponge cake
glace ice cream
macarons macaroons
miel honey
mignardise same as *petits fours*
parfait frozen mousse
sablé shortbread
yaourt yoghurt

Fromage (Cheese)

chèvre goat's cheese
doux/fort mild/strong
fromage de brebis sheep's cheese
plateau de fromage cheese (board)

Cooking Terms and Sauces

bien cuit well-done steak
à point medium steak
saignant rare steak
bleu very rare steak
aigre-doux sweet and sour
aiguillette thin slice
à la provençale cooked with tomatoes, garlic and olive oil
au feu de bois cooked over a wood fire
au four baked
broche roasted on a spit
chaud hot
congelé frozen
cru raw
émincé thinly sliced
en croûte cooked in a pastry crust
en papillote baked in buttered paper
épices spices
farci stuffed
feuilleté flaky pastry
flambé set aflame with alcohol
forestière with bacon and mushrooms
frais, fraîche fresh
frappé with crushed ice
frit fried
froid cold
fumé smoked
garni with vegetables
pané breaded
pâte pastry, pasta
paupiette thin slices of fish or meat, filled and rolled
pavé slab

piquant spicy hot
salé salted
sucré sweet
tranche slice
vapeur steamed

Miscellaneous

addition bill (check)
beurre butter
carte non-set menu
confiture jam
couteau knife
cuillère spoon
formule set menu
fourchette fork
fromage cheese
huile (d'olive) (olive) oil
menu set menu
pain bread
œufs eggs
poivre pepper
sel salt
service compris/non compris service included/not included
sucre sugar
vinaigre vinegar

Boissons (Drinks)

bière (pression) (draught) beer
café coffee
café au lait white coffee
café express *espresso* coffee
chocolat chaud hot chocolate
eau (minérale, non-gazeuse ou gazeuse) water (mineral, still or sparkling)
glaçons ice cubes
infusion or ***tisane*** herbal tea
jus juice
lait milk
pastis anis liqueur
pichet carafe
pression draught
thé tea
verre glass

Planning Your Trip

06

When to Go

Climate

Languedoc-Roussillon has a basically Mediterranean climate, one wafted by **winds** that give it a special character. The most notorious is the *mistral* (from the Provençal *mistrau*, or master – supposedly sent by northerners jealous of the south's climate), rushing down the Rhône and gusting west as far as Narbonne. On average the *mistral* blows 100–150 days a year, nearly always in multiples of three, except when it begins at night. It is responsible for the dryness in the air and soil (hence its nickname, *mangio fango*, or mud-eater). Besides the Master, there are 22 other winds, most importantly: the *levant*, the east or southeasterly 'Greek' wind, which brings the much desired rain; the *pounent*, or west wind; and the suffocatingly hot *sirocco* from Africa. The region from the Spanish border to Montpellier is occasionally bulldozed by the *tramontane*, the 'Catalan wind' from the northwest; heading west, it's the *autan* wind that sweeps across the Lauragais.

Rainfall varies widely. The higher Pyrenees get more rain than most places on this planet – over 2m a year (Prats de Mollo once got 838mm in 16 hours, the European record). Other upland regions, Cévennes and the Montagne Noire, also get their share, including the occasional *orage* or *épisode cévenol* – massive but fortunately rare downpours in autumn or winter that can lead to massive flooding in the Hérault and Gard. On the other hand, the coasts are one of the driest and sunniest regions in France.

Each season has its pros and cons. In **January** and **February** all the tourists are in the Alps or Pyrenees. **April** and **May** bring lots of flowers, capricious weather, and an agreeable lack of crowds. By **June**, the *mistral* is slowing down and the resorts begin to fill; walking is safe in the highest mountains. **July** and **August** are bad months, when everything is crowded, temperatures and prices soar (Perpignan has the highest average summer temperatures in France) and tempers flare; but it's also the season of concerts and festivals. Once French school holidays end in early **September**, prices and crowds decrease along with the temperature. In **October** the weather is traditionally mild on the coast, although torrential downpours and floods are not unknown; the first snows fall in the Pyrenees. Mid- to late **November** is another bad time to travel; it often rains and many museums, hotels and restaurants close down after the 11 November national holiday. **December** brings Christmas tourists and the first skiers.

Festivals

Languedoc-Roussillon offers everything from international culture festivals to the village *fête*. The latter may come with a Mass, bumper cars, a *pétanque* tournament, a feast (anything from sardines to *cassoulet* to paella) and an all-night dance. Bullfights, either traditional ones or the non-lethal *course camarguaise* (*see* p.121) play a part in many *fêtes* or *férias*, in which much of the merriment is carried on in *bodegas* – tents furnished by groups or families. A *corso* is a parade with carts or floats. In the Hérault, many towns and villages possess a kind of totem animal (a donkey in Gignac, a camel in Béziers, a colt in Pézenas), often associated with the patron saint.

Another Hérault speciality, at least around the coast, is the *joutes nautiques* – jousting, but carried on from boats (*see* p.167). Like the bullfights, these may coincide with local festivals or they may not.

St John's Night (23 June) is a big favourite, especially in Roussillon, and often features bonfires and fireworks. The midsummer bonfires around Mt Canigou have been part of the culture since ancient times, or at least since the Visigoths. At Catalan *festas* you're bound to see the national dance, the *sardana*,

Average Temperatures in °C (°F)

	Jan	Feb	Mar	April	May	June	July	Aug	Sept	Oct	Nov	Dec
Nîmes	7 (44)	7 (44)	11 (52)	15 (59)	17 (62)	21 (70)	23 (73)	25 (77)	23 (73)	16 (61)	10 (50)	8 (45)
Perpignan	12 (54)	12 (54)	13 (55)	17 (62)	20 (69)	23 (73)	28 (82)	28 (82)	26 (79)	20 (69)	16 (61)	14 (56)

a complex, circular dance that alternates 16 long steps with eight short ones, properly accompanied by a *cobla*, a band of a dozen instruments, some unique to Catalunya. In the southern Rhône valley, people still like to celebrate with a *farandole*, a dance in 6/8 time with held hands or a handkerchief, which may be as old as the ancient Greeks. One-man musical accompaniment is provided by a *galoubet*, a little three-holed flute played with the left hand, and a *tambourin*, a drum played with the right.

Calendar of Events

Towns and villages here lay on over 2,000 events each year, so this is a selective list. Dates may change from year to year; consult local tourist office websites for precise ones.

January

Early Winter fireworks and circus at the Pont du Gard

Mid-month Truffle festival, Uzès

Mid-month Flamenco Festival, Nîmes

Mid-Jan into March *Los Fecos*, the world's longest carnival, sees lavish costumes and a 400-year-old dance performed by different groups in the area every weekend in Place de la République, Limoux

February

2 Feb and mid-Feb *Fête de l'Ours*: men dressed as bears are chased through the village, Prats-de-Mollo and Arles-sur-Tech

Carnival Limoux, and big doings in Nîmes, Pézenas (*Le Poulain*) and Perpignan.

Second Sun: Mimosa festival, Roquebrun

14 *Fête des Amoureux*, Roquemaure

Late Feb *Fête du Cochon*, celebrating pork in all its glories, St-Pons-de-Thomières

March

Four weeks before Easter *Féria de Printemps*, with *corridas*, Nîmes

April

First weekend *La Grande Ourse*, teddy bear festival, Arpaillargues

Good Friday *Procession de La Sanch*, Perpignan, Collioure and Arles-sur-Tech

Late April *Toques et Clochers*, wine, gastronomy and music (*see* p.212), Limoux); *Médiévales*: big medieval celebrations in Sommières

Last week *Fête de St-Aphrodise*, with procession of the 'camel', Béziers

Late Week-long 'Confrontation' film festival, Perpignan

May

Ascension weekend *L'âne Martin*: fête in honour of the donkey who saved Gignac from the Arabs, Gignac

5 days at Pentecost *Féria de Pentecôte*, the biggest of the city's *férias*, with *corridas* and everything else, Nîmes

Late May: *Fête du Drac*, Beaucaire

June

First week: International Festival of Extreme Sports, Montpellier

First/second week Music festival, early/ Baroque, Maguelone

Mid-month *Festival de la Nouvelle Danse*, Uzès; also Sand Sculpture Festival, Cap d'Agde

Mid-June–Aug *Festival de Carcassonne*, dancing, music and theatre, including medieval spectacles in early Aug, Carcassonne

21 *Fête de la musique*, with outdoor concerts, celebrated all over France

23–24 *Fête de la St-Jean*, with bonfires and *sardanas* across Roussillon, with fireworks in Perpignan, Céret and Villefranche-de-Conflent

Last weekend *Fête des pêcheurs*, Gruissan; *Festival Les Nuits d' Encens*, Arab song and dance, and more, Aigues-Mortes

Late June–early July *Festival International de Danse*, Montpellier

July

Most of the month *Musique Sacrée*, St-Guilhem-le-Désert

All month *Fugue en Aude Romane*, classical music in churches and abbeys of the Aude; also the famous chamber music festival, *Les Nuits Musicales*, Uzès; Jazz Festival in Sète, and *Les Estivales* in Perpignan, with theatre, song and dance

Mid-July to mid-Aug *Festival d'Opérettes*, an international festival of operettas and operas, Lamalou-les-Bains

14 Fireworks and celebrations in many places for Bastille Day, superb in Carcassonne, Narbonne and Gruissan

Mid–late July *Festival de Radio France*, two weeks of classical music, Montpellier

Mid-July–early Aug *Nuits Musicales d'Uzès*, Uzès

Late July Olive festival, Bize-Minervois

Late July Folklore festivals in Quillan; *Les Estivales*, Beaucaire, evoking the famous market

Late July Poetry and art festival, Lodève

Late July–mid-Aug *Fiest'à* music festival, massive celebrations of world music, around the Bassin de Thau and Sète

August

Late July–early Aug *Festival Pau Casals*, chamber music in the medieval abbeys, Prades

Second week International Folklore Festival, an important event since 1936, Amélie-les-Bains

15 *Féria*, four days of music, *corridas* and wine in Béziers – the biggest one in Languedoc

Mid-Aug St-Vincent, huge *fête* with famous fireworks, Collioure

Late Aug (around the 25th) *Fête de Saint-Louis*, with historical re-enactment, Aigues-Mortes; *joutes nautiques* championship, Sète

Late Aug–mid-Sept *Visa Pour l'Image*, Perpignan, festival of international photo-journalism

Last week Cassoulet festival, Castelnaudary; Southern Cultures festival, Carcassonne

September

Mid-Sept *Féria des vendanges*, wine harvest festival, Spanish-style, with *corridas*, Nîmes; *Festa Major de Sant-Ferriol*, dancing, folklore, sports, dinners, Ceret; Roman wine harvest, Beaucaire

Third weekend *Journées du patrimoine*, to showcase national treasures; free entry to museums, all over France

October

Early Oct *Fête des vendanges* to celebrate grape harvest, various locations; one of the best is at Banyuls-sur-Mer

Mid-Oct *Fête votive*, with bullfights, Aigues-Mortes

Late Oct–early Nov International Mediterranean Film Festival, Montpellier

November

Every weekend Major jazz festival in tiny Cornilhac-Corbières; *Nimagine* Arts and Crafts Fair, Nîmes

December

Mid-Dec Christmas market, Carcassonne and Perpignan; also *Foire au Gras*, Castelnaudary, with a goose fat competition; *Salon des Antiquaires*, massive antiques fair, Nîmes

Tourist Information

Every city and town, and most villages, has a tourist information office, usually called an *Office de/du Tourisme/Maison de/du Tourisme/Syndicat d'Initiative*. Most offices, even in the small villages, have a website, with information on local events and much more.

French Tourist Offices Abroad

UK: Lincoln House, 300 High Holborn WC1V 7JH, **t** 09068 244 123 (calls charged at 60p/min), *uk.franceguide.com*.

Ireland: **t** 15 60 235 235 (90 cents a minute), *http://ie.franceguide.com*.

Australia and New Zealand: Level 13, 25 Bligh Street, Sydney, 2000 NSW, **t** (61) 02 9231 5244, *au.franceguide.com*.

USA: New York: 825 Third Avenue, 29th floor, New York, NY 10022, **t** (212) 838 7800; Los Angeles: 9454 Wilshire Bd, Suite 210, 90212 Beverly Hills, California, **t** (514) 288 1904; and Chicago: 205 N. Michigan Ave, Suite 3770, 60601 Chicago, Illinois, **t** (514) 288 1904; *us.franceguide.com*.

Canada: 1981 Avenue McGill College, Suite 490, Montréal, Québec QC H3A 2W9, **t** (514) 876 9881, *ca.franceguide.com*.

Consulates and Embassies

Foreign Embassies, etc. in France

UK: British Consulate-General, 24 Avenue de Prado, 13006 Marseille, **t** 04 91 15 72 10, *www.fco.gov.uk*.

Ireland: 4 Rue Rude, Paris, **t** 01 44 17 67 00, *www.ireland.visahq.com/embassy/France*.

Australia: 4 Rue Jean Rey, 75724 Paris, **t** 01 40 59 33 00, *www.france.embassy.gov.au*.

USA: Consulate-General, 12 Place Varian Fry, 13286 Marseille, **t** 04 91 54 92 00, *marseille.usconsulate.gov*.

Canada: Canadian Embassy in France, 35 Ave Montaigne, 75008 Paris, **t** 01 44 43 29 00, *www.amb-canada.fr*.

French Consulates and Embassies Abroad

UK: 6a Cromwell Place, London SW7 2EW, **t** 0845 7300 118; 11 Randolph Crescent, Edinburgh EH3 7TT, **t** (0131) 225 7954, *www.ambafrance-uk.org*.

Ireland: 36 Ailesbury Rd, Ballsbridge, Dublin 4, **t** (01) 277 5000, *www.ambafrance-ie.org*.

Canada: Toronto: 2 Bloor Street East, Suite 2200, Toronto, ON, M4W 1A8, **t** (416) 847 1900 *www.consulfrance-toronto.org;* Montréal: 1501 Av McGill College, 10ᵉ étage, Bureau 1000, Montréal, (QC) H3A 3M8, **t** (514) 878 4385, *www.consulfrance-montreal.org;* Vancouver: Suite 1100, 1130 West Pender St, Vancouver, BC, V6E 4A4, *www.consulfrance-vancouver.org*.

USA: Washington DC: 4101 Reservoir Rd NW, 20007-2185, **t** (202) 944 6195, *www.consulfrance-washington.org*; Chicago: 205 North Michigan Avenue, Suite 3700, Chicago, IL 60601, **t** (312) 327 5200, *www.consulfrance-chicago.org;* Los Angeles: 10390 Santa Monica Blvd 410, Los Angeles, CA 90025, **t** (310) 235 3200, *www.consulfrance- losangeles.org;* New York: 934 Fifth Av, New York, NY 10021, **t** (212) 606 3600, *www.consulfrance-newyork.org;* Atlanta: 3399 Peachtree Road NE, Suite 500, Atlanta, GA 30326, **t** (404) 495 1660, *www.consulfrance-atlanta.org;* Boston: Park Square Building, Suite 750, 31 Saint James Avenue, Boston, MA 02116, **t** (617) 832 4400, *www.consulfrance-boston.org;* Houston: 777 Post Oak Blvd, Suite 600, Houston, Texas 77056, **t** (713) 572 2799, *www.consulfrance-houston.org*; Miami: Espirito Santo Plaza, Suite 1050, 1395 Brickell Avenue, Miami FL 33131, **t** 305 403 4150, *www.consulfrance-miami.org*; New Orleans: 1340 Poydras Street, Suite 1710, New Orleans, LA 70112, **t** (504) 569 2870, *www.consulfrance-nouvelleorleans.org*; San Francisco: 540 Bush Street, San Francisco, CA 94108, **t** (415) 397 4330, *www.consulfrance-sanfrancisco.org*.

Entry Formalities

Passports and Visas

Holders of EU, US, Canadian, Australian, New Zealand and Israeli passports do not need a visa to enter France for stays of up to three months; most other nationals do (see *www.diplomatie.gouv.fr*). Apply at your nearest French consulate before leaving home.

Customs

Those over the age of 17 arriving from another **EU country** do not have to declare goods imported into France for personal use if they have paid duty on them in the country of origin. In theory, you can buy as much as you like, provided you can prove the purchase is for your own use and not for other purposes (e.g. selling on to friends). In practice, customs will be more likely to ask questions if you buy in bulk, e.g. more than 3,200 cigarettes or 400 cigarillos, 200 cigars or 3kg of tobacco; plus 10 litres of spirits, 90 litres of wine and 110 litres of beer. Travellers caught importing any of the above for resale will have the goods seized along with the vehicle they travelled in, and could face imprisonment for up to seven years.

Travellers from **outside the EU** must pay duty on goods worth more than €175 that they import into France.

Travellers from the USA are allowed to take home, duty-free, goods to the value of $400, including 200 cigarettes or 100 cigars; plus one litre of alcohol. For more information, call the US Customs Service. You're not allowed to bring back absinthe or Cuban cigars. Canadians can take home $300 worth of goods in a year, plus their tobacco and alcohol allowances.

French Customs, *www.douane.gouv.fr*.

UK Customs, **t** 0845 010 9000, *www.hmce.gov.uk*.

US Customs, **t** (202) 354 1000, *www.customs.gov*.

Disabled Travellers

France has improved greatly in the past few years with regard to accessibility. The Eurostar, TGVs and most SNCF trains are fully equipped to transport disabled people; alternatively you can ask for an assistant to accompany you on your journey (although you will have to pay for them). Eurostar has a special area reserved for wheelchair-users and their assistants (who can travel at

Specialist Organizations

In France

Association des Paralysés de France, Siège National, 17 Bd Auguste Blanqui, 75013 Paris, **t** 01 40 78 69 00, *www.apf.asso.fr*. A national organization with offices in all *départements*, that publishes an annual holiday guide for disabled travellers.

Organizations in the UK

Access Travel, 6 The Hillock, Astley, Lancashire M29 7GW, **t** (01942) 88 88 44, *www.access-travel.co.uk*. Travel agent for disabled people.

RADAR (Royal Association for Disability and Rehabilitation), Unit 12, City Forum, 250 City Rd, London EC1V 8AF, **t** (020) 7250 3222, *www.radar.org.uk* (*open Mon–Fri 10–4*).

RNIB (Royal National Institute of the Blind), 105 Judd St, London WC1H 9NE, **t** 0303 123 9999, *www.rnib.org.uk*.

Tourism for All, Shap Road Industrial Estate, Shap Road, Kendal, Cumbria LA9 6NZ, **t** 0845 124 9971, *www.tourismforall.org.uk*.

Organizations in the USA

American Foundation for the Blind, 2 Penn Plaza, Suite 1102, New York, NY 10121, **t** 800 232 5463, *www.afb.org*.

Mobility International USA, 132 E. Broadway, Suite 343, Eugene, OR 97401, **t** (541) 343 1284, *www.miusa.org*.

SATH (Society for Accessible Travel and Hospitality), 347 Fifth Ave, Suite 605, New York, NY 10016, **t** (212) 447 7284, *www.sath.org*.

reduced rates; call **t** 08705 186 186, *www.eurostar.com*). For more general information, **t** 0890 640 650, *www.accessibilite.sncf.com*.

Ferry companies offer special assistance if contacted beforehand. Vehicles modified for disabled people are charged reduced tolls on *autoroutes*. For more information contact the **Ministère des Transports**, Grande Arche, Paroi Sud, 92055 La Défense Cedex, Paris, **t** 01 40 81 21 22, *www.transports.equipement.gouv.fr*.

Gîtes accessibles aux personnes handicapées, by Gîtes de France (*www.gites-de-france.fr*), lists self-catering accommodation. Hotels with facilities for the disabled are listed in Michelin's *Red Guide to France*.

Insurance and EHIC Cards

Citizens of the EU who bring along their **European Health Insurance Card** (in the UK available by calling **t** 0845 606 2030, or online at *www.ehic.org.uk*, or by post using the forms available from post offices) are entitled to the same health services as French citizens. You must apply for a card for every member of the family (you'll need passports and National Insurance numbers). The EHIC must be stamped and signed to be valid, and the card must be renewed annually.

The EHIC covers 70% of the costs of visits to doctors and dentists, 80% of hospital costs, and 15–100% of the price of prescription drugs, although fees must be paid for up front; you'll be given a treatment form (*feuille de soins*). In hospitals, the EHIC will keep you from having to pay refundable fees up front, though you will still have to pay around 20% as well as a flat fee of €16 per day as an outpatient, and €18 per day as an inpatient. Some or all of this may be refundable back home.

Before you leave France, you can reclaim reimbursements from the local CPAM office (Caisse Primaire d'Assurance Maladie). Bring the *feuille de soins*, copies of receipts and prescriptions, a copy of your EHIC, your address and bank details, including IBAN and BIC. Confirmation of your refund will be sent to your home address.

If you were unable to claim a refund in France, contact the Overseas Healthcare Team (Newcastle) on **t** 0191 218 1999 on your return to the UK.

As an alternative, consider a **travel insurance** policy, covering theft and losses and offering 100% medical refund; check to see if it covers expenses if you get bogged down due to airport or train strikes or Icelandic volcanoes. Beware that accidents resulting from sports are rarely covered by ordinary insurance.

Canadians are usually covered in France by their provincial health coverage; Americans and others should check their policies.

Money and Banks

The currency of France is the euro. The wide acceptance of **credit cards** in ATM machines for withdrawing cash makes them by far the most convenient way of carrying cash. Check to see if your bank has a partnership with a French bank, allowing you to withdraw money without paying the fee. Also, some US credit cards lack the microchip required to work automatic machines such as petrol station pumps and *autoroute* toll booths.

Visa (Carte Bleue) is by far the most widely recognized credit card, followed by **MasterCard** and **American Express**. It must also be said that smaller establishments (especially *chambres d'hôtes* and *fermes-auberges*) tend to accept only cash, and that there are few ATMs outside the main towns.

If your card is lost or stolen in France, ring the company as soon as possible to block it:

American Express: call collect, **t** 00 1 905 474 0870

Diner's Club: **t** 0810 31 41 59 (French office hours)

Master Card: **t** 0800 90 13 87

Visa: **t** 0800 90 11 79

The police will provide you with a certificate called the *Récépissé de déclaration de vol* to give to your bank or insurance company.

Banks are generally open 8.30am–12.30pm and 1.30–4pm; they close on Sunday, and most close either on Saturday or Monday as well. Many no longer exchange bank notes or traveller's cheques (although the central post office of a major city just might), so if you need to change cash to euros do it at a *bureau de change* as you enter France. Visa's pre-paid travel currency cards have taken the place of traveller's cheques.

Getting There

By Air

The **airports** in the region are Montpellier, Nîmes, Carcassonne, Béziers and Perpignan –

Airline Carriers

UK and Ireland

Aer Lingus, *www.aerlingus.com*. Dublin to Marseille and Toulouse; Bristol to Perpignan.

Air France, *www.airfrance.co.uk*. Via Paris to Toulouse, Marseille and Montpellier.

bmiBaby, *www.bmibaby.com*. Manchester to Montpellier and Perpignan.

British Airways (BA), *www.ba.com*. London Heathrow to Toulouse.

City Jet, *www.cityjet.com*. London City to Avignon.

easyJet, *www.easyjet.com*. London Gatwick to Montpellier, Marseille and Toulouse; Bristol to Toulouse and Marseille.

Flybe, *www.flybe.com*. Birmingham to Toulouse and Avignon; Southampton to Perpignan, Béziers, Avignon; Exeter to Avignon.

Jet2, *www.jet2.com*. Belfast to Toulouse.

Ryanair, , *www.ryanair.com*. To Nîmes from London Luton and Liverpool. To Montpellier from Leeds and Birmingham. To Béziers from London Luton and Bristol. To Perpignan from London Stansted. To Carcassonne from Stansted, Dublin, Cork, East Midlands, Liverpool, Leeds, Glasgow and Nottingham. To Marseille from Dublin, Edinburgh, and London Stansted.

USA and Canada

Numerous airlines offer direct flights from the United States and Canada to Paris: also look into flights by way of other European hubs (London, Frankfurt, Munich and Amsterdam) to Toulouse and Marseille.

Air France, *www.airfrance.com*. Regular services to Paris from numerous cities.

Air Transit, *www.airtransat.com*. From Montreal to Toulouse and Marseille.

American Airlines, *www.aa.com*. To Paris from Boston, Chicago, Dallas, New York JFK and Miami.

Continental, *www.continental.com*. Flights to Paris from Newark, Orlando, New Orleans, Houston, Boston, Washington DC, Chicago, San Francisco and Los Angeles.

Delta, *www.delta.com*. Flights to Paris from Boston, Detroit, Atlanta, Chicago, Cincinnati, Salt Lake City and Minneapolis.

United Airlines, *www.united.com*. To Paris from Montreal, Newark, Philadelphia, Charlotte, Houston, Toronto and Chicago.

US Airways, *www.usairways.com*. Flights to Paris from Atlanta, Charlotte, Chicago, Miami, Philadelphia, San Francisco, and Washington DC.

XL, *www.xl.com*. To Paris from New York and Las Vegas.

with Toulouse, Avignon and Marseille as other possibilities; those going to the Gard are near Marseille, while travellers to Roussillon often fly into Girona (*see* Perpignan, p.249) for bus links. While they are served by (mostly) low-cost flights from UK regional airports, from most other points of departure – North America, Australia, etc. – flights are only to Paris, from where you can catch a connecting flight to Montpellier, Marseille or Toulouse, or a high-speed train to Languedoc-Roussillon. Note that while London, with its many cheap flights to regional airports, may seem like a good bet, getting across the city from one airport to another can take up to 3hrs and end up costing more than you might think.

Domestic flights on Air France from Paris-Orly fly to Toulouse and, less frequently, to Montpellier, Perpignan and Nîmes.

By Train

Airport awfulness makes France's high-speed **TGVs** (*trains à grande vitesse*) an attractive and environmentally sound (but not necessarily cheaper) way of reaching Languedoc-Roussillon. **Eurostar** trains leave from London St Pancras, Ashford and a new station in north Kent, Ebbsfleet International (near Dartford). Check out the **Railteam** (*www.railteam.co.uk*) website for the fastest routes to Nîmes (6 hours from London), Montpellier (7 hours), or Perpignan (8 hours); many involve a handy change in Lille, which saves crossing Paris to change stations.

As with airlines, fares are cheaper if booked as far in advance as possible (up to 90 days before travel). Children up to age 3 can travel free if they share a seat. Two or more people travelling together are entitled to a 25% *Découverte à Deux* discount on return tickets on TGVs (subject to availability), and other trains as long as their journey starts during a blue period (*see* p.67); the same reduction applies to a group of up to four people travelling with a child under 12 (*Découverte Enfant Plus*), to under-26-year-olds (*Découverte 12–25*), over-60s (*Découverte Senior*), and for anyone who books a return journey of at least 200km in distance, including a Saturday night away (*Découverte Séjour*).

It may be worth investing in a **rail pass** if your plans include Languedoc-Roussillon as part of a longer journey. European residents of at least six months are eligible for a one- or multi-country **InterRail** pass, valid for 3, 4, 6 or 8 days of unlimited travel within a month through **Rail Europe** (*www.raileurope.com*). Passes include travel on high speed and overnight trains (as long as you make reservations), and include reduced fares on Eurostar and up to 30% discount on Irish Ferry connections to France. There are half-prices passes for ages 4–11, and discounts for 12–25-year-olds as well.

Non-Europeans are eligible for a similar **Eurail Pass** (*www.eurail.com* or *www.raileurope.com*). There are quite a few options to choose from, including a two-country Regional Pass (for instance France and Italy), the Select Pass (valid in 3–5 countries), or the Global Pass (valid in 22 countries). The Eurail pass also offers up to 30% discount on Irish Ferry connections to France, as well as free RER connections from Paris Charles de Gaulle to the Gare du Nord, and discounts on hotel vouchers. Passes can be purchased online, with free delivery (if you order them far enough in advance).

You can book regular tickets online on the **French railways** website in English (*www.tgv-europe.com*), and have them sent to addresses outside France, if ordered far enough in advance. Otherwise it's easy to pick them up at the station, through a machine or at a ticket booth.

For more, *see* ***www.seat61.com*** – an incredibly informative, reliable, independent train travel website.

By Car

A car entering France must have its **registration and insurance papers**, and carry them at all times, while the driver needs to carry a full licence and passport. **Green cards** are no longer compulsory, but do make sure your insurer covers you in France. Some policies cover breakdowns but many do not: the AA and RAC offer special European cover and have helplines. Drivers with a valid licence from an EU country, Canada, the USA or Australia don't need an **international licence**.

Carrying a reflective waistcoat and a warning triangle inside the car (not in the boot) is mandatory; it should be placed 50m behind the car if you have a breakdown. If you're coming from the UK or Ireland, pick up **headlamp adjusters**.

The *autoroutes* will get you south the fastest, but be prepared to pay some €70–100 in **tolls**; the N7 south of Paris takes longer, but costs nothing. For **toll charges** and route information, see *www. autoroutes.fr*. For information on driving in France, *see* 'Getting Around', pp.68–9.

By Channel Tunnel

Taking your car on Eurotunnel is a convenient way of crossing the Channel between the UK and France. It takes only 35mins to get through to Calais; you remain in the car, although you can get up to stretch your legs. Fares are competitive with the ferries, rising substantially in summer and other high seasons. The price is by car and for up to nine passengers (there are special carriages for caravans and other high vehicles).

Eurotunnel, *www.eurotunnel.com*.

By Car and Sea

If you prefer a dose of bracing sea air, you've plenty of choice; France is served by several ferry and catamaran companies sailing from the UK and Ireland. **Brittany Ferries** sail from Portsmouth to Caen (6 hours or overnight), Plymouth to Roscoff (6 hours or overnight), Poole to Cherbourg (high speed, 2.5 hours) and Cork to Roscoff (only one a week, 14 hours). **LD Lines** sail from Newhaven to Dieppe (5 hours) and Portsmouth to Le Havre (3 hours, 15 minutes). **Condor** sail from Plymouth to Cherbourg on Sundays (offering special deals for campers and caravans) and from Weymouth and Poole to St-Malo (6 hours). **P&O Ferries** offer crossings from Dover to Calais in about 90 minutes and from Hull sailing overnight to Zeebrugge in Belgium, a short drive on motorways from France. **SeaFrance** offer frequent 90-minute ferry links between Dover and Calais. **Norfolkline** ferries link Dover and Dunkirk (2 hours) and Newcastle overnight to Amsterdam – about five hours from Paris.

Ferry Operators

Brittany Ferries: *www.brittany-ferries.co.uk*.

LD Lines: *www.ldlines.co.uk*.

Condor Ferries: *www.condorferries.co.uk*.

P & O Ferries: *www.poferries.eu*.

SeaFrance: *www.seafrance.com*.

Norfolkline: *www.norfolkline.com*.

Prices vary considerably according to season and demand, so shop around for the best deal.

Getting Around

By Train

SNCF nationwide information number, **t** 36 35 (€0.34/min), *www.sncf-voyages.com*, or **TGV**, *www.tgv-europe.com*.

The SNCF runs an efficient network of trains through the major cities of Languedoc-Roussillon, with an added service called the **Petit Train Jaune** (*see* p.269) from Villefranche-de-Conflent to Latour-de-Carol in the Pyrenees, with bus connections at either end to Perpignan and Andorra.

If you plan on making only a few long hauls, **international rail passes** (*see* p.66) may save you money. Other possible discounts hinge on the exact time of your departure. The SNCF has divided the year into **blue** (off-peak; *bleue*) and **white** (peak; *blanche*) **periods**, based on demand; white periods run from Friday noon to midnight Saturday, and from Sunday 3pm to Monday 10am and during holidays. There is then a complicated system of ***découverte*** discounts aimed mainly at French residents but which may just fit your circumstances – also discounts on tickets booked in advance; *see* p.66 and the SNCF websites for details.

Tickets (valid for two months after purchase) must be stamped in the little orange machines by the entrance to the lines that say *Compostez votre billet* (this puts the date on the ticket). Any time you interrupt a journey until another day, you have to revalidate your ticket. TGVs and long-distance trains (*trains Corail*) have snack trolleys and bar/cafeteria cars; some have play areas.

Local trains (TER) within Languedoc-Roussillon have their own website: *www.ter-sncf. com/regions/languedoc_roussillon/fr*.

Nearly every city station has large computerized **lockers** (*consigne automatique*) which take a while to puzzle out the first time, although any threat of terrorist activity in France tends to close them down across the board.

By Bus

Do not count on seeing much of rural France by public transport. The bus network is barely adequate between major cities and towns (places often already well served by rail) and usually rotten in rural areas, where the one bus a day fits the school schedule, leaving at the crack of dawn and returning in the afternoon; more remote villages are linked to civilization only once a week or not at all. The exception to the rule is Roussillon, where the *département* runs an efficient €1 bus system – *see www.cg66.fr/553-plan-et-horaires.htm*; services are also pretty good in the Hérault (*www.herault-transport.fr*).

Other buses are run either by the **SNCF** (replacing discontinued rail routes) or **private firms**. Rail passes are valid on SNCF lines, which generally coincide with trains. Private bus firms, especially when they have a monopoly, tend to be a bit more expensive than trains.

Some towns have a ***gare routière*** (coach station), usually near the train station, though many lines start from any place that catches their fancy.

By Car

Unless you plan to stick to the major cities and beaches, a car is unfortunately the only way to see most of Languedoc. This has its drawbacks: relatively high car rental rates and petrol prices, and an accident rate double that of the UK (and much higher than the USA).

Though **roads** are generally excellently maintained, anything of lesser status than a departmental route (D-road) may be uncomfortably narrow. Mountain roads, though, are reasonable, even in the Pyrenees.

The cheapest place to buy **petrol** is at the big supermarkets; the most expensive is on motorways. Petrol stations keep shop hours (most close Sun and/or Mon, plus lunchtimes) and are rare in rural areas, so replenish your fuel supply before making any forays into the mountains. Unleaded is *sans plomb*; diesel is *gazole* or *gasoil*. Automated machines functioning outside these hours accept foreign debit/credit cards as long as they have a microchip. **Speed limits** are 130km/80mph on the *autoroutes* (toll motorways); 110km/69mph on dual carriageways (divided highways); 90km/55mph on other roads; 50km/30mph in an 'urbanized area' – as soon as you pass a white sign with a town's name on it and until you pass another sign with the town's name barred.

There are more and more speed cameras all the time, and no longer any signs warning drivers of their presence. **Fines** for speeding, payable on the spot, are high (from €200), and can be astronomical (up to €4,500) if you fail a breathalyser test.

In some places you still need to give **priority to the right** at unmarked intersections. Watch out for the *cédez le passage* (give way) signs, and, wherever there aren't any, be very careful.

When you (inevitably) get lost in a town or city, the *toutes directions* or *autres directions* signs are like Get Out of Jail Free cards. Blue **'P'** signs will infallibly direct you to a village or town's already full car park. Watch out for the tiny signs that indicate which streets are meant for pedestrians only (with complicated schedules in even tinier print); and for Byzantine street parking rules (which would take pages to explain – do as the natives do, and be careful about village centres on market days).

For more information on driving in France, contact:

AA: *www.theaa.com*.

RAC: *www.rac.co.uk*.

AAA (USA): *www.aaa.com*.

Accidents and Breakdowns

If you wind up in an **accident**, the procedure is to fill out and sign a *constat amiable* (European Accident Statement; if you don't have one, download several copies from the internet). One copy should be filled in with personal, insurance and vehicle details, a sketch of the accident, and indications of damage. Both drivers sign this and keep a copy, which must be posted to your insurer within five days. Summon the police if someone is hurt or there is a disagreement, or call an ambulance in case of a serious accident, on **t** 15 or **t** 18.

If you have a **breakdown**, dial the European emergency number (**t** 112) to help find the nearest garage to tow you. **Europ Assistance**, **t** 0844 338 5533, *www.europ-assistance.co.uk*, will help with car insurance for abroad.

Useful Websites

Route planners: *www.mappy.com*, *www.rac.co.uk*, *www.theaa.com*.

Autoroute information: *www.autoroutes.fr* (includes information in English).

Car Hire

The minimum age for hiring a car in France is often 21 (though younger drivers with a year's experience can sometimes get a car with the payment of an insurance supplement), and the maximum around 70. Before booking a car with your flight, check the numerous car hire websites to compare deals; you can also book a car through the SNCF website. In high season it's essential to book one in advance.

Drivers coming from outside the EU who intend to spend three weeks or more driving in France can save money on the **TT Car Transit scheme**, which includes a new car, unlimited mileage, full risk insurance without waiver and 24-hour, 7 days a week road assistance: see *www.ttcar. com/uk*.

By Boat

One of the most congenial ways of visiting Languedoc is on a *péniche* or canal barge, chugging along at 5mph on the Canal du Midi and the connecting Canal de la Robine (through Narbonne) and the Canal Rhône-Sète to Beaucaire, winding through some of the region's loveliest countryside. There is a wide choice of boat rentals. Hiring a fully equipped barge sleeping four runs between €800–1,500 a week depending on season and comfort, with no prior boating experience required. *See* the box above for barge rental firms. Most come with optional bike hire for explorations along the way.

Canal Barges

Connoisseur, *www.connoisseur.ie*.

Crown Blue Line, *www.crownblueline.co.uk*.

France Fluviale, *www.francefluviale.com*.

LeBoat, *www.leboat.com*.

Locaboat Plaisance, *www.locaboat.com*.

Rive de France, *www.rivedefrance.com*.

By Bicycle

Much of Languedoc-Roussillon is ideal for cycling, with quiet little roads and as many hills as you care to try – the Pyrenees for Tour de France moments or the towpath of the Canal du Midi for car-free calm. If you mean to cycle in the summer, start and stop early to avoid the heat.

French drivers, not always courteous to fellow motorists, usually give cyclists a wide berth; and yet on any summer day half the patients in hospital are from accidents on two-wheeled transport. Consider a helmet, and beware that bike thefts are fairly common. Avoid the busy N roads as far as possible.

Getting your own bike to France can be expensive, as most now charge a fee from €100–200. In general, if you fit a bike in a suitcase that meets the size and weight requirements, you will not be charged extra. On Eurostar cross-Channel trains, passengers (in summer only) may take a bike with them provided it can be folded and carried on board in a bicycle bag (front wheel removed, etc.). The bike will count as one item of your baggage allowance; otherwise it can travel with you or be sent ahead as registered baggage. For further information see *www.eurostar.com*.

Many French trains, especially regional TER trains, carry bikes for free; otherwise you have to send them as registered luggage and pay a fee of around €50 for delivery within 48hrs (though delays are common). For cycling holidays, *see* the list of special-interest companies, pp.72–3. For cycle-friendly itineraries, have a look at **Bikely** (*www.bikely.com*) or **Bikemap** (*www.bikemap.net*).

Fédération Française de Cyclotourisme, *www.ffct.org*. Maps and cycling information in France.

Bike Hire

Main towns and holiday centres always seem to have at least one shop that hires them out – local tourist offices have lists, or see **Holiday Bikes** (*www.holiday-bikes.com/fr*). A *vélo tout terrain* (abbreviated to VTT) is a mountain bike. You may want to enquire about theft insurance.

You can also hire bikes from most SNCF train stations in major towns; they vary in quality, so check them. The advantage of hiring from a station is that you can drop the bike back off at another, as long as you specify where when you hire it. For more information, *see* **Train + Vélo**, *www.velo.sncf.com*.

On Foot

A network of long-distance paths or ***Grandes Randonnées*** (**GRs**; marked by red and white signs, or splodges of red and white paint; at path junctions, an 'X' denotes this is not the right one to take) take in some of the most beautiful scenery in Languedoc-Roussillon. Each GR is described in a *Topoguide*, with maps and details about camping sites, *refuges* and so on, available in local bookshops or from the **Fédération Française de la Randonnée Pédestre**, *www.ffrandonnee.fr*; for general info on each route, see *www.gr-infos.com*. Local tourist information offices have maps and leaflets on walks in the area.

One of the more popular walks here is **Le Chemin de Saint Guilhem le Désert** (GR 74) an optional route to Compostela for pilgrims starting in Le Puy-en-Velay, who wanted to pay their respects to St-Guilhem (*see* p.155) before picking up the branch via Montpellier, Narbonne and Toulouse. It's also near the GR 7, a route which crosses much of Languedoc-Roussillon. St-Jean-du-Gard marks the end of the GR 70, the famous **Chemin Stevenson** across the Cévennes (*see* p.104), still a popular road, with or without a donkey to carry your bags.

The Pyrenees and their foothills are magnificent walking country. The ideal way to slowly drink in the beauties of the Corbières and Cathar castles from Padern, Peyrepertuse and Puilaurens to Montségur in the Hautes-Pyrénées is by way of the **Sentier Cathare** (*www.lesentiercathare.com*), a path shared by walkers and riders, and well marked and endowed with places to eat and stay. A number of firms offer self-guided and guided walking tours along these and other trails, and will arrange all your accommodation, food and transport your bags; *see* listings on pp.72–3.

Where to Stay

Hotels

French hotels are graded by their facilities (not by charm or location) with **stars** from five to one, although recent regulations have seen many of the old basic ones close down, while chain hotels (Campanile, Ibis, Formule 1, etc.) have expanded exponentially; although not included in the text, you can presume any town of consequence will have at least one or two. It's become rare to find a hotel without en-suite bathrooms throughout.

Many hotels offer a wide range of rooms and prices. In some, every single room has its own personality, and the difference in quality and price can be enormous: a large room with a balcony overlooking the sea will cost much more than a poky back room in the annexe of the same hotel. The coastal resorts are much pricier than the rest of the region, but even here you can find deals in the off-season.

Single rooms are relatively rare, and usually two-thirds the price of a double; rarely will a hotelier give you a discount if only doubles are available. Increasingly hotels offer **family rooms**, some with interconnecting rooms, others with bunk beds on a mezzanine, while others offer triples or quads.

Hotel Price Categories

Note that prices listed here and elsewhere in this book are for a double room in high season.

luxury	€€€€€	€230+
very expensive	€€€€	€150–230
expensive	€€€	€100–150
moderate	€€	€60–100
inexpensive	€	under €60

Breakfast is nearly always optional: you'll do as well for less in a bar. As usual, rates rise in the busy season, when many hotels with restaurants will require that you take **half-board** (*demi-pension* – breakfast and a set lunch or dinner). Many hotel restaurants are superb and non-residents are welcome. In the off-season, board requirements vanish into thin air.

Your holiday will be much sweeter if you **book ahead**, especially from May to October. July and August are the only really impossible months; otherwise it usually isn't too difficult to find something. Many hotels will only confirm a room reservation with a credit card number to cover the first night. Tourist offices have lists of accommodation in their given areas; many will even call around and book a room for you on the spot for free or for a nominal fee.

Don't confuse chain hotels with the various umbrella organizations like **Logis** (*www.logishotels.com*), which includes reliable inns mostly in villages and smaller towns; **Relais du Silence** (*www.relaisdu silence.com*) for peaceful hotels; **Châteaux & Hotels** (*www.chateauxhotels.com*) for hotels in historic buildings; or the prestigious **Relais et Châteaux** (*www.relaischateaux.fr*), which promote and guarantee the quality of independently owned hotels and their restaurants. Many of these are recommended in the text.

Apartment Hotels

If you plan on spending a few days in a city, an apartment hotel with a kitchenette can be good value, especially when travelling with a family. Prices are competitive with classic hotels. Most belong to one of these chains, where you'll find complete listings:

Citadines: *www.citadines.com.*

Adagio: *www.accorhotels.com.*

Appart City: *www.appartcity.com.*

ResidHome : *www.residhome.com.*

B&Bs (*Chambres d'Hôtes*)

These have become quite the thing in Languedoc-Roussillon, as more and more people are setting up cosy and often very stylish accommodation in town houses, *châteaux* or farms. Many offer evening meals as well as breakfast; some offer airport pick-ups and other personalized services. Many are listed in the text, but for complete listings *see* the box above.

B&B Organizations

Chambres d'Hôtes.Org: *www.chambres dhotes.org.*

Chambres en France: *www.chambres-en-france.com.*

Clévacances: *www.clevacances.com.*

Fleurs de Soleil: *www.fleursdesoleil.fr.*

Gîtes de France: *www.gites-de-france.com.*

Samedi Midi Editions: *www.thebestbedand-breakfastfrance.com.*

Youth Hostels

Most cities and resort areas have youth hostels (***auberges de jeunesse***) that offer simple dormitory accommodation and rooms with breakfast to people of any age for around €15–25 a night. Many offer kitchen facilities as well. They are the best deal going for people travelling on their own; for people travelling together, a one-star hotel can work out just as cheap. Another downside is that many are in the most ungodly locations – in the suburbs where the last bus goes by at 7pm, or miles from any transport at all in the country.

Gîtes d'Etape and *Refuges*

A ***gîte d'étape*** is a simple shelter with bunk beds and a rudimentary kitchen set up by a village along GR walking paths (*see* p.70) or cycling paths. In the mountains, similar rough shelters along the GR paths are called ***refuges***, and most of them open in summer only. Both charge around €15 a night, and many provide meals if you book ahead – as you should in the summer. For complete listings, *see* **Le Guide Gîtes d'Etape et Refuges**: *www.gites-refuges.com.*

Camping and Holiday Villages

Camping is extremely popular in Languedoc-Roussillon. Campsites, like hotels, are graded with stars from four to one, and there's at least one campsite in or near every town, from inexpensive, no-frills places run by the town itself (*camping municipal*) to top-of-the-line sites with their own water parks, a huge range of sporting options, kids' clubs, evening entertainment and even air-conditioned mobile homes. All but the most basic have some kind of self-catering accommodation to rent, generally by the week (or less, if they aren't busy), along with their pitches for tents and camper cars.

The **Fédération Française de Camping et de Caravaning** (*www.ffcc.fr*) lists their 11,000 members on their site, *www.campingfrance.com*; they also sponsor Camping Qualité (*www.campingqualite.com*), which means that designated sites are certified to meet certain standards: a warm welcome, cleanliness, truth in advertising, private pitches, and respect for the environment. Wherever you go, in July and August it's essential to book, especially if you want to stay by the sea; alternatively consider some more peaceful sites by Languedoc's major rivers.

A cheaper option is staying on a **farm**, or Camping à la Ferme: *see www.bienvenue-a-la-ferme.com* for listings.

A number of UK holiday firms offer camping holiday packages to some of the fancier campsites in the region:

Canvas Holidays, *www.canvasholidays.co.uk*.
Eurocamp, *www.eurocamp.co.uk*.
Keycamp Holidays, *www.keycamp.co.uk*.
Yello!, *www.yellohvillage.co.uk*.

Languedoc-Roussillon is also fairly well endowed with **holiday villages** (known as *villages vacances* or *résidences clubs*), designed for families. These offer accommodation in self-catering bungalows or apartments, with restaurants and cafés on site; rooms are cleaned and linens provided, and there are pools, crèches, kids' clubs and entertainment. Most of these are run by several companies:

Pierre et Vacances: *www.pv-holidays.com*.
Belambra: *www.belambra.fr*.
Odalys: *www.odalys-vacances.com*.
M Vacances: *www.mvacances.com*.

Gîtes de France and Other Self-catering Accommodation

Languedoc-Roussillon offers a vast range of self-catering: inexpensive farm cottages, history-laden châteaux with gourmet frills, sprawling villas, flats in modern beach resorts and canal boats.

The **Fédération Nationale des Gîtes de France** offers a wide range of accommodation by the week, mostly in rural areas. Lists with photos arranged by *département* are available at *www.gites-de-france.fr*. Prices depend very much on the time of year as well as facilities; nearly always you'll be expected to begin your stay on a Saturday. Many *départements* also have a second (and usually less expensive) listing of *gîtes* in the guide *Clévacances* (*www.clevacances.com*). Or try getting back to nature, with a Panda Gîte in Haut-Languedoc or the Roussillon in one of a network of about 250 rural *gîtes* and B&Bs in collaboration with Gîtes de France, WWF France and the Federation of French Nature Reserves (*www.gites-panda.fr*).

For private *gîte* rentals booked directly with the owners, try *www.frenchconnections.co.uk*, which also offers ferry discounts, and *www.abritel.fr*.

Special-interest Holidays

Based in France

Agly Walking Tours, *www.aglyrando.com*. Self-guided walking tours in the region.

Altitude Adventure, *www.altitudeadventure.com*. Mountain bike and ski holidays, based in Font-Romeu in the Pyrenees.

Brezilou Horse Riding Stables, *www.quillan-horseriding-southfrance.com*. Short- or long-distance rides in the Aude.

Domaine de Fraisse, *www.domaine-de-fraisse.com*. Riding holidays based near Carcassonne.

Dragon Ceramic Studios, *www.dragonceramic.com*. Ceramics courses in a village near Uzès.

Feuilla Nature, *www.feuillanature.com*. Walking, birdwatching, wild flower-themed and cultural heritage holidays in the Corbières.

Gardoussel, *www.gardoussel.com*. Yoga and Ayurveda holidays and writing workshops in the northern Gard.

Gastronomicom, *www.gastronomicom.fr*. In-depth cookery, French pastry and wine classes, along with French lessons – from one month to two years – located at Cap d'Agde.

Hidden Gardens Hidden France, *www.hiddengardensfrance.com*. Garden tours, botanical walks.

La Maison Verte, *www.lamaisonverte.co.uk*. Singing courses near Pézenas.

Languedoc Nature, *www.languedoc-nature.com*. Vast range of active holidays, rock climbing in Le Caroux, walks with donkeys, caving, canoeing, canyoning, etc. based in the Hérault.

La Petite Pépinière, *www.lapetitepepiniere.com*. Gardening courses and tours, based in Caunes-Minervois.

Les Ânes de Licorne, *www.mari-ane.com*. Eight-day treks in the eastern Pyrenees with donkeys, based in Mosset.

Mas Saurine, *mas-saurine.com*. Located near Prades, offering cookery, stained glass, painting, digital photography and creative writing courses.

Miam-Miam, *www.stage-cuisine.com*. Unique cooking *atelier* near Le Vigan in the Cévennes, specializing in the use of 80 spices; weekend or day courses.

Paint France, *www.paintfrance.com*. All media from drawing to oils taught in Lodève.

Painting Holidays France, *www.painting-holidays-france.com*. Watercolour holidays in the Hérault.

Petra Carter, *www.petracarter.com*. Weekend cookery, photography, yoga and painting courses based at Mirepeisset, between Béziers and Narbonne.

Sentiers de France, *www.sentiersdefrance.com*. Self-guided walking tours of the Côte Vermeille, Cathar trail, and Cathar castles.

Vinécole, *www.vinecole.com*. Based near Limoux, offering Wine & Spirit Education Trust (WSET) courses as well as wine-tastings. *See* p.54.

Viveka Yoga Holidays, *www.franceyogaretreats.com*. Various yoga holidays in a rural retreat in the Aude.

Walking in Languedoc, *www.walking-languedoc.com*. Self-guided walking holidays through many parts of the region.

From the UK and US

Abercrombie & Kent, *www.abercrombiekent.com*. Luxury canal and river cruises.

Active Gourmet Holidays, *www. activegourmetholidays.com*. Three- to seven-day cooking classes in Languedoc, and other activities besides.

Arblaster and Clarke, *www.arblasterandclarke.com*. Gourmet wine tours and cruises.

Art & Yoga Holidays, *www.acy-holidays.com*. With studios based near Nîmes and Carcassonne.

Belle France, *www.bellefrance.co.uk*. Self-guided walking, walking with donkeys and snow-shoeing, and luxury barges on the Canal du MIdi.

Discover France, *www.discoverfrance.com*. Self-guided walking and bicycle tours.

French Cycling Holidays Ltd, *www.frenchcyclingholidays.com*. For serious cyclists.

French House Party, *www.frenchhouseparty.eu*. Masterchef cookery, creative writing, song-writing, and digital movie-making, based near Carcassonne.

Golf Par Excellence, *www.golfparexcellence.com*. Golf holidays on the best Languedoc courses.

Sherpa Expeditions, *www. sherpa-walking-holidays.co.uk*. 'Inn-to-inn' walking tours in Roussillon.

Tastes of Languedoc, *www.tastesoflanguedoc.com*. Wine and food tours, based in La Tour-sur-Orb.

Unicorn Trails, *www.unicorntrails.com*. Riding holidays around Carcassonne and the Pyrenees.

World Walks, *www.worldwalks.com*. Walks along the coast of Roussillon.

Self-catering

In France/From the UK

A.I.P.L.V., *www.pour-les-vacances.com*. French site that matches you with villa owners.

Bowhills, *www. bowhills.co.uk*. Luxury villas and farmhouses, mostly with pools.

Chez Nous, *www.cheznous.com*. Villas, *gîtes* and holiday cottages across Languedoc-Roussillon.

Crème de Languedoc, *www.creme-de-languedoc.com*. Apartments, villas, cottages, town houses, and more.

Dominique's Villas, *www.dominiquesvillas.co.uk*. Large villas and châteaux with pools.

French Connections, *www.frenchconnections.co.uk*. Large listing of *gîtes* and villas, and ferry discounts.

French Country, *www.frenchcountry.co.uk*. Small selection of listings placed by owners.

Holiday Lettings, *www.holidaylettings.co.uk*. Extensive listings.

Midi Hideaways, *www.midihideaways.com*. Properties in and around St-Chinian in the Hérault.

Pézenas Properties, *www.pezenasproperties.com*. Villas in the Hérault.

VFB Holidays, *www.travelzest.com*. A few rustic *gîtes*, luxurious farmhouses and hotels.

Villa Renters, *www.villarenters.com*. A selection of mostly moderately priced accommodation around the region.

VRBO, *www.vrbo.com*. Stands for 'vacation rentals by owner', a website where owners list their properties, including a wide range of cottages, villas, châteaux, lodges and apartments.

From the USA/Canada

France by Heart, , *www.francebyheart.com*. Hundreds of properties.

Home Away, *www.homeaway.com*. With over 7,500 places to choose from in Languedoc-Roussillon.

Vacances Provençales, *www.europeanhome-rentals.com*. Luxury villas, country homes, châlets and apartments.

Practical A–Z

07

Conversions: Imperial–Metric

Length (multiply by)

Inches to centimetres: 2.54
Centimetres to inches: 0.39
Feet to metres: 0.3
Metres to feet: 3.28
Yards to metres: 0.91
Metres to yards: 1.1
Miles to kilometres: 1.61
Kilometres to miles: 0.62

Area (multiply by)

Inches square to centimetres square: 6.45
Centimetres square to inches square: 0.15
Feet square to metres square: 0.09
Metres square to feet square: 10.76
Miles square to kilometres square: 2.59
Kilometres square to miles square: 0.39
Acres to hectares: 0.40
Hectares to acres: 2.47

Weight (multiply by)

Ounces to grams: 28.35
Grammes to ounces: 0.035
Pounds to kilograms: 0.45
Kilograms to pounds: 2.2
Stones to kilograms: 6.35
Kilograms to stones: 0.16
Tons (UK) to kilograms: 1,016
Kilograms to tons (UK): 0.0009
1 UK ton (2,240lbs) = 1.12 US tonnes (2,000lbs)

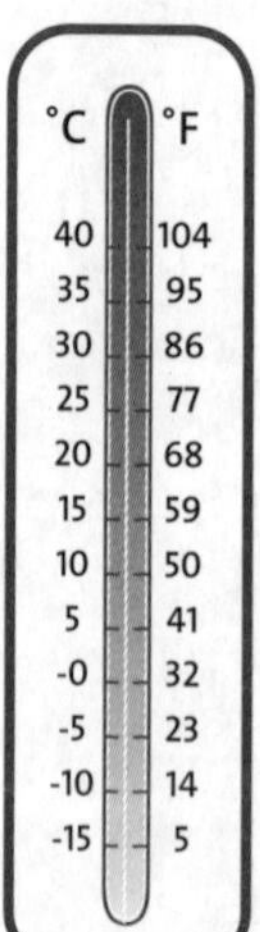

Volume (multiply by)

Pints (UK) to litres: 0.57
Litres to pints (UK): 1.76
Quarts (UK) to litres: 1.13
Litres to quarts (UK): 0.88
Gallons (UK) to litres: 4.55
Litres to gallons (UK): 0.22
1 UK pint/quart/gallon = 1.2 US pints/quarts/ gallons

Temperature

Celsius to Fahrenheit: multiply by 1.8 then add 32

Fahrenheit to Celsius: subtract 32 then multiply by 0.55

France Information

Time Differences

Country: + 1hr GMT; + 6hrs EST

Daylight saving from last weekend in March to end of October

Dialling Codes

France country code 33

To France from: UK, Ireland, New Zealand 00 / USA, Canada 011 / Australia 0011 then dial 33 and then the number without the initial zero

From France to: UK 00 44; Ireland 00 353; USA, Canada 001; Australia 00 61; New Zealand 00 64 then the number without the initial zero

Directory enquiries: 118 218

Emergency Numbers

Police: 17
Ambulance: 15
Fire/rural ambulance (pompiers): 18
EU emergency number: 112

Embassy emergency numbers

UK: 04 91 15 72 10; **Ireland** 01 44 17 67 00; **USA**: 01 43 12 22 22; **Canada** 00 1 613 996 8885; **Australia** 00 61 2 6261 3305; **NZ** 00 1 64 4 439 8000

Shoe Sizes

Europe	UK	USA
35	2½ / 3	4
36	3 / 3½	4½ / 5
37	4	5½ / 6
38	5	6½
39	5½ / 6	7 / 7½
40	6 / 6½	8 / 8½
41	7	9 / 9½
42	8	9½ / 10
43	9	10½
44	9½ / 10	11
45	10½	12
46	11	12½ / 13

Women's Clothing

Europe	UK	USA
34	6	2
36	8	4
38	10	6
40	12	8
42	14	10
44	16	12

Crime and the Police

Police t 17

Though it isn't widely publicized, Montpellier, Perpignan and Nîmes rank among the very highest crime cities of France.

Don't be alarmed. Violent crime rates are much lower than in British or American cities, and you're probably safer here than you would be at home. Take the usual precautions concerning your valuables and your car. Insure your property, especially if you're driving.

Report **thefts** to the nearest *gendarmerie* – not a pleasant task but the reward is the bit of paper you need for an insurance claim. If your **passport** is stolen, contact the police and your nearest consulate for emergency travel documents. Carry photocopies of your passport, driver's licence, etc.; it makes it easier when reporting a loss.

By law, the police can stop anyone anywhere and demand to see ID; in practice, they only tend to do it to harass minorities and the scruffy.

The **drug** situation is the same in France as anywhere in the West: soft and hard drugs are widely available and the police only make an issue of victimless crime when it suits them. Smuggling any amount of marijuana into the country can mean a prison term.

Eating Out

In this guide, price ranges are based on the cost of a set menu for one person, or for an average three-course meal for one without wine (*see* box).

For more on food and local specialities, *see* **Food and Drink**, pp.51–8. The chapter also contains further details on the wine regions of the area, as well as a menu reader.

Restaurant Price Categories

For full meal, per person, but not including wine, based on set menus.

very expensive	€€€€	over €60
expensive	€€€	€30–60
moderate	€€	€15–30
inexpensive	€	below €15

Electricity

French electricity is 220V. British and Irish appliances need an adapter with two round prongs; North American 110V appliances usually need a transformer as well.

Health and Emergencies

Ambulance (SAMU) **t** 15; **Fire t** 18

According to the UN, France has the best medical system in the world. If you need an English-speaking doctor, local tourist offices should be able to help. Most doctors manage basic English.

If you don't need an ambulance but it's urgent, local **hospitals** are the place to go in an emergency (*urgence*). **Doctors** take turns on duty at night and on holidays, even in rural areas: ring one to listen to the recorded message to find out who to call.

If it's not an emergency, **pharmacists** are trained to administer first aid and dispense advice for minor problems. In rural areas there is always someone on duty if you ring the bell; in cities pharmacies are open on a rota on Sundays and holidays, and addresses are posted in their windows.

The biggest health menace in rural Languedoc-Roussillon are likely to be insect bites or stings. In July and August, tiny chiggers (harvest mites, or *aoûtats*) can be a real nuisance in rural areas, leaving itchy bites around the ankles (wash the area well in warm soap and water as soon as possible; ask in the pharmacy for Aspivenin, Ascabiol or Tiq'Aouta to relieve the itch. In the forests, beware of ticks: if you find one, pull it out with fine tipped tweezers.

For information on **EHIC cards** and health and travel **insurance**, *see* p.64.

National Holidays

On national holidays, banks, shops and businesses close; some museums do too, but most restaurants stay open.

The French have a healthy approach to holidays: if there is a holiday near a weekend, they often 'make a bridge' (*faire le pont*) to the weekend, and take the extra day in between off too.

1 January New Year's Day
Easter Sunday and Monday (Mar or April)
1 May *Fête du Travail* (Labour Day)
8 May VE Day, Victory 1945
Ascension Day (usually end of May)
Pentecost (Whitsun) and following Monday (early June)
14 July Bastille Day
15 August Assumption of the Virgin Mary
1 November All Saints' Day
11 November Remembrance Day (First World War Armistice)
25 December Christmas Day

Opening Hours

Shops: While many shops and supermarkets in large cities now open Mon–Sat 9–7 or later, businesses in smaller towns still close for lunch from 12 or 12.30pm to 2 or 3pm. Smaller shops tend to shut on Mon.

Markets (daily in cities, weekly in villages): usually run mornings only, except clothes, flea and antiques markets.

Banks: Banks generally open 8.30–12.30 and 1.30–4. They close on Sun, and most either on Sat or Mon as well.

Museums: Smaller ones close for lunch, and often all day Mon or Tues, and sometimes for all of Nov or the entire winter. If you're making a special trip out of season, ring ahead. Most museums give **discounts** for children, students and seniors.

Post offices: Generally open Mon–Fri 9–12 and 2–4.30, and Sat 9–12. In larger cities they remain open during lunch.

Churches: Churches are either open all day, or closed all day and only open for Mass. Notes on the door may direct you to a house to pick up the key. There are often admission fees for cloisters, crypts and special chapels.

Post Offices

Branches of **La Poste** are discernible by their sign of a blue bird on a yellow background. Larger offices are equipped with special machines for you to weigh and stamp your package, letter or postcard. You can also purchase **stamps** in tobacconists (*tabacs*).

Sports and Activities

Bullfights

The Roman amphitheatre at Nîmes had hardly been restored in the early 1800s when it once again became a venue for *tauromachie*. The *corrida* or bullfights are now more popular than ever, with massive annual *ferias* in Nîmes and Béziers. Still, not a few were surprised in April 2011, when the bullfights of southern France (and not Spain!) were granted World Heritage status.

Not all bullfights in Languedoc are bloody. The *courses*, as they are called, can be traced back to the bull games described by Heliodorus in ancient Thessaly. Played by daring young men dressed in white called *razeteurs*, the sport demands grace, daring and dexterity; for more information, *see* p.121.

Canoeing and Kayaking

Languedoc-Roussillon is well-endowed with rivers and gorges that make for calm or exciting canoeing or kayaking. You'll find outfitters along the Gardon (allowing you to kayak right under the Pont du Gard), the Vidourle, the Hérault, the Orb and the Aude; you can also canoe along the Canal Rhône à Sète and the Canal du Midi. For white water, head to upper stretches of many of the above rivers, as well as the Cèze in the Gard and the Têt and Tech rivers in Roussillon. You can also sea-kayak in the coastal lagoons and in many spots along the Mediterranean.

Comité Régional de Canoë-Kayak du Languedoc-Roussillon, *www.crck.org/languedocroussillon*.

Extreme Sports

Several companies in the Conflent valley (*see* p.277) in the Pyrenees offer canyoning, rock climbing, caving, via ferrata, mountain biking, and more.

Fishing

You can fish in the sea without a permit as long as your catch is for local consumption. Freshwater fishing requires an easily obtained (if expensive) permit; tourist offices can tell you where to find them. The Lac du Salagou in the valley of the Hérault (*see* p.158) is one of the best spots.

Golfing

There are 20 courses in the region, all listed here: *www.sudfrancegolf.com*, which also offers the chance to purchase a Golf-Pass (high season €150, low season €120), covering greens fees on at least two different courses.

Horse-riding

Each tourist office has a list of riding stables (*centres hippiques* or *centres équestres*), or check the website of the **Comité Régional du Tourisme Equestre** (*www.telr.net*).

The Camargue, with its many ranches, cowboy traditions and open spaces, is the most popular place to ride in the region.

Pétanque

Boules, or *pétanque*, is one of the essential ingredients of the Midi; even the smallest village has a rough, hard *boulodrome* under the plane trees for its practitioners – nearly all male, although women are welcome to join in.

Rugby Union

Rugby is the national sport of southwest France, cradle of most of the players on the national team (although movements to change the national team's name to 'Occitania' have so far fallen flat). You can watch fiery matches in Perpignan, Narbonne, Béziers (the town has three rugby schools) and Carcassonne. In some places they play heretical 'Cathar rugby' – 13 a side instead of 15.

Skiing

Although not endowed with the world's most challenging downhill slopes, skiing in the Pyrenees of Roussillon is enjoyable and an excellent bet for intermediate and beginning skiers, families and snowboarders, with good facilities and excellent cross-country skiing and snow-shoeing. Most of the resorts (Bolquère, Font Romeu, Les Angles and others) have joined forces to create the **Neiges Catalanes Ski Area** (*www.neiges catalanes.com*), with 203 pistes, including 31 black runs, mostly above 2000m with reliable snow; the biggest resort, Font-Romeu, has snow cannons, and plenty of *après-ski* fun.

Spas

Appreciated since ancient times, the region's many naturally therapeutic springs (the vast majority are in Roussillon) now have up to date facilities: Lamalou, Amélie-les-Bains, Rennes-les-Bains, Vernet, Moltig, Prats-de-Mollo, Alet-les-Bains, and the little hot springs up in the Cerdagne, which are especially fun in the snow. For sea treatments, try the plush thalassotherapy spas at La Grande Motte, Cap d'Agde, and Banyuls-sur-Mer.

Walking

Languedoc-Roussillon is well endowed with lovely walks and long distance trails; for more *see* p.71.

Water Sports and Beaches

Languedoc-Roussillon has more miles of free sandy beaches than anywhere in the western Mediterranean, stretching into the horizon on either side of its scores of small resorts. Areas are always set aside for *les naturistes*: Cap d'Agde is Europe's biggest naturist resort, and the enormous beach at Le Grau du Roi in the Camargue has large naturist and gay sections.

The best windsurfing in the region is around Cap Leucate; the best diving (and snorkelling) is off Cap d'Agde and in the Côte Vermeille's marine reserve.

Inland, many of the rivers have pebble beaches and shady swimming.

Telephones and Internet

For dialling codes, *see* p.76.

Public telephones are rare apart from in train stations and airports. They use ***télécartes*** (phonecards), which you can buy at any post office or news-stand. The newer ones also take **credit cards**.

Mobile phone coverage is good, but you may hit a black spot in the mountains or rural areas. European phones work normally in France, but if you mean to do a lot of calling in France it may be worthwhile 'unlocking' your phone to accept a French SIM card from Orange, SFR or Bouygues. Cards may be purchased on line before you leave, and you will be given a French mobile number (starting with 06).

US tri-band cellphones with GSM will work in France (ring your carrier to have it unlocked before you leave for France). When you arrive in France, pick up a pre-paid SIM card.

Many cafés (and all McDonald's) offer free Wi-fi, while some charge a fee. Increasing numbers of hotels and B&Bs offer free Wi-fi in the rooms as well, while campsites usually have a designated area.

Nîmes and the Gard

Like most French départements, *the Gard is named after a river – a river made famous by a feat of Roman engineering that symbolizes the Midi as boldly as the Eiffel Tower does Paris. Its spirit, or at least something intangibly Classical, lingers in the Gard's luminous, sun-blond landscapes and clear air; note how often a solitary windswept pine or cypress dominates the view, as if lifted straight from a painting by Claude Lorrain.*

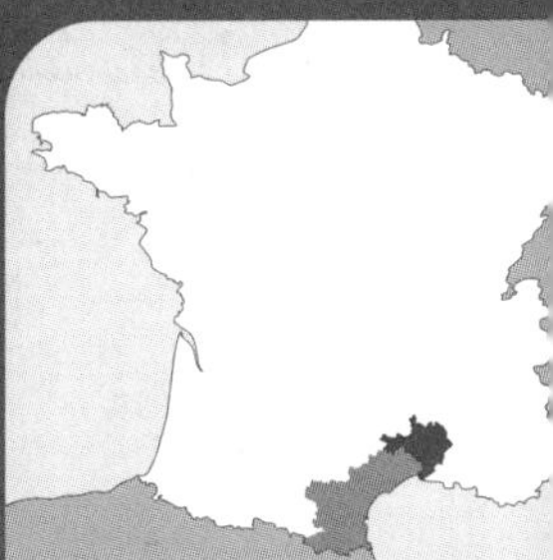

08

Don't miss

1. City of the crocodile and palm tree
   Nîmes **p.83**
2. A legendary Roman aqueduct
   Pont du Gard **p.94**
3. A ducal beauty
   Uzès **p.97**
4. Saint Louis' walled city
   Aigues-Mortes **p.122**
5. Lawrence Durrell's old haunts
   Sommières **p.125**

See map overleaf

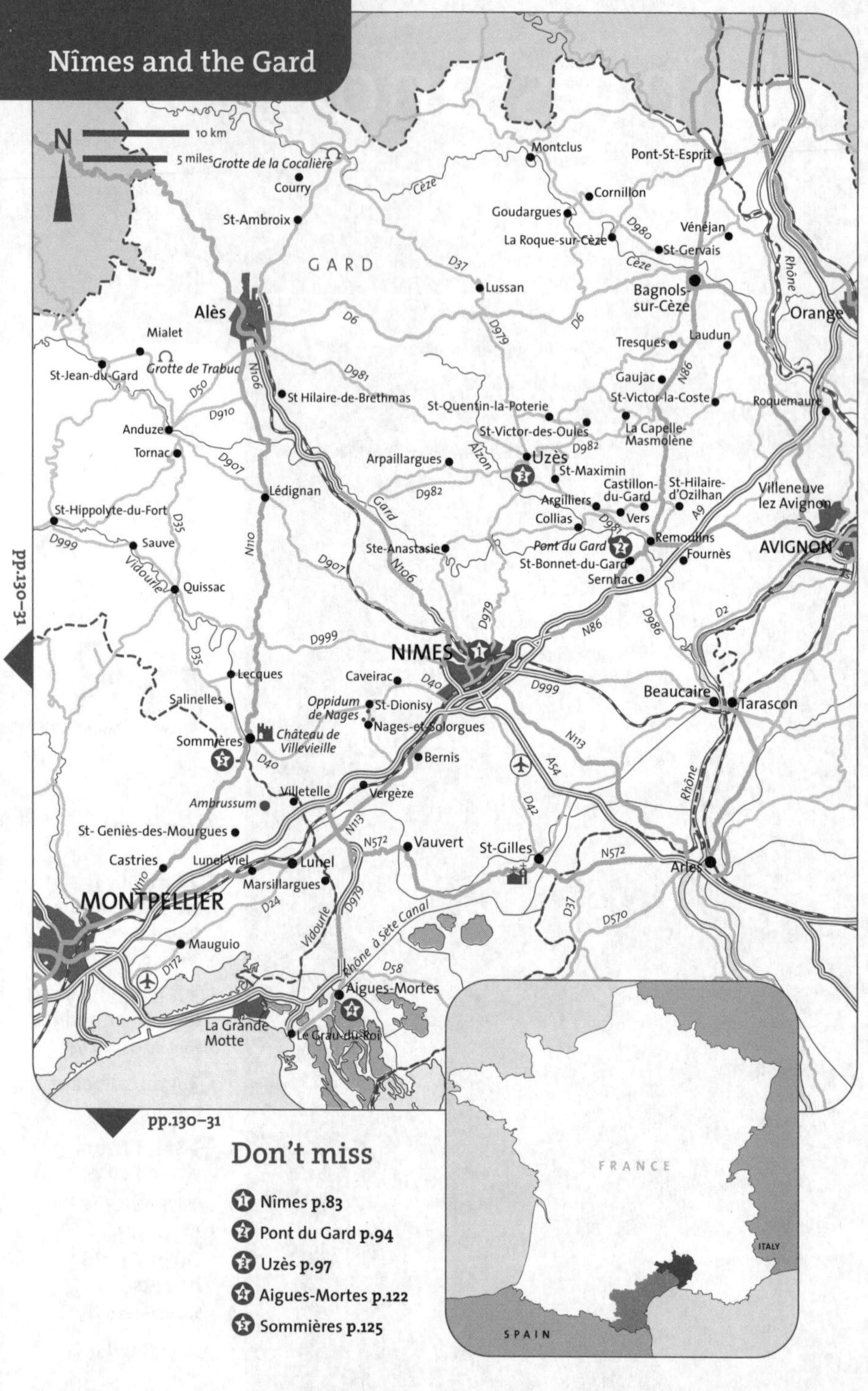

Nîmes and the Gard
N
10 km
5 miles
Grotte de la Cocalière
Courry
St-Ambroix
GARD
Alès
Mialet
St-Jean-du-Gard
Grotte de Trabuc
Anduze
Tornac
St Hilaire-de-Brethmas
Lédignan
St-Hippolyte-du-Fort
Sauve
Quissac
Vidourle
Lecques
Salinelles
Sommières
Château de Villevieille
Ambrussum
Villetelle
St- Geniès-des-Mourgues
Castries
Lunel-Viel
Lunel
Marsillargues
MONTPELLIER
Mauguio
La Grande Motte
Le Grau-du-Roi
Aigues-Mortes
Rhône à Sète Canal
Vauvert
Vergèze
Bernis
Oppidum de Nages
St-Dionisy
Nages-et-Solorgues
Caveirac
NIMES
St-Gilles
Arles
Beaucaire
Tarascon
AVIGNON
Villeneuve lez Avignon
Orange
Roquemaure
Fournès
Remoulins
Sernhac
St-Bonnet-du-Gard
Pont du Gard
Collias
Vers
Argilliers
Castillon-du-Gard
St-Hilaire-d'Ozilhan
St-Maximin
Uzès
Arpaillargues
St-Victor-des-Oules
St-Quentin-la-Poterie
La Capelle-Masmolène
St-Victor-la-Coste
Gaujac
Tresques
Laudun
Bagnols-sur-Cèze
Lussan
St-Gervais
Vénéjan
La Roque-sur-Cèze
Goudargues
Cornillon
Montclus
Pont-St-Esprit
Cèze
Rhône
Gard
Alzon
Ste-Anastasie
D37
D6
D979
D981
D980
D982
D907
D910
D50
N106
N110
D35
D999
D40
N113
A54
D42
N572
D37
D570
D986
N86
D2
A9
D24
D919
D58
D172
pp.130–31
FRANCE
ITALY
SPAIN
Don't miss
1 Nîmes p.83
2 Pont du Gard p.94
3 Uzès p.97
4 Aigues-Mortes p.122
5 Sommières p.125

The Gard's capital, Nîmes, was especially coddled by Rome and still has a full share of grand monuments; Sommières, one of the *département*'s most charming (and most flooded) towns, stands by its Roman bridge. The Gard is also home to Uzès, *ville d'art* and the 'First Duchy of France', to the lush southern Cévennes, to Bagnols-sur-Cèze, with its exceptional little museum of modern art, and to the natural charms and vineyards of the lower valley of the Cèze. The *département* also owns a slice of the Camargue, the romantically swampy delta of the Rhône that includes the once-great medieval towns of St-Gilles and Aigues-Mortes.

Nîmes

★ Nîmes

Built of stone the colour of old piano keys, lively Nîmes is 'the Rome of France' – the Rome of the Caesars, of course, not of the popes: neither the Church nor, for that matter, bossy old Paris have ever gone down well in this mercantile, Protestant town. But after the passions of the Wars of Religion, Nîmes fell into a doze that lasted for centuries. Travellers in the 1800s found it the quintessential dusty southern city; they came to marvel at the city's famous Maison Carrée, the best-preserved Roman temple in the world, and wrote that it was so neglected that it looked as if it was dedicated to the goddess of sewage.

The city saw some spectacular changes under its dynamic mayor in the 1980s, Jean Bousquet, who wakened Nîmes from its daydreams, devoting nearly 14 per cent of its budget to culture in an effort to rival upstart Montpellier. The opening of Sir Norman Foster's Carré d'Art threw down the gauntlet to the then mayor of Montpellier, Georges Frêche. Bousquet then signed up Foster to redevelop Nîmes' old centre, and built a new university, specializing in law, literature and medicine. Just like the one in Montpellier. The current mayor, Jean-Paul Fournier, first elected in 2001, isn't resting on his laurels and among his other accomplishments has at long last restored the Maison Carrée (*see* p.88) in time for its 2,000th birthday.

Most Nîmois view the battle for avant-garde supremacy in this corner of France with detached amusement, for what really makes the juices flow here is not modern architecture but bulls. Nîmes is passionate about its three major annual *ferias*, so much so that – forget Rome – its nickname should be the 'Spain of France'.

History

Geography dealt Nîmes a pair of trump cards: first, a mighty spring, whose god, Nemausus, was worshipped by the first recorded residents, the Celtic Volcae-Arecomici, and secondly, a

Getting to and around Nîmes

By Air

Ryanair flies direct from the UK and Brussels to Nîmes, *see* **Planning Your Trip**. Nîmes-Garons **airport**, **t** 04 66 70 49 49, *www.nimes-aeroport.fr*, is 8km from Nîmes along Rte de St-Gilles (A54). *Navettes* (shuttle buses) coincide with flights and run between the airport and Nîmes' train station and other parts of town; call **t** 04 66 29 27 29.

By Train

Nîmes' train station, at the south end of Av Feuchères on Bd Sgt Triaire, is a kind of arcaded train-aduct that perfectly suits *la Rome française*. There are direct trains to Carcassonne, Montpellier, Arles and Marseille; and TGVs to Paris (4hrs) and Lille (5hrs).

By Bus

The *gare routière* is just behind the train station in Rue Ste-Félicité, **t** 04 66 29 49 02; there are services to the Pont du Gard, Uzès, St-Gilles, Aigues-Mortes, Le Grau-du-Roi, La Grande Motte, Avignon and Montpellier.

Bike Hire

HIre bikes from Commavélo, 28 Rue Emile Jamais, **t** 04 66 29 19 68, *www.commavelo.com.*

---

position on the main route from Italy to Spain, a trail blazed by Hercules himself during his Tenth Labour when he herded Geryon's cattle back to Greece from the Pillars that bear his name. The Romans paved his route in 118 BC and called it the **Via Domitia**, and made Celtic Nîmes into their 'Colonia Nemausensis'. The Volcae-Arecomici Celts, unlike Astérix and Obélix, thought the Romans were just swell, and Augustus reciprocated by endowing Nîmes with the Maison Carrée, a sanctuary for the spring, an aqueduct (the Pont du Gard) to augment the spring, and four miles of walls. The Nîmois celebrated Augustus' conquest of Egypt, and the arrival of a colony of veterans from the Battle of Actium, by minting a coin with a crocodile chained to a palm, a striking image which François Ier adopted as the city's coat of arms in 1535.

Nîmes declined along with Rome; the city contracted, and, after a brief Arab occupation in the 8th century, Frankish viscounts took over and restored some of the town's former prestige by dominating Narbonne and Carcassonne; the Roman amphitheatre was transformed into a fort, the *castrum arenae*, whose knights played a major role in urban affairs. Nîmes, like much of Languedoc, got into trouble with the Church in the early 13th century by taking up the Cathar heresy, although at the approach of the terrible Simon de Montfort the city surrendered without a fight.

Catholicism never went down well in Nîmes, and, when the Protestant alternative presented itself in the 16th century, three-quarters of the population took to the new religion immediately and attacked the other quarter's churches and prelates. The terror reached a peak with the **Michelade**, the massacre of 200 priests, monks and nuns in 1567, but continued off and on until the Edict of Nantes (1598); this brought Nîmes enough peace for its Protestants

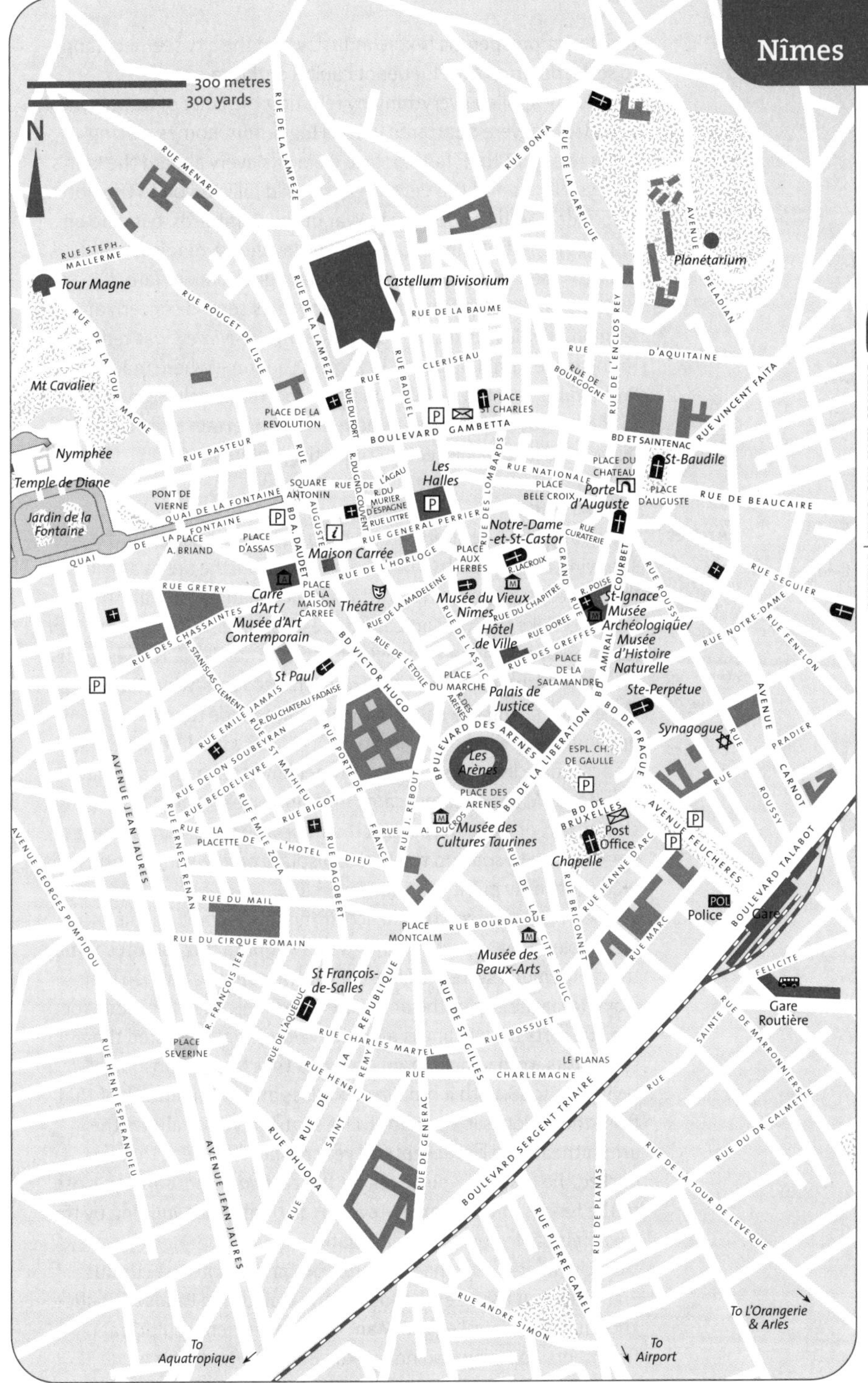

300 metres
300 yards
N
Rue Menard
Rue de la Lampeze
Rue Bonfa
Rue de la Garrigue
Avenue Peladian
Planétarium
Rue Steph. Mallerme
Tour Magne
Castellum Divisorium
Rue Rouget de Lisle
Rue de la Baume
Rue de la Tour Magne
Rue de l'Enclos Rey
Rue Cleriseau
Rue Baduel
Rue d'Aquitaine
Rue de Bourgogne
Mt Cavalier
Place de la Revolution
Rue du Fort
Place St Charles
Boulevard Gambetta
Rue Vincent Faita
Bd et Saintenac
Rue Pasteur
Nymphée
Temple de Diane
Jardin de la Fontaine
Les Halles
Rue Nationale
Place du Chateau
St-Baudile
Pont de Vierne
Quai de la Fontaine
Square Antonin
R. du Gnd Couvent
Rue de l'Agau
R. du Murier d'Espagne
Rue Littre
Place Bele Croix
Porte d'Auguste
Place d'Auguste
Rue de Beaucaire
Place A. Briand
Place d'Assas
Bd A. Daudet
Rue Auguste
Rue General Perrier
Rue des Lombards
Notre-Dame -et-St-Castor
Rue Curaterie
Quai de la Fontaine
Maison Carrée
Rue de l'Horloge
Place aux Herbes
R. Lacroix
Grand Rue
Rue Courbet
Rue Roussy
Rue Seguier
Rue Gretry
Carré d'Art/ Musée d'Art Contemporain
Place de la Maison Carree
Théâtre
Rue de la Madeleine
Musée du Vieux Nîmes
Rue du Chapitre
R. Poise
St-Ignace
Musée Archéologique/ Musée d'Histoire Naturelle
Rue Notre-Dame
Rue Fenelon
Rue des Chassaintes
R. Stanislas Clement
Hôtel de Ville
Rue Doree
Rue des Greffes
Bd Amiral
Place de la Salamandre
Rue de l'Etoile
Rue de l'Aspic
St Paul
Bd Victor Hugo
Place du Marche
Rue des Arenes
Palais de Justice
Ste-Perpétue
Avenue Carnot
Rue Emile Jamais
R. du Chateau Fadaise
Rue Porte de France
Boulevard des Arenes
Bd de la Liberation
Bd de Prague
Synagogue
Rue Pradier
Les Arènes
Espl. Ch. de Gaulle
Rue Delon Soubeyran
Rue St Mathieu
Rue Becdelievre
Rue Emile Zola
Rue Bigot
Rue J. Reboul
Place des Arenes
Rue A. Ducros
Musée des Cultures Taurines
Bd de Bruxelles
Post Office
Avenue Feucheres
Rue Roussy
Avenue Jean Jaures
Rue Ernest Renan
Rue la Placette
Rue de l'Hotel Dieu
Rue Dagobert
Chapelle
Rue Jeanne d'Arc
Rue Briconnet
Rue de la Cite Foulc
Police
Gare
Boulevard Talabot
Avenue Georges Pompidou
Rue du Mail
Rue du Cirque Romain
Place Montcalm
Rue Bourdaloue
Musée des Beaux-Arts
Rue Marc
Rue Felicite
Gare Routière
St François-de-Salles
Rue de la Republique
R. François 1er
Rue de l'Aqueduc
Rue de St Gilles
Rue Sainte
Rue de Marronniers
Place Severine
Rue Charles Martel
Rue Bossuet
Le Planas
Rue Henri IV
Rue Remy
Rue Charlemagne
Rue Henri Esperandieu
Rue de Saint
Rue de Generac
Boulevard Sergent Triaire
Rue du Dr Calmette
Rue Dhuoda
Rue de la Tour de Leveque
Rue de Planas
Rue Pierre Gamel
Rue Andre Simon
To L'Orangerie & Arles
To Aquatropique
To Airport

to set up a prosperous textile industry, and the city seemed happy to settle down as the Huguenot capital of the south.

Louis XIV spoiled everything by revoking the Edict of Nantes in 1685; troops were quartered in the Huguenots' homes, forcing them to abjure their faith or face exile or slavery aboard the king's galleys. Nîmes and the Cévennes, the wild hilly region to the north, responded with the desperate **War of the Camisards**, tying up an important part of the French army by inventing, or reinventing, many of the techniques used in modern guerrilla warfare.

After the troubles, Nîmes went back to its second concern after religion: textiles. Its heavy-duty blue *serge 'de Nîmes'* was reduced to the more familiar 'denim' in 1695 in London – where many of the Protestants went in exile – and was exported widely. Some of it found its way to California, where in 1848 a certain Levi Strauss discovered it to be perfect for outfitting goldrushers.

The Arènes

Arènes
t 04 66 21 82 56, www.arenes-nimes.com; open summer 9–7 (tickets until 6.30); winter 9.30–5 (tickets until 4.15); free audioguide with ticket; closed during events (see website); adm

Ranking only twentieth in size but the best preserved of the 70 surviving amphitheatres of the Roman world, the arena at Nîmes (late 1st century AD) is just a little smaller than its twin at Arles in Provence. Like the Maison Carrée, it escaped being cannibalized for its stone by being put to constant use: as a castle for the Visigoths and the knightly militia of the Frankish viscounts, who bricked up the arches facing the Palais de Justice and made them their headquarters; then, after union with France, as a slum, where some 2,000 people lived in shanties jammed into the arches, seats and *vomitoria*. When restorers came in 1809 to clear it out, they had to shovel 20ft of rubbish to reach the floor where the sands (*arènes*) were spread to soak up the blood; displays on the various kinds of gladiators now put it all in context.

When new, the arena could accommodate 24,000 people, who were able to reach or leave their seats in only a few minutes thanks to an ingenious system of five concentric galleries and 126 stairways. Near the top of the arena are holes pierced in the stone for the supports of the canvas awning (*velum*) that sheltered the spectators from sun and rain – an idea that Mayor Bousquet revived in 1988, with a mobile plexiglass and aluminium roof that from the air looks like a giant toilet seat, but which allows the amphitheatre to host events all year round. The event that has packed the crowds in since 1853 is the *corrida*, a sport always close to the hearts of the Nîmois – even in ancient times, judging by the two bulls carved over the main gate.

On the nearby Esplanade Charles de Gaulle, note the curious Siamese-twin figure embedded in the wall of the Palais de Justice, known as the '**Four-Legged Man**', made of ancient sculptural fragments. You may also notice Rue Bigot, named after a

19th-century fable writer from Nîmes. The name is particularly pertinent to local attitudes in the Wars of Religion. 'Bigot', after all, comes from the Old French and refers to the first religious intolerance to shake Nîmes – the conflict between the Catholicism of the Franks and the Arianism of the Visigoths, or *Bigothi*.

Crocodiles Galore, the Maison Carrée and the Carré d'Art

The *hôtels particuliers* in the historic centre – the area between the Arènes, the Maison Carrée and the cathedral – date from the 17th and 18th centuries, when Nîmes' textile magnates and financiers enjoyed their greatest prosperity. Beginning at the Four-Legged Man, **Rue de l'Aspic** (which in French evokes vipers as well as jelly) is one of the candidates for the *cardo*, the shorter of the two main streets of a Roman town. The city's most charming square, the **Place du Marché**, opens up to the left, and is the site of a charming **crocodile fountain** designed by Martial Raysse. Four more examples of the city's saurian emblem (donated by well-wishers to the city between 1597 and 1703) can be seen stuffed and dangling high over the stair in the high-tech designer interior of the 18th-century **Hôtel de Ville**, to the right of Rue de l'Aspic.

Around the corner, at 16 Rue Dorée, Nîmes' very own Académie meets behind the elaborate portal of the 17th-century **Hôtel de l'Académie**. This body was granted the same privileges as the Académie Française in 1682 by Louis XIV, and even today the Académiciens of Nîmes may sit with their fellows in Paris.

To the south, the amphibian community is represented in **Place de la Salamandre**, named after François Ier's totem animal. Many Renaissance rulers had similar emblems, and used to represent them in works of art; François chose the salamander for the belief that it could survive in fire – the first fabrics woven of asbestos were called 'salamander skins'. The salamander sculpture that once adorned this square now stands in the courtyard of the Archaeology Museum, but note the square's 17th-century **Hôtel de Chazelles**, another fine example of civic architecture.

To the north stands Nîmes' **Cathédrale Notre-Dame-et-St-Castor**, which was consecrated in 1096 but almost completely flattened by rampaging Huguenots in 1597 and 1622, who spared only the campanile to use as a watchtower. A vigorous frieze of the Old Testament runs across the façade, while lower down, and sadly damaged, are reliefs of Samson and the lion, and Alexander the Great being pulled up to heaven by a pair of griffons, coaxed by a piece of liver dangled over their heads – a favourite medieval fancy. Another Romanesque frieze nearby adorns a rare 12th-century house, the **Maison Romane**, on the corner of Place aux Herbes and Rue de la Madeleine.

Maison Carrée
www.arenes-nimes.com; open summer 10–8; spring and autumn 10–6; winter 10–1 and 2–4.30; adm

What an infatuation in modern architects, that can overlook the chaste and elegant simplicity of taste manifest in such a work, and yet rear such piles of laboured foppery and heaviness as are to be met with in France.

Arthur Young, *Travels*, 1787

Musée d'Art Contemporain
t 04 66 76 35 70, www.nimes.fr; open Tues–Sun 10–6; closed Mon; free; library open Tues and Thurs 10.30–7, Wed, Fri and Sat 10.30–6; museum library open mid-Aug–mid-July Tues–Sat pm only plus Sat am

Of course, more remarkable still is the state of that graceful little 1st-century BC temple known as the **Maison Carrée**, just off the Via Domitia in Place de la Maison Carrée. The best-preserved Roman temple anywhere, it was built by General Agrippa (who also built the Pantheon in Rome) and was dedicated to the Imperial cult of Augustus' grandsons, Caius and Lucius, the 'Princes of Youth' – their 'deification' a form of flattery to the emperor. Called *carrée*, or square, because of its right angles and 'long' square shape (85ft by 50ft), its *cella* (or cult sanctuary) is perfectly intact, as are the Corinthian columns of the porch. Nîmes always found it useful for something, most notably as the meeting hall of the consuls and least notably as a stable, and now for a cheesy 3D film about gladiators. Some locals have complained that the temple's restoration was so thorough that it now looks fake!

In the 1990s, Sir Norman Foster was given the chance to make a modern riposte in Place de la Maison Carrée – the **Carré d'Art** (1993). The ancient columns of the Maison Carrée are reflected in Foster's slender columns of steel; the walls and even the stairways are of glass to let light stream through the building. Inside, the **Musée d'Art Contemporain** on the first floor contains over 250 post-1960 works, plus temporary exhibitions; other floors house a library strong in two local obsessions – Protestantism and bullfighting – and a smaller library of art, while the top floor is home to a lovely café.

Water and Other Mysteries

A block north of the Carré d'Art, **Place d'Assas** was designed by Martial Raysse in 1989 as a kind of expiatory gesture to the two religions that went down in Nîmes without a fight: that of the Celts (the two figures in the central fountain represent the indigenous gods, 'Nemausa' and 'Nemausus') and the Cathars (the mysterious seven-pointed stars, etc.). The statue at the west end is of Ernest Denis of Nîmes, whose writing championed the founding of Czechoslovakia in 1918. Nearby in the **Square Antonin**, a 19th-century statue of Emperor Antoninus Pius (whose family was from Nîmes) holds his hand out, as the Nîmois say, to see if it's raining.

A short walk north of here will bring you to Rue Lampèze and a basin 18ft in diameter called the **Castellum Divisorium**, where the five million gallons of water gushing in from the Pont du Gard was distributed to the city through 10 pipes of lead. The only other one to survive is at Pompeii. Like so much in Nîmes it was built under Augustus, and to him was dedicated the city's east gate on the Via Domitia (Rue Nationale), the **Porte d'Auguste**. Built in 15 BC, it had two entrances for vehicles, and two smaller ones for pedestrians.

But before Augustus there was Nemausus the water god, and the leafy Quai de la Fontaine west of Square Antonin leads to his spring, domesticated as the **Jardin de la Fontaine** in the 18th century – making it one of the very first public gardens in France, complete with a neo-Roman *nymphaeum* and a maze of balustrades and urns and canals; altogether, the ensemble is one of the loveliest city parks in France. In ancient times a complex of temples and sanctuaries stood here, of which only the so-called **Temple de Diane** (perhaps originally a library) remains.

Tour Magne
www.arenes-nimes.com; viewing platform open summer daily 9.30–6.30; winter daily 9.30–1 and 2–4.30, spring and autumn daily 9.30–6; adm

Paths wind up among the flowerbeds and leafy arbours of Mont Cavalier to the oldest Roman monument in Gaul, the octagonal **Tour Magne**. No record of its origin or purpose has survived, though some speculate that it may have been a trophy dedicated to the opening of the Via Domitia, or a signal tower, or simply the mightiest of the 30 towers in the city wall – a sort of 'homage tower' like those of Aigues-Mortes and other medieval cities. Although 106ft high today, the tower was once half as big again; stairs spiral up to the viewing platform. The Tour Magne made news in 1601, when a gardener named François Traucat read Nostradamus' prediction that a gardener would uncover an immense buried treasure. As it was commonly believed that the Romans, like leprechauns, hid pots of gold in their ruins, Traucat decided the treasure must be buried under the Tour Magne. Henri IV gave him permission to dig (at his own expense, and with two-thirds of the loot going to the crown), but instead of finding gold he found another pre-Roman tower around which the even larger Tour Magne had been built. No one could identify the rubble at the time, and the Consul of Nîmes, fearing that any more digging would undermine the Tour Magne, ordered the now bankrupt Traucat back to his garden.

Museum-crawling

The former Jesuit college at 13 bis Boulevard Amiral Courbet was, after the Edict of Nantes, diplomatically divided between Protestants and Catholics. Nowadays, the division is between pot-shards and possums, the first half devoted to archaeology and the second to natural history. The **Musée Archéologique** is filled with odds and ends for the expert, such as a vast collection of ancient inscriptions, but there are some crowd-pleasers as well: the 4th- to 3rd-century BC figure of the *Guerrier de Grézen*, in his curved hood-helmet and belt, and nearby a rare Celtic lintel, the *Linteau de Nages*, found near the *oppidum*'s spring (*see* 'Nages', p.124). The lintel has a frieze of galloping horses and human heads – favourite Celtic motifs, but rarely carved with such pizzazz. Upstairs is a fine collection of ancient glass and everyday Roman items, Greek vases, bronze figurines and miniature altars, some bearing the mallet of the Celtic god Sucellus, whom the Romans adapted to become their Silvanus.

Musée Archéologique
t 04 66 76 74 80; open Tues–Sun 10–6; closed Mon; adm

Wine: Costières-de-Nîmes

Covering 24 *communes* between Estézargues and Vauvert, the AOC Région des Costières de Nîmes rides the high terraces and hills of the Rhône, where the vineyards are planted amid round pebbles (*les grès*). Near Nîmes, the rough landscape is tempered by the sea, and, although the district is best known for rosés, the reds (similar to Côtes du Rhône) and whites (made from clairette, grenache blanc, maccabeo and marsanne) are good, inexpensive, fresh young wines; the reds are only aged two or three years at the most.

For more information, visit the **Syndicat Vignerons des Costières de Nîmes**, 19 Place Aristide Briand, Quai de la Fontaine, **t** 04 66 36 96 20.

Musée d'Histoire Naturelle
t 04 66 76 73 45; open Tues–Sun 10–6; closed Mon

The other half of the college is the charmingly old-fashioned **Musée d'Histoire Naturelle**, home to a collection of those mysterious menhirs-with-personality, the statue-steles. Carved with stylized faces, and sometimes with arms, a knife and a belt (*c.* 2000 BC), they are similar to those found in the Hérault, and also in Tuscany and Corsica. Large glass cases of scary masks and spears and early 20th-century photographs fill the ethnographic hall, and beyond is a brave little natural history collection featuring a 9ft stuffed moose, a beaver foetus, a wide selection of faded bats, two-headed lambs and deformed kittens, pine-cone-shaped pangolins, stuffed *corrida* bulls from the 1890s, two baby rabbits in formaldehyde retrieved from the belly of a snake, and an armadillo 'captured near the Pont du Gard'.

Adjacent, the Jesuit church **St-Ignace** (1678) is a fine piece of Baroque architecture with an unusual pattern of vaults and openings, now used for exhibitions.

Musée du Vieux Nîmes
t 04 66 76 73 70; open Tues–Sun 10–6; closed Mon

For the **Musée du Vieux Nîmes** in Place aux Herbes, follow Grand-Rue behind the museums, north to Rue Lacroix. It has an exceptional collection of 19th-century textiles and 500 print designs – a real eye-opener for anyone who thought the paisley design was invented in the 1960s. There are 17th-century carved *armoires*, a Charles X billiard table, a 19th-century bed supported by weightlifters, and ceramics and an abundance of curios.

Musée des Beaux-Arts
t 04 66 67 38 21; open Tues–Sun 10–6; closed Mon; adm

The **Musée des Beaux-Arts** is on the other side of the Arènes, on Rue de la Cité-Foulc, in a charming 1907 building by a local architect, who chiselled the façade with the names of Nîmes' painters and sculptors, and optimistically left plenty of room for future geniuses. It was opulently restored by Jean-Michel Wilmotte in 1986–7. In the centre of the ground floor is an enormous Roman mosaic, *The Betrothal of Admetus*, surrounded by a frieze of scenes. Upstairs, look out for two Venetian paintings: an example of 15th-century retro in Michele Giambono's *Mystic Marriage of St Catherine*, and one of Jacopo Bassano's finest works, *Susanna and the Elders* (1585), with a serene bunny rabbit in the corner. As usual, it's the Dutch paintings, with their buxom wenches and oyster-slurping sessions, that one would most like to be in. Of the

French offerings, the outstanding painting is Paul Delaroche's *Cromwell Looking into the Coffin of Charles I*, an 18th-century painting as memorable as it is odd.

Planétarium
Avenue Peladan, **t** *04 66 67 60 94; public shows Sat and Sun 3pm; adm*

If you are tired of terrestrial culture, Nîmes' small **Planétarium** off Avenue du Mont Duplan takes you to the stars with glittering displays of the universe.

Musée des Cultures Taurines
t *04 66 36 83 77; open mid-May–early Nov Tues–Sun 10–6; closed Mon; adm*

Appropriately located near to the Arena, the **Musée des Cultures Taurines** at 6 Rue Alexandre Ducros is one of only a few museums dedicated to bullfighting in France. Over 8,000 exhibits illustrate the different forms of the fight, the history of the *tauromachie*, the famous *toreros*, and the culture of the *corridas*.

Aficionados of modern architecture won't want to miss **Nemausus**, the subsidized housing project commissioned by Mayor Bousquet from Jean Nouvel in 1987. It's south of the station, on the Route d'Arles, and resembles a pair of beached ocean liners from the future. You wouldn't want to live there, but in 2008 it was awarded 20th-century heritage status, so it's there to stay.

Market Days in Nîmes

Daily: Les Halles, 5 Rue des Halles.
Mon am: Av Jean Jaurès, flea market.
Fri am: Bd Jean Jaurès Sud, organic and farmers' market.

Festivals in Nîmes

See Nîmes at its most exuberant during its two major *ferias*: during the six-day ***Feria de Pentecôte*** (Whitsun), which draws even bigger crowds than Munich's *Oktoberfest*, or during the ***Feria de Vendages***, the third weekend of September. As in Seville, people open up their homes as *bodegas* to take the overflow of aficionados from the cafés, and the drinking and music go on until dawn. In July, the Arènes come alive with music at the ***Festival de Nîmes***, *www.festivaldenimes.com*.

Where to Stay in Nîmes

Nîmes >
6 Rue Auguste, near the Maison Carrée, **t** *04 66 58 38 00, www.ot-nimes.fr; open daily all year*

Nîmes ✉ 30000

Reservations are essential during the *ferias*, when prices are higher.

Very Expensive (€€€€)

****__Hôtel Impérator Concorde__, Quai de la Fontaine, **t** 04 66 21 90 30, *nimes.concorde-hotels.com*. A 19th-century dowager with a facelift, a lovely garden, and good restaurant to boot.

Jardins Secrets >>

****__Jardins Secrets__, 3 Rue Gaston Maruejol, **t** 04 66 84 82 64, *www.jardinssecrets.net*. A romantic oasis that lives up to its name, plus a spa and a pool.

Expensive (€€€)

***__L'Hacienda__, Le Mas de Brignon, Marguerittes ✉ 30320 (8km northeast on N86), **t** 04 66 75 02 25, *www.hotel-hacienda-nimes.com*. A large farmhouse in the *garrigue*, converted into a hotel with a spacious swimming pool, terraces and an excellent restaurant (€€€; *dinner only*).

Cheval Blanc >>

Cheval Blanc, 1 Place des Arènes, **t** 04 66 76 05 22, *www.lechevalblanc-nimes.com*. Chic rooms, nearly all with views of the Arènes, in a former denim factory; self-catering available.

***__L'Orangerie__, 755 Rue de la Tour de l'Evêque, **t** 04 66 84 50 57, *www.orangerie.fr*. Best Western hotel 1km from the centre with a garden, pool and restaurant (€€).

Moderate (€€)

__Hôtel des Tuileries__, 22 Rue Roussy, **t 04 66 21 31 15, *www.hoteldestuileries.com*. Lovely little central hotel with Wi-fi, a garage, and friendly staff.

__Majestic__, 10 Rue Pradier, **t 04 66 29 24 14, *www.hotel-majestic-nimes.com*.

Colour-drenched rooms (including some for families) with Wi-fi and air-conditioning.

****Hôtel de l'Amphithéâtre**, 4 Rue des Arènes, **t** 04 66 67 28 51, *www.hotel-amphitheatre.pagesperso-orange.fr*. Sweetly restored 18th-century building in the old town, with antique furniture and nice big bathrooms.

Inexpensive (€)

Acanthe du Temple, 1 Rue Charles Babut, **t** 04 66 67 54 61, *www.hotel-temple.com*. Nîmes' best bargain, a friendly family hotel in a 17th-century building in the centre of town, all 20 rooms en suite and equipped with fans.

***Hôtel Brasserie des Arènes**, 4 Bd des Arènes, **t** 04 66 67 23 05, *www.brasserie-arenes.com*. Not very quiet, but it's central and has Wi-fi, and a brasserie serves Provençal cuisine (€€).

Auberge de Jeunesse, 257 Chemin de l'Auberge de Jeunesse, **t** 04 66 68 03 20, *www.fuaj.org/Nimes*. On a hill 2km from the centre (bus I from the station, direction Alès or Villeverte, get off at stop '*Stade*' and follow signs).

★ A la Table de Clair >>

Eating Out in Nîmes

Nîmes claims some delicious specialities: *brandade de morue* (pounded cod mixed with fine olive oil), a recipe said to date back to Roman times, and *tapenade*, an appetizer made of olives, anchovies and herbs. Its *pélardons*, the little goat's cheeses from the *garrigues*, are among the best anywhere. The city is also proud of its *croquants Villaret*, almond biscuits cooked by the same family in the same oven since 1775, available at **Maison Villaret**, 13 Rue de la Madeleine, **t** 04 66 67 41 79.

Alexandre, 1 Rue Xavier Tronc, **t** 04 66 70 08 99, *www.michelkayser.com* (€€€€). Michelin-starred chef Michel Kayser mans the hob at Nîmes' top restaurant, featuring ever-evolving market cuisine; the setting is a delight, too, in a contemporary house with a beautiful garden. *Closed July and Aug Sun and Mon; Sept–June Sun eve, Mon and Tues.*

Le Darling, 40 Rue Madeleine, **t** 04 66 67 04 99, *www.ledarling.com* (€€€€). As the name suggests, it's a romantic place to bring your honey, to savour the fresh, original cuisine invented by the New Caledonia-born chef. *Closed Wed.*

Aux Plaisirs des Halles, 4 Rue Littré, **t** 04 66 36 01 02. *www.auxplaisirsdeshalles.com* (€€€–€€). Exquisite little bistro near the market. Ask the chef for *aïoli* with vegetables or *brandade* with truffles and black olives. *Closed Sun, Mon.*

Le Lisita, 2 Bd des Arènes, **t** 04 66 67 29 15, *www.lelisita.com* (€€€). Next to the amphitheatre, decorated with bullfighting memorabilia, serving regional and gastronomic cuisine. *Closed Sun and Mon.*

Le Jardin d'Hadrien, 11 Rue de l'Enclos Rey, **t** 04 66 21 86 65, *www.lejardindhadrien.fr* (€€€–€€). A favourite, with its beamed dining room and veranda; try the cod with olive oil, or courgette flowers stuffed with *brandade*. *Closed Sun eve–Tues lunch.*

A la Table de Clair, Place des Esclafidous, **t** 04 66 67 55 61 (€€€–€€). Self-taught chef Clair has the culinary instincts of a master – try the succulent steaks of Camargue beef with ravioli, flavoured with white truffles. *Eves only, closed Sun.*

Nicolas, 1 Rue du Poise (off Bd Amiral Courbet), **t** 04 66 67 50 47 (€€€–€€). One of the more affordable fine restaurants in town, and always busy. *Closed Sat lunch, Mon and Tues.*

Le Petit Bec, 87 bis Rue de la République, **t** 04 66 38 05 83, *www.restaurant-lepetitbec.fr* €€). A tempting selection of seasonal dishes to eat in the garden. *Closed Sun eve, Mon, most of Aug and of Feb.*

Au Flan Coco, 21 Rue Grand Couvent, **t** 04 66 21 84 81, *www.auflancoco.com* (€€). Handsome, atmospheric restaurant; try their speciality, the Pat' à Coco – a potato and meat pie with a *salade composée. Closed Mon and Sun.*

Wine Bar Le Cheval Blanc, 1 Place des Arènes, **t** 04 66 76 19 59 (€€). Stylish and popular place to sip Languedoc's wines with well-prepared steaks and seafood dishes. *Closed Sun.*

Le Chapon Fin, 3 Place du Château-Fadaise (behind St Paul's church), **t** 04 66 67 34 73, *www.chaponfin-restaurant-nimes.com* (€€). Excellent informal *bistrot* seving local, filling dishes. *Closed Sat and Sun.*

Entertainment and Nightlife in Nîmes

Clubs and Bars

The Pelican, 54 Rte de Beaucaire, **t** 04 66 29 63 28, *www.thepelican.fr*. Lively bar with a Louisiana theme, playing great music. *Closed Mon.*

Le Rezo, 2 Rue Notre-Dame, **t** 04 66 64 79 40. Lively bar just outside the centre.

La Bodeguita, 3 Bd Alphonse Daudet, **t** 04 66 58 28 29. A *tapas* and music bar (jazz, tango, flamenco and salsa) especially popular during *feria* time.

La Comédie, Rue Jean Reboul, **t** 06 76 99 42 50. The hip in-town in-club, near the Arènes. *Open Thurs, Fri and Sat night.*

Lulu Club, 10, Rue de la Curaterie, **t** 04 66 36 28 20. Nîmes' gay disco, with lots of funk and soul.

Classical Music and Theatre

Théâtre de Nîmes, 1 Place de la Calade, **t** 04 66 36 65 10, *www.theatredenimes.com*. Full schedule of opera, dance and concerts.

Cinema

Le Sémaphore, 25 Rue Porte de France, **t** 04 66 67 83 11, *www.semaphore.free.fr*. Sometimes shows films in their original language (*v.o.*).

Leisure

Aquatropic, 39 Chemin de l'Hostellerie, near the *autoroute* exit Nîmes-Ouest, **t** 04 66 38 31 00, *http://aquatropic-equalia.fr*. Indoor/outdoor water park, with sauna, tennis and keep-fit centre.

North of Nîmes

The Pont du Gard and Around

...when one sees the thing, all that is said of it comes true. Its isolation, its dignity, its weight, are all three awful. It looks as though it had been built long before all record by beings greater than ourselves, and was intended to stand long after the dissolution of our petty race.
Hilaire Belloc

By 19 BC the fountain of Nemausus could no longer slake Nîmes' thirst, and the search was on for a new source. The Romans were obsessed with the quality of their water, and, when they found a crystal-clear spring called the Eure near Uzès, the fact that it was 48km away hardly posed an obstacle to antiquity's star engineers. The resulting aqueduct, built under Augustus' son-in-law Agrippa, was like a giant needle hemming the landscape, piercing tunnels through hills and looping its arches over the open spaces of the *garrigue*, and all measured precisely to allow a slope of 0.07 centimetres per metre. Where the water had to cross the gorge of the unpredictable River Gardon, the Roman engineers knuckled down, ordered a goodly supply of neatly dressed stone from the nearby quarries at Vers and built, without a speck of cement, the Pont du Gard, at 157ft the highest of all Roman aqueducts and, along with the span in Segovia, the best preserved in the world.

The Discovery Centre, nature paths and kayaking under the big arches can easily take up much of the day here; bring your swimsuit.

North of Nîmes

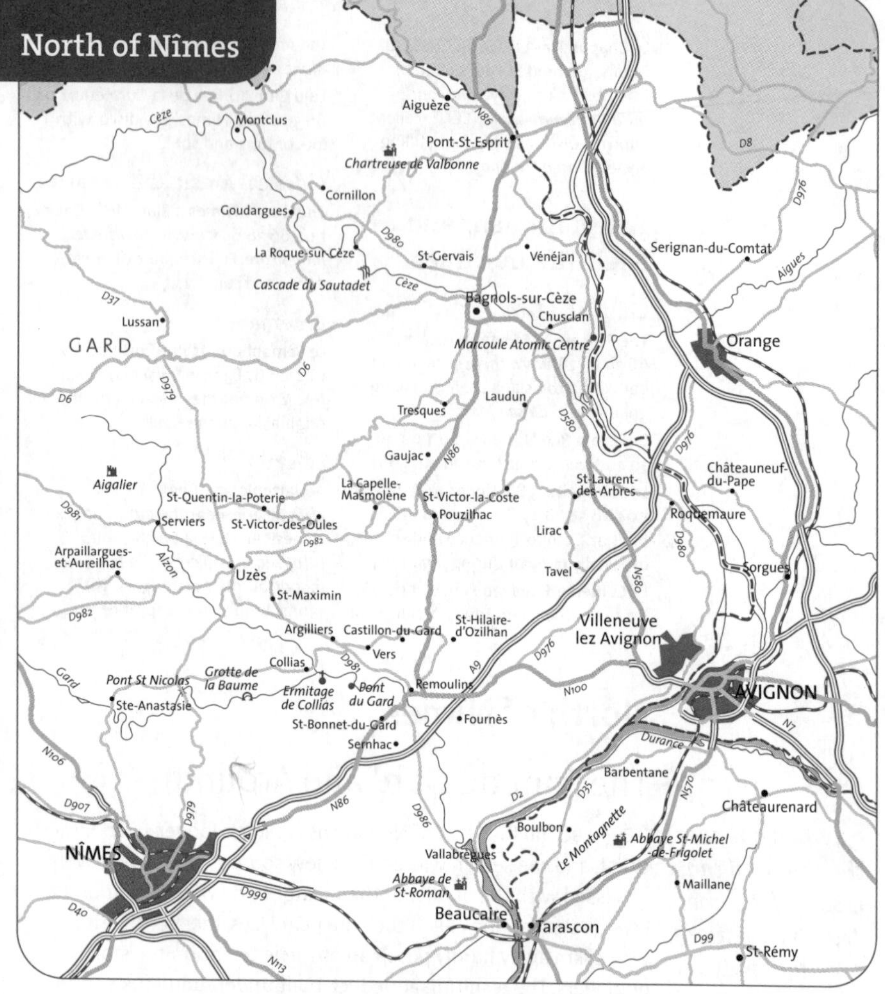

The Pont du Gard

Pont du Gard
www.pontdugard.fr; open year-round

No matter how many photos you've seen before, the aqueduct's three tiers of arches of golden stone without mortar make a brave and lovely sight; since the 1920s the natural setting and river have been maintained as intact as possible. In summer it's beautifully illuminated, its arches glowing magically in the night.

What the photos never show are the two million people who come to pay it homage every year (it's one of the five most visited sites in France), so you may well find it more evocative if you arrive very early in the morning or about an hour before sunset. As you walk over it, notice how it's slightly curved (the better to stand up to floods) and how the Roman engineers left cavities and protruding stones to support future scaffolding. In the 18th

Getting around North of Nîmes

Edgard bus B21 from Nîmes, Uzès and Bagnols-sur-Cèze pass within a kilometre of the Pont du Gard (**t** 08 10 33 42 73, *www.edgard-transport.fr*). The Pont du Gard has pay **car parks** on either side.

Canoes and **kayaks** for paddling under the Pont du Gard are available for hire upstream at Collias; just try to avoid the summer afternoon rush hour (**Kayak Vert, t** 04 66 22 80 76, *www.canoe-france.com/riviere-gardon-canoe-france.html)*.

For **bike** hire in Uzès, try Les Cycles d'Uzès, 4 Av du Maréchal Foch, **t** 04 66 57 41 15, or **Village Vélo** at St-Quentin-la-Poterie, **t** 06 86 45 13 10, *www.villagevelo.org*.

century, the bottom tier was expanded to take a road that was used until 1996.

As testimony to the skill of its engineers, the Pont du Gard has stood up to some terrific floods that destroyed far younger bridges over the Gardon, including one in 1958 that reached the second tier. Devastating floods in 1998 and 2002 prompted a major renovation project: new visitors' centres and car parks were built on either side of the bridge, along with a pedestrianized promenade and restaurants and shops.

The Pont du Gard Discovery Centre

Pont du Gard Discovery Centre
t 04 66 37 50 99; open April–Oct 9–5.30 (May–Sept till 7); closed Mon am; adm; entrances on both banks; closed Nov–Mar

The Discovery Centre explains everything you could possibly want to know about the big bridge, with special archaeological and engineering projects for children, films, permanent exhibitions and a cafeteria offering sandwiches and light lunches. Ring ahead to book one of the 90-minute **guided tours**, which is the only way to walk through the upper channel. There are marked botanical trails through the surrounding *garrigue*, and other paths around Vers that explore the ancient quarries and tracks used by the ancient engineers to bring the stone to the building site. For the restoration, the ancient Estel quarries were reopened. Some of the original blocks weigh six tonnes; many have inscriptions, a few left by the Roman builders, but most left by the *compagnons*, French journeyman masons who, as part of their training, travelled about France studying its most important monuments.

Wine Villages Around the Aqueduct

Just north, hilltop **Castillon-du-Gard** exudes medieval atmosphere, even if it was mostly rebuilt in the 16th century. It offers views down to the Pont du Gard and a Romanesque chapel, St-Caprais, a setting for summer concerts and art exhibitions. East of Castillon, 11th-century **St-Hilaire-d'Ozilhan** is another charming village with an even older chapel, the Clastre, standing on its own just to the south. If it's *supermarchés* or bustling sprawl you're after, there's **Remoulins**, the area's market town and the gateway to the **Fosses de Fournès**, a weirdly eroded lunar landscape to the east.

Southwest of Remoulins, explore traces of the aqueduct in the hills around **Sernhac** (the local IGN map may come in handy here). Here the Romans dug two impressive tunnels, one for the water and one for maintenance, still bearing the grooves left by the hammers that excavated them, stroke by stroke. The extraordinarily hard calcium deposits that accumulated in the water channels were chiselled out as a prized building material in the Middle Ages: some went into the walls of the fortified Romanesque church of **St-Bonnet-du-Gard**, near Sernhac.

Columns, Columns, Columns and a Bridge

The Roman quarries that produced the Pont du Gard are just off the Uzès road in **Vers**, another pleasant little village with another Romanesque church. Here, by the level crossing on the D227 and down the white road a couple of hundred yards to the south, stand a few aqueduct arches in a state of romantic abandon; other vestiges may be seen between Vers and Argilliers, just off the D3B, taking the side road that veers sharply to the left. At **Argilliers**, a Romanesque chapel and a neoclassical colonnaded funeral chapel dedicated to Saint Louis (Louis IX) on the D981 mark the entrance to one of Languedoc's most curious follies, the **Château de Castille** (visible from the exterior), the private mania of Froment Fromentès, Baron de Castille (1747–1829). One of the great travellers of his day, the baron was afflicted by a serious case of columnitis in Rome, and on his return to his estates in the Gard he erected over 200 pillars and columns, of which only some 50 survive, incorporated into garden follies, porticoes and hemicycles inspired by Bernini.

South of Argilliers, down on the banks of the river, **Collias** has a popular beach, kayak rental and paths going up and down the river from the Pont du Gard to Pont St-Nicolas. The dramatic, wild beauty of the sheer-walled **Gardon gorge** around Collias inspired an awe of religious proportions in the past, and there are several old hermitages in caves, one near the **Grotte de la Baume**, with an 11th-century chapel (an hour's walk), and another, the **Ermitage de Collias**, in a place so beautiful that it has been classed like a historic monument. People have worshipped here since prehistoric times – there's a little chapel by the cave, a Roman bridge and fountain dedicated to Minerva. Further west, the D112 will take you to **Pont St-Nicolas**, where an impressive 13th-century bridge takes the scenic old Nîmes–Uzès road over the Gardon gorge. Just above it to the west, the 12th-century church of **Ste-Anastasie** is all that survives of the Priory of St-Nicolas de Campagnac; built with exquisite care, the church is unusually large, sober, pure and empty.

Remoulins >>
Place des Grands Jours (by the eastern roundabout), **t** *04 66 37 22 34, www.ot-pontdugard.com; open July and Aug daily; June and Sept Mon–Fri and Sat am; Oct–May Mon–Fri*

Where to Stay and Eat near the Pont du Gard

Pont du Gard ✉ 30210

Le Vieux Moulin, left bank, **t** 04 66 37 14 35, *www.vieuxmoulinpontdugard.com* (€€€). Idyllic setting, especially in the evening overlooking the illuminated Pont du Gard, and a menu that changes according to the season, with good vegetarian choices. *Closed Nov–Mar.*

Les Terrasses, left bank, **t** 04 66 37 50 88 (€€). Simple Mediterranean cuisine, snacks and teas. *Open summer daily; winter Thurs–Sun.*

Castillon-du-Gard ✉ 30210

****Le Vieux Castillon**, Rue Turion Sabatier, **t** 04 66 37 61 61, *www.vieuxcastillon.com* (€€€€€–€€€€). A Relais & Châteaux hotel with rooms in several village houses connected by patios; there are tennis courts, a stunning swimming pool, and an excellent restaurant (€€€€) featuring dishes with truffles (the Gard produces 15% of France's crop) and *langoustines*. *Closed Jan–mid-Feb; restaurant closed for lunch Mon and Tues.*

Remoulins ✉ 30210

Le Colombier, Rte du Pont du Gard, **t** 04 66 37 05 28, *www.lecolombierdugard.com* (€). With 18 comfortable rooms behind its broad awnings, and a restaurant (€€).

Pouzilhac ✉ 30210

La Closeraie, **t** 04 66 37 12 66, *www.lacloseraie.com* (€). North of Castillon, off the N86. Comfortable rooms, some with balcony or private garden, and a friendly welcome. Ample grounds, parking and a pool. Restaurant (€€) with a terrace.

Collias ✉ 30210

***Le Castellas**, Grand-Rue, **t** 04 66 22 88 88, *www.lecastellas.fr* (€€€). A friendly Art Deco hotel spread out in two large houses, with a good and stylish restaurant (€€€€–€€€), plus a very pretty garden and deep enclosed pool. Cookery lessons are available. *Closed Jan, Feb and one week Dec; restaurant closed Wed except in July and Aug.*

Uzès, the First Duchy of France

Uzès

Et nous avons des nuits plus belles que vos jours. (Even our nights are more beautiful than your days.)
Jean Racine, writing to Paris from Uzès, 1662

Few towns of 8,000 souls have so bold a skyline of towers, or so little truck with the modern industrial world. Uzès seems to have been vacuum-packed when its wealthy Protestant merchants of cloth and silk stockings picked up their bags and left at the Revocation of the Edict of Nantes. 'O little town of Uzès,' wrote André Gide (whose father was an Uzétien), 'were you in Umbria, the Parisians would flock to visit you!' Now they do, more or less, ever since 1962, when Uzès was selected as one of France's 50 *villes d'art*, entitling it to dig into the historical preservation funds set aside by De Gaulle's culture minister, André Malraux. Houses tumbling into ruin have been repaired, creating the perfect set for films like *Cyrano de Bergerac*.

Duché
t *04 66 22 18 96, www.duche-uzes.fr; daily guided tours July–Aug 10–12.30 and 2–6.30; Sept–June 10–12 and 2–6; English translation available; adm exp*

The Duché and Around

Café life in Uzès engulfs most of the available space in and around Place Albert Ier, just under the residence of the dukes, the **Duché**. The de Crussols of Uzès, claiming a family tree that sent out its first shoots under Charlemagne, became the first dukes and peers of the realm when the Duc de Montmorency forfeited the title (along with his head) in 1632. The current title-holders, a handsome young couple (he can often be spotted messing about with his car collection, she shopping with the kids in the local Carrefour supermarket), open their grand fortified home to visitors. The oldest section, the rectangular *donjon* called the **Tour Bermonde**, was built over a Roman tower in the 10th or 11th century; its crenellations were designed by the inevitable Viollet-le-Duc (*see* p.198) to replace the originals destroyed in the Revolution. The **Renaissance façade** in the central courtyard, a three-layered classical cake of Doric, Ionic and Corinthian orders, was constructed in 1550 and bears the motto of the dukes: *Ferro non auro* ('iron, not gold' – i.e. they were warriors, not financiers). This didn't keep the women of the family from sometimes donning the trousers: in 1565 the Duchess of Uzès became the first woman to be sent abroad as an ambassador, and then there's the amazing Duchess Anne, heiress to the Veuve Clicquot fortune, talented sculptress, enthusiastic huntress who rode until the age of 86, feminist, friend of anarchist Louise Michel (of Paris Commune fame) but still an ardent monarchist (she personally financed General Boulanger's attempt to overthrow the Republic to the tune of three million gold *écus*), the first woman in France to get a driving licence – and the first to get a speeding ticket. The tour of the Duché includes several furnished rooms.

Across Place du Duché is the attractive 18th-century **Hôtel de Ville**, while to the left of the Duché is a rock-cut **crypt** that lost its church (the Jesuits discovered it under their monastery); it is believed to date from the 4th century and has some primitive bas-reliefs of St John the Baptist and a convert. Uzès is a lot smaller than it seems, and a short wander will soon bring you to the irregular, arcaded, perfectly delightful **Place aux Herbes**, with its old plane trees, for centuries the centre of public life. The nearby church of **St-Etienne**, with an attractive Baroque façade, was rebuilt in the 18th century after destruction in the Wars of Religion two centuries earlier, and contains a handful of good paintings.

The Cathedral and Tour Fenestrelle

Set apart from the rest of the old town on a terrace, the **Cathédrale St-Théodorit** was built in 1663, the third to occupy the site after its predecessors were destroyed in the Albigensian Crusade and the Wars of Religion. The quaint neo-Romanesque façade was tacked on in 1875, with the idea of making a better partner to the stunning 12th-century **Tour Fenestrelle**, spared by the Protestants only because they found it useful as a watchtower. Unique in France, the 137ft tower is encircled by six storeys of double-lit windows, inspired by the Romanesque campaniles of Ravenna and Lombardy.

The cathedral's once splendidly ornate interior was severely damaged during the Revolution, when it was converted into a Temple of Reason, leaving only the peculiar upper gallery with its wrought iron railing (erected right after the revocation of the Edict of Nantes, to make room for the former Protestants) and the cathedral's pride and joy: a splendid **organ** of 1670, the only one in France to have retained its original painted shutters. Restored, it is the centrepiece of the mid-July/beginning-of-August festival, *Nuits Musicales d'Uzès*.

Adjacent, the 1671 **Ancien Palais Episcopal** was the seat of the powerful bishops of Uzès (64 reigned here between the 5th century and the Revolution). A restoration attempt in the 1970s caused the interior to cave in behind the façade, although the right wing is in good enough nick to hold the eclectic collections of the **Musée Georges Borias**, with its fossils, paintings, and memorabilia of the Gide family.

Musée Georges Borias
t 04 66 22 40 23; open July–Aug Tues–Sun 10–12 and 3–6; Mar–June and Sept–Oct Tues–Sun 3–6; Nov–Feb Tues–Sun 2–5; adm

Behind it stretches the **Promenade des Marronniers**; the funny little domed building abutting the belvedere is the so-called **Pavillon Racine**, named after the playwright and poet who, in spite of popular belief, never sat there, because it was built a quarter of a century too late. In 1661, at the age of 22, Racine spent a year with his uncle, the Vicar-General of Uzès, during which time his family hoped he would forget his foolish love of poetry and turn to the priesthood. Luckily for French theatre, the climate, friendly welcome and charming girls conspired to defeat their plans.

Jardin Médiéval
t 04 66 22 38 21; open July and Aug daily 10.30–12.30 and 2–6; April–June and Sept Mon–Fri 2–6, Sat and Sun 10.30–12.30 and 2–6; Oct daily 2–5; closed Nov–Mar; adm

The odd building at the busy crossroads below the terrace is the **Hôtel du Baron de Castille**, its façade adorned with the baron's beloved columns (*see* p.96) – tall slender ones that don't conform to any classical order but which have a charm all their own. There is also a lovely herb garden near here in the Impasse Port Royal, the **Jardin Médiéval**, with a collection of carefully labelled local plants, and medicinal and culinary herbs used since the Middle Ages.

Within walking distance of Uzès (from Parc du Duché, follow the Chemin André Gide), the **Vallée de l'Alzon** is the arcadian setting of the **Fontaine d'Eure**, the spring that fed the Roman aqueduct to Nîmes; you can see the large basin that regulated the flow down the canal, excavated in 1993.

Musée du Bonbon
t 04 66 22 74 39, www.haribo.com; open July–Aug daily 10–7; Sept–June Tues–Sun 10–1 and 2–6; closed most of Jan

Haras Nationaux d'Uzès
t 04 66 22 68 88, www.haras-nationaux.fr; open Mon–Sat 8.30–12 and 2–5; mid-June–mid-Sept Tues and Thurs guided visits only; adm

La Bouscarasse
t 04 66 22 50 25, www.bouscarasse.fr; open June–Aug Mon–Fri 10–7, Sat and Sun 10–8; adm

If you've brought the kids, it might be hard to avoid the Haribo company's **Musée du Bonbon**, south of town at Pont des Charrettes, a kids' paradise where you can watch them make little jelly crocodiles and much much, more in a brightly coloured orgy of sugar (one poll of children rated it the best museum in France). Horse-lovers can meet the 65 stallions at the national stud, the **Haras Nationaux d'Uzès** at the Mas des Tailles, Route d'Alès, or carry along the same road to **La Bouscarasse** in **Serviers,** one of the most beautiful water parks in France, where you can float about on inner tubes under the trees among other splashy delights – especially useful for kids on a Haribo sugar-high.

Around Uzès: The Uzège

The countryside around Uzès – where fields of asparagus, cherry orchards, forests of truffle oaks and vineyards alternate with *garrigues* – is dotted with delightful old villages. **Arpaillargues**, 4km west on the D982, has the added attraction of the **Musée 1900** at Moulin de Charlier, one man's amazing 30-year accumulation of period cars, motorcycles, gramophones, movie posters, locomotives and more; there is also a **Musée du Train et du Jouet**, with model trains and toys. Just west of Arpaillargues, the walled hilltop hamlet of **Aureilhac** has a superb view of Uzès' skyline. Nine kilometres northwest of Uzès, off the road to Alès, **Aigaliers**, with its medieval lanes, dungeons, Saracen wall and Romanesque church all piled under a ruined castle, has long been a favourite subject of local painters.

Musée 1900/ Musée du Train et du Jouet
t 04 66 22 58 64, www.moulin-de-chalier.fr; open July–Aug daily 10–7; Mar–June Tues– Sun 10–12 and 2–6; Sept–Oct plus school hols in Feb, Nov and Dec Tues–Sun 10–12 and 2–6; rest of Nov and Dec ring ahead; closed Jan, and Feb outside hols; adm

The clay-rich soil north of Uzès has provided **St-Quentin-la-Poterie** with its vocation since the cows came home, and in some strange tangential way inspired its most famous son, Joseph Monier (1823–1906), to invent reinforced concrete. After producing thousands of amphorae, roof tiles, bricks, ceramic pipes and all the glazed tiles for the floors of the Popes' Palace in Avignon, the last ceramic factory closed in 1974; but in 1983 the kilns were fired up again as the village made a concerted effort to bring the potters back. Fifteen now live in the village year-round; you can visit their workshops or get an overview of their work at the **Maison de la Terre**, 5 Rue de la Fontaine. The adjoining **Musée de la Poterie Méditerranéenne** has a wonderful selection of examples of pottery from all over the Mediterranean, in a beautiful variety of glazes.

Maison de la Terre/Musée de la Poterie Méditerranéenne
t 04 66 03 65 86, www.musee-poterie-mediterranee.com; open July–Aug daily 10–1 and 3–7; June Wed–Sun 10–1 and 3–7; Sept Wed–Sun 10–1 and 3–6; Feb–May and Oct Wed–Sun 2–6; Nov–Jan by appt; adm

Lovely **Lussan** is 18km north of Uzès, but well worth the detour: a nearly perfect, unspoiled medieval *village perché* below a 13th-century château. Near Lussan, the sheer gorge of the river Aiguillon, **Les Concluses**, makes a magnificent and easy walk in the summer when the river is dry, with potholes (*marmites*) formed by the river, eagle's nests and a remarkable steep and narrow **Portail** that closes in on top. Leave your car in one of the car parks along the D643; the walk takes about 30 minutes.

Northeast of Uzès, strange sandstone formations and quarzite quarries mark the environs of **St-Victor-des-Oules**, 'of the pots', another pottery village, this one specializing in stoneware (*grès*). Paths lead up **Mont Aigu**, for scant ruins of a 5th-century BC *oppidum* and superb views of the Cévennes to the west. Further east, the 12th-century château in **La Capelle-Masmolène** was the summer palace of the bishops of Uzès.

Market Days in Uzès

Uzès: Wed, and a massive general one on Sat. Also a *marché aux truffes*, Sat in Dec–Mar, Av de la Libération.

Where to Stay and Eat in and around Uzès

ⓘ Uzès > *Chapelle des Capucins, Place Albert 1er, t 04 66 22 68 88, www.uzes-tourisme.com; open June–Sept daily; Oct–May Mon–Fri and Sat am*

Uzès ✉ 30700

Between December and March, look for fresh truffles on the menus.

******Hôtel du Général d'Entraigues**, Place de l'Evêché, **t** 04 66 22 32 68, *www.hoteldentraigues.com* (€€€–€€). A fine old hotel in a 15th-century building, with a roof-top pool; try to get a room near the top. The restaurant, **Les Jardins de Castille** (€€€–€€), has a classy lunch menu.

★ Mas Laurent >

Mas Laurent, Route de Bagnols, **t** 04 66 03 00 55, *www.maslaurent.com* (€€€). A lovely Australian couple run this B&B in a handsome farmhouse near Uzès, immersed in lavender and lovely landscapes.

****Hostellerie Provençale**, 1-3 Rue de la Grande Bourgade, **t** 04 66 22 11 04, *www.hostellerieprovencale.com* (€€). This charming inn has stylish, air-conditioned rooms and one of the town's best restaurants (€€).

****Le St-Geniès**, Route de St-Ambroix, **t** 04 66 222 999, *www.hotel-saintgenies.com* (€€). An oasis of tranquillity half a mile from the centre, with a charming pool and three-star rooms. You can hire bikes here, too. *Closed mid-Nov–Feb.*

★ Les Sardines aux Yeux Bleus >>

****La Taverne**, 7 Rue Sigalon (just off Place Albert Ier), **t** 04 66 22 13 10, *www.lataverne-uzes.com* (€€). Renovated rooms with beamed ceilings and Wi-fi; you can dine on a pretty terrace (€€). *Closed Jan.*

★ L'Artemise >

L'Artemise, Chemin de la Fontaine aux Bœufs, **t** 04 66 63 94 14, *www.lartemise.com* (€€€€–€€€). Brilliant young chef Guillaume Foucault, trained at Lucas Carton, regales diners with his top-notch cuisine in a gorgeous 16th-century *mas*, surrounded by an enormous park. *Summer closed Tues and Wed and Sat lunch; winter closed Tues–Thurs, closed Feb and Nov.*

Millézime, 6 Bd Gambetta, **t** 04 66 22 27 82, *www.restaurant-millezime.fr* (€€). In the historic centre, dine on well-prepared classic dishes of the Gard from *brandade de morue* to *gardianne de taureau* in this stylish restaurant. *Closed Sun eve and Mon.*

Hôtel de l'Ancienne Gare, on the Remoulins road, **t** 04 66 03 19 15, *www.anciennegare.eu* (€€). In a former train station; refined cooking and frequently changing menus; specialities include *tête de veau*.

Around Uzès ✉ 30700

*****Château d'Arpaillargues**, 4km west of Uzès at Arpaillargues, **t** 04 66 22 14 48, *www.chateaudarpaillargues.com* (€€€€–€€€). Sleep in an antique bed (or just dine) at this 18th-century hotel. Marie d'Agoult was Liszt's muse and Wagner's mother-in-law, and a frequent guest. There's a pool and tennis courts, and courtyard restaurant (€€€) serving truffles in season. *Closed mid-Oct–mid-April.*

Clos du Léthé, 6km from Uzès in St-Médiers, **t** 04 66 58 37, *www.closdulethe.com* (€€€€). Stunning, luxuriously equipped five-room B&B in an old stone *mas* (unsuitable for kids under 10) with an infinity pool, fitness centre and steam bath.

Les Sardines aux Yeux Bleus, Hameau de Gattigues, Aigaliers, **t** 04 66 74 03 10 04, *www.les-sardines.com* (€€€–€€). Lovely laid-back B&B in a 17th-century farmhouse, with idyllic rustic-chic rooms, gardens and a pool and Wi-fi. They also offer two self-catering apartments.

The Cévennes Gardoises

West of the Pont du Gard and north of Nîmes, you can follow the Gardon upstream into the Cévennes, the granite southern stretches of the Massif Central, marked by lush valleys covered in

Getting to and around the Cévennes Gardoises

Trains from Nîmes or Montpellier go to Alès, and from there local **buses NTECC** (*www.ntecc.fr*) go to Anduze, St-Jean-du-Gard and St-Hippolyte-du-Fort; **Edgard bus A12** links Nîmes to Anduze and St-Jean-du-Gard.

---

chestnut groves and fragrant scrub. It provided a handy refuge for Protestants after the Revocation of the Edict of Nantes (1685) when its many secret caves, ravines and forests became their 'desert', similar to the Hebrews in the Book of Exodus or Jesus's forty days in the wilderness; their determined resistance culminated in the War of the Camisards (*see* **History**, p.28) and only ended afterwards with the French Revolution. Even today the region has a strong Protestant identity, with temples in every town, and old houses still equipped with secret hiding places for pastors (who risked execution if they were caught), many still sporting burgundy or grey shutters – the Protestant colours. The history of protecting the persecuted continued into the Second World War, when an extraordinary number of Protestants hid Jews.

Although today one of the more peaceful, rural corners of Languedoc, the Cévennes once supported a booming silk industry that by the 1850s was producing half of all France's stockings – just before a parasitical worm completely devastated the industry. Louis Pasteur came down in person in the 1860s to see what could be done, and after five years of research located the problem and prescribed isolating and destroying infected worms – studies which marked the beginning of his important work on germs and infectious diseases. Outside many towns, keep an eye peeled for abandoned *magnaneries*, the buildings where they used to raise silkworms.

Alès and Anduze

Mine Temoin
t 04 66 30 45 15, www.mine-temoin.fr; open July–Aug daily 10–7; mid-Feb–June and Sept–11 Nov daily 9.30–12.30 and 2–6. In summer, special evening theme visits (ring ahead); adm

Alès is the biggest town in these parts but, rather than silk, this was a coal town; mining in the Cévennes began in the 13th century and reached its apogee during the Industrial Revolution, before closing down in 1960, a story recalled in the **Mine Témoin** on the Chemin de la Cité Sainte-Marie; the visit includes a ride down into the mines. Alès is also home to the Grand Ecole des Mines, where the *crème de la crème* of French engineers learn their stuff.

Les Camellias de la Prairie
t 04 66 52 67 48, www.camellia.fr; open Tues–Sun with guided visits at 10, 2 and 4; closed Sun in Aug; adm

Above ground, the warm but wet climate of the Cévennes is auspicious for flowers. Between October and June 200 different varieties of rare camellias bloom at **Les Camellias de la Prairie** at 2396 Chemin des Sports in the Quartier Prairie Sud. The garden also has ancient olives and rare fruit trees – a delight for gardeners on the guided tour (epecially if they understand a bit of French).

Grotte de la Cocalière
t 04 66 24 34 74, www.grotte-cocaliere.com; open July–Aug daily 10–6; mid-Mar–June and Sept– early Nov daily 10–12 and 2–5; adm includes the mini-train ride to the entrance

Yet the underworld beckons: just off the D904, 26km north of Alès, the **Grotte de la Cocalière**, the 'diamond cave', is made of sparkling stone; it's one of the three most beautiful in France, adorned with rare circular concretions, a cave pearl in formation, 'macaroni' stalactites, translucent draperies, and enchanting staggered pools (*gours*).

Southwest of Alès, set amid the cliffs of the Gardon, **Anduze** is a charming ceramics town of little squares, plashing fountains (the colourful, tiled **Fontaine Pagode** of 1649 is the town symbol) and kids swimming in the river on summer afternoons. Its high-quality clay has been used to make *vases d'anduze* – large honey or blue garden pots decorated with garlands and splashes of colour – ever since 1610, when a local potter spotted some at the *Foire de Beaucaire* (*see* p.115) destined for the Medici, and started to reproduce them. The pots received their own *lettres de noblesse* when they were purchased for the orangerie in Versailles, and the rest is history. Anduze's nine potteries still make them; the tourist office has a complete list.

La Bambouseraie de Prafrance
t 04 66 61 70 47, www.bambouseraie.com; open Mar–15 Nov daily 9.30–dusk; adm

Musée du Désert
t 04 66 85 02 72, www.museedudesert.com; open July and Aug daily 9.30–6; Mar–Nov daily 9.30–12 and 2–6; adm

Just north of Anduze, the beautiful, exotic park of **La Bambouseraie de Prafrance** in Générargues is a perfect oasis on a hot day, planted in 1856 by a spice merchant who brought back over 150 kinds of bamboo from the east, and created a little paradise amid bananas, sequoias and much more – so much more that the garden drove him into bankruptcy. Further north in Mialet, the **Musée du Désert** is located in Le Mas Soubeyran, in the house of the great Camisard leader Pierre Laporte (*nom de guerre* Rolland, who was betrayed and killed in 1704. One of the key sites of French and Swiss Protestanism (on the first Sunday in September some 20,000 faithful gather here in remembrance), this house-museum created in 1911 houses France's most extensive collection of original items related to French Protestantism, the Camisards and the subterfuges they often had to resort to to keep their faith alive: secret pulpits, maps, forbidden books and Bibles, weapons, paintings and manuscripts.

Grotte de Trabuc
www.grotte-de-trabuc.com; guided tours July and Aug daily 10.15–6; April–June and Sept daily 10.30 and 11.30 and 2.30–5.30; Oct daily 2.30–5.30; Feb and Nov Sun and school hols 2.30–4.30; closed Dec and Jan; adm

Les Safaris Souterrains
t 04 67 66 11 11, www.grottes.com; tours depart if there are 6 people minimum

Just a couple of minutes to the north, the vast **Grotte de Trabuc** was a famous bandit hideout (a *trabuc* is a kind of firearm, much favoured by local highwaymen). During the War of the Camisards, royal troops walled up the entrance to prevent Protestants from hiding in it. Geologically, it has its share of marvels, including cave pearls, red 'waterfalls' of stone and a mysterious formation called the 100,000 Soldiers, a massive army of what look like mini-stalagmites, but geologically are something completely different. If you've always wanted to don a head lamp and have a prowl in the bowels of the earth, **Les Safaris Souterrains** offer four- or six-hour guided excursions into the depths.

St-Jean-du-Gard

Train à vapeur des Cévennes
t 04 66 60 59 00, www.trainavapeur.com; runs April–Oct; check schedules and book tickets online

Anduze is also the terminus of the **Train à vapeur des Cévennes**, a steam train that chugs in 40 minutes to St-Jean-du-Gard through lovely Cévennes scenery (when you book, note that some trains are pulled by less romantic diesel engines). The train stops at La Bambouseraie (*see* above) while at St-Jean-du-Gard you can visit the vast, privately run ethnographic collection in the **Musée des Vallées Cévenoles** at 95 Grand Rue, in an 18th-century postal relay station, containing exhibits on everything from silk to chestnuts to the kitchen sink. On Av de la Résistance are the colourful tanks of the **Aquarium de St-Jean-du-Gard**, with fish from around the world: come on Sundays at 3pm to watch the feeding of the sharks.

Musée des Vallées Cévenoles
www.museedes valleescevenoles. pagesperso-orange.fr; open July–Aug daily 10–7; April–June and Sept–Oct daily 10–12.30 and 2–7; Nov–Mar Tues and Thurs 9–12 and 2–6, Sun 2–6; adm

Aquarium de St-Jean-du-Gard
t 04 66 85 40 53, www.aquarium-cevennes.com; open June–Aug daily 11–7; April, May, Sept and Oct Tues–Sun 11–6; closed Nov–Mar; adm

St-Jean-du-Gard marks the end of the 252km GR70 from Le Puy-en-Velay in the Haute Loire – a path known as the **Chemin Stevenson** ever since it was trodden by Robert Louis Stevenson and immortalized in his delightful *Travels with a Donkey in the Cévennes*, the first ever account of someone roughing it for pleasure, published in the hope of raising enough money to get to California and the woman he loved. He invented the precursor of the sleeping bag for the occasion, but it was so heavy that it required the services of a strong-willed little mouse-coloured donkey named Modéstine. The book was a success (and did indeed get him to the United States and his future wife). You too can hire a donkey and retrace his steps – RLS took 12 days to complete the entire walk, although some do it in as few as eight.

Chemin Stevenson
for information on the route, with or without a donkey, see www.chemin-stevenson.org

Southwest of Anduze, **St-Hippolyte-du Fort** sits on the banks of the famously unpredictable River Vidorle. It was a Protestant stronghold (its temple, or Protestant church, rivals Anduze for the title of the biggest in France) and the fort of its name was built in the 17th century by the king to keep a close eye on its citizens. It has more than its share of sundials, and the **Musée de la Soie** will tell you everything you've always wanted to know about the industry, from mulberry leaf-munching worms to stockings, with hands-on activities for the kids.

I travel not to go anywhere, but to go. I travel for travel's sake. The great affair is to move.
Robert Louis Stevenson

Musée de la Soie
t 04 66 77 66 47, www.museedelasoie-cevennes.com; open July–Aug daily 10–12.30 and 2–6; April–June and Sept–Nov Tues–Sun 10–12.30 and 2–6; adm; call for hours of guided visits

Heading back towards Nîmes on the D999 you'll go through the striking medieval village of **Sauve**, with its 12th-century bridge spanning the Vidourle, tall houses and artists' colony, which includes underground cartoonist legend Robert Crumb and Rolling Stone Charlie Watts. Most of all, it's a great place to pick up a handmade nettle tree pitchfork – the local speciality, some say – since the Saracens invaded in the 8th century and taught the locals how to make them.

ⓘ St-Jean-du-Gard >>
Place Rabout Saint-Etienne, **t** *04 66 85 32 11, www.tourisme-saintjeandugard.fr; open Mon–Sat, also on Sun in July and Aug*

ⓘ Sauve >>
Rue des Boisseliers, **t** *04 66 77 57 51, www.ville-de-sauve.fr; open winter Mon–Fri; spring and autumn Mon–Sat; summer also Sun am*

ⓘ Anduze >
Plan du Brie, **t** *04 66 61 98 17, www.ot-anduze.fr; open Mon–Sat, plus Sun in June–Aug*

★ Domaine du Soleil >>

★ Le Ranquet >

Market Days in the Cévennes Gardoises

Anduze: Thurs.
St-Jean-du-Gard: Tues.
St-Hippolyte-du-Fort: Tues.
Sauve: Sat.

Where to Stay and Eat in the Cévennes Gardoises

St-Hilaire-de-Brethmas ✉ 30560

Comptoir St-Hilaire, southeast of Alès, **t** 04 66 30 82 65, *www.comptoir-saint-hilaire.com* (€€€€). Gorgeous luxury designer B&B – choose a theme from *la dolce vita* to the Highlands, set in 50ha of rolling *garrigue* country, with a pool, tennis and spa. Superb breakfast and gourmet meals – all perfect for a honeymoon in the Cévennes.

Anduze ✉ 30140

******Le Ranquet**, Rte de St Hippolyte du Fort, 30140 Tornac, **t** 04 66 77 51 63, *www.leranquet.com* (€€€€–€€€). Delicious retreat in the woods, with beautiful rooms and one of the Gard's best restaurants (€€€€), using produce from local organic gardens; check the website for its offers of romantic gourmet weekends. *Restaurant closed Mon lunch (and eves in winter), Tues and Wed.*

****La Porte des Cévennes**, Rte de St-Jean-du-Gard, **t** 04 66 61 99 44, *www.hotel-restaurant-porte-cevennes.com* (€€). Modern Logis de France in a beautiful setting amid the lush green hills, with well-equipped rooms, a heated covered pool and playground – perfect for families – and a good restaurant with its own vegetable garden.

****La Régalière**, Rte de St-Jean-du-Gard, **t** 04 66 25 22 01, *www.la regaliere-anduze.fr* (€€–€). Excellent value for money in this atmospheric little hotel in a villa from the early 1900s, with a charming, helpful owner, a pool and park, plus fine *table d'hôtes* meals.

St-Jean-du-Gard ✉ 30270

****Les Bellugues**, 13 Rue Pelet de la Lozère, **t** 04 66 85 15 33, *www.hotel-bellugues.com* (€€–€). Located in a former silk mill, this has 16 rooms in a charming sunny garden with a pool.

St-Hippolyte-du-Fort ✉ 30170

****L'Auberge Cigaloise**, Rte de Nîmes, **t** 04 66 77 64 59, *www.auberge cigaloise.fr* (€€). Little stone Logis de France with a pool and fine restaurant (€€), serving succulent lamb, surprises such as kangaroo, and dishes in pastry.

Sauve ✉ 30140

Domaine du Soleil, Route de Villesèque **t** 04 66 80 45 14 or 06 80 33 19 14, *www.domaindusoleil.fr* (€€). In a house dating back to the 12th century on the outskirts of Sauve, this a fine B&B for couples or families, with a pool and jacuzzi; owners Karin and Eric can arrange riding holidays, a massage and even a haircut. Good *table d'hôtes* meals and wines.

La Magnanerie, Quartier Evesque, **t** 04 66 77 57 44, *www.lamagnanerie.fr* (€€). Seven pleasant rooms in a 17th-century silk barn, still set amongst the mulberries; there's a pool and a superb creative restaurant (€€€–€€) with a Mediterranean menu that changes every three months. *Closed Mon and Tues.*

Le Bossens, Place de la Révolution, **t** 06 47 06 85 62 (€€). Find a table under the three enormous plane trees and enjoy tasty Mediterranean cuisine; not much choice, but it's all delicious.

Northeastern Gard

Bagnols-sur-Cèze

Defined in the north by the river and gorges of the Ardèche, the river Cèze and the Rhône, the northeastern Gard throws up some surprises. Its main town, Bagnols-sur-Cèze, is the traditional gateway to – or exit from – Languedoc. The Romans named it for its sulphur baths, but these days Bagnols is more famous for its green beans (*les bagnolais*) and the nearby nuclear power plant at Marcoule, the construction of which led Bagnols' population to quadruple. Yet the narrow lanes of the old town have changed little; every now and then you'll see the city's quaint emblem of three golden pots.

The prettiest square in Bagnols, central, arcaded **Place Mallet**, has a tower, the **Tour de l'Horloge**, erected by Philippe le Bel, and a delightful 18th-century Hôtel de Ville housing the only real reason for visiting Bagnols: the **Musée Albert André**. In 1854, Léon Alègre, a local humanist and Sunday painter, set up a museum to instruct his fellow citizens, with everything from Roman pots to paintings to stuffed animals. In 1918, Albert André, a painter friend of Renoir's, became volunteer curator and gave the museum the first provincial collection of contemporary art in France – only to have the whole thing go up in smoke in 1924, when the local firemen set it alight during their annual ball. It proved to be a blessing in disguise when André sent out a message to France's artists: 'I am the curator of a museum of naked walls. Help me fill them!' They did. The eight rooms blaze with colour, filled with Fauvist Albert Marquet's famous *14 Juillet au Havre* (1906); Pierre Bonnard's *Bouquet de fleurs des champs*; Matisse's *La Fenêtre ouverte à Nice* (1919); and works by Renoir, Van Dongen, Paul Signac, Gauguin, Jongkind and Picasso, as well as a room of Albert André's own paintings. If you crave more, Bagnols also has the **Musée Léon Alègre** at 24 Av Paul Langevin, with archaeological finds from the Iron Age to the Romans. Or learn all about the wonders of nuclear power and other sources of energy (in French) at Marcoule's **Visiatome.**

Musée Albert André
t *04 66 50 50 56, www.gard-provencal.com/musees/aandre.htm; open Mar–Jan Tues–Sun 10–12 and 2–6; 3–7 in July–Aug; closed Mon and Feb; adm*

Musée Léon Alègre
t *04 66 89 74 00, www.gard-provencal.com/musees/alegre.htm; open Mar–Jan Thurs–Sat 10–12 and 2–6; 3–7 in July and Aug; closed Feb; adm*

Visiatome
t *04 66 39 78 78, www.visiatome.fr; open Mon–Fri 10–6, Sat and Sun 2–6; adm*

Wine: Côtes du Rhône Gardoises

Bagnols is the centre of Languedoc's Côtes du Rhône production, while three villages, Chusclan, Laudun and St-Gervais, take pride in bottling their own Côtes du Rhône-Villages. Try the **Cave des Vignerons de Chusclan**, at Chusclan, **t** 04 66 90 11 03, *www. vigneronsdechusclan.com* (*open 9–12 and 2–6.30*), for bottled or by-the-litre wines; and the exceptional wines of **Domaine Ste-Anne**, at Les Celettes in St-Gervais, **t** 04 66 82 77 41 (*open 9–11 and 2–6; closed Sun*), especially the Cuvée Notre-Dame and their pure syrah Côtes du Rhône. One of the finest white Côtes du Rhône is made by **Luc Pelaquie**, at Laudun, *www.domaine-pelaquie.com* (*open Mon–Sat 9–12 and 2–6*); Pelaquie's wine has a natural freshness that is unusual for such a hot area. It has great depth and will age well for several years.

The *domaine* produces a good range of other wines, too, including Tavel, Lirac red and rosé, and Côtes du Rhône red; the **Vignerons d'Estézargues** produce a delightful, fresh, fruity red under the Terra Vitis label. Producers signing up to Terra Vitis undertake to produce wine in an environmentally friendly way (see *www.terravitis.com*).

If you are near Bagnols in mid-July, ask the tourist office about the ***Festival des Vins et Saveurs du Gard***, an opportunity to taste many local wines and delicacies.

Around Bagnols

Many of the items in Bagnols' archaeology museum were found at the lofty *oppidum* of **St-Vincent de Gaujac**, 13km south of Bagnols and then a 2km walk up from the car park. Dating from the 5th century BC to the 6th century AD, it became a holy site in Gallo-Roman times, and has the foundations of temples and a bath complex from the 3rd century AD. If you're in the vicinity, don't miss medieval **St-Victor-la-Coste**, a picturesque village gathered around its ruined castle, with a pair of 11th-century chapels.

Laudun, between St-Victor-la-Coste and Bagnols, is another handsome medieval village, with a 14th-century church, Renaissance château and above, on a high plateau with superb views, the **Camp de César**, a 40-acre archaeological site. After its start as a Celtic *oppidum* in the 5th century BC, it grew into a Roman city and was abandoned in the 7th century: Cyclopean walls, towers, a forum, a basilica, some houses and a few other buildings have so far been excavated. Other items found on the site are on permanent exhibition in Laudun's **town hall**.

Camp de César
t 04 66 50 55 79, www.ville-laudun.fr; call for guided tours

The Romans built villas in the surrounding area: around **Tresques**, just southwest, many were converted into Romanesque chapels. One, **St-Martin de Jussan**, on the north end of Tresques, is Lombard in inspiration – companies of builders from the banks of Lake Como roved far and wide in the Middle Ages – and has a carved portal. Another church, **St-Pierre de Castres**, 4km northeast, is one of the oldest, with archaic chapels.

Five kilometres north of Bagnols, there are more fine views over the Rhône valley from **Vénéjan**; and 2km northeast from there the charming 11th-century **Chapelle de St-Pierre** is decorated with Lombard-style bands of stone and a little square bell-tower. If you're lucky and find it open, you'll see the interior has curious, primitive sculptural decoration: six-pointed stars, concentric circles, solar discs, birds, animals and two praying figures.

The Cèze valley is even more rural than the Cévennes, dotted with isolated farms and hamlets. It's lovely hill-walking country. Bagnols is also a good base for exploring the scenic lower valley of the Cèze, beginning with **St-Gervais**, a wine village set under steep cliffs. Further upstream, **La Roque-sur-Cèze**, a member of 'the most beautiful villages in France' club, is piled on a hill opposite a 13th-century bridge, with streets too narrow for cars. La Roque overlooks the **Cascade du Sautadet**, where the Cèze flows through a mini-canyon that looks as if it was clawed out of the rock by a giant bear.

Further up at **Goudargues**, the saintly warrior St Guilhem (*see* p.155) founded an abbey in the early 9th century, which Louis the Pious gave to the abbey of Aniane: the ruins of St Guilhem's original Chapelle St-Michelet still stand over the village, while the later abbey church, built in the 12th century and remodelled in the 18th and 19th centuries, is particularly grand. The Benedictines drained the marsh that once surrounded Goudargues into canals, to water their crops and make the village, with no little exaggeration, 'the Venice of the Gard'; in high summer it often has more water in it than the Cèze. Across the Cèze, **Cornillon** is a 17th-century village with a ruined château and a grand view. Little **Montclus**, further up, is prettily set in a tight loop of the Cèze, with a ruined castle keep.

Further up along the Cèze, keep an eye open for anything that glisters – in this case it may well be gold. In 1889 a 543g nugget was found here, and, prices being what they are, don't be surprised to see people panning along the banks. There are gorges upstream and lovely hill walks; pick up maps and explore.

North of Bagnols

Chartreuse de Valbonne
t 04 66 90 4124, www.chartreusedevalbonne-monument.com; open July–Aug daily 10–7; Sept–June daily 10–12 and 1–5.30; for guided tours and wine tastings by appt

North of Bagnols, in a beautiful old oak forest between the Cèze valley and the Gorges de l'Ardèche, the **Chartreuse de Valbonne**, 'of the good valley', was founded in 1204. It was rebuilt in grand Baroque style with a beautiful tile roof after the Wars of Religion, then restored after the Revolution. In 1901 it was abandoned, like all the other charterhouses in France, when a new law put religious orders under the control of the state; the Carthusians preferred exile in Spain. In the 1920s Valbonne found a new use as a hospital for tropical diseases and leprosy: today it makes wine and does rehabilitation work. Tours include the church, with its stuccoes and stone vaults, and the huge cloister.

Musée d'Art Sacré du Gard
t 04 66 39 17 61, www.gard-provencal.com/musees/artsacre.htm; open July–Aug Tues–Sun 10–7; Sept– Jan and Mar–June Tues–Sun 10–12 and 2–6; closed Mon and Feb; adm

Musée Paul-Raymond
t 04 66 39 09 98, www.gard-provencal.com/musees/praymond.htm; open June–Sept Tues–Sun 10–12 and 3–7; Oct–May Wed, Thurs and Sun 10–12 and 2–6

To the east, **Pont-St-Esprit** was named for its famous bridge over the Rhône, erected between 1265 and 1309 by a confraternity of builders called the Brothers of the Holy Ghost. Nineteen of the 25 arches are original, but the mighty towers that once controlled access from either bank are long gone. There are fine views of the bridge from the terrace by the 15th-century parish church, once part of the influential Cluniac abbey of St-Saturnin-du-Port. Pilgrims to Santiago de Compostela would cross the bridge, stop at the church and head down Rue St-Jacques, a street that has preserved many of its medieval houses. Appropriately enough for a town named Holy Ghost Bridge, one of these (No.2) houses the **Musée d'Art Sacré du Gard**, displaying a wide range of works from the 15th to the 19th centuries, from paintings to *santons* (handpainted clay figures). The house itself, the Maison des Chevaliers, was built in the 12th century by a family of merchants, who kept on enlarging their home until the 18th century. Just up the street in Place de l'Ancienne Mairie, the **Musée Paul-Raymond** has a collection of paintings of landscapes and scenes from the Psalms by the Russian artist Benn (1905–89).

Market Days in Northeastern Gard

Bagnols: Wed and Thurs.
Laudun: Mon.
Pont-St-Esprit: Sat.
Goudargues: Wed.

Where to Stay and Eat in Northeastern Gard

Bagnols-sur-Cèze ✉ 30200

********Château de Montcaud****, Route d'Alès, in Sabran, **t** 04 66 89 60 60, *www.chateau-de-montcaud.com* (€€€€€). In a leafy 27-acre park, with comfortable, air-conditioned rooms, a gym and Turkish bath, a pool, and an equally exquisite restaurant (€€€€) and cheaper *bistrot*. *Closed mid-Oct–early April; restaurant closed lunch, bistrot closed Sat and Sun.*

*****Château du Val de Cèze**, 69 Route d'Avignon, **t** 04 66 89 61 26, *www.sud-provence.com* (€€€). Bagnols' most luxurious hotel, with individual bungalows around a 13th-century château. In a park, with tennis and a pool. No restaurant. *Closed Nov–Mar.*

****Le St-Georges**, 210 Av Roger Salengro, **t** 04 66 89 53 65, *www.restaurantlesaintgeorges.com* (€). A small, typical provincial hotel.

Les Grignotte des 5 Continents, 18 Place Mallet, **t** 04 66 89 14 53, *www.lagrignottedes5continents.com* (€). Great little spot with an outdoor terrace near the Hôtel de Ville, and tasty exotic dishes. *Closed Wed and Sat lunch.*

Pont-St-Esprit 30130

****Le Mas d'Olivier**, 138 Av de Gaulle, **t** 04 66 89 12 38, *www.mas-olivier.com* (€€). Modern, tranquil air-conditioned rooms in a large garden with a pool and Provençal cuisine in the restaurant.

Goudargues/Cornillon ✉ 30630

*****La Vieille Fontaine**, Cornillon, **t** 04 66 82 20 56, *www.lavieillefontaine.net* (€€€). In the walls of the castle, with eight rooms, each furnished with antiques. Garden terraces descend to a pool. The restaurant (€€€) is delightful. *Closed Nov–early Mar; restaurant closed lunch exc. Sun.*

ⓘ **Bagnols-sur-Cèze >**
*Espace St-Gilles, Av Léon Blum, **t** 04 66 89 54 61, www.tourisme-bagnolssurceze.com; open Mon–Sat, also Sun am in June–Sept*

ⓘ **Goudargues >>**
*4 Rte de Pont-St-Esprit, **t** 04 66 82 30 02, www.tourisme-ceze-ardeche.com; open July–Aug Mon–Fri and Sat/Sun am; Sept–June Mon–Fri and Sat am*

'Among the stricken, delirium rose: patients thrashed wildly on their beds, screaming that red flowers were blossoming from their bodies, that their heads had turned to molten lead.'
Time magazine, August 1951

In 1951, Pont-St-Esprit unintentionally made the headlines, with a mystery that has gone down in the history books as *Le Pain Maudit*, the 'cursed bread'. Beginning on 16 August, a day that began like any other day, there was a widespread outbreak of insanity that led to five deaths and dozens committed to asylums. The madness was originally blamed on ergot poisoning in the bread from the local bakery. In 2009, author Hank Albarelli discovered evidence suggesting that the villagers were the unwitting victims of a top secret Cold War mind-control experiment – the CIA had sprayed the air and contaminated food with diethylamide, one of the ingredients in LSD (at the time manufactured only by Sandoz, in Switzerland) to see what would happen. The inhabitants of Pont-St-Esprit are keen to learn more, but it remains to be seen if they'll get their wish.

Just north of Pont-St-Esprit, the Ardèche flows into the Rhône. Medieval **Aiguèze**, the last town in the Gard, hangs over the cliffs looking up towards the gorges of the Ardèche, guarded by two towers left over from the Hundred Years' War. Cross the bridge for St-Martin-d'Ardèche, where you can hire canoes to paddle up the gorge.

The West Bank of the Rhône

The eastern Gard, across the river from Orange and Avignon in Provence, is an austere land, its knobby limestone hills and cliffs softened by crowns of silver olives and the green pinstripes of vines, especially in the river-bend north of Villeneuve lez Avignon along the D976. The landmark here is **Roquemaure**, where Pope Clement V died from eating a plate of ground emeralds (prescribed by his doctor for stomach ache) in its now-ruined castle. Even so it's not his ghost who haunts it, but that of a lovely but leprous queen who was quarantined in the tower. After she died, Rhône boatmen would see her on summer nights, flitting along the bank, dressed in white and sparkling with jewels. Roquemaure's church of **St-Jean-Baptiste**, opened by Clement V in 1329, has sheltered since 1868 the relics of a certain St Valentine, whom it celebrates with the *Fête des Amoureux*, which dons its 19th-century threads to celebrate the patron saint of lovers, with plenty of smooches and barrel organ serenades. The church also houses a superb real organ of 1680, built for the *Cordeliers* in Avignon and transferred here in 1800, with all of its original pipes.

From here, the D976 continues southwest past the charming little village of **Tavel**, a place that is equally haunted – in this instance by wine fiends come to slake their thirst on the pale ruby blood of the earth. **Lirac**, situated 2km to the north, is even smaller; a pretty kilometre's walk west from the village leads to the **Sainte-Baume**, a cave holy since time immemorial, where a miraculous statue of the Virgin was discovered in 1647 and a hermitage built. To the north, little **St-Laurent-des-Arbres** used to be owned by the medieval bishops of Avignon, and has a fortified Romanesque church of 1150, a tower and a castle keep.

If you cross over to Provence from this corner of the Gard, you'll be in the famous (but tiny) wine region of **Châteauneuf-du-Pape**.

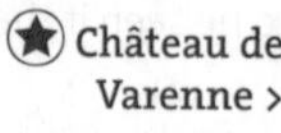
Château de Varenne >

Where to Stay and Eat on the West Bank of the Rhône

Roquemaure ✉ 30150

*****Château de Varenne**, Place St-Jean, Sauveterre, 4km from Roquemaure, **t** 04 66 82 59 45, *www.chateaudevarenne.com* (€€€€). A stunning 18th-century building set in a beautiful park with a pool. *Closed Jan–mid-Feb.*

****Le Clément V**, 6 Rue Pierre Sémard (Route de Nîmes), **t** 04 66 82 67 58, *www.hotel-clementv.com* (€€). An excellent, moderately priced hotel complete with a pool. *Closed Jan.*

Tavel ✉ 30126

*****Auberge de Tavel**, Voie Romaine, **t** 04 66 50 03 41, *www.auberge-de-tavel.com* (€€€–€€). Charming, quiet, well-equipped rooms and a good elegant restaurant (€€€). *Closed Wed and Thurs lunch.*

La Louisia, north of Tavel near St-Laurent-des-Arbres, at crossroads on N580, **t** 04 66 50 20 60 (€€€–€€). Reliable good food and a great place to try *gâteau de rascasse à l'américaine* (scorpion fish). *Closed Tues.*

Wine: Tavel and Lirac

The sun-soaked, pebbly limestone hills on the left bank of the Rhône are celebrated for their rosés – including Tavel. The original pink wine, Tavel has been beloved of kings since the 13th century, when Philippe le Bel declared, 'It isn't good wine unless it's Tavel.' By the 1930s, the vine stocks – grenache, cinsault, bourboulenc, carignan and red clairette – were so old that Tavel nearly went the way of the dodo. Since revived to the tune of 825 healthy hectares, it remains the universal, harmonious summer wine that goes with everything from red meat to seafood.

Some growers add syrah and mourvèdre to give their Tavels extra body and colour, including the two best-known producers in the village, open by appointment: the de Bez family at the **Château d'Aquéria**, **t** 04 66 50 04 56, *www.aqueria.com*, and the prize-winning **Domaine de la Mordorée**, **t** 04 66 50 00 75, *www.domaine-mordoree.com*.

The Lirac district begins 3km to the north of Tavel and encompasses four *communes* – Roquemaure, Lirac, St-Laurent-des-Arbres and St-Geniès-de-Comolas. Its pebbly hills are similar to those of Tavel, and the *appellation* differs in the addition of two grape varieties – white ugni and maccabeo – and the fact that everything doesn't come up rosé: Lirac produces fruity whites, with a fragrance reminiscent of the wildflowers of the nearby *garrigue*, and well-structured reds. Try it on weekdays by appointment at **Domaine Duseigneur**, St-Laurent-des-Arbres, **t** 04 66 50 02 57, *www.domaineduseigneur.com*, and at **Château St-Roch**, Roquemaure, **t** 04 66 82 82 59, *www.chateau-saint-roch.com*.

Just beyond it lies **Orange**, a drab town with some remarkable relics, including a triumphal arch and the best-preserved Roman theatre in the world.

Villeneuve lez Avignon

Just across the Rhône rises **Avignon**, the city of the popes with its famous half-bridge and its wealth of medieval and Renaissance art and architecture. It's in Provence and there's no room to include it here, but if you cross over, don't miss the Palais des Papes, and the great collections of the Musée du Petit Palais and Musée Calvet.

Here on the Languedoc side, a wealthy abbey grew into the King of France's bastion on the Rhône. It began in 586, on Puy Andaon, the rock that dominates Villeneuve lez Avignon, where a Visigoth princess-hermit named Casarie died in the odour of sanctity (holiness smells like crushed violets, apparently). In the 10th century, Benedictines built the abbey of St-André to shelter her bones and lodge pilgrims on the route to Compostela. St-André grew to become one of the mightiest monasteries in the south of France, and in 1226, when Louis VIII besieged pro-Albigensian Avignon, the abbot offered the king co-sovereignty of the abbey in exchange for royal privileges. And so what was once an abbey town became a frontier-fortress of the king of France, a new town (*ville neuve*), heavily fortified in case the pope over the river should start feeling his oats. But Villeneuve was soon invaded in another way; wanton, squalid 'Babylonian' Avignon didn't suit all tastes, and the pope gave permission to his cardinals who preferred it not-so-hot to retreat across the Rhône into princely *livrées cardinalices* (palaces 'freed' from their original owners by the Curia).

Though something of a dormitory suburb these days, Villeneuve still maintains a separate peace, with well-fed cats snoozing in the sun, leisurely afternoons at the *pétanque* court and some amazing works of art.

Around Town

In 1307, when Philip the Fair ratified the deal that made Villeneuve royal property, he ordered that a citadel be built on the approach to Pont St-Bénezet, named after guess who. As times grew more perilous, this bright white **Tour Philippe-le-Bel** was made higher and higher to keep out the riff-raff, and from its terrace, reached by a superb winding stair, it offers splendid views of Avignon and Mont Ventoux.

Tour Philippe-le-Bel
t 04 32 70 08 57; open May–Sept Tues–Sun 2.30–6.30; Mar and April and Oct, Tues–Sun 2–5; closed Nov–Feb; adm

From here, Montée de la Tour leads up to the 14th-century **Collégiale Notre-Dame**, once the chapel of a *livrée* and now Villeneuve's parish church. From Villeneuve's Chartreuse (*see* below) it inherited an elaborate marble altar of 1745; it also contains a copy of Enguerrand Quarton's famous *Pietà de Villeneuve lez Avignon* (the original is in the Louvre).

Collégiale Notre-Dame
t 04 90 27 49 23; open April–Sept daily 10–12.30 and 2–6.30; Oct–Mar daily 10–12 and 2–5

The church's most famous work, a beaming, swivel-hipped, polychrome ivory statue of the Virgin, carved in Paris out of an elephant's tusk *c.* 1320, has been removed to safer quarters in the nearby **Musée Pierre-de-Luxembourg**, which is housed in yet another *livrée*. The museum's other prize is the masterpiece of the Avignon school: Enguerrand Quarton's *Couronnement de la Vierge* (1454), one of the greatest works of 15th-century French painting. It was originally commissioned for the Chartreuse and rather unusually portrays God the Father and God the Son as twins, clothed in sumptuous crimson and gold, like the Virgin herself, whose fine sculptural features were perhaps inspired by the ivory Virgin. Around these central figures the painting evokes the spiritual route travelled by the Carthusians through vigilant prayer, to purify the world and reconcile it to God. St Bruno, founder of the Order, plus saints, kings and commoners are present, hierarchically arranged, while the landscape encompasses heaven, hell, Rome and Jerusalem, and local touches such as the Montagne Ste-Victoire and the cliffs of L'Estaque just over the Rhône in Provence.

Musée Pierre-de-Luxembourg
t 04 90 27 49 66; open May–Sept Tues–Sun 2.30–6.30; Jan, Mar, April and Oct–Dec Tues–Sun 2–5; closed Feb; adm

Other notable works in the museum include a curious 14th-century double-faced Virgin, the 'Eve' face evoking original sin and the 'Mary' face human redemption; Simon de Châlon's 1552 *Entombment*; and, amid the 17th-century fluff, Philippe de Champaigne's *Visitation*.

La Chartreuse and Fort St-André

Just up from the museum at 53 Rue de la République is the **Livrée de la Thurroye**, the best-preserved Cardinal's palace in Villeneuve; a prelate would maintain a household of a hundred or so people here. Further up the street, and up the scale, rises what used to be the largest and wealthiest charterhouse in France, the **Chartreuse du Val de Bénédiction**.

Chartreuse du Val de Bénédiction
t 04 90 15 24 24; www.chartreuse.org; open July–Sept daily 9–6.30; April–June daily 9.30–6.30; Oct–Mar daily 9.30–5; adm

This began life as the *livrée* of Etienne Aubert who, upon his election to the papacy in 1352 as Innocent VI, deeded his palace to the Carthusians for a monastery. For 450 years it was expanded and rebuilt, acquired immense estates on either side of the Rhône from kings and popes, accumulated a precious library, two more cloisters and various works of art, and in general lived high on the hog by the usual Carthusian standards. In 1792, the Revolution forced the monks out, and the Chartreuse was sold in 17 lots; squatters took over the cells and outsiders feared to enter after dark. Now beautifully restored, the buildings house the **CNES** (Centre National des Ecritures du Spectacle), where playwrights and others are given grants to work in peace in some of the former cells; it hosts seminars, exhibitions and performances, especially during the Avignon Festival.

Still, the sensation that lingers in the charterhouse is one of vast silences and austerity, the hallmark of an order where conversation was limited (at least at the outset) to one hour a week; monks who disobeyed the rule of prayer, work and silence ended up in one of the seven prison cells that are set around the laundry in the Great Cloister, each with a cleverly arranged window on the prison chapel altar. Explanations (in English) throughout offer an in-depth view of Carthusian life: one cell has been furnished as it originally was. Pierre Boulez discovered that the dining hall, or ***tinel***, has some of the finest acoustics in the whole of France, designed so that everyone could hear the monk who read aloud during mealtimes. In the *tinel*'s **chapel** are some ruined 14th-century frescoes by Matteo Giovannetti and his school: originally their work covered the walls of the huge **church**, now bare except for their masons' marks and missing its apse, which collapsed. The artistic highlight is **Innocent VI's tomb**, with its alabaster effigy under a fine Gothic baldachin. Innocent was solemnly reburied here in 1960: a century ago the tomb was being used as a rabbit hutch. Popes who took the name Innocent have tended to suffer similar posthumous indignities: the great Innocent III was found stark naked in Perugia cathedral, a victim of poisoned slippers, while the corpse of Innocent X – the last of the series – was dumped in a toolshed in St Peter's.

Fort St-André
t 04 90 25 45 35, www.fort-saintandre.monuments-nationaux.fr; open mid-May–mid-Sept daily 10–1 and 2–6; April–mid-May and mid–end Sept daily 10–1 and 2–5.30; Oct–Mar daily 10–1 and 2–5; adm

Gazing down into the charterhouse from the summit of Puy Andaon are the bleached walls of **Fort St-André**, built by the French kings around the old abbey in the 1360s, not only to stare down the pope over the river but to defend French turf during the heyday of the *Grandes Compagnies*, a rather glorious name for bands of

Market Days in Villeneuve lez Avignon

Thurs: Place Charles David.

Sat am: Place Jean Jaurès.

Where to Stay in Villeneuve lez Avignon

Villeneuve lez Avignon ✉ 30400

Villeneuve's history as a haven for cardinals has translated into some fine places to stay.

****Le Prieuré, 7 Place du Chapitre, **t** 04 90 15 90 15, *www.leprieure.com* (€€€€€–€€€€). An exquisite, centrally located hotel that gives you the option of sleeping in a 14th-century *livrée*, where the rooms are furnished with antiques, or in the more comfortable annexe by the large swimming pool. Further attractions are its gardens, tennis court and splendid restaurant. *Closed Nov–mid-Mar.*

******Hostellerie La Magnaneraie**, 37 Rue Camp-de-Bataille, **t** 04 90 25 11 11, *www.hostellerie-la-magnaneraie.com* (€€€€€–€€€€). A Best Western hotel with old-fashioned rooms in a former silkworm nursery, and a modern annexe, plus a swimming pool, gardens and Le Prieuré's rival for the best restaurant in town. *Closed Jan; restaurant closed Wed, Sat lunch and Sun eve.*

Aux Ecuries des Chartreux, 66 Rue de la République, **t** 04 90 25 79 93, *www.ecuries-des-chartreux.com* (€€€–€€). Nicely decorated B&B in a 17th-century building with studios next to the Chartreuse.

*****L'Atelier**, 5 Rue de la Foire, **t** 04 90 25 01 84, *www.hoteldelatelier.com* (€€€–€€). A charming, beautifully restored 16th-century building with stylishly furnished rooms and a walled garden, in the centre.

****Les Cèdres**, 39 Av Pasteur Bellevue, **t** 04 90 25 43 92, *www.lescedres-hotel.fr* (€€). A 17th-century building with a swimming pool, restaurant and bungalows. *Closed Nov–mid-Mar.*

UCJG Centre YMCA, 7 bis Chemin de la Justice, **t** 04 90 25 46 20, *www.ymca-avignon.com* (€). A hostel with superb views of the Rhône and a pool.

Eating Out in Villeneuve lez Avignon

La Maison, 1 Rue Montée-du-Fort, **t** 04 90 25 20 81 (€€). A friendly old favourite with traditional Provençal food. *Closed Tues, Wed and Aug.*

La Guinguette du Vieux Moulin, 1 Rue du Vieux Moulin, **t** 04 90 94 50 72, *www.guinguettevieuxmoulin.com* (€€). Fun riverside restaurant with grilled dishes, seafood and lots of jazz nights. *Closed Dec–Easter Mon lunch, open eves only Fri and Sat; other times closed Sun eve and Mon, daily July and Aug.*

ⓘ **Villeneuve lez Avignon >**
1 Place Charles David, t 04 90 25 61 33, www.tourisme-villeneuvelezavignon.fr; open daily all year

★ **Le Prieuré >**

★ **La Guinguette du Vieux Moulin >>**

unemployed mercenaries who pillaged the countryside and held towns to ransom. The two round towers afford a famous vantage point over Avignon; the southwestern tower is called the **Tour des Masques** (or Tour des Sorcières, or Tour des Fées); no one remembers why. Jumbly ruins are all that remain of the once splendid **Abbaye St-André** amid beautiful Italian gardens – sumptuous in springtime – restored and presided over by Roseline Bacou, former curator at the Louvre.

Abbaye St-André
t 04 90 25 55 95, www.abbaye-saint-andre.com; open April–Sept Tues–Sat 10–12.30 and 2–6; Oct–Mar Tues–Sat 10–12.30 and 2–5

Beaucaire

South of Avignon, twin towns glower at each other across the Rhône, or Malabar, the 'strong man' of French rivers. Each has its castle, and each has its particular monster. In **Tarascon** in Provence, it's the Tarasque, a mustachioed armadillo that gobbled up locals before St Martha put an end to it in the 9th century. Languedocien Beaucaire's is a river monster, called the **Drac** – a dragon in some versions, or a handsome young man who liked to stroll invisibly through Beaucaire, before luring his victims into the Rhône by holding a bright jewel just below the surface. When the Drac became a father, he kidnapped a washerwoman to nurse his baby for seven years, during which time the woman learned how to see him when he was invisible. Years later, during one of his town prowls, she saw him and greeted him loudly. He was so mortified that he was never seen again, although like the Tarasque he makes an annual reappearance by proxy, on the first weekend in June. Beaucaire was also the setting of one of the most charming medieval romances: of **Aucassin**, son of the count of Beaucaire, and his 'sweet sister friend' Nicolette, daughter of the king of Carthage, whom Aucassin loved so dizzily that he fell off his horse and dislocated his shoulder, among other adventures.

But in those days Beaucaire was on everyone's lips. It was here, in 1208, that a local squire assassinated Pope Innocent III's legate, who had come to demand stricter measures against the Cathars. It gave Innocent the excuse he needed to launch the **Albigensian Crusade** against Beaucaire's overlords in Toulouse, and all their lands in Languedoc. In 1216, when the war was in full swing, Raymond VII, the son of the count of Toulouse, recaptured the town from the Crusaders, who took refuge in the castle. As soon as word reached Simon de Montfort, he set off in person to succour his stranded men and to teach Beaucaire a lesson, besieging the town walls, while his troops took up the fight from inside the castle, sandwiching Beaucaire in a double attack. The siege lasted 13 weeks before the troops in the castle ran out of food and surrendered and de Montfort admitted a rare defeat. In gratitude, Raymond VI granted Beaucaire the right to hold a duty-free fair. But five years later the town was gobbled up by France along with the rest of Languedoc.

In 1464, Louis XI restored its freedoms and fair franchise; before long its *Foire de la Ste-Madeleine* became one of the biggest in western Europe. For 10 days in July, merchants from all over the Mediterranean, Germany and England would wheel and deal in the *pré*, a vast meadow on the banks of the Rhône; by the 18th century, when the fair was at its height, Beaucaire (with a population of 8,000) attracted some 300,000 traders, as well as acrobats, thieves and sweethearts, who came to buy each other rings of spun glass as a symbol of love's fragile beauty. So much money changed hands that Beaucaire earned as much in a week as Marseille did in a year.

The loss of Beaucaire's duty-free privileges just after Napoleon lost at Waterloo put an end to the fair, and since then Beaucaire has had to make do with traffic on the Rhône and tourism along the Rhône–Sète Canal (an extension of the Canal du Midi), its quarries and its wine, ranging from good plonk to AOC Costières du Gard. But in the spring you can try one last legacy of the great fair in Beaucaire: the *pastissoun*, a patty filled with preserved fruits, introduced by merchants from the Levant.

The Château and Historic Centre

Louis XI's restoration of Beaucaire's rights paid off for a later Louis (XIII); in 1632, when the **château** was besieged by the troops of the king's rebellious brother, Gaston d'Orléans, the loyal citizenry forced them out. To prevent further mishaps, Richelieu ordered Beaucaire's castle be razed to the ground. But after the south wall had been demolished, the shell was left to fall into ruins romantic enough for an illustration to *Aucassin et Nicolette*, and filled with trees. There are sweeping views of the Rhône and the old fairgrounds, the Champ de Foire, from the 80ft **Tour Polygonale**.

Musée Municipal Auguste Jacquet
t 04 66 59 90 07; open April–Oct Wed–Mon 10–12.30 and 2–6; Nov–Mar Wed–Mon 10–12 and 2–5; closed Tues; adm

In the castle gardens, the **Musée Municipal Auguste Jacquet** houses finds from Roman Beaucaire (then clumsily called Ugernum), including a fine statue of Jupiter on his throne, and another of the lusty Priapus found in a villa. There's a geological collection, popular arts, and advertising posters and mementos from the fair, when thousands of brightly coloured cloths swung over the streets, each bearing a merchant's name, his home address and his address in Beaucaire; it was the only way in the vast, polyglot throng to find anyone.

From the château, arrows point the way to the delightful **Place de la République**, and to the grand, elegant Baroque church of **Notre-Dame-des-Pommiers** (1744), which perhaps more than anything proves how many visitors this now rather quiet town once expected. It replaced a smaller Romanesque church but conserves, on the wall facing Rue Charlier, a superb 12th-century frieze depicting Passion scenes in the same strong, lively style as the reliefs at St-Gilles (*see* pp.119–21).

The stately French classical **Hôtel de Ville** (1683), in Place Georges Clemenceau, was designed by Jacques Cubizol and bestowed on Beaucaire by Louis XIV, who wanted to give the town a monument worthy of its importance: note Louis' sun symbols on the façade, the town's coat of arms set in the Collar of St Michael (the French equivalent of the Order of the Garter – Beaucaire was the only town in France awarded the honour), and Beaucaire's motto: 'Renowned for its Fair, Illustrious for its Fidelity'.

If it's a holiday, there will probably be some dramatic bull follies in the **Arènes**: 100 bulls are brought in for the *Estivales*, a week-long re-creation of the medieval market and other celebrations in late July. Beaucaire's *razeteurs* have a reputation as the most daring of them all; statues of Clairon and Goya, the bulls that gave them the best sport in the Courses Camarguaises, greet visitors respectively by the Rhône bridge and in Place Jean Jaurès.

Around Beaucaire

Le Vieux Mas
t 04 66 59 60 13, www.vieux-mas.com; open July–Aug daily 10–7; April–June and Sept daily 10–6; Oct–Mar Wed, Sat, Sun and hols 1.30–6; adm

Le Vieux Mas, 8km south on the road to Fourques, is a living evocation of a Provençal farmhouse at the turn of the 19th century, complete with a working blacksmith and other artisans, plus farm animals, and regional products to buy.

Mas Gallo Romain des Tourelles
t 04 66 59 19 72, www.tourelles.com; open July–Aug Mon–Sat 10–12 and 2–7, Sun 2–7; April–June and Sept–Oct daily 2–6; Nov–Mar Sat 2–5.30, other days by appt

The **Mas Gallo Romain des Tourelles**, 4km southwest at 4294 Route de Bellegarde, is far older: on the 210-acre vineyard of the Château des Tourelles (which has been owned by the Durands since the 18th century) archaeologists excavated a huge 1st-century AD agricultural estate that produced olives, wheat and wine, complete with a vast and efficient pottery factory capable of producing 4,000 amphorae a day. It inspired the Durands to re-create a Gallo-Roman winery – in September the grapes are pressed in the Roman way and bottled, or rather amphora-ed, in jars ranging in size from five to 1,000 litres, wrapped in straw to keep them from breaking in transit. You can taste and buy the result, although there's no way of knowing how close it comes to the stuff quaffed by Nero – the Romans added lime, egg whites, plaster, clay, mushroom ashes and pig blood to 'improve' their wines, and Durand, thankfully, does not.

Beaucaire's Roman incarnation made its living transferring goods (including its wine) along the Roman 'superhighway', the **Via Domitia** that linked Rome to Spain. An 8km stretch of this ancient roadway has come through in remarkably good nick, especially in a place known as **Les Bornes Milliaires** (take the D999 1km northwest past the train tracks, turn left and continue for 800m, following the Enclos d'Argent lane). Nowhere else along the route have the milestones survived so well: these three, on the 13th mile between Nîmes and Ugernum, were erected by Augustus, Tiberius and Antoninus Pius.

Abbaye Troglodytique Saint-Roman de l'Aiguille
t 04 66 59 19 72, www.abbaye-saint-roman.com; open July–Aug daily 10–1 and 2–7; April–June and Sept Tues–Sun 10–1 and 2–6; Oct and Mar Tues–Sun 2–5; Nov–Feb Sun and school hols Tues–Sun 2–5; adm

In the same area, the unique and vaguely spooky **Abbaye Troglodytique Saint-Roman de l'Aiguille**, 4km up the D999, was founded in a cave during the perilous 5th century and was laboriously carved out of the living rock. It was mentioned in the chronicles in 1363, when Pope Urban V made it a *studium*, a school open even to the poorest children; but by 1537 it had lost its importance and was engulfed in a fortress. When the fortress in

Market Days in Beaucaire

Beaucaire: Thurs am and Sun am, Pl de la Mairie and Cours Gambetta.

Where to Stay and Eat in Beaucaire

Beaucaire ✉ 30300

***Les Doctrinaires**, 6 Quai du Général de Gaulle, **t** 04 66 59 23 70, *www.hoteldoctrinaires.com* (€). Old-fashioned inn set in the home of the Doctrinaire fathers of Avignon (1650). Under the stone vaults, it also has a good restaurant (€€) with a pretty summer patio.

***Robinson**, 2km north of town on Route de Remoulins (D986), **t** 04 66 59 21 32, *www.hotel-robinson.fr* (€€). Thirty rooms set in acres of countryside, with a swimming pool, tennis court, playground and restaurant (€€). *Closed Feb.*

Auberge de l'Amandin, 1076 Chemin de la Croix de Marbre, **t** 04 66 59 55 07, *www.auberge-amandin.com* (€€€–€€). Featuring the classic dishes of Provence (after all, just over the river) on a lovely terrace. *Closed Sun eve and Mon.*

L'Ail Heure, 43 Rue Château, **t** 04 66 59 67 75 (€€). Excellent little restaurant with a limited menu and affable owner; great food, prepared with finesse.

ⓘ **Beaucaire >**
*24 Cours Gambetta, **t** 04 66 59 26 57, www.ot-beaucaire.fr; open July Mon–Sat and Sun am; Easter–June and Aug–Sept Mon–Sat; Oct–Easter Mon–Fri; guided tours in English*

turn lost its importance in the 19th century and was destroyed, the abbey was rediscovered: you can see the chapel, with its remarkable abbot's chair; the subterranean cells; the water cisterns and wine press; and 150 rock-cut tombs in the necropolis on the upper terrace, from where the dead monks had better views than the live ones down below.

Musée de la Vannerie et de l'Artisanat
t 04 66 59 48 14; open April–Oct Wed–Sun 3–7; Nov–Mar Wed–Sun 2–6; adm

Northeast of Beaucaire, **Vallabrègues**, 'the most Provençal town of Languedoc', was cut off from the rest of the Gard when the Rhône changed its bed. Surrounded by clumps of osier, it still makes its living from wicker and basketry: learn all about the long-standing local craft in the **Musée de la Vannerie et de l'Artisanat**.

South of Nîmes: The Petite Camargue

The Rhône finishes its long journey south in the Camargue, the delta swampland that is France's salt cellar, home to its greatest concentration of waterfowl and some of its most exotic landscapes. The Languedoc end is known as the Petite Camargue, part of the delta of a distributary called the Petit-Rhône, but like the big Camargue it has white Camargue horses, flamingo-filled lagoons and herds of very special cows looked after by the French cowboys, the *gardians*. The two attractions on its edge, St-Gilles and Aigues-Mortes, were in the Middle Ages among the most flourishing towns in the south; both have long since been marooned by the advancing delta.

St-Gilles

In medieval times and earlier, much nearer the sea, St-Gilles was a port, site of a Phoenician merchant colony, a Greek-Celtic *oppidum* and, in the 7th century, the refuge of a Greek hermit named Aegidos or Gilles, who was most famous for a doe who gave him her milk. When the king wounded the doe in a hunt, the hermit scolded him for harming a defenceless beast; and the king, impressed by his goodness, built an early monastery. In the 11th century, the popes, the monks of Cluny and the counts of Toulouse (whose family originally came from St-Gilles) promoted it as a major clearing house for pilgrims from the north, who would walk from Ile de France to Le Puy-en-Vélay, then take the Route de St-Gilles or the Régordane over the Cévennes to St-Gilles, and from there walk or sail to Rome, Compostela or Jerusalem. It boomed with the onset of the Crusades, and both the Templars and Knights Hospitallers (who owned large tracts in the Camargue) built important *commanderies*. In 1116 the abbey church of St-Gilles was begun, one of the most ambitious projects ever undertaken in medieval Languedoc.

Destiny, however, soon began making it clear that this was not the place. As the delta gradually expanded, the canals silted up and St-Gilles could no longer function as a port. The real disaster came with the Wars of Religion, when the town became a Protestant stronghold; the leaders of the Protestant army thought the church, that obsolete relic from the Age of Faith that took 200 years to build, would look much better as a fortress, and they demolished nearly all of it to that end. It was rebuilt, in a much smaller version, after 1650. What was left suffered more indignities during the Revolution – the loss of many of the figures' faces is nothing short of tragic – but it is a miracle that otherwise one of the greatest ensembles of medieval sculpture has survived more or less intact.

The Abbey of St-Gilles

Abbey of St-Gilles-de-Gard
guided visits of the crypt and Vis; call the tourist office on **t** *04 66 87 33 75; adm*

This is the masterpiece of the Provençal school of 12th-century sculptors, the famous work that was copied, life-size, in the Cloisters Museum in New York. Created roughly at the same time as the façade of St-Trophime in Arles, it is likewise inspired by ancient Roman triumphal arches.

Instead of Roman worthies and battle scenes, the 12 Apostles hold place of honour between the Corinthian columns. This is a bold, confident sculpture, taking delight in naturalistic detail and elaborately folded draperies, with little of the conscious stylization that characterizes contemporary work in other parts of France. In this, too, the Romans were their masters. The scheme is complex, and worth describing in detail.

The Church Façade (*see diagram, below*)

Left portal: tympanum of the Adoration of the Magi (1); beneath it, Jesus' entry into Jerusalem (2); flanking the door, a beautiful St Michael slaying the dragon (3); and on the right the first four Apostles, SS Matthew and Bartholomew, Thomas and James the Lesser (4–7).

Central portal: tympanum of Christ in Majesty (8), with symbols of the Evangelists; underneath, a long frieze that runs from one side portal across to the other: from left to right, Judas with his silver (9); Jesus expelling the money-changers from the temple (10); the resurrection of Lazarus (11); Jesus prophesying the denial of Peter and the washing of the Apostles' feet (12); the Last Supper (13); the Kiss of Judas, a superb, intact work (14); the Arrest of Christ (15); Christ before Pilate (16); the Flagellation (17); Christ carrying the Cross (18). Left of the door, saints John and Peter (19); right of the door, saints James the Greater and Paul, with the soul-devouring Tarasque under his feet (20). Beneath these, at ground level, are small panels representing the sacrifices of Cain and Abel and the murder of Abel (21); a deer hunt and Balaam and his ass, and Samson and the Lion (22).

Right portal: tympanum of the Crucifixion (23), and, beneath it, two unusual scenes: the three Marys purchasing spices to anoint the body of Jesus, and the three Marys at the tomb. To the left of this, the Magdalen and Jesus (24); to the right, Jesus appearing to his disciples (25). Left of the door, four more unidentifiable Apostles (26–29; note how the 12 represented here are not the canonical list – better-known figures such as John the Evangelist and Paul were commonly substituted for the more obscure of the original Apostles). To the right of the door, Archangels combat Satan (30).

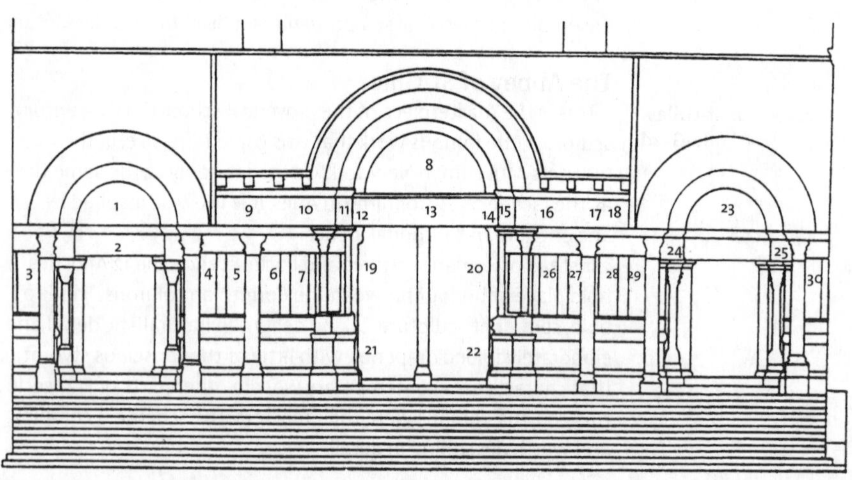

The Vis de St-Gilles

The 17th-century interior of the rebuilt church holds little of interest, but its original, wide-vaulted **crypt** or lower church survives (so many pilgrims came to St-Gilles that upper and lower churches were built to hold them). Behind the church, amid the ruins of the **choir** and **apse** of the original, which was much longer than the present structure, is the ***Vis*** or 'screw' of St-Gilles, a spiral staircase of 50 steps that once led up one of the bell-towers. Built about 1142, it is a *tour de force*. The stones are cut with amazing precision to make a self-supporting spiral vault; medieval masons always tried to make the St-Gilles pilgrimage just to see it. Its author, Master Mateo of Cluny, also worked on the church of Santiago de Compostela, where he is buried.

The Maison Romane

Maison Romane
t 04 66 87 40 42; open July and Aug Mon–Sat 9–12 and 3–7

The rest of the town shows few traces of its former greatness, although opposite the façade of the church, on Place de la République, is a fine 13th-century mansion, claimed to be the birthplace of Guy Folques, who became Pope Clement IV. Today this Maison Romane houses sculptures and architectural fragments from the church, and collections on the folklife and nature of the Camargue.

The Camargue: Flora and Fauna

Nature and man co-exist fairly well in the Camargue. Salt has been panned here since Neolithic times, but agriculture in the rich alluvial soil only began in the Middle Ages, when Cistercian and Benedictine monks started to build dykes to drain and cultivate the land, which now produces cereals, grapes (*vin de sables*), as well as serving as France's only rice-growing region, of late specializing in a relatively new red variety that has earned the thumbs-up from gourmets. Rice-growers, however, have to contend with the Camargue's iconic pink flamingos, who like nothing better than trampling the young shoots (the Parc Naturel has started a programme of planting trees around the paddies to keep the flamingos out). Reeds, sea wort, tamarisks and sea lavender thrive in the Camargue's briny marshes.

Besides flamingos, some 400 bird species have been spotted in the Camargue. The famous little white horses, the Camarguis, are a breed that dates back to prehistoric times; born black, they become white by the time they are four. They live, like the black bulls, in *manades*, or semi-feral herds, fending for themselves. Once a year the *gardians*, the Camargue cowboys, round them up for health checks and branding. Many of the native black cattle are raised similarly in *manades*; this is essential for their meat to qualify as AOC Taureau de Camargue, the key ingredient in the classic stew, *gardiane de taureau*, served (naturally) with rice.

Camargue bulls are fast and can weigh up to 450kg. The late spring round-ups or *ferrades* are festive occasions, when the year-old bulls are branded and the likeliest, cleverest ones chosen to participate in the bloodless *course camarguaise* or *course libre*. Beaucaire, one of the great centres of the sport, claims to have invented the rules in the 19th century, which pits teams of agile, white-clad *razeteurs* against a bull, which wears *attributs* (threads) around its horns and a ribbon cocade between them. The *razeteurs* have 15 minutes (to the tune of Bizet's Carmen, naturally) to cut the *attributs* and pluck off the cocade from the annoyed bull; they avoid its charges by leaping over wooden barricades. A good bull earns piles of money; exceptional ones, at least in Beaucaire, earn statues (*see* p.117).

The Camargue's least popular creature is the mosquito – bring buckets of repellant.

Market Days in St-Gilles

St-Gilles: Thurs and Sun am.

Where to Stay and Eat in St-Gilles

St-Gilles ✉ **30800**

****Le Cours**, 10 Allée François Griffeuille, **t** 04 66 87 31 93, *www.hotel-le-cours.com* (€€–€). A typically traditional Logis de France, with a shady restaurant terrace (€€) where you can try the likes of Camargue *pilaf* and frogs' legs. *Closed mid-Dec–Feb.*

*****L'Héraclée**, 30 Quai du Canal, **t** 04 66 87 44 10, *www.hotel-heraclee.com* (€€). Unexciting but well run, and has free Wi-fi.

ⓘ St-Gilles >
Place Frédéric Mistral, t 04 66 87 33 75, www.ot-saint-gilles.fr; open Mon–Fri; on Sat go to Point Annexe, Place de l'Eglise

Aigues-Mortes: Salt and Walls

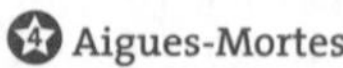

Every French history book has a photo of Aigues-Mortes, and every French person carries in their mind the haunting picture of the great walled port from which Saint Louis sailed off to the Crusades, now marooned 5km inland by the muck of the advancing Rhône delta. It is as compelling a symbol of time and fate as any Roman ruin, and as evocative of medieval France as any Gothic cathedral.

In 1241 the Camargue was the only stretch of Mediterranean coast held by France, and St Gilles was rapidly silting up. To solidify this precarious strip, Louis IX (Saint Louis) began construction of a new port and a town, laid out in an irregular grid to stop the wind from racing up the streets. In 1248 the port was complete enough to hold the 1,500 ships that carried Louis and his knights to the Holy Land on the Seventh Crusade, which was to bring Louis disasters both at home and abroad (the town was the last he saw of France – he died in Tunis of the plague in 1270). His successor, Philippe III, finished Aigues-Mortes and built its tremendous walls. Being the only French Mediterranean port, by the late 13th century it was booming, with perhaps four times as many inhabitants as its present 4,800, its harbour filled with ships from as far away as Constantinople and Antioch.

Aigues-Mortes means 'dead waters', and it proved to be a prophetic name. The sea deserted Aigues and, despite efforts to keep the harbour dredged, it declined after 1350. Attempts to revive it in the 1830s failed, ensuring Aigues' demise, but allowing the works of Louis and Philippe to survive undisturbed. Forgotten and nearly empty by the early 1900s, Aigues now makes its living from tourists.

Towers and ramparts
t 04 66 53 61 55, http://aigues-mortes.monuments-nationaux.fr; open May–Aug daily 10–7; Sept–April daily 10–5.30; adm

Aigues-Mortes' **walls** are more than 1.5km in length, streamlined and almost perfectly rectangular. Pick up tickets at the Logis du Gouverneur to visit the **towers and ramparts**, most notably the **Tour de Constance**, an enormous cylindrical defence tower used to guard the northeastern land approach to the town. After the Crusades, the tower was turned into a prison, first for Templars and

Getting to and around Aigues-Mortes

For **trains** from Nîmes, contact **t** 08 00 88 60 91; for buses **t** 08 10 33 42 73. There are also buses from Montpellier, **t** 08 25 34 01 34.

---

later for Protestants. One of them, Marie Durand, spent 38 years here in unspeakable conditions. On her release in 1768, she left her credo, *register* ('resist' in Occitan) chiselled into the wall, where it can still be seen.

The tower to the south was used as a temporary mortuary in 1431, during the Hundred Years' War, when the Bourguignons, who held the city, were suddenly attacked and decimated by their arch-enemies, the Armagnacs. There were so many gruesome bodies lying around that the Armagnacs simply stacked them up in the tower, covering each with a layer of salt: hence its name – the **Tower of the Salted Burgundians** – and hence, too, the French nursery rhyme:

Bourguignon salé,
L'épée au côté,
La barbe au menton,
Saute! Bourguignon!
(Salted Burgundian/Sword at your side/Beard on your chin/ Jump! Burgundian!)

Salins d'Aigues-Mortes
t 04 66 73 40 24, www. visitesalinsde camargue.com; 75min tours July–Aug 10–5.50, Mar–June and Sept–Oct 10.30–4; adm; they also run 3.5hr 4x4 salt and nature tours twice a day (adm exp); book ahead

And salt there was in plenty. Half of France's supply is collected here, at the pink-tinted 10,000-hectare **Salins d'Aigues-Mortes** pans just to the south, which you can tour in a *petit train*. Now the sea wants to return, and attempts to keep the tides from draining the saltpans could be futile, or at least very expensive.

Seaquarium
t 04 66 51 57 57, seaquarium-grau-du-roi.fr; open July–Aug daily 9.30am–11.30pm; April, May, June and Sept daily 9.30am–7.30pm; Nov–Mar daily 9.30–6.30; adm exp; ticket office closes an hour before

Eight kilometres southwest, **Le Grau-du-Roi** with its 18th-century lighthouse started as an old fishing port, in the midst of endless beaches. In the 1960s, it was given an artificial playground neighbour, **Port-Camargue**, a Florida-style nest of holiday homes and marinas that has since gobbled it up; it has a *de rigueur* flashy fish show, **Seaquarium**, on Av du Palais de la Mer, with seals and orcas, a glass tunnel through the shark tanks, and a small museum dedicated to Le Grau-du-Roi. To the south stretches the **Plage de l'Espiguette**, a remarkable seven-mile stretch of natural sand dunes, where the only building in sight is a lighthouse by the car park – after about half an hour's walk you'll come to the naturist section, and beyond that the gay beach.

Market Days in Aigues-Mortes

Aigues-Mortes: Av Frédéric Mistral: Wed and Sun am.

Activities in Aigues-Mortes

Pescalune, t 04 66 53 79 47, *www. pescaluneaiguesmortes.com*, offer barge tours of the Petite Camargue.

Hotel Canal >>

In Le Grau-du-Roi, **Pierrot le Camarguais, t** 04 66 51 90 90, *www.pierrot-le-camarguais.fr*, runs 4x4 safaris through the delta's wilds. Or explore on horseback and splash through the sea with the **Abrivado Ranch** in Le Grau-du-Roi (**t** 04 66 53 01 00, *www. abrivadoranch.fr* (*mid-April–mid-Oct*). For nature and off-the-beaten-track tours contact **la Maison du Guide de Camargue, t** 04 66 73 52 30 or **t** 06 12 44 73 52, *www.maison duguide. camargue.fr*.

Where to Stay and Eat in Aigues-Mortes

Aigues-Mortes >
Place Saint-Louis, t 04 66 53 73 00, www. ot-aiguesmortes.fr; open daily all year; offers historical tours of the town, year-round

Aigues-Mortes ✉ 30220

Villa Mazarin, 35 Bd Gambetta, **t** 04 66 73 90 48, *www.villamazarin.com* (€€€€–€€€). A romantic hotel in a 15th-century villa within the town walls, with enchanting rooms, a pool and restaurant (€€€€).

***Le Saint-Louis**, 10 Rue de l'Amiral Courbet, **t** 04 66 53 72 68, *www. lesaintlouis.fr* (€€€). A distinguished and beautifully furnished 18th-century building just off Place Saint-Louis, with gracious staff and a restaurant. *Closed mid-Nov–April.*

***Hotel Canal**, 440 Route de Nîmes, **t** 04 66 80 50 04, *www.hotelcanal.fr* (€€€–€€). Stylish, contemporary canal-side hotel with great staff and Wi-fi.

Marie Rosé, 13 Rue Pasteur, **t** 04 66 53 79 84 (€€). Some of Aigues-Mortes' best food (lamb, seafood and organic veg) is prepared without fuss or muss in this restaurant housed in a former *presbytère. Closed Sun–Wed in winter.*

La Camargue, 19 Rue de la République, **t** 04 66 53 86 88, *www.restaurantla camargue.com* (€€). The place where the Gypsy Kings got their musical start, and still the liveliest place in town, with flamenco guitars strumming in the background. Eat in the garden in summer.

Port-Camargue ✉ 30220

***Le Spinaker**, Point de Môle, **t** 04 66 53 36 37, *www.spinaker.com* (€€€). Idyllic oasis overlooking the yachts, built around a palm garden and pool, with a romantic gastronomic restaurant, **Le Carré des Gourmets** (€€€).

Between Nîmes and Montpellier

There are three routes between the two cities: the *autoroute*; its southern parallel, the N113; or the longest, prettiest route – the D40 from Nîmes to Sommières, then the N110 to Montpellier.

Via Nages and Sommières

Nages: A Celtic *Oppidum*

The D40 from Nîmes passes through lush, hilly country and slumberous villages like **Caveirac** and **St-Dionisy**. Above the latter, off the D737, is the 3rd-century BC *oppidum* of **Nages**, one of the outstanding pre-Roman sites in the south (easy access on foot, signposted from the village of **Nages-et-Solorgues**). Like Nîmes, Nages was built around a spring, entirely of dry stone, with a temple, and walls punctuated by round towers; on top of the tallest, the **Tour Monumentale**, a cache of stones for slings was discovered. The streets, with their rectangular houses, were laid out in a tidy grid – long before the Romans introduced their waffle-shaped city plans. The first floor of Nages-et-Solorgues' *mairie* has been converted into a small **archaeology museum**.

Archaeology museum
t 04 66 35 05 26; open by request

Sommières

It is a pity indeed to travel and not get this essential sense of landscape values. You do not need a sixth sense for it. It is there if you just close your eyes and breathe softly through your nose; you will hear the whispered message, for all landscapes ask the same question in the same whisper. 'I am watching you – are you watching yourself in me?'

Lawrence Durrell, *Spirit of Place: Letters and Essays on Travel*

Sommières

Hidden under the cliffs of the River Vidourle, Sommières suffers only moderately from the usual plagues besetting picturesque southern villages: the Parisians, the English, the trinket shops – it has even had to do without a famous writer since long-time resident Lawrence Durrell died in October 1990.

Huge plane trees, a little bullring and an enormous *boulodrome* (for *pétanque*) line the river, and swans and mallards float calmly by, except during the *vidourlades*, the local name for the Vidourle's seasonal floods, when it pours down hell-for-leather from the Cévennes: recent measures have dampened some of its impetuosity, but it still floods badly from time to time.

Before Sommières, there was Sommières' **bridge**, built by Tiberius between AD 19 and 31. Its 17 arches have withstood centuries of *vidourlades*; they carry road traffic to this day and still look in mint condition. The top was restored in 1715. Oddly, almost half of the bridge is now hidden inside the town; medieval Sommières expanded into the dry parts of the riverbed and eventually an embankment was built. The **Tour de l'Horloge**, the entrance to the town, was built over the bridge's fifth arch in 1659.

The other arches of the bridge lie under Rue Marx Dormoy, the street leading to **Place des Docteurs Dax** (natives of Sommières who discovered the exact spot in the brain in charge of language), a lovely 12th-century market square that everyone still calls by its old name, the **Marché-Bas**. It preserves the Pierre d'Inquant, where slaves were once made to stand when they were being sold. The houses are all built on stone arcades: in the old days, the square

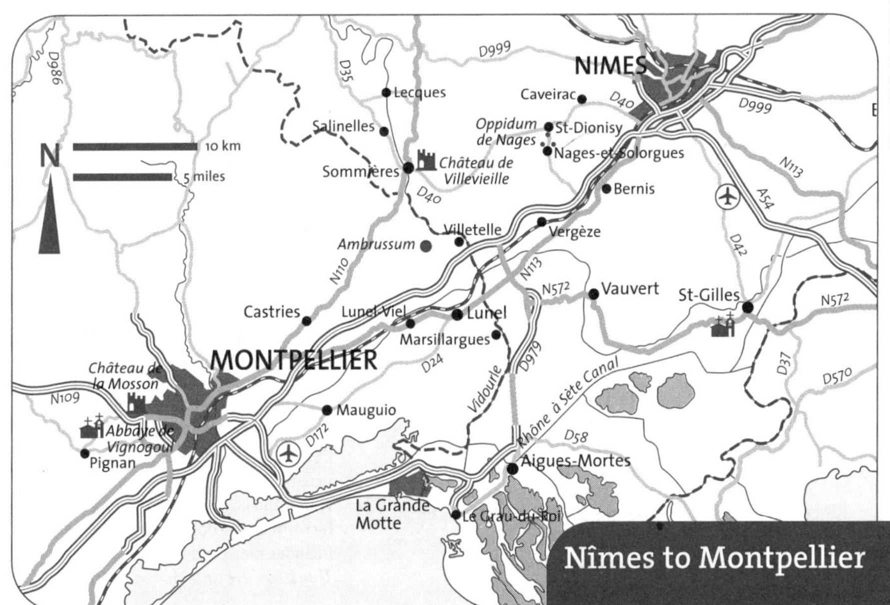

would be underwater every spring, forcing the market up two streets to the **Marché-Haut** (now Place Jean-Jaurès). The lanes radiating from these squares have their share of handsome *hôtels particuliers*. An enthusiastically Protestant town, Sommières was destroyed during the Wars of Religion after two terrible sieges, in 1573 and 1575, then again in 1622, so most of what you see is from the 17th-century rebuilding.

Rue de la Taillade, cut into the cliffs by the Romans for the Nîmes–Lodève road, is one of the most attractive streets, with well-preserved old shops; the former Ursuline convent here, now the **Espace Lawrence Durrell**, is used for temporary exhibitions. From here, the Montée des Régordanes leads up to the half-ruined **Château de Sommières** and the **Tour Bermond**, with its views, as far as Pic St-Loup and Aigues-Mortes.

Tour Bermond
open July–Aug Tues, Wed, Thurs 10–1 and 3–7; adm

Around Sommières

Château de Villevieille
t *04 66 80 01 62, www.placedelacom.net /clients/villevieille; open July–Sept daily 2–8; April–June and Oct–Nov Sat and Sun 2–7; adm*

A mile away, on a hill above Sommières, the **Château de Villevieille** was first built in the 11th century by the lords of Sommières, the Bermond de Sauve, whose most famous scion was a Cathar and brother-in-law of Raymond VII of Toulouse – excuse enough for Saint Louis to confiscate their estate in 1243. He divided the vast property in two, leaving a bit for the family's daughter and trading the remainder to the monks of Psalmody in exchange for the site of Aigues-Mortes. In 1527 the château was ceded to the Pavée family, who have owned it since. It escaped being sold off in the Revolution, thanks to the Marquis de Villevieille's friendship with Mirabeau and Voltaire. You can count on one hand the châteaux in France that have preserved their original family furnishings – this is one.

★ **Hôtel de l'Orange >>**

ⓘ **Sommières >**
5 Quai Frédéric Gaussorgues, **t** *04 66 80 99 30, www.ot-sommieres.fr; open July–Aug daily; Sept–June Mon–Fri, Sat am*

★ **Auberge du Pont Romain >**

Market Day in Sommières

Sommières: Sat.

Where to Stay and Eat in Sommières

Sommières ✉ 30250

***Auberge du Pont Romain, 2 Rue E. Jamais, **t** 04 66 80 00 58, *www.aubergedupontromain.com* (€€€–€€). Lovely, spacious rooms in a 19th-century herbal distillery close to the river, with a pool and a gourmet restaurant (€€€) serving the house *foie gras* and other delights on a peaceful garden terrace. *Closed Nov and mid-Jan–mid-Mar.*

Hôtel de l'Orange, 7 Rue des Beaumes, **t** 04 66 77 79 94, *www.hotel.delorange.free.fr* (€€€ €€). A 17th-century building, lovingly converted into a guesthouse, with a pool and a garage but only five rooms, so book early in the summer; ask to see the *baume* (cave). There's also a bungalow for weekly self-catering rental.

L'Olivette, 11 Rue Abbé Fabre, **t** 04 66 80 97 71 (€€). This restaurant in the centre is a local favourite, serving regional cuisine with an original twist, such as snails *à la sommiéroise*. *Closed Tues summer, Tues eve and Wed winter.*

L'Evasion, 6 Rue Paulin Capmal, **t** 04 66 77 74 64 (€). At lunchtime, watch the life of the Marché-Bas pass by from an outdoor table; the menu includes pizza and mussels. *Closed Thurs, Sun eve and Mon in winter.*

Four kilometres northwest of Sommières, along a Roman road, is the pretty country chapel of **St-Julien-de-Montredon**, at **Salinelles**, a lovely setting among vines. First mentioned in 813, it was rebuilt by the monks of Psalmody in the 11th century and decorated with archaic carvings of animals and birds. Salinelles also has a **beach** along the Vidourle; others are nearby at Lecques and Villetelle.

Nîmes to Montpellier by Way of Perrier and Lunel

This faster route along the N113 has its own rewards, especially if you combine it with a detour to historic Aigues-Mortes (*see* p.122).

Fizzy Water and a Statue of Liberty

Bernis, 7km southwest of Nîmes, offers the first potential stop, for the sake of its 12th-century church, once a possession of the abbey of St-Gilles. Though mostly rebuilt after the Wars of Religion, its façade is intact, carved in a style archaic back in the 12th century, especially the Carolingian-inspired decorations by the door. The capitals are carved with people, birds, animals, a dragon and a mermaid.

Just off the the N113 at **Vergèze**, fizzy water fans can make a pilgrimage to the **Source Perrier**. Surprisingly, the vast water-producing complex was established by an Englishman in 1903, and looks less like a natural spring than an obsessively tidy aeroplane factory, with immaculate gardens; the green bottles come whizzing off the line in their billions.

Source Perrier
t *04 66 87 61 01; gardens, museum, Hall du Docteur Perrier open July–Aug Mon–Fri 9.15–7; April–June and Sept Mon–Fri 9.30–6; Feb–Mar and Oct–Dec Mon–Thurs 9.30–6; closed Jan; free; ring in advance for the tour*

The big town along this route is **Lunel**, and a peculiar place it is. Legend has it that Lunel was founded by Jews from Jericho under the reign of Vespasian – a story now dismissed as a play on words (Jericho was the city of the moon, the *ville de la lune*). Historians now say the first Jews probably settled in the 11th century and, until their expulsion in 1306, Lunel was their educational centre in France, with well-known schools of everything from medicine (predating even Montpellier's) to the Kabbala. For decades it was known as 'little Jerusalem'.

Today, the town raises bulls for bloodless *course carmarguaise*. Its cops wear star-and-crescent badges just like those of New Orleans, and one of its biggest businesses is dog food research and development. It has a copy of the Statue of Liberty (erected in 1989 to commemorate the bicentenary of the French Revolution) as well as a new statue celebrating the nursery rhyme about the local who fished for the moon with a hole in his creel, derived from the Occitan name of the inhabitants, *les Pescalunes* (literally 'moon-fishers'). Little remains of medieval Lunel: some bits of the Jewish schools on Rue Ménard, and a vaulted alley called the Passage des Caladons that once was part of a Templar commandery.

Château de la Tour de Farges
t 04 67 83 01 69 www.latourdefarges.com; open for tastings daily 9am–7pm

In the 19th century, Lunel Viel was the holiday retreat of a man who hardly seemed the type to take a vacation in the south of France – Karl Marx. Marx suffered from asthma, and had just completed the *Communist Manifesto* when he came to spend a few days at the **Château Tour de Farges** (off the road to St-Geniès-des-Mourgues), owned by the husband of opera diva Caroline Ungher. Another guest was Gustave Courbet, who immortalized it in his *Vue de la Tour de Farges*. It's one of several in the area that produce natural sweet Muscat de Lunel.

Musée Pastre
t 04 67 83 52 10; open Wed 3–6

South of Lunel, the charming and shady village of **Marsillargues** has an elegant Renaissance château. The rooms, with their marble and plaster relief decoration of the 1570s and later, are lovely, but empty; it's sad that this château, one of the few undamaged in the Revolution, should have lost most of its furnishings in a fire in 1936. Recently, four of the rooms have been filled up with the contents of the villagers' attics as the **Musée Pastre**. There are various events and theatre performances at the château.

Château de Teillan
open afternoons 15 July–15 Aug, by appt only, t 04 66 88 02 38

The **Château de Teillan**, at **Aimargues**, on an unpaved road across the River Vidourle from Marsillargues, has a large park with fragmentary Roman ruins, milestones, the largest *noria* (hydraulic machine) in Languedoc and a gigantic *pigeonnier*, once part of a 7th-century military depot.

By the *autoroute* north of Lunel in **Villetelle**, a single arch (there were originally 11) of a Roman bridge stands in the middle of the Vidourle at **Ambrussum**; you can see what it looked like 150 years ago when it still had two in Courbet's painting in Montpellier's Musée Fabre. Ambrussum was a Celtic *oppidum* from the same period as Nages (*see* p.124) and later became a way-station on the Via Domitia; archaeologists have uncovered 200 metres of paved Roman road (the deep grooves near the bridge mark the spot where the wagons and chariots stopped to pay their toll), as well as villas and public buildings.

ⓘ Lunel >>
16 Cours Gabriel Péri, t 04 67 71 01 37, www.ot-paysdelunel.com; open Mon–Sat, and Sun am

★ La Passiflore >

Market Days around Lunel

Lunel: Tues–Sun food, Halles, Cour G. Péri; Thurs and Sun, mixed market; Sat am, flea market.
Marsillargues: Tues, Thurs and Sat.

Where to Stay and Eat around Lunel

Vergèze ✉ 30310

La Passiflore, 1 Rue Neuve, **t** 04 66 35 00 00, *www.lapassiflore.com* (€€–€). Well placed for the *autoroute* and the Camargue, this gorgeous little hotel with an enclosed courtyard is run by an English couple. It's beautifully decorated and has Wi-fi. The service is friendly, and they like kids.

Lunel ✉ 34400

****Les Mimosas**, Av du Vidourle, **t** 04 67 71 25 40, *www.hotelmimosas.fr* (€€). Just outside the centre. Bright air-conditioned rooms. *Open year-round.*

Didier Chodoreille, 140 Rue Lakanal, **t** 04 67 71 55 77, *www.chodoreille.fr* (€€€–€€). Dine well on French classics; it's by the station, with a pretty garden terrace that makes Lunel's traffic seem far away. *Closed Mon, Sun.*

Montpellier and the Hérault

For devotees of rural France, the Hérault may be the ultimate find. Just enough tourists come for there to be plenty of country inns and fermes-auberges, *though in some villages foreigners are still a novelty. The food is good, and there's enough wine to make anyone happy. That's an understatement – the Hérault is the most prolific wine-producing region in France. It can be a perfect alternative to overcrowded and overpraised Provence: just as beautiful, more real and relaxed, full of things to see – and considerably less expensive.*

In this region, some 150km across at most, the diversity is tremendous: a microcosm of France, from mountain forests of oak and pine, and limestone cirques *and* causses, *to the endless beaches of the coast and the rolling hills around the Canal du Midi.*

09

Don't miss

1. Urban dynamo
Montpellier **p.132**

2. A fishing port with a museum of modest arts
Sète **p.165**

3. A town scarcely changed since Molière's day
Pézenas **p.173**

4. A stately canal for boating down
The Canal du Midi **p.181**

5. A seven-sided church
Rieux-Minervois **p.188**

See map overleaf

Montpellier and the Hérault

pp.192–3

pp.192–3

France isn't the sort of country that allows itself to be neatly dissected for the benefit of geographers and travel writers. So it is only for convenience's sake that the rugged *garrigue* of the upper Hérault, the green hills of the Espinouse and the flat expanses of the Béziers coast are combined together in one chapter (along with an adjacent corner of the Aude *département*, the Minervois).

p.82

pp.192–3

Don't miss

1. Montpellier **p.132**
2. Sète **p.165**
3. Pézenas **p.173**
4. The Canal du Midi **p.181**
5. Rieux-Minervois **p.188**

Beaches

The sands of the Camargue continue around the elbow of the French coast. The Golfe d'Aigues-Mortes washes against immense swaths of sand, much of which is being eaten up by concrete development, such as the resort of **La Grande Motte. Palavas** is Montpellier's summer cruising zone – trendy and overpopulated. For more space and fewer frills, head south past Sète, or stop at the tranquil **Plage des Aresquiers**, accessible only by a dead-end road from Frontignan. Other top beaches are:
Maguelone: long, narrow and sandy, one of the best near Montpellier.
La Tamarissière: just outside Cap d'Agde, long sands backed by an ancient pine forest.
Marseillan: fine sands, usually not too crowded, near Béziers.

Montpellier

Montpellier

If that town could suck as hard as it can blow, it could bring the ocean to it and become a seaport.

Although an old saying (*see* left) originally referred to the brash, booming, braggart Atlanta of the 1880s, it applies just as fairly to France's eighth and fastest-growing city. The public relations geniuses in Montpellier have managed to outdo even Atlanta: their beloved city has been cockadoodled as the *Technopole*, the *Surdoué* (the Specially Gifted), the 'Synergetic Euro-cité', the 'Capital of Southern Europe', rightful 'heir to the Florence of the Medicis', the 'French California', and indeed nothing less than 'the Rome of Tomorrow'. Unlike Atlanta, Montpellier has actually sucked hard enough to get a port (or at least a marina) by widening its puny river Lez, a feat that gave it a new horn to toot: *Montpellier la Méditerranée!*

Until 1977 and the election of the irrepressible socialist Mayor Georges Frêche (*see* pp.46–8), Montpellier was a sleepy university backwater of 100,000, one that could put forth the modest claim that Stendhal found it the 'only French city of the interior that doesn't look stupid'. The population of the metropolitan area now approaches 600,000, making it the eighth biggest city in France, including the large staff of IBM and more than 60,000 students from around the world who come to study where Rabelais and Nostradamus learned medicine. With his huge development projects, notably the monumental modern quarter of Antigone, Frêche made Montpellier a European model for innovative and effective city government.

History

Compared with its venerable Roman neighbours, Narbonne, Béziers and Nîmes, Montpellier is a relative newcomer, tracing its roots back a mere thousand years, to 985, when the count of Mauguio bestowed a large hamlet at Monspestelarius on the Guilhems, related to the counts of Toulouse. It was defensible, and it had a key early medieval location: near the Via Domitia, the *Cami Salinié* (salt route) and *Cami Roumieu* (the pilgrimage route between St-Gilles and Compostela); and above all it had access to the sea through its port, Lattes, on the river Lez.

Getting to and around Montpellier

By Air

The **airport**, Montpellier-Méditerranée, is 8km southeast of the centre on the D21 (**t** 04 67 20 85 00, *www.montpellier.aeroport.fr*). There are flights from the UK and Paris. The airport **shuttle bus** travels to and from Place de l'Europe, in the Antigone quarter, at roughly one-hour intervals, **t** 04 34 88 89 99, or see the airport website.

By Train

The **train station** is in Place Auguste Gibert, just south of the Ecusson. You can race there from Paris in 4hrs 40mins on the TGV, or catch direct trains to or from Avignon, Nîmes, Marseille, Nice, Perpignan, Béziers, Narbonne, Agde, Lunel, Sète and Carcassonne.

By Bus

The train station is linked by an escalator to the *gare routière* in nearby Rue du Grand St-Jean (**t** 04 67 92 01 43), which has buses to Nîmes, La Grande Motte, Béziers, Aigues-Mortes, etc. For information, **t** 04 34 88 89 99, *www.herault-transport.fr*.

By City Bus/Tramway

Montpellier has two sleek tram lines and a third 'Haute Couture line' plan slated for completion in April 2012. For bus and tram plans and schedules, contact **TaM**, **t** 04 67 22 87 87, *www.montpellier-agglo.com/tam*.

Bike Hire

The city's **Vélomagg** bike scheme allows visitors to hire a city bike for €1 for four hours, or €2 for a day, leaving ID as security from Véostation Centrale TaM, 27 Rue Maguelone (tramway station St-Roch, open daily 8am–8pm).

The hamlet quickly grew into a village of merchants, who made their fortunes by importing spices from the Levant. Many of the imported spices had medicinal uses taught to the merchants by their Arab and Jewish trading partners and by graduates of the medical school of Salerno; by the year 1000 the Guilhem lords had issued laws allowing doctors to lecture as much as they pleased; the university was officially founded in 1160. By the late 12th century, the town was big enough to need a wall with 25 towers, shaped like an escutcheon, or *écusson* (as the old town is still known). It lost its independence when Guilhem VIII failed to produce a son and gave his only daughter, Marie, to King Pere II of Aragon. Montpellier was her dowry, just in the nick of time to spare the town from the Albigensian Crusade. When Marie and Pere's son, Jaume the Conqueror, divided Aragon between his two sons, Montpellier joined the Kingdom of Majorca.

In 1220 the teachers of medicine formed a *Universitas Medicorum*, and began to attract students from all over Europe; in 1250 it was supplemented by a *studium* of law, both of which were given Pope Nicholas IV's seal of approval in 1289. Another impetus behind Montpellier's huge growth in the 13th and 14th centuries was dead bugs – cochineal beetles found on oaks in the nearby *garrigue*, used as a natural red dye (even today France is the world's largest producer). The spice and gold-working trades thrived, particularly after those mega-consumers, the popes, moved to Avignon.

In 1349 the Kings of Majorca sold Montpellier to France for 120,000 golden *écus*. A period of relative peace and prosperity continued until the 1560s, when the university academics and tradesmen embraced the Reformation. For the next 70 years much of what Montpellier had achieved was wiped out; churches and suburbs were destroyed, building and art came to a halt. In 1622, Louis XIII came in person to besiege the rebellious city and reassert royal authority; he built a citadel to watch the Montpellerains, then transferred here from Pézenas the Estates-General of Languedoc, with all its nobles, prelates and deputies, who built themselves the patrician *hôtels particuliers* that still dominate the old city.

Putting its merchant republic days behind it, Montpellier settled down to the life of a university town and regional capital. The Revolution closed the university, but otherwise passed without kicking up much dust; a far bigger crisis for Montpellier occurred in the 1890s, when phylloxera knocked out the wine-making industry – an economic blow from which it only began to recover in the 1950s. In the 1960s the population was given an instant 35 per cent boost with the arrival of large numbers of French Pieds Noirs from Algeria. And once Georges Frêche was elected mayor, it never looked back.

With the French mania for categorizing, Montpellier pigeonholes its booming economy into five 'poles': *Euromédecine* (including its numerous labs and pharmaceutical industries), *Héliopolis* (tourism), *Informatique* (IBM has been here since 1965), *Agropolis* (it boasts the first European research centre of agronomy in hot climates, among other institutes) and *Pole Antenna*, for its role as the telecommunications centre of Languedoc. Frêche's successor since 2004, Socialist mayor Hélène Mandroux, has kept up his breakneck momentum: new tram lines are planned, and a new Hôtel de Ville by Jean Nouvel has just gone up at Port Marianne, to be followed shortly, in the district of La Paillade, by Zaha Hadid's Pierresvives, a building evoking a petrified tree trunk that will house some of the Hérault's busy bureaucrats.

A Place Named Comédie

The various personalities of Montpellier all come together in the lively, café-lined **Place de la Comédie**, locally known as *l'Œuf*, or the Egg, owing to the shape it had in the 18th century, and still outlined in the pavement. Now flattened into an omelette, its centre is watered by the fountain of the *Three Graces* (1796). Other ornaments of the square include a *doppelgänger* of the Paris Opéra, and various 19th-century larded bourgeois buildings with domes reminiscent of bathyspheres, while opposite the square

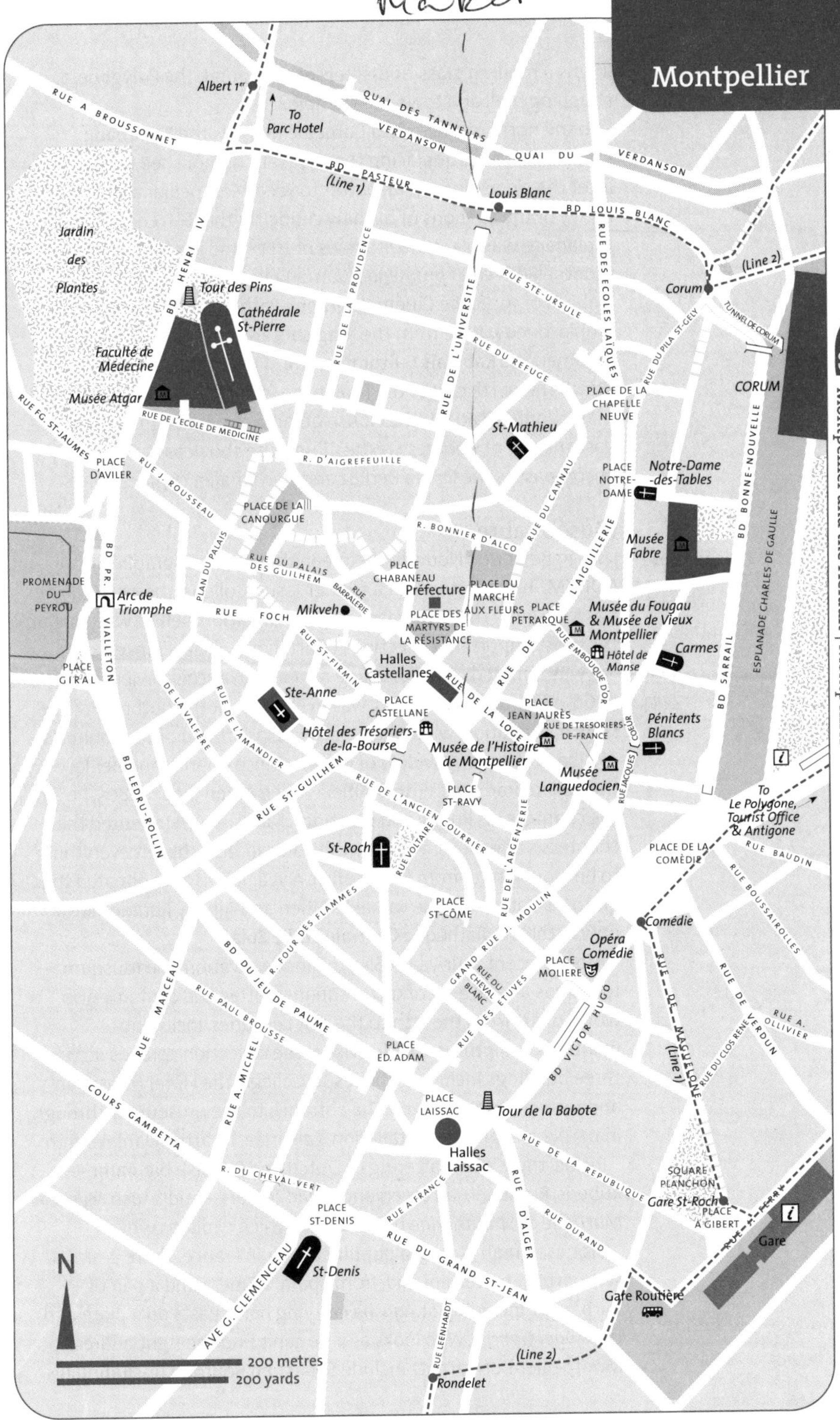
Albert 1er
To
Parc Hotel
RUE A BROUSSONNET
QUAI DES TANNEURS
VERDANSON
QUAI DU VERDANSON
BD PASTEUR
(Line 1)
Louis Blanc
BD LOUIS BLANC
(Line 2)
Corum
TUNNEL DE CORUM
CORUM
Jardin
des
Plantes
BD HENRI IV
Tour des Pins
Cathédrale
St-Pierre
Faculté de
Médecine
Musée Atgar
RUE DE L'ECOLE DE MEDICINE
RUE FG. ST-JAUMES
PLACE
D'AVILER
RUE J. ROUSSEAU
RUE DE LA PROVIDENCE
RUE DE L'UNIVERSITE
RUE STE-URSULE
RUE DU REFUGE
RUE DES ECOLES LAÏQUES
RUE DU PILA ST-GELY
PLACE DE LA
CHAPELLE
NEUVE
St-Mathieu
R. D'AIGREFEUILLE
PLACE DE LA
CANOURGUE
PLACE
NOTRE-
DAME
Notre-Dame
-des-Tables
BD BONNE-NOUVELLE
ESPLANADE CHARLES DE GAULLE
R. BONNIER D'ALCO
RUE DU CANNAU
RUE DE L'AIGUILLERIE
Musée
Fabre
PROMENADE
DU
PEYROU
BD PR. VIALLETON
Arc de
Triomphe
PLAN DU PALAIS
RUE DU PALAIS
DES GUILHEM
RUE BARRALERIE
PLACE
CHABANEAU
Préfecture
PLACE DU
MARCHÉ
AUX FLEURS
RUE FOCH
Mikveh
PLACE DES
MARTYRS DE
LA RÉSISTANCE
PLACE
PETRARQUE
Musée du Fougau
& Musée de Vieux
Montpellier
Hôtel de
Manse
RUE EMBOUQUE D'OR
Carmes
BD SARRAIL
PLACE
GIRAL
RUE ST-FIRMIN
Halles
Castellanes
RUE DE LA LOGE
Ste-Anne
PLACE
CASTELLANE
PLACE
JEAN JAURÈS
RUE DE TRESORIERS-
DE-FRANCE
Pénitents
Blancs
RUE JACQUES COEUR
DE LA VALFÈRE
RUE DE L'AMANDIER
Hôtel des Trésoriers-
de-la-Bourse
Musée de l'Histoire
de Montpellier
Musée
Languedocien
BD LEDRU-ROLLIN
RUE ST-GUILHEM
RUE DE L'ANCIEN COURRIER
PLACE
ST-RAVY
To
Le Polygone,
Tourist Office
& Antigone
St-Roch
RUE VOLTAIRE
RUE DE L'ARGENTERIE
PLACE DE LA
COMÈDIE
RUE BAUDIN
RUE BOUSSAIROLLES
PLACE
ST-CÔME
R. FOUR DES FLAMMES
GRAND RUE J. MOULIN
Comédie
Opéra
Comédie
PLACE
MOLIERE
RUE DU CHEVAL BLANC
RUE DES ETUVES
BD VICTOR HUGO
RUE DE MAGUELONE
(Line 1)
RUE DE VERDUN
RUE A. OLLIVIER
RUE DU CLOS RENE
BD DU JEU DE PAUME
RUE MARCEAU
RUE PAUL BROUSSE
RUE A. MICHEL
PLACE
ED. ADAM
COURS GAMBETTA
PLACE
LAISSAC
Tour de la Babote
Halles
Laissac
RUE DE LA REPUBLIQUE
SQUARE
PLANCHON
Gare St-Roch
PLACE
A GIBERT
RUE J. FERRY
Gare
R. DU CHEVAL VERT
PLACE
ST-DENIS
RUE A FRANCE
RUE D'ALGER
RUE DURAND
RUE DU GRAND ST-JEAN
AVE G. CLEMENCEAU
St-Denis
Gare Routière
N
RUE LEENHARDT
(Line 2)
200 metres
200 yards
Rondelet

looms a modern glass-and-steel semi-ziggurat, the **Polygone**, a shopping mall and town hall complex.

To the north of Place de la Comédie extends the **Esplanade Charles de Gaulle**, replacing the city walls demolished by Louis XIII after the siege of 1622, the better to keep Montpellier at the mercy of the cannons of his new citadel. In the 18th century the Esplanade was planted with rows of trees and became Montpellier's chief *promenade*; among its monuments is a rare survival of 1908, the **Cinématographe Pathé**, a little cockerel-emblazoned palace from the magical early days of cinema (now renamed the **Rabelais Cultural Centre**, it often shows foreign films). The north end of the Esplanade is flanked by the mastodontic **CORUM**, 'the House of Innovation' designed by Claude Vasconi, one of Georges Frêche's Euro-Cité showcases, which encompasses the Opéra Berlioz and two smaller congress halls.

Musée Fabre

Musée Fabre
t 04 67 14 83 00, http://museefabre.montpellier-agglo.com; open Tues, Thurs, Fri and Sun 10–6, Wed 1–9, Sat 11–6; closed Mon and hols; adm

At 39 Bd Bonne Nouvelle, between the Cinématographe and CORUM, in the fastness of a former Jesuit College, the Musée Fabre has long been the main reason for visiting Montpellier, with one of the most important collections of art in provincial France.

It was founded on a Florentine romance. François Xavier Fabre (1766–1837), a pupil of David, was in Florence at the outbreak of the French Revolution, where he became a close friend of the countess of Albany, the merry widow of Bonnie Prince Charlie, and her lover, the Italian dramatist Vittore Alfieri. When Alfieri died in 1805, he left the countess his library and paintings. Fabre in turn inherited the countess's affections, and when she died in 1824 she left everything to her young man from Montpellier. A year later, Fabre donated the lot to his native city; the valuable Alfieri and Albany libraries are now in the **Médiathèque Centrale Emile Zola**.

After a recent four-year, €62.5 million renovation, the museum today has a total area of 9,200 square metres and contains 900 works of art from the 15th to the 21st centuries, including paintings, sculptures and drawings. The collection spreads across three buildings including the Jesuit College, the Hôtel Massillian and 19th-century annexes. The entrance to the museum is through a marble and granite installation: *La Portée*, by artist Daniel Buren.

Inside, there's a smattering of Dutch and Flemish big names – Rubens, Ruysdael, Jan Steen and David Teniers – and a lush *Mystic Marriage of St Catherine* by Veronese, which explains why 'Veronese green' is such a popular colour in France. There is also a self-portrait by Bernini and, from Spain, a Ribera and a pair of Zurbarans, including *St Agatha* carrying her breasts on a plate and the *Angel Gabriel*, who looks as if he can't find the right address. Montpellier-born artists include Sébastien Bourdon (including his best known work *Homme aux Rubans Noirs*, painted while he was in the city in 1657–8), Jean Ranc and Jean Raoux, and Fabre himself, who proves to be as romantic in art as in his life (*St Sébastian* and *The Death of Narcissus*).

What makes the Fabre unique, however, are the paintings donated by the museum's other great benefactor, Alfred Bruyas (1821–77). Born into a Montpellier banking family, Bruyas resolved the frustration of not being able to paint himself by befriending many of the artists of his day and asking them to paint him instead – as a result there are 24 portraits of the red-bearded Bruyas to contemplate, including examples by Delacroix and Alexandre Cabanel of Montpellier (1823–89). Four are by Gustave Courbet (1819–77), who became the great man's friend and whose works are the museum's great treasures: the *Baigneuses*, which caused such a scandal in the Paris Salon of 1853 with its out-of-doors non-goddess bare buttocks that Napoléon III ordered it to be removed (Bruyas immediately snapped it up, and it wasn't long before artists came expressly to Montpellier to study it; it became a model for dozens of later French skinny-dipping scenes). Then there's the delightful, sun-drenched *Bonjour, Monsieur Courbet* (1854) in which the jaunty Courbet, strutting down a country lane with easel and paints strapped to his back, meets who else but Alfred Bruyas?

Other paintings cover the artistic movements on either side of Courbet: the later cold classicism of Ingres' *Stratonice* (1866) and David's clean, unbloodied *Dead Hector*, which stand as the antithesis of the warm, exotic romanticism of Delacroix's *Mulatress and Algerian Odalisques* (1849) or the melting landscapes of Corot. Southern painters of the period contribute big historical and exotic scenes and landscapes. The gloomy young romantic Théodore Géricault (1791–1824) is represented by an idealized *Portrait of Lord Byron* and a surreal *Study of Arms and Legs*, cannibal leftovers painted in a medical school while students dissected the corpses.

On the second floor there's a room dedicated to the early impressionist Frédéric Bazille, who died at war aged only 28. He was a friend of Renoir and Monet, whose best works glow with the strong sun of Languedoc: *Les Remparts d'Aigues-Mortes* and *La Vue du Village* (Castelnau, now engulfed by Montpellier). Eugène Castelneau (1827–94) painted bright landscapes around Languedoc such as the *Vue du Pic Saint-Loup* (1859). There are also works by Berthe Morisot, Robert Delaunay, Kees Van Dongen and Nicolas de Stael, and over 30 pieces dating from 1951 to 2005, donated by artist Pierre Soulages, that explore the artistic possibilities of the colour black. Other modern artists are represented back on the first floor, including Claude Viallat, Vincent Bioulès and other followers of the movement '*Supports-Surfaces*'.

Since 2010, the museum's rich collection of furniture, decorative pieces, ceramics and *objets d'art* have been housed at the nearby **Hôtel Sabatier d'Espeyran** (6 bis Rue Montpelliéret). There's also a restaurant, Insensé, run by the city's celebrity chefs, the Pourcel twins (*see* Eating Out, p.144).

Into the Ecusson

There is nothing else as compelling as the Musée Fabre in Montpellier's historic centre; much was lost in the Wars of Religion, and even many of the 17th- and 18th-century *hôtels particuliers*, stuccoed and ornate inside though many of them are , are fairly plain outside. But few cities in the south of France manage to be as pleasant and lively. Instead of gaggles of tourists, Montpellier has students; this is the second-biggest university town in the south after Toulouse. Mayor Frêche made the entire Ecusson a pedestrian zone, and it is a delightful place for walking.

Most of the foot traffic naturally funnels up the high street, Rue de la Loge, to café-filled Place Jean Jaurès with its friendly statue of the popular Socialist leader assassinated in 1914. Originally the 10th-century church, Notre-Dame-des-Tables ('of the money changers'), stood here, where Montpellier's early bankers did business with pilgrims on route to Compostela, but only the crypt survived the fires of the Wars of Religion; this is now the **Musée de l'Histoire de Montpellier**, with audiovisuals telling the city's history.

Musée de l'Histoire de Montpellier
t 04 67 54 33 16; open Tues–Sat 10.30–12.30 and 1.30–6; last entry 11.50 and 5.20; adm

Inns once lined the old pilgrims' way (now Rue de l'Aiguillerie). Follow it up to Place Pétrarque, where the **Hôtel de Varennes**' beautiful façade (1758) conceals a pair of Gothic halls. Upstairs, there's a pair of small museums devoted to the good old days. The **Musée du Fougau** ('the Foyer') was founded to preserve the arts and traditions of old Montpellier by the local Félibres, members of the artificially contrived literary movement founded by Frédéric Mistral in 1854 to safeguard the seven 'grand dialects' of Occitan. The **Musée du Vieux Montpellier** exhibits portraits of notables, and plans and views of the city from the 16th century on, along with some peculiar relics, such as the model of the Bastille carved from one of its stones after it was demolished in 1789.

Musée du Fougau
t 04 67 84 31 58; open Wed and Thurs 3–6; adm

Musée du Vieux Montpellier
t 04 67 66 02 94; open Tues–Sat 9.30–12 and 1.30–5; adm

Around the corner, at 4 Rue Embouque-d'Or, the **Hôtel de Manse** (1670) is famous for its richly decorated openwork staircase, designed by Italian architects – a stair that became the prototype for a score of others in Montpellier, including the one in the handsome Renaissance courtyard of the nearby **Hôtel de Lunaret**, at 5 Rue des Trésoriers-de-France. This, combined with the adjoining **Hôtel des Trésoriers de France**, around the block at 7 Rue Jacques Cœur, was the residence of the famous merchant and financier Jacques Cœur, whose motto was 'flies can't enter a closed mouth'. In 1441 he was appointed a treasurer of Charles VII, and charged with obtaining royal subsidies from Languedoc. Reasoning that the wealthier the land, the easier it is to tax, Cœur became one of Montpellier's greatest benefactors, among other things building a merchants' exchange and dredging the outlets of the Lez to make them navigable; this town house originally had a tower so high that he could scan the sea and its traffic. His career ended abruptly in 1451, when he was accused of poisoning the king's mistress, Agnès Sorel; he escaped prison in 1454 and died on the Greek island of Chios, while leading a fleet against the Ottomans for the pope.

Musée Languedocien
t 04 67 52 93 03, www.musee-languedocien.com, open mid-June–mid-Sept Mon–Sat 3–6; mid-Sept–mid-June Mon–Sat 2.30–5.30; adm

Although much renovated since Jacques Cœur's day, most of the contents predate him, as it's now the **Musée Languedocien**, housing all kinds of treasures: Greek vases, dolmens, funeral steles and other prehistoric finds from the Hérault; an excellent collection of Romanesque sculpture salvaged from the 11th-century version of Notre-Dame-des-Tables and from surrounding abbeys; the rock-crystal seal of King Sancho of Aragon; and three 12th-century Islamic funeral steles discovered in Montpellier, a rare relic of the city's cosmopolitan spice-trading days. From Jacques Cœur's day there are two fine paintings, an anonymous Catalan *SS. Apolline and Guilhem* and, from the Clouets' workshop, *Gabrielle d'Estrées and her Sister in their Bath*. A major collection of 16th–18th-century faïence made in Montpellier rounds things off, together with a grand ceiling painting of 1660, *Justice Discovering Truth with the Help of Time* by Jean de Troy. A plaque nearby in Rue des Trésoriers-de-France recalls that another of the city's colourful cast of characters lived here: that great wanderer Rabelais, who enrolled at Montpellier's medical school in 1530 at the age of 40, and became a doctor as well as a priest, although he later wrote that 'physicians always smelled of enemas, like old devils' (*Pantagruel*, 1532).

Amphithéâtre Anatomique St-Côme
accessible only on a tourist office guided tour

To the south, Rue Jacques Cœur becomes **Grand-Rue Jean Moulin**, one of the city's most elegant streets. On guided visits organized by the tourist office you can see the **Amphithéâtre Anatomique St-Côme** built in 1757 with funds left by Louis XV's surgeon, François Gigot de Lapeyronie. Turn left at the foot of Grand-Rue Jean Moulin for the **Tour de la Babote**, a recently restored medieval tower topped by an astronomical observatory in 1741.

Around Place Castellane

Halles Castellanes
open Mon–Sat 7.30am–7.30pm, Sun 7.30–2

In the heart of the Ecusson, at the top of Rue de la Loge, **Place Castellane** with its bustling covered market or **Halles Castellanes** (1869) is a main vortex of daily life. The charming squares on either side of the nearby **Préfecture**, the Place du Marché aux Fleurs and the Place Chabaneau, are favourite places to watch the world go by in pavement cafés. The handsome **Hôtel des Trésoriers-de-la-Bourse** (1631–93) is nearby on the street of the same name.

Montpellier's fame in heaven's circle hinges on Roch, the pious son of a wealthy merchant, who was born around 1350 and abandoned all of his worldly goods to make the pilgrimage to Rome in 1367. On his way home, he came to an Italian village decimated by plague; after miraculously curing a number of victims, Roch went down with the disease himself, and retreated to the country where no one could hear his groans. Nourished by a friendly dog who stole food for him from its master's table, Roch recovered and returned to Montpellier, so ravaged by his illness that he wasn't recognized and was thrown into prison as a spy, where he died in 1379. Only then did his grandmother recognize him by a birthmark in the shape of a cross. News of Roch's reputation reached plague-torn Venice, and, even though he had yet to be canonized, Venetians disguised as pilgrims stole his bones and built the magnificent Confraternity of San Rocco in his honour. Nevertheless, as patron saint of Montpellier, St Roch came through for his home town in the cholera epidemics of 1832 and 1849, and finally a church of **St-Roch** was built, in Viollet-le-Duc's Ideal Gothic, in the medieval quarter of the Ecusson.

Rue Voltaire leads up to the socializing centre of the neighbourhood, **Rue de l'Ancien Courrier**, which carries on to another neo-Gothic church, dedicated to **Ste-Anne**; now deconsecrated and used for exhibitions, it stands in the centre of a neighbourhood of violin-makers, a craft first documented here in 1768.

Rue Foch and the Promenade du Peyrou

Mikveh
accessible with the tourist office's guided tour

From the centre of the Ecusson, **Rue Foch** was sliced out in the 18th century as a grand formal boulevard, just missing a rare, very well preserved Jewish ritual bath, or **Mikveh**, at 1 Rue Barralerie. Dating from *c.* 1200, it was once in the midst of a large, active Jewish quarter. Since the late 17th century, however, this loftiest edge of Montpellier has been devoted to tons of mouldy fol-de-rol glorifying Louis XIV, beginning with the recently restored **Arc de Triomphe** (the triumphs referred to include the Canal du Midi, wrestling the English lion to the ground and conquering heresy – with the Revocation of the Edict of Nantes, a nasty piece of bigotry that went down like a lead balloon in Montpellier). You can climb its 103 steps inside on a guided visit from the tourist office.

Beyond stretches the **Promenade du Peyrou**, featuring an equestrian statue of his megalomaniac majesty as big as the Trojan horse. It was brought laboriously by sea and river from Paris in 1718, fell into the Garonne on the way and had to be rescued with great difficulty, then set up here, only to be smashed to bits in the Revolution – a fact that didn't prevent the erection of the present exact copy in 1838. At the edge of the promontory, the elegant **Château d'Eau** is a neoclassical temple designed by Jean Giral to disguise the reservoir of the **Aqueduc St-Clément** (1771) snaking below in curious perspective, a triple-tiered work inspired by the Pont du Gard.

The Cathedral and the Jardin des Plantes

Faculté de Médecine
can be visited on a tourist office tour

Musée Atgar
***t** 04 67 41 76 40; open Mon, Wed and Fri 1.30–5.45, free*

Jardin des Plantes
*www.jardindesplantes.univ-montp1.fr, **t** 04 67 63 43 22; open June–Sept Tues–Sun 12–8; Oct–May Tues–Sun 12–6*

The waters of the aqueduct feed the unicorn fountain in the nearby **Place de la Canourgue**, a charming 17th-century square. It looks down on the medieval monastery college of St-Benoît, on Rue de l'Ecole de Médecine, built by papal architects from Avignon, currently (since 1795) Montpellier's venerable **Faculté de Médecine**, housing an enormous medical library. Within it, at 2 Rue de l'Ecole-de-Médecine, the **Musée Atgar** offers an excellent collection of Flemish, Italian, Dutch and German grand master drawings.

St-Benoît's chapel has been Montpellier's **Cathédrale St-Pierre** ever since the see was transferred here from Maguelone in 1563, although its status didn't spare it the usual depredations in the Wars of Religion and the Revolution. Its greatest distinction is its porch, supported by two rocket-shaped turrets.

Boulevard Henri IV, running alongside the Faculté, descends to the tree-topped **Tour des Pins**, a last vestige of the medieval walls. Beyond lies the lovely **Jardin des Plantes**, France's oldest botanical garden, founded by a decree of Henri IV in 1593 to instruct students on native and exotic plants used for remedies. It has several magnificent 400-year-old trees, exotic succulents, *garrigue* plants, and an *orangerie*; in a spot celebrated for its exquisite melancholy, there's a plaque with the inscription *Placandis Narcissae Manibus*. The Narcissa is said to be the consumptive 18-year-old daughter of the poet Edward Young (best known for his gloomy *Night Thoughts*, probably the most bizarre text ever illustrated by William Blake). In 1734 he brought Narcissa to France, hoping the warm climate would cure her; instead the exertion of travelling killed her, and she was buried either in Lyon or here 'in the garden she loved' – a story that made this a favourite rendezvous for romantic students like Paul Valéry and André Gide. At the highest point of the garden is the Tree of Secrets, its trunk pitted with niches where lovers would leave *billets d'amour*.

Antigone

East of the Place de la Comédie lies another of the jewels in the Euro-Cité's crown: Antigone, a mostly moderate-income quarter with housing for 10,000 people, and shops and restaurants, all designed by Barcelona architect Ricardo Bofill in 1979 and spread along a huge formal axis down to the river Lez, on 50 hectares of vacant land. Bofill understood just what a Rome of Tomorrow needed: 'a parody of neo-Classicism', as Robert Hughes wrote – Mannerist neo-Roman arches, cornices, pilasters, and columns as big as California redwoods, built around the **Place du Nombre d'Or** and the **Place du Millénaire**, the squares of the 'Golden Number' and the 'Millennium' – celebrating the city's first thousand years – that link Montpellier to its newly dredged-out Tiber, the Lez. Does Antigone work? Even though it stretches nearly to the centre of the city, there was no attempt to relate the project to the rest of town – as you'll discover when you try to find it (from Comédie, the only way to reach Antigone is to pass through the 1970s Polygone shopping mall and walk out of the back door of the Galeries Lafayette department store).

On a bad day, Antigone looks like the surreal background to a De Chirico painting; and yet on a good day it seems delightful – and increasingly central on the plan of France's fastest-growing city. The newest parts of the project lie along the Lez: a gargantuan semicircle of apartments with a vaguely Stalinist air called the **Esplanade d'Europe**, decorated with a huge blue 'M' for Montpellier on the pavement. This part of the river has been blocked off by two bridges that hug the waterline, forming a space for paddling canoes; across the river, and closing the long axis, stands the sharp glass and stone castle arch of the **Hôtel de Région**, where Frêche held office as president of Languedoc-Roussillon, and had just been elected to his second term when he died of a heart attack in October 2010.

Tram 1 continues from here to Port Marianne, site of an urban watersports centre and Jean Nouvel's new Hôtel de Ville, before continuing to the Odysseum, a shopping mall, ice-skating and cinema complex, which also contains the state-of-the-art **Aquarium Mare Nostrum**, with 300 different species of marine creatures, deep sea tanks, a simulated cargo boat ride, and much more for the kids.

Aquarium Mare Nostrum
t 04 67 13 05 50, www.aquariummarenostrum.fr; open July–Aug 10am–10pm; Sept–June Sun–Thurs 10–7, Fri–Sat 10–8; adm exp

Around Montpellier

Montpellier is spreading its tentacles to suck in all that surrounds it, and has already gobbled up a number of 18th-century châteaux and gardens that were the country retreats of its élite. One of the oldest is 3km east of Antigone on the D24: the **Château de Flaugergues**. Begun in the 1690s, the place is filled with 17th- and 18th-century furnishings and tapestries, and a collection of optical instruments. It also produces wine.

Château de Flaugergues
t 04 99 52 66 37, www.flaugergues.com; guided tours June, July and Sept Tues–Sun 2.30–6.30, otherwise phone; gardens open year-round Mon–Sat 9.30–12.30 and 2.30–7, closed Sun; adm

A bit further east (take the D172), **Château de la Mogère** is a refined *folie* of 1716, with period furnishings, family portraits and, in the garden, a delightful Baroque *buffet d'eau*, a fountain built into a wall.

Château de la Mogère
t 04 67 65 72 01, www. lamogere.com; guided tours June–Sept daily 2.30–6.30 (ring ahead to check for Sat); Oct–May Sat, Sun and hols only, by appt; adm

North of the centre, the excellent **Parc Zoologique de Lunaret** is one of the nicest urban zoos in France, filled with exotic and regional fauna, amid woodlands and *garrigue*. Its Serre Amazonienne is a greenhouse partnered with a park in French

Parc Zoologique de Lunaret
www.zoo.montpellier.fr; take Tram 1 to St-Eloi, and then catch the Agropolis Lavalette shuttle bus; open Easter–Nov school hols Tues–Sun 9–7; winter till 5; the zoo is free, but adm charged to the Serre Amazonienne

Guyana encompassing the main eco-systems and fauna of the region, with thunderstorms every half-hour in the rainforest.

West of Montpellier, bus 109 from the Mas Drevon tram stop halts in front of the remarkable church of the Cistercian **Abbaye St-Martin-du-Vignogoul** (1250) in Pignan. Believed to be the first attempt at Gothic in Languedoc, the church is small in size but grand in vision, a lofty, single-naved, pint-sized cathedral decorated with a trefoil arch, finely sculpted capitals (still more Romanesque than Gothic), and a unique polygonal choir, lit by a row of bull's-eye windows.

Abbaye St-Martin-du-Vignogoul
t 04 67 42 76 68; open Mon–Fri 10–12 and 2–6

Tourist Information in Montpellier

The **tourist offices** offer a bouquet of guided tours of the city centre in English, every Sat at 5.30 in season.

A **City Card** can be bought for between one and three days which gives free transport plus entrance to certain sights plus reductions on concerts and activities.

ⓘ Montpellier >
***Town centre**: Allée Jean de Lattre de Tassigny, Esplanade de la Comédie, **t** 04 67 60 60 60, www.ot-montpellier.fr; open daily*

***Also at the airport**, Arrivals hall, between doors A and B*

Market Days in Montpellier

At Espace Mosson (La Paillade), there is a **flower** market on Tues and a **flea** market on Sun am. Daily **food** markets take place in Halles Castellanes (Rue de la Loge); Tues–Sat there's a market at Bd des Arceaux, by Rue Marioge; and at Antigone a market of **farmers' produce** every Wed, Place du Nombre d'Or.

Festivals in Montpellier

The city hosts many festivals: among them are theatre in June and early July, during the ***Printemps des Comédiens*** at Château d'O, *www.printempsdescomediens.com*; dance performances of all kinds, including whirling dervishes, films and workshops, at the ***Festival International Montpellier Danse***, *www.montpellierdanse.com*, also June and July; and all-star music from opera to jazz at the ***Festival de Radio France et Montpellier***, *www.festivalradiofrancemontpellier.com*, in the last three weeks of July. The end of October sees the ***Festival International du Cinéma Méditerranéen***, *www.cinemed.tm.fr*.

Shopping in Montpellier

Antiques shops cluster around Place de la Canourgue and the district of Ste-Anne.

Le Bookshop, 8 Rue Bras de Fer, **t** 04 87 88 20 90, *www.lebookshop.com*. An English bookshop and café.

Maison Régionale des Vins et des Produits du Terroir, 34 Rue St-Guilhem, **t** 04 67 60 40 41. A good range of local wines and food products from olive oil to caviar. *Open Mon–Sat 9.30–8.*

Pomme de Reinette, 35 Rue de l'Aiguillerie, **t** 04 67 60 52 78. Exceptional toy shop, filled with antique and modern toys, board games, you name it.

Where to Stay in Montpellier

Montpellier ✉ 30400

*******Domaine de Verchant**, 1 Bd Phillipe Lamour, just north of town in Castelnau le Lez, **t** 04 67 07 26 00, *www.domainedeverchant.com* (€€€€€). The most decadent place to stay – a combo wine estate dating from the 14th century, deluxe spa, and hotel full of sleek Parisian chic and a gourmet restaurant overseen by the Pourcel twins – all near the city centre but far from all the hubbub. There's an apartment for families as well.

******Le Jardin des Sens**, 11 Av St-Lazare. a 10-minute walk from the centre, **t** 04 99 58 38 38, *www.jardindessens.com* (€€€€€–€€€€). Modern Relais & Châteaux rooms owned by the Pourcels, with a pool and restaurant. *See* 'Eating Out'.

Baudon de Mauny ›

Demeure des Brousses ›

Le Jardin des Sens ››

La Maison de la Lozère: Cellier Morel ››

Baudon de Mauny, 1 Rue de la Carbonnerie, **t** 04 67 02 21 77, *www.baudondemauny.com* (€€€€). Palatial B&B in an elegant *hôtel particulier* of 1777 in the historic centre, preserving many of its original features integrated with contemporary design and lots of mod cons. Two nights minumum stay.

***__Aragon__, 10 Rue Baudin, **t** 04 67 10 70 00, *www.hotel-aragon.fr* (€€€). Lovely, fully equipped, full service boutique hotel, a stone's throw from Place de la Comédie.

***__Demeure des Brousses__, Rte des Vauguières (4km east of town on the D24 and D172E), **t** 04 67 65 77 66, *www.demeure-des-brousses.fr* (€€€–€€). If you have a car, the most charming place to stay is this 18th-century ivy-covered *mas* in a vast park, a few minutes from the city or the sea. There's no restaurant, but next door is the gastronomic haven of **Le Mas des Brousses**, **t** 04 67 64 18 91 (€€€€–€€). *Restaurant closed Sat lunch, Sun eve and Mon.*

***__La Maison Blanche__, 1796 Av de la Pompignane (off the route to Carnon), **t** 04 99 58 20 70, *www.hotelmaison blanche.fr* (€€€–€€). Another gem requiring your own transport: a big, balconied house that looks as if it has escaped from the French quarter of New Orleans, surrounded by a park. *Restaurant closed Sat lunch and Sun.*

__Parc__, 8 Rue Achille Bégé, **t 04 67 41 16 49, *www.hotelduparc-montpellier.com* (€€). An 18th-century *hôtel particulier* fitted out with Wi-fi, air-conditioning, TV, etc.

__Palais__, 3 Rue Palais des Guilhem (just off Rue Foch), **t 04 67 60 47 38, *www.hoteldupalais-montpellier.fr* (€€). Comfortable rooms with Wi-fi in a recently restored building.

__Arceaux__, 33–5 Bd Arceaux, **t 04 67 92 03 03, *www.hoteldesarceaux.com* (€€). Attractive and comfortable, with Wi-fi, a small garden and terrace. Internet discounts.

Majestic, 4 Rue du Cheval Blanc, **t** 04 67 66 26 85, *www.hotelmajestic.hostel.com* (€€–€). Around the corner from the Etuves.

*__Les Fauvettes__, 8 Rue Bonnard, **t** 04 67 63 17 60 (€). Good value for money near the Jardin des Plantes, with quiet rooms overlooking interior courtyards.

Etuves, 24 Rue des Etuves, **t** 04 67 60 78 19, *www.hoteldesetuves.fr* (€). Cheap and comfortable; 100m from Place de la Comédie.

Auberge de Jeunesse, Impasse Petite Corraterie, Rue des Ecoles-Laïques, **t** 04 67 60 32 22, *www.fuaj.org/Montpellier* (€). In the student area; take the tramway to Louis Blanc. This is a very popular place to stay: be sure to book to get a bed in one of the dormitories; they also have triples and quads.

Eating Out in Montpellier

Le Jardin des Sens, 11 Av St-Lazare (off the N113 towards Nîmes), **t** 04 99 58 38 38, *www.jardin-des-sens.com* (€€€€). Montpellier is home to one of the most celebrated restaurants in the southwest. It is run by local twins Jacques and Laurent Pourcel, who are devoted to the *cuisine* of Languedoc and the Med. Try the squid stuffed with ratatouille and crayfish tails, *bourride* soup, fish soup and traditional *oreillette* pastries. *Closed Sun, Mon lunch and Wed lunch in July and Aug; Sun, Mon, Tues lunch, and Wed lunch in Sept–June; also 2 weeks Jan.*

La Maison de la Lozère: Cellier Morel, 27 Rue de l'Aiguillerie, **t** 04 67 66 46 36, *www.celliermorel. com* (€€€). Chefs Eric Cellier and Pierre Morel prepare gastronomic delights based on local produce in a 13th-century vaulted dining room. *Closed Sun all day, Mon lunch, Wed lunch and Sat lunch.*

La Réserve Rimbaud, 820 Avenue Saint-Maur, **t** 04 67 72 52 53, *www.reserve-rimbaud.com* (€€€). Lovely (especially in summer) contemporary restaurant with modern dishes, on the banks of the Lez, on the site of a 19th-century *guingette*. Tram station Les Aubes. *Closed Sun, Mon, and Sat lunch.*

Morceau de la Lune,14 Rue du Pila Saint Gély, **t** 04 67 52 80 59, *www.restaurant-morceau-de-lune.fr* (€€€). WIne bar with creative dishes to match; very popular, especially at weekends, so book. *Open lunch Wed–Fri, eves Tues–Sat.*

Divine et Sens, 2 Impasse Perier, **t** 04 67 54 12 30, *www.divine-et-sens.fr* (€€€). In a romantic setting under 12th-century vaults near the Corum, slurp on bivalves at the oyster bar or plump for something more elaborate, from Corsican *figatelli* to fillets of Carmargue beef. Those with light appetites can opt for a simple *plat du jour*, even in the evening. *Closed Sun.*

Le Petit Jardin, 20 Rue J-J Rousseau, **t** 04 67 60 78 78, *www.petit-jardin.com* (€€€–€€). Remarkably quiet restaurant in the centre of town, with a delightful large shady garden with a view of the cathedral. Good local fish, salads and fresh pasta with vegetables. *Closed Mon.*

★ L'Air du Temps >

L'Air du Temps, 55 bis Rue de la Cavalerie, **t** 04 99 58 18 91, *www.lairdutemps-restaurant.com* (€€€–€€). Contemporary-styled, award-winning restaurant near the Beaux Arts tram stop, serving creative Mediterranean cuisine (lamb baked for four hours, *gambas* roasted in garlic) with an exceptional children's menu and play area with chalkboards and colouring books. *Closed Sun eve–Tues lunch.*

Le Volodia, 29 Rue Jean-Jacques Rousseau, **t** 04 99 61 09 17, *www.volodiarestaurant.com* (€€). Sleek black and white dining room in the Ecusson, with an Art Deco touch and gourmet treats like a 'hambur-Gers' made with duck *magret*. *Closed Sat lunch, Sun and Mon.*

Le Dilemme, 12 Rue Farges, **t** 04 67 69 02 13 (€€). Good choice of French classics on affordable menus, and a young informal atmosphere. *Eves only.*

Les Saveurs du Liban, 7 Rue Faubourg Figuerolles, **t** 04 30 10 83 36, *www.lesaveursduliban.com* (€). Tasty informal Lebanese dishes, just off Cours Gambetta.

Lively Rue des Ecoles Laïques and Place de la Chapelle Neuve make up Montpellier's **Latin Quarter**, where the colours and smells from the assorted Turkish, Greek, Spanish and Tunisian restaurants collide in gleeful culinary discord.

Tripti-Kulai, 20 Rue Jacques Cœur, **t** 04 67 66 30 51, *www.triptikulai.com* (€). A vegetarian restaurant and tea room near the Musée Languedocien that offers some exotic dishes. *Closed Sun.*

Entertainment and Nightlife in Montpellier

Montpellier is a great town for cinema, both recent releases and classics; complete listings for these, as well as clubs, theatre and music, can be found in the city weekly *La Gazette*. FNAC, in the Polygone, sells tickets for events.

Most **bars** and **clubs** do not heat up until after 11pm.

Rockstore Odéon, down from Place de la Comédie at 20 Rue de Verdun, **t** 04 67 06 80 00, *www.rockstore.fr*. Still the place to be, with the red Cadillac sticking out of the façade. A café, five bars, concert hall and disco. *Open Mon–Sat till 4am.*

Le Twins, 13 Rue du Grand Saint-Jean, **t** 04 67 29 78 69, *www.letwins77.com* (€€). Trendy late-night restaurant and disco in the city centre. *Eves until 4am; closed Mon.*

JAM, 100 Rue Ferdinand de Lesseps, **t** 04 67 58 30 30, *www.lejam.com*. Montpellier's jazz school puts on frequent concerts from October to July.

La Villa Rouge, at Lattes, **t** 04 67 06 50 54, *www.la-villarouge.fr*. Buzzy place on the beachfront – gay/straight disco, concerts and themed evenings. *Closed Mon and Tues..*

Montpellier's Coast

West of the Camargue (*see* pp.118–24), the lagoons continue for another 80km, skirting the coast like beads on a string. Almost all of this coast is easily accessible by car. There are beaches and resorts in abundance; at the east end they begin with a bang, with

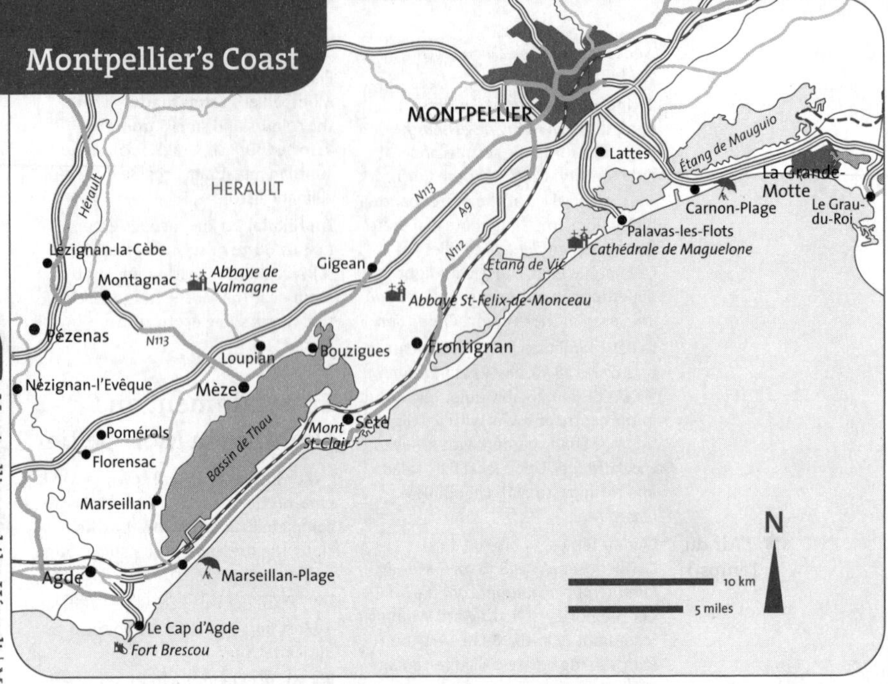

an uncanny skyline of tall ziggurats – a resort town straight from science fiction.

La Grande Motte

When concocting their grand Languedoc resort plan in 1963, designed to lure the French away from the new mass tourism wonderland of the Costa Brava, De Gaulle's planners in their wisdom decided that one of the new holiday towns was to be boldly modernist, and they picked 'the big lump', an empty swath of sand on the Golfe d'Aigues-Mortes, for the experiment.

Jean Balladur, the original architect, and his successors gave them perhaps more than they bargained for. La Grande Motte looks like no other resort in the world, its hotels and apartments rising in colourful triangles and roller-coaster curves, its public buildings in jarring, amoeboid shapes like a permanent 1960s World Fair. The 'modernism' of the Motte is more surface than substance; there are no real innovations in architecture or design. The original buildings themselves, like all the experiments of the kitschy 1960s, already look dated. Although peripheral bits have been abandoned to weeds, graffiti and mildew, the core of La Grande Motte proved a great success as a resort, a proper city with room for over 100,000 space-age holidaymakers.

The fun starts at **Point Zéro**, the name Balladur whimsically gave the central square on the waterfront. In season 'little train' tours around the town start from here. The first clutches of ziggurats (the Grande Mottois prefer to call them *pyramides*) rise to the west, around the marina; to the east are the outlandish buildings of the civic centre, including the *mairie* and congress hall. Beyond that, stretch broad beaches, thalassotherapy, tennis courts, golf courses (three, designed by Robert Trent Jones), marinas, windsurfing, diving, a big water park, a casino and all the rest. Summer is packed with festivals, concerts and sporting events.

West of La Grande Motte, a narrow strip of land separates the sea from the **Etang de Mauguio**. It's in easy striking distance of Montpellier, whose citizens fill up the more traditional resorts of **Carnon-Plage** and **Palavas-les-Flots**. Built around a narrow canal full of boats, Palavas offers some 8km of good beaches and a wowser casino. The old centre has a wonderfully casual air about it, toured by a silly tourist train dedicated to French humorist Albert Dubout, whose works, if you are sufficiently curious, are displayed in the **Musée Albert Dubout**, in the 18th-century Redoute de Ballestras, built to defend Palavas' fishermen. Palavas is proud of its modern 128ft **Phare de la Méditerranée** (formerly a water tower) with panoramic views from the restaurant at the top and the tourist office in the bottom. You can also see bullfights in the arena.

Musée Albert Dubout

t 04 67 68 56 41; www.dubout.fr; open July–Aug daily 10–12 and 4–9; Mar–June and Sept–Dec Tues–Sun 2–6; Jan–Feb school hols and weekends only; adm

Inland, the village of **Lattes** at the mouth of the river Lez has been absorbed into Montpellier's expanding agglomeration, but has far older credentials than the big noise of Languedoc. The proof of the pudding is the Roman necropolises and the **Musée Archéologique Henri Prades** at 390 Avenue de Pérols, with recent discoveries from the ongoing excavations at the adjacent site of **Lattara**, one of the most important ports of the indigenous Iberian-Celts, dating back to the 8th century BC; finds show that they had a thriving trade with the Etruscans and Greeks.

Musée Archéologique Henri Prades

t 04 67 99 77 20, www.museearcheo.montpellier-agglo.com; open Mon and Wed–Fri 10–12 and 1.30–5.30; Sat, Sun and hols 2–6; closed Tues; adm

Maguelone

To balance La Grande Motte, a town without a history, here we have a history without a town. Maguelone, 4km from Palavas, may have begun as a Phoenician or Etruscan trading post. It prospered under the Romans and Visigoths, becoming the seat of a bishop. After that the history is obscure. Old maps show the place as 'Port Sarrasin', suggesting that Arab corsairs were using it as a base in the 8th century, and there is a record of Charles Martel coming down from Paris to chase them out, destroying the town in the process. But Maguelone still had one attraction – salt – and the rights were owned by a powerful and progressive multi-national, the Church. In the 1030s, when demand was high, a cleric named Arnaulf oversaw the town's rebuilding and added a monastery. The enterprise prospered; Urban II, the first of many popes to visit (1096), called Maguelone the 'second church of Rome', and gave its restored bishops special privileges. Later, Maguelone became a papal holding, a key base both politically and ideologically in the difficult 12th century. It gradually dwindled after that, and the see moved to Montpellier in 1536.

Though almost no trace of the town remains today (its very stones were hauled off by the canal-builders), the impressive **Cathédrale de Maguelone** was saved from ruin and restored in the 1870s. Built, and built well, by Lombard masons in the 1170s, it is an austere building. The main decorative feature – reliefs around the main portal – show Christ in Majesty with the four Evangelists. Inside, there are fragments of the bishops' tombs, inscriptions and furnishings, and you can climb the surviving bell-tower for views down the coast.

Cathédrale de Maguelone
t 04 67 50 63 63, www.compagnons-de-maguelone.org; open June–Sept daily 9–9; Oct–May daily 9–7; audio guides available

Except at the height of summer, Maguelone is remarkably peaceful; there are plenty of beaches around it, a bit rocky but good for seashells. The lagoons stretching from La Grande Motte to Frontignan are rich in waterfowl, especially pink flamingos, but little else. Most are stagnant and lack oxygen; decomposing water plants in hot summers cause a phenomenon called the *malaïgue*, making the air smell like rotten eggs. The vineyards (*vin de sable*, 'sand wine', and others, run by the Compagnons de Maguelone) don't mind the occasional pong; the Magasin du Prévôt, Route de la Cathédral, offers tastings and shellfish.

Frontignan

From Maguelone, you'll need to backtrack to Palavas and continue around the landward side of the lagoons, rejoining the coast at Frontignan, an industrial town with a good 12th-century church, **St-Paul**, with a frieze of fish and boats over the door. Frontignan claims to be nothing less than the world capital of muscat, beloved by the ancient Romans and Thomas Jefferson. It comes in a screwy bottle, in honour of Hercules, who stopped here for a drink while performing his Twelve Labours; the big fellow liked the wine so much that he twisted the bottle to squeeze out the last drop.

Market Days around La Grande Motte

Palavas-les-Flots: Sun am April–Nov, Mon, Wed and Fri; Sat am, flower market and flea market.

La Grande Motte: Sun am, and Thurs am June–Sept.

Festivals around La Grande Motte

Palavas-les-Flots: *Feria*, first weekend of May and last weekend of Sept.

ⓘ La Grande Motte >
*Place de la Mairie, **t** 04 67 56 42 00, www.ot-lagrandemotte.fr; open daily all year*

ⓘ Palavas-les-Flots >>
*Phare de la Méditerranée, **t** 04 67 07 73 34, www.palavaslesflots.com; open daily all year*

Where to Stay and Eat near La Grande Motte

La Grande Motte ✉ 34280

The bad news about La Grande Motte is that you can't stay there; all the hotels in the centre are absurdly overpriced.

******Les Corallines***, Quartier Point Zéro, **t** 04 67 29 13 13, *www.thalasso-grandemotte.com* (€€€€). Right on the front, with a thalassotherapy centre and balconied rooms with good sea views.

*****Le Mediterranée**, 277 Allée du Vaccarès, **t** 04 67 06 54 68, *www.hotellemediterranee.com* (€€€€–€€€) Set in a park of magnolias 200m from the beach, this boutique hotel offers rooms designed by artists, a piano bar and the resort's most fashionable restaurant, **Le Prose** (€€€€).

*****Mercure Port**, 140 Rue du Port, **t** 04 67 56 90 81, *www.mercure.com* (€€€€–€€€). The splashy status address on the Big Lump, looming over the marina like a concrete refugee from Miami Beach; rather charmless, but a chance to meet that segment of the fast crowd who choose to avoid the Riviera, and it does have a nice terrac[e] and a regional food restaurant.

Alexandre, Esplanade Maurice Justin, **t** 04 67 56 63 63, *www.alexandre-restaurant.com* (€€€€–€€€). A splurge for refined regional specialities in an especially elegant setting. *Closed Mon.*

Palavas-les-Flots ✉ 34250

L'Escale, 5 Bd Sarrail, north of the canal on the seafront, **t** 04 67 68 24 17, *www.restaurant-lescale.com* (€€€). Sit by the sea and enjoy *sèche à la rouille* for starters, or extravaganzas like the mixed shellfish plate they call *panaché de coquillages* – beware: the bill can skyrocket. *Closed Wed.*

La Passerelle, Quai Paul Cunq, **t** 04 67 47 39 90 (€). This couldn't be simpler, its menu limited to piles of fresh, inexpensive shellfish. *Closed Oct–April.*

Lattes ✉ 34250

****Mas de Couran**, Route de Fréjorgues, **t** 04 67 65 57 57, *www.mas-de-couran.com* (€€€€–€€€). It's worth coming inland to Lattes for this 19th-century mansion, set in a beautiful park, with pool and restaurant (€€€). *Closed Sun eve.*

The Northern Hérault

North of Montpellier: The *Garrigue*

On a map, you'll notice lots of blank space in this region. It is a geographer's textbook example of *garrigue*, a dry limestone plateau with sparse vegetation, where even sheep only just get by. *Garrigue* is an old Occitan word for the holly oak, and these scrubby would-be trees grow everywhere, along with thyme and lavender-scented *maquis* and, increasingly, vines, which not only thrive but are also quickly changing the local economy. The windblown landscapes are as romantic as anything in Provence, although a shade more sombre. The few villages seem huddled, closed into themselves.

Pic St-Loup, St-Martin-de-Londres and Cambous

From Montpellier, the best approach to the *garrigue* is by way of the D17 to **St-Mathieu-de-Tréviers**, where you can pick up the D1/D122 west, a scenic high road that passes below the ruined **Château de Montferrand**. Montferrand was one of the first castles

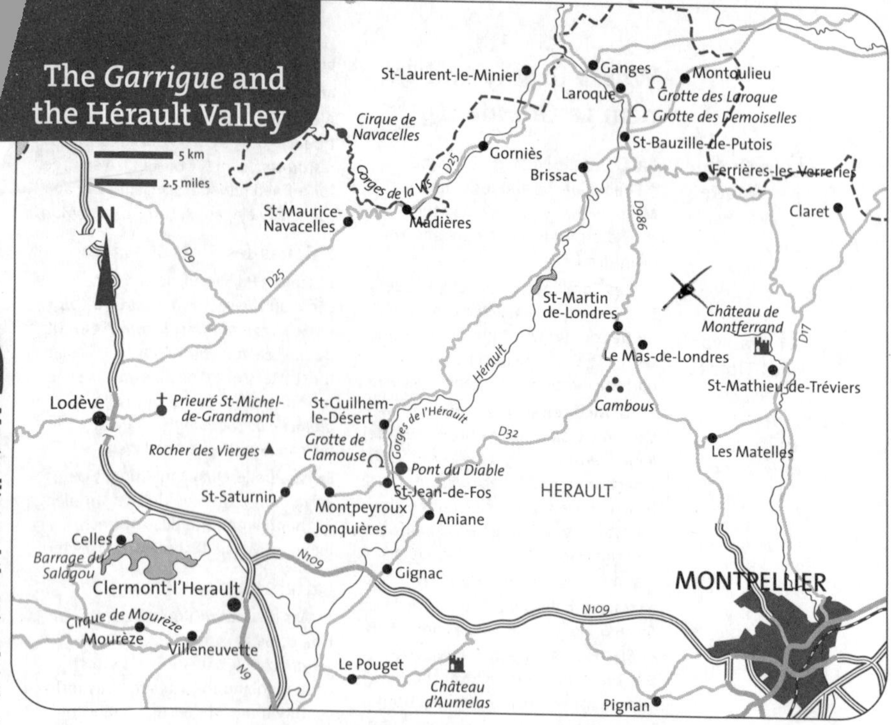

to fall to the Albigensian Crusade, but the real damage was done by Louis XIV, as part of his general royal policy of cleaning up unnecessary and possibly dangerous castles. It's a long climb up, but the view takes in the striking 2,110ft exclamation point of **Pic St-Loup** and cliff-rimmed lump of the **Montagne d'Hortus** just in front, two of the great limestone landmarks of the *garrigue*, rising out of tidy rows of vines.

The D122 passes through the typical *garrigue* village of **Le Mas de Londres** before arriving at **St-Martin-de-Londres**. St-Martin is a surprise package. Passing the tiny, densely built village on the road, you would never guess that it conceals an exquisite medieval square, picturesquely asymmetrical and surrounded by houses that haven't changed for centuries. The ensemble has a church to match, an architecturally sophisticated 11th-century building with a rare elliptical cupola. A recent restoration, clearing out the

Wine: Pic Saint-Loup

By the time Caesar conquered Gaul, the vineyards in the hills and the great plain of Languedoc (north and west of modern Montpellier) were already well established, thanks to the Greeks. Dramatic *garrigue* landscapes characterize one of the top areas, Pic Saint-Loup (*www.pic-saint-loup.com*), which is applying to be its own little AOC area. The hills and valleys around the landmark mountain create varying microclimates able to grow such diverse varietals as mourvèdre, syrah and grenache. There are three dozen or so producers, all tuned into new styles and producing excellent meaty red wines that can take considerable ageing. Try the **Domaine de L'Hortus**, in Valflaunès, **t** 04 67 55 31 20 ; and the **Château La Roque**, at Fontanès, **t** 04 67 55 34 47, *www.chateau-laroque.fr*.

Getting around the Hérault

Except along the coast, public transport is rudimentary at best. There is a **train** service from Béziers to Bédarieux.

Olargues is connected by **bus** to Bédarieux, St-Pons and Montpellier. From the *gare routière* in Montpellier there are regular bus services to Gignac, Clermont l'Hérault and Lodève, less frequently to other villages; there are buses to tourist attractions (like St-Guilhem-le-Désert) in summer. See *www.herault-transport.fr* for plans and schedules.

---

dross of a brutal 19th-century remodelling, has uncovered some charming fragments of the original decoration: St Martin on horseback, carved Celtic spirals, and neo-Byzantine capitals. 'Londres' is a local place name for the surrounding dried-out swamp, and has nothing to do with the big town on the island over the Channel.

Cambous
visits April–Oct; call the Société Languedocienne de Préhistoire, **t** *04 67 86 34 37, www.archeologue.org, for further information*

South of St-Martin, in a military zone just off the D32, a 5,000-year-old settlement was discovered at **Cambous** in 1967. With considerable intelligence and dedication, the archaeologists have made the site into a veritable re-creation of ancient life. They have reconstructed a communal house of this 'Fontbouisse civilization' and gathered together enough artefacts to make you feel entirely at home among the Fontbouissians. These peaceful folk knew both farming and husbandry, and were just learning about copper tools. They also had a well-developed cultural life, as evidenced by their geometrically decorated pottery and stone statue steles.

La Halle du Verre
t *04 67 59 06 39; www.halleduverre.fr; open mid-June–mid-Sept daily 10–12.30 and 2–7; mid-April–mid-June and mid-Sept–Oct Wed, Sat and Sun 2–6; closed Nov–mid-April; adm*

Distillerie des Cévennes
t *04 67 59 02 50, www.distilleriedes cevennes.com*

In the 13th–18th centuries, the country north of the **Causse d'Hortus** was famous for its 'Gentlemen Glassblowers', who passed their secrets down through the generations. Their history is recalled in the new **Halle du Verre** at **Claret**, with a museum on glass and glass-blowing; there is still a glass-blower in action opposite the site. The Halle has information on the **Chemin des Verriers**, a route set up to explore the tiny villages once attached in some way to the trade, including **Ferrières-les-Verreries**, where the Renaissance-era glassmakers, the Verrerie de Couloubrines, was restored in 1989. In Claret you can also visit Europe's only family-run cade oil mill, the **Distillerie des Cévennes**; the fragrant oil of cade (*Juniperus oxycedrus*, the prickly juniper native to northern Languedoc) has been used for embalming since antiquity, and the mill offers a range of modern products made from the stuff.

Ganges, Caves and the Cirque de Navacelles

From St-Martin, the D986 leads northwards towards the deeply forested Cévennes to the village of **St-Bauzille-de-Putois** (a *putois* is a polecat, although residents are quick to say that the name actually derives from *Saint Bauzille ad puteum*, or 'St Bauzille of the wells'). From here a steep side road climbs to an important Protestant hideout during the War of the Camisards (1702–04) called the Cave of the Fairies or **Grotte des Demoiselles**, which also

Grotte des Demoiselles
t 04 67 73 70 02, www.demoiselles.com; open for tours July–Aug hourly 10–6; April–June and Sept hourly 10–5.30; Mar and Oct 2.30–4.30, plus 10–1.45 on Sun and school hols; Nov–Feb Mon–Fri hourly 2–4, plus Sun 10 and 11; adm

Canoë Le Moulin
t 04 67 73 30 73, www.canoe-france.com/herault

has one of France's most spectacular displays of pipe-organ stalactites and stalagmites in the staggeringly enormous 'Cathedral of the Abysses'. Visits take an hour by subterranean funicular; bring a sweater.

Geologically, this is folded country; along the Hérault you can clearly see the lines of stratification of limestone and schist in the cliffs. See them from river level by floating down the Hérault in a canoe (hire one in St-Bauzille-de-Putois at **Canoë Le Moulin**) to **Brissac**, which is guarded by a ruined castle perched on a pinnacle of rock.

Ganges is the only real town for miles, closed in between the river Hérault and *maquis*-carpeted hills. In the 18th century it was France's capital of silk stockings. Like most of the Cévennes, Ganges was and remains a mostly Protestant area; the old part of town is crisscrossed by *chemins de traverse*, labyrinthine passes laid out to confuse Catholic troops, and it has an imposing, peculiar seven-sided Protestant temple, built in 1850.

Ganges makes a good base for exploring this pretty region, between the *garrigue* and the lofty limestone plateau, the Causse du Larzac, that extends south from the Massif Central to Lodève. The D25 leads west into the **Gorges de la Vis**, passing a waterfall and favourite local swimming hole and a 17th-century château at **St-Laurent-le-Minier**. The gorge continues for another 34km; the best parts, beyond **Madières**, can only be reached on foot.

Signs, however, point an easier way up the *causse* to the **Cirque de Navacelles**. Just when you begin to think it's all a wild goose chase, you suddenly come to the enormous lunar crater of a loop scooped out of the limestone by the meandering river Vis. Of all the many *cirques* in the Midi this is the most striking, with steep walls and a rocky 'island' in the centre, occupied by the sweet little village of Navacelles. Get there by way of the winding road from the belvedere-café at **St-Maurice-de-Navacelles**, and bring a picnic to eat by the waterfall, where you can also go for a dip.

Musée Cévenol
t 04 67 81 06 86; open April–Oct Wed–Mon 10–12 and 2–6; otherwise Wed only; adm

Observatoire Météo du Mont Aigoual
t 04 67 82 60 01, www.aigoual.asso.fr; open July–Aug 10–7; May–June and Sept 10–1 and 2–6

Heading north of Ganges into the Cévennes (*see* pp.101–105) you could stop in **Le Vigan** for its picturesque 12th- century bridge and the **Musée Cévenol** in an 18th-century silk mill, with exhibits on the region's trades from silk to *boules*-making. Or carry on 30km from Ganges to the **Observatoire Météo du Mont Aigoual** (5,141ft). Aigoual is the source of the Hérault (its name means 'the watery one' with good reason: it gets soaked with some 2,250mm – over 7ft – of rain a year). The observatory is the last manned weather station in France, the training ground for France's weather forecasters since 1887: on a clear day the view extends from Mont Blanc to Canigou in the Pyrenees. Inside, a museum of meteorology has photos, information on the work of the observatory, and old and high-tech new weather instruments.

Market Days North of Montpellier

Ganges: Tues and especially Fri am, when the lively market takes over half the town.

Where to Stay and Eat North of Montpellier

St-Martin-de-Londres ✉ 34380

****Hostellerie Le Vieux Chêne**, Causse de la Selle, west of St Martin, **t** 04 67 73 11 00, *www.hotel-restaurant-vieuxchene.com* (€€–€). Three double rooms, pool and a good restaurant (€€€–€€) serving French classics on a pretty terrace. *Closed Wed and Sun eve.*

Auberge de Saugras, in remote little Argelliers, south of St-Martin, off the D 127, **t** 04 67 55 08 71, *www.aubergedesaugras.fr* (€€–€). A stone *mas* with several rooms and gourmet menus (€€€–€€). Book ahead. *Closed Tues and Wed.*

Les Muscardins, 19 Route des Cévennes, **t** 04 67 55 75 90, *www.les-muscardins.fr* (€€€€–€€€). Gourmets from Montpellier drive up especially to feast on the fancy *terrines* and pâté, game dishes, formidable desserts and a selection of the best regional wines on a choice of menus. *Closed mid-Feb–mid-Mar, plus Mon and Tues.*

Ferrières les Verreries ✉ 34190

Mas des Baumes, **t** 04 66 80 88 80, *www.oustaldebaumes.com* (€€€). Seven attractive rooms, but this place is best known for its excellent restaurant (€€€), using fresh ingredients from the *garrigue*.

St Bauzille-de-Putois ✉ 34190

Mas de Coulet, Rte de Montpellier, **t** 04 67 83 72 43 (€€). Pretty place off the main road, serving old-fashioned classics with local wines. They also have *chambres d'hôtes* rooms (€€). *Restaurant open July–Aug; closed Sun eve and Wed in April–June and Oct; Oct–Mar open Fri eve–Sun lunch only.*

Ganges ✉ 34190

******Château de Madières**, 17km west of Ganges towards the Cirque de Navacelles, **t** 04 67 73 84 03, *www.chateaumadieres.com* (€€€€–€€€). If you want to combine the austerity of the *garrigue* with style and creature comforts, this hotel has 12 super-luxurious rooms in a 14th-century fort. Park, pool, fitness centre/gym and beautiful vaulted dining room (€€€). *Closed Nov–Easter.*

*****Les Norias**, 254 Av des 2 Ponts, Cazilhac, just south of Ganges on the D25, **t** 04 67 73 55 90, *www.les-norias.fr* (€€–€). The dining room and terrace overlook the Hérault river and the restaurant (€€€–€€) features Mediterranean cooking. *Closed mid-Nov–early Dec and part of Feb; restaurant closed Mon, and Tues lunch, except July and Aug.*

****Hôtel de la Poste**, 8 Plan de l'Ormeau, **t** 04 67 73 85 88, *www.hoteldelaposteganges.com* (€). A prettily restored hotel with Wi-fi.

Ferme-Auberge Domaine de Blancardy, Moules et Baucels, 7km east of Ganges on the D999, **t** 04 67 73 94 94, *www.blancardy.com* (€). With 14 rooms in a distinctive old *mas* from the 12th century, where home-made *confits* and pâté accompany fine wine (€€€–€€).

ⓘ **Ganges >>**
Plan de l'Ormeau, t 04 67 73 00 56, www.ot-cevennes.com; open Mon–Sat

ⓘ **St-Martin-de-Londres >**
Place de la Mairie, t 04 67 55 09 59, www.tourismed.com; open July and Aug daily; Sept–June Sat am

★ **Ferme-Auberge Domaine de Blancardy >>**

The Valley of the Hérault: The Haut Pays d'Oc

The Hérault river slices dramatically through the *garrigue*, and the atmosphere is clear, luminous, otherworldly – the perfect landscape for saints and pilgrims, and for wine.

St-Guilhem-le-Désert

'Desert' might seem a little unfair to the rosemary-scented jumble of *garrigue* around St-Guilhem, northwest of Montpellier; there are plenty of green, shady spots for a picnic, and even forests of pines. But *desert*, in French or English, originally meant deserted or uninhabited, as in 'desert island', and this is still as lonely a region as it was when the hermit St Guilhem came here during the reign of Charlemagne. Besides being a delightful place to visit, St-Guilhem is a living history lesson, evoking the time when the 'desert' was a troubled frontier between Frank and Saracen, and later, when it became a key cultural outpost in the process of making the south of France Christian and French.

Maison du Grand Site
t 04 99 61 73 01 or t 04 67 57 58 83, www.saintguilhem-valleeherault.fr; open July–Aug 10–7.30; April–June and Sept–Oct 10.30–6; free shuttles to St-Guilhem and the Grotte de Clamouse weekends in May, June and Oct, and daily in July and Aug

To cope with the crowds of summer visitors, a pay car park, shop, café and visitor centre, the **Maison du Grand Site**, has been set up to the south downriver from the spectacular stone Pont du Diable of 1030, spanning the gorges of the Hérault (and a favourite spot for a swim). From here a shuttle will take you to the village of St-Guilhem, stretched on the edge of a ravine, little changed since medieval times. On the the main street, some modest Romanesque palaces survive from the 13th century, an especially picturesque one housing the *mairie*; at the opposite end, facing the D4, the church of **St-Laurent** (now the tourist office) has a fine apse like that of the abbey church of St-Guilhem.

The Abbaye de Gellone

Abbaye de Gellone
open July–Aug 8–6.30, Sept–June Mon–Sat 8–6, Sun and hols 11–2.30; museum open Oct–Mar Sat and Sun 1–5; April–Sept Mon–Sat 10.30–12 and 1–6, Sun 1–6; adm

For 30 years Guilhem, the second Count of Toulouse, nicknamed Court-Nez ('short nose') after a giant Sarcacen lopped off the tip of it in battle, campaigned from the Atlantic to the Alps, mostly against the Arabs, whose wave of 8th-century expansion through Spain had washed up in Languedoc as far as Narbonne and Orange. In 803, he liberated Barcelona at the side of Charlemagne's son Louis the Pious, and was given a piece of the True Cross by his grateful cousin Charlemagne. His friend Benedict, the monastic reformer from Aniane, had also been a warrior fighting with Charlemagne in Italy, and convinced Guilhem to follow his example and renounce the world. Guilhem spent his last six years in a humble cell here, near the gorges of the Hérault (then called the Gellone); his abbey was originally known as Sancta Crucis de Gellone, and he was canonized soon after his death in 812. The abbey also had an early reputation for its library and scholarship.

It wasn't long before pilgrims began to visit. For his early work in the Reconquista, Guilhem was a popular saint with the Spaniards and, not long after, with northerners going in the opposite direction to Compostela. The original community of hermit cells grew into a wealthy monastery. Construction of the current great

The Elusive William of Gellone

Guilhem or WIlliam (755–814) was the son of Aldane d'Austrasia, a daughter of Charles Martel, and was raised in the court of his cousin Charlemagne. His father's side is the murky one – Theodoric (Thierry IV), Count of Autun and first Count of Toulouse, was argued by some at the end of the 20th century to be of Merovingian and even (so went the theory) of Jewish descent; his real name was said to have been Makhir Todros ben Judah Zakkai and it was posited that he was recognized as 'the seed of the royal house of David' by Pepin the Short (Charlemagne's father) as well as the Caliph of Baghdad (for more, see *A Jewish Princedom in Feudal France* (1972) by Arthur Zuckermann, incidentally one of the most important sources for the authors of *Holy Blood, Holy Grail*). One of Guilhem's (or 'Nathan Kalonymus') many sobriquets was William of David-Toulouse; he spoke fluent Gothic, Latin, Arabic and Hebrew (some say he learned in the schools of Toledo), and he is said to have borne the Lion of Judea on his battle shield; his first wife was Cunegonde, daughter of Charlemagne's brother Carloman; his second wife was Guibourc, according to some, a Saracen convert. Montpellier, the nearest city to the Abbaye de Gellone, would soon become an important study centre of the Cabala.

Charlemagne made Guilhem the first count of Orange after a great victory over the Arabs during the holy war led by the Emir of Cordoba, Hisham I, in 800; he was also made the Count of Razès (the present region of Rennes-le-Château, *see* p.214) and the first Duke of Septimania (or Gothia, later to be known as Languedoc and Catalonia). He was the subject of a number of medieval Chansons de Geste, and according to some accounts he may have been the original source of the most famous: his student Flegetanis was the one whose stories inspired the enigmatic troubadour 'Kyot of Provence', who gave Wolfram von Eschenbach the story of Parsifal and the Holy Grail. Eschenbach wrote another epic, sadly left unfinished, called Willeham – about William himself.

abbey church began about 1050, and in 1066, as a sign of his lofty celestial ranking, Guilhem was (unusually) canonized yet again.

It didn't last. Already in decline during the Wars of Religion, the abbey was sacked by the Protestants in 1569; its celebrated library was burnt down in the process. The final indignity came not during the Revolution, surprisingly, but a decade before, when clerics from Lodève and other towns succeeded in having the monastery suppressed, apportioning its treasures and holy relics among themselves. One of these was the beautiful, priceless *Sacramentaire de Gellone*, the most extant Merovingian liturgy to survive (now in the Bibliothèque Nationale in Paris). Written in Carolingian minuscule in *c.* 790 (just before Charlemagne's church reforms) for Bishop Hildoard of Cambrai, the *Sacramentaire* is believed to have been a gift to the new monastery from Louis the Pious or Duke William of Toulouse.

Yet the **abbey church** has survived as a remarkably grand and lovely specimen of Lombard architecture, with its blind arcading and trademark cross-shaped window. The best part, the broad, arcaded apse, recalls the contemporary churches of Milan or Pavia. The façade, facing an ancient, colossal plane tree in the Place de la Liberté, is somewhat blighted by an ungainly tower of cheap stone, built in the 14th century more for defence than for bell-ringing. The interior, lofty and dark, has lost almost all of its original decoration. Some fragments of frescoes survive in the side chapels, along with the marble altar of 1076, sadly damaged in all the abbey's vicissitudes, plus St-Guilhem's reliquary in the left aisle and the

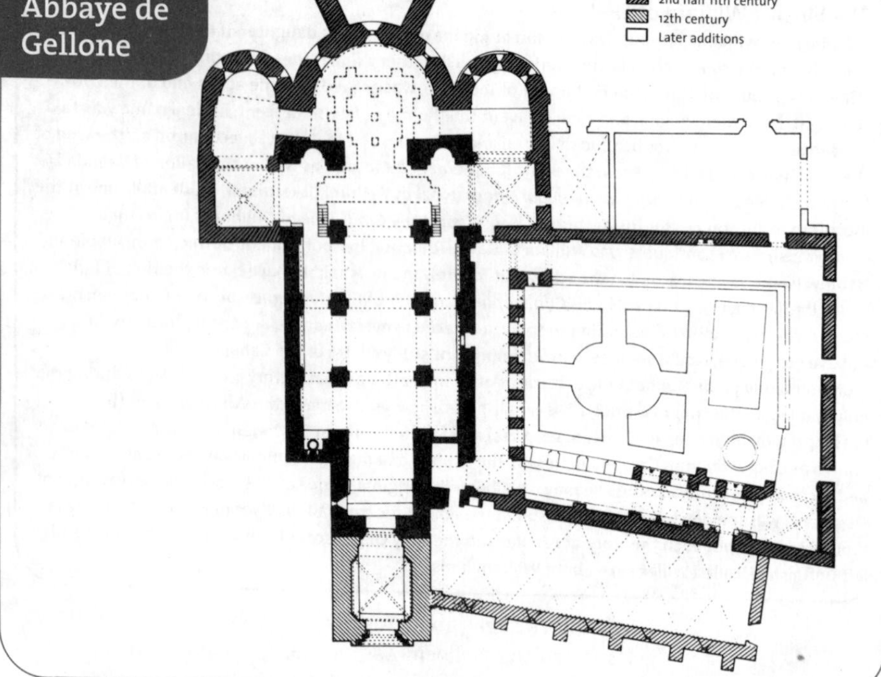

silver reliquary of the True Cross from Charlemagne to the right of the choir. The organ, built in 1782, is the focus of a series of Baroque concerts in July. The cloister is ruined, and most of its capitals have ended up at the Cloisters Museum in New York. The museum in the old refectory contains pieces from the church and cloister.

Around St-Guilhem

Other medieval relics from the abbey's heyday can be seen along the Hérault: medieval mills, for grain and for oak bark (used in tanning leather), set near the modern trout hatcheries by the river. The hills around St-Guilhem are fine walking country – there's a ruined castle and other fortifications, and the **Rue du Bout du Monde** that leads from the back end of the village to a lovely spot with a flowing spring.

Grotte de Clamouse
t 04 67 57 71 05, www.clamouse.com; open July–Aug daily 10.30–6.20; June and Sept 10.30–5.20; Feb–May and Oct–Nov 10.30–4.20; closed Dec and Jan; adm

With all this eroded limestone about, you would expect caves, and there are several. The most impressive, 3km south, is the **Grotte de Clamouse**, 'the Cathedral of Time', with its lovely glittering white aragonite crystals, set off with LED lights and music.

Aniane and Gignac

Everyone who studies medieval history has trouble untangling the two Benedictine Benedicts. The first, Benedict of Norcia, founded the order and wrote its rule around 530. In the time of

Charlemagne, Benedict of **Aniane** (*c.* 747–821), born as Witiza, the son of of the Visigothic Count of Maguelone, raised in the Frankish court of Pepin and friend and mentor of St Guilhem, reformed it, forcing the poor Benedictines back to the original precepts of obedience and hard work. As important and influential as the abbey Benedict built in his home town was, it was thoroughly wrecked by the Protestants and rebuilt in the 17th century; it's now occupied by a school. The church, **St-Sauveur**, was rebuilt under Louis XIV, and in drab little Aniane it comes as quite a shock, with a glorious Baroque façade framed in big volutes and an interior still divided into two parts: one for the monks and one for the villagers. Nearby is 12th-century Romanesque **St-Jean-Baptiste des Pénitents**. For all that, pilgrims who wend their way to Aniane today tend to have more hedonistic aims (*see* box, below).

South of Aniane on the D32, the market town of **Gignac** enjoyed a period of prosperity in the 17th and 18th centuries, embellishing itself with Baroque churches and palaces to go with its medieval **Tour de l'Horloge**; its best-known monument, however, is outside town, over the Hérault: the **Pont de Gignac**. Begun in 1776, it's every inch a product of the Age of Enlightenment, strong and functional without a trace of Bourbon curlicues.

Mouldering Castles

The monasteries of St-Guilhem and Aniane brought considerable prosperity to the area. Villages like **St-Jean-de-Fos** and **St-Saturnin** have fine Romanesque churches and buildings; the latter also has a ruined early 11th-century castle on the **Rocher des Vierges**.

There are two other fascinating if ruined castles in the vicinity: **Montpeyroux**, between St-Jean and St-Saturnin, grew up around a

More Wine, and a 'Grand Cru'

Along with Pic Saint-Loup, the region just west of Montpellier is hallowed wine ground. Among the many excellent vineyards, there's **Château de l'Engarran** at Lavérune, **t** 04 67 27 60 89, *www.chateau-engarran.com* (*open all year 9–7*), part of the *terroir* St-Georges d'Orques (AOC Languedoc Grès de Montpellier), which produces fine red wines with a scent of dried herbs. In Jonquières, west of Gignac, Olivier Jullien has a fine array of white and red wines on the Larzac plateau and the Pic Baudille at the **Mas Jullien, t** 04 67 96 60 04 (*open April–end Dec*).

In nearby Aniane, you can find the legendary **Mas de Daumas Gassac**, off the D32 (**t** 04 67 57 88 45, *www.daumas-gassac.com* (*open Mon–Sat 10–12 and 2–6, July and Aug 9.30–6.30*), founded almost serendipitously in 1972 by Aimé Guibert, a Parisian glovemaker, who was told by a friend – the famous oenologist Professor Henri Enjalbert – that the land by the farmhouse he bought was ideal for growing grapes. He was right; and Daumas Gassac has gone on to become perhaps the most important of the great pioneering estates in the region, producing a wine classified as a *vin de pays d'Hérault* but nicknamed the 'Château Lafite of Languedoc', a 'Grand Cru' that often needs decades in the cellar. The reds are mainly cabernet sauvignon but the estate also grows surprises such as tannat, merlot, nebbiolo, cabernet franc, barbera, dolcetto and pinot noir; the whites, also exceptional, are mainly chardonnay, viognier, chenin blanc and petit manseng. Guibert went on to become one of the heroes of the wine documentary *Mondovino* (2005).

mysterious abandoned pile called the **Castel Viel**, a long, impressive circuit of walls with nothing inside. Its history is utterly unknown; it may be from the 11th century, the 16th century or anywhere in between, and it was probably less a military post than a protection for livestock in times of war. Southeast of Gignac, off the main N109, the **Château d'Aumelas** occupies a romantically isolated hilltop. This castle, built some time before 1036 by the lords of Montpellier, is on a dirt track and hard to reach, but it's a wonderful place to explore; parts of the noble residence, chapels and other buildings are still quite intact.

The castle is located in the Commune d'Aumelas, one of the biggest completely blank spots on the French map. South of the château on a rocky track is a beautiful and austere Romanesque church, **St-Martin-de-Cardonnet**, set amidst the ruins of the monastery that once surrounded it. To the west, back towards civilization on the D139, the circular fortified village of **Le Pouget** is just north of the colossal **Dolmen Gallardet**.

Clermont-l'Hérault to Lodève

Clermont is a peacefully bovine and prosperous town, living off the wine and table grapes of this more fertile part of the Hérault valley. Its medieval centre, on a hilltop, is large and well preserved, including a tall and graceful Gothic church, **St-Paul**, begun in 1276. The 10th–11th-century **castle** around which the town grew up is also in good shape, with gates, prisons and keep. Clermont holds the big weekly market in this region, every Wednesday, and has done so since the year 1000.

West of Clermont, you leave the green valley for more peculiar landscapes around the **Lac du Salagou**, a man-made sheet of water surrounded by hills that is much more natural-looking and attractive than most artificial lakes. Circumnavigating it, you'll pass some singular cliffs and weirdly eroded rock formations, and also the village of **Celles**, on the water's edge, now almost completely abandoned. The oddest formations lie to the south, in the **Cirque de Mourèze**, a long, stretched-out *cirque* with the dusty village of **Mourèze** and its ruined castle at the centre.

Villeneuvette
guided tours in summer,
t *04 67 96 00 06*

Between the *cirque* and Clermont lies **Villeneuvette**, founded only in 1670. The 'little new town' was a manufacturing centre for *londrins* (fine woollen cloth, imitating London fabrics) founded by a local merchant and elevated by Louis XIV's minister Colbert from 1677 to 1703 into a Royal Manufacture. It boomed in the 19th century with exports to the Ottoman empire, employing some 800 workers, and, although the works closed in 1954, Villeneuvette is still the very picture of an old French paternalistic company town. The manufactories remain – behind the gate with the big inscription '*Honneur au Travail*' – along with some of the workers' housing, a school, a church, bridges and aqueducts, warehouses and gardens, all slowly being restored by a local association.

North of Clermont, the N9 heads into the *causses* of deepest France, passing **Lodève**, a comfortable, somewhat isolated town wedged between two rivers. Like Clermont-l'Hérault, Lodève has an impressive Gothic church with a lofty tower as its chief monument: **St-Fulcran**, named after a 9th-century bishop who became the city's patron, was begun in 1280 and turned into a fortress during the Hundred Years' War. It is one of the few churches in France with a chandelier – a present from Queen Victoria to Napoléon III. Lodève has a distinguished wool-manufacturing past – under Louis XV it had a monopoly on making all the uniforms for the French army, thanks to prime minister and native son Cardinal André Hercule de Fleury – maintained to this day in the Gobelins-La Savonnerie's only workshop outside Paris, the **Manufacture de la Savonnerie** at Impasse des Liciers. Lodève was Celtic Luteva, and later Roman Forum Neronis; its **Musée Fleury** in the Cardinal's birthplace on Square Georges Auric has antiquities, along with dinosaur bones and footprints, and fossil trilobites, as well as a beaux-arts section with paintings and sculptures that puts on exceptional special exhibitions.

St-Fulcran
open summer 9–7; winter 9–5.30

Manufacture de la Savonnerie
t 04 67 96 41 34; guided tours by appt only, Thurs 10.30, 2 and 3.30; Fri 10.30 and 2; adm

Musée Fleury
t 04 67 88 86 10, www.lodevoisetlarzac.fr; open Tues–Sun 9.30–12 and 2–6; closed Mon; adm

East of Lodève, a pretty country road, the D153, leads in 9km to the **Prieuré St-Michel-de-Grandmont**. The Order of Grandmont, founded in the Limousin in the 12th century, was a monastic reform movement like that of Cluny or Cîteaux; it faded away five centuries ago and no one even remembers it today. This priory is its only surviving monument, gradually restored by private owners over the last century. The austere church and cloister, begun in the 12th century, are well preserved, and there are concerts and art exhibitions and an animal park, but the real attraction here is a group of dolmens in the grounds, colossal works shaped like *cèpe* mushrooms, from *c.* 2000 BC – one has an unusual little 'oven door'.

Prieuré St-Michel-de-Grandmont
t 04 67 44 09 31, www.prieure-grandmont.fr; open for guided tours June–Sept daily at 10.30, 3, 4 and 5; Oct–mid-Dec and Feb–May at 3; closed mid-Dec–Jan; adm

Today one of the most active religious institutions in the area is the striking Tibetan Buddist temple and retreat **Lerab Ling** in Roqueredonde (take the D902 northwest of Lodève), founded in 1991 by Sogyal Rinpoche and twice visited by the Dalai Lama. There's a visitor centre and temple visits on Sundays.

Lerab Ling
t 04 99 62 00 18, www.lerabling.org; temple visits (ring ahead, audioguides in English) April–Oct Sun 2–5; Mar and Nov Sun at 2; adm

ⓘ St-Guilhem-le-Désert >>
2 Rue Font du Portal, t 04 67 57 44 33, www.saint-guilhem-le-desert.com; open daily all year

★ Guilaum d'Orange >>

Market Days in the Valley of the Hérault

Gignac: Sat.
Clermont-l'Hérault: Wed.

Where to Stay and Eat in the Valley of the Hérault

St-Guilhem-le-Désert ✉ 34150

In St-Guilhem, rooms are scarce.

Guilaum d'Orange, **t** 04 67 57 24 53, *www.guilhaumedorange.com* (€€).

ⓘ **Lodève**
7 Place de la République, t 04 67 88 86 44, www.lodeve.com; open Mon–Fri and Sat am

ⓘ **Gignac >**
3 Parc d'Activités de Camalce, t 04 67 57 58 83; open Mon–Fri

ⓘ **Clermont-l'Hérault >>**
Place Jean Jaurès, t 04 67 96 23 86, www.clermont-l-herault.com; open Tues–Sat

★ **Auberge Campagnarde de la Vallée du Salagou >>**

★ **Le Mimosa >**

Charming little 10-room hotel in the village, and a good restaurant, **La Table d'Aurore**.

****Hostellerie St-Benoit**, Aniane, **t** 04 67 57 71 63 , *www.hostellerie-saint-benoit.com* (€€). A comfortable motel with a pool and a good restaurant (€€) using local produce. *Closed for a month in winter.*

***La Taverne de l'Escuelle**, 11 Grand Chemin du Val de Gellone, **t** 04 67 57 72 05, *www.hotel-lataverne.fr* (€€). Six rooms with Wi-fi and a good little restaurant; parking available.

Gignac ✉ 34150

Restaurant de Lauzun, 3 Bd de l'Esplanade, **t** 04 67 57 50 83, *www.restaurant-delauzun.com* (€€€–€€). Popular restaurant with a terrace, worth a visit for its inventive regional and seasonal cooking. *Closed Mon and Sat lunch, Sun eve.*

Ferme-Auberge de Pélican, Domaine de Pélican, **t** 04 67 57 68 92, *www.domainedepelican.fr* (€€). This place (which also has handsome rooms in an 18th-century building, €€) offers wonderful dishes on a set menus with choices – *pintade* (guinea hen) stuffed with olives, duck in honey vinegar – and their own wines. *Closed Sept and Oct; restaurant open Mon–Wed and Fri–Sat eves and Sun lunch in July and Aug; Nov–June open Sat eve and Sun lunch.*

St-Saturnin ✉ 34725

Le Mimosa, 10 Place de la Fontaine, **t** 04 67 88 62 62, (€€). A gorgeous small hotel run by a British couple, all tastefully restored stones and tiles and modern furniture. Very comfortable bedrooms. *Closed Nov–mid-Mar.* Its restaurant, in nearby St-Guiraud, **t** 04 67 96 67 96 (€€), has long been a pilgrimage for *cognoscenti* from Montpellier. An 18th-century wine-grower's house, it's beautifully decorated and offers superb cuisine, prepared by Bridget Pugh, a former prima ballerina. *Closed Mon, Tues–Sat lunch and Sun eve, plus late Oct–mid-Mar.*

Montpeyroux ✉ 34150

La Terrace du Mimosa, 33 Place de l'Horloge, **t** 04 67 44 49 80, *www.laterrassedumimosa.blogspot.com* (€€). Newly reopened wine bar branch of the Mimosa network, serving tapas and light dishes based around the wines of the Terrasse du Larzac; check website for jazz events. *Closed Tues and Wed.*

Clermont-l'Hérault ✉ 34800

Clermont-l'Hérault will be the most likely place to find a room if you haven't booked.

****La Source**, Place Louis XIV, Villeneuvette, 4km southwest, **t** 04 67 96 05 07, *www.hoteldelasource.com* (€€–€). A charming rural retreat with Wi-fi, pool and tennis courts, and a restaurant (€€€–€€) serving salmon and truffles. *Closed Nov–early April; restaurant closed Wed lunch and Tues.*

Auberge Campagnarde de la Vallée du Salagou, at Salasc on the D8, **t** 04 67 88 13 39, *www.aubergedusalagou.fr* (€). A comfortable B&B with lovely views; the restaurant (€€) serves a filling menu, offering grilled lamb or steaks and wine from nearby Octon.

The Northern Fringes: Monts de l'Espinouse

If you continue along the northern fringes of the Hérault, you'll get an idea of what France is like for the next hundred miles northwards, through the Aveyron and Lozère into the Auvergne – rough canyons and rough villages, an occasional dusting of snow, trout streams and chestnut groves. The natural beauty of the Espinouse did it little good in former times; even 40 years ago, this was a poor area, losing its population to the cities. The creation of the Parc Naturel Régional du Haut-Languedoc in the 1960s has

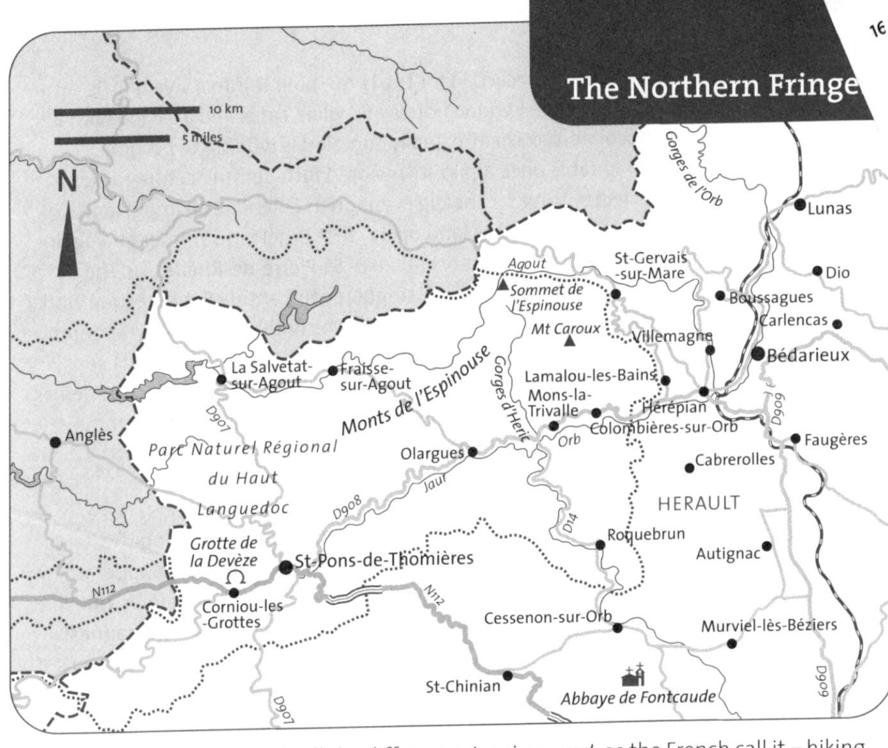

made all the difference; *tourisme vert*, as the French call it – hiking and canoeing or just relaxing under the pines – increases every year. It's no strain on the hospitable folk in the villages, and right now the Espinouse is as happy and content as a patch of mountains can be.

Bédarieux and Lamalou-les-Bains: the Pays d'Orb

The only big road in this region, the D908, runs west from Clermont-l'Hérault across the base of the mountains, following the valleys of the Orb and the Jaur. The first town on the way is **Bédarieux**, a humble enough agricultural centre and market town. Humility stops, however, with Bédarieux's famous son, Pierre-Auguste Cot, one of the 19th-century kitsch-realist artists so popular with the Academicians, the sort that made the Impressionist revolution necessary. They've named the main square after him, and you can see his work in the **Espace Culturel**, created on the site of an old hospice; it includes a modern art centre, the Maison des Arts (where you can find Cot's work along with fossils, railway memorabilia and exhibitions re-creating past country life and costumes).

Espace Culturel
t 04 67 95 48 27; open Mon–Fri 3-5; adm

Lamalou-les-Bains, 10km further west, is a sort of museum in itself. A thermal spa since the 17th century, Lamalou made it big when the railroad came through in 1868. The prosperity of the next three decades – dukes and counts, famous actresses, even a sultan of Morocco checked in for the *cure* – built it into a sweet little resort of Belle Epoque hotels and villas, cafés and a casino with a chocolate-box theatre. Today, Lamalou is bidding to become fashionable once again. Its restored 19th-century centre makes a perfect setting for the big event on its calendar, an important festival of operettas (and opera) that is held in summer and again in winter. The cemetery church of **St-Pierre-de-Rhèdes**, on the eastern edge of town, is a singular 11th-century Romanesque work with a sculpted portal (unusually, the lintel under the tympanum has a stylized but impossible-to-read inscription in Arabic) and apse, marked by a crude figure with a staff and gourd, identified as a pilgrim – quite possible, as the church is on the road from Toulouse to St-Guilhem-le-Désert.

The Eastern Espinouse

Either of the above towns is a good base for exploring the eastern half of the Espinouse. North of Bédarieux, the upper valley of the Orb starts out plagued by industry and power lines, but you can escape into the hills on either side, to **Dio** or to **Boussagues**, both delightful medieval villages with ruined castles; the latter's highly picturesque, stone-roofed Renaissance **Maison du Bailli** once belonged to Toulouse-Lautrec. Persevere northwards and you'll come to the **Gorges de l'Orb**, ending in a big dam and artificial lake at **Avène**. East of Bédarieux, there's another pretty village, **Carlencas**, famous for chickpeas; to the south is **Faugères**, centre of a small wine region (*see* box below).

Fonderie de Cloches
t *04 67 95 07 96; open for guided tours (French only) July–Aug Mon–Sat 10–12 and 2–6; shop open the rest of the year Mon–Thurs 10–12 and 2–6; Fri 10–12*

Hérépian, between Bédarieux and Lamalou, has the only bell foundry in the south of France, the **Fonderie de Cloches**, in business since 1605. Hérépian offers another medieval detour, north on the D922 to **Villemagne**. Villemagne-L'Argentière it was in the 12th century, when a Benedictine abbey here looked after a rich silver

Wine: AOC Faugères and St-Chinian

It's the mix of limestone and schist in this beautiful, mountainous corner of Languedoc that creates the dark, beefy red wines of Faugères and St-Chinian. The French currently view these wines as the ascendant stars of the country's lesser-known regions, views borne out by the concentration of talented wine-makers to emerge from the area.

The wines require a few years in the cellar to reveal their true personalities; AOC Faugères, *www.faugeres.com*, has a high percentage of syrah, as well as grenache, old carignan stock and mourvèdre grapes. Pick up a few bottles at **Domaine Gilbert Alquier**, Route de Pézenas, in Faugères, **t** 04 67 95 15 21, *www.gilbert-alquier.fr* (*open afternoons*); and **Château des Estanilles**, in Cabrerolles, **t** 04 67 90 29 25, *www.chateau-estanilles.com* (*call ahead; closed Sun*), which produces delightful variations in all three colours (including a fine white AOC Languedoc of maccabeu and grenache).

St-Chinian encompasses 20 villages, but you can try nearly all the labels of fruity, dark, cherry-red St-Chinian at the 18th-century **Maison des Vins**, Avenue de la Promenade St-Chinian, **t** 04 67 38 11 69, *www.saint-chinian.com* (*open Mon–Sat 9–12 and 2–6.30, plus July and Aug Sun 10–12, when there are daily tastings*); they also have a wine road, and sponsor a variety of tours and weekends in the area. Or visit the **Château Cazal-Viel**, in Cessenon-sur-Orb, **t** 04 67 89 63 15, *www.laurent-miquel.com*.

mine owned by the Trencavels of Béziers and Carcassonne. Most of the abbey and its fortifications are in ruins, and sadly neglected. There are two lovely churches, Romanesque **St-Grégoire**, which has an **archaeology museum**, and Gothic St-Majan, along with a richly decorated 13th-century building believed to have been the mint, the **Hôtel des Monnaies**. Just to the north of Villemagne is a humpbacked medieval bridge called, like that of St-Guilhem and so many others, the **Pont du Diable** – it must have been hard for the medieval peasant imagination to see how such things could stand up without divine or infernal aid.

St-Grégoire archaeology museum
t 06 73 75 29 83; open May–mid-Oct Wed, Sat and Sun 3–6

Continuing west from Lamalou, at **Colombières-sur-Orb** there's a wild gorge to explore, framed on the west by wild Mt Caroux, the granite massif known as the 'mountains of light' for its shimmering mica. On the other side of Le Caroux, there another canyon, the enchanting **Gorges d'Héric** stretching north of Mons-la-Trivalle, where walkers can stroll under cliffs and cool off in the rockpools, or pick up a canoe or raft from **Atelier Rivière Randonnée** at the nearby watermill Moulin de Tarassac in Mons, to paddle south through another gorge or even all the way to **Roquebrun**.

Atelier Rivière Randonnée
t 04 67 97 74 64, www.canoe-tarassac.com

Sheltered by the mountains, this village calls itself 'Petit Nice' and is famous for its mimosas (celebrated with a festival on the second Sunday in February); cacti grow in its **Jardin Mediterranéen Cade de Roquebrun** on Rue de la Tour. If you get too hot, go for a dip in the Orb, swimming and canoeing under its stone bridge. South of Roquebrun, it's a clear shot along to Béziers and the sea, with nothing to detain you along the way.

Jardin Mediterranéen Cade de Roquebrun
open July–Aug daily 9–7; other times 9–12 and 12.30–5.30; closed mid-Nov–mid-Feb; adm

The Parc Naturel Régional du Haut-Languedoc

The loveliest village of the Espinouse, **Olargues** sits in a curl of the River Jaur, dominated by two medieval monuments, a romantic 11th-century bell-tower set up above on a hill surrounded by swooping swifts, and another spectacular Pont du Diable. Its **Centre Cebenna,** on Avenue du Champ des Horts, is a research centre on the area's ecosystem, with information on the wildlife and fascinating geology of the Haut-Languedoc.

Centre Cebenna
t 04 67 97 88 00, www.cebenna.org; open July–Aug Mon–Fri 9–12 and 3–7, Sat 10–1 and 4–7; Sept–June Tues–Fri 9–12 and 2–6

Next to the west, **St-Pons-de-Thomières** is the little capital of the Espinouse, surrounded by forests. St-Pons probably gets more snow than anywhere in Languedoc east of the Pyrenees, giving it a decidedly Alpine air. Its landmarks are a **cathedral**, with a Romanesque portal and a tremendous 18th-century organ, and its **Musée Municipal de Préhistoire Régionale**, installed in the abbey building opposite the cathedral on the Grand Rue. Never suspecting they were in a future Regional Park, Neolithic people made St-Pons and the Espinouse one of their favourite haunts in France; archaeologists even speak of a *civilisation saintponienne*. This museum documents their career, but the star attractions are

Musée Municipal de Préhistoire Régionale
t 04 67 97 22 61, www.pays-saintponais.com; open April–June Thurs–Sun 3–6; July–mid-Sept Tues–Sun 10–12 and 3–6; closed mid-Sept–Mar; adm

the statue menhirs, the true cultural totems of this part of the Mediterranean (some 70 have been found in the valley of the Agout) similar to those found in the Gard, in Tuscany and in Corsica, dating from 3000 BC to Roman times. A film evokes local Neolithic life.

St-Pons is the perfect base for visiting the Parc Naturel Régional du Haut-Languedoc, spread over a wide area of the Espinouse on the borders of the Hérault, Tarn and Aveyron. It also has the **Maison du Parc** with information on trails in the mountains through wild areas that have, appropriately enough, the largest population of *mouflons* in Europe, decendants of Neolithic sheep. These were introduced here from Corsica in 1954 – some 19 individuals who have literally thousands of great-great-great-grand curly-horned descendants frisking over the slopes.

Maison du Parc Naturel Régional du Haut-Languedoc
t 04 67 97 38 22, www.parc-haut-languedoc.fr

From **Prat-d'Alaric**, the valley of the Agout spreads across the heart of the park; the roads that follow it, the D14 and D53, make a delightful tour, through beautiful villages such as **La Salvetat-sur-Agout** and **Fraisse-sur-Agout**, which has a curious **statue-menhir** *in situ*, carved with a serpent and egg, a universal symbol found as far afield as the prehistoric Indian mounds in Ohio. The D53 continues towards the summit of the Espinouse (3,652ft). A little further on – over the Lauze pass on the D180 – there is a stone enclosure, a vestige of a Roman army camp, and beyond – on the D922 – **St-Gervais-sur-Mare**, full of medieval and Renaissance buildings.

Much closer to St-Pons, the rocky hills are pocked with caves around Corniou-les-Grottes, the most important of which is the **Grotte de la Devèze**, another gorgeous cave of delicate stalactites and shining crystals, nicknamed the 'Palace of the Glass Spinner'. To climb down from the Espinouse, there is the choice of the D907 out of St-Pons towards Minerve, or the N112 for Béziers and the Canal du Midi (*see* pp.177–86). On this route, you'll pass through **St-Chinian** and its wine region (*see* p.162); about 9km east of that village is the Romanesque **Abbey of Fontcaude**.

Grotte de la Devèze
t 04 67 97 03 24; open July–Aug 10–6; April–June and Sept 2–5; Oct–Mar Sat, Sun and hols 2–5, closed Jan; adm

Market Days in the North Hérault

Lamalou-les-Bains: Tues.
La Salvetat: Thurs and Sun.

ⓘ Lamalou-les-Bains >
1 Av Capus, t 04 67 95 70 91, www.ot-lamaloulesbains.fr; open June–mid-Sept Mon–Sat and Sun am; mid-Sept–May Mon–Fri and Sat am

Where to Stay and Eat in the North Hérault

Lamalou-les-Bains ✉ 34240

Le Couvent d'Hérépian, 2 Rue du Couvent, just east of Lamalou, **t** 04 67 23 36 30, *www.garrigae-resorts.com* (€€€€€). Luxurious 17th-century convent converted into a resort with all the bells and whistles.

*****L'Arbousier**, 18 Av A. Daudet, **t** 04 67 95 63 11, *www.arbousier hotel.com* (€€–€). This 100-year-old hotel has been prettily renovated; it serves old French favourites in the restaurant (€€).

****Belleville**, 1 Av Charcot, **t** 04 67 95 57 00, *www.hotel-lamalou.com* (€). Excellent value for relative luxury: some bathrooms come with Jacuzzi and there's a restaurant (€€).

ⓘ **St-Pons-de-Thomières >>**
*Place du Foirail, **t** 04 67 97 06 65, www.saint-pons-tourisme.com*

ⓘ **Bédarieux**
*Rue de la République, **t** 04 67 95 08 79, www.bedarieux.fr*

ⓘ **Olargues >**
*Av de la Gare, **t** 04 67 97 71 26, www.olargues.org; open winter Tues–Sat; summer daily*

★ **Domaine de Rieumégé >**

Faugères ✉ 34600

La Vigneronne, Rte de Pézenas, **t** 04 67 95 78 49, *www.shopics.be/vigneronne* (€€). Handsome B&B with a pool and *boulodrome*, in the centre of the wine region. Evening meals available (€€). *Mid-June–mid-Sept min. 3 nights.*

Villemagne l'Argentière ✉ 34600

Auberge de l'Abbaye, next to the church, **t** 04 67 95 34 84, *www.aubergeabbaye.com* (€€€–€€). Dine on seasonal dishes in the garden or in the 12th-century dining room. Specialities include *profiteroles de foie gras* and truffles in season; they also have three pretty rooms (€€). *Closed Mon, Tues lunch and Nov–early Feb.*

Olargues ✉ 34390

*****Domaine de Rieumégé**, 3km out on the St-Pons road, **t** 04 67 97 73 99, *www.domainederieumege.fr* (€€€–€€). Enchanting 17th-century building set in a 20-acre estate – peace guaranteed. Twelve nice rooms, two pools and tennis, and a separate farmhouse with its own pool. If you don't stay, at least eat in the superb restaurant (€€) in the beautifully restored *grange*. *Closed mid-Oct–Feb.*

St-Pons-de-Thomières ✉ 34220

****Les Bergeries de Ponderach**, about 1km outside St-Pons towards Narbonne, **t** 04 67 97 02 57, *www.bergeries-ponderach.fr* (€€€–€€). A haven of peace in the hills, with a rustic restaurant, serving Belgian and French dishes (€€). Rooms with terraces, country views, a pool, summer concerts and an art gallery.

****Le Cabaretou**, on the D907 towards La Salvetat, **t** 04 67 95 31 62 (€). Up in the heart of the mountains, 10km from St-Pons, this plain, comfortable old post house has a surprisingly ambitious restaurant (€€), its cuisine based entirely on seasonal ingredients.

La Route du Sel, 15 Grand-Rue, **t** 04 67 97 05 14 (€€–€). A little restaurant specializing in original dishes such as *foie gras* with Jerusalem artichokes (*topinambours*) when they're in season. *Closed Sat and eves in winter.*

Ferme-Auberge du Moulin, Le Soulié, on the D150 4km from La Salvetat, **t** 04 67 97 22 27 (€€). Good farm cooking, specializing in cold meats, farm veal and mushrooms. Book ahead. *Closed Dec–Easter and Wed.*

The Hérault Coast: Sète and Cap d'Agde

Seafood, sun and sand are the big attractions along this stretch of coast, but it offers much more – from ancient Greek bronzes to jousting on water.

Sète: the Venice of Languedoc

② Sète

Amid the glitzy candy-land of the planned 1960s resorts, you may have despaired by now of finding anything authentically Mediterranean on these shores, but just in time, there's gritty, salty, workaday Sète, France's biggest Mediterranean fishing port. After the rather depressing and sometimes smelly town entrance, you can stroll along the Canal Maritime and watch businesslike freighters carrying French sunflower and rapeseed oil to every corner of the globe, along with dusty cement boats, gigantic tankers of Algerian natural gas (if one ever goes off, it will take the

Getting around the Hérault Coast

Except along the coast, public transport is rudimentary at best; the coastal **SNCF line** runs from Montpellier through Frontignan, Sète, Agde and Béziers on its way to Narbonne and Perpignan, with around six **trains** a day.

whole town with it), and rusty trawlers jammed full of woebegone sardines or some of the 138 other fish caught by Sétois fishermen. After that, perhaps a leisurely tour of the city's historic monuments? Go ahead and try; in this infant city, younger than Boston or New York, there isn't a single one.

For entertainment, there are the sailors' bars, or the thrills of the city's favourite summer sport, the *joutes nautiques*, or **water-jousting**. If you can stand a little modern madness, Sète will be great fun. It's an attractive town, laced with canals, and livelier and more colourful than any place on Languedoc's coast.

Along the Grand Canal

The city's arms show a field of *fleurs-de-lis* with a whale – *cetus* in Latin – one of the possible explanations for the name, which is first mentioned in a Carolingian document of 814. As previous Languedocien ports such as St-Gilles and Aigues-Mortes had all silted up, it had long been considered as a possible replacement, but action was only taken in 1666, when Louis XIV's minister, Colbert, began construction of the port as the terminus for the Canal du Midi. Even then not everyone was convinced; to encourage people to move in, he built a fake cardboard and wooden town to show just what the future held. It worked, notably among Italians who moved here in droves; in 1673 the new town was declared a free port. The pesky English first came to visit in 1710, occupying the city during the War of the Spanish Succession; out in the harbour, you can see **Fort St-Pierre**, which failed to keep them out. Little has happened since. Despite its booming port, Sète never grew into a major city; hedged between Mont St-Clair, the lagoons and sea, there simply isn't room.

Sète should be the twin city of Livorno in Italy. Both grew up at the same time; both have canals (Sète likes to call itself the 'Venice of Languedoc'), a lot of Italians and a winsome architectural anonymity. And they have both made their contributions to modern culture: Livorno was the birthplace of Modigliani, Sète of the poet Paul Valéry, Georges Brassens and Jean Vilar, father of the Avignon festival. The bustling centre is its 'Grand Canal', lined with quays where the ambience ranges from boatyards and ship's chandlers to banks and boutiques and waterside cafés. In Place Aristide Briand in front of the *mairie*, Sète has what is undoubtedly the world's biggest cast-bronze octopus, writhing over a modern fountain.

Joutes Nautiques

A direct descendant of the sea battles or *naumachia* that took place in the flooded amphitheatres across the Roman empire, nautical jousts are fought in several regions of France, including the lakes of the Franche Comté. None, however, can match the enthusiasm that Languedoc has had for these mock water battles since 1270, when legend has it that bored Crusaders revived the sport at Aigues-Mortes while waiting to sail to Tunisia with St Louis.

Today nine towns practise the sport according to the *méthode Languedocienne*: Sète, with six jousting fraternities, a school (children can start learning the ropes at age seven) and its climactic *tournament de la Saint Louis* on 25 August, is the centre of the sport. Each *fraternité* or club has eight to ten oarsmen, a helmsman, a drummer and an oboe player, and a high platform (*la tintaine*) built on the stern of the blue or red boats, where the jouster (each team has several) stands with a small shield and an 8ft lance. All are dressed in white. Rousing jousting songs are played on the banks of the canals as the boats race towards each other, while each jouster tries to knock the other into the drink. You can usually find some action on summer weekends in Sète – and it's not to be missed.

At 23 Quai Maréchal de Lattre de Tassigny, two local artists – Hervé Di Rosa (b. 1959), known internationally as the leader of the lively, playful *Figuration Libre* movement, and equally quirky artist Bernard Belluc – have created the **Musée International des Arts Modestes**, an eclectic Ali Baba's cavern of day-to-day useless items, baubles, and kitsch from over the past 50 years, imaginatively displayed; special exhibitions cover aspects of popular culture.

Musée International des Arts Modestes
t 04 99 04 76 44, www.miam.org; open April–Sept daily 9.30–7; Oct–Mar Tues–Sun 10–12 and 2–6; adm

Far more serious (but rarely as fun) exhibitions take place in the **Centre Régional d'Art Contemporain Languedoc-Roussillon**, at 26 Quai Aspirant Herber.

Centre Régional d'Art Contemporain
t 04 67 74 94 37, www.crac.lr.free.fr; open Mon and Wed–Fri 12.30–7, Sat and Sun 2–7

At the southern end of the canal, the **Vieux Port** handles most of the fishing fleet. From here, it's a bit of a climb up to the **Cimetière Marin**, celebrated in a famous poem by Paul Valéry (1871–1945), who was buried here in his family tomb (under the name Grassi – like Brassens, his mother was Italian) bearing an inscription from the poem (*Ô récompense après une pensée/Qu'un long regard sur le calme des dieux*). The adjacent, recently renovated **Musée Paul Valéry** not only contains exhibitions on his life (elected to the Académie in 1925, he was not only known as 'the last great Symbolist' poet for his musical, meditative verse, but also wrote essays and represented French culture in the League of Nations), but also covers the history of Sète. There's a good collection of art, mostly from the 19th (Courbet, Cabanel, Jongkind and Marquet) and 20th centuries (Desnoyer, Couderc and Robert Combas and Hervé Di Rosa); another section concentrates on the *joutes nautiques*. Just below, the open-air **Théâtre de la Mer**, with a lively programme of summer concerts, is dedicated to Jean Vilar; just above begins a network of paths up to **Mont St-Clair** (600ft), once the Sunday promenade of the Sétois.

Musée Paul Valéry
t 04 99 04 76 16, www.museepaulvalery-sete.fr; open April–Sept Tues–Sun 9.30–7; Oct–Mar Tues–Sun 10–6; closed Mon; adm

Sète's major contribution to culture, the greatest of modern French troubadours Georges Brassens (d. 1981), is buried in the **Cimetière de Py**, under the Pierres Blanches, overlooking the Etang

Espace Georges Brassens
t 04 99 04 76 26, www.sete.fr/brassens; open July–Aug daily 10–12 and 2–7; June and Sept daily 10–12 and 2–6; Oct–May Tues–Sun 10–12 and 2–6; adm

de Thau; fans or the merely curious can learn and hear all about him in the nearby **Espace Georges Brassens** at 67 Boulevard Camille Blanc, with photos and exhibits relating to Brassens' life, accompanied by his songs and a film from one of his concerts.

A few years ago, in the course of a literary discussion, someone asked who was the best poet at the moment in France. I responded without hesitation: Georges Brassens.

Gabriel García Márquez

★ Hotel Venezia >>

Market Days in Sète

Daily: Les Halles, Rue Gambetta.

Wed am: Place A. Briand, Place Léon Blum and Rue A. Lorraine.

Fri am: Av V. Hugo, opposite station.

Sun am: Place de la République, flea market.

Festivals in Sète

Summer is busy in Sète with its water jousts and events in the Theatre de la Mer, *www.theatredelamer.fr*.

Mid-July: Jazz Festival.

Late July–Aug: ***Fiest'A Sète***, with world music and dance.

Aug 25: Saint Louis water jousting finals.

Guided Tours

Sète Croisières, **t** 04 67 46 00 46, *www.sete-croisieres.com*. Cruises of the canals in electric boats, of the coast and Bassin de Thau. In July and Aug at 3.30 and 4.30 they offer a fascinating look at the Criée des Poissons, the wholesale fish market (book in advance with the tourist office).

Where to Stay in Sète

Sète ✉ **34200**

*****Grand Hôtel**, 17 Quai Maréchal de Lattre de Tassigny, **t** 04 67 74 71 77, *www.legrandhotelsete.com* (€€€–€€). Right on Sète's 'Grand Canal', it almost deserves its name, with plenty of original décor from the 1920s. If you can't swing the Danieli in Venice, this will do fine. The hotel's **Quai 17** restaurant, **t** 04 67 74 71 91 (€€€), is refined and serves rewarding menus.

*****L'Orque Bleue**, 10 Quai Aspirant Herber, **t** 04 67 74 72 13, *www.hotel-orquebleue-sete.com* (€€). Renovated hotel in central Sète beside the Royal canal. Parking for a small charge.

*****Terrasses du Lido**, Rond-Point de l'Europe, along the Corniche road, **t** 04 67 51 39 60, *www.lesterrassesdulido.com* (€€). A pretty Provençal-style villa with a pool and near the beach, with a good restaurant (€€€) open to non-residents, serving authentic Mediterranean dishes from *bourride* to *bouillabaisse*. *Closed Sun eve and Mon except in July and Aug.*

Hotel Venezia, 20, La Corniche de Neuburg, **t** 04 67 51 39 38, *www.hotel-sete.com* (€€). A minute from the beach, this is a tidy little budget choice with Wi-fi and parking and a lovely owner.

Auberge de Jeunesse Villa Salis, 7 Rue du Général Revest, **t** 04 67 53 46 68, *www.fuaj.org/Sete* (€). Youth hostel located near the top of the town on the slopes of Mont Saint-Clair. Take bus 1,2 or 4 to the stop 'Paul Valéry' and walk 300m. *Closed Dec and Jan.*

Eating Out in Sète

La Palangrotte, Rampe Paul Valéry, **t** 04 67 74 80 35 (€€€–€€). Quality seafood on the lower end of the Canal de Sète: grilled fish and several styles of fish stew, including the local *bourride sétoise*. *Closed Sun eve, Wed eve and Mon, except in July and Aug.*

Paris-Mediterranée, 47 Rue Pierre-Semard, **t** 04 67 74 97 73 (€€€–€€). The décor isn't much, but the creative dishes served in the *bistrot* are among the city's best. *Closed Sat lunch, Sun and Mon, and early July.*

L'Esquisse, 90 Rue Mario Roustan, **t** 04 67 74 14 97 (€€). One of Sète's most popular restaurants, for its delicious, wide variety of dishes on a menu that changes each month. Best to book. *Eves only, closed Sun.*

Monte-Christo, 31 Quai Général Durand, **t** 04 67 51 95 65 (€€). Reliably good fresh seafood. *Closed Wed dinner and Thurs out of season.*

ⓘ **Sète >**
*60 Grand-Rue Mario Roustan, **t** 04 99 04 71 71, www.ot-sete.fr; open daily all year*

★ L'Esquisse >>

The Bassin de Thau

The largest and deepest la
21km Bassin de Thau has al
most of the lagoon has fo
huge oyster (the famous
some 18 kinds of shellf

There are two roads
quickly through the
narrow grey beach n
development, this is a good
don't mind the cars.

The longer route from Sète follows the ba… the way it passes a small, modern thermal resort, … **Bains**, with its ancient parent up on a hill above, the medi… village of **Balaruc-le-Vieux**. North of here towards Gigean, the 11th–13th-century Benedictine (later Cistercian) **Abbaye St-Félix du Monceau** stands in romantic ruins on its hill overlooking the lagoon. The abbey includes both a Romanesque and a Gothic church, and since 1970 has been an archaeological restoration project run by an association of volunteers, who have recently replanted the monastic gardens.

Abbaye St-Félix du Monceau
www.saintfelix-abbaye.fr

In Languedoc's oyster capital, the picturesque port of **Bouzigues**, you can learn everything about shellfish-breeding and -fishing, both today and yesteryear, at the **Musée de l'Etang de Thau**. Loupian, an attractive village with remnants of its old walls and palaces, has an unusually vaulted 12th-century church; the real attraction here, however, is a **Gallo-Roman villa** that once stood along the Via Domitia. As with many such villas in France, this one started out as a modest rural manor and gradually grew to palatial proportions – a reminder of how the land-owning families burgeoned through the imperial centuries until they owned nearly everything in Gaul. This family, whose initials were MAF, exported so much wine they made their own amphorae on the estate. Many villas eventually became feudal castles or abbeys; others, like this one, disappeared completely, though the excavations here have brought to light an exceptional set of mosaics, covering what was the villa's entire ground floor. These are largely geometric decorative patterns, in the style of Roman Syria, though they also include a peach tree, and an allegory of the Four Seasons. A museum contains finds from the site and explains the history and economic role of the villa.

Musée de l'Etang de Thau
t 04 67 78 33 57, www.bouzigues.fr; open July–Aug 10–12.30 and 2.30–7; Mar–June and Sept–Oct 10–12 and 2–6; Nov–Feb 10–12 and 2–5; adm

Gallo-Roman villa
t 04 67 18 68 18, www.ccnbt.fr; site open July–Aug 1.30–7, with guided tours of mosaics at 11; Sept–June Wed–Mon 1.30–6, guided tours of the mosaics Sat and Sun at 11; closed Jan; adm

Further south, the ancient lagoon port of **Mèze** still makes a go of it as a fishing village, though nowadays the money comes from the less romantic chores of oyster-farming. It's a quiet place, with a pleasant harbour lined with cafés and a small beach. On the N113 just north of Mèze, the **Musée-Parc des Dinosaures** is a kids'

Musée-Parc des Dinosaures
t 04 67 43 02 80, www.musee-parc-dinosaures.com; open July–Aug daily 10–7; Feb–June daily 2–6; Sept–Jan daily 2–5; adm

[W]here to Stay and Eat around the Bassin de Thau

Bouzigues ✉ 34140

***Côte Bleue**, Av Louis Tudesq, **t** 04 67 78 30 87, *www.la-cote-bleue.fr* (€€). A large, historic family-owned hotel with stylish rooms and a pool, and a restaurant (€€€) overlooking the Bassin de Thau. A great place to sample a vast variety of shellfish, mussels, langoustines and local oysters. *Closed Wed in winter, plus Jan and mid-Feb–early Mar.*

Mèze ✉ 34140

La Marmitiere, 38 Rue du Port, **t** 04 67 43 84 99, *www.lamarmitiere.fr* (€€€–€€). In a narrow street in old Mèze, with evidence of the village's past in its old stone arches. The harbour is nearby and you can eat fish, but also traditional meat dishes such as *filet de bœuf au beurre persillé*. A small terrace faces the street. *Closed Mon–Fri lunch, Sun eve and Mon in winter.*

Marseillan ✉ 34140

Chez Philippe, 20 Rue de Suffren, **t** 04 67 37 36 80 (€€€–€€). Riviera style under the pines, lots of choice and good value on the fixed menus; try the poached oysters and courgette *beignets*. *Closed lunch and Sun eve, and Mon out of season; also mid-Nov–mid-Feb.*

La Paillotte, 705 Av des Camping, **t** 04 67 01 62 55, *www.lapaillotte.net* (€€). Lively Creole cuisine under the palms, set back from the sea; try excellent accras, colombos and over 50 kinds of rum. No credit cards. *Open June–Aug eves and Sun lunch; April–Oct Fri and Sat eves and Sun lunch.*

[...] Chez [Ph]ilippe >>

favourite, marking the spot where in 1996 palaeontologists found the biggest cache of dinosaur eggs ever discovered in Europe. Life-size models and skeletons are hidden amid the trees, including a complete skeleton of a brachiosaurus.

At the southern end, the fishing/oyster port of **Marseillan** was founded in the 6th century BC by the Greeks and marks the spot where the Canal du Midi meets salt water. By the port at 1 Rue Noilly you can find out the secrets of Marseillan's famous straw-coloured vermouth, **Noilly-Prat**, on the very popular tour of the distillery, in place here since 1813 and unique in that the wooden barrels spend a year soaking up the sun.

Noilly-Prat visits
t 04 67 77 20 15, www.noillyprat.com; guided tours May–Sept 10–12 and 2.30–7; Mar–April and Oct–Nov 10–11 and 2.30–4.30; closed Dec–Feb; adm

Marseillan has a 17th-century covered Halles, but also has one of the newest landmarks in the region – its once nondescript **Château d'Eau** or water tower. In 2007, local château owner Alain Liedts came up with the idea of making it into a monument celebrating the local delicacy, and in a period of six months it was covered with a mosaic made of 200,000 local oyster shells, creating a shimmering, textured mother-of-pearl effect. An expanse of partly overgrown dunes between the sea and the south end of the lagoon marks the small resort of **Marseillan-Plage**.

Agde, the 'Black Pearl of Languedoc'

If Sète is a brash young upstart, Agde has been watching the river Hérault flow into the sea for some 2,500 years. Founded by Greeks from Phocis, not long after Marseille, its name was originally

Agatha, after Agatha Tyche, the 'good spirit' of popular Greek religion, usually portrayed as a goddess carrying a cornucopia; the people of Agde are still called Agathois. In medieval times it was an important port, despite occasional visits by Arab sea-raiders. The last few centuries have left Agde behind, but it is still a good town, and a grey one – built almost entirely of volcanic basalt from nearby Mont St-Loup. Its road system can be a little bemusing.

A Stroll Around Town

The tiny **old quarter** or ***cité*** is defined by its walls, now largely demolished for a promenade; a bit of the old **ramparts** remains, near the river, resting on Greek foundations (now below street level). Overlooking the Hérault, Agde's stern basalt **Cathédrale St-Etienne** was begun about 1150. Its appearance – it looks like a baddie's castle in a Hollywood movie – is no accident; Agde's battling bishops used it as their citadel. Previous cathedrals had been wrecked in battles, once at the hands of Charles Martel himself. The only original feature is the 12th-century marble altar.

From the quay along the Hérault, Rue Chassefière leads into the *bourg*, or medieval addition to the city. On Rue de la Fraternité, the **Musée Agathois** is one of the best of Languedoc-Roussillon's town museums, encapsulating nearly everything about Agde's history and traditions in a few well-arranged rooms: archaeological finds, religious art, costume exhibits, dances and festivals, an old-fashioned kitchen and fishermen's gear. Behind the museum, Agde's market shares Place Gambetta with the church of **St-André**, where important Church councils were held in the days of the Visigoths; of the present building, though, the oldest part is the 12th-century tower. Another church, **St-Sever** on Rue St-Sever, contains a fine Renaissance painting of Christ on wood, a little the worse for wear from having been thrown into the Hérault during the Revolution.

Musée Agathois
t 04 67 94 82 51; open June–Sept daily 9.30–6; Oct–May Mon and Wed–Sat 9–12 and 2–6, closed Tues; adm

With the massive new tourist development at nearby Cap d'Agde, this lovely town does not get much peace in summer. **Le Grau d'Agde**, where the Hérault meets the sea, is a pleasant village along the riverbanks, with fishing boats and fishermen. From 15 June to 15 September, it's linked by a little ferry to Agde and **La Tamarissière**, a gorgeous stretch of sand by a 200-year-old pine forest; another boat, the ***Provence III***, leaves from Le Grau's Quai Commandant Méric and goes out to the Bassin de Thau and the **Ile du Brescou**, site of one of Vauban's 17th-century forts.

Provence III
t 04 67 21 38 72; boat trips July–Aug (in July–Aug call **t** *04 67 21 09 88), www.brescou croisieres.com*

A Fishy Saint and a Synthetic Resort

The road to Cap d'Agde, only 4km away, passes the ancient, extinct volcano **Mont St-Loup**, its top disfigured by pylons. Agde's black basalt comes from here. Whoever St Loup, or 'Holy Wolf', might have been is not clear (although there is a northern saint by that name, a 5th-century bishop of Troyes). *Loup* is also the name for sea bass, the favourite fish in Agde's restaurants; at its base is lovely **La Grande Conque**, a black basalt sand beach and black cliffs, where the underwater lava formations make for fascinating snorkelling along a designated shallow water nature trail.

Cap d'Agde, built around a small harbour with miles of sandy beaches on all sides, is the biggest and most fashionable beach playground in Languedoc and another triumph of French holiday efficiency. Like La Grande Motte, it began in the 1960s as a planned resort fostered by the government, and it looks it: a freshly built pastel-coloured 'traditional' centre, with plenty of parking, broad boulevards and everything in its place. The original plan accommodated naturists, in a camp called **Héliopolis** on the northern edge of town at Port-Ambonne. Over the last 20 years, this has become the real story at Cap d'Agde; the camp has grown into a **Quartier Naturiste**, 'Naked City', the biggest nudist colony in Europe, with a futuristic semicircular central building that includes shopping malls, banks and a supermarket. It attracts people from all over the world – as many as 40,000 of them on any given day in July and August. Lifestyles of all sorts are welcome, and the nightlife, both gay and straight, is legendary: swingers' clubs, S&M clubs and everything else. Anything goes here, though in daytime the families, the old folks and the faster crowd each keep to their own parts of the beach.

Cap d'Agde has plenty of other attractions: a **casino** and a first-rate golf course, championship tennis courts, and other sports facilities. There's a wildlife sanctuary at the nearby **Etang de Bagnas** with rare waterfowl (purple heron, grand bittern), and the **Fort de Brescou**, built off shore on a bit of volcanic cone. First built in 1586, destroyed in 1632, rebuilt, perhaps by Vauban, only to serve as a prison – this was Languedoc's Alcatraz until 1851. Boats visit from the port (*see* p.171).

Aquarium

t 04 67 26 14 21, www.aquarium-agde.com; open July–Aug daily 10am–11pm; June–Sept daily 10–7; Oct–May daily 2–6; adm

Cap d'Agde's **Aquarium** at 11 Rue des Deux Frères specializes in live coral and other local sea life. Kids will like the **Luna Park** and the inevitable **Aqualand**.

Musée de l'Ephèbe

t 04 67 94 69 60; open June–Sept daily 9.30–6; Oct–May Mon and Wed–Sat 9–12 and 2–6, closed Tues; adm

One surprising attraction is the remarkable archaeological collection at the **Musée de l'Ephèbe**, named for its star attraction, the *Ephèbe d'Agde*, a magnficent Hellenistic bronze of a young man believed to be Alexander the Great, discovered in 1964 in the bed of the Hérault. Since then he has been joined by other finds from shipwrecks: a bronze Eros and a bronze 'royal child', possibly the son of Caesar and Cleopatra, a rare bronze Etruscan tripod and scores of amphorae from around the Mediterranean – as well as far more recent finds.

Market Days in Agde

Agde: Thurs am.

Cap d'Agde: June–Sept Mon am, Tues am, Wed am and Sat am, and a flea market Sun am.

Where to Stay and Eat in Agde

Agde ✉ 34300

****Le Donjon**, Place Jean Jaurès, **t** 04 67 94 12 32, *www.hotelagde.com* (€€–€). Near the centre, with old-fashioned, rather basic rooms – but one of the only hotels in the *cité*. Half-board in July and Aug. Parking is available.

La Table de Stéphane, 2 Rue des Moulins-à-Huile, **t** 04 67 26 45 22, *www.latabledestephane.com* (€€€€–€€€). A creative young chef prepares little works of art (scallop and red mullet tart, duck cooked in two manners, etc.) at this welcoming restaurant; fine wine list too. *Closed Sat lunch and Mon.*

Le Grau d'Agde ✉ 34300

Hotel Le Voilis, Bd Front de Mer, **t** 04 67 94 24 35, *www.voilis.com* (€€). Tidy air-conditioned rooms by the beach, many with sea views, and a wonderful terrace for just lazing about; the good restaurant (€€) and music lounge are added pluses.

L'Astori, 8 Quai du Commandant Méric, **t** 04 67 94 13 78 (€€€–€€). Le Grau is famous for its seafood restaurants, and this is one of the best, with a terrace right on the water. *Closed Nov–Mar.*

Cap d'Agde ✉ 34300

*****Hotel du Golfe**, Ile des Loisirs, **t** 04 67 26 87 03, *www.hotel-du-golf.com* (€€€). Bright fruity colours, lush gardens under the palms, outdoor pool and a free wellness centre are some of the charms of this medium-sized hotel near Richelieu beach. *Open April–Sept.*

*****Les Grenadines**, Impasse Marie-Céleste, Plage Richelieu Ouest, **t** 04 67 26 27 40, *www.hotelgrenadines.com* (€€€–€€). Plain on the outside, this affable hotel has big air-conditioned rooms with Wi-fi (including family rooms), a pool and path straight to the beach.

*****Capao**, 1 Rue des Corsaires, Plage Richelieu Centre, **t** 04 67 26 99 44, *www.capao.com* (€€€–€€). Stylish, family-orientated hotel right on the beach, with lawns and a pool and sea views; all rooms have Wi-fi and air-conditioning. *Open mid-April–mid-Oct.*

****Azur**, 18 Av des Iles d'Amérique, **t** 04 67 26 98 22, *www.hotelazur.com* (€€€–€€). At the lower end of the price range, a cheerful little hotel with colourful sound-proofed rooms and a pool near the centre of the action, but only a short walk from the Plage Richelieu. Private parking.

ⓘ **Cap d'Agde >>**
*Rond-Point du Bon Accueil, **t** 04 67 01 04 04, www.capdagde.com (also covers Agde and Le Grau d'Agde); open daily all year*

The Southern Hérault

Pézenas

The area inland from Agde, behind the Bassin de Thau, is one of the duller stretches of the Hérault, a rolling plain dotted with agricultural villages – up-to-date and businesslike rather than picturesque and cosy. Right in the centre is Pézenas. If Carcassonne is Languedoc's medieval movie set, this town has often been used for costume dramas set in the time of Richelieu or Louis XIV (most famously, *Cartouche*). Few cities have a better ensemble of buildings from what the French (rather over-enthusiastically) used to call the 'Golden Age'. In summer, the Piscénois live out a lingering *ancien régime* fantasy, with a series of festivals, concerts and exhibitions put on by the ***Mirondela dels Arts***.

Mirondela dels Arts
www.mirondeladelsarts.com

History

Roman Piscenae was known for wool, the best in Gaul. In the 13th century, it became a possession of the French Crown and renewed its prosperity by royally chartered merchants' fairs. Later, the troubles of Béziers and Narbonne in the Albigensian Crusade and the Hundred Years' War would prove lucky for Pézenas. Besides draining off their trade and commerce, the royal town replaced Narbonne as seat of the Estates-General of Languedoc after 1456. The royal governors of the region followed in 1526, bringing in their wake a whole wave of wealthy nobles, clerics and jurists, who rebuilt Pézenas in their own image with new churches, convents, government buildings and scores of refined *hôtels particuliers*. For the next two centuries they remained, preferring their aristocratic little enclave to decaying Narbonne or to Montpellier, full of untidy industry and Protestants.

All this came to an end with the Revolution. Since then, Pézenas has done its best to keep up its monuments while making a living from agriculture and tourism.

A Walk around Town

Jean-Baptiste Poquelin was born in Paris. Molière was born in Pézenas.
Marcel Pagnol

With its 70-odd listed historical buildings, from the Renaissance through to the 18th century, Pézenas really did develop and maintain a distinctive architectural manner. This can best be seen in the ***hôtels particuliers***, with their lovely arcaded courtyards and external staircases. It was an eclectic style, incorporating elements as diverse as Gothic vaulting and Italian Renaissance balustrades, tasteful, if not ambitious.

The **tourist office**, in the Hôtel de Peyrat, was also once the shop of a barber named Gély. A certain young actor playwright named Jean-Baptiste Poquelin – who changed his name to Molière, most likely to spare his family the shame of having produced an actor – spent some seasons in Pézenas in the 1650s, when his troupe was employed by the governor, the Prince de Conti, and he liked passing the afternoons in Gély's salon, doing research for his comedies (in particular, *Tartuffe* and *Don Juan*), watching the comings and goings and listening to the conversations. Today it houses a new 3D attraction, the **Scénovision Molière**, which endeavours to recreate the playwright's 17th-century life and times in 55-minute shows.

Scénovision Molière
t 04 67 98 35 39, www.scenovisionmoliere.com; open July–Aug Thurs and Sat–Tues 9–7, Wed and Fri 9–8; Sept–June daily 9–12 and 2–6; adm

Across Place Gambetta, the former government palace, the **Maison Consulaire**, has been rebuilt so many times since the 13th century that it is in itself a little museum of Pézenas architecture. Around the corner on Rue Alliés, the **Musée de Vulliod-St-Germain**

Musée de Vulliod-St-Germain
t 04 67 98 90 59; open July–Oct Tues–Sun 10–12 and 3–7; Sept–June Tues–Sun 10–12 and 2–5; adm

Wine: AOC Languedoc and Picpoul de Pinet

Another pocket of this wide-flung AOC label is in Pézenas, home of some excellent wines, including **Prieuré de St-Jean de Bébian**, *www.bebian.com*, purchased in 2010 by a Swiss investment group. For a unique, golden-hued clairette wine from the fragrant, thyme-covered slopes to the north, try the **Château St-André**, Route de Nizas at Pézanas, **t** 04 67 98 33 46, *www.vins-languedoc-saint-andre.com* (*ring ahead*).

Pomérols, near Pézenas, is the centre of a traditional but minuscule growing area on the west shore of the Bassin de Thau called Picpoul (literally 'lip stinger') de Pinet, producing in spite of its name an unusual soft white wine with sea-green highlights that goes well with fish; try some at the **Cave Coopérative Les Costières**, in Pomérols, **t** 04 67 77 01 59, *www.cave-pomerols.com* (*open Mon–Sat 8.30–12 and 2–6*). In Florensac, just west of Pomérols, **Vinipolis**, 5 Av des Vendanges, **t** 04 67 77 00 20, is a contemporary, interactive wine-tasting centre that opened in 2007 next door to the local co-operative and a bistrot: the aim to make the region's wines accessible to all (*open Mon–Thurs 9–6, Fri and Sat 9–7.30*).

Lézignan-la-Cèbe, just north of Pézenas, is the mild onion capital of France and also has the **Château Domaine Olivier d'Ormesson**, **t** 04 67 98 12 95 (*ring in advance*), run by a count devoted to perfecting his white and red *Vins de Pays d'Oc* that have surpassed not a few proud AOC labels – especially a red called L'Enclos made of merlot and cabernet sauvignon.

contains a display of the fancy furnishings, faïence and art that the *hôtels particuliers* would have contained, but nothing of Molière until 2009, when it bagged the very chair he sat on *chez* Gély.

West of Place Gambetta are some of the best streets for peeking inside the courtyards of the *hôtels particuliers*: Rue Sabatini, Rue François-Oustrin (the **Hôtel de Lacoste**, with an elegant staircase and courtyard, is at No.8 and can be entered during opening hours by way of its current occupant, a branch of the Société Générale bank) and Rue de Montmorency (where there's an amusing **Musée du Jouet** with the 'marvels of yesteryear' at No. 2bis).

Musée du Jouet: Jouets et Merveilles d'Antan
t 0467 35 92 88, http://museedujouetpezenas.jimdo.com; open July–Sept daily 10–8; Oct–June Tues–Sun 2–7, daily during French schools hols; adm

Fanciest of all was **Rue de la Foire**, the status address of the old days, with a number of palaces, including the Renaissance **Hôtel de Carrion-Nizas** at No.10. Just down the street, note the charming relief of child musicians at No.22. At the northern end of the street, a left takes you into Rue Emile Zola; the **Hôtel de Jacques Cœur** (the famous merchant of Montpellier; *see* pp.138–9) is at No.7, with an allegorical sculpted façade. It faces the **Porte Faugères** (1597), a remnant of the town walls, and the nearby entrance to the small Jewish **Ghetto**, a single poignant lane closed in by two gates in the 14th century. At 5 Rue Montmorency, in keeping with the town's architectural heritage, there is a **museum of doors and ironwork**.

Museum of Doors and Ironwork
t 04 67 98 35 05; open Tues–Sun 2–5

The broad **Cours Jean Jaurès**, site of the market, divides Pézenas in two. It, too, has its palaces: an especially good row of them at Nos.14–22. The Cours leads into Place de la République, and the church of **St-Jean**, with profuse 17th- and 18th-century marble decoration that proves Pézenas' artistic instincts were much sounder in secular matters. South of the Cours, seek out the **Hôtel de Malibran** and **Hôtel de l'Epine**, with a lavish sculptural façade, both on Rue Victor Hugo; the **Hôtel Montmorency**, on Rue Reboul, was the Pézenas home of the First Dukes of France and the governors of Languedoc, until the leading member rebelled and lost his head in Toulouse and the Dukes of Uzès moved up to first place; and, best of all, the **Hôtel d'Alfonse** on Rue Conti, which has a delightful courtyard loggia on three levels, built in the 1630s.

Abbaye de Valmagne

Abbaye de Valmagne
t 04 67 78 06 09, www.valmagne.com; open for guided tours and wine tasting Easter–mid-June Mon–Fri 2–6, weekends 10–6; mid-June–Sept daily 10–6; Oct–mid-June daily 2–6; closed Jan

Thirteen km east of Pézenas, Valmagne was an early Cistercian foundation, begun in 1138 and financed by Raymond Trencavel. Being one of the richest houses, it also became one of the most decadent; the records mention a certain 16th-century Florentine abbot named Pietro da Bonzi, who built himself a palace on the site, plus a French garden with a statue of Neptune, and who threw the best dinner parties in Languedoc. Thoroughly trashed in the Revolution, the abbey has survived only by good luck: one owner proposed to dismantle it to provide building stone for a new church in Montpellier, but the canons fortunately found the price too high. For the past century, the vast church has served as the biggest **wine cellar** in the Hérault, with some of the best AOC Languedoc, both red and a traditional lemon-coloured white and rosé.

Valmagne is not your typical Cistercian church. St Bernard would have frowned on architectural vanities like the porch, the big bell-towers and the sculpted decoration – grapevines, representing less the scriptural 'labourer in the vineyard' than the real vineyards that made Valmagne so rich. Its size is astonishing: a 370ft nave, and great pointed arches almost as high as Narbonne cathedral's. Most of the work is 14th-century, in a straightforward but sophisticated Late Gothic; note how the nave columns grow slightly closer together towards the altar, a perspective trick that makes the church seem even longer (St Bernard wouldn't have fancied that either). The relatively few monks who lived here would hardly have needed such a church; here, too, architectural vanity seems to have overcome Cistercian austerity. Both the chapterhouse and the refectory are well preserved, around a pretty cloister that contains the loveliest thing in the abbey, an octagonal Gothic pavilion with a tall flowing fountain inside, a fantasy straight from a medieval manuscript or tapestry. An 18th-century poet, Lefranc de Pompignan, named it right: a *fontaine d'amour*.

Market Days in Pézenas

Pézenas: Sat.

Festivals in Pézenas

Few towns in Languedoc are *en fête* as often as Pézenas, beginning in February and March with festivities for patron saint Blaise and Carnival: the *poulain* or 'foal' has been Pézenas' totem animal ever since 1226, when the favourite mare of King Louis VIII gave birth in the town. A mock version of wood and canvas is the star of the town's three-day Carnival, and leads a colourful parade in medieval costume. In mid-June, Pézenas reverts to its golden days in the time of Molière, with costumes, markets and performances of his comedies, 17th-century style.

Where to Stay and Eat in Pézenas

ⓘ **Pézenas >**
Place Gambetta, t 04 67 98 36 40, www.pezenas-tourisme.fr; open July–Aug daily; Sept–June Mon–Sat and Sun pm

★ **Hostellerie de St-Alban >**

Pézenas ✉ 34120

15 Grand Rue, Caux, **t** 04 67 37 50 61, *www.15grandrue.com* (€€€). Five minutes from Pézenas, this beautiful restored house offers four elegant, well-equipped B&B suites, run by Abi, a great source of knowledge about the area.

***Hostellerie de St-Alban**, 31 Route d'Agde, Nézignan l'Evêque, just south of Pézenas, **t** 04 67 98 11 38, *www.saintalban.com* (€€€–€€). A quiet 19th-century villa in the vines, with a pool, tennis and one of the top restaurants in town (€€€). *Closed mid-Nov–mid-Feb.*

Hotel de Vigniamont, 5 Rue Massillon, **t** 04 67 35 14 88, *www.hoteldevigniamont.com* (€€€–€€). Luxurious little 17th-century *hôtel particulier*, with a peaceful inner courtyard and cosy lounge bar.

Villa Juliette, 6 Chemin de la Faissine, **t** 04 67 35 25 38, *www.villajuliette.com* (€€). In the centre, overlooking pretty Sans Souci park, offers five B&B rooms in a pretty garden with a pool.

Le Pré St-Jean, 18 Av du Maréchal Leclerc, **t** 04 67 98 15 31 (€€€–€€). Has a pretty terrace and serves stuffed squid and *carré d'agneau. Closed Sun eve, Mon, and Thurs eve.*

L'Oustal, 15 Rue Anatole France **t** 04 67 11 08 68 (€€). The new chef prepares exciting dishes, inspired by the market and season.

Maison Alary, 5 Rue St-Jean, **t** 04 67 98 21 39. This *boulangerie* makes Pézenas' spool-shaped *petits pâtés*. They often take French visitors by surprise ('What is this, half sweet and half mutton?'), but if you're British you may not find them that shocking: the recipe was introduced in 1770 by the Indian chef of Lord Clive, Governor of India. Eat them warm. *Closed Mon.*

Béziers

Béziers is older than the Romans; its site, a commanding, defensible hill on a key part of the Mediterranean coast, high over the river Orb, was promising even for Julius Caesar to found a colony called Victrix Julia Septimanorum Baetarae. Its promise in the Middle Ages, however, was cut rudely short, leaving one famous anecdote behind.

Béziers was ruled by the tolerant Viscount Roger-Raymond Trencavel of Carcassonne, and its 200 Cathars and thousands of Catholics lived together in harmony. In 1203, the Bishop of Béziers disobeyed Innocent III's order to excommunicate the Cathars, so the Pope sent his Legate, Pierre de Castelnau, to convert the heretics. Instead, the Biterrois ran him out of town, not long before he was assassinated in Beaucaire.

So Béziers wasn't exactly in the Church's good books in 1209, when Simon de Montfort's Albigensian Crusaders besieged the city. He ordered the Catholics to leave the city, but they refused, preferring to fight alongside their fellow citizens. When the Crusaders stormed the city, they found that the entire population

Getting to and around Béziers

Aéroport Béziers Cap d'Agde, t 04 67 80 99 09, is off the E80, 16km east of Béziers and has buses to Béziers bus station, Agde train station and Marseillan coinciding with flight times.

Béziers is on the main coastal **rail** line, and it's easy to get from Narbonne, Sète, Montpellier or points beyond, with trains never much more than two hours apart.

The ***gare routière*** is on Place du Général de Gaulle, t 04 67 28 36 41, with regular **bus** connections to Pézenas, and less regular ones to villages of the eastern Hérault. City bus 16 runs from here to nearby Valras, the popular lido of the Biterrois.

'Today, your Holiness, twenty thousand citizens were put to the sword, regardless of rank, age, or sex.'
Arnaud-Amary's letter to Pope Innocent III

When the town was taken Catholic citizens sought refuge in a Church dedicated to Mary Magdelene./ Hurriedly they took refuge in the high church./ The priests and clerics put on vestments/ And had the church bells rung as for a funeral/ And started a mass for the dead.
Song of the Cathar Wars

had taken refuge in the churches. The Crusaders' ayatollah, the new papal legate Arnaud-Amary, ordered the massacre of all the Cathars. Asked how to distinguish them from the Catholics, he replied, 'Kill them all; God will know his own.' The churches were set ablaze; the papal legate boasted of all the people, even newborn babies, put to death.

Not surprisingly, Béziers languished for centuries. The second chance came in the 1660s, with the building of the Canal du Midi (*see* pp.44–6), when it grew to become, by the 19th century, the 'World Capital of Wine'. Today its 70,000 souls put on the biggest party in Languedoc – a four-day *Feria* in August – grow wine, and support a crack rugby squad and bullfights. Its pigeon-grey streets may not be quite as grand as its heroic hilltop skyline suggests, but there's plenty to see and three good museums.

Allées Paul Riquet and the Cathedral

Life in Béziers centres around the the **Allées Paul Riquet**, a broad promenade of plane trees named after the city's great benefactor, the builder of the Canal du Midi. Besides a statue of Riquet, there is a handsome 19th-century theatre, and a monument to Resistance hero Jean Moulin (another Biterrois) at the top of the **Plateau des Poètes**, a romantic garden with ponds and swans and statues by local sculptor Jean-Antoine Injalbert that descends gracefully down to the train station. From the other end of the Allées Paul Riquet, any of the streets to the west will take you up to the top of the hill and the medieval centre.

Someone must have been left in Béziers after 1209, for the city spent the next two centuries working on its huge **cathedral**, replacing the Romanesque original that split 'like a pomegranate' when set ablaze by the Crusaders. Its grim, fortress-like exterior seems a foreign presence, the citadel of an occupying force, built in their northern Gothic style. The inside is more graceful; in clean, warm ashlar masonry with plenty of stained glass, it creates a light and airy effect, especially in the apse, where large windows of blue and white decorative glass (behind a dreadful Baroque altar) are the prettiest feature in the church. In two chapels (second right and second left) there are fragments of Giotto-esque frescoes, and, at the west front, there is a magnificent organ almost as good as the one in Narbonne, carved in walnut in 1623 by Guilhaume Martois, who is buried next to it. Architectural fragments from the earlier church can be seen in the beautiful vaulted cloister, a work of the late 14th century.

Musée des Beaux-Arts
t 04 67 28 38 78, www.ville-beziers.fr/culture; open July–Aug Tues–Sun 10–6; April–June and Sept–Oct Tues–Sun 9–12 and 2–6; Nov–Mar Tues–Sun 9–12 and 2–5; closed Mon; adm

Behind the cathedral, the Hôtel Fabrégat, in Place de la Révolution, houses Béziers' **Musée des Beaux-Arts**, founded in 1859, with something for every taste: a 16th-century *Virgin and Child* by Martin Schaffner of Ulm, a portrait by Hans Holbein the Younger, 17th-century Italian works (including a Domenichino), a Richard Bonington *Storm*, and 18th- and 19th-century French paintings. Many of the modern works (by Soutine, Dufy and De Chirico) were purchased by Jean Moulin; the great Resistance leader posed as a designer and art dealer under the name of Romanin.

Hôtel Fayet
t 04 67 49 04 66, www.ville-beziers.fr/culture; open July–Aug Tues–Sun 10–6; April–June and Oct Tues–Sun 9–12 and 2–6; Nov–Mar Tues–Sun 9–12 and 2–5; closed Mon; adm

Just north, the **Musée des Beaux-Arts/Hôtel Fayet**, in a delightful 17th-century *hôtel particulier* at 9 Rue du Capus, contains several rooms of 18th- and 19th-century paintings and decorative arts, and several rooms dedicated to the sculptures of Injalbert.

Madeleine
open Wed and Fri 10–12, Thurs 3–6, Sat 10–12 and 2–5, Sun 10–12.30 and 2–4, but check with tourist office as times change often

If you have time for more churches, the Romanesque **Madeleine**, north of the cathedral and halles on Place de la Madeleine, was rebuilt after 7,000 people who sought to take refuge in its walls were burnt alive in 1209.

St-Aphrodise, further north, hidden behind newer buildings in Place St-Aphrodise, was Béziers' cathedral in the 8th century. 'St Aphrodise', if it isn't Aphrodite herself, would be the legendary first bishop, who rode into Béziers one day on a camel (now the city's symbol). The Romans naturally chopped off his head and threw it into a well – but the water rose miraculously to the surface, floating the head with it. Aphrodise fished it out and carried it under his arm to the site of this church, and then disappeared into the ground. It's more likely, however, that pagan Aphrodite had a temple on or near this site. Almost nothing remains of the original building, but a 4th-century sarcophagus has been recycled for use as a baptismal font.

Musée du Biterrois
t 04 67 36 81 61; open July–Aug Tues–Sun 10–6; April–June and Sept–Oct Tues–Sun 9–12 and 2–6; Nov–Mar Tues–Sun 9–12 and 2–5; closed Mon; adm

Espace Taurin
t 04 67 35 28 46; open July–Aug Tues–Sun 10–6; April–June and Sept–Oct Tues–Sun 9–12 and 2–6; Nov–Mar Tues–Sun 9–12 and 2–5; closed Mon; adm

A third Romanesque church, 12th-century **St-Jacques**, has an intricately worked apse, and sits on a belvedere on the south side of Béziers, overlooking the Orb. From here, Rue St-Jacques passes by the **Arènes**, a Roman amphitheatre that once sat 15,000, now surrounded by houses. Here too is a third museum, the **Musée du Biterrois**, housed in an 18th-century barracks on Rampe du 96ème (from the top of Avenue Gambetta, turn down Avenue de la Marne). The museum divides its space between regional archaeological finds, medieval capitals and other bits (including St Aphrodise with his head), ethnography, science and ceramics. If you like bullfighting half as much as the locals do, visit the **Espace Taurin** at 1 Avenue President Wilson.

Towards the Sea

Head down the Orb from Béziers, and a surprise waits in the village of **Sérignan**: the new **Musée Régional d'Art Contemporain Languedoc-Roussillon** at 146 Avenue de la Plage. Occupying a recently refurbished former winery, it changes its collection annually and offers four to five special exhibitions every year. Its stretch of five sandy beaches and dunes are among the prettiest and most peaceful on the coast. The main Biterrois beach, **Valras-Plage** at the mouth of the Orb, is a laid-back resort with wide sands, a casino and plenty of restaurants.

Musée Régional d'Art Contemporain Languedoc-Roussillon
t 04 67 32 33 05, www.ville-serignan.fr; open Tues–Fri 10–6, Sat and Sun 1–6; closed Mon and hols; adm

★ Hotel des Poètes >>

ⓘ Béziers >
Palais des Congrès, 29 Av St-Saëns, t 04 67 76 84 00, www.beziers-tourisme.fr; open mid-June–Aug daily; Sept–June Mon–Sat; also Information Point Centre Ville, Place Lavabre (Rue du 4 Septembre), t 04 67 36 06 27

★ Octopus >>

★ Château de Raissac >

Market Days in Béziers

Fri: flowers, antiques, food and clothes in Allées Paul Riquet, Place David d'Angers, and around.

Sat and Sun: Place de la Madeleine, flea and produce markets.

Where to Stay in Béziers

Béziers ✉ 34500

Le Clos de Moussanne, Rte de Pézenas, **t** 04 67 39 31 81, *www.leclosde maussanne.com* (€€€). This 17th-century convent has been converted into a delightful five-room boutique *chambres d'hôtes* with a pool, charming veranda and delicious set dinners.

Château de Raissac, 2km from Béziers on Rte de Lignan, **t** 04 67 28 15 61, *www.raissac.com* (€€€). Delightful B&B in an early 19th-century wine château, run by a truly lovely couple of artists, Jean and Christine Viennet, whose works and spirit of *joie de vivre* give it a special magic.

L'Appart des Anges, on the Canal du Midi in Cers (just east of Béziers), **t** 04 67 26 05 57, *www.appartdesanges.com* (€€€). Sheltered under giant plane trees, three delightful cosy cabin-style bedrooms on a Freycinet barge, with free Wi-fi, bicycles and lounging space on deck; rates include breakfast.

*****Impérator**, 28 Allées Paul Riquet, **t** 04 67 49 02 25, *www.hotel-imperator.fr* (€€). This has the best location in town, and there's a garage.

****Hotel des Poètes**, 80 Allees Paul Riquet, **t** 04 67 76 38 66, *www. hoteldespoetes.net* (€€). Charming little hotel by the park, offering well-equipped modern rooms and free bikes for guests.

Eating Out in Béziers

L'Ambassade, 22 Bd de Verdun (opposite the train station), **t** 04 67 76 06 24, *www.restaurant-lambassade.com* (€€€€–€€€). Dine well and elegantly while watching the progress of your meal (the kitchen has a large window). Menus start at €29. *Closed Sun and Mon.*

Octopus, 12 Rue Boieldieu, **t** 04 67 49 90 00, *www.restaurant-octopus.com* (€€€€). Gourmet rival to L'Ambassade, the Octopus in the centre of Béziers is run by a young trio from the Bristol in Paris who create wonderfully imaginative dishes; there are a number of intriguing *menus dégustations* to choose from and a €22 lunch *formule*. Be sure to book.

La Maison de Petit Pierre, 22 Av Pierre Verdier, **t** 04 67 30 91 85, *www.la maisondepetitpierre.fr* (€€€–€€). The French love cooking shows on television; book a table on this pretty garden terrace and see what French 'Top Chef' champion Pierre Auge comes up with. *Open lunch Mon–Sat, and dinner Thurs–Sat.*

Le P'tit Semard, 13B Place Semard, **t** 04 67 80 31 04, *www.leptitsemard-beziers.com* (€€–€). A popular place by the cathedral, just opposite the market; the tender Charolaise steak with home-made *frites* is a favourite. *Closed Mon and Sun eve.*

The Hérault-Aude Borders

The Canal du Midi

Canal du Midi

A World Heritage site since 1996, the Canal du Midi (*see* **Topics**, pp.44–6) is one of the jewels of Languedoc, idyllically winding through the countryside – you can always spot it from the distance by its parallel rows of plane trees, planted to hold the soil and help keep the canal from silting up, as well as to shade the boatmen and their cargo. The canal Paul Riquet built is also an early monument of economic planning, from the days of Louis XIV's great minister Colbert, when everything in France was being reformed and modernized. Begun in 1667, as many as 12,000 men worked on the project for 14 years, linking the 145 miles between the Mediterranean and Toulouse. Riquet died a few months before the opening.

No one has shipped any freight on the Canal du Midi since 1979, but it wasn't long before British holidaymakers arrived, pioneering the idea that chugging slowly along a canal could be fun, especially when it passes near vineyards and châteaux built with the money the canal earned local winegrowers in the 18th and 19th centuries. All the locks are tended (although the lock-keepers take an hour off for lunch), but can be avoided if you stick to the 53km pound (the longest lock-less stretch on any French canal) beyond the Ecluses de Fonséranes (*see* below). You can cruise slowly from Béziers to Toulouse or just rent a boat for a few hours and spend a drowsy day under the plane trees. Sadly, these ancient trees are now endangered due to an incurable canker stain disease, a fungus partly spread by people tying barges to trees. The World Heritage teams are taking out infected specimens, so if you see gaps in the rows, that may well be the reason why.

The Canal West of Béziers

The canal connects Sète, its purpose-built port on the Mediterranean, with Toulouse – and thence to the Atlantic by way of the Garonne river, and since 1856 by way of the Canal Latéral à la Garonne. The best parts of it are west of Béziers, where it passes through a score of lovely old villages, fitting so well into the landscape that it seems to have been there all the time. Pick it up just outside Béziers at the **Ecluses de Fonséranes,** just off the N113. This is a remarkable 312m 'stair' of nine locks, which facilitated the biggest drop in altitude along the canal's length. In 1858, the Pont-Canal de l'Orb was built – a bridge for the canal over the unruly river Orb – which cut the required locks down to seven.

Getting around the Canal du Midi

By Car or Bike

You'll need a **car** to get around here, or better still a **mountain bike** (*VTT* in French); the shady towpaths are lovely for cycling. Hire a bike from **Mellow Vélos**, 3 Place d'Eglise Paranza, **t** 04 68 43 38 21, *www.mellowvelos.com*.

By Boat

Best of all, hire a small **boat**, or spend a week on a **barge** – off-season prices are quite reasonable. For a list of firms (most are British) *see* p.69 No previous experience is required, and most people bring or hire bikes for outings along the way. Most luxurious of all are the barge hotels (*péniches hôtels*); see *www.midicruises.org*.

No one road follows the canal for long, but with a good map and some careful navigation you can stay close to it, on the back roads through **Colombiers**, first of the canal villages, then to **Nissan-lez-Ensérune**, a busy place with a 14th-century Gothic church. You will already have noticed the next landmark in the flat countryside; one of the most important pre-Roman towns of southern Gaul, the **Oppidum d'Ensérune**. The site is a relic of the time when these coasts were first coming into the mainstream of Mediterranean civilization. Initially settled in the 6th century BC, it began as a fortified trading village under Greek influence, closely connected to Marseille. By 250 BC it may have had as many as 10,000 people, though later in that century it was wrecked, possibly by Hannibal on his way to Italy during the Punic Wars. Under Roman rule it revived again, refounded as a Roman colony, but in peaceful, settled times it could not survive. The cramped, difficult site was good for defence; when this was no longer necessary, people and trade gradually moved down to the plains and the coast, and Ensérune was largely abandoned by the 1st century AD.

Oppidum d'Ensérune
t 04 67 37 01 23, enserune.monuments-nationaux.fr; open May–Aug daily 10–7; April and Sept Tues–Sun 10–12.30 and 2–6; Oct–Mar Tues–Sun 9.30–12.30 and 2–5.30; last entry 1hr before closing; adm

Not much remains of the town: just the foundations of the wall, cisterns and traces of habitations. The excellent **museum** has a collection of ceramics, including some fine Greek and Etruscan works, along with local pieces that show the strong influence of the foreigners. Just outside the town, where an ancient column with an unusual trapezoidal capital has been re-erected, you can take in one of the oddest panoramas in France, a gigantic surveyor's pie, neatly sliced. This was the **Etang de Montady**, a roughly circular swamp reclaimed in the 13th century, when the new fields were precisely divided by drainage ditches radiating from the centre.

Both the Via Domitia and the Canal du Midi pass right under Ensérune, the latter by way of the 567ft Malpas tunnel (1679), the first canal tunnel ever, dug by Riquet, who knew best, in spite of considerable controversy at the time. Find out more at the **Maison de Malpas**, a multimedia centre with exhibitions, information and a shop.

Maison de Malpas
Route de l'Oppidum, t 04 67 32 88 77, www.lemalpas.com; open Mar–Sept daily 10–7; Oct Tues–Sun 10–5; Nov–Feb Tues–Sat 10–5; also guided tours (adm) of the Canal du Midi, Etang de Montady, and Malpas tunnel

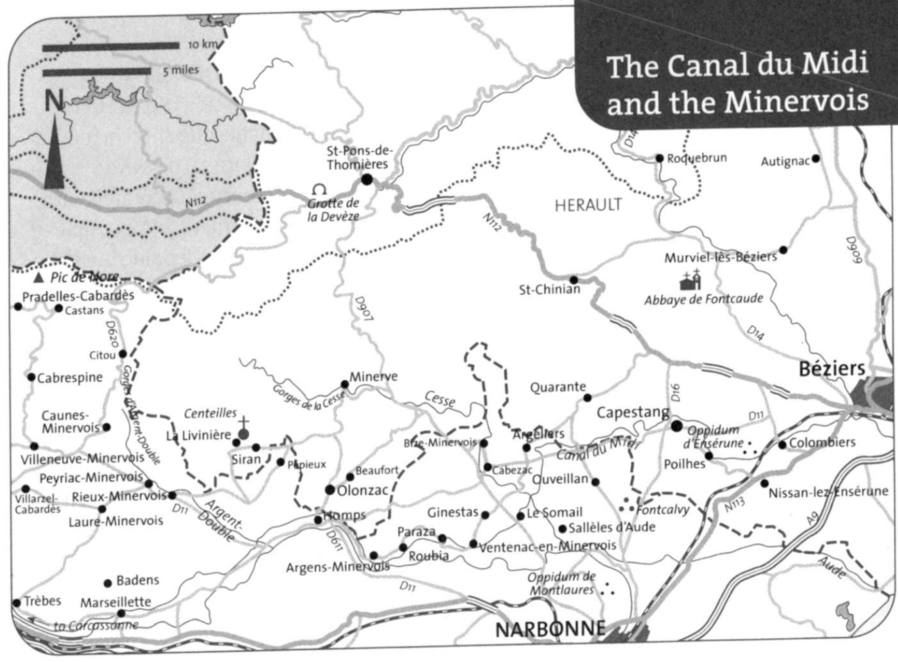

The Canal du Midi and the Minervois

Canal Villages

Most of these have at least one restaurant, some have guest-houses and boat rentals; all are agreeable spots to while away an afternoon. From Nissan, the D37 heads to **Poilhes**, a lovely, sleepy village built around one of Paul Riquet's graceful brick canal bridges. **Capestang**, the next one, has a landmark visible for miles around: the tall, unfinished Gothic **Collégiale St-Etienne**, a monument to unfulfilled ambition, like Narbonne cathedral, which indeed is believed to have been the work of the same architect. Capestang's rugged **château** is the summer home of the Archbishop of Narbonne; the interior includes a Renaissance ceiling fancifully painted with caricatures; ask at the tourist office about guided visits. A detour south of Capestang and just west of the village of **Ouveillan** will take you to an unusual medieval monument, the **Grange de Fontcalvy**. A testament to the wealth of the Cistercian order, this was a key stronghold of Fontfroide Abbey (*see* p.235), a fortified barn of considerable architectural sophistication, 66ft square, with ogival vaulting. Today it hosts the summer theatre and music Festival de Fontcalvy (*www.festival-fontcalvy.com*).

Collégiale St-Etienne
open June–Sept 10–12 and 4–7; tower visits by guided tour, summer 11, 5 and 6; adm

A Detour to Quarante

All along, the lands around the canal have been packed with vineyards. Further west, this continues but the countryside becomes lusher, with some of the cosiest landscapes in the Languedoc. Quarante isn't on the canal (although there's an impressive aqueduct nearby, one of Vauban's last works (1693), over the river Quarante), but it is worth a 4km side trip, north on D36/D37E, for its severe and dignified Romanesque church, the **Abbatiale Ste-Marie**, built between 982 and 1053. The *trésor* contains a marble sarcophagus of the 3rd century, decorated with angels and portraits of the deceased, and a remarkable example of Montpellier silversmithing from the 1440s: a very leonine bust of St John the Baptist with almond eyes and a Gallic nose.

Le Somail and Bize-Minervois: Hats and Olives

Librarie Ancienne du Somail
28 Allée de la Glacière, t 04 68 46 21 64, www.le-trouve-tout-du-livre.fr; open April–15 Nov 10–12 and 2.30–6.30; closed Tues exc in July and Aug; Dec–Mar closed mornings

Musée du Chapeau
3 Rue de la Bergerie, t 04 68 46 19 26; open Mar–Oct Mon–Sat 9–12 and 2–7; Nov–Feb 2–6; adm

L'Oulibo
t 04 68 41 88 88, www.loulibo.com

Back on the canal, across the Hérault border into the *département* of Aude, the string of villages continues with **Argeliers** and **Le Somail**, a sweet hamlet where the bargemen stop to take their afternoon naps. It has a great second-hand bookshop, the **Librarie Ancienne du Somail**, founded in 1960 in a building disassembled in Paris and brought here; there's also a barge supermarket, an ice house, chapel and a quirky **Musée du Chapeau**, with thousands of hats.

Just north of Le Somail, another diversion beckons: **Bize-Minervois,** a charming village with a delightul pebble beach on the river Cesse, complete with a lifeguard on summer afternoons. Once famous for garlic, Bize is now best known for its long, pale green, creamy dreamy Lucques, one of the world's best table olives, grown only in Languedoc-Roussillon; the region's biggest co-operative, **L'Oulibo,** founded in 1942, is 2km away at the hamlet of Cabezac. After a terrible frost in 1956 that destroyed 95 per cent of France's groves, Lucques olives have made a remarkable comeback (in 2011 they won a gold medal in Paris); at L'Oulibo you can pick up the locally made olives, oils, *tapenades* and cosmetics – all celebrated in July at Bize's olive festival. The striking 11th-century **Château de Cabezac** nearby with its four turrets is a favourite wedding venue (otherwise no adm).

Sallèles to Trèbes

Musée nphoralis
t 04 68 46 89 48, www.sallelesdaude.fr; open July–Sept daily 10–12 and 3–7; April–June Tues–Fri 2–6, Sat and Sun 10–12 and 2–6; closed Oct–Mar; adm

East of Le Somail, on the branch of the Canal de la Robine that leads to Narbonne, **Sallèles d'Aude** thinks you might like to see its dusty old pots at the **Musée Amphoralis**. It's more interesting than that. Archaeologists have excavated a large factory complex on this site from the 1st to 3rd centuries AD, one that made everything ceramic from roof tiles to amphorae. The Romans of those days complained that the Gauls were underselling local Italian production in everything from wine to pottery: evidence of a little bit of globalization even in antiquity. Old traditions are maintained with a potters' market in August.

Further west, on the main branch of the Canal du Midi are **Ventenac-en-Minervois**, **Paraza**, **Roubia** and **Argens-Minervois**, a once-fortified village with a ruined castle. The canal at this point runs parallel to the river Aude, and in places the two are only a few hundred feet apart. Near Roubia, the canal passes over a small stream on the **Pont-Canal de Répudre**. Paul Riquet designed this, too; it is the oldest canal bridge in France.

Further west comes **Homps**, with another ruined castle, built by the Knights Hospitallers, and the chance to take a two-hour jaunt on the canal with **Croisières du Midi**. There's a long, empty scenic stretch of the canal towards **Marseillette** in the Minervois, followed by **Trèbes**, a fortified village that has become a canal boating hub, with a triple set of locks and an impressive canal bridge over the Orb built by Vauban in 1686. Have a look inside the village church, **St-Etienne**; its impressive single nave holds a real curiosity: high up on the corbels that support the roof, where only God can see them well, are 320 small paintings of human and animal faces from the 14th century. No one knows who painted them or why; they were only discovered in 1977 when the plaster that covered them fell. Now they are restored, and a few of the best have been detached and displayed in one of the chapels.

Croisières du Midi
t 04 68 91 33 00, www.croisieres-du-midi.com; cruises run early April–Oct; ring ahead to book

Market Days by the Canal du Midi

Capestang: Wed and Sun am.

Where to Stay and Eat by the Canal du Midi

Nissan-lez-Ensérune ✉ 34440

****Résidence**, 35 Av de la Cave, **t** 04 67 37 00 63, *www.hotel-residence.com* (€€). Antiquated charm, with a pool and exceptionally good restaurant (€€€–€€) and a more modern annexe. *Closed mid-Dec–Jan; restaurant closed lunch, Sat and Mon.*

Le Somail ✉ 11120

Bed and breakfast, Le Somail, **t** 04 68 46 16 02, *www.canalmidi.com/bernabeu.htm* (€). In a charming 17th-century house. There is also a *gîte*. *Closed Nov–Feb.*

Bize-Minervois ✉ 11120

*****La Bastide Cabezac**, Cabezac, **t** 04 68 46 6610, *www.la-bastide-cabezac.com* (€€€–€€). Once an 18th-century post house, this delightful hotel has a dozen rooms and suites, a pool, and gastronomic restaurant, **L'Olivier** (€€€), with an excellent regional wine cellar. *Restaurant closed Sun eve and Mon.*

Homps ✉ 11120

****Auberge de l'Arbousier**, 50 Av de Carcassonne, Homps, **t** 04 68 91 11 24, *www.auberge-canaldumidi.com* (€€–€). A charming hotel-restaurant in an old *mas* on the banks of the canal; the kitchen specializes in cooking with local Minervois wine. *Closed Mon and Tues lunch and Sun eve.*

En Bonne Compagnie, 6 Quai des Negociants, **t** 04 68 91 23 16, *www.in-good-company.com* (€€). Friendly, British-run, serving good food right on the canal. *Closed Sun and Mon lunch.*

Trèbes ✉ 11800

*****Château de Floure**, 1 Allée Gaston Bonheur, Floure, **t** 04 68 79 11 29, *www.chateau-de-floure.com* (€€€€€). Just east of Trèbes, this ivy-covered château was a Romanesque abbey converted into a home by writer Gaston Bonheur. Now a Relais du Silence hotel, it has an elegant French garden, with pool and tennis, comfortable rooms and a good restaurant (€€€). *Closed mid-Nov–Feb.*

ⓘ Nissan-lez-Ensérune >
Square René Dez, t 04 67 37 14 12, www.office-detourisme-nissanlezenserune.fr; open Mon–Fri and Sat am

ⓘ Capestang
Maison Cantonnière, t 04 67 37 85 29, www.tourismecanaldumidi.fr; open Mon–Sat 9.30–12 and 2–5.30

North of the Canal: The Minervois

Half in the Hérault and half in the Aude, this is a *pays* with plenty of character, though not many people. With typical French irony, the Minervois suffered grievously from poverty and rural depopulation throughout the 20th century – then, just when everyone was gone, vintners improved the quality of their Minervois wines. They have become popular across France and the region's prosperity has returned. The Corbières (*see* pp.218–26) tells much the same story. In other ways, too, the Minervois is a prelude to the Corbières: the sharp contrast of tidy vineyards with ragged country and outcrops of eroded limestone, the sense of strangeness and isolation – in a region of France that has been inhabited for more or less 200,000 years.

Olonzac and Siran

Olonzac is the centre of the wine district and the closest thing the eastern Minervois has to a town. It is an attractive place with cafés under the trees and a holiday feel on warm days.

To the northwest, some of the most civilized landscapes in the Minervois lie around the village of **Siran**, with three remarkable if little-known attractions. Start in the east, with the biggest passage tomb in the south of France, the **Dolmen des Fadas** ('fairy dolmen') on a pine-covered hill, signposted just off the D52, 1km east of Siran (or 1.5km north of Pépieux, which has a mini version of the tomb on a roundabout). With a single 8ft-high capstone surviving *in situ*, it's a stunning sight, stretching 79ft through the remains of its mound, lined with slabs and dry stone walling; there are remnants of a 'porthole' entrance into its antechamber.

Chapelle de Centeilles
t 04 68 91 62 25; open 15 Mar–Nov Sun only 3–5

Then there's the 12th-century country church of **St-Germain-de-Cesseras**, with a beautifully sculpted apse (signposted off the D168), and the rare **Chapelle de Centeilles**, north of Siran, entirely covered inside with frescoes from the 13th to the 15th centuries, with a fragment of Roman mosaic. It stands by a now-capped holy well, believed to date to Megalithic times, whose juju perhaps exerts a beneficial influence on the wines made next door at the Clos Centeilles (*see* box, opposite) .

Minerve

From Olonzac, the narrow D10 leads into the heights of the Minervois, to **Minerve**, a town as old as any in Languedoc. Minerve is a natural place for a defensible settlement, on a steep rock between two rivers, but that does not explain why the area around it should have been so popular for so long. Traces of habitation dating back 170,000 years have been found in its caves, and Neolithic dolmens abound. The Celts and the Romans built the

Wine: Minervois

Rough and arid, protected from the cold winds of the north by the mountains, the sun-bleached region of AOC Minervois stretches from Carcassonne almost to St-Chinian. Its glories are supple but powerful red wines, dominated by mourvèdre, grenache, syrah and carignan, and with a lingering bouquet reminiscent of the *maquis*, that have long been one of the gems of Languedoc – the finest wines may require several years in the cellar to reach their best.

If you're passing by the Canal du Midi, you can stop to try some Minervois wines right by the canal at two spots: the **Domaine de Sérame, t** 04 68 27 02 47, *www.chateaudeserame.com*, an old *mas* just outside Argens, or the *cave coopérative* at the **Château de Ventenac**, Ventenac-en-Minervois **t** 04 68 43 27 34, *www.chateaude ventenacminervois.com*. Another excellent estate is **Château de Paraza**, high above the canal in Paraza, ✉ 11200 Lézignan, **t** 06 75 50 38 69, purchased in 2006 by the Danglas family. Towards Minerve in La Caunette, the **Domaine de Blayac**'s prize reds sell out quickly (**t** 04 68 91 26 70). The white wines of Minervois are among the revelations of recent years, clean and packed with character. Good examples are to be found at **Château La Grave** at Badens, **t** 04 68 79 16 00, *www.chateau-la-grave.net*. If you're short on time, head for **Le Chai de Port Minervois**, 35 Quai des Tonneliers, Port-Minervois (near Homps), **t** 04 68 91 29 48, *www.lechai-portminervois.com*.

Otherwise head west to seek out wines from the *appellation* **Minervois La Livinière**, a sunny, spicy red, and to a lesser extent white, wine based in seven villages in the semi-arid limestone plateau around La Livinière; try the wines from the excellent co-operative there or **Clos Centeilles** (in Centeilles, north of Siran, **t** 04 68 91 52 18, *www.closcenteilles.com*), owned by wine pioneer Patricia Boyer-Domergue, or at La Livinière the wines produced by the **Château Ste-Eulalie** (**t** 04 68 91 42 72, *www.chateausainte eulalie.com*) and **Château Laville Bertrou** (**t** 04 68 91 49 20, *www.gerard-bertrand.com*), one of former rugby man Gérard Bertrand's vineyards. At Laure-Minervois, taste the dark, exquisite Cuvée Alexandre at **Château Fabas**, on the Rieux road, **t** 04 68 78 17 82, *www.chateaufabas.com*. One of the most innovative producers in Minervois is **Château Maris**, based at La Livinière, **t** 04 68 91 42 63, *www.maris wine.com*, whose wines are notable for their depth and purity of flavour.

town itself, and in the Middle Ages it was a feudal stronghold with a Cathar slant. Minerve accepted refugees from the sack of Béziers in 1209; Simon de Montfort followed them and took the town after a two-month siege, followed by the usual butchery and burning of 140 Cathars at the stake. A full-size replica of a catapult by the ravine stands as a solemn reminder.

Minerve archaeology and palaeontology museum
t 04 68 91 22 92; open July–15 Sept 10.30–7; April–June and 15 Sept–mid-Nov 1.30–5.30; also open afternoons on Sun and during school holidays in winter

Musée Hurepel
t 04 68 91 12 26, www.ocmusic.org/hurepel.htm; open April–Sept daily 10.30–12.30 and 2–6; adm

Minerve today counts little over a hundred inhabitants; nothing has been done or built since Unspeakable Simon's visit, and the medieval relic on its dramatic site has become a peaceful and unambitious tourist attraction, with potters, artists and souvenir stands filling the spaces left by all the folk who have moved to the cities in the last 80 years. Parts of the walls are still in good nick, but all that is left of the château is a single, slender octagonal **tower**; the Minervois call it the '*candela*'. There are narrow medieval alleys, gates and cisterns, a simple 12th-century **church** with a white marble altar from 456, said to be the oldest in Europe, and a small **archaeology and palaeontology museum** with some fossils and prehistoric finds, across from a *caveau de dégustation* of Minervois wines. The **Musée Hurepel** in Rue des Martyrs tells the Cathar story (*see* pp.41–3) with figurines.

The real attractions, however, are out in the country. A short walk from town, there are 'natural bridges' – really more like tunnels, eroded through the limestone by streams. To the west extends the narrow, blushing pink **Canyon de la Cesse**, and determined hikers can seek out a collection of caves and dolmens north of this, at **Bois Bas**, off the D147.

The Seven-Sided Church of Rieux-Minervois

Rieux-Minervois
t 04 68 78 13 98; open 9–12 and 2–6

West of Siran, the Minervois flattens into the valley of the Argent-Double ('silver water'; *dubron* was a Celtic word for water, and the Romans made it *Argentodubrum*). An old bridge spans it for the village of Rieux, built around one of France's more uncanny medieval monuments.

The seven-pointed star is the recurring mystic symbol of the Midi. The Cathar castle at Montségur, in Ariège, was laid out subtly to fit inside its angles, the Félibres of Provence used it as part of their emblem, and it has been a recurring theme in folk art. Just what it means has never been adequately explained; neither has anyone ventured an explanation for the presence in this unremarkable Minervois village of what may be the only seven-sided church anywhere. Dedicated to the Virgin, the church was built some time in the late 12th century, exactly when, why and by whom, no one knows. A medieval scholar would have cited Scripture: 'Wisdom has built her house; she has set up her seven pillars' (*Proverbs* 1:9), also recalling that the Divine Wisdom was identified (at the time) with the Virgin Mary. Clearly, this temple opens a deep vein of intellectual medieval mysticism, full of geometry and allegory and not entirely recoverable by our minds. Its builders, pressed to explain why the central heptagon around the altar has four squat pilasters and three columns, might have mumbled something about the 'Marriage of Heaven and Earth' – the four-square world and the spiritual triangle. Modern investigators have also discovered various series of ley lines based on this site; according to them, the line of the midsummer sunrise passes from an altar inside the church through a (now closed-up) window and begins an alignment that goes as far as Minerve and St-Guilhem-le-Désert, passing several chapels dedicated to St John along the way.

The ambition of the builders of this church, and their resources, are seen in the sculptural detail inside, entrusted to the Master of Cabestany. Most of the capitals carved with fanciful foliage are by his workshop, while the Master himself is believed to have done the capitals with the reliefs of lions and the Assumption of the Virgin. Building in heptagons certainly must have tried the patience and mathematical know-how of a 12th-century mason; we can admire their careful work, especially the seven-sided belfry, directly over the altar, and the tricky toroid vaulting that connects the heptagon with the 14-sided exterior wall. Over the centuries, a

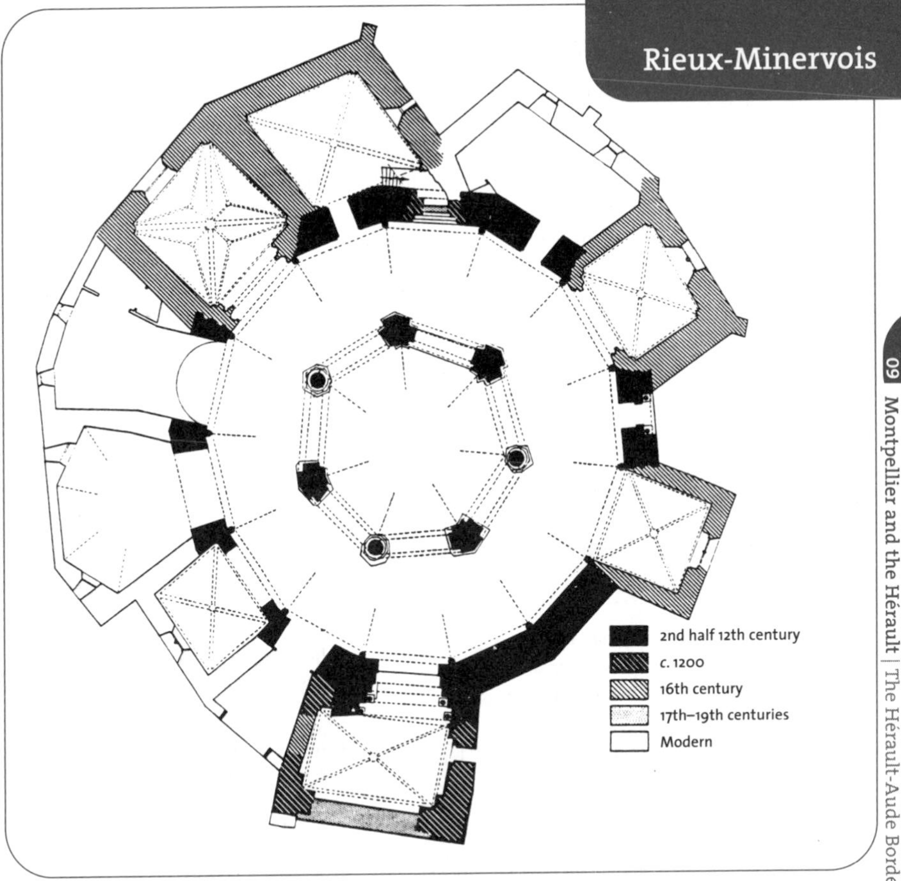

number of chapels have been built along the edges of the church; its exterior aspect, along with the original portal, are now lost.

Caunes-Minervois

The marble for Rieux's church came from **Caunes-Minervois**, just up the Argent-Double, which is also the source of the marble for the Great Mosque of Cordoba, St Peter's in Rome, the Paris Opera, and the Trianon at Versailles. It is rare for good stone in so many tints, from green to pink to reddish-orange, to occur in one place, and the **quarries**, in neatly geometrical excavations around Caunes, make an unusual sight. There is a path along the edge of the quarries with huge chunks of marble left lying around (signposted from the village). Over the centuries they have made Caunes more prosperous and open to the world than its neighbours. Its streets show some modest palaces, such as the Hôtel d'Alibert on the main square, along with the former abbey church of **St-Pierre-et-St-Paul**, founded in the 8th century by Benedict of Aniane, a hotchpotch of Gothic, Romanesque and later styles, conserving

St-Pierre-et-St-Paul
t 04 68 78 09 44, www.mairiedecaunes.fr; open summer 10–12 and 2–7; winter 10–12 and 2–5; adm

some odd capitals from the Carolingian original. a good 13th-century portal, and cloister.

North of Caunes, the D620 leads past the quarries into the narrow and scenic Gorge de l'Argent-Double. Onion lovers should stop to pay homage at **Citou**, the cradle of France's sweetest 'no-more tears' onions.

South of Caunes towards Carcassonne, on a hill just outside **Laure-Minervois**, the 49ft **Allée Couverte de St-Eugène** is the third largest dolmen in the south, and makes a nice companion piece to the Dolmen des Fadas (*see* p.186), similarly built of slabs and drystone walls, set in a circular stone cairn. Laure-Minervois is also the home of the **Domaine Vignalet,** a wine estate that gave up its tractors and runs on horse power; you can combine a horse-drawn carriage ride through the vines with a wine-tasting tour. They also have rooms.

Domaine Vignalet
t 04 68 78 12 03, www.vignalet.com; tours May–mid-Sept at 5pm (allow two hours); adm

Market Days in the Minervois

Olonzac: Tues.

Rieux-Minervois: Tues, Thurs and Sat.

Laure-Minervois: Sun.

Where to Stay and Eat in the Minervois

Olonzac ✉ 34210

Restaurant du Minervois, 2 Rue des Ecoles, **t** 04 68 91 20 73, *www.belminervois.com* (€€). Dine on gourmet treats (*cappuccino de cèpes* with truffles) near the lake on the shady patio. *Closed Sat lunch, and eves in winter.*

Siran ✉ 34210

******Château de Siran**, Av du Château, **t** 04 68 91 55 98, *www.chateau-de-siran.com* (€€€–€€). Offers charming, comfortable rooms and an excellent restaurant with new owners as of 2010 (€€€). See their website for an array of special packages and wine workshops.

Minerve ✉ 34210

***Relais Chantovent**, 17 Grand-Rue, Minerve, **t** 04 68 91 14 18, *www.relaischantovent-minerve.fr* (€). The only hotel in Minerve, with seven rooms; it also has a fine restaurant (€€€–€€) with a terrace overlooking the gorge, serving truffles. *Closed mid-Nov–mid-Mar; restaurant closed Sun eve and Mon.*

Auberge de St-Martin, south of Minerve in Beaufort, **t** 04 68 91 16 18 (€€). A sweet old *mas* with a shady terrace, offering wood-fire grilled meat and fish and a variety of regional dishes (such as artichoke flan with parmesan) which change seasonally. *Closed Mon May–Sept; Sun eve, Mon, and Tues eve Oct–April.*

Rieux-Minervois ✉ 11160

Logis de Mérinville, Av Georges Clemenceau, Rieux-Minervois, **t** 04 68 78 12 49 (€€€–€€). An atmospheric 19th-century stone inn in the village centre, serving good food. *Closed Nov, Jan–Mar, Tues eve and Wed.*

Caunes-Minervois ✉ 11160

****Hôtel d'Alibert**, Place de la Mairie, **t** 04 68 78 00 54, *www.caunesminervois.com* (€€). A sweet little place to stay, with seven rooms in a romantic *hôtel particulier*, and good regional food in the restaurant. *Closed mid-Nov–mid-Mar, and Sun eve and Mon.*

★ **Auberge de St-Martin >>**

ⓘ **Rieux-Minervois >>**
5 Rue Saint Blaise, t 04 68 78 13 98; open daily all year

ⓘ **Minerve >**
9 Rue des Martyrs, t 04 68 91 81 43, www.minerve-tourisme.fr; open Tues–Sat

Carcassonne and the Aude

The Aude is famous for wine and castles – and it has plenty of both. Western Languedoc traditionally fills an ample bay of the European Union's wine lake, and after centuries of complacency it is also beginning to produce some really good wine. The castles, on the other hand, have always been strictly AOC.

Before the border with Spain was definitively drawn in 1659, the Languedoc was a hotly contested region for a thousand years, disputed first by Visigoths and Saracens, and finally by Madrid and Paris. The French determination to hold it has left us Carcassonne, queen of all medieval castles, cloud-top Cathar redoubts like Aguilar and Quéribus, and over a hundred others, in every shape, colour and style known to military science.

10

Don't miss

See map overleaf

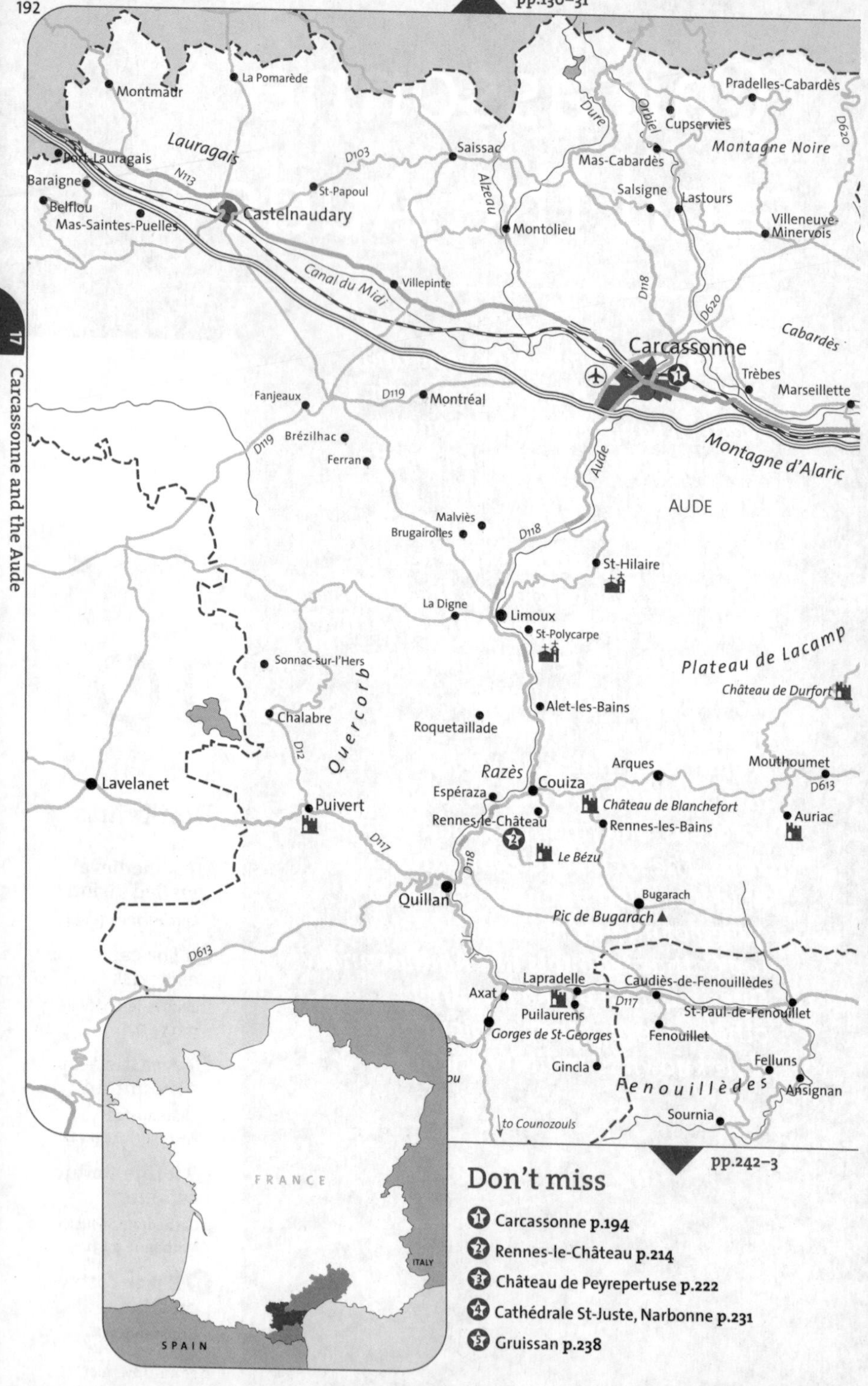

Don't miss

1. Carcassonne **p.194**
2. Rennes-le-Château **p.214**
3. Château de Peyrepertuse **p.222**
4. Cathédrale St-Juste, Narbonne **p.231**
5. Gruissan **p.238**

pp.130–31

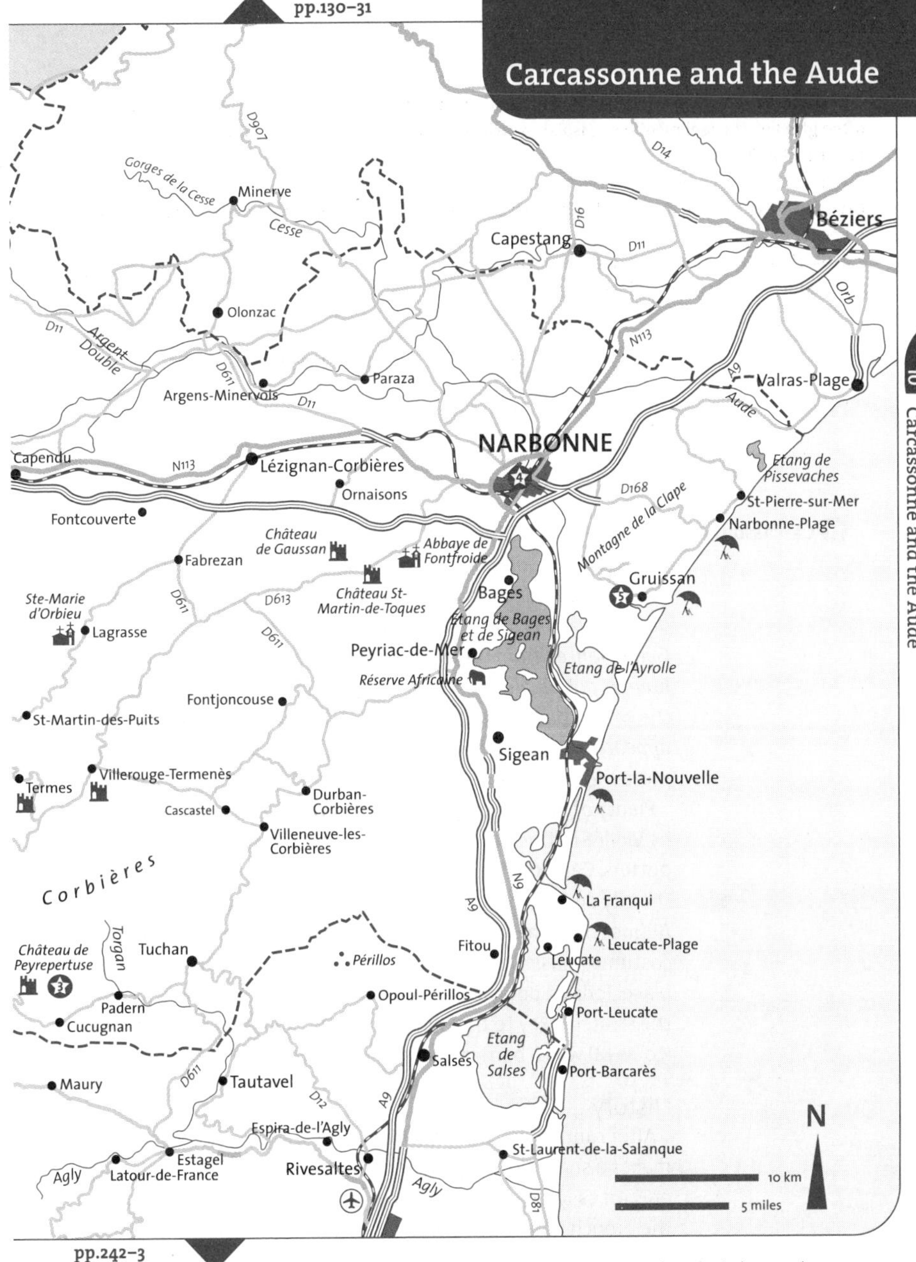

pp.242–3

The modern fascination with the Cathars has led the Aude to brand itself the *pays Cathar*, or Cathar country, attracting thousands of visitors, many to keen to learn more and perhaps get in touch with some of the bushels of esoterica that have emerged around them in recent years: and Rennes-le-Château is only the beginning of it. But there's a strange beauty to the Aude as well: seldom does the Midi offer a greater jumble of landscapes, with

Beaches

From Narbonne south into Spain is really just one long beach. The sand is perfect and the lagoons often give you the feeling of being isolated on a desert island, amongst sand dunes and flocks of summer flamingos.

The best beaches are:

Gruissan Plage: setting for the cult film *Betty Blue*; a wide expanse of sand populated by curious raised houses on stilts.

Port-la-Nouvelle: un-chic; watch the tankers roll by.

La Franqui: a simple, old-fashioned family beach.

wild mountain gorges just an hour's ride from sandy coastal lagoons where the *tramontane* can blow your hat off.

Carcassonne

Standing before the great eastern gate of the walled city, the writer had his notebook out and was scribbling furiously. It was market day, and rustic villeins in coarse wool tunics were offering hung pheasants and great round cheeses from their wooden carts. Geese honked from cages made of twigs and rushes, while pigs and hounds poked about in the cobbled gutters. 'This is medieval indeed,' the writer mused – and just then the director and his entourage appeared over the drawbridge. 'Lovely, everyone, but we'll want more sheep; lots more sheep!'

Plenty of obscure costume dramas have been shot here, drawn by Viollet-le-Duc's romantic restoration. Even without pigs in the gutters, Carcassonne is the Middle Ages come to life. The people of the city do their best to heighten the medieval atmosphere: every August there are various medieval-themed events with artisans in costume, music and jousts. Reality intrudes in the history of the place. Today a dour manufacturing town, Carcassonne was once the strategic key to the Midi; the castle built here by Saint Louis (Louis IX) was a barrier to invaders greater than the Pyrenees.

History

After running north down from the Pyrenees, the river Aude makes a sharp right turn for the sea, conveniently providing not only an easy natural route into the mountains, but also one across the 'French isthmus', between the Mediterranean and the Atlantic. The river's angle, one of the crossroads of France since prehistoric times, is an obvious site for a fortress; there seems to have been one nearby since the 8th century BC. The Tectosage Gauls occupied the site of the present Cité in the 3rd century BC; a century later the Romans established a fortified veterans' colony on it called Carcaso, which gradually grew into a town. With the coming of the Visigoths in the Germanic invasions of the 5th century AD,

Getting to and around Carcassonne

By Air

Carcassonne's airport is 5km west of town, **t** 04 68 71 96 46, *www.carcassonne.aeroport.fr*. There are direct flights from the UK (*see* **Planning Your Trip**) and Ireland; a shuttle service links the **airport** to the Cité, Place Gambetta and the station.

By Train and Bus

From the **train station**, on Av du Maréchal Joffre at the northern edge of the Ville Basse, there are regular connections to Toulouse, Narbonne, and from there to all the coastal cities; other trains go down the Aude valley to Limoux and Quillan.

There are several **bus** companies going to towns and villages outside Carcassonne; contact **Cars Teissier**, **t** 04 68 25 85 45, *www.teissier.fr*, or **Agglo' Bus**, **t** 04 68 10 56 00, *www.agglocarcassonnais.fr*.

To get up to the Cité from the lower town, take the no.8 city bus from Place Gambetta.

By Car

There is a huge **car park** outside Porte Narbonnaise, but expect to pay €6 a day. Otherwise, you need to be up at the crack of dawn to find a space in summer.

Bike and Boat Hire

Hire **bicycles** at **Evasion 2 Roues**, 85 Allée d'Iéna, **t** 04 68 11 90 40, or a **canal boat** by the weekend or week from **Canaolous**, 15 Quai Riquet, **t** 04 68 71 88 95, *www.canalous-canaldumidi.com*. **Lou Gabaret** offers barge rides and picnics on the Canal du Midi from the port, April–Oct (except Mon out of season), **t** 04 68 71 61 26, *www.carcassonne-croisiere.com*.

Other Ways of Seeing the Cité

Carriage rides leave from Porte Narbonnaise for a trot around Les Lices, April–mid-Nov, **t** 04 68 71 54 57, *www.carcassonne-caleches.com*; a **tourist train** leaves from the same area for a visit of the towers and ramparts, May–Sept, **t** 04 68 24 45 70, *www.petit-train-cite-carcassonne.com*.

Carcassonne began to assume its historic role as a border stronghold between France and Spain – the Frankish and Visigothic kingdoms. The action started as early as AD 506, when the Frankish King Clovis unsuccessfully besieged the town.

Arabs from Spain arrived about 725, one of the high-water marks of the Muslim tide in Europe. Pepin the Short chased them out 30 years later. Not that the Franks could hold it either. With the collapse of the Carolingian Empire, local viscounts attained a *de facto* independence. From 1084 to 1209, Carcassonne enjoyed a glorious period of wealth and culture under the Trencavels, a family who were also viscounts of Béziers and Nîmes. Under them, the cathedral and the Château Comtal were begun.

Simon de Montfort, realizing the importance of the town, made it one of his first stops in the Crusade of 1209. The last viscount, Raymond-Roger Trencavel, was no Cathar but a gentleman and a patriot, determined to oppose the planned rape of Languedoc by the northerners. His famous declaration is still remembered today: 'I offer a town, a roof, a shelter, bread and my sword to all the persecuted people who will soon be wandering in Provence.' Unfortunately, Trencavel allowed himself to be tricked outside the Cité walls on pretence of negotiation; he was put in chains and the leaderless town surrendered soon after. Raymond-Roger died in

Gare
Port
AV MARECHAL JOFFRE
AV MARECHAL FOCH
RUE TOURTEL
BOULEVARD OMER SARRAUT
RUE ANTOINE MARTY
ALLEE D'IENA
Canal du Midi
RUE DE LA LIBERTE
RUE DE LA LIBERTE
VILLE BASSE
BOULEVARD JEAN JAURES
BOULEVARD DE VARSOVIE
RUE DE 4 SEPTEMBRE
RUE DE 4 SEPTEMBRE
Gare Regionale
St-Vincent
RUE ALBERT TOMEY
RUE DE LA REPUBLIQUE
RUE DE LA REPUBLIQUE
RUE VICTOR HUGO
RUE VICTOR HUGO
PLACE CARNOT
RUE JULES SAUZERE
ALLEE D'IENA
RUE DE VERDUN
RUE DE VERDUN
BD VARILLA
PL DAVILLA
To Airport
BOULEVARD MARCOU
Maison des Mémoires
Halles aux Grains
Musée des Beaux Arts
SQUARE GAMBETTA
RUE AIME RAMOND
BOULEVARD CAMILLE PELLETAN
RUE DU PONT
Cathédrale St-Michel
RUE VOLTAIRE
BOULEVARD BARBES
BOULEVARD BARBES
BOULEVARD CDT ROUMENS
R. DES TROIS COURONNES
Aude
N
250 m
250 yds

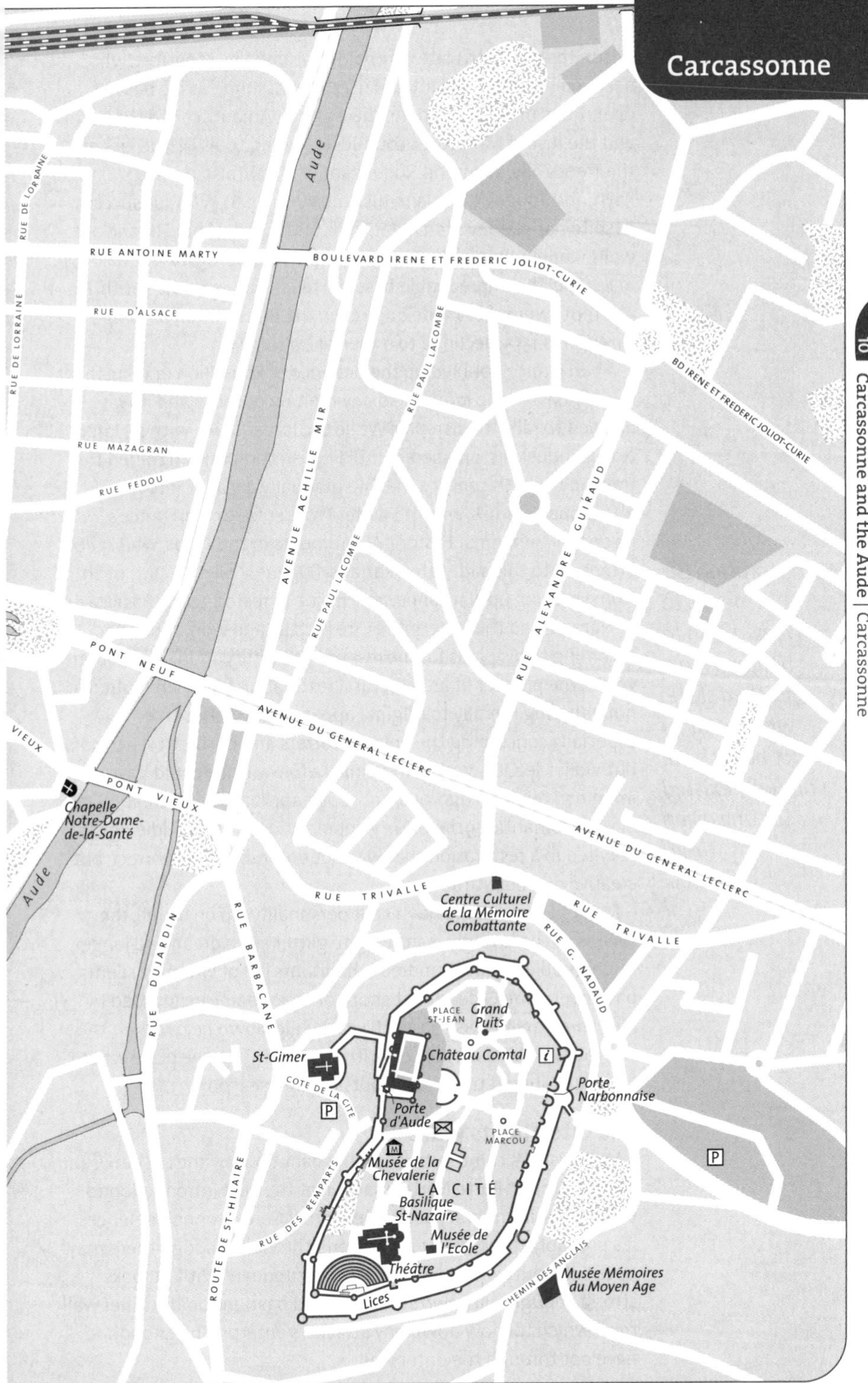
RUE DE LORRAINE
RUE ANTOINE MARTY
BOULEVARD IRENE ET FREDERIC JOLIOT-CURIE
RUE D'ALSACE
Aude
RUE PAUL LACOMBE
BD IRENE ET FREDERIC JOLIOT-CURIE
RUE MAZAGRAN
RUE FEDOU
AVENUE ACHILLE MIR
RUE ALEXANDRE GUIRAUD
PONT NEUF
AVENUE DU GENERAL LECLERC
PONT VIEUX
Chapelle Notre-Dame-de-la-Santé
RUE TRIVALLE
Centre Culturel de la Mémoire Combattante
RUE DUJARDIN
RUE BARBACANE
RUE G. NADAUD
PLACE ST-JEAN
Grand Puits
St-Gimer
Château Comtal
Porte Narbonnaise
COTE DE LA CITE
Porte d'Aude
PLACE MARCOU
Musée de la Chevalerie
LA CITÉ
Basilique St-Nazaire
RUE DES REMPARTS
ROUTE DE ST-HILAIRE
Musée de l'Ecole
Théâtre
CHEMIN DES ANGLAIS
Musée Mémoires du Moyen Age
Lices

prison three months later, probably poisoned by Montfort, who declared himself viscount and used Carcassonne as his base of operations until his death in 1218. His son, Amauri, ceded the town and the rest of Montfort's conquests to King Louis IX. The last of the Trencavels, Raymond-Roger's son and heir, also named Raymond, fought to reclaim his lands until 1240, without success despite popular revolts. Under Louis and his son, Philip III, the outer walls were built, making the entire town into the greatest fortress in Europe, the impregnable base of French power in the south. No attempts were ever made on it; even the Black Prince, passing through in 1355, declined to undertake a siege.

When France gobbled up the province of Roussillon in 1659, this mighty bastion no longer had any military purpose and it was allowed to fall into disrepair. While the lower town, with its large textile industries, prospered until English competition ruined the trade in the 19th century, the Cité gradually decayed into a half-abandoned slum. It was the writer Prosper Mérimée, France's Inspector-General of Historic Monuments in the 1830s, who called attention to this sad state of affairs. Eugène Viollet-le-Duc, fresh from sprucing up Narbonne, got the job of restoring the Basilica de St Nazaire, and then the entire Cité in 1844, and work continued according to his plans for the rest of the century. As in all his other works, the pioneer of architectural restoration has been faulted for not adhering literally to original appearances. This is true, especially concerning the pointed turrets and northern slate roofs, but Viollet-le-Duc worked in a time before anyone could have imagined our own rigorous, antiseptic approach to re-creating the old. His romantic, 19th-century appreciation of the Middle Ages resulted in a restoration that was not only essentially correct, but creative and beautiful.

restoration is… 'a means to reestablish [a building] to a finished state, which may in fact never have actually existed at any given time.'
Viollet-le-Duc

Today's Carcassonne has a split personality: up on its hill, the 52 towers of the lovingly restored Cité glitter like a dream, no longer impregnable; its few hundred inhabitants (all of whom, it seems, have opened Ye Olde tourist shops or snack bars) are invaded by over three million visitors each year, while, down below, the workaday Ville Basse gets on with the job. This is one place where you really should try to come outside high season.

The Cité and its Walls

Most visitors come in through the back door, by the car parks and the bus stop at **Porte Narbonnaise**. Not the best introduction to the impressive military sophistication of Carcassonne's defences, it's probably the weakest point along the walls, though there may have been outworks that have since disappeared. Still, it looks strong enough, with two stout rounded bastions on the inner wall from which to mow down any attackers enterprising enough to have got through the outer wall.

Between the two walls, you can circumnavigate the Cité by the open space called **Les Lices**, the 'lists', where knights trained and where tournaments were held. The **outer wall** is Louis IX's work; note how it is completely open on the inside, so attackers who stormed it would have no protection from the defenders on the **inner wall**. Parts of this date back to the Romans – wherever you see large, irregular blocks without mortar, or layers of smaller stones interspersed with courses of thin brick. The ground level within the lists was slightly lowered by the French, so that you will often see their rectangular stones, either smooth or rusticated, beneath Roman work, where they had to underpin the towers.

To the right of the Porte Narbonnaise, the first large tower is the mighty **Tour du Trésau**. Beyond it, the northern side of the inner wall is almost completely Roman, begun in the 1st century and rebuilt in the Imperial decline of the 4th century, like the walls of Rome itself, with the characteristic rounded bastions used all over the Empire. Near the second-last of them is a Roman postern gate. The walls to the left of the Porte Narbonnaise were almost completely rebuilt under Philip III, a long stretch of bastions culminating in the great **Tour St-Nazaire**.

Atop both the inner and outer walls, almost everything you see – the crenellations, wooden galleries (*hourds*) and pointed turrets that make up Carcassonne's memorable skyline – is the work of Viollet-le-Duc.

Château Comtal

Approaching the Cité from the western side, above the river, you pass the Gothic church of **St-Gimer**, ascending to the **Porte d'Aude**. In the old days, you couldn't come empty-handed; the Cité has no natural source of water and commoners from the Ville Basse had to bring up two buckets each time to get in. The Porte d'Aude was the ultimate discouragement for an attacker, employing every trick in the medieval bag. Note, for example, how the approach comes from the right; to protect themselves, soldiers on the way up would have to keep their shields in their right hand, making it difficult to do anything else. The winding path made it impossible to use a battering ram on the gate, and attackers would be under fire from the walls the entire way; there is another gate inside, and if anyone got through the first they would find themselves trapped in a box, under fire from all sides.

Château Comtal
t 04 68 11 70 70, www.carcassonne.monuments-nationaux.fr; open April–Sept daily 9.30–6.30; Oct–Mar daily 9.30–5; closed most public hols; adm exp; audioguides available; guided tours last 40 or 90mins, usually on the hour, schedule posted at the entrance

The protection is strongest on the western side because here the Cité's three lines of defence are closely compressed – the outer ar inner walls and the citadel, the **Château Comtal**. Probably the of the Roman governors' palace, the château was rebuilt by Trencavels for their own palace, and expanded by King Lc protect his seneschal from the locals. The guided tour and towers begin with a room-sized model and continue, in fascinating, excruciating detail, through an advanced course in medieval military architecture. Louis' builders laid as many traps for invaders inside the walls as without – for example, the stairways where each riser is a different height. Be careful.

The château houses ancient and medieval fragments: from Roman inscriptions and milestones to Merovingian sarcophagi and country roadside crosses (in local folklore, erroneously believed to be tombstones of the Cathars). Old prints and paintings give an idea of the half-ruined state of the Cité before Viollet-le-Duc went to work on it, with houses half-filling Les Lices and windmills along the walls. Two medieval works saved from the town's churches are especially worth a look: an unusual 15th-century English alabaster of the Transfiguration, and an excellent sculpted altarpiece, with a host of expressive faces in attendance.

Near here, a little square holds the impressive Grand Puits, the largest of the Cité's 22 wells, and one reputed to hold the legendary treasure of Solomon, stuffed down there by the Visigoths. If anyone has actually found it over the centuries, they've not told.

Basilique St-Nazaire

Basilique St-Nazaire *open summer daily 9–12 and 2–7; winter Mon–Sat 9–12 and 2–5; Sun Mass 11am*

The epitaph says, for those who can read it,
That he is a saint and martyr who shall breathe again
And shall in wonderous joy inherit and flourish
And wear a crown and sit on a heavenly throne.
And I have heard it said that this must be so –
If by killing men and spilling blood,
By ruining souls, and preaching murder,
By following evil counsels, and raising fires,
By ruining noblemen and besmirching honour,
By pillaging the country, and by exalting Pride,
By stoking up wickedness and stifling good,
By massacring women and their infants,
A man can win Jesus in this world,
then Simon surely wears a crown, respondent in heaven.

13th-century Cathar Wars song, on Simon de Montfort's tomb

In 1096 (the year after he declared the First Crusade), Pope Urban V visited Carcassonne, giving his blessing to the beginning -f the works. The building took shape as an austere, typically ›uthern Romanesque cathedral, and stayed that way until 1270. ne French conquerors had more ambitious plans, and rebuilt the ansepts and choir in glorious perpendicular Gothic. The best eatures can be seen from outside: two vast rose windows, a tall pse with acres of windows, and gargoyles projecting like cannons.

The windows illuminate the interior with beautiful 16th- and 7th-century stained glass depicting the Tree of Jesse and Life of

Christ. In the right aisle, pay your respects to the devil himself at the **tomb of Simon de Montfort**, marked by a small plaque. Understandably, Montfort is no longer present; six years after his death, his descendants took him back up north, where he would be less in danger of desecration. The plaque is near a 13th-century stone relief of a siege, perhaps the one of Toulouse where de Montfort got his come-uppance.

There are several small private museums in and around the Cité. The **Musée de l'Ecole** recreates a 19th-century French school, at 3 Rue du Plô. Museums dedicated to all things medieval include the **Musée de la Chevalerie**, in 2 Rue Porte d'Aude, the collection of a former castle-owning enthusiast, who often consults on films about the Middle Ages – and sells replica medieval gear as well, in case you feel like making your own knight and fair maiden adventure. There's also the **Musée Mémoires du Moyen-Age**, just outside the Cité, near Porte Narbonnaise, with videos and models of the Cité, costumes, weapons and so on – great fun for kids. Rushing forward in history, there's the **Centre Culturel de la Mémoire Combattante**, a museum on French military exploits from 1870 on, outside the Cité at 102 Rue Trivalle.

Musée de l'Ecole
t 04 68 25 95 14; open summer daily 10–7; winter daily 10–6; closed Jan

Musée de la Chevalerie
t 04 68 72 75 51, www.musee-chevalerie.com; open April–Oct Tues–Sun 10–1 and 3–7; closed Mon; adm

Musée Mémoires du Moyen-Age
t 04 68 71 08 65; open all year except Xmas hols daily 10–7; adm

Centre Culturel de la Mémoire Combattante
t 04 68 72 40 16; open Mon–Fri 9–12 and 2–6; free

The Ville Basse, or Bastide Saint-Louis

Before Saint Louis (Louis IX), the Cité was surrounded by long-established suburbs. In 1240 these were occupied by Raymond Trencavel, son of the last viscount. With the help of the townspeople, he besieged the Cité and nearly took it back. Louis pardoned the rebels, but did find it necessary to knock their houses down, to deprive any future attackers of cover. To replace the old *bourg*, he laid out a new town across the river, in the strict (and here, rather drab) grid pattern of a *bastide*, a medieval new town, one of hundreds built by the French and English rulers during the Hundred Years' War.

Descending from the Cité through the Porte d'Aude, you'll pass some streets of houses that managed to creep back despite the royal decree. **Rue Trivalle**, with a pair of elegant Renaissance *hôtels particuliers*, leads down to the long, 14th-century **Pont Vieux** and one of the finest views of the Cité. At the far end, there once was a sort of triumphal arch, as can be seen in the old prints in the Château Comtal. Now there remains only the chapel of **Notre-Dame-de-la-Santé**, built in 1538.

The Ville Basse proper begins two streets further down, with a circle of boulevards that replaced the old walls. In 1355, during the Hundred Years' War, the walls failed to keep out the Black Prince, who burned the *bastide* to the ground after he was unable to take the Cité. Only the street plan survived and, at the north and south ends, two huge, mouldering Gothic churches: **St-Vincent** and **St-Michel**, both begun under Louis IX, both on Rue Dr Tomey.

Centre for Cathar Studies
t 04 68 72 45 55; open Tues–Sat 9–12 and 2–6; free

Musée des Beaux Arts
t 04 68 77 73 70; open mid-June–mid-Sept daily 10–6; mid-Sept–mid-June Tues–Sat 10–12 and 2–6, first Sun of month 2.30–5.30

Parc Australien
t 04 68 25 05 07; www.leparcaustralien.wifeo.com; open July–Aug daily 10.30–7.30; April–June and mid-Sept–mid-Nov daily 2–7

Parc Acrobatique Forestier
t 06 07 96 04 55, www.wanside2.wordpress.com; open June–Aug daily 1–6; winter Wed, Sat, Sun and hols 1–6; closed Dec–Feb; adm

St-Michel was restored by Viollet-le-Duc and serves as co-cathedral with St-Nazaire in the Cité.

A *bastide* was always built around a central market square (here, pretty **Place Carnot** with a fountain of Neptune), while one street over, off Rue de Verdun, you can see the handsome 18th-century **Halles aux Grains**.

You can learn all about the famous heretics at the **Centre for Cathar Studies** in the **Maison des Mémoires**, 53 Rue de Verdun, in the Ville Basse; this was the home of Carcassonne's contribution to Surrealism, Joë Bousquet, and there's a display about him, and another organization dedicated to the study of folk traditions in the Aude. At 1 Rue de Verdun, the 17th-century **Présidial** houses the **Musée des Beaux Arts**, with paintings and decorative arts from the 17th–19th centuries, including works by Corot, Chardin and Courbet.

Outside Carcassonne, learn about animals, art and music from Down Under at the well-signposted **Parc Australien**, Chemin des Bartavelles, on the way out to Lac de la Cavayère. And in the same direction there's the **Parc Acrobatique Forestier** for playing Tarzan in the trees at the **Complexe de Loisirs Raymond Chésa**, where there's also a lake, pedalos, picnic area and mini-golf.

Market Days in Carcassonne

Tues, Thurs and Sat: Pl Carnot, flowers, fruit and veg, and Bd Barbès, clothes.

Shopping

Le Vieux Lavoir, 11 Rue de Plô, **t** 04 68 71 00 04, *levieuxlavoir.canalblog.com*. Handmade arts and crafts from around Languedoc-Roussillon.

In most of Carcassonne's *pâtisseries* you can satisfy your sweet tooth on the local favourite, *boulets de Carcassonne*, which are made with peanuts and honey. There's also a Vin de Pays de la Cité de Carcassonne.

Where to Stay in Carcassonne

Carcassonne ✉ 11000

Luxury (€€€€€)

********Hôtel de la Cité**, Place Auguste-Pierre Pont, **t** 04 68 71 98 71, *www.hoteldelacite.com*. In a pretty garden beside the walls of the Cité, this hotel (now part of the Orient Express group) occupies the former episcopal palace, grandly restored in 1909, and filled with wonderful medieval details (Walt Disney stayed here while thinking up plans for Sleeping Beauty's castle in Disneyland); families welcome, and there's a pool and three restaurants.

********Domaine d'Auriac**, Rte St-Hilaire, south of town, **t** 04 68 25 72 22, *www.domaine-d-auriac.com*. This Relais & Châteaux hotel is a stately, ivy-covered 18th-century mansion set in a large park. There's a pool, tennis court and a golf course close by. Also an elegant and highly rated restaurant (€€€€), featuring mostly traditional dishes of the Aude, such as pigeon, served here with truffles. *Closed Jan; restaurant closed Mon lunch, Tues lunch, Wed lunch, plus Sun eve and Mon eve out of season.*

Expensive (€€€)

*******Hôtel du Donjon**, Rue du Comte Roger, **t** 04 68 11 23 00, *www.hotel-donjon.fr*. An atmospheric old mansion in the Cité filled with suits of armour, with a small garden and a fine restaurant.

ⓘ **Carcassonne >**
Ville Basse: 28 Rue de Verdun, t 04 68 10 24 30, www.carcassonne-tourisme.com; open daily
Cité: Porte Narbonnaise, t 04 68 10 24 36; open daily

★ 42 Rue Victor Hugo >

★ Le Parc Franck Putelat >>

★ Demeure Saint-Louis >

*****Hôtel du Château**, 2 Rue Camille St-Saens, **t** 04 68 11 38 38, *www.hotelduchateau-carcassonne.com*. Just outside the gate of the Cité, this cosy boutique hotel has a heated pool, private parking, and a nearby spa – but no restaurant.

42 Rue Victor Hugo, **t** 09 77 52 44 36, *www.42ruevictorhugo.com*. Two designer apartments and a B&B suite for couples in this lovely home away from home just off Place Carnot, run by the delightful Debrah Smith and Peter Woodcock; special gourmet breaks available.

*****Trois Couronnes**, 2 Rue des Trois Couronnes, **t** 04 68 25 36 10, *www.hotel-destroiscouronnes.com*. Modern hotel by the river in the lower town; makes up for its unprepossessing appearance with a superb view of the Cité, an indoor pool on the 4th floor and a very good restaurant.

*****Château de Cavanac**, Cavanac, 4km south on the Rte St-Hilaire, **t** 04 68 79 61 04, *www.chateau-de-cavanac.fr*. A big old wine-maker's house in a quiet garden, with an excellent restaurant in the former stables that serves a unique four-course menu, starting with a peach kir. You can also taste and buy their wines. *Closed Jan–Feb and 2 weeks Nov; restaurant closed Sun eve and Mon.*

Moderate (€€)

*****Bristol**, 7 Av Foch, **t** 04 68 25 07 24, *www.hotelbristol-carcassonne.com*. Recently rennovated grand 19th-century hotel near the station, with rooms overlooking the Canal du Midi; restaurant and brasserie.

****Hôtel du Pont Vieux**, 32 Rue Trivalle, **t** 04 68 25 24 99, *www.lacitedecarcassonne.fr*. One of the best and closest hotels to the Cité; some rooms in the inexpensive range. No restaurant.

Demeure Saint-Louis, 2 Rue Michel Sabatier, **t** 04 68 72 39 04, *www.demeure-saint-louis.fr*. Four cushy B&B rooms and a splendid breakfast on Limoge porcelain, midway between the Cité and Ville Basse.

Inexpensive (€)

Le Grand Puits, 8 Place du Grand Puits, **t** 04 68 25 16 67, *legrandpuits.free.fr*. Atmospheric rooms in the heart of the Cité; book well in advance.

****Hôtel Central**, 27 Bd Jean Jaurès (Ville Basse), **t** 04 68 25 03 84, *www.hotelcentral-carcassonne.com*. Pleasant hotel with family rooms, 500m from the station.

***Astoria**, 18 Rue Tourtel (Ville Basse), **t** 04 68 25 31 38, *www.astoriacarcassonne.com*. A friendly, family-run place, with comfy décor.

Auberge de Jeunesse, Rue Raymond Trencavel, **t** 04 68 25 23 16. In the Cité, a friendly place, with free Wi-fi. Reserve in summer, or book online at *www.fuaj.org*. *Closed mid-Dec–Jan.*

Eating Out in Carcassonne

Le Parc Franck Putelat, Chemin des Anglais, **t** 04 68 71 80 80, *www.leparcfranckputelat.com* (€€€€). Zen serenity in the dining room and garden, featuring some of the region's top creative and occasional whimsical cuisine. €25 lunch menu. *Closed Sun, Mon.*

La Barbacane, Pl Auguste-Pierre-Pont, **t** 04 68 71 98 71, *www.hoteldelacite.com* (€€€€). Superb medieval atmosphere and top-notch cuisine in the Hôtel de la Cité. *Closed Tues, Wed, Feb–mid-Mar.*

Atelier Robert Rodriguez, 39 Rue Coste-Reboulh, **t** 04 68 47 37 80, *restaurantrobertrodriguez.com* (€€€). Robert Rodriguez has a moustache nearly as big as Dalí's, and prepares some of the region's best traditional dishes prepared with top organic ingredients. Try his less pricey **Cantine de Robert**, Place de Lattre-de-Tassigny (same phone). *Atelier closed Sun, Mon, Wed and Aug–Feb. Cantine closed Sun and Wed dinner.*

Château St-Martin, Montredon (take Bd Jean Jaurès to Rue A. Marty and follow the signs), **t** 04 68 71 09 53, *www.chateausaintmartin.net* (€€€). This handsome *gentilhommière* with a huge terrace and bucolic park offers a choice of traditional dishes and fresh market cuisine; delicious seafood salad, *cassoulet* and langoustines. *Closed Wed, plus Sun eve in winter.*

Brasserie Le Donjon, 4 Rue Porte d'Aude (Cité), **t** 04 68 25 95 72, www.brasserie-donjon.fr (€€). The best of Languedoc cooking – here the humble *cassoulet* reaches new heights. *Closed Sun eve from Nov–Mar.*

★ Dame Carcas >

Dame Carcas, 3 Place du Château-la-Cité, **t** 04 68 71 23 23, *www.damecarcas.com* (€€–€). Delicious wood-fired cooking, with Provençal options like grilled piglet with honey sauce. *Closed mid-Jan–mid-Feb.*

L'Escalier, 23 Bd Omer Sarraut (Ville Basse), **t** 04 68 25 65 66 (€€). Something of an institution, a lively late-night restauant with pizza, Tex-Mex and moussaka. *Closed Sun lunch.*

Le St-Jean, Place St-Jean (Cité), **t** 04 68 47 42 43, *www.le-saint-jean.eu* (€€–€). A varied menu at this popular lunchtime restaurant serving *cassoulet*, meat and fish dishes. The *cassoulet* has hearty chunks of meat. *Closed Tues Sept–June.*

Bloc G, 112 Rue Barbacane, **t** 04 68 48 58 20, *www.bloc-g.com* (€€–€). Trendy black and white restaurant and wine bar with a terrace at the foot of the Cité, serving market-fresh dishes on a frequently changing menu. *Closed Sun, Mon out of season.*

Comptoir des Vins et Terroirs, 3 Rue du Comte Roger in the Cité, **t** 04 68 26 44 76, *www.comptoir-vins.fr* (€). Excellent wine bar in the Cité, with tasty dishes to accompany your glass of Corbières (also sales and tastings). *Closed Sun eve, Mon out of season, Jan.*

North of Carcassonne: The Montagne Noire

The southern end of the Massif Central tails off into the bleak, brooding Black Mountain, an 18-mile-wide stretch of peaks, taller than their neighbours and difficult to access until modern times. The long ridge in fact divides two climates: its north face has an Atlantic climate, while the south is Mediterranean. Its slate-roofed villages have a solemn air, and their people are bent to serious mountain pursuits – mining and quarrying, logging and paper-making. In the old days they scratched iron and copper out of the mountain; this still continues, along with a bit of silver and gold – the deposits at Salsigne, discovered a century ago, yield around a tonne of gold each year. The trees are even more important: chestnut groves, some planted in the Middle Ages when chestnuts were a mountain staple, and also stands of foreign intruders – Scots pine and Douglas fir, grown for the lumber business.

An area this dramatic and authentic in the UK would attract day-trippers by the thousand in the summer, with traffic jams to match. But here you can drive the winding mountain roads in August and hardly see a soul. In the larger tourist offices, look out for the guide *Balades et Randonnées a pied et à VTT Montagne Noire* published by Chamina.

The Clamoux Valley

All the routes into the mountains follow narrow parallel valleys leading up from the river Aude; the first is the Argent-Double, from Caunes, part of the Minervois (*see* p.189). Next comes the Clamoux (on the D112), with equally impressive gorges extending north of Villeneuve-Minervois; 6km up the Clamoux and a 20-

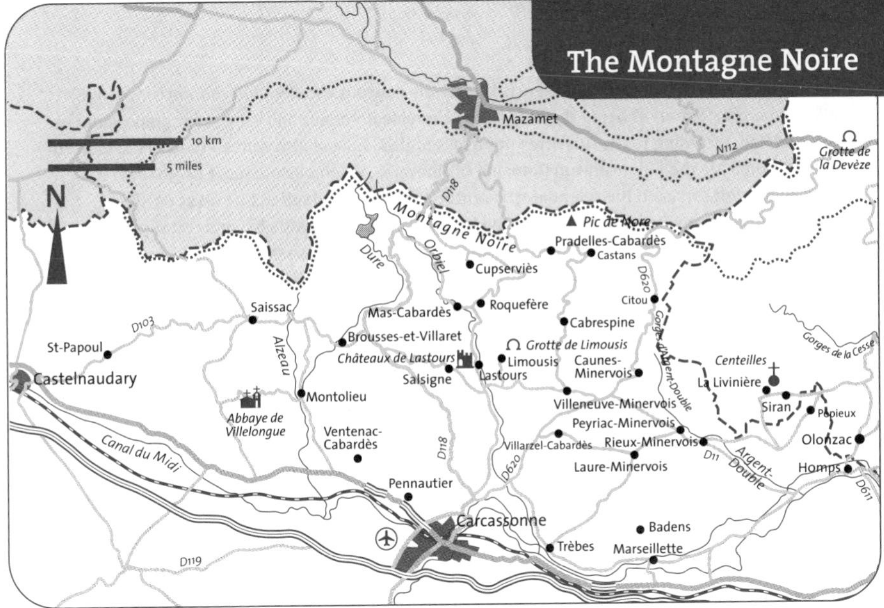

Gouffre Géant de Cabrespine
t 04 68 26 14 22, www.gouffre-cabrespine.com; guided tours July–Aug 10–7; April–June and Sept–Oct 10–11.30 and 2.30–5.30; Feb, Mar, Nov and Dec self-guided interactive tours 2–5.30; closed Christmas–Jan

Les Safaris Souterrains
t 04 67 66 11 11, www.grottes.com

Les Lamas de la Montagne Noire
t 04 68 26 60 11, www.lamabalade.free.fr; open year-round

Châteaux de Lastours
t 04 68 77 56 02, www.les4chateaux-lastours.lwdsoftware.net; open July–Aug daily 9–8; April, May, June and Sept daily 10–6; Oct–mid-Nov daily 10–5; Nov and Dec see website; Feb and Mar weekends and hols only 10–5; closed Jan; adm

minute drive from Carcassonne is **Cabrespine** with its lofty castle (Simon de Montfort slept here) and its deep abyss, the **Gouffre Géant de Cabrespine**, part of it accessible to all, including wheelchairs, and part of it left as it was, which you can explore in four–five-hour excursions guided by **Les Safaris Souterrains**. Further up is the **Gorge de Clamoux** in **Pradelles-Cabardès**, where the people used to make a living by shipping ice down to the cities of the valley. Their sunken ice chambers are still a feature of the landscape.

Above Pradelles looms the **Pic de Nore**, at 3,937ft the highest point of the Montagne Noire, while the D9 leads to **Castans**, a collection of seven hamlets, with seven springs, and a church with seven bells. This is fine walking country, and you can do it (why not?) with a llama, from **Les Lamas de la Montagne Noire** in the hamlet of Les Vernedes.

The Orbiel Valley and Châteaux de Lastours

The next valley, that of the **Orbiel** (D101), is the most populous of the region, and perhaps the most beautiful. It also contains the region's landmark, the **Châteaux de Lastours** – not one but four castles, in various romantic states of picturesque ruin, all on the same hilltop to defend the Montagne Noire's mineral richness. The lords of Cabardès, bosses of the Montagne Noire before the arrival of Simon de Montfort in 1211, built the first of them, the castles of **Cabaret** and **Quertinheux**; the two between these, **Surdespine** and **Tour Régine**, were added by the French kings in the 13th century. Remember the Drac, in Beaucaire? (If not, *see* p.115.) Apparently, after his embarrassment there he took refuge here. The legendary

Wine: AOC Cabardès

In this area north of Carcassonne there is a relatively new but excellent *appellation* (since 1998) called Cabardès, famous as being the only one to combine Bordeaux and Languedoc grape varieties (half and half, according to the rules), resulting in rounded, quite stylish wines. Producers to look out for in this area are the American-run **Domaine O'Vineyards**, Villemoustaussou, **t** 06 30 18 99 10, *www.ovineyards.com*, and the splendid 17th-century **Château Pennautier**, **t** 04 68 25 63 48, *www.vignobles-lorgeril.com*, at Pennautier, which also has rooms, a wine bar and restaurant.

knight Roland himself was on his trail near Lastours, and his horse left a hoof-print in a great boulder near the châteaux, a place still called the *Saut de Roland*. Don't miss the belvedere 2km away.

Grotte de Limousis
t 04 68 26 14 20, www.grotte-de-limousis.com; open July–Aug daily 10–6; April–June and Sept daily 10.30–5.30; Mar and Oct daily 2.30–5.30; Nov Sun and hols 2.30–4.30; closed Dec–Feb; adm

Salsigne, with its gold mine, lies just to the west of Lastours. To the east is a remarkable cave, the **Grotte de Limousis**, with unique formations of gleaming white aragonite crystals, one of which, the *Lustre* (chandelier), is over 30ft across.

Further up the valley are two of the most beautiful and unspoiled villages of the region: **Roquefère** and Mas-Cabardès; north of Roquefère, a 5km detour leads up to a high, lovely waterfall at a place called **Cupserviès**. **Mas-Cabardès** has some half-timbered houses and a 16th-century church with a rugged octagonal belfry. In the village centre, note the pretty, carefully carved stone cross, a typical decoration of Montagne Noire villages. This one was a 16th-century gift of the weavers' guild; with its abundance of water, this region had a thriving textile trade before the black-hearted English Industrial Revolutionaries started underselling them in the 18th century. Another water-powered trade was paper; in **Brousses-et-Villaret**, west of Mas-Cabardès, you can visit Languedoc's last paper mill, learn the history of paper and how to make it by hand at the 18th-century **Musée du Moulin à Papier**.

Musée du Moulin à Papier
t 04 68 26 67 43, www.moulinapapier.com; open for guided tours in French July–Aug daily on the hour 11–6; Sept at 11 and hourly 2.30–5.30; Oct–June Mon–Fri 11 and 3.30, Sat, Sun and hols 11am and hourly 2.30–5.30; adm

Finally, back towards Carcassonne in **Villarzel-Cabadès**, anyone intrigued by the Visigoths should stop at the **Musée Archéologique Claude Journet** at Impasse du Clôcher. Decorated with a colourful mural of what the region might have looked like 1,600 years ago, the museum was born after 1966, when two locals discovered a Visigothic necropolis known as the Mourel dels Morts; there are Visigothic tombs (made out of Roman stone roof tiles) and skulls and grave goods, including late Roman-early Christian pottery, coins and jewellery that may have belonged to a princess. A 6.5km path from the museum leads to the Mourel dels Morts and the pre-Romanesque chapel of **Notre-Dame de la Lauze**, which goes back at least to the 9th century.

Musée Archéologique Claude Journet
*t 04 68 77 17 36 (out of season **t** 04 68 77 02 11); open daily – just ring ahead*

The Western Montagne Noire

Further west, the crown of the Montagne Noire is dotted with artificial lakes, part of a big hydroelectric scheme; the Bassin de Lampy is particularly attractive. In the valley of the Vernassonne, **Saissac** is another lovely village, built over a ravine and surrounded

Where to Stay and Eat in the Montagne Noire

Accommodation is limited: Carcassonne is close enough for the Montagne to be an easy day trip.

Lastours ✉ 11600

Le Puits du Trésor, Route des Quatre Châteaux, **t** 04 68 77 50 24, *www.lepuitsdutresor.com* (€€€€–€€€). For a Michelin-starred splurge, visit this renovated textile factory by the river Orbiel, which is partly an elegant restaurant (there is also a cheaper *auberge*). Chef Jean-Marc Boyer offers mouthwatering seasonal dishes. *Closed Sun eve–Wed lunch.*

Saissac ✉ 11310

Montagne Noire, Av Maurice Sarraut, **t** 04 68 24 46 36 (€). Has rooms and serves tasty food under its century-old trees. *Closed Oct–April.*

Montolieu ✉ 11170

Abbaye de Villelongue, St-Martin-le-Vieil, west of Montolieu, **t** 04 68 76 92 58, *www.abbaye-de-villelongue.com* (€€). Antiques-furnished *chambres d'hôtes. Book at least 2 weeks ahead in summer.*

★ Le Puits du Trésor >

by forests, with yet another romantically ruined, overgrown fortress, and a 10ft menhir, just to the north off the D4.

To the south, **Montolieu,** balanced over the gorges of the Alzeau and Dure, has become the '*Village du Livre*', a centre of the local book-making trade: in the middle of this pretty floral village the **Musée Michel Braibant** traces the history of bookbinding and printing, and there are a dozen or so bookshops, and summer book fairs. West on the D64, the 13th-century Cistercian **Abbaye de Villelongue** is one of the best preserved monastic complexes in Languedoc; its current owner adores gourdes and sells them in the shop. And you can stay here, *see* box, above.

Musée Michel Braibant
t 04 68 24 80 04; open April–Dec Mon–Sat 10–12.30 and 2–6, Sun 2–6; Jan–Mar daily 2–5; adm

Abbaye de Villelongue
t 04 68 76 90 38, www.abbaye-de-villelongue.com; open May–Oct 10–12 and 2–6.30, Sat until 4; closed Nov–April; guided tours, English spoken; adm

North of Pic de Nore, the Montagne Noire descends to rolling hills, in a vast forested area that is part of the Parc Régional Naturel du Haut-Languedoc.

The Aude's Northwest Corner: The Lauragais

West of Carcassonne and the Montagne Noire lies a region called the Lauragais, an undulating expanse of serious farming of the humbler sort: beans, barley and pigs, and in some villages a substantial chicken-plucking trade. Windmills are a chief landmark, as is the shady, blue and nearly straight ribbon of the Canal du Midi en route to Toulouse.

Rugby makes the juices flow in these parts, but in the old days it was religion: here stands St-Félix-de-Caraman (today 'de-Lauragais'), where the doctrines of Catharism were born.

Castelnaudary, Famous for Beans

To be authentic, a *cassoulet* requires four things: 'white beans from Lavelanet, cooked in the pure water of Castelnaudary, in a casserole made of clay from the Issel, over a fire of furze from the Black Mountain'. Having finally penetrated to deepest France, what you find is not always what you might expect. Here, the precious insight into the folk soul is a cherished mess of beans, lard, goose fat and miscellaneous pork parts. The clay pot of *cassoulet* in Castelnaudary's kitchen is the town's Eiffel Tower, its Acropolis, its very identity, and in August, celebrated in an annual four-day *Fête du Cassoulet*. Back in the 1570s, Castelnaudary's *cassoulet* was prescribed to Queen Margot as a cure for sterility, unfortunately without success.

With *cassoulet*, the charms of Castelnaudary are nearly exhausted. There is the 14th-century church of **St-Michel**, with a tall steeple dominating the city; the **Moulin de Cugarel**, a restored 17th-century windmill, only survivor of 32 that once spun in the vicinity, and the port and turning basin of the Canal du Midi. Next to the **Présidial** (now a school) you can visit the **local museum** in the old prison, with annual special exhibitions. There's also an 18th-century **apothecary** with its original pots and utensils, at the hospital on Avenue Monseigneur de Langle.

Moulin de Cugarel
open July–mid-Aug; ask tourist office for times

Musée du Lauragais
t 04 68 23 00 42; open July–mid-Sept Tues–Sun 2.30–6.30; closed Mon; adm

The Medieval Lauragais

In the Middle Ages, **St-Papoul**, 8km east of Castelnaudary on the D103, was the centre of the Lauragais and the home of its bishop. An **abbey** has been here since the time of Charlemagne; in 1317 Pope John XXII turned the abbot into a bishop and the monks into canons – the better to keep an eye on local heretics. In decline for centuries, this forgotten town still has some of its walls and half-timbered houses, as well as a fine Romanesque **cathedral** – from the 14th century, a typically archaic building in a region that disdained the imported Gothic of the hated northerners. Although remodelled in trashy Baroque inside, the exterior has remained largely unchanged, including a beautiful apse with carved capitals attributed to the Master of Cabestany. Other good Romanesque churches with carvings are west of Castelnaudary at **Mas-Saintes-Puelles** and **Baraigne** (take the D33 and D218 from Castelnaudary), and at **Montmaur**, north of the D113 on the D58; the latter two preserve examples of small circular roadside crosses. In medieval times this region had hundreds of them; almost all have been destroyed or moved.

Abbaye de St-Papoul
t 04 68 94 97 75, www.saintpapoul.fr; guided tours July–Aug 10–6.30; April–June and Sept 10–11.30 and 2–5.30; Oct 10–11.30 and 2–4.30; Nov–Mar Sat, Sun and hols 10–11.30 and 2–4.30; closed Sun mornings and all Jan; adm

West of Castelnaudary, the Canal du Midi loses most of its tranquillity, as both the *Autoroute des Deux Mers* and the N113 move in to keep it company on the way to Toulouse. On the borders of the *département*, at **Port-Lauragais**, the canal passes its highest point. Figuring out how to cross it was Paul Riquet's biggest challenge; he solved it with an elaborate system of smaller canals and reservoirs, carrying water to the locks from as far as 30 miles away, in the Montagne Noire. Near Port-Lauragais there is a large obelisk in Riquet's honour (erected by his descendants in 1825, the year the canal turned in a profit!) and a small museum-cum-information centre about the canal, accessible from the *autoroute*.

South of Castelnaudary are more reminders of the Cathars and their oppressors. **Fanjeaux**, on the D119, began its career as Fanum Jovis, from an ancient temple of Jupiter; from that you can guess that the town, like almost all the sites dedicated to the god of thunder and storms, is on a commanding height, with a wide view over the Lauragais plains. Fanjeaux was a hotbed of Catharism and gained its fame in 1206, when St Dominic himself came from Spain to live here as a missionary to the heretics – quite peacefully and sincerely, although his Dominican followers would be the Church's chief inquisitors and torture-masters for centuries to come. They bequeathed Fanjeaux a 14th-century Gothic church, in the former Dominican monastery; a better work, the parish church of 1278, has a *trésor* full of unusual old reliquaries. St Dominic founded a monastery in nearby **Prouille**, after a vision in Fanjeaux, and it became a pilgrimage site. Unfortunately, it was wrecked in the Revolution and charmlessly rebuilt in the 19th century.

South of Fanjeaux, on the way to Limoux, the villages are often laid according to a circular or even elliptical plan: **Ferran**, **Brézilhac** and **La Digne**, among others. They are medieval new towns, or *bastides*; no one knows exactly why the medieval planners decided to depart from their accustomed strict rectangularity here, but there are clusters of them in Languedoc. They even have their own association, the **Association des Villages Circulaires**.

Association des Villages Circulaires
Mairie de Paulhan ✉ 34230, **t** *04 67 25 31 42, www. circulades.com*

Market Day in the Lauragais

Castelnaudary: Mon.

Where to Stay and Eat in the Lauragais

Castelnaudary ✉ 11400

****Centre et du Lauragais**, 31 Cours République, **t** 04 68 23 25 95, *www. hotel-centre-lauragais.com* (€€). A family-run hotel in the centre, with nice big rooms, a terrace and a restaurant (€€–€) serving *cassoulet*, of course. *Restaurant closed Sun eve.*

***Grand Hôtel Fourcade**, 14 Rue des Carmes, **t** 04 68 23 02 08 (€). Family-run, remodelled but still nicely old-fashioned. Its restaurant (€€) is the best in town: gourmet *cassoulet* with goose *confits*, and the like. *Closed Sun eve and Mon out of season, and Jan.*

Le Tirou, 90 Av Monseigneur-Delangle, **t** 04 68 94 15 95, *www.letirou.com/fr* (€€). Classic beanery since 1993 with a terrace (next to a llama) and a reputed *cassoulet*, roast pigeon, duck dishes and more. *Open Tues–Sun lunch, and Sat eve.*

Around Castelnaudary

******L'Hostellerie de la Pomarède**, La Pomarède, ✉ 11400, **t** 04 68 60 49 69, *www.hostellerie-lapomarede.fr* (€€€€–€€). North of Castelnaudary, stylish, tranquil rooms, either in an 11th-century Cathar castle or an old *presbytère* with a spa and outdoor pool in a peaceful wooded setting; creative gourmet restaurant run by talented chef Gérald Garcia; weekday lunch menu €17, otherwise (€€€€). *Closed Sun eve, Mon, and Tues lunch; in summer closed Mon, Tues, Wed lunch.*

ⓘ **Castelnaudary** >
Place de la République, **t** *04 68 23 05 73, www. castelnaudary-tourisme.com; open Mon–Sat*

★ **Grand Hôtel Fourcade** >

Auberge Le Cathare, Château de la Barthe, Belflou ✉ 11410, **t** 04 68 60 32 49, *www.auberge-lecathare.com* (€). West of Castelnaudary, on an artificial lake off the D217. Home cooking, *cassoulet*, and a campsite with mobile homes and chalets to rent. *Closed Fri eve and Sat lunch in winter.*

Les Deux Acacias, Villepinte (11km southeast of Castelnaudary on N113), **t** 04 68 94 24 67, *www.les-deux-acacias.com* (€). Another highly respected pot of beans is dished up here; they also have pleasant rooms (€€–€). *Closed Fri.*

South of Carcassonne

The Limouxin and Quercorb

Before its right turn at Carcassonne, the Aude traverses a lovely, modest stretch of open rolling country, the Limouxin. Most of the roads here are still graced with their long arcades of plane trees – there isn't enough traffic yet to threaten them.

Limoux

Even before you notice the vineyards, the civilized landscapes suggest wine. Limoux, the capital, is an attractive town, with a medieval bridge across the Aude, the **Pont Neuf**; this meets the apse and steeple of **St-Martin**, a good piece of Gothic, if anachronistic – although the church was begun in the 14th century, most of the work is from three centuries later. The centre is the arcaded **Place de la République.** Like Carcassonne's Ville Basse, Limoux was a *bastide*, and this was its market square, as well as the stage for *Los Fecos* (*see* p.212). Rue Blanquerie, named for the tanneries that once were Limoux's main business, is one of the streets with 15th- and 16th-century houses, like the 1549 **Hôtel de Clercy**, with a lovely and unusual courtyard of interlocking arches.

Musée Petiet
t 04 68 31 85 03, www.limoux.fr; open July–Aug Tues–Fri 9–12 and 2–6, Sat 9–12 and 2–5, closed Sun and Mon; Sept–June Wed–Fri 9–12 and 2–6, Sat 10–12 and 2–5, closed Sun, Mon and Tues; adm

Musée du Piano
t 04 68 31 85 03; ring for times

La Bouichère
t 04 68 31 49 94, www.labouichere.com; open mid-July–mid-Aug Wed–Sun 10–6; May–mid-July and mid-Aug–Sept Wed–Sun 1–6; adm

On the Promenade du Tivoli, a broad boulevard that replaced the town walls, the tourist office shares the home of the Petiet family with the **Musée Petiet**, which contains a collection of 19th-century paintings, and canvases by the museum's founder, Marie Petiet, a talented, neglected artist of the 1880s. A woman painter, and a woman's painter, her work brings a touch of magic to very domestic subjects, nowhere better than in the serene, luminous composition called *Les Blanchisseuses* (*The Washerwomen*). There is also a **Musée du Piano** at the Chapelle St-Jacques, Place du 22 Septembre, with over 100 instruments; at the time of writing the acoustics are being improved for concerts. On the outskirts of town, you can spend a peaceful hour or two at **La Bouichère**, on Rue Dewoitine, a garden of 2,500 plants especially chosen for their fragrance, run by a charming couple with very green thumbs.

In the sculpted countryside around Limoux, you can combine picnics and piety with a tour of three sites. The chapel of **Notre-Dame-de-Marceille**, just to the northeast, houses a 'Black Virgin',

Wine: Blanquette de Limoux

Available in London or New York, you may have already met Blanquette de Limoux, popularly recognized as the poor man's champagne. The Limouxins wouldn't care to hear it put that way; they would point out that their Blanquette was the world's first sparkling wine, first recorded in 1531 – long before anyone ever heard of champagne. Made from local grape mauzac, plus chenin and chardonnay, Blanquette may not have the depth or ageing ability of its celebrated rival, but you should certainly give it a try, especially as it is excellent value. Locals like to drink it as an *apéritif*, with little cakes called *pebradous*, flavoured with pepper.

You'll have little trouble finding Blanquette (along with the other, non-classified *vins de pays*, white and red) on the roads around Limoux. Among the best producers is **Antech**, at Domaine de Flassian, on the D118 towards Carcassonne, **t** 04 68 31 15 88, *www.antech-limoux.com* (*closed weekends*). For excellent organic Blanquette, visit **Cave Beirieu** at Roquetaillade, **t** 04 68 31 60 71, *www.domaine-beirieu.com* (contact them first).

Over 80 per cent of Limoux's wines are grown by the powerful co-operative that bottles them under the names **Aimery** and **Sieur d'Arques**, Av Mauzac (from Limoux, follow signs to Chalabre, **t** 04 68 74 63 00, *www.sieurdarques.com*). They have a big tasting room (be sure to try their excellent, slightly less sparkling Crémant de Limoux) and offer tours, and sponsor the renowned *Toques et Clochers* festival (*see* p.212), dedicated to some of the finest still chardonnays grown in France.

Northwest of Limoux, an estimable but little-known red wine called La Malepère only received AOC status in 2007. It is produced in a small area (in Malepère, Brugairolles, Malviès and Lauraguel) but the closest one in Languedoc to Bordeaux – hence the use of varieties like cot, merlot and cabernet franc. A good one is **Château Guilhem**, in Malviès, **t** 04 68 31 14 41, *www.chateauguilhem.com*, while in Brugairolles you can taste and learn about all of Languedoc-Roussillon's wines at the wonderful **Vinécole**, run by master of wine Matthew Stubbs (**Domaine Gayda**, Chemin de Moscou, **t** 04 68 31 64 14, *www.vinecole.com*).

Abbaye de St-Hilaire
t 04 68 69 62 76, www.abbayedesainthilaire.pagesperso-orange.fr/; open July–Aug daily 10–7; April–June and Sept–Oct daily 10–12 and 2–6; Nov–Mar daily 10–12 and 2–5; closed Christmas; adm

an 11th-century icon. To the east, an exceptionally pretty side road (the D104) leads to the **Abbaye de St-Hilaire**, founded in the 8th century; its Benedictine monks invented the *méthode ancestrale* for making bubbly Blanquette de Limoux. A graceful, double-columned Gothic cloister survives, along with the Romanesque abbey church, containing the white marble sarcophagus of St Sernin (d. 250), the patron of Toulouse, one of his masterpieces by the Master of Cabestany. The refectory has a hollowed-out stone lectern you can climb into, and the capitulary has a fascinating 16th-century painted ceiling of secular scenes.

South of St-Hilaire, the monastery of **St-Polycarpe** was founded around the same period by the Visigoth Witiza, later known as St Benedict of Aniane (*see* pp.156–7), whose head is preserved in a reliquary on the altar, along with that of St Polycarpe. Its Romanesque church retains some bits of early frescoes and a pair of Visigothic marble altars, decorated with reliefs of interlacing designs and the 'Cross of Silence' with an alpha and omega – similar to the one in Rennes-le-Château. The narthex has an impressive wooden stair.

The Quercorb

Southwest of Limoux, you may venture into one of the most obscure *pays* in all France. Very few French people, even, have heard

Château Chalabre
t 04 68 69 37 85, www.chateau-chalabre.com; open French school holidays 12–6.30; July–Aug Sun–Fri 12–6.30, and May, June and Sept Sun 2–5.30; adm

Musée du Quercorb
t 04 68 20 80 98, www.quercorb.com/musee; open mid-July–Aug daily 10–7; April–mid-July and Sept daily 10.30–12.30 and 2–6; Oct daily 2–5; adm

Château de Puivert
t 04 68 20 81 52, www.chateau-depuivert.com; open April–Sept daily 8–8; Oct–Mar daily 10–5; adm

of the **Kercorb** (or Quercorb), a sleepy region with plenty of sheep and plenty of trees. **Quercorb** is known for its apple cider, and little else. **Chalabre**, an attractive village of old stone houses with overhanging windows, is its capital, and like any village in the Aude worth its salt it has a castle, the **Château Chalabre**, although this one is a bit different – it's a medieval theme park, where locals in costumes offer tips on medieval calligraphy, building, dancing, archery and displays of jousting, etc.

At **Puivert**, 8km south, the **Musée du Quercorb** will tell you everything there is to know (a reconstructed kitchen and other rooms, cow bell manufacturing, and crafts). It also includes reconstructions of 14th-century musical instruments, based on the sculptures of musicians found in the *donjon* of the **Château de Puivert**; its lords were famous as patrons and protectors of the troubadours. Puivert also has a popular lake.

Festivals in the Limouxin

Les Fecos, Limoux' carnival, is steeped in local folklore and is the earliest and the longest-running in France (weekends Jan–mid-Mar), with music, songs in Occitan, dances and seven tonnes of confetti.

In late April, the *Toques et Clochers* festival celebrates local chardonnays; Sieur d'Arques, the sponsors, auction off 82 barrels of their finest wines in a different Limouxin village every year. The *toques* (chef's hats) refer to the Michelin-starred guest chef, who prepares a meal for 1,000 wine-growers; the *clochers* are the bell towers repaired with the proceeds of the auction. Visitors buy a glass and go wine-tasting, with lots of food, music and merriment.

Market Days in the Limouxin

Limoux: Fri; flea market 1st Sun.
Chalabre: Sat.

Where to Stay and Eat in the Limouxin

Limoux ✉ 11300

***Grand Hôtel Moderne et Pigeon**, Place Général Leclerc, **t** 04 68 31 00 25, *www.grandhotelmodernepigeon.fr* (€€€–€€). The most luxurious choice. It has served as a convent, a *hôtel particulier* and a bank. The restaurant (€€€) has a charming terrace and appropriately serves pigeon (and other dishes, too). *Closed Jan; restaurant closed Mon, Tues lunch and Sun eve.*

Hôtel des Arcades, 96 Rue St-Martin, just off Place de la République, **t** 04 68 31 02 57 (€). With comfortable rooms and a restaurant (€€). *Closed mid-Dec–Jan; restaurant closed Wed.*

***Auberge de la Corneilla**, just off the D118 at Cournanel, south of Limoux, **t** 04 68 31 17 84, *www.aubergedelacorneilla.fr* (€). An unpretentious restored farmhouse with nice rooms, a restaurant (€€) and a garden and pool. *Restaurant closed Sat lunch and Sun eve out of season.*

Maison de la Blanquette, 46 bis Promenade du Tivoli, **t** 04 68 31 01 63 (€€€–€€). Wine-sampling and relaxed home cooking, from Limoux's *charcuterie* to *confits* to the people's choice, a variation on *cassoulet* called *fricassée* (Limoux even has an 'Association pour la Promotion de la Fricassée'). *Closed Sun eve.*

Maison Gayda, Brugairolles (10km north of Limoux) **t** 04 68 20 65 87, *www.maisongayda.com* (€€€€–€€€). Part of the Vinécole complex, this restaurant amid the vines serves contemporary cuisine to complement its wide range of wines, and does occasional jazz evenings. Lunch menu

★ **Maison de la Blanquette** >>

ⓘ **Limoux** >
Promenade du Tivoli, t 04 68 31 11 82, www.limoux.fr

Chalabre >
Cours d'Aguesseau, t 04 68 69 65 96, www.tourisme chalabrais.com

Le Trésor >

€22. *Open Wed–Sun, and some eves out of season.*

Chalabre ✉ 11230

Le Trésor, 20 Place de l'Eglise, at Sonnac sur l'Hers, t 04 68 69 37 94, *www.le-tresor.com* (€€). Charming little B&B run by Tilly and Will, two young refugees from London; excellent *table d'hôte* meals on weekends. *Closed Nov–Mar.*

The Razès

South of Limoux is a *pays* called the **Razès**, a sparse, scrubby, haunted region, the back door to the Corbières. As Rhedae, it has been known to history since the time of the Visigoths. According to author Henry Lincoln, the uncanniness begins with the Razès' sacred geometry: its five most prominent peaks, including the perch of Languedoc's conspiracy headquarters, Rennes-le-Château, describe a unique, perfect natural pentangle. The precise measurements were repeated in the Middle Ages, in the geomantic placing of churches around Espéraza. Even in the off season you'll see cars with numberplates from faraway countries, cruising about looking for goodness knows what.

Alet-les-Bains

Benedictine abbey
open July–Aug daily 10–12 and 2.30–7; Sept–June Mon–Sat 10–12 and 2.30–6; closed Sun

Continuing south up the Aude from Limoux, Alet-les-Bains is one of the most beautiful and best-preserved medieval villages of Languedoc. A small spa since Roman times, Alet owes its prominence to the popes, who made it a bishopric in 1318. Its two jewels are the 14th-century church of **St-André**, with frescoes and a fine west portal, and the impressive **Benedictine abbey**, founded in the 9th century and wrecked in the Wars of Religion. The narrow streets of the village itself are an equal attraction, with a score of 13th- and 14th-century buildings, such as the colonnaded house called the **Maison Romane**. Alet is still a thriving spa; it bottles its water to clean out your digestive tract, and runs a casino to clean out your pockets. There's a pretty river to paddle in.

Couiza and Espéraza

The Razès' biggest town, gritty and peculiar **Couiza**, makes shoes and plastic panelling. Its landmark is the imposing Renaissance **château** of the Ducs de Joyeuse, who made nuisances of themselves on the Catholic side during the Wars of Religion; their descendants have turned the old homestead into a hotel (*see* p.218).

Dinosauria
t 04 68 74 26 88, www.dinosauria.org; open July–Aug daily 10–7; Feb–June and Sept–Nov daily 10.30–12.30 and 1–5.30; adm

Dinosaurs were fond of the Aude valley and especially **Espéraza**, just north, where Jurassic-era souvenirs fill the only museum in France entirely dedicated to dinosaurs, **Dinosauria**. Most come from the Bellevue site, 3km away in Campagne-sur-Aude; the richest in France, it's yielded 35 different species so far, and in July and August you can watch volunteers unearth new ones.

Musée de la Chapellerie
t 04 68 74 00 75, www.museedelachapellerie.fr; open July–Aug daily 10–7; Feb–June and Sept–Oct daily 10–12 and 2–6; Nov–Dec daily 1.30–5.30; adm

Espéraza also takes pride in being 'the world's second-greatest maker of hats in the first half of the 20th century' and curses the day JFK set the fashion for going without. The village's glory days are recalled in the nearby **Musée de la Chapellerie**.

Château d'Arques
t 04 68 69 84 77; www.chateau-arques.fr; open July–Aug daily 10–7; April–June and Sept daily 10–1 and 2–7; Mar, Oct and Nov daily 10–1 and 2–5; closed Dec–Feb; adm

Maison de Déodat Roché
t 04 68 69 85 62; same hours as the Château

To the east of Couiza are **Rennes-les-Bains**, a charming small spa in business since the time of the Romans (finds from the ancient baths are in the Villa Marie), and **Arques**, where a few Cathars are still said to go about their business. Arques has a tall, elegant, Gothic 13th-century **château** – or just the keep of one, framed in turrets, as Simon de Montfort took it from the Termes family in 1231 and gave it to one of his lieutenants. The same ticket admits you to the **Maison de Déodat Roché**; a famous Cathar historian, Roché (1877–1978) was born in Arques, and his house in the centre of the village has a permanent exhibition on Catharism in the 19th and 20th centuries.

Rennes-le-Château

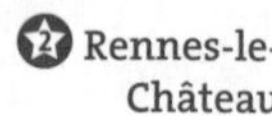

Rennes-le-Château

Whatever is haunting the Razès, much of it resides here, in a woebegone mountaintop village above Couiza that is possibly familiar to more people in Britain and America than in Carcassonne. The fun began in the 1890s, when the young parish priest Bérenger Saunière began spending huge sums of money on himself and on embellishing his church. The story, and the speculation, hasn't stopped unfolding since. In a nation addicted to secret conspiracies, preferably with a medieval pedigree, every sort of shadowy religious cult and fantastico-political faction has got its oar in, from neo-fascists to neo-Jews, along with monarchists, satanists, dilettante Cathars and dress-up Templars.

With its few dusty streets and spectacular views over the Aude valley, Rennes-le-Château is an unsurpassed vortex of weirdness: so many people turn up in season now that you'll need to park in one of the car parks on the road and take the little tourist train to the village. Besides a couple of restaurants, its one permanent business is an occult bookshop, where you can pick up a copy of the 1970s bestseller *Holy Blood, Holy Grail*, the first account in English that attracted international attention to Rennes, describing Jesus' problematical but well-publicized western European tour, an escape from Palestine after a faked crucifixion. It's been a recurring theme in French and English legend from the beginning ('And did those feet in ancient time,' etc.). Here, the idea is that Jesus came to Gaul with his wife Mary Magdalene; both may have been buried in Rennes and their descendants were the French Merovingian kings, deposed in the 8th century by a shady deal between the popes and Carolingians. Supposedly, the bloodline survives to this day.

It hardly matters that the story has been revealed as a hoax, perpetrated on the poor authors of *Holy Blood, Holy Grail* by some devilishly clever Frenchmen. The success of Dan Brown's novel *The Da Vinci Code* got the whole occult machine wound up and running again. Did Saunière discover proof of Jesus' tomb in Rennes-le-Château and make his fortune by blackmailing the Vatican to keep his mouth shut? Or did he find the Holy Grail, or perhaps the treasure of the Jews, pillaged from Jerusalem by Titus in AD 10, and pillaged in turn by the Visigoths, who carted it off to Toulouse or Carcassonne in the 5th century?

When Clovis, king of the Franks, captured Toulouse in 507, the treasure was supposedly removed for safekeeping to the Visigoths' impregnable fortress and secret capital, Rennes-le-Château (today, the whole area around the village is lined with stern 'no digging' signs). Rennes became the capital of the Razès when Amairic, a Visigothic prince, married a Frankish princess, and it is claimed to have eventually had a population of 30,000 – 3,000 would be closer to reality – before it was definitively sacked by the Aragonese in 1170, only to be destroyed again for good measure in Simon de Montfort's *blitzkrieg*.

Interest in the Razès began in the 17th century, after a humble shepherd found a gold treasure in the area, but never revealed exactly where; there is some evidence that artist Nicolas Poussin used landmarks of the region (including the hill of Rennes-le-Château) in the background of his enigmatic painting *Et in Arcadia Ego* (1638–40), generally understood to mean death is present, even in idyllic Arcadia. Or some say it as a rather juicier anagram: '*I Tego Arcana Dei*' ('Begone! I hide the Secrets of God!').

When Bérenger Saunière was appointed parish priest of Rennes-le-Château, the village was in a sorry state; even the 12th-century church was falling over. During the repairs in 1891, Saunière supposedly found, somewhere in or around a pillar carved with a Visigothic 'Cross of Silence' (very similar to the one in St-Polycarpe, p.211), a parchment in a glass phial. Not long after, Saunière was spotted digging furtively in the local cemetery. One of his activities was the systematic defacement of the inscription on the tomb of the last Lady of Rennes-le-Château, Hautpoul de Blanchefort (d. 1781), not knowing that someone had already copied it out in the early 1820s (it had Greek letters reading '*Et in Arcadia ego*'). Hautpoul, who died without heirs, had in her last hours of life confided some great secret to the parish priest, who left the enigmatic epitaph on her tomb.

Ste-Marie-Madeleine

open July–Sept daily 10–7.15; May–June daily 10–6.15; mid-Mar–April daily 10–1 and 2–5.15; Oct–mid-Nov daily 10–1 and 2–5.15; Nov–mid-Jan Sat and Sun 10–1 and 2–5.15; adm

After his nocturnal digs, Saunière asked the Louvre for a copy of Poussin's painting, then began spending money like nobody's business (an estimated €2.5 million) paving the road up to Rennes, and redoing the **church**, dedicated (naturally) to Mary Magdalene, in a style the French have labelled 'St-Sulpicien' after the garish church in Paris. Over the door he wrote *Terribilis est locus iste* ('This is a terrible – or awesome – place') – along with, around the arches below the rest of the inscription, *hic domus Dei est et porta coeli* ('This is God's house and the gate of heaven'), all part of the traditional entrance antiphon for the dedication of a church, and not a secret message.

Saunière's somewhat unorthodox imagery of his bevy of plaster statues apparently distils a secret message to the initiated (note, for instance, that in the Holy Family both Mary and Joseph hold babies). Even Saunière got into hot water with the Church over the demonic figure that supports the font, representing not Satan but Asmodeus, the guardian of the treasure of Solomon. Eventually he was suspended from the priesthood for his unwillingness to account for the origin of all his money.

Domaine de l'Abbé Saunière
t 04 68 31 38 85, www.rennes-le-chateau.fr; same hours as church; adm

Adjacent is the **Domaine de l'Abbé Saunière**, the genteelly dilapidated bourgeois villa and garden that Saunière built with his secret loot – although he never actually lived in it. Exhibits include the Visigothic pillar and the curious Carolingian-era *Dalle des Chevaliers*. Saunière died in 1917 (they say the priest who heard his deathbed confession refused to grant him the last rites) and left everything to his housekeeper, Marie Dénaraud, who promised to tell his sercrets to the new owner of the Domaine before she died, but had a fit and went speechless to her grave in 1953. Three years later, a local paper picked up the story about Saunière, and the story might have died there had it not inspired a novel, *L'Or de Rennes*, by Gérard de Sède in 1966 – which in turn inspired two tricksters to plant documents about a secret 'Priory of Sion' in the Bibliothèque Nationale...

From Rennes' belvedere you can see several towers, forts and other ruins, their origin and purpose a matter of conjecture, although they may well have been first built by the Visigoths to relay signals; the largest of them, the **Château de Blanchefort**, was probably wrecked by Simon de Montfort. Another, **Le Bézu**, to the south (on a road from Espéraza) was another Cathar castle, abandoned before Simon got there, although others say it was a stronghold of the Templars, who were sent in to keep an eye on the mysterious treasure, which it is said was actually buried here (the castle is ruined now, but you can hike up for excellent views over Rennes-le-Château and the Pic de Bugarach).

More Strangeness: Bugarach

Honestly, that should be enough strangeness for one little corner of France, but there's more. South of Rennes-les-Bains, the little village of Bugarach (pop. 189) lies under the striking limestone Pic de Burgarach, where you can join hundreds if not thousands of New Agers and UFOlogists who believe it to be sacred. Why? Because hidden in its depths there's a dormant alien spacecraft (you can hear it softly humming, if you know how to listen) that a local man (now dead) saw, which will lift off and just maybe may take them along for a ride to the stars as Armageddon destroys the rest of the world. Actually, it's a bit deeper than that, although, as in the case of Rennes-le-Château, answers are few and far between – but throw in dollops of Cathar mysticism and suggestions that it's not a spaceship hidden here, but the Ark of the Covenant... Jules Verne apparently set his *Journey to the Centre of the Earth* here, and the site is said to have inspired Steven Spielberg's *Close Encounters of the Third Kind*.

Further up the Aude, and Down into the Earth

Heading south of Couiza, next up is **Quillan**, a town that makes its living from manufacturing shoes and Formica; it has an odd, perfectly square castle from the 1280s, a ball and three *quilles* (bowling pins) on its coat of arms. From here the D117 joins the course of the Aude, passing northwards through a spectacular canyon, the **Défilé de Pierre-Lys**. At **Axat**, at its end, you can go **white-water rafting** on the Aude with **Pyrene**. Take the narrow road threading the dramatic **Gorges de St-Georges**; at its end are two options. The D118 leads to a cave (unlike the mysterious one at Bugarach) that you can actually visit, the **Grotte de l'Aguzou**. This is a spectacular stalactite cave, full of lovely delicate formations and crystals, but, unlike most others open to the public, it hasn't been fitted out with walkways and lights; rather, small groups from eight to 10 (children must be at least 10 years old) are taken in with lighted helmets, overalls, belts and lights to explore. Die-hard couch potatoes should abstain.

Pyrene
Camping du Pont d'Aliès, **t** *04 68 20 52 76, www.pyrenerafting.com*

Grotte de l'Aguzou
t *04 68 20 45 38, www.grotte-aguzou.com; visits strictly by appt, with one-day tours, including lunch, for small groups, and half-day tours for individuals*

Your other option is take the narrow D17, switchbacking its way up to the Col de Jau (5,022ft) on its way to Mosset in Roussillon (*see* p.274). Along the way, in a remote setting near **Counozouls**, the last village before the pass, you can see the nothing less than the tallest standing stone in the south of France, the 29ft (8.9m) **Grand Menhir de Counozouls**, spectacularly set against a backdrop of mountains, and weighing in at an estmated 50 tonnes.

Or stay on the main D117 at Axat and head east 6km to one of the five 'sons of Carcassonne' and the southernmost of the Aude's mountaintop Cathar castles, **Puilaurens**, open for those with the puff to climb (in about 20 minutes from the car park). Even Simon de Montfort couldn't get into this one, built in the 10th century by the powerful abbey of St-Michel-de-Cuxa (*see* p.272). After giving up his own castle, Guillaume de Peyrepertuse and many other Cathars came here. By 1255, after Montségur's fall, it was in the hands of Saint Louis – the records don't say how. Its fortifications, the most complete and sophisticated of any in the region, mostly date from French rebuilding; the southwesternmost tower is the Tour de

Château de Puilaurens
t *04 68 20 65 26; open daily Feb, April, and Oct–mid-Nov 10–5; Mar Sat, Sun and school hols only 10–5; May 10–6; June and Sept 10–6; July–Aug 9–8; closed mid-Nov–Jan; adm*

Market Days in the Razés

Espéraza: Thurs and especially Sun.
Couiza: Tues and Sat.
Quillan: Wed and Sat.

Where to Stay and Eat in the Razès

Alet-les-Bains ✉ 11580

****L'Hostellerie de l'Evêché**, **t** 04 68 69 90 25, *www.hotel-eveche.com* (€€). The riverside former bishop's mansion; rather plain, it has a huge garden with century-old cypresses and a restaurant. *Closed Nov–Mar.*

Couiza ✉ 11190

Château des Ducs de Joyeuse, off the main road, set amid playing fields, **t** 04 68 74 23 50, *www.chateau-des-ducs.com* (€€€). A handsome 16th-century place with attractive rooms, some with canopied beds; the elegant restaurant serves the best meals around. *Closed mid-Nov–Feb; restaurant closed Sun eve and Mon eve.*

Quillan ✉ 11500

*****La Chaumière**, 25 Bd Charles de Gaulle, **t** 04 68 20 02 00, *www.pyren.fr* (€€). Cosy rooms and mountain food featuring trout.

****Hôtel Cartier**, 31 Bd Charles de Gaulle, **t** 04 68 20 05 14, *www.hotelcartier.com* (€). Century-old hotel with basic air-conditioned rooms, free Wi-fi and a good restaurant (€€).

****La Pierre Lys**, Av François Mitterrand, **t** 04 68 20 08 65 (€). At the north end of town, this modern hotel offers comfort, quiet and some of the best meals in the town (€€€–€€), with sea perch, *confits*, etc. *Closed mid-Nov–mid-Dec.*

Les Eaux Tranquilles, 9 Quartier de la Condamine, Belvianes-et-Cavirac (south of Quillan, off the D117), **t** 04 68 20 82 79, *www.chambresdhote.com* (€€–€). Tranquil B&B set in a private park with a pool, and tasty evening meals; vegetarians catered for, but no children under 14.

Gincla ✉ 11140

****Hostellerie du Grand Duc**, 2 Route de Boucheville, **t** 04 68 20 55 02, *www.host-du-grand-duc.com* (€€). A handsome old mansion near Puilaurens with elegant rooms and a shady garden; the restaurant (€€€) serves tasty French classics. *Closed Nov–Mar; restaurant closed Wed lunch except July and Aug.*

ⓘ **Alet-les-Bains >**
Av Nicolas Pavillon,
t *04 68 69 93 56,*
http://info.aletlesbains.free.fr

ⓘ **Quillan >**
Square André Tricoire,
t *04 68 20 07 78,*
www.aude-pyrenees.fr;
open May–Sept Mon–Sat; Oct–April Mon–Fri

Dame Blanche, recalling that stay of Blanche de Bourbon, not long before her murder at the hands of her husband Pedro the Cruel; her ghost is occasionally sighted wandering on top of the wall.

The Corbières: Wine and Cathars

Thanks to wine, the Corbières has finally found its vocation. This scrubby, mountainous area, where landscapes range from classic Mediterranean to rugged Wild West, has been the odd region out since ancient times. As a refuge for disaffected Gauls, it was a headache to the Romans. In the early Middle Ages, it was part of the *Marca Hispanica*, the patchwork of little feudal counties ruled by military élites, and a permanent zone of combat. Local *seigneurs* littered the landscape with castles on incredible, impregnable mountaintop sites. Somewhat surprisingly, many of these were begun by the lords of Besalú in northern Catalonia – a now-tiny but once ambitious town whose Count Guifré unified Catalonia and became Count of Barcelona in the 9th century.

Getting around the Corbières

SNCF rail lines make a neat square around the Corbières – but none of them ventures inside the region. The only useful one is from Carcassonne, following the Aude and then turning east through the Fenouillèdes, stopping at Limoux, Alet-les-Bains, Couiza and Quillan on its way to Perpignan. A local association, the **TPCF**, runs the narrow-gauge **Train du Pays Cathare et des Fenouillèdes**, offering excursions from Rivesaltes or Espira de l'Agly (*see* p.245).

The **Sentier Cathare** (*www.lesentiercathare.com*) is one of several trails passing through here; you can arrange to have your baggage carried for you with **Balade Cathare** (**t** 06 07 89 57 42, *www.balade-cathare.com*).

If you're **driving**, keep the tank full. The Corbières is the badlands of France, and its unique fascination comes from traversing spaces as empty as central Anatolia with all the specific charms of France close at hand. There are few good roads.

By the 13th century, many of the local bosses were Cathars, and when Carcassonne fell to the Albigensian Crusaders they took refuge in their impossible castles in the air, holding on in some cases into the mid-13th century. Languedoc's new rulers, the kings of France, refortified them and called the biggest ones 'the five sons of Carcassonne' to defend their new frontier from Aragonese ambition, a back-and-forth battle that only ended in the 17th century when France annexed Roussillon and moved her frontier troops to the Pyrenees. Nearly all the castles are ruined today, but, for anyone with clear lungs and a little spirit, exploring them will be a challenge and a delight. And amid the lonely landscapes of limestone crags and *maquis*, the vineyards advance tenaciously across every dusty, sun-bleached hectare of arable ground.

Lézignan-Corbières and Lagrasse

The Corbières' 'capital', **Lézignan-Corbières**, lies halfway between Carcassonne and Narbonne, on the border between the Minervois and Corbières wine regions. Documented back in 806 as Licinianus, it offers the busiest weekly market on Wednedays, a few places to flop, and a good introduction to what the *pays* does best: the **Musée de la Vigne et du Vin**, at 3 Rue Turgot. There are good Romanesque churches to seek out in nearby **Escales** (with three bijou apses and an altar made from a Roman sarcophagus) and in **Montbrun-des-Corbières**, an old village perched among the ruins of its castle. The church, the pretty 11th-century **Notre-Dame de Colombier**, is 2km away. The story goes that when the local lord went off crusading, he returned so changed that his son didn't recognize him and set the dogs on him. The father died of his injuries, and in the morning, when the grief-stricken son found the body, he saw a dove alight nearby and, taking it as a sign of forgiveness, built this chapel to mark the spot.

Musée de la Vigne et du Vin
t 04 68 27 07 57; open daily 9–12 and 2–7

Just south of Lézignan, **Fabrezan** remembers the Corbières' most famous son in the **Musée Charles Cros** in the *mairie*. Cros (1842–88) was a poet and would certainly be better known had he not also

Musée Charles Cros
t 04 68 27 81 44; open 9–12 and 2–6

been the unluckiest inventor ever. In 1869 he invented a process of colour photography at exactly the same time as Ducos de Hauron, who got the credit for it, and in 1877 he invented the phonograph and discovered how to record sounds at the same time as Edison, who beat him to the patent office.

Dominating the countryside here, looming over the Aude valley and the *autoroute* between Carcassonne and Narbonne, is the massive lump of the **Montagne d'Alaric** (1,968ft), with its distinctive layers of rock; many historians believe that it was here (and not Poitiers) where Alaric II of the Visigoths had his fortress and buried his treasure, and was defeated by the Frankish king Clovis in 508. The GR 77 goes up to the summit, or a rough track for 4x4s leads up from Moux to the fire tower, for grand views over the Corbières.

This northern part of the Corbières has more monasteries than castles. 'One of the most beautiful villages in France', **Lagrasse** is a walled medieval gem that grew up around an important Benedictine abbey, even older than its charter of 799 from Charlemagne himself, given, or so they say, after the emperor saw

Wine: Corbières, and Some Others

One of the biggest AOC areas in France, the Corbières has a singular microclimate, swept by the *tramontane* and with a sparse, irregular rainfall. Under its vines and *maquis* lies a geological jigsaw puzzle of Liassic, Triassic, Urgonian and who-knows-what-other kinds of rocks, not to mention the Urgo-Aptian debris and Villefranchean scree. There are just as many variations of soil, often giving wines from one village a completely different character from that of its neighbour: one reason why the Corbières region is subdivided into 11 *terroirs*.

Wine has always been made here – the land isn't good for much else – but only in the past 30 years have producers tried to exploit its unique possibilities. The results have been more than encouraging. Corbières red (mostly carignan, grenache and cinsault) varies widely, but will always be dark ruby red, full-bodied and intense. There is also white and rosé Corbières, although you won't often see them; good rosé (as well as red) comes from the **Château La Baronne**, near Fontcouverte, **t** 04 68 43 90 20, *www.chateaulabaronne.com*.

Corbières is a stronghold of the village co-operative cellar, and has been ever since the troubles in 1907. There are, nevertheless, a number of strictly private producers. Some of the best, such as the excellent organic **Domaine Haut Gléon** in Durban (t 04 68 48 85 95, *www.hautgleon.com* – *see also* 'Where to Stay', p.226) are in the aptly named Vallée du Paradis along the D611. Along the D611A, visit **Château Gléon-Montanié**, west of Portel-des-Corbières, **t** 04 68 48 28 25, *www.gleon-montanie.com*, a lovely estate behind an old stone bridge, which makes a fine, very traditional red and a striking Corbières white based on 100 per cent malvoisie, as well as rosé.

Nearby, the vast **Château Lastours**, Portel-des-Corbières, **t** 04 68 48 64 74, *www.chateaudelastours.com*, is set among the *garrigue* and canyons where motor-heads train for the Paris–Dakar rally – you too can have a go in a four-wheel-drive. Château Lastours has grown wine since the 12th century, and was revived in 1970 by a group in Marseille in order to produce wines according to the most modern methods, and at the same time to offer employment and independence to people with mental disability (try the unusual Vendange Tardive harvested at the end of October, perfumed and rich). The **Château de Boutenac**, Maison des Terroirs en Corbières, **t** 04 68 27 84 73, is a showcase for Corbières AOC wines, *www.aoc-corbieres.com*, with a wide range of wines to taste and buy, along with other local products.

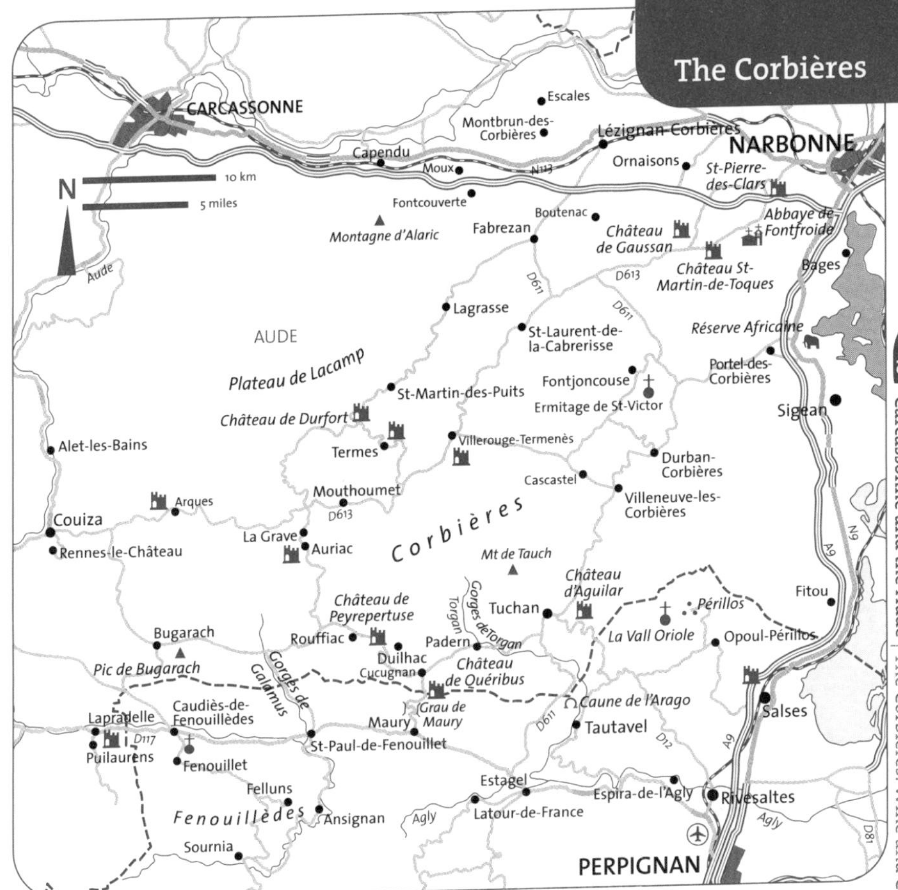

seven local hermits reproduce Christ's miracle of the bread and fish; it was one of several he founded to offer people protection in an area that by then had been devastated by centuries of war with Franks, Visigoths and Muslims. Some of the houses around the central *halles* date back to the 14th century, while the walls and the graceful hump-backed **Pont Neuf**, the older of its two picturesque bridges, are from the 12th. There's a new little museum, the **Musée 1900 AD** at 13 Bd de la Promenade, depicting life at the turn of the last century, with shop-fronts and workshops along with dolls and toys, plus a wine-tasting at the end.

Musée 1900 AD
t 04 68 32 18 87; open April–mid-Oct Tues–Sun 10–12.30 and 2–6; other times open bank and school holidays, same hours; adm includes self-guded audio tour and half a bottle of wine

The bridge leads to the **Abbaye de Ste-Marie d'Orbieu**, divided into two properties after the last 14 monks were shown the door during the Revolution. One part became an orphanage for decades, while the church half is now home to a monastic community, the Canons Regular of the Mother of God. Part of the transept dates from the 9th century, and in the Chapelle Abbatiale (1296) are fragments of a mural of the Tree of Life and the Last Judgment. There are two picturesque cloisters, from the 13th and 17th

Abbaye de Ste-Marie d'Orbieu
t 04 68 43 15 99, www.chanoines-lagrasse.eu; open June–Sept Fri–Wed 3.15–5.25 (last entry), closed Thurs; Oct–May Sat, Sun and hols; adm

centuries. Take the 16th-century tower's 230 steps up for the charming view over Lagrasse and the surrounding hills; if it's hot there will be local families swimming in the clear green waters of Orbieu just below.

St-Martin-des-Puits
ask at the mairie, **t** *04 68 43 11 66, for the key*

Southwest of Lagrasse, in one of the remotest corners of the Corbières, there is a remarkable country church at **St-Martin-des-Puits**. The oldest part, the apse, was built in the 9th century, and has a horseshoe arch supported on a pair of Visigothic colums and the nave has some still recycled Merovingian pieces. Picasso made a special visit to see the fanciful frescoes, added in the 11th century.

Termes and Villerouge-Termenès

Château de Termes
t *04 68 70 09 20, www.chateau-termes.com; open July–Aug daily 9.30–7.30; April–June and Sept–Oct daily 10–6; Nov–mid-Dec and Mar Sat, Sun and hols 10–5; closed mid-Dec–Feb; adm*

Château de Villerouge-Termenès
t *04 68 70 09 11; open July–Aug daily 10–7.30; April–June and Sept–Oct daily 10–6; Nov–mid-Dec and Mar Sat, weekends and hols 10–5; closed Jan–Feb; adm*

Near here, the Termenès is the wildest, least-travelled part of the Corbières; its name comes from the Latin *terminus* – the end of cultivatable land. The castles at **Termes** and **Durfort** are less than 5km apart. Both were the strongholds of local barons – Termes belonged to the Viscount Raymond, brother of the Cathar *parfait* Benoît de Termes, who in 1207 debated religion with St Dominic at the famous Colloquy of Montréal. Both castles were besieged and taken by Simon de Montfort during the Albigensian Crusade; Termes held out for four months, until lack of water forced the defenders to sneak out one night through a secret passage, although the elderly viscount was captured and died imprisoned in Carcassonne.

His son Olivier de Termes was one of the greatest knights of the day. He joined in the fight to regain Carcassonne for the Trencavels in 1240, but then swore allegiance to Saint Louis. He led the Seventh Crusade and accompanied the king out of Aigues-Mortes on his disastrous Eighth Crusade to Tunis, then died in Acre in 1274. His castle at Termes was blown up in the 1600s, but the surviving walls and vertiginous views still impress.

Montfort also conquered the **Château de Villerouge-Termenès**, 14km east, which has been restored to its 13th-century glory. Inside, an audiovisual display, 'The World of Guilhem Bélibaste, the last Cathar *parfait*', evokes the story of the Cathars, life in the Middle Ages and the story of Guilhem Bélibaste, who was burned at the stake here in 1321.

There's yet another castle at **Auriac**, an old copper-mining village; nearby, at **La Grave**, is an unusual 9th- to 12th-century country church, the Chapelle St-André.

★ Château de Peyrepertuse
t *04 82 53 24 07, www.chateau-peyrepertuse.com; open July–Aug daily 9–8; April–June and Sept daily 9–7; Oct 10–6; Nov–Dec and Feb–Mar daily 10–5; closed Jan at the end of the Christmas holidays; adm; note that the château may close in bad weather, especially in thunderstorms*

Château de Peyrepertuse

Castles atop mountains will be nothing new by now, but nowhere else, perhaps, is there a bigger castle atop a taller, steeper mountain. If the air is clear, and you know where to look, you can spot Peyrepertuse ('pierced rock' in Occitan) from any bit of high ground as far away as the coast. From Rouffignac, on the road from Auriac, it is an unforgettable sight – a white limestone cliff rising vertically up to the clouds, crowned by a stretch of walls and towers over 777ft long. Close up, from Duilhac or the bottom of the cliff, you can hardly see it at all.

Begun in the 9th century by the Count of Besalú, Peyrepertuse was abandoned by its owner, Guillaume de Peyrepertuse, after the son of Raymond-Roger Trencavel failed to re-take Carcassonne in 1240. Not long after, it was expanded to its present dimensions by Saint Louis. As important to the defence of France's new southern border as Carcassonne, Peyrepertuse was intended as an unconquerable base, big enough (incredibly, it's the same size of Carcassonne's Cité) to hold a large force that could come down and attack the rear of any Aragonese invader. Attacking it would be madness; no one ever tried, although it's a fairly easy 15-minute hike up from the car park.

The entrance leads into the **Château Vieux**, the original castle, rebuilt by Saint Louis. Here you'll discover one of Peyrepertuse's secrets: the castle may indeed be long, but, conforming to its narrow site, in places it is only a few yards across, resembling a huge prow on the rock. Nearly everything is in ruins, although the keep is still in good shape, along with a large cistern and the ruined chapel directly behind it. Further up is a vast open space that held most of the barracks and stores; and above this, Louis added yet another citadel called St Jordi, a castle in a castle, with another keep and chapel. There is a medieval festival in August, and falconry demonstrations in summer.

There are no easy roads in any other direction from Peyrepertuse, but, if you're heading west, rejoin the main route by way of the D7 and the white cliffs of the **Gorges de Galamus**, the most impressive natural wonder of the Corbières, a deep gorge with wonderful stone pools for swimming and canyoning.

Cucugan and Quéribus

Southeast of Peyrepertuse, **Cucugnan** is a colourful little village with a windmill, offering a scenic detour through the spectacular **Grau de Maury**, the Corbières' back door through Roussillon. Its landmark is obvious from a distance, the picture-postcard **Château de Quéribus**, balancing nonchalantly on a pinnacle, half a mile in the air over the gorge, reached in a rather steep 20–25-minute climb from the car park. Quéribus was the very last redoubt of the Cathars; a small band of bitter-enders, protected by the castle's master Pierre de Cucugnan, held out here until Olivier de Termes persuaded them to surrender in 1255 – 11 years after their fiery Alamo at Montségur. In easy signalling distance of Peyrepertuse, the views are simply spectacular, taking in the Mediterranean and the Pyrenees.

Château de Quéribus
t 04 68 45 03 69; open July–Aug daily 9–8; April–June and Sept daily 9.30–7; Oct daily 10–6.30; Nov–Jan daily 10–5; Feb daily 10–5.30; Mar daily 10–6; closed Jan except school hols; adm

Admission to the castle includes a stop at the Achille Mir theatre to hear the famous repent-and-be-saved speech of the parish priest of Cucugnan, from the story in Alphonse Daudet's *Lettres de mon moulin*. And who was Achille Mir? He was the local scribe who wrote the story that Daudet shamelessly plagiarized for his own, to the extent that most readers are surprised that Cugugnan is here and not in Provence. Pop into Cucugnan's church to see an unusual statue worthy of Rennes-le-Château – a rare pregnant Virgin, holding a baby – and visit the **Miellerie des Deux Châteaux** to pick up a jar of the Corbières' other speciality – its sublime honey.

Miellerie des Deux Châteaux
t 04 68 45 02 88; open Mar–Oct daily 10–1 and 2–7; other times ring ahead

Padern just east has another 11th-century **castle**, once the property of the abbey of St-Marie d'Orbieu in Lagrasse, captured by de Montfort's bunch in 1210. Despite rebuilding work in the 18th century, it stands as a strikingly romantic ruin balanced on a precipice; its nickname is the Gate of Paradise (there's an easy path up from the south). The village also offers the chance of a scenic detour through the **Gorges du Torgan**.

Tuchan, Aguilar and Durban-Corbières

To the east of Padern, the humble, two-lane D611 was the medieval main route through the Corbières, connecting with the passes over the Pyrenees to Spain. Castles occur with the frequency of petrol stations on a motorway; before the kings of France asserted their authority, one wonders how many times the poor merchants had to pay tolls. Even the landscape is suggestive of castles, with limestone outcrops resembling ruined walls and bastions. Below are dry stone terraces and *capitelles* (dry stone huts) recalling the time when, instead of vines, this was the land of shepherds, who brought their flocks down from the Pyrenees to graze in the winter.

All the real strongholds are in ruins today. **Tuchan**, another typically stark and dusty Corbières village in the shadow of 2,800ft Mount Tauch (the heartland of AOC Fitou, *see* box), has no fewer than three ruined castles. The best of them, the **Château d'Aguilar**, is the most domestic-looking of the 'five sons of Carcassonne', along with Puilaurens, Quéribus, Peyrepertuse and Termes, but it saw plenty of action: Simon de Montfort stormed it in 1210, but the French had to take it again from rebellious barons 30 years later; over the next 200 years the Spaniards knocked at the gate with regularity. Two walled enclosures survive, along with the Romanesque chapel of Ste-Anne, the keeper's residence and guards' room, and gorgeous views over the hills and vines.

Château d'Aguilar
t 04 68 45 51 00; open April–mid-June 10–6; mid-June–mid-Sept 9–7; mid-Sept–early Nov 11-5; adm

From Tuchan, you can (in good weather) drive much of the way up a dirt track to the austere Romanesque chapel of Notre-Dame de Faste, and then carry on to the summit and the **Tour des Géographes**, a tower built for the Académie des Sciences on the

Wine: AOC Fitou

Fitou, near the border of Roussillon, gave its name to one of Languedoc's finest wines, although its heartland is inland, along the stretch of D611 between Villeneuve and Tuchan. Strong and fragrant with the scent of the *garrigue*, dominated by carignan (mixed with grenache and syrah), Fitou was the first AOC-designated wine in the region (1948). It isn't sold until after a year or more of maturation, and after five years or longer in the bottle takes on a spicy, wild aroma. At the **Château de Nouvelles**, on a side road north of Tuchan, **t** 04 68 45 40 03, try the delicious Fitous, Rivesaltes and Muscat. Another good bet is **Château L'Espigne** in Villeneuve-les-Corbières, **t** 04 68 41 92 46 , *www.chateaulespigne.fr*. This ancient estate, originally a '*moulin à huile*', is planted with 90-year-old vines that produce tiny amounts of grapes, resulting in wines of enormous concentration and complexity. Award-winning Corbières, *vins de pays* and over 90 per cent of the Fitou sold in the UK comes from the co-operative **Les Vignerons de Mont Tauch** in Tuchan, who have recently opened a new visitors' centre at 2 Rue de la Coopérative, **t** 04 68 45 44 73, *www.mont-tauch.com* (*open winter Mon–Sat 9–12 and 2–6; summer daily 9–1 and 2–7*). Or visit the **Caves des Vignerons de Fitou**, on the N9, **t** 04 68 45 71 41, or **Les Maitres Vignerons du Paradis**, Grand Rue, Cascastel, **t** 04 68 45 91 74, *www.cascastel.com* (*open Mon–Fri 8–12 and 2–6*), who produce a red Fitou, Château d'Arse, which despite its unfortunate name is a real fruity delight.

order of the Revolutionary government in Paris, with a very special task: to calculate with absolute precision the line of the meridian from Dunkerque to Barcelona, to help determine a unit of measure one ten-millionth of the distance from the Pole to the Equator. After six years of work, the astronomers presented the standard metre, cast in platinum in 1799.

One of the smaller models of Corbières castles, built by the kings of Aragon, is at the wine-heartland **Durban-Corbières**; it was made into a residence of the Barons of Gléon until they died out in 1787, and then cannibalized for its stone. North of here, the landscapes are so empty they attracted hermits; some of these religious athletes, who apparently did not get on with their brethren at the Abbaye de Fontfroide (*see* p.235) lived up at the **Ermitage de St Victor**, north of Durban, and enjoyed some of the region's finest views. Modern visitors have the option of retiring to little **Fontjoncouse** – and in this rather unlikely tiny villae, enjoying some of the finest food in all France (*see* 'Where to Stay and Eat in Corbières', below).

Terra Vinea
t 04 68 48 64 90, www.terra-vinea.eu; guided tours (in French) Mon–Sat at 1.45, 3.15 and 4.45; Sun and hols at 11, 1.45, 2.30, 3.15, 4 and 4.45; adm

Overlooking the Mediterranean, **Portel-des-Corbières** offers up wine and Mediterranean history with theme park panache at **Terra Vinea**, run by the Caves Rocbère (the name used by three local co-operatives): there's a film, a little train ride, a sound and light show with wine barrels in the startling cathedral-like confines of a former gypsum quarry, and a visit through historical eating and wine-making from ancient Rome to the present wine-tasting.

Market Days in the Corbières

Lézignan-Corbières: Wed.
Lagrasse: Mon.
Tuchan: Thurs.

Where to Stay and Eat in the Corbières

Hotels and restaurants are few and far between in the Corbières, which makes it all the more surprising that a village of 137 souls boasts one of the finest restaurants in France.

ⓘ **Lézignan-Corbières >**
*9 Cours de la République, **t** 04 68 27 05 42, www.lezignan-corbieres.fr; open July–Aug Mon–Sat and Sun am; Sept–June Mon–Fri*

★ **Maison Allenne >**

★ **Château Haut Gléon >>**

ⓘ **Lagrasse >**
*16 Rue Paul Vergnes, **t** 04 68 43 11 56, www.lagrasse.com; open daily*

★ **Auberge du Vieux Puits >>**

Lézignan-Corbières ✉ 11200

*****Relais du Val d'Orbieu**, on the D24 in Ornaisons (east of Lézignan), **t** 04 68 27 10 27, *www.relaisduvald orbieu.com* (€€€€-€€). Amid the vines north of the village, it has tennis, a pool and all amenities, including an excellent restaurant (€€€) serving fish baked with rosemary and more. *Closed Dec and Jan; restaurant eves only.*

Maison Allenne, 6 Rue du 24 Février, **t** 04 68 27 14 48, *www.maison allene.com* (€€). Charming B&B with delightful knowledgeable owners in the village centre; great breakfast too.

Balade Gourmande, Bd Léon Castel, **t** 04 68 27 22 18 (€). There's a buffet of starters and desserts, and in between well prepared main courses, all for under €20.

Coco Sweet, 4 Place Salvadore Allende, **t** 04 68 33 56 28, *www.cocosweet.net* (€). Popular for its laid-back atmosphere, and delicious crêpes, salads and grilled steaks. *Closed Wed and Sun lunch.*

Lagrasse ✉ 11220

L'Hostellerie des Corbières, 9 Bd de la Promenade, **t** 04 68 43 15 22, *www. hostellerie-des-corbieres.com* (€€). A Logis de France hotel in a *maison de maître*, with a decent restaurant looking out over the vines (€€). *Closed Jan; restaurant closed Thurs.*

Duilhac-sous-Peyrepertuse ✉ 11350

L'Hostellerie du Vieux Moulin, 24 Rue Fontaines (entrance to the village), **t** 04 68 45 02 00 (€€–€). Run by the same people as the Auberge in Cucugnan. They have entirely renovated this old house near Peyrepertuse to create equally welcoming rooms. No restaurant, but breakfast available. *Closed mid-Nov– Easter.*

Cucugnan ✉ 11350

****Auberge du Vigneron**, 2 Rue Achille Mir, **t** 04 68 45 03 00, *www.auberge-vigneron.com* (€€–€). Just six cosy rustic rooms and a restaurant (€€) in a former wine cellar. *Closed mid-Nov–Feb; restaurant closed Mon.*

Durban-Corbières ✉ 11360

Château Haut Gléon, **t** 04 68 48 85 95, *www.hautgleon.com* (€€). Stay on a wine estate in the Corbières hills, with comfortable stylish rooms and *gîtes* in the renovated stable wing and works of art in the garden. There's breakfast but no restaurant (most go to the Auberge du Vieux Puits, *see* below).

Le Domaine Grand Guilhem, 6km west from Durban at Cascastel, **t** 04 68 45 86 67, *www.grandguilhem.com* (€€). A fine wine estate offering four warm and welcoming B&B rooms with period furnishings in a 19th-century *maison de maître* and *gîtes*; lovely breakfast, pool and garden.

Le Clos de Cascastel, 28 Quai de la Berre, Cascastel, **t** 04 68 45 06 22 (€€). Hearty regional cuisine served in a former school building.

Fontjoncouse ✉ 11360

Auberge du Vieux Puits (**Gilles Goujon**), Av St-Victor, Fontjoncouse (off the D611), **t** 04 68 44 07 37, *www.aubergeduvieuxpuits.fr* (€€€€). Feast on the gorgeous cuisine of Gilles Goujon, who learned a trick or two at the Moulin de Mougins and was chosen by 6,000 French chefs as chef of the year in 2011 – as well as earning his third Michelin star and five *toques* from Gault-Millau. There are also 14 spacious rooms (€€€€–€€€) and a pool. *Closed June–Sept Mon lunch; Oct–May Sun eve, Mon and Tues; plus Jan and Feb.*

Narbonne

Narbonne gave birth to the last of the troubadours, Guiraut Riquier (d. 1292). A melancholy soul, like many men of his time, Riquier never seemed to earn his lady's affection, or the apprecia-tion of his patrons, and he grew to a bitter old age watching his world unravel. '*Mas trop suy vingutz als derriers*' ('But I was born too

Getting to and around Narbonne

By Train

Narbonne's **station**, just north of the centre on Bd Frédéric Mistral is, an important rail junction, in the middle of the main Bordeaux–Toulouse–Nice route across the Midi; there are frequent connections to Perpignan, Toulouse, Béziers and other coastal cities.

By Bus

Citibus (**t** 04 68 90 18 18, *www.citibus.fr*) provides links to greater Narbonne, including Narbonne-Plage and Gruissan.

By Boat

If you haven't any particular destination in mind, take a trip on the **canal boat** with the **Coches d'eau du Patrimoine** that traverses the Canal de la Robine for a tour of the nature reserve of Ile Ste-Lucie, departing from Cours Mirabeau (**t** 04 68 90 63 98; book). Otherwise, in mid-June–mid-Sept you can hire an **electric boat**, from Cours de la République, **t** 06 03 75 36 98.

---

late') he mourned in one of his last songs. If he had lived longer, he would have seen his own proud city become a symbol for the eclipse of the Midi and its culture. Narbonne, Languedoc's capital and metropolis since Roman times, suffered some outrageous fortune in the decades after Riquier's death, enough to plunge it into a centuries-long decline. The symbol for Narbonne's own particular eclipse is its majestic unfinished cathedral, the arches and truncated columns of its skeletal nave haunting the square in front of the plain brick façade thrown up when ambition died.

Fortunately, the Narbonne of today has no interest in melancholy whatsoever. Thanks to roads and railroads, trade has come back for the first time since the Middle Ages. The local economy is still largely fuelled by wine – the bountiful vineyards of the Corbières and other nearby regions. The city is also finding a new vocation as an industrial centre, and its outskirts have developed accordingly. With a population of only 50,000, Narbonne can nonetheless sometimes fool you into thinking it a metropolis. With its impressive medieval monuments, boulevards and lively streets, it is quite a happy and contented town – one of the Midi's most agreeable urban destinations – with an excellent museum and the best cathedral in the south.

History

Colonia Narbo Martius, a good site for a trading port along the recently built Via Domitia, began by decree of the Roman Senate in 118 BC. The colony rapidly became the most important city of southern Gaul, renowned for its beauty and wealth. Under Augustus it was made the capital of what came to be known as the province of Gallia Narbonensis. After 410, it briefly became the headquarters of the Visigoths, and continued as their northernmost provincial capital until the Arab conquest of Spain in the 8th century; the Arabs took Narbonne but could not hold it, and

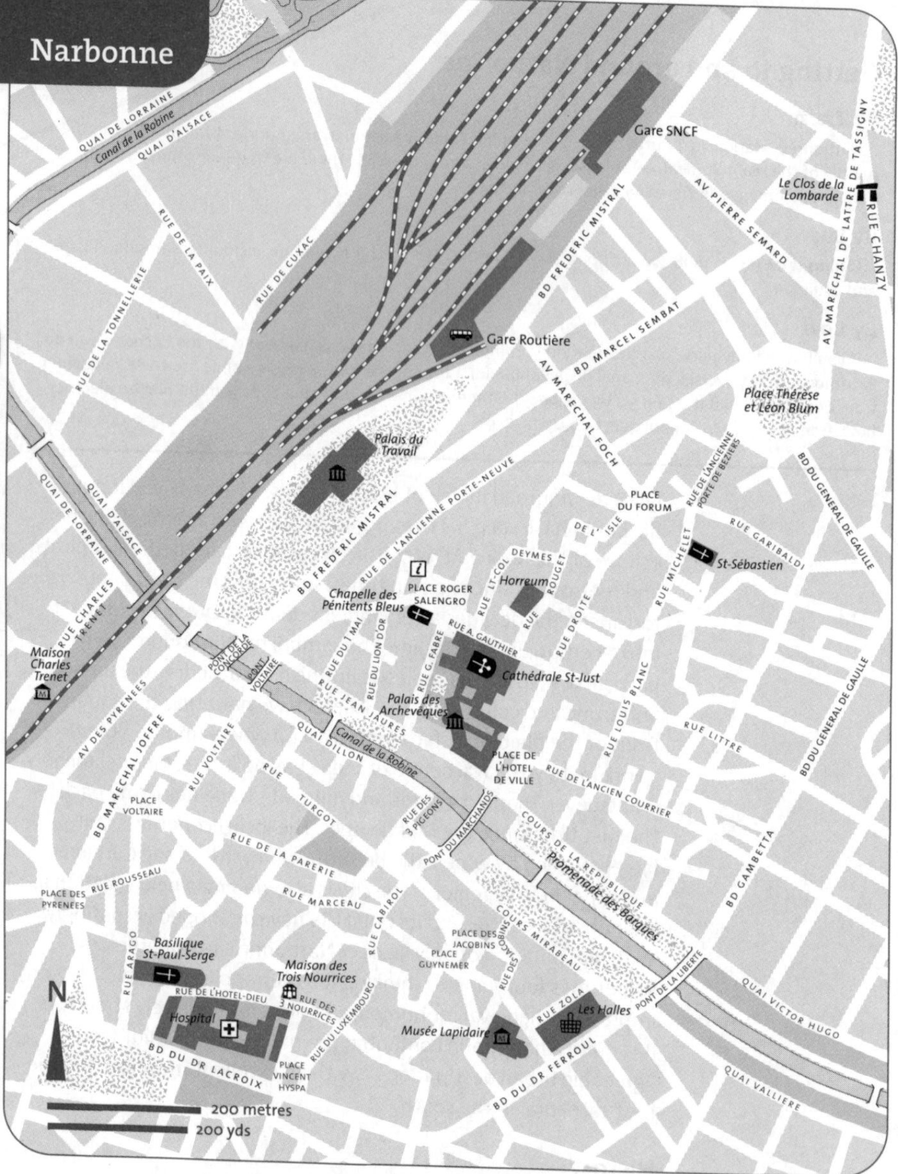

Pepin the Short reclaimed it for the Frankish Kingdom in 759, although so many Visigoths remained that until the 10th century Gallia Narbonensis was known as Gothia.

In the 12th century, Narbonne entered its second golden age. Under a native dynasty of viscounts the city maintained its independence for two centuries and began its great cathedral (1272). The famous Viscountess Ermengarde, who ruled for five decades after 1134, managed the ship of state with distinction while presiding over a 'court of love' graced by troubadours such as

Bernart de Ventadorn. The troubled 14th century was murder on Narbonne, however. As if wars and plagues were not enough, the harbour began to silt up; finally, even the river Aude decided to change its course and desert the city, ruining its trade. By the end of the century, the city had shrunk to a mere market town, albeit one with an archbishop and a very impressive cathedral.

Stagnation continued until the 20th century, despite the efforts of the indefatigable Paul Riquet in the 1680s; though his Canal du Midi (*see* pp.44–6 and 181) met the sea further north, Riquet began a branch canal, the Robine, that followed the old course of the Aude through Narbonne. Powerful interests in Béziers and Sète, however, kept it from being completed until 1786; the man who finally saw it through was Narbonne's last archbishop, an Irishman, Arthur Dillon, who played an important role in the city's history (his remains were returned to Narbonne cathedral in 2007, after his coffin came to light during excavation work for the Eurostar station in London's St Pancras). Only in the last hundred years has Narbonne started to revive, thanks to industry and the wine trade; since the Second World War it has overtaken the Aude's capital Carcassonne as the largest city in the *département*.

The City Centre

Narbonne is a city of surprises. Arriving by train or bus, the first thing you're likely to see is the gargantuan, horrific **Palais du Travail** on Bd Frédéric Mistral, a full-blown piece of 1930s Stalinist architecture. Turn the corner on to Rue Jean Jaurès and you'll be following the **Canal de la Robine** into the centre of the city, lined with a delightful park called the **Jardin Entre Deux Villes**. Behind the Hôtel de Ville, the **Pont des Marchands** is covered with shops, a charming miniature version of Florence's Ponte Vecchio.

Palais des Archevêques

Narbonne's centre is the busy **Place de l'Hôtel de Ville** – and always has been; a section of the Via Domitia is cleverly displayed in its original bed and alignment. Standing over this and looking at the entrance to the Rue Droite on the northeast side of the square and the Pont des Marchands opposite, you see a pair of steel strips, set in the ground, tracing the edge of the old highway to the two streets. This gives the rather eerie feeling that only a dust cover has been thrown over ancient Narbo Martius.

Facing the square, the twin façades of the **Palais des Archevêques** were blessed with a romantic Gothic restoration by the master himself, Viollet-le-Duc, in the 1840s; opinion is divided over whether this 19th-century fancy was an improvement on the austere 13th-century original it replaced. The passage between the two buildings (the **Palais Neuf** on the left, and the **Palais Vieux** on the right) leads to a small courtyard, and the entrances to Narbonne's two excellent museums of art and archaeology. The parts of the Archbishops' Palace not used for museums house Narbonne's **Hôtel de Ville**. In the Palais Neuf, the 1628 Hall of the Synods has original Aubusson tapestries. Now a reception room for the city, it was once the political centre of the region; Narbonne's archbishop had the right of presiding over the *Etats-Généraux*, or parliament, of Languedoc, although it moved to Pézenas in 1456.

Musée d'Art et d'Histoire

Musée d'Art et d'Histoire
t 04 68 90 30 54; www.amisdesmusees-narbonne.org; open mid-July–Oct daily 10–1 and 2.30–6; April–mid-July Wed–Mon 10–12 and 2–5; Nov–Mar Wed–Mon 2–5; joint adm with Musées Archéologique, Horreum and Lapidaire valid for three days

This museum occupies the old archbishops' apartments; it is reached by an elegant stair from the 1620s, decorated with a bust of Venetian historian Andrea Morosini and a bronze Capitoline Wolf, sent by the city of Rome for Narbonne's 2,000th birthday. These reminders of Italy are perfectly fitting, for this museum could easily pass for one of the great aristocratic galleries of Rome. Most of the collection belonged to the archbishops; they must have acquired a Roman taste on sojourns there. Their sumptuous rooms have been well preserved, beginning with the chapterhouse, or **Salle des Audiences**, where there is a portrait of the redoubtable Archbishop Dillon (the last of the line – his period of office was rudely interrupted by the Revolution in 1792), and an *Equestrian Louis XIV* by Van der Meulen – a pompous, offensive portrait, typical of the Sun King's use of art as propaganda. Louis slept here in 1642, in the adjacent **Chambre du Roi**. The 1632 ceiling frescoes are by local talent the Rodière brothers: harmless *Muses* that look more like nursery-school teachers. Note the floor, a restored Roman mosaic in a labyrinth pattern.

The **Grande Galerie** contains some of the best paintings: a gloomy landscape by Gaspard Dughet and an intense *St Jerome* by Salvator Rosa (both artists were favourites in Rome), a Canaletto and, among many Dutch and Flemish pictures, *Wedding Dance* by Pieter Breughel the Younger. The 16th- and 17th-century enamelled plaques come from Limoges, with portraits of French kings. Opposite these, a collection of lovely faïence apothecary jars from Montpellier makes a proper introduction to the next room, the **Salle des Faïences**. These 18th-century painted ceramics come mostly from well-known centres like Moustiers and Varange, though many are from cities such as Marseille and Montpellier, where the art has since died out.

The archbishops' chapel, the **Oratoire**, harbours a few surprises: 14th-century carved alabaster from Nottingham, an odd Byzantine icon from the Aegean, and a perfect, incandescent 15th-century Florentine *Madonna*; though anonymous (once falsely attributed to Piero della Francesca), it gracefully upstages everything else in the museum. The rest of the apartments are a grab bag: Archbishop Dillon's library, with his well-thumbed St Augustine, and his dining room; an *azulejo* tile floor from Portugal, François Ier's vinegar pot, Beauvais tapestries with scenes from La Fontaine's fairytales, a luscious Veronese (*The Anointing of King David*), portraits by Nattier and by Venice's favourite 18th-century celebrity portraitist Rosalba Carriera, a sprinkling of native and foreign followers of Caravaggio, and a tortured *St Andrew* by Ribera. There are also 19th-century works, and the Orientalist art of the age, charmingly displayed in a decor inspired by a North African palace and the Great Mosque of Cordoba.

Donjon Gilles Aycelin
open mid-July–Oct daily 10–1 and 2.30–6; April–mid-July Wed–Mon 10–1 and 2.30–6; Nov–Mar Wed–Mon 2–5; adm

If you don't mind tackling the 162 steps, you can climb the palace's 13th-century **Donjon Gilles Aycelin**, a Gothic defence tower with a collection of medieval sculpture and good views from the top.

Musée Archéologique

Musée Archéologique
t 04 68 90 30 65, same hours as Musée d'Art et d'Histoire; joint adm

It is only luck that made Nîmes the 'French Rome' while none of Narbonne's monuments has survived; the ambitious viscounts and archbishops of medieval Narbonne obviously had a greater appetite for recycling old building stone. There is, however, no shortage of remaining bits and pieces, and the best have been assembled here: reliefs from Narbonne's three triumphal arches and the gates of its walls, milestones from the Via Domitia, funeral monuments and a model of a Roman house. The **Chapelle de la Madeleine**, where Greek and pre-Greek ceramics are displayed, retains some fragments of its original 14th-century frescoes; it also offers the best view of the apse and buttresses of the adjacent cathedral, which is almost completely surrounded by buildings.

Christianity seems to have come late to Narbonne; the first bishop, Paul, is recorded in the 3rd century. Nevertheless, there are some Christian sarcophagi, and an unusual reliquary in the form of the Church of the Holy Sepulchre in Jerusalem. The products of other faiths here are more interesting: a Greek statue of a *Drunken Silenus*, altars dedicated to Cybele and Attis, and an image of Priapus, that mythological embarrassment, this time at least decently covered. Recent excavations in and around the city have enriched the Roman collection greatly, with sculptures, mosaics, and some of the finest examples of Roman painting in France from the Clos de la Lombarde (*see* p.234).

Cathédrale St-Just

(4) Cathédrale St-Just
open July–Sept daily 10–7; Oct–June daily 10–12 and 2–6

This can be entered through the 14th-century **cloister**, near the entrance to the museums, a Gothic quadrangle with gargoyles. A better way, though, is to circumnavigate the huge bulk of the cathedral and palace complex towards the west front and the **Cour St-Eutrope**, a spacious square that occupies the unfinished two-thirds of the cathedral itself. On every side rise truncated pilasters, walls and arch-bases, witness to medieval Narbonne's ambition and the 14th-century disasters that stopped it cold.

This is the third church to occupy the site; the first was a basilica from the reign of Emperor Constantine, the second a Carolingian rebuilding of AD 890. The present church was begun in 1272, at the height of the city's fortunes. Funds were hardly lacking; the cornerstone was sent by Pope Clement IV, a former Archbishop of Narbonne, and he probably contributed a little more besides. To extend the new cathedral to its planned length, it would have been necessary to rebuild a section of the city wall; in 1340 a lawsuit over this broke out between the city and the Church – a good, old-fashioned French lawsuit, just what was needed in those bad times to put an end to construction forever.

Just the same, this one-third of a cathedral is by any measure the finest in the Midi, the only one comparable to the magnificent Gothic structures of the Ile-de-France. The short nave, in fact, heightens the exuberant verticality of the 130ft apse and choir, exceeded in height only by those of Amiens and Beauvais. Throughout, the structural lines are accented with ribbing or with protruding stone courses, as if the builders wanted to leave a gentle reminder of the extraordinary technical skill that made such a building possible. The whole is done in a clean and elegant stone, grey perhaps, but a grey that here bids to be included among the colours of the spectrum.

Inside, most of the best features are in the ambulatory and its chapels. Near the altar, facing the chapels, are two remarkable archiepiscopal tombs. The **tomb of Cardinal Briçonnet** (1514) is a mix of Renaissance refinement and ghoulish, grinning skeletons, typical of that age. The other, the **tomb of Cardinal Pierre de Jugie**, is an exquisite Gothic work of 1376; though much damaged, some of the original paint remains. The ambulatory chapels are illuminated by lovely 14th-century glass: the *Creation* (left chapel), the *Infancy of Christ* in the centre, and *Sts Michael, Peter and Paul* (right chapels). Some faded original frescoes can be seen in the far right chapel, and also around the main altar. Behind this is something really special: rare polychrome reliefs of a late 14th-century Gothic retable. Ruined and covered in a Baroque remodelling of 1732, these were rediscovered in the 19th century. On the upper band (left to right): an *Annunciation* and *Kings of France*, the *Presentation at the Temple, Palm Sunday* and *Crucifixion*. Lower band: *Purgatory*, *Hell* and *Limbo*. The side chapels provide little to see but tapestries; in the first right is a 16th-century polychrome *Entombment of Christ* from Bavaria. Almost the entire west wall is covered by a spectacular **organ**, a mountain of carved wood and statuary that took over 100 years to complete (1741–1856).

Cathedral Treasury

Cathedral Treasury
open mid July–Oct Mon–Sat 10–12 and 2–5.45, Sun 2–6; Nov–mid-July Wed–Mon 2–5.45, closed Tues; adm

Don't miss the entrance to the treasury, through a tiny door in the right ambulatory chapel. Arranged in a domed chamber with odd acoustics, formerly housing the cathedral archives, the collection includes medieval reliquaries, books and a 10th-century ivory plaque. Here also are the most outlandish of all Narbonne's surprises: two early 16th-century Flemish **tapestries** from a set of 10, belonging to Archbishop François Fouquet (the other eight and a half have disappeared, probably ending up as insulation, mattress-stuffing and a bed for the dog). The half-tapestry depicts Adversity, from an *Allegory of Prosperity and Adversity*. Amidst a landscape of shipwrecks and earthquakes you'll find Cleopatra, Antiochus Seleucis and other celebrities of antiquity who met bad ends (all conveniently labelled), while Vulcan grinds out strife on his forge and a grinning Penury exults over the unfortunates. Part of the centrepiece also survived (on the left), dominated by an uncanny Goddess of Fortune on horseback, her face veiled.

The other tapestry is a strange account of the *Creation*. The seven days of Genesis are arranged in tableaux, each with figures of the Holy Trinity, represented as three crowned, bearded old men. The iconography is unorthodox in the extreme; the symbolism seems to hint at some concealed vein of medieval mysticism. In any case, the artists who created it produced a true *tour de force*, filling every corner with delightful naturalistic detail – a forest, the firmament, spring flowers and the Kingdom of the Sea. Bring the children, and see if they can spot the elephant.

Roman Narbonne

Horréum
open April–mid-July Wed–Mon 10–12 and 2–5, closed Tues; mid-July–Oct daily 10–1 and 2.30–6; Nov–Mar Wed–Mon 2–5, closed Tues; adm

There isn't much of it. The centre of the ancient city, north of the cathedral, is a dowdy, blank-faced quarter. Signs on the street corners point to the **Horréum** on 7 Rue Rouget de Lisle. Typical of the state-run warehouses of any Roman city, this is the only complete one anywhere. So far the north and west wings of tiny chambers has been excavated; the original structure was over 500 feet long. Among the fragments displayed in the evocatively illuminated rooms is a charming relief of bear trainers and their bears bathing together.

From the Place de l'Hôtel-de-Ville, Rue Droite runs northeastwards, roughly following the route of the Roman main street; it ends at **Place du Forum** – the former Forum, though nothing remains but some re-erected columns and a copy of a 17th-century fountain. One block east is the 15th-century Flamboyant church of **St-Sébastien**, built over the (apocryphal) birthplace of the saint himself. A favourite of artists across southern Europe (nearly always depicted, porcupine-line, stuck full of arrows), Sebastian was always a popular saint owing to the belief that he could intercede against the plague.

Further north, beyond the charming Square Thérèse et Léon Blum, on Rue de Chanzy, excavations continue at **Le Clos de la Lombarde**, a row of Roman houses, excavated since 1974, where the murals in the archaeology museum were found.

Le Clos de la Lombarde
t 04 68 90 26 38; open July–Aug 10–12 and 3–7, other times by appointment only

The Bourg

This is Narbonne's medieval extension across the river (now across the canal). Cross over by the bridge in the **Promenade des Barques**, the elegant park along the canal. On the other side, the city's covered **Halles** is a rare sensory experience even by French market standards. The Narbonnais take great pride in it, and it once won an annual award as the best in France.

Behind it, the 13th-century church of Notre-Dame-de-Lamourguie now houses the remarkable, newly refurbished **Musée Lapidaire**, a large collection of architectural fragments from ancient Narbonne, displayed more or less at random. They are here thanks to François Ier; on a visit, he recommended to the Narbonnais that they incorporate the vast heaps of antique rubble, column drums, inscriptions and tombstones lying about into the new walls they were building. The walls themselves thus became an open-air museum, much commented on by travellers, until they were demolished in the 19th century and the old bits assembled here – now the subject of an astonishing high-tech *son-et-lumière* show evoking the history of Narbonne and the Mediterranean.

Musée Lapidaire
t 04 68 65 15 60; open mid-July–Oct daily 10–1 and 2.30–6; April–mid-July Wed–Mon 10–12 and 2–5, closed Tues; Nov–Mar Wed–Mon 2–5, closed Tues; adm

Follow the boulevards west, along the course of the demolished medieval walls; the modern city hospital on Boulevard du Dr Lacroix incorporates the old one, the **Hôtel-Dieu**, with a grand Baroque chapel decorated by Narbonnais painters of the 1780s. Behind this, the **Maison des Trois Nourrices**, on the street of the same name, is the best surviving example of a Renaissance palace in the city; the 'three nurses' are the three classical caryatids holding up the main window.

Narbonne's other ancient church, the **Basilique St-Paul-Serge**, was first built in the 5th century, and dedicated to the first bishop of Narbonne. The present building was begun in 1229, an imposing monument that was one of the first in the south to adopt the new Gothic architecture. Three Christian sarcophagi from AD 250 (the oldest in Gaul) remain from the first church, and there's a famous frog squatting in a stoop – petrified, so legend has it, by an archbishop, in punishment for having croaked heresy during the Mass.

The catacomb-like **cemetery-crypt** (ask for the key from the vestry) was begun in the time of Constantine. Such burials were not peculiar to the Christians. In Rome, pagan and Christian catacombs exist side by side; parts of this one are decorated with pagan symbols, raising the possibility that this cemetery was for a time non-denominational.

Narbonne's Singing Fool

Maison Natale de Charles Trenet
t 04 68 90 30 65; guided musical visits mid-July–Oct daily 10–1 and 2.30–6; April–mid-July Wed–Mon 10–12 and 2–5, closed Tues; Nov–Mar Wed–Mon 2–5, closed Tues; adm

Follow the Canal de la Robine north, to the other side of the tracks, and you'll soon find the **Maison Natale de Charles Trenet** on 14 Av Charles Trenet, where the jolliest of all French singer-songwriters, known as the *Fou Chantant* ('the singing fool'), was born on 18 May 1913. Trenet left the house to the city when he died in 2001 on the condition that it didn't become a museum, so it's been left the way it was, with its old piano and furniture, filled with his songs.

Market Days in Narbonne

Daily am: Les Halles.
Thurs: outdoor market.

Shopping in Narbonne

Local Wine

For a wide selection of Languedoc wines, the **Cave du Palais** at Domaine de St-Crescent on the Route de Perpignan outside Narbonne, **t** 04 68 41 49 67, *www.lacavedupalais.com*, can't be beaten.

Activities in Narbonne

On a wet day (especially if you have kids) you could do worse than head out of town on the N9 towards Perpignan to **Espace de Liberté** (**t** 04 68 42 17 89, *www.espace liberte.com; open daily*), a giant aquatic park with three huge swimming pools, slides, tenpin bowling and ice skating.

Where to Stay in Narbonne

ⓘ Narbonne ›
31 Rue Jean Jaurès, t 04 68 65 15 60, www.mairie-narbonne.fr; open daily

Narbonne ✉ 11100

***__Château l'Hospitalet__, Rte de Narbonne-Plage, **t** 04 68 45 36 00, *www.chateau-lhospitalet.com* (€€€–€€). Ten minutes south of Narbonne, this wine *domaine* on the Clape Massif incorporates a contemporary hotel with 22 rooms, a *bistrot*-style restaurant, pool, *caves* and wine-tastings in an idyllic setting of vineyards overlooking the sea.

***__La Résidence__, 6 Rue du 1er Mai, **t** 04 68 32 19 41, *http://hotelresidence.fr* (€€). Near the cathedral in an old *hôtel particulier*, with calm, well-equipped rooms and a garage. *Closed mid-Jan–mid-Feb.*

***__Hôtel du Languedoc__, 22 Bd Gambetta, **t** 04 68 65 14 74, *www.hoteldulanguedoc.com* (€€). A gracious old establishment of 1855 near the station, now a little down-at-heel but recently refreshed, with free Wi-fi in the rooms. It has a good restaurant and bar-crêperie.

__France__, 6 Rue Rossini, **t 04 68 32 09 75, *www.hotelnarbonne.com* (€€–€). Cosy little hotel in a quiet side street near the covered market.

__Will's Hôtel__, 23 Av Pierre Sémard, **t 04 68 90 44 50, *http://willshotel-narbonne.com* (€€). It's not run by a Will, and the owners can't imagine who Will might have been, but it is still a comfortable and friendly place.

__Le Régent__, 13 Rue Suffren, **t 04 68 32 02 41, *www.leregent-narbonne.com* (€). Central, pleasantly renovated rooms in a 19th-century *hôtel particulier*.

Eating Out in Narbonne

★ Le 26 ››

La Table St-Crescent, 68 Avenue du Gén-Leclerc, **t** 04 68 41 37 37, *www.la-table-saint-crescent.com* (€€€€–€€€). Narbonne's top restaurant is just outside town at the Palais du Vin, where top culinary whiz Lionel Giraud holds court. A vine-covered terrace shelters a modern stylish dining room – even the humble sardine is transformed into a work of art here, accompanied by the region's top wines. Book. *Closed Sat lunch, Sun eve and Mon.*

Le 26, 8 Bd Docteur Lacroix, **t** 04 68 41 46 69, *www.restaurantle26.fr* (€€€–€€). Lovely market cuisine, warm welcome, and cooking classes if you're inspired to try it at home. *Closed Mon.*

Le Petit Comptoir, 4 Bd du Maréchal Joffre, **t** 04 68 42 30 35 (€€€–€€). A 1930s-style *bistrot* for some adventurous dishes with a Catalan touch. *Closed Sun and Mon.*

Le Billot, 22 Rue de l'Ancienne Porte de Béziers, **t** 04 68 32 70 88, *www.lebillot.com* (€€€). Northeast of the centre, near Square Thérèse et Léon Blum. Specializes in meats – beef, lamb, duck and pork. *Closed Mon, and Tues lunch.*

L'Ecrevisse d'Alsace, 2 Av Pierre Sémard, **t** 04 68 65 10 24, *www.restaurant-narbonne.com* (€€€–€€). This friendly brasserie with a veranda is a good source of fresh seafood. *Closed Sun and Wed.*

Aladin, 51 Rue de la Parerie, **t** 04 68 42 17 44, *www.restaurant-aladin.com* (€). Excellent couscous, *tagine* and *pastillas*.

Around Narbonne: Inland

Before there was Narbonne there was the **Oppidum de Montlaures**, 11km to the north, the hilltop town founded around 800 BC by the Elisycs, the Bronze Age people who occupied the Aude valley from Narbonne to Carcassonne before the invasion of the Iron Age Tectosage Celts. Like Ensérune, which it resembles, it survived into Roman times.

If you take the N113 west of Narbonne and turn south on the D613, the first sight, to the left, is the derelict, frequently overlooked castle of **St-Pierre-des-Clars**. In its grounds, Roman coins with the images of Pompey and Brutus have been found, but the present building probably dates from the late 12th or 13th centuries. The purpose of this ineffably romantic ruin was probably to protect sheep in wartime. This is not as daft as it may sound: after iron, sheep were the most valuable commodity of the Middle Ages, the wool-on-the-hoof that made the banking fortunes of so many medieval cities.

Three kilometres further down the D613, you'll see another impressive castle in the distance, madly perched on a perpendicular cliff. A perfect introduction or final bow to the fortified wilderness of the Corbières (*see* pp.218–26), **St-Martin-de-Toques** was gradually built between the 10th and 13th centuries by the viscounts of Narbonne. Recently restored, it is now a private residence.

Abbaye de Fontfroide

Abbaye de Fontfroide
t 04 68 45 11 08, www.fontfroide.com; open daily for hour-long guided tours only (audioguides in English) every 45mins except 1pm from 10–4; adm

A side road off the D613 leads to the Abbaye de Fontfroide. When the tour reaches the monks' **refectory**, the guide will take pains to point out that the fireplace is a recent addition; heating of any kind was a little too posh for medieval Cistercians. On the other hand, after inspecting the lavish church, courtyard and grounds it is hard to believe the monks were giving much away to the poor – a typical medieval enigma: power and wealth, without the enjoyment of them.

One of the most important abbeys in the south, Fontfroide w. founded in 1093 by the Viscount of Narbonne, and after a person. visit by St Bernard, adopted his Cistercian rule in 1145. It soon became one of the richest and most influential of all Cistercian houses: one of its abbots was the Papal Legate Pierre de Castelnau, whose murder in Beaucaire in 1209 led the pope to start the Albigensian Crusade; a century later, another abbot was the papal legate who testified against the Knights Templar at their trial in Paris; another would become Pope Benedict XII in Avignon. After its suppression in 1791, the abbey was largely in ruins until a local family, the Fayets, bought it in 1908 and have been restoring it ever since.

One of the loveliest corners of Fontfroide is its 13th-century **cloister**; its style of broad arches inset with smaller ones was much copied in later cloisters in Languedoc. The 12th-century **church** impresses with its proportions and Romanesque austerity: following Cistercian custom, simple floral patterns constitute the only decoration. The art of making stained glass, once one of France's proudest achievements, had nearly died out by the 19th century. There has been a modest revival in the last century; one of its first productions was the excellent set of windows here, a *Last Judgment* and signs of the zodiac done in the 1920s. More glass can be seen in the **dormitory** – fascinating abstract collages of old fragments, brought here from northern French churches wrecked during the First World War. Behind the cloister is a **rose garden**, where medieval varieties are grown by a local firm. The abbey has an excellent, moderately priced restaurant, **La Table de Fontfroide**, in the 18th-century *bergerie*; it also produces its own wine, which you can taste and buy.

To protect the produce of its vast estates, the abbey maintained a network of fortified farms and storehouses all over the region. The most impressive is near Capestang (*see* p.183); the closest, 8km west of Fontfroide, is the **Château de Gaussan** (4km south of Bizanet). Followers of Viollet-le-Duc restored it in the 19th century, with plenty of neo-Gothic ornament and frescoes inside. In 1994 it became the home of Benedictine monks from the abbey of Fontgombault in Indre; the **Château Gaussan Kozine** opposite makes fine Corbières.

Château Gaussan Kozine
t 04 68 45 18 07

Narbonne's Coast

The coastal road, more or less along the path of the Roman Via Domitia, cannot follow this complicated shoreline, a miasma of marshes and lagoons; some detours on the back roads will be necessary to see it. One big obstacle is the mouth of the Aude, northeast of Narbonne; this pretty and amiable river comes all the way from the high Pyrenees to meet an inglorious end in a boggy landscape called the Etang de Pissevaches, (literally) 'Piss-cow Swamp'.

Narbonne-Plage and Gruissan

South of the Etang de Pissevaches, one of the rare fishing villages in these parts, **St-Pierre-sur-Mer**, has been swallowed up by the bright, modern, characterless resort of **Narbonne-Plage**, with plenty of sand and its full whack of seaside amusements. Just to the north, near **Oustalet**, is Languedoc's answer to the Fontaine de Vaucluse, a 'bottomless' pool called the **Gouffre de l'Œil Doux** – the 'seductive eye' – always full of pure, fresh water, though only a mile from the sea. Beyond Narbonne-Plage, the landscape rises into the **Montagne de la Clape**, once an island and still a world in itself. Parts are lush and pine-clad, others rugged and desolate, reminiscent of a Greek island. Near the top, the 13th-century chapel of **Notre-Dame-des-Auzils** has or rather had a fascinating collection of sailors' *ex votos* – ship models, paintings and the like, many of which were stolen in 1960. Since then the priest has had the walls decorated with *trompe l'œil* paintings. Notre-Dame also has a unique, body-less marine cemetery, where all the monuments recall sailors lost at sea.

Notre-Dame-des-Auzils
key from Gruissan tourist office, generally open July and Aug 3–6

Gruissan

Most of those sailors came from **Gruissan**, south of La Clape. One of Narbonne's ports in the Middle Ages, Gruissan today is surrounded by lagoons and piles of salt from pans harvested every autumn; the charming village is set in concentric rings around a ruined 13th-century castle, built to defend the approaches to Narbonne. Its tower, the **Tour de Barbarousse**, possibly takes its name from a visit by the famous Turkish pirate-admiral Barbarossa; in the 1540s the Ottoman sultan's fleet was briefly based in Toulon, helping the French against the Holy Roman Emperor Charles V. To Gruissan's fine beaches the government has added a marina, resulting in one of the Aude's more agreeable resorts.

Gruissan's other landmark is the **Plage des Pilotis** (or Plage des Chalets) where neat rows of beach cottages hang in the air. The sea regularly covers the sand, so over a century ago people began the

Wine: AOC La Clape

The lower slopes of the La Clape are covered with vines producing small quantities of very good AOC Languedoc-La Clape (*www.laclape.com*), an increasingly exciting area for wine-lovers. The top-rated **Château de la Negly**, Fleury d'Aude, **t** 04 68 32 36 28, produces excellent whites as well as reds; the top of their line is named the 'Door to Heaven', Porte du Ciel. Other estates to look out for are **Château de Pech Redon**, **t** 04 68 90 41 22, *www.pech-redon.com*, where one of the first Languedoc pioneers, the late Jean Demolombe, produced his superb L'Epervier wines, and **Château l'Hospitalet**, **t** 04 68 45 36 00 (with a hotel/restaurant, *see* 'Where to Stay in Narbonne'). **Château Rouquette-sur-Mer**, off the D168 southwest of Narbonne-Plage in Gruissan, **t** 04 68 49 90 41, *http://chateaurouquette.com*, prouduces both AOC Languedoc and La Clape and rents out *gîtes*.

habit of building their holiday retreats on stilts. The houses and beach gained romantic notoriety as the setting for Jean-Jacques Beineix's cult 1986 film, *Betty Blue*; many have since been tarted up with aluminium siding.

Around the Etang de Bages et de Sigean

To carry on down the coast, you'll have to return to Narbonne and circle around the **Etang de Bages et de Sigean**. This broad lagoon, with its many islands and forgotten, half-abandoned hamlets, is especially rich in waterfowl, including flamingos, cormorants, egrets and herons. For the best view, drive across part of the Etang on the narrow D105 between the charming villages of **Bages** (now a fashionable haunt of art galleries and fish restaurants) and **Peyriac-de-Mer**. Near the latter, visit the little **Etang de Doul**, the saltiest of Languedoc's seaside lagoons, where people come to float and pretend they're at the Dead Sea. **Boat trips and windsurfing** on the big lagoon can be arranged, starting from the dock of a vanished medieval village, **Port-Mahon**, near **Sigean**, a pleasant if rather forgotten village that began as an Iron Age *oppidum*, Pech Maho, and a station on the Via Domitia. Finds are in Sigean's **Musée des Corbières** in Place de la Libération, which also offers guided tours of the *oppidum* (ring ahead). Excavations were relaunched in 2004 after the discovery of the remains of a massive ritual sacrifice of 25 horses, dated around the 3rd century BC and mixed in with a human body (perhaps sacrified as well). They also found the remains of a massive funeral pyre of ten individuals, burned with their jewellery and grave goods and just left on the spot. Not long afterwards, Hannibal and his elephants marched passed, followed by Pech Maho's destruction – by the Romans, leading researchers to suspect it was revenge for aiding the enemy.

Boat trips
contact the Cercle Nautique des Corbières **t** *04 68 48 44 52, www.port-mahon-voile.com*

Musée des Corbières
t *04 68 41 59 89; open July–Aug Tues–Fri 9–1; Sept–June Tues and Thurs 9–12 and 2–6, Mon, Wed and Fri 2–6*

Wildlife of an entirely different sort co-exists peacefully nearby at the **Réserve Africaine** north of Sigean: a big zoo, flamingo lake and drive-through safari park with the only white rhinoceroses, most likely, in all Languedoc-Roussillon, not to mention more Tibetan bears than in all Tibet.

Réserve Africaine
t *04 68 48 20 20, www.reserveafricainesigean.fr; open daily summer 9–6; closes earlier out of season; adm exp*

Port Nouvelle and Leucate

When the builders of the Canal de la Robine laid out their coastal port in 1820, they gave it the strikingly original name of **Port-la-Nouvelle**. Now France's third-largest Mediterranean port, it is a gritty, no-nonsense town of Communist stevedores, where the waterfront promenade takes in a panorama of shiny oil tanks. It has good beaches, and doubles as a bustling resort. If you didn't fancy the palms and ice cream of La Grande Motte or Cap d'Agde (*see* pp.146–7 and 172), a day on the beach here, watching cement barges and tankers sail past, might be just the thing. If you're

ⓘ **Gruissan >>**
1 Bd Pech Maynaud,
t *04 68 49 09 00,*
www.gruissan-mediterranee.com

ⓘ **Sigean**
Pl de la Libération,
t *04 68 48 14 81,*
www.sigean.fr;
open summer Mon–Fri plus Sat am and Sun am; winter Tues–Sat am

Tourist Information on Narbonne's Coast

The tourist office at **Sigean** includes a little museum with stuffed birds and archaeological titbits.

Where to Stay and Eat on Narbonne's Coast

Narbonne-Plage ✉ 11100

****Hôtel de la Clape**, 4 Rue des Fleurs, **t** 04 68 49 80 15, *www.hoteldelaclape.com* (€€€–€€). Hardly upmarket, but a a charming, family-run hotel and great address from which to write home, and it does have family rooms and a pool. *Closed Jan–mid-Mar.*

Gruissan ✉ 11430

****Le Corail**, Quai Ponant in Gruissan Port, **t** 04 68 49 04 43, *www.monalisahotels.com*. Little hotel on the port (€€€–€€). *Closed Nov–Jan.*

L'Estagnol, Quai de l'Etang, **t** 04 68 49 01 27 (€€). Popular converted fisherman's cottage at the entrance to the village, offering sumptuous seafood and fish. *Closed Sun eve, Mon and Tues lunch, and Feb.*

Bages ✉ 11100

Portanel, Passage du Portanel, **t** 04 68 42 81 66 (€€€). One of the best fish restaurants here, Portanel specializes in serving eel in every imaginable way. *Best to reserve.*

Domaine de Jugnes et sa Baleine
t *04 68 48 00 51;*
open daily 10–12 and 3–7

sticking around, don't miss on Avenue de Catalogne the **Domaine de Jugnes et sa Baleine**, housing a skeleton of a dead whale that washed up on the beach in 1989, which owner M. Fabre hauled home with the aid of a tractor, a 2CV and a few friends, then carefully reconstructed in an old wine warehouse. If you know your plants, cross the Canal de la Robine to the Ile Ste-Lucie, overgrown with 100 rare specimens.

For something completely different, continue south past another lagoon to **La Franqui**, a rare blossom on this coast: a holiday resort from the 1930s, with its stately houses and palms sheltered by the headland of Cap Leucate. **Leucate** itself is squeezed between its beach and lagoon, bursting with all the holiday essentials from casino to mini golf; at modern **Port Leucate**, holiday home owners can park their boats in front of their houses on canals, while the long stretch of sand between them is popular with naturists. The area is renowned among windsurfers: the blustering *tramontane* makes it one of the gustiest corners in the entire Mediterranean. To continue along the coast, *see* p.244).

Roussillon

Cross the Agly river into the southernmost angle of the French hexagon, and you'll begin to notice a certain non-Gallic whimsy in the names of the towns. The further south you go, the stranger they become: Llivia, Llous and Llupia, Eus and Oms, Molitg, Politg and Py, Ur and Err. You'll also notice that some malcontents have decorated the yellow diamond 'priority road' signs with four red stripes, making them into little escutcheons of the long-ago Kingdom of Aragon. Street signs appear in two languages. On menus, sweet wines and peculiar desserts will appear, and you may begin to suspect that you are not entirely in France any more.

You are in fact among the Catalans, in the corner of Catalonia that, for military considerations in the 17th century, was destined to become part of France. As a département, *it's officially known as the Pyrénées-Orientales (or P-O for short), but it prefers its more melodic ancient name, Roussillon.*

11

Don't miss

See map overleaf

pp.192–3

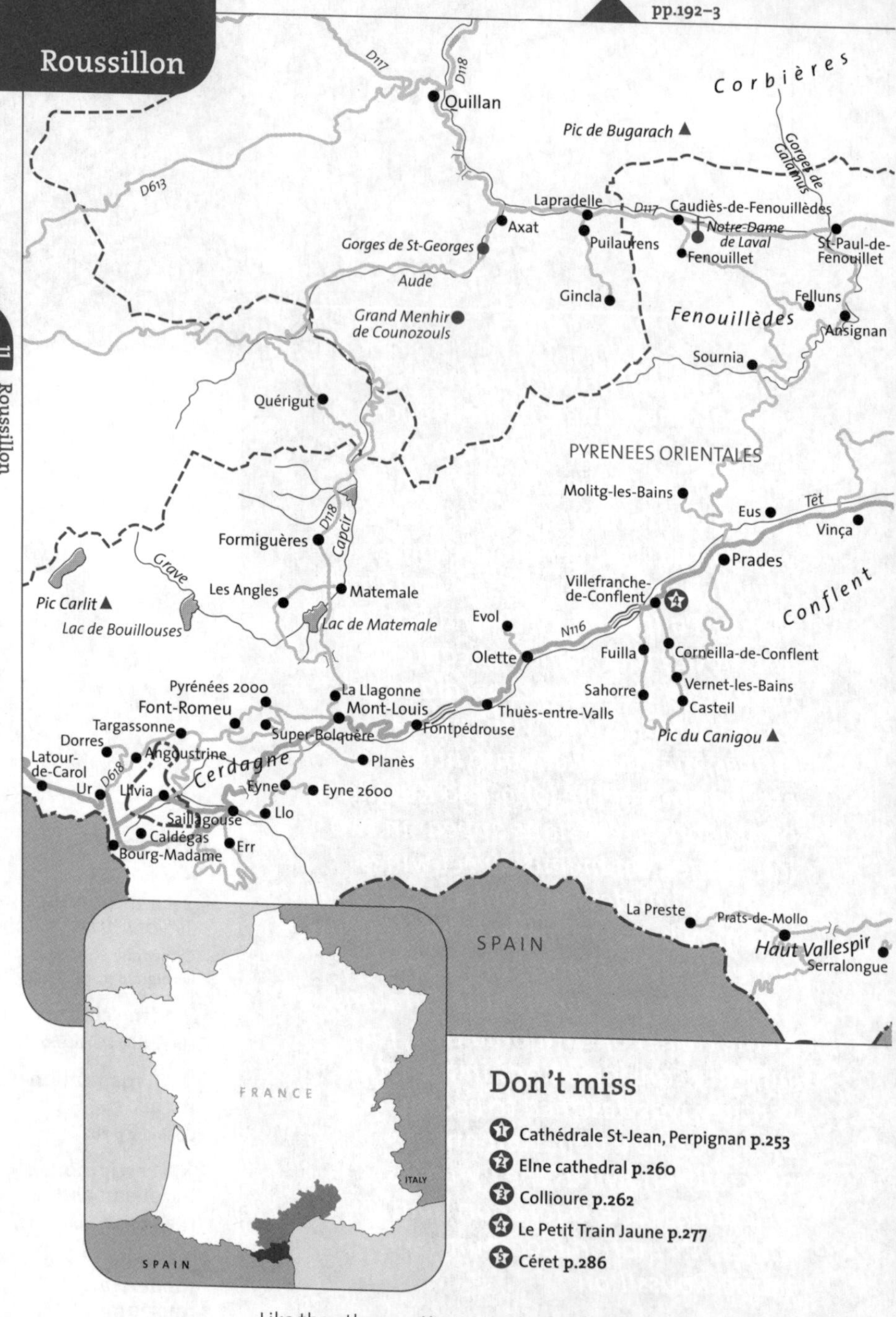

Don't miss

1. Cathédrale St-Jean, Perpignan p.253
2. Elne cathedral p.260
3. Collioure p.262
4. Le Petit Train Jaune p.277
5. Céret p.286

Like the other captive nations of the Hexagon – the Bretons and Corsicans, for example – most of Roussillon's people have rationally decided that being French isn't such a terrible fate. Catalan is spoken by relatively few, but this culturally passionate people stays

in close touch with the rest of 'southern' Catalonia; and they still perform the *sardana*, the national dance and symbol of Catalan solidarity.

Perpignan is the capital; around it stretches the broad Roussillon plain, crowded with the dusty, introverted villages that make all that sweet wine. The real attractions are on the periphery: Collioure and the delectable Côte Vermeille on one side and, on the other, valleys that climb up into the Pyrenees. The sun shines 300 days a year and the scenery is tremendous, even an hour's drive from the coast; among the pine forests and glacial lakes you can visit Vauban fortresses, ride the famous Little Yellow Train (*see* p.269), and get an introduction to the surprising early medieval

Beaches

The sand continues into Roussillon, to beaches favoured by beach bum Pablo Picasso. From Port-Barcarès southwards, beach follows beach, some less accessible than others (these tend to be haunted by overweight nudists). Picasso's favourite was Collioure, with its three small stretches of sand.

The best beaches are:

South of Port-Barcarès: empty miles of sand.

Collioure: for the bell-tower and because Picasso can't be wrong, but be prepared to share the space.

monuments of Catalonia, which compared to the rest of the region's are fairly intact – after all, Roussillon was still part of Spain during the Wars of Religion, and remained far enough out of the Revolutionary mainstream for its citizens to ever get the urge to take cudgels or torches to its beautiful churches.

Northern Roussillon

A geographical oddity, this run of coastline is almost perfectly straight and runs due north–south for 40km from Port-Barcarès to Argelès. It isn't the most compelling landscape, but it is almost solid beach, and has been much developed since 1960s, when De Gaulle's government decided to try to keep the French masses holidaying in France (but not on the elite Côte d'Azur) instead of spending all their hard-earned francs on the Costa Brava.

Port-Barcarès

Heading down the coast from Leucate (*see* p.240), there's more seaside la-la-land at **Port-Barcarès**, where the landmark is the *Paquebot Lydia*, a 1930s steamship brought over in 1967 by an entrepreneur and converted into a casino; in 2011 it was purchased by the town and awaits a new destiny. Further south, the beaches are less cluttered but harder to reach; back roads lead off the D81 to **Torreilles-Plage** and **Ste-Marie-Plage**.

The alternative to traversing beach-land is a voyage through the back end of the lagoon, the **Etang de Salses** (or **de Leucate**), on the same route tramped by Hannibal and his elephants. The divorce of land and sea here is startlingly complete. Until the 1960s (and DDT), the malarial coast was utterly deserted and no one in the region gave it a second thought; from the landward side of the lagoon, in a few minutes you can be up in the rugged, dusty hills of the Corbières (*see* pp.218–26) and Opoul (*see* p.246) where it is hard to believe any sea could be within a hundred miles. The only village on this side of the lagoon is **Fitou**, justifiably famous for one of the finest wines of Languedoc-Roussillon (*see* p.225).

Forteresse de Salses
t 04 68 38 60 13, www.salses.monuments-nationaux.fr; guided tours June–Sept 9.30–7; Oct–May 10–12.15 and 2–5; adm

Forteresse de Salses

After another 7km of emptiness appears the last, lowest and least spectacular of all this region's many castles – but the

Getting around Northern Roussillon

By Train

Local trains from Narbonne to Perpignan call at Salses and Rivesaltes; at the latter you can pick up the **Train Touristique du Pays Cathare et des Fenouillèdes** (**t** 04 68 59 99 02, *www.tpcf.fr*), revived in 2001. It offers rides in open-air carriages through some lovely scenery to St-Paul-du-Fenouillet, Caudiès, Puilaurens and as far as Axat in the Aude (*see* p.217) (*weekends April–Oct, daily July–Aug; reservations essential*).

By Bus

Buses (all fares €1) run by the Conseil Général (**t** 04 68 80 80 80, *www.cg66.fr/252-les-bus-departementaux.htm*) provide services to the main towns.

Forteresse de Salses was the most important of them all. Built in 1497 by Ferdinand the Catholic, first king of united Spain, Salses was the last word in castles for its time, the budget-busting masterpiece of a great military architect named Ramiro Lopez. Set squarely on the then French–Spanish border, Salses was meant to house 1,500 men to guard Perpignan and the vital coastal road. It finally had a chance to do so in 1639 – and failed. The Spaniards, caught by surprise, had only a small garrison at Salses; nevertheless, it required 18,000 Frenchmen and a month's siege to take it. The same year, a Spanish army spent three months winning it back. Both sieges were serious operations; until recently, the locals would go out cannonball-hunting for fun in the surrounding hills. When France acquired Roussillon in 1659, Salses no longer had a role to play. The famous Vauban, perhaps jealous, wanted to knock it down, but it was too expensive and survived to become a national monument in 1886.

At first glance, Salses looks strikingly streamlined and modern. It is a product of a transitional age, when defenders were coming to terms with the powerful new artillery that had made medieval castles obsolete. Salses is all curves and slopes, designed to deflect the cannonballs; its walls are not only incredibly thick (28ft on average, 50ft thick at the base), but also covered with heavy stone barrel vaulting to protect the walkway at the top.

The region around Salses and **Rivesaltes**, to the south, is famous for its sweet wines, sold throughout France. Rivesaltes was the home of Marshal Joffre, and now houses the small **Musée du Maréchal Joffre**, dedicated to the Battle of the Marne.

Musée du Maréchal Joffre
t 04 68 64 04 04; open mid-June–mid-Sept Tues–Sat 9.30–12.30 and 3–7; adm

In nearby **Espira-de-l'Agly** stands the impressive fortified Romanesque church of **Ste-Marie**, built in 1136 as part of a monastery by the bishops of Urgel in Spain (powerful Catalan clerics whose successors, along with the presidents of France, are still the joint tributary lords of Andorra). The businesslike exterior has one fine carved portal, but the lavish interior (unfortunately usually locked) still comes as a surprise, with polychromed marbles and elaborate altarpieces from the 16th century.

Wine: Rivesaltes and Côtes du Roussillon

Catalans have a notoriously sweet tooth, and some 90 per cent of the dessert wine (*vin doux naturel*) of France comes from this *département*, spilling over into the Corbières to the north. Mostly from grenache, muscat or maccabeu grapes, these wines are made simply by stopping the fermentation at the right moment, leaving more sugar in the wine; usually a small amount of pure alcohol is added as well. Since the 13th century, Rivesaltes (*www.rivesaltes.com*) has been known for its fruity muscat, a wine to be drunk young, with sorbets or lemon tarts. Its AOC status, awarded in 1972 along with other Rivesaltes red and white *apéritif* wines, covers 99 *communes* in the eastern Pyrenees. Try some in Rivesaltes itself, at the **Domaine Cazes**, 4 Rue Francisco-Ferrer, **t** 04 68 64 08 26, *www.cazes-rivesaltes.com*; the talented brothers Bernard and André Cazes not only produce some of the finest muscat but also AOC Côtes du Roussillon and Côtes du Roussillon Village, plus some excellent white, rosé and red *vin de pays*. In the past, few wine writers ever had anything good to say about this old *vin de pays* but, as in Languedoc, a number of producers like the Cazes brothers have been creating notable, individualistic wines from fine blends of syrah, carignan, grenache and mourvèdre.

Côtes du Roussillon is made all over the *département*, often in village co-operatives that also produce Rivesaltes or sweet muscat. In the hot corner around Perpignan, **Domaine Sarda-Malet**, Chemin de Ste-Barbe, **t** 04 68 56 72 38, *www.sarda-malet.com*, puts out three labels of red, two whites, a rosé, several *vins de table* and four dessert wines. Or visit the **Château de Jau** on the D117 in Cases-de-Pène, **t** 04 68 38 90 10, *www.chateaudejau.com*, which produces Côtes du Roussillon of surprisingly high quality. In summer they also host art exhibitions and have a restaurant that offers good value fixed-price menu lunches (*mid-June–Sept only, book at* **t** *04 68 38 91 38*), featuring local specialities and a wide range of wines. Some of the finest red and white wines , full of local character, can be found at **Domaine Gauby** in Calce, **t** 04 68 64 35 19, *www.domainegauby.fr*. The **Cellier des Albère** at St-Genis-des-Fontaines, **t** 04 68 89 81 12, *www.vignerons-des-alberes.com*, produces a honey-sweet, fresh, lively rosé, Château Montesque des Albères.

Inland: The Plateau d'Opoul

Just above Salses, the long rocky wall of the southern Corbières spreads into a *plateau* that happens to be one of the most barren and isolated places in France. Don't be surprised to find tanks and suchlike growling across your path. The western half of the Plateau d'Opoul is one of the French Army's zones for manoeuvres, the closest France can get to desert conditions. Most of the time, however, you won't see anyone, save old farmers half-heartedly trying to keep their ancient Citroëns on the road, on their weekly trip to the village to get a haircut or a goose.

The village is **Opoul-Périllos**, a cosy place that shuts itself off from the surrounding void. It is a relatively new settlement; its predecessor, **Périllos**, is an eerie ruined village higher up on the plateau, now inhabited by praying mantises, with another castle nearby. Both castle and village have enormous stone cisterns. Water was always a problem here – indeed, everything was a problem, and the 14th-century Aragonese kings who built both village and castle had to bribe people with special privileges to live on the plateau. Today there are vineyards, but until recently the only real occupation was smuggling.

Near the castle, a rocky side road leads west into the most desolate part of the plateau; at a spot called **La Vall Oriole** stands a massive, lonely limestone outcrop with a locked door at the bottom. It seems that some time in the early Middle Ages th… was hollowed out by a community of cave-dwelling monks, lik… famous Cappadocia ones in Turkey. There are plenty of other stran… things up on this plateau, and in its history: connections with Bérenger Saunière and André Malraux, dragon legends, ley lines, an odd ruin called the 'Seat of Death', a lord of Périllos who became grand master of the Knights of Malta, a mysterious plane crash and UFO sightings, rumours of secret government installations. Enough material, in fact, for Périllos to have become a little vortex of mystery, a kind of bargain-basement Rennes-le-Château (a website, *www.perillos.com*, provides a suitably murky introduction).

Tautavel and the Fenouillèdes

Descending from Opoul to the southwest, the D9 passes through some romantically empty scenery towards **Tautavel**, a pretty village under a rocky escarpment. Throughout Europe, prehistoric man picked the unlikeliest places to park his carcass. Around Tautavel, human bones have been found from as far back as 450,000–680,000 BC, making 'Tautavel Man' a contender for the honour of First European when discovered in 1969 (although his grandad status has since been usurped by the discovery in 2008 of a 1.2 million-year-old humanoid jaw at Atapuerca in northern Spain). Back then, the climate was quite different, and Tautavel Man had elephants, bison and even rhinos to keep him company. Palaeolithic bones have become a cottage industry – over 430,000 have been found, especially in a cave called the Caune de l'Arago north of the village – the best being displayed in the **Musée de Tautevel: Centre Européen de Préhistoire**, in Avenue Léon Jean Grégory. From April to September, during the excavation season, there's a camera link to the cave so you can watch the palaeontologists at work.

Musée de Tautevel
t 04 68 29 07 76, www.tautavel.com; open July–Aug daily 9–7; Sept–June 10–12.30 and 2–6; adm

From Tautavel, the D611 continues south into the valley of the Agly. This and surrounding mountains make up the **Fenouillèdes** – the northernmost region of medieval Catalonia. The scenery makes a remarkable contrast to the dry and windswept Corbières. Here, limestone gradually gives way to granite, the true beginning of the

The Wines of Maury

As in neighbouring Roussillon, the area around Maury and Estagel produces sweet dessert and *apéritif* wines called VDNs, or *vins doux naturels* – but it makes what many consider the best of them: Maury. Like its chief rival Banyuls, Maury is made from grenache noir, but it has a distinctive character of its own, a more consistent colour and spicy, leathery aroma, especially as it ages; a fragrant well-aged Maury Chabert is one of the few French wines that goes well with curries. Most of the 40,000 hectolitres produced each year pass through Maury's village co-operative, the **Vignerons de Maury**, on Av Jean Jaurès, **t** 04 68 59 00 95, *www.vigneronsdemaury.com*. Also look out for wines from the excellent estate of **Mas Amiel**, **t** 04 68 29 01 02, *www.masamiel.fr*, isolated in the middle of the dry schist vineyards surrounded by cypress and olive trees under the grey jagged peaks. You can see the Maury being exposed to the sun in a collection of glass jars (*bonbonnes*) *(visits Mon–Sat 9–6)*.

Pyrenees. Some of it is covered by ancient virgin forest, broken by quick-flowing streams and ravines. The first likely stop along the D117 is **Maury**, famous for its dessert wines and its pottery of deep blues and greens; next is **St-Paul-de-Fenouillet**, known for almond cookies.

The next village, **Caudiès-de-Fenouillèdes**, has become something of an art centre, especially in summer. Three kilometres to the south, **Fenouillet** is guarded by three more ruined castles, all within a few hundred yards of each other (for the crow, anyhow). Beneath them, the simple medieval chapel of **Notre-Dame-de-Laval** has a wonderful polychrome wooden altarpiece, dated 1428.

The D619 south from St-Paul-de-Fenouillet is the only good road through the Fenouillèdes, passing through **Sournia** on the Desix river, the only real town. Along the way, be sure to stop at **Ansignan** to see its Roman **aqueduct**, a rustic, seldom-visited version of the famous Pont du Gard. An arcade of 551ft, with 29 arches, carries it over the Agly; it is still in use, carrying water to the vineyards, and you can walk over it, or follow the channel towards the village. The question is why the Romans built it, with no nearby towns. It is unlikely that agriculture on the coastal plains was ever so intensive as to merit such a work. One possibility is a patrician villa – such things were often cities in themselves – but no traces of one have been discovered. Signs in Ansignan point the way up to a dolmen and to **Felluns**; there are wide-ranging views over the mountains just beyond, on the D7 south to Sournia.

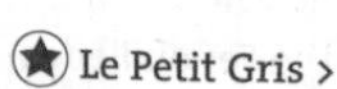

Le Petit Gris >

Port-Barcarès
Pl de la République, **t** *04 68 86 16 56, www.portbarcares.com; open daily*

St-Paul-de-Fenouillet >>
26 Bd Agly, **t** *04 68 59 07 57, www.st-paul66.com; open July–Aug Mon–Sat; Sept–June Tues–Sat*

Where to Stay and Eat in Northern Roussillon

Tautavel ✉ 66720

Le Petit Gris, Route d'Estagel, **t** 04 68 29 42 42 (€€). A very popular family restaurant with great views of the plain from big windows; they serve traditional Catalan fare, including *petit gris* (snails), *gambas* and more. *Closed Mon.*

Maury ✉ 66460

Pascal Borrell, La Maison du Terroir, Avenue Jean-Jaurès, **t** 04 68 86 28 28, *www.maison-du-terroir.com* (€€€). Simple decor and a terrace amid the vines; contemporary Mediterranean cuisine from a chef trained at Arpège, and a €25 lunch *formule* Mon–Fri.

Caramany ✉ 66720

Auberge du Grand Rocher, Rue Eloi Tresserres, **t** 04 68 84 51 58, *www.auberge-du-grand-rocher-66.com* (€€€–€€). Simply furnished restaurant in a pretty hill town, a 20min drive from Maury; the terrace has valley views. Local specialities such as boar casserole. Book. *Closed Sun eve and Mon in summer; Mon, Tues and Sun–Thurs eves in winter.*

St-Paul-de-Fenouillet ✉ 66220

****Le Châtelet**, Rte de Caudiès, **t** 04 68 59 01 20, *www.hotel-lechatelet.com* (€€–€). A Logis de France hotel, with a pool and restaurant (€€). *Closed Nov–Mar; restaurant closed lunch.*

****Relais des Corbières**, 10 Av Jean Moulin, **t** 04 68 59 23 89, *www.lerelaisdescorbieres.com* (€). Smaller, central, with a restaurant (€€).

Getting to and around Perpignan

By Air

Perpignan's **airport**, **t** 04 68 52 60 70, *www.perpignan.cci.fr*, is 5km northwest of the city and linked by shuttles (*navettes*) from the bus station an hour before each flight (**t** 04 68 55 68 00 and schedules on the airport website). There are regular flights from the UK, although there are far more frequent ones to Girona, in Spain; two companies, **Frogbus** (*www.frogbus.com*) and **Perpicat** (*www.perpicat.com*) provide links.

By Train

The **train station** is at the end of Av du Général de Gaulle and has frequent slow services down to the Spanish border at Port Bou and high speed links to Paris, Figueres and Barcelona (due in 2012).

By Bus

Perpignan's city bus service, CTPM (**t** 04 68 61 01 13, *www.ctpmperpignan.com*), links the urban area to most of the beaches in summer. Bus lines across the *département* (**t** 04 68 80 80 80, *www.cg66.fr/252-les-bus-departementaux.htm*) leave from the ***gare routière*** north of the city, on Av du Général Leclerc, **t** 04 68 35 29 02.

Perpignan

There's a little craziness in every Catalan soul. In *Perpinyà* (as its residents call it), former capital of the kings of Majorca and the counts of Roussillon, this natural exuberance was until recently suppressed by French centralization; of late, however, it's been feeling its oats, with a major rugby championship under its belt (2009), new high-speed train links with Paris and Barcelona and a busy calendar of festivals.

'a true mental ejaculation... suddenly I saw it with the brightness of lightning: in front of me I saw the centre of the Universe'

Dalí describes his vision at the Gare de Perpignan

The king of kookiness himself, Salvador Dalí, set off the first sparks in 1963, when he passed Perpignan's train station in a taxi (he would frequently visit to ship his paintings abroad, not trusting the train station in his native Figueres) and realized it was the great hinge of existence. He painted a picture of it, one of his last masterpieces, called *Mystique de la Gare de Perpignan* (1965), which shows, among other things, Dalí himself being sucked into a vortex of light; a later revelation showed in 1983 that the entire Iberian Peninsula rotated precisely at Perpignan station 132 million years ago – and might some day break off, a theory which he illustrated in one of his final drawings, the *Topological Abduction of Europe – Homage to René Thom*. Perpignan's otherwise ordinary Gare SNCF (with its new terminal for the TGV which puts Figueres and the Dalí Museum only 20 minutes away) has been a hot destination for Surrealist pilgrims ever since.

History

Perpignan is named after Perperna, a lieutenant of the great 1st-century BC populist general Quintus Sertorius. While Rome was suffering under the dictatorship of Pompey, Sertorius governed most of Spain in accordance with his astonishing principle that one should treat Rome's provinces decently. The enraged Senate sent out five legions to destroy him, but his army, who all swore to die if he was killed, defeated each one until the villainous Perperna invited his boss to a banquet in the Pyrenees and murdered him.

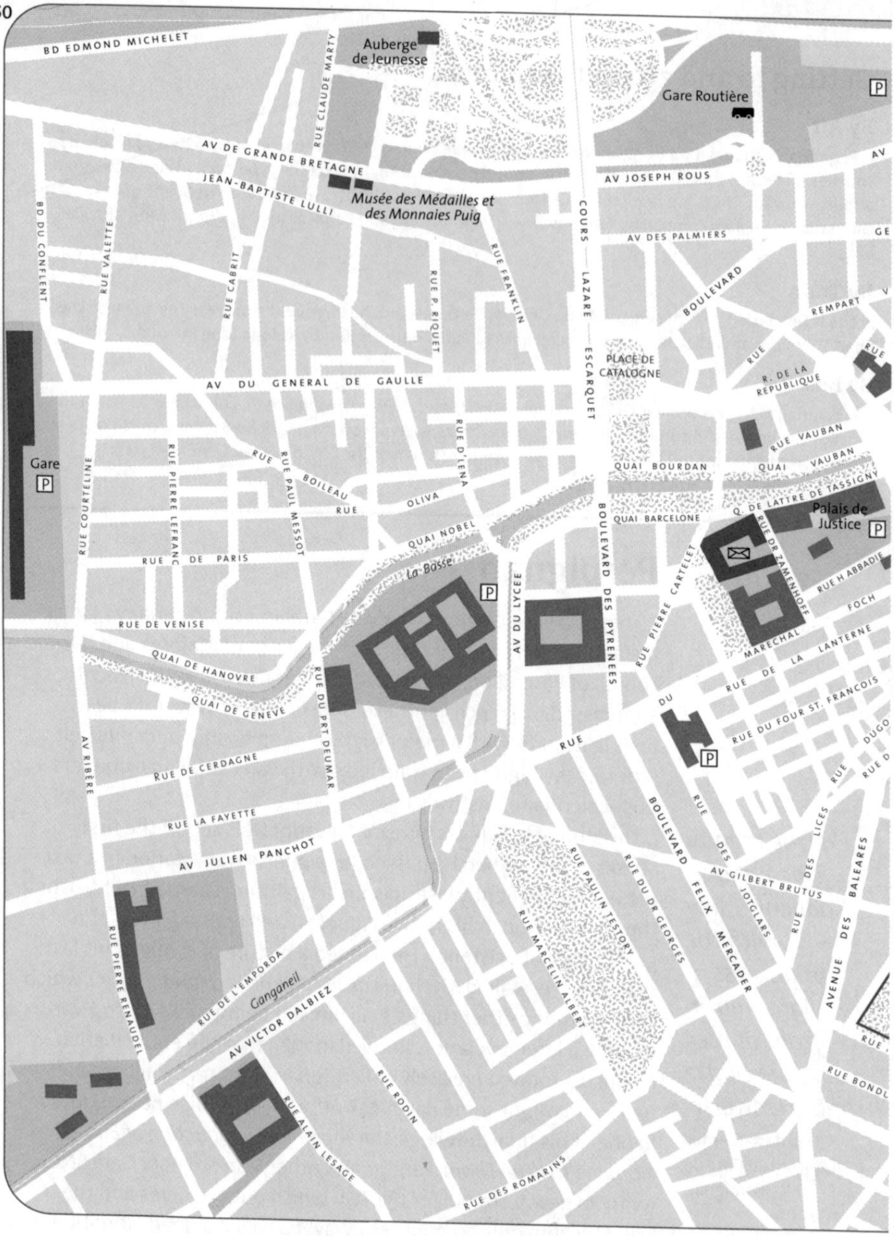

In 1197, Perpignan became the first Catalan city granted a municipal charter, and governed itself by a council elected by the three estates or 'arms'. Its merchants traded as far abroad as

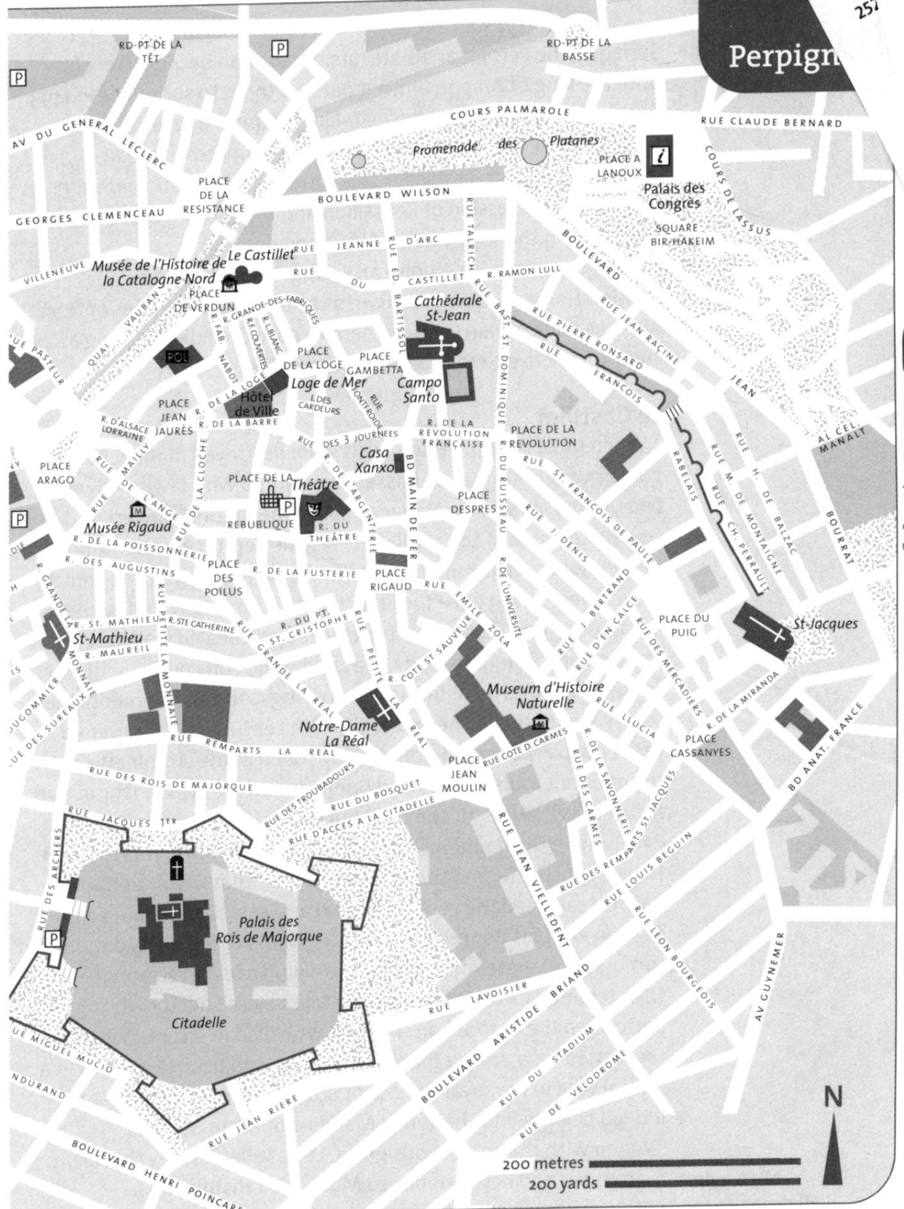

Constantinople, and the city enjoyed its most brilliant period in the 13th century when Jaume I, king of Aragon and conqueror of Majorca, created the Kingdom of Majorca and County of Roussillon for his younger son, Jaume II. This little kingdom was absorbed by the Catalan kings of Aragon in the 14th century, but continued to prosper until 1463, when Louis XI's army came to claim Perpignan and Roussillon as payment for mercenaries sent to Aragon.

Besieged, the Perpignanais ate rats rather than become French, until the king of Aragon himself ordered them to surrender. In 1493, Charles VIII, more interested in Italian conquests, gave Perpignan back to Spain. But in the 1640s Richelieu pounced on the first available chance to grab back this corner of the mystic Hexagon, and French possession of Roussillon and the Haute-Cerdagne was cemented in the 1659 Treaty of the Pyrenees.

Perpignan made little noise after that. Recent troubles over immigration and rivalries between the city's communities of North Africans and Catalan Gypsies seem to have dwindled, leaving a sunny, attractive town, popular with visitors.

Le Castillet

When most of Perpignan's walls were destroyed in 1904, its easy-going river-cum-moat, **La Basse**, was planted with lawns, flower-beds, mimosas and Art Nouveau cafés. The fat brick towers and crenellated gate of **Le Castillet** in Place de Verdun were left upright for memories' sake; built in 1368 by Aragon to keep out the French, it became a prison once the French got in, especially during the Revolution. In 1946 a mason broke through a sealed wall in Le Castillet and found the body of a child, which on contact with the air dissolved into dust; from the surviving clothing fragments the corpse was dated to the end of the 18th century. And for over 50 years, people wondered: could it have been Marie-Antoinette's son, the dauphin Louis Charles and briefly, before he died in 1795 at age 10, Louis XVII? After all, the child buried in the Temple prison in Paris, where the dauphin was said to have died of TB, was thought to be a substitute, and there were rumours that Revolutionaries had instead used the young dauphin as a secret bargaining chip in dealing with his Bourbon relatives in Spain. All the many dauphin rumours and pretenders' claims were put to rest in 2000, when DNA testing of a desiccated heart stolen by the doctor who performed the autopsy on the child who died in Temple, which had resurfaced in 1975 after many adventures, and been deposited in a crystal vase in the royal Basilica of St-Denis, proved that it had indeed belonged to the son of Marie-Antoinette.

Musée de l'Histoire de la Catalogne Nord
t 04 68 35 42 05; open Tues–Sun 10.30–6; closed Mon; adm

Along with this mysterious ghost, Le Castillet houses the newly rearranged and newly renamed **Musée de l'Histoire de la Catalogne Nord**, with items ranging from casts of Pau (Pablo) Casals' hands to a kitchen from a Catalan *mas*, complete with a hole in the door for the Catalan cat. The religious section includes religious poems carved on wood known as *goigs*, which people would commission to mark important events, plus a 'Cross of Insults', and a folksy 17th-century carving of the *Last Supper*. **Place de Verdun**, nearby, is one of Perpignan's liveliest squares, while just outside the gate the **Promenade des Platanes** is lined with rows of magnificent, never pruned plane trees.

Loge de Mer to the Musée des Beaux Arts

From Le Castillet, Rue Louis Blanc leads back to **Place de la Loge**, the medieval centre, where the cafés provide a grandstand for contemplating Aristide Maillol's voluptuous bronze *Venus* and the beautiful Gothic **Loge de Mer** or Llotja, built in 1397 by the king of Aragon to house the exchange and the Consolat de Mar, a branch of the Barcelona council founded by Jaume I to resolve trade and maritime disputes. This proud and noble building, with its Venetian arches, loggia and ship-shaped weathercock, fell on hard times and was used as a fast food outlet; it has now moved a bit upmarket, with a proper *bistrot*.

The neighbouring 13th-century **Hôtel de Ville** has been spared the Llotja's humiliation, probably because it still serves its original purpose: on Saturday mornings, when its courtyard fills with blushing brides posing for photos by Maillol's allegory of the Mediterranean (as a naked woman, of course). It is built of rounded river pebbles and bricks in the curious layer-cake style of medieval Perpignan; three bronze arms sticking out of the façade symbolize old Perpignan's three estates. To the right, the **Palais de la Députation Provinciale** (1447) is a masterpiece of Catalan Renaissance, built for Roussillon's parliament but now housing dismal municipal offices. **Rue des Fabriques-d'en Nabot**, opposite the palace, was once the street of drapers: note the **Hôtel Julia** (No.2), a rare survival of a 15th-century town house, with a Gothic courtyard.

Musée des Beaux Arts Hyacinthe Rigaud
t 04 68 35 43 40; open Tues–Sun 10.30–6; closed Mon; adm

South of the Députation, at 16 Rue de l'Ange, the **Musée des Beaux Arts Hyacinthe Rigaud** is named after the hometown boy who became portrait-painter to Louis XIV. Hyacinthe (1659–1743), master of raising the mediocre and unworthy to virtuoso heights of rosy-cheeked, debonair charm and sophistication, is well represented, most famously in his portrait of the Cardinal de Bouillon, who beams with self-satisfaction with his overflowing chest of loot (he was Grand Almoner of France) and the golden hammer he used to open the Holy Door at St Peter's in 1700. Note that he has a slight squint; because Rigaud painted it, the Cardinal refused to pay him for the picture, so Rigaud kept the hammer instead. Another masterpiece is the *Retable de la Trinité* (1489) by the Master of Canapost, painted for the 100th anniversary of the Consolat de Mar and showing, underneath, a fanciful scene of the sea lapping at the base of the Llotja. Other works are by Picasso, Dufy, Maillol, Miró and others; among them, don't miss the works on Spanish Civil war exiles by Catalan-American artist Pierre Daura.

Cathédrale St-Jean and the *Dévôt Christ*

(1) Cathédrale St-Jean
t 04 68 51 33 72; open 7.30–6

Just east of Place de la Loge unfolds Place Gambetta, site of Perpignan's pebble and brick cathedral, topped by a lacy 19th-century wrought-iron campanile with a four-octave carrillion.

Begun in 1324 but not ready for use until 1509, the interior is a success because the builders stuck to the design provided in the 15th century by Guillem Sagrera, architect of the great cathedral of Palma de Mallorca. Typical of Catalan Gothic, it has a single **nave**, 157ft long, striking for its width rather than its soaring height.

The wave of sacred fountain smothers the hill of the guilty serpent
Latin inscription on the font

The **chapels**, wedged between the huge piers, hold some unique treasures along with their ornate retables, the oldest of which is a mysterious marble **baptismal font** (first chapel on the left). Pre-Romanesque, perhaps even Visigothic, and carved from the drum of a Roman column to look like a tub bound with a cable, it bears a primitive face of Christ over an open book. Further up the left aisle, the massive **organ** of 5,075 pipes was decorated in 1504 with painted shutters (now displayed in a side chapel) and sumptuous carvings. On the pendentive under the organ, note the Moor's head – a common Catalan conceit symbolizing wisdom, taken from the Templars, who exerted a powerful influence over the kings of Aragon. The jaw was articulated, to vomit sweetmeats or stick out its tongue at the children on holidays; now it's stuck, gaping open.

Beyond the Moor's head is the entrance into the chapel of **Notre Dame dels Correchs**, a survivor of the original cathedral of St Jean le Vieux (consecrated in 1025), filled with reliquaries and the effigy of the cathedral's founder, Jaume's son Sancho, his feet resting on a Chinese lion. The rest of the church was converted into an electrical generating station in 1890; it is closed to visitors, but you can see the portal with its image of Christ in Majesty just outside the present cathedral.

The cathedral is proudest of its exquisite **retables**: on the high altar, the marble *Retable de St-Jean*, carved in a late Renaissance style in 1621 by Claude Perret; at the end of the left crossing, the *Retable des Stes Eulalie et Julie* (1670s); in the apsidal chapels, the painted wood *Retable de St-Pierre* (mid-16th century), and, to the right, the lovely *Notre-Dame de la Mangrana* (1500) – its name, 'of the pomegranate', comes from an earlier statue of the Virgin, which held a pomegranate, a symbol of fertility.

Recent work on the cathedral revealed that it still has a rare 'Pentecostal hole' in the roof; on Pentecost Sunday a priest would climb on the roof and, at the appropriate moment in the Mass, light branches of dry broom and drop them through the hole on the congregation to symbolize the tongues of flame that appeared over the apostle's heads when they were filled with the Holy Spirit. So far there has been no talk of reviving the old custom.

A door in the right aisle leads out to a 16th-century chapel constructed especially to house an extraordinary wooden sculpture known as the ***Dévôt Christ***. Carved in the Cologne region in 1307, this wasted Christ, whose contorted bones, sinews and torn flesh are carved with a rare anatomical realism, is stretched to the limits of agony on the Cross. Almost too painful to behold, it con straight from the gloomy age when Christendom believed that pain, contemplated or self-inflicted, brought one closer to God. It is an object of great veneration, and the Perpignanais claim that when the Christ's bowed head sags another quarter-inch to touch His chest, the world will end. A door from the cloister leads into the striking 15th-century **Salle Capitulaire**, its complex ogival vaulting attributed to Guillem Sagrera.

Campo Santo
open Oct–April Tues–Sun 11–5.30; closed Mon

Nearby in Rue Amiral Ribeill is the cathedral's **Campo Santo** of 1300–30, the only cloister-cemetery of its kind of France, the Gothic tomb niches (*enfeux*) decorated with bas-reliefs; this being Perpignan, until the late 1980s it was occupied by the local *gendarmerie*. Today it forms the perfect setting for the city's summer concerts.

Casa Xanxo
t 04 68 62 37 98; open May–Sept Tues–Sun 12–7; Jan–April Tues–Sun 11–5.30; closed Mon, and Oct–Dec

South of the cathedral at 8 Rue de la Main de Fer, the Gothic **Casa Xanxo** was built in 1507 by draper Bernat Xanxo, keen to show off his new wealth, although he made sure to decorate his proud new house with a relief of the Seven Deadly Sins. Portraits of Bernat and his wife decorate one of the doors, and there's an impressive fireplace but otherwise little else has survived, although there is a model of Perpignan in 1686, with the fortifications planned for the city by Vauban. It frequently hosts special exhibitions.

Quartier St-Jacques

The piquant neighbourhood south of the cathedral, built on the slopes of **Puig des Lépreux** (Lepers' Hill), was once the *aljama*, or Jewish quarter of Perpignan. In its happiest days, in the 13th century, it produced a remarkable body of literature – especially from the pen of the mathematician and Talmudic scholar Gerson ben Salomon (author of the philosophical *Gate of Heaven*) – as well as rare manuscripts and calligraphy, all now in Paris. After the Jews were exiled, the quarter was renamed St-Jacques, and inhabited by working men's families, Gypsies, and most recently by North Africans. Its landmark, the 12th- to 14th-century church of **St-Jacques** is opulent and rich inside: there's a 'Cross of Insults' covered with the symbols of Christ's Passion, a statue of St James in Compostela pilgrimage gear (1450), and more fine retables, especially the 15th-century *Notre-Dame de l'Espérance*, featuring a rare view of the pregnant Virgin. Even today it's a hotbed of stalwart Catholic tradition, performing Masses in Latin since the Pope gave the nod in 2007.

St-Jacques
open Tues–Sun 11–5

Museum d'Histoire Naturelle
t 04 68 66 33 68, www.mediterranees.net/museum/index.html; open Mon–Sat 9.30–5; adm

Below St-Jacques, the **Museum d'Histoire Naturelle** on 12 Rue Fontaine Neuve was created for Perpignan's university in 1770, and displays creatures now rare or extinct in the eastern Pyrenees, including a plaster mould of a giant prehistoric tortoise, 'Perpiniana du Pliocene', discovered just outside the city at Serrat

La Sanche

In the early 15th century, while the fire-eating Dominican preacher St Vincent Ferrer was in Perpignan to advise in the dispute between Antipope Benedict XIII and Rome, he founded in the church of St-Jacques the confraternity of the Holy Blood (de la Sanch) to bring religious comfort to prisoners condemned to death. As in Seville, the confraternity reaches a wider audience on Good Friday afternoons, when it dons spooky black and red Ku Klux Klan-like robes and hoods called *orcaparutxe* (en route to an execution, the prisoner, judges and executioner were all dressed in *caparutxe*, to prevent anyone with enemies from being lynched along the way). Penitents in the procession carry the *misteri*, life-size statues representing scenes of the Passion (each one weighs up to 50kg, so carrying them really is an act of penitence); others crawl on their knees. A tambourine, and the occasional bell break the solemn silence, along with the chanting of traditional Easter *goigs*, or verses. Similar processions take place in the evening at Arles-sur-Tech and Collioure.

d'en Vaquer. The mummy was a gift from Ibrahim Pasha, sent over in 1847 after he took the cure at Vernet-les-Bains.

The Palace of the Kings of Majorca

Palace of the Kings of Majorca
t 04 68 34 48 29; open daily June–Sept 10–6; Oct–May 9–5; adm

Enclosed in a vast extent of walls, originally medieval and later enlarged by Vauban, the Palais des Rois de Majorca (entrance in Rue des Archers) is the oldest royal palace in France, begun in the 1270s by Jaume the Conqueror and occupied by his son Jaume II after 1283. Yet for all its grandeur, only three kings of Majorca were to reign here before Roussillon, Montpellier, the Cerdagne and the Balearic islands were reabsorbed by Aragon in 1349. The scale of magnificence that they intended to become accustomed to survives, but not much else.

The throne room, with its three vast fireplaces, and the double-decker chapels in the **Donjon**, with the queen's chapel on the bottom and the king's on top, both offer hints of the exotic splendour of the Majorcan court. The **sacristy** was the entrance to a network of underground passageways that connected the palace to its enormous 147ft-deep wells, which also afforded Jaume II the chance to escape should his fierce and unwelcome older brother, Pere III of Aragon, come to call. The palace once stood in the midst of what the archives call 'Paradise' – partly enclosed terraced gardens, inspired by Moorish gardens on Majorca. A few traces remain to the right of the mightiest tower, the **Tour de l'Hommage**. The narrow grid of streets below the palace, around the church of **St-Mathieu**, were designed by the Templar tutors of Jaume the Conqueror, although most of the buildings are 18th-century.

Musée des Médailles et des Monnaies Puig
t 04 68 62 37 64; open daily 9.30–6; adm

Lastly, on the northwest side of town at 42 Avenue de Grande-Bretagne, the **Musée des Médailles et des Monnaies Puig** has an excellent collection of coins and medals from antiquity to modern times, with a section on Catalan money.

Perpignan Environs: Cabestany

Of all the villages ingested by Greater Perpignan, none has the star power, at least among medievalists, as Cabestany (Cabestanh),

4km to the southeast, for lending its name to the highly original Romanesque sculptor known as the Master of Cabestany. The Michelangelo of his day, he was in demand as far afield as Tuscany. In Cabestany's church **Notre Dames des Anges** he left a remarkable **tympanum** of the *Dormition and Assumption of the Virgin*, and a scene of the Virgin in heaven, handing her girdle down to St Thomas, rediscovered during renovations in 1930 (now removed and displayed inside the transept). The anonymous master's itinerant life is explored in the **Centre de Sculpture Romane Maître de Cabestany** in Parc Guilhem, which has over 60 casts of his finest works.

Centre de Sculpture Romane Maître de Cabestany
t 04 68 08 15 31, www.maitre-de-cabestany.com; open May–Sept Tues–Sun 10–12.30 and 1.30–6.30; Oct–April 10–12.30 and 1.30–6; adm

Cabestany was also the home of the troubadour Guilhem de Cabestanh, who wrote some of the most popular love poems of the Middle Ages. He is most famous for the legend of his demise, that Boccaccio inserted in *The Decameron* (Day 4: 9). Guilhem loved and was loved by the wife of a knight, one Raymond of Castel-Rossello. When Raymond learned of their affair, he ambushed Guilhem, murdered him and cut out his heart, which he gave to his cook to prepare with plenty of pepper. His wife ate it and praised the dish. 'I am not surprised,' said her husband, 'as you loved it so well when it was alive.' And he told her what she had eaten. 'Sir,' the lady replied, 'you have given me such an excellent thing to eat that God forbid any other food should again pass my lips.' And she leapt out of the window to her death.

Festivals in Perpignan

In September, Perpignan hosts **Visa pour l'Image**, *www.visapourlimage.com*, the annual world festival of photo-journalism.

Perpignan Market Days

Daily am: Place Cassanyes.
Sat am: Place de la République, regional produce.

Shopping in Perpignan

Maison Quinta, 3 Rue Grande des Fabriques, **t** 04 68 34 41 62, *www.maison-quinta.com*. If it's Catalan – food, fabrics, art, toys – they have it in this fun and colourful shop.

ⓘ Perpignan >
Palais des Congrès, Place Armand Lanoux, t 04 68 66 30 30, www.perpignantourisme.com; open mid-June–mid-Sept daily; mid-Sept–mid-June Mon–Sat and Sun am
***Information point**: Pl Arago; open Mon–Sat*

Where to Stay in Perpignan

Perpignan ✉ 66000

********La Villa Duflot**, Rond-Point Albert Donnezan, **t** 04 68 56 67 67, *www.villa-duflot.com* (€€€€–€€€). Near the Perpignan-Sud-Argelès motorway exit, in the middle of an industrial zone! However, you can pretend to be elsewhere in the comfortable air-conditioned rooms and garden, or in the popular restaurant (€€€) overlooking the pool.

★ Château La Tour Apollinaire >>

Château La Tour Apollinaire, 15 Rue Guillaume Apollinaire, **t** 0468 92 43 02, *www.latourapollinaire.com* (€€€€–€€€). The French-Russian poet Apollinaire's cousin built this mansion packed full of character, now stylishly restored with a po-mo flair and sense of fun. Choose between rooms and apartments with loads of mod-cons, and relax in the pool in the subtropical gardens. All only a 10-minute walk from the centre.

******La Faucelle**, 860 Chemin de la Faucelle, **t** 04 68 21 09 10, *www.lafauceille.com* (€€€). 5km south of the centre towards Argelès, colourful contemporary rooms with a pool, spa and fine restaurant.

*****Park Hôtel** , 18 Bd Jean Bourrat, near tourist office, **t** 04 68 35 14 14, *www.*

parkhotel-fr.com (€€€–€€). Plush, traditional, soundproofed rooms with air conditioning and Wi-fi and the beautiful **Le Chap** restaurant (€€€), famous across the region but currently undergoing a rethink, with fewer bells and whistles.

****Hôtel de la Loge**, 1 Rue des Fabriques-d'en Nabot, **t** 04 68 34 41 02, *www.hoteldelaloge.fr* (€€–€). The nicest in the centre, in a 16th-century building, this has pretty rooms, some with TV and air-conditioning, and a lovely inner courtyard.

***Aragon**, 17 Av Gilbert Brutus, **t** 04 68 54 04 46, *www.aragon-hotel.com* (€). Close to the centre, with air conditioning, Wi-fi and affordable parking.

Auberge de Jeunesse, Parc de la Pépinière, Av de Grande-Bretagne, **t** 04 68 34 63 32, *www.fuaj.org* (€). A small youth hostel, with breakfast available. Book in summer. *Closed mid-Nov–mid-Mar.*

Eating Out in Perpignan

La Galinette >

La Galinette, 23 Rue Jean Payra, **t** 04 68 35 00 90 (€€€–€€). Christophe Comes' gastronomic restaurant delights palates with fresh and seasonal products including vegetables from the chef's own garden. Excellent value. Book first. *Closed Sun and Mon, plus mid-July–mid-Aug.*

La Casa Sansa >

La Casa Sansa, 3 Rue Fabriques Couvertes, near Le Castillet, **t** 04 68 34 21 84 (€€€–€€). Lively, with excellent food served in a 14th-century cellar – with dishes from Catalan *escargots* to rabbit with *aïoli*; occasional live music, and more than its share of Catalan flair. Book Fri and Sat nights.

Les Antiquaires, Place Desprès, **t** 04 68 34 06 58 (€€€–€€). A local favourite for reliable, excellent French specialities. *Closed Sun eve and Mon, and 3 weeks in June.*

Le Grain de Folie, 71 Avenue Général Leclerc, **t** 04 68 51 00 50 (€€). Excellent value for money seasonal dishes, with a menu that changes every month. *Closed Sun eve and Mon.*

Le Barathym, 7 Rue des Cardeurs, **t** 04 68 50 98 14 (€€). Central and classy, with excellent seafood dishes with a south-of-the-border flair.

Lou Grilladou, 7 Place de Belgique (5mins' walk from the train station), **t** 04 68 34 86 81 (€€). Affordable creative cuisine (scallops and chorizo on a spit, etc.). *Closed Sat lunch, Sun and Mon.*

La Pitcholina, 12 Rue Lazare Escarguel, **t** 04 68 34 02 01 (€€–€). Delicious Corsican specialities and good value menus. *Closed Sun and Mon.*

Nature et Gastronomie, 37 Quai Vauban, **t** 04 68 59 00 38, *www.natureetgastronomie.fr* (€). Great place for a quick, wholesome lunch.

Entertainment and Nightlife in Perpignan

The lively bars around Place de la Loge, and the surrounding streets are where much of the city's nightlife unfolds. There's free music of all kinds on Thursday nights in summer.

Le Zinc, 8 Rue Grande des Fabriques, **t** 04 68 35 08 80. Jazz and cocktails; especially animated during the Perpignan Jazz Festival in October, called ***Jazzèbre***.

Le Habana Club, 5 Rue Grande des Fabriques, **t** 04 68 34 11 00. Music, dancing and food with a Latin touch.

Perpignan's Coast

Perpignan's suburbs have sprawled out to meet the sea and the continuation of Roussillon's die-straight sands, while Elne, just inland, has one of the south's greatest Romanesque cloisters, not only surviving, but surviving *in situ*.

Getting to and around Perpignan's Coast

The slow **trains** from Perpignan to Cerbère stop in Elne, Collioure and Banyuls, the same route followed by **bus** 400 from Perpignan. Canet-Plage is linked by city buses, while St-Cyprien is on bus 420.

Canet-Plage and St-Cyprien-Plage

The beach extention of **Canet-en-Roussillon** has long been the favourite resort of the Perpignanais. After taking a beating in the last war, it has been rebuilt without much distinction. To add to the joys of the beach and endless water-based sports there's an **Aquarium** by the port, where the star attraction is that impossibly unlovely living fossil from the depths of the Indian Ocean, the coelacanth. The tourist office organizes tours of the Canet's medieval **castle** in summer.

Aquarium
t 04 68 80 49 64, www.aquarium-canet.com; open July–Aug daily 10am–11pm; Sept–June Tues–Sun 10–12 and 2–6; closed mornings Christmas–New Year; adm

South of Canet the distinctive profile of the Pic du Canigou looms as prominently as Fiji over the flamingo-filled Etang de Canet, while the road and bike path runs down a lido of wild beaches and dunes, complete with a reconstructed reed hut fishermen's village. At the end lies **St-Cyprien-Plage**, which looks just like Canet only more so, with fancier restaurants, an enormous Aqualand water park, a 27-hole golf course, and a summer chamber music festival. Set back in **St-Cyprien** proper, 3km from the beach in Place de la République, the **Musée François Desnoyer** has works by Catalan artists such as Maillol, Delfau and Bone, and a small collection of paintings by Picasso, Dufy, Chagall and Miró once owned by François Desnoyer (1894–1972), along with several of Desnoyer's own colourful, figurative works.

Musée François Desnoyer
t 04 68 21 32 07, www.collectionsdesaintcyprien.com; open July–mid-Sept daily 10–12 and 3–7; mid-Sept–June Wed–Mon 10–12 and 2–6, closed Tues; adm

Elne

Just inland from St-Cyprien, atop a steep hill, the citadel of Elne has guarded the Roussillon plain for at least 2,700 years. Its ancient name, Illiberis, is said to be Iberian. Hannibal sojourned here on his way to Italy, waiting to negotiate an alliance with the Celts to guard his rear; the locals, apparently unimpressed even with the elephants, made him pay a toll to pass through. The name-change came in the time of Constantine, to Castrum Helenae, after the emperor's mother, St Helen, legendary discoverer of the True Cross. Throughout the Middle Ages and into the 16th century, Elne was one of the most important cities in Roussillon, the seat of the archbishops. The town is now reduced to some 6,000 souls, having lost all its honours and status to Perpignan.

But they couldn't take away its fortified **cathedral** at the top of the town. Begun in 1069, it has a wonderful stage presence, with its crenellated roof-line and stout, arcaded tower. Inside, the stone masons pulled some optical techniques straight out of the magic hat of antiquity to accentuate the beauty – the cornice along the nave slopes and the pillars gently lean outwards. In a chapel on the right is an Italianate 14th-century altarpiece of St Michael and there are some fine tombs, especially that of Ramon de Costa (1310). The **cloister** is perhaps the best in the Midi, and also the best preserved, its capitals and pillars decorated with imaginative, exquisitely carved arabesques and floral patterns. What makes Elne's cloister particularly interesting is the fact that its four sides were completed in different periods, at roughly 50-year intervals; that closest to the cathedral is the earliest, from the 12th century, and its capitals show the influence of the sculptors of St-Michel-de-Cuxa (*see* p.272). Oddly, each generation of sculptors chose to repeat the subjects of their predecessors: all but the north gallery have central pillars carved with serpentine dragons and mermaids (who may well have been introduced in the region by the Visigoths) spreading their forked tails; other capitals repeat scenes from the Old Testament. The little **museum** tells the history of the cathedral and cloister, including its lost upper gallery, dismantled in 1827 and sold off at an auction in 1960.

Cathedral cloister
t 04 68 22 70 90; open daily except during services June–Sept 9.30–6.45; April–May 9.30–5.45; Oct 9.30–12.15 and 2–5.45; Nov–Mar 9.30–11.45 and 2–4.45; adm

Admission to the cloister includes admission to the **Musée Terrus** a short walk away; the painter Etienne Terrus (1857–1922) was a friend of Matisse and Derain and the museum contains mainly his landscapes.

Musée Terrus
t 04 68 22 88 88, http://museeterrus.over-blog.com; open May–Sept Tues–Sun 10–7; Oct–April Tues–Sun 10–12 and 2–6; adm

Argelès, Romanesque art and Tortoises

South of St-Cyprien, big bland **Argelès** (divided into the old town Argelès-sur-Mer and Argelès-Plage) has 7km of sand and makes some claim as the European Capital of Camping, with 56 sites and a capacity for 100,000 happy campers. When you can't stand any more beach fun, head 4km inland to **St-André**, in the foothills of the coastal Albères mountains. It has a lofty 12th-century church with a sculpted lintel of 1030; opposite, the small **Maison Transfrontalière de l'Art Roman** is dedicated to sculpture from this and from other Romanesque churches in Roussillon and Catalonia. One of these is just west of St-André: the Benedictine monastery of **St-Genis-des-Fontaines**, founded around the year 800. Its church has a remarkable carved lintel dated 1020 (the earliest ever with a date) decorated with a Christ *Majestat* and stylized apostles shaped like bowling-pins; the pretty late 13th-century cloister was dismantled and sold off in 1924, one of the final scandals of France's traditional lack of concern for its medieval heritage. In 1988 it was rebuilt as it was, using a mix of originals and copies of its capitals.

Maison Transfrontalière de l'Art Roman
t 04 68 89 04 85; open mid-June–mid-Sept Tues–Sun 10–12 and 2.30–7; mid-Mar–mid-June and mid-Sept–mid-Nov Tues–Sat 10–12 and 3–6; closed mid-Nov–mid-Mar; adm

St-Genis-des-Fontaines
t 04 68 89 84 33; open June–Aug Mon–Fri 10–12 and 3–7; May and Sept 9–12 and 2–6; Oct–April daily 9.30–12 and 2–5

Just south of St-André, in Sorède and the Vallée Heureuse ('Happy Valley') filled with cork groves, rare Hermann's tortoises and 30 other species inhabit **La Vallée des Tortues**, a tortoise refuge (visit at the cooler times of day, when the animals are more active). The adjacent Fun Valley offers plenty of activities for the small fry.

Vallée des Tortues
t 04 68 95 50 50 or t 06 74 18 92 11, www.lavalleedestortues.fr; open April–mid-May and mid-Aug–Sept daily 10–6, mid-May–mid-Aug 9–7; Oct 11–5; Nov–Mar, open by appt (ring the mobile number); adm

Where to Stay and Eat on Perpignan's Coast

Canet-en-Roussillon ✉ 66140

★ **Le Don Quichotte >**

Le Don Quichotte, 22 Av de Catalogne, **t** 04 68 80 35 17, *www.ledon quichotte.com* (€€€). For over a quarter of a century this restaurant with its elegant white dining rooms has been serving a small but choice selection of seafood and meat dishes; opt for the menu *'3 assiettes en trilogie'* to try three starters, three fish courses and three desserts (each in small portions). *Closed Mon and Tues, except hols.*

St-Cyprien ✉ 66750

ⓘ St-Cyprien >

Quai Arthur Rimbaud, **t** *04 68 21 01 33, www.tourisme-saint-cyprien.com; open daily*

Two of the area's class resort hotels are here.

★ **L'Ile de la Lagune >**

****L'Ile de la Lagune, Bd de l'Almandin, **t** 04 68 21 01 02, *www.hotel-ile-lagune.com* (€€€€). Air-conditioned rooms, tennis and a swimming pool, all set on its own little island, L'Ile de la Lagune. The restaurant, **L'Almandin** (€€€€–€€€), is considered one of the best on the coast, with a stylish treatment of Catalan dishes, such as *blinis aux anchois de Collioure à la tapenade et caviar d'aubergine. Restaurant closed Mon and Tues in Oct–mid-April.*

***__Le Mas d'Huston__**, Rue Jouy d'Arnaud **t** 04 68 37 63 63, *www.golf-st-cyprien.com* (€€€€–€€€). By the golf course and an easy walk to the beach, with a pool, smart restaurant and cheaper brasserie. A modern, relaxing place. *Restaurant closed lunch; brasserie closed eves.*

Elne ✉ 66201

ⓘ Elne >>

Place Sant Jordi, **t** *04 68 22 05 07, www.ot-elne.fr; open July–Aug daily; June and Sept Mon–Fri and Sat pm; Oct–May Mon–Fri*

__Hôtel Logis Elne__, 10 Bd Illibéris, **t** 04 68 22 10 42, *www.hotelcarasol.com* (€€). Hotel with eight rooms set in the old ramparts of the town. Bedrooms have views across the Roussillon plain to the mountains, and the restaurant (€€), serving Mediterranean dishes, has a lovely terrace.

Argelès-sur-Mer ✉ 66700

***__Auberge du Roua__**, Chemin du Roua, **t** 04 68 95 85 85, *www.auberge duroua.com* (€€€–€€). Away from the hubbub, a luxurious little stone *auberge* with a pool and terrace restaurant (€€€). *Closed mid-Nov–Feb.*

The Flowers, 59 Rue Victor Hugo, **t** 04 68 81 05 79, *www.leflowers.net* (€€–€). World cuisine – choose between North African, Asian or Catalan, with a lunch buffet and chance to choose your own veggies, fish or meat for the chef to whip up in the wok and serve with noodles or rice.

The Côte Vermeille

After Argelès, Roussillon's long, straight shoreline undergoes a dramatic change, climbing into the Pyrenees and a delicious southern world of crystalline rock, olive trees and uncanny sunlight, a 30km prelude to Spain's Costa Brava. Forgive yourself for cynically thinking that the name 'Vermilion Coast' might have been cooked up by promoters – of course it was. The red clay soil of the ubiquitous olive groves does lend the area a vermilion tint, but as far as colours go that is only the beginning.

Every point or bend in the Mediterranean coast is a sort of meteorological vortex, given to strange behaviour: the Fata Morgana at the southern tip of Italy, the winds of the Mani in the Peloponnese or the glowing, subdued light of Venice. The Côte Vermeille gets a strong dose of the *tramontane* wind that can shriek like a monster in a B movie, but also has a remarkable mix of light and air, inciting the coast's naturally strong colours into an unreasonably heady and sensual Mediterranean spectrum. André Derain and Henri Matisse spent one summer here, at Collioure, and the result was a milestone in the artistic revolution known as Fauvism.

Collioure : Fauves and Anchovies

37 Collioure

Sempre endavant, mai morirem (Always forward, we'll never die)
Collioure's motto

If the tourists would only leave it in peace, Collioure would be quite happy to make its living in the old way, filling up barrels with anchovies. As it is, the town bears their presence as gracefully as possible, though in summer parking is nigh on impossible. In a way, Collioure *is* unspoiled – though it has 17 hotels, it does not have mini-golf or a water slide, or all the hype projected on St-Tropez, that other unaffectedly beautiful port discovered at the beginning of the 20th century by the Fauves. Instead, you'll find every other requisite for a civilized Mediterranean resort: a castle, a pretty church by the sea, three small beaches, a shady market square with cafés – and warehouses full of anchovies. Its narrow streets are lined with boutiques and tall, shuttered houses painted in pink, green, blue and yellow.

It's hard to believe, looking at the map, but in the Middle Ages this was the port for Perpignan; with no good harbours on the (then) unhealthy sandy coast to the north, Perpignan's fabrics and other goods had to come to the Pyrenees to go to sea. In the 14th century, Collioure was one of the biggest trading centres of Aragon, yet nearly the whole town was demolished by the French after they took possession in 1659. They weren't angry with the Colliourencs; the town was merely in the way of modernizing its fortifications. Our own century has no monopoly on twisted military logic: Collioure had to be razed in order that it could be better defended.

No sky in all France is more blue than that of Collioure
Henri Matisse

Espace Fauve
t 04 68 98 07 16; open June–Sept daily 9.30–12.30 and 3–7; Oct–May Tues–Fri 10–12 and 3–6, Sat and Sun 3–6; guided tours in July and Aug, departing from Quai de L'Amirautée, Tues and Thurs at 10am

Musée d'Art Moderne
t 04 68 82 10 19; ring ahead for hours; adm

The population moved into the part that survived, the steep hillside quarter called the Mouré, where they have made the best of it ever since. Collioure was discovered in 1905 by Matisse and Derain. Many other artists followed, including Picasso, but these two were the most inspired by the place, and they put a little of Collioure's vermilion tint into the deep colours of their first Fauvist experiments. Fourteen sketches by Matisse are in Céret 30km away, and his best works from Collioure are in private collections, or in the Hermitage in St Petersburg. Collioure has none. To rectify the lack, the village has created the *Chemin du Fauvisme*, placing copies of Matisse and Derain's works on the spots where the two set up their easels. The **Espace Fauve** is on Av Camille Pelletan; there is also the **Musée d'Art Moderne**, in a peaceful villa on the road to Port-Vendres with a terraced olive grove, which has works by lesser-known artists in the style of the Fauves, as well as an intriguing collection of Moorish ceramics.

Collioure (or as the locals call it, Cotllures) is a thoroughly Catalan town, and the red- and yellow-striped Catalan flag waves proudly

Château Royal
t 04 68 82 06 43; open June–Sept daily 10–5.15; Oct–May daily 9–4.15; adm

over the **Château Royal**, which dominates the harbour. With its outworks it is nearly as big as the town itself. First built by the Templars in the 13th century, it was expanded by various Aragonese kings, and used as a summer palace by the kings in Perpignan. The outer fortifications, low walls and broad banks of earth were state-of-the-art in 1669. The great Vauban, Louis XIV's military genius, oversaw the works and the demolition of the old town. Collioure's fate could have been even worse; Vauban had wanted to level it completely and force everyone to move to Port-Vendres. The older parts of the castle have been restored and are open for visits, along with several small exhibitions on local specialities from whip-making to espadrilles.

From the castle, cross the small stream called the Douy (usually dry and used as a car park) into the **Mouré**, the old quarter that is now the centre of Collioure. There is an amiable shorefront, with a small beach from which a few anchovy fishermen still ply their trade; several brightly painted fishing smacks are usually pulled up to complete the effect. At the far end you'll see Collioure's landmark, painted by Matisse and many others: the church of **Notre-Dame-des-Anges**. The Colliourencs built it in the 1680s to succeed the original church destroyed by Vauban; they chose the beach site to use the old cylindrical lighthouse as a bell-tower. The best thing about the church is that you can hear the waves of the sea from inside, a profound *basso continuo* that makes the celebration of Mass here unique. The next best are the retables, five of them, done between 1699 and 1720 by Joseph Sunyer and others. Catalan Baroque at its eccentric best, influenced by the Spanish *churrigueresque*, often concentrated its finest efforts on these towering constructions of carved wooden figures, dioramas of scriptural scenes with intricately painted stage-backdrop backgrounds. Sunyer's are especially lifelike.

Notre-Dame-des-Anges
open daily 9–12 and 2–6

The second of Collioure's beaches lies right behind the church; really an old sand bar that has become part of dry land, it connects the town with a former islet, the **Ilôt St-Vincent**, crowned with a tiny medieval chapel. A scenic footpath called the Sentier de la Moulade leads from near the church along the rocky shore north of Collioure. High above, you'll see **Fort Miradoux**, the Spanish King Philip II's addition to Collioure's defences, and still in military use. You can however tour the **Fort Ste Elme** built by Charles V in 1552 as a key link in Spain's coastal defences; and, if that's not high enough, a road leads up to the 13th-century **Tour de Madeloc** (2,100ft; for more fortresses, *see* below).

Fort Ste Elme
t 06 64 61 82 42; guided tours April–Sept 2.30–7

Collioure's cemetery has its share of celebrities: the Spanish poet Antonio Machado died here in 1939, after escaping Franco's forces in the Civil War (an annual poetry competition is held in his honour), as is translator and historical novelist Patrick O'Brian (d. 2000), who moved to Collioure with his wife in 1949.

Collioure marks the northern tip of the great Catalan 'Anchovy Coast' that extends south to the Gulf of Roses on the Costa Brava. Few of us, probably, give any thought to how the little fish are apprehended in the open sea. It isn't, in fact, a terribly difficult operation. The diabolical Catalans have boats called *lámparos*, with big searchlights. They sneak out on warm summer nights, when the normally shy anchovies are making their promenade, and nab the lot. After spending a few months in barrels of brine, the unfortunate fish reappear, only to be stuffed into olives; and it must be said a proper fat brown Catalan anchovy is a very different beast from the dinky silvery salt bomb that can sneak onto your pizza. Find out more (and buy some) at **Anchois Roque**, 17 Route d'Argelès.

Anchois Roque
t 04 68 82 04 99, www.anchois-roque.com; open Mon–Fri 8-6.30, Sat and Sun 8–12 and 2–6.30

Port-Vendres and Banyuls-sur-Mer

Even more of this doubtful anchovy business goes on in **Port-Vendres**. This is a real port, with few of the charms of Collioure, even though in ancient times it was nothing less than *Portus Veneris*, the Port of Venus. Louis XVI's government had big plans for developing it which were scuppered with the Revolution. A few grandiose neoclassical buildings from this programme managed to get built around the central **Place de l'Obélisque**, along with a 98ft obelisk decorated with propaganda reliefs celebrating poor Louis' glorious reign (it is one of few to survive the furious hammers of the Revolution).

Every town on the Côte Vermeille has its artist, and the one who spent the last two winters of his life (1925–6) rambling the hills and painting vibrant watercolours here was Charles Rennie Mackintosh, the great Scottish architect and designer, who loved the area so well that he had his ashes scattered in the sea off Port-Vendres. In the garden of the Dôme on Route de Collioure, a new **Interpretation Centre** has an exhibition and photos on his life and paintings; there's also an **art walk**, with 13 copies of his works.

Mackintosh Interpretation Centre
t 04 68 82 60 99, www.crmackintoshfrance.com, open June–Sept Tues, Wed and Fri 4–6; mid-Feb–mid-April Fri 3–5; mid-April–May and Oct–mid-Nov Tues and Fri 3–5; closed mid-Nov–mid-Feb

The coast juts out east here, with a picturesque little promontory called **Cap Béar**, topped by another of this area's many Baroque fortresses. Its monument to Sidi-Ferruch was originally erected in Algiers in 1930 to celebrate the centenary of French colonization; after 1962, when the Algerians didn't want it any more, it was set up inside here; it's opened only for group visits via the tourist office.

There are many isolated **beaches** in the vicinity, though they are hard to reach; most are south of the cape, including three at Paulilles, where the landmark is a dynamite factory (a mildly historic one, because it belonged to Alfred Nobel, inventor of

Maison du Site de Paulilles
t 04 68 95 23 40; open daily July–Aug 9–9; May, June, Sept 9–8; April and Oct 9–7; Nov–Mar 9–5

Aquarium de Banyuls-sur-Mer
t 04 68 88 73 39, www.biodiversarium.fr; open July–Aug daily 9–1 and 2–9; Sept–Dec and Feb–June 9–12 and 2–6.30; closed Jan; adm

Réserve Naturelle Marine de Cerbère-Banyuls
18 Av du Fontaulé, t 04 68 88 09 11

dynamite and plywood, who used the profits to finance his prizes), which operated from 1870 to 1984; you can visit the factory, director's house and interpretation centre, the **Site de Paulilles**.

Banyuls-sur-Mer (Banyuls de la Marenda in Catalan) is the next town along the picturesque coastal N114. It's a resort with a beach and thalassotherapy centre, the heart of the Banyuls wine region, but also the home of the **Fondation Arago**, an oceanographic laboratory affiliated to the University of Paris. Their excellent **Aquarium**, on Av du Fontaulé, was built in 1883; don't miss the grandaddy lobster and sea anemones and 250 kinds of birds. Since 1974, 650ha of coast between Banyuls and Cerbère has been protected as the **Réserve Naturelle Marine de Cerbère-Banyuls**, the oldest in France and said to be the only one entirely underwater. You can snorkel along the **Sentier Sous-Marin** (Underwater Trail) – there's an information point on Banyuls' quay and at the Plage de Peyrefitte – or explore it with local diving clubs (*see* p.268). To show

Wine: Banyuls and Collioure

Sweet and spicy and AOC since 1936, Banyuls is mainland France's southernmost wine *appellation*. Growing vines on its steep schisty slopes, swept by the *tramontane* winds, with long sunny summers and torrential rains in winter, was first done by the Knights Templar in the 11th century, who built the stone terraces, dug drainage trenches to keep them from being washed away and stone walls to keep them from being blown away, and planted the dark grenache noir grapes that were best suited for the difficult conditions. But what made Banyuls into the Banyuls we know today was their adoption of the vinification process proposed in the 13th century by Arnau de Villanova, a Catalan alchemist and physician to the Popes. While studying in Muslim Cordoba, Arnau learned the secrets of distillation and transmitted it to the West; in particular he invented the principle of wine fortification and stablization with a dollop of neutral *eau de vie*, which preserves some of the wine's natural sugar and its aroma. Afterwards the wine is aged for 3–15 years, sometimes in barrels right under the roof of a winery, or out in the full sun, to subject it to extreme variations in temperature, resulting in a distinctive rich amber wine with a raisiny taste. A fine old Banyuls is claimed to be the only wine that can accompany chocolate desserts, but be warned: a cheap young bottle may hardly do justice to a Mars bar.

Collioure, Port-Vendres, Cerbère and Banyuls are the only places allowed to wear the AOC label, and 75 per cent of their wine, as well as the delightful dry red, rosé and white wines of Collioure, pass through the **Grande Cave du Cellier des Templiers** co-operative, Route de Mas-Reig, **t** 04 68 98 36 92, *www.banyuls.com* (*open April–Oct daily 10–7.30; Nov–Mar tastings Mon–Sat 10–1 and 2.30–6.30, visits Mon–Fri 2.30–6*), a large concern happy to receive visitors for tastings and a tour of their magnificently vaulted 13th-century *grande cave*; their *cave souterraine* (*open July and Aug only*) just below has enormous hundred-year-old oak barrels, and a film on the wine. If you have a car you can take 2hr guided tours for €28 by ringing ahead.

The **Cave de l'Etoile**, 26 Av du Puig-del-Mas in Banyuls, **t** 04 68 88 00 10, *www.caveletoile.com*, is a co-operative where everything is done lovingly in the old-fashioned way; up the same street, one can visit the excellent **Domaine de la Rectorie, t** 04 68 88 13 45, *www.la-rectorie.com*.

A good selection of Collioure wine can be found at **Domaine du Mas Blanc**, 9 Av Général de Gaulle, **t** 04 68 88 32 12, *www.domaine-du-mas-blanc.com* (*open by appt only out of season*) and in Collioure at **Cellier des Dominicains**, Place Orphila, **t** 04 68 82 05 63, *www.dominicain.com*. If you wish to try the local wines with local food in a delightful setting, book dinner (*May–Sept only*) at the *ferme-auberge* **Les Clos de Paulilles** at the **Domaine de Valcros**, Port-Vendres, **t** 04 68 98 07 58, *www.domainedevalcros.com* – different wines accompany each course.

there's nearly as much natural diversity in this magical niche, the Aquarium has set up the **Jardin Méditerranéen du Mas de la Serre** located on a hill overlooking Banyuls (take Rue Jules Ferry-Rout to Mas Roig to the Route des Crêtes).

Jardin Méditerranéen
t 04 68 88 73 39, www.biodiversarium.fr; open July–Aug daily 9–1 and 2–9; mid-April–June and Sept–mid-Oct Wed–Sun 2–6; winter groups only; adm

As for art, Banyuls has a good 11th-century Romanesque church, **La Rectorie** on Rue Charles de Foucault, and takes credit for giving the world Aristide Maillol, perhaps the best-known French sculptor of the last century after Rodin, who was born here in 1861. He contributed the town's War Memorial, but in general expressed everything through the medium of the stylized, voluptuous female form. His tomb and a few copies of works are displayed in his old farmhouse, La Métairie, now the **Musée Aristide Maillol**, 4km up the Col de Banyuls road.

La Rectorie
open Sat 10.30–12 and 2–6, Sun 3–6; guided visits arranged by tourist office

Musée Aristide Maillol
t 04 68 88 57 11, www.musee-maillol.com; open May–Sept Tues–Sun 10–12 and 4–9; Oct–April Mon, Wed–Sun 10–12 and 4–7; closed hols; adm

If you don't care to go to Cerbère, or to Spain, there is an alternative to retracing your steps along the coast – an extremely scenic route through the mountains back to Collioure, along the steep and narrow D86. It begins from the back of Banyuls, beyond the railway overpass, and climbs through ancient olive groves on the lower slopes of the **Monts-Albères**. Several abandoned fortresses come into view, although none is especially easy to reach. This border region rivals even the Corbières for quantity of castles per square

Maillol and his Muse

Aristide Maillol had a lifelong fixation: young, nude women. This is not so uncommon, mind you, but Maillol (1861–1944) cast his idée fixe *in bronze with sufficient conviction to have it lodge in museums and art history books and on the pedestals of monuments all over France.*

Vicki Goldberg, *New York Times*, 1996

Maillol started off as a painter influenced by Gauguin, Puvis de Chavannes and Maurice Denis, before opening up a tapestry workshop in Banyuls, becoming one of the first to revive the art. By the early 1900s he had turned to sculpture, using his wife as a model, and introduced his first simplified, serene classical female nude, *Méditerranée*, to the world in 1905 – ironically, just as the Fauves up the road in Collioure were taking the first steps of turning representative art on its head. Rodin was impressed.

Although he lived in Paris, Maillol loved Banyuls, and was proud of his Catalan heritage – he proudly wore his *birretina* (Catalan cap) and espadrilles. But by 1934 he was in the doldrums, when a friend discovered 'a living Maillol', Dina Veirny, then a 15-year-old student. Within a couple of years, posing in between her school work, she had become devoted to him, and herself offered to pose in the nude (he apparently was far too shy to ask!), inspiring a whole new period of creativity. Their relationship by mutual agreement was platonic, but it didn't stop Madame Maillol from complaining long and bitterly.

In 1939 Maillol took refuge in Banyols, and was eventually followed by Dina, who in spite of the danger (she was Jewish) was working with the Resistance, and in particular with Varian Fry in Marseille, who ran an organization dedicated to smuggling Jews out of France. Maillol showed her all the secret paths around Banuyls. When she was arrested, Maillol hired a lawyer who won her freedom, then sent her to Nice for her own safety, to Henri Matisse, where she posed for him, before Maillol, nervous of losing her, summoned her back. When Dina was arrested again, this time by the Gestapo, Maillol managed to free her after six months by appealing to Hitler's favourite sculptor.

After Maillol's death in a car accident in 1944, Dina was made one of the executors of his will. She became the greatest promoter of his art, buying up all she could and opening a Musée Maillol in Paris; her foundation, run by her sons since her death in 2009, also runs the little museum in Banyuls.

Le Chemin Walter Benjamin

There is no document of culture that is not at the same time a document of barbarism.

Walter Benjamin

One of the old smugglers' trails that Maillol showed Dina Veirny (*see* box opposite) begins near 'old Banyols' – the hamlet of Puig d'el-Mas – then crosses over the Col de Rumpissa. It was used by Republican refugees fleeing Spain during the Civil War, and then by refugees fleeing France and the Nazis. The most famous of these was the 48-year-old Jewish German philosopher Walter Benjamin, who got out of Paris in the nick of time. Out of shape, a heavy smoker with a bad heart, and weighed down by a heavy briefcase holding a precious manuscript, he set off from Banyuls with two companions on a hot September day in 1940. They made it to Port Bou, exhausted, where Benjamin was retained by the police; told he would be repatriated to France the next day, he (apparently) committed suicide. Benjamin's precious briefcase was entrusted to a fellow refugee – who lost it on the train to Madrid. In Port Bou, Benjamin is remembered with the memorial *Passages* (1994) by the Israeli sculptor Dani Karavan in the town cemetery, where he was buried anonymously.

mile. There is also a ruined monastery, the **Abbaye de Valbonne**, on the heights to the west; the track to it begins at the pilgrimage chapel of **Notre-Dame-de-Consolation**. A little before this, the **Tour Madeloc** is the climax of the trip; it was a signal tower, part of the sophisticated communications network that kept the medieval kings of Aragon in close contact with their borders.

Cerbère and Beyond

You may well have already been here, but Cerbère, once the busiest rail crossing into Spain, won't bring back any pleasant memories – being herded from one train to another in the middle of the night under the gaze of soldiers with sub-machine-guns and impossible customs men who do their best to make this seem like an old Hitchcock spy film. No one has ever seen Cerbère in daylight, but you might give it a try. The coast here is at its most spectacular and there are a few pebble beaches. With its handful of hotels, Cerbère is a minuscule resort with a World's End air about it – an impression reinforced by its solar lighthouse, '*le phare du bout du monde*'.

There is a lot to be said for pressing on even further, into southern Catalonia (the signs at the border still say 'Spain' for courtesy's sake). If you liked the Côte Vermeille, continue south for more of the same on the **Costa Brava**. Or try **Figueras**, a short hop by train or a pleasant 50km drive along the C252, site of the remarkable Dalí Museum, in the artist's home town.

Market Days on the Côte Vermeille

Collioure: Wed, and Sun am.

Port-Vendres: Sat am.

Banyuls: Thurs and Sun am.

Festivals and Activities on the Côte Vermeille

Collioure's mid-August **Festival de Saint Vincent** is celebrated with dance, music and an unforgettable fireworks display. On July and August evenings the streets fill with jazz.

There are several **sea excursions** available from Port-Vendres, including catamaran cruises, fishing trips, and a day on a sailboat; the tourist office website has a complete list.

Diving clubs include:

CIP-Collioure, 15 Rue de la Tour d'Auvergne, Collioure, **t** 04 68 82 07 16, *www.cip-collioure.com*.

Aqua Blue Plongée, 5 Quai Georges Petit, Banyuls-sur-Mer, **t** 04 68 88 17 35, *www.aquablue-plongee.com*.

Where to Stay and Eat on the Côte Vermeille

★ Le Neptune >>

ⓘ Collioure > *Place du 18 Juin, **t** 04 68 82 15 47, www.collioure.com; open daily; Oct–Mar Mon–Sat*

★ Caucoliberi >>

★ Hostellerie des Templiers >

ⓘ Banyuls-sur-Mer >> *Av de la République, **t** 04 68 88 31 58, www.banyuls-sur-mer.com; open July–Aug daily; Sept–June Mon–Sat*

★ Les Elmes >>

ⓘ Port-Vendres *1 Quai François Joly, **t** 04 68 82 07 54, www.port-vendres.com; open July–Aug daily; rest of the year closed Sun*

Collioure ✉ 66190

***__La Casa Païral__**, Impasse des Palmiers, **t** 04 68 82 05 81, *www.hotel-casa-pairal.com* (€€€–€€). Charming, dignified, mansard-roofed mansion offering a wide choice of rooms, from the simple to the luxurious; also a pool and enclosed garden. No restaurant. *Closed Nov–Mar.*

****Hostellerie des Templiers**, 12 Quai de l'Amirauté, **t** 04 68 98 31 10, *www.hotel-templiers.com* (€€€–€€). Rooms have been refurbished with air-conditioning and Wi-fi since the days when Picasso, Matisse, Dufy and Dalí all stayed here. Original works cover the walls, although the Picassos have been locked away since several were stolen by a 'guest'. The bar is a friendly local hangout, and the restaurant (€€) is excellent, with terrace and imaginative, good-value dishes like their own *bouillabaisse*. *Closed Jan; restaurant closed Mon–Fri in Feb and Mar.*

****La Frégate**, Av Camille Pelletan, **t** 04 68 82 06 05, *www.fregate-collioure.com* (€€€–€€). This pink and jolly place is on the busiest corner of Collioure, but has been soundproofed and air-conditioned; it has a good restaurant (€€€–€€), mostly serving seafood. *Closed Dec–Jan.*

Saint-Pierre, 16 Av Gen de Gaulle, **t** 04 68 82 19 50, *www.hotel.saint-pierre@wanadoo.fr* (€€–€). *Sympathique* little hotel in easy walking distance of the centre with helpful staff

Boramar, 19 Rue Jean Bart, on the Plage du Faubourg, **t** 04 68 82 07 06 (€€–€). A simple, sweet hotel overlooking the busiest beach. *Closed Dec–Mar.*

Ermitage, Notre-Dame-de-Consolation, above Collioure on the D86, **t** 04 68 82 17 66, *www.ermitage.consolation.free.fr* (€). Rustic, peaceful B&B around a medieval hermitage. *Call to confirm which months they close.*

Dinner in Collioure need not necessarily include anchovies, but the rest of the catch merits attention.

Le Neptune, 9 Rte Port-Vendres, **t** 04 68 82 02 27, *www.leneptune-collioure.com* (€€€€–€€€). One of the best in town, with wonderful canopied sea views and the full *nouvelle* Catalan cuisine; menus change seasonally but you might be offered *salade chemin des Fauves*, which combines eggs, artichokes, *tapenade* and tomato *confit* in highly decorative style, or lobster ravioli with cardamom vinaigrette; desserts are delicious. *Closed Tues.*

Caucoliberi, 17 Rue Jean Bart, **t** 0468 88 86 65 (€€). A seafood-lover's dream – a family-run place serviving superbly fresh fish and *gambas*, wine without huge mark-ups and a view to die for.

Can Pla, 7 Rue Voltaire, **t** 04 68 82 10 00, *www.restaurant-can-pla-collioure.com* (€€). Relaxed family restaurant with a nice terrace – one of the best for traditional Catalan dishes, and lots of seafood.

L'Insolite, Place de l'Eglise, **t** 04 68 82 08 61 (€€–€). Suntrap by the beach, serving a mix of salads, crêpes, seafood and tapas. *Open all day.*

Banyuls-sur-Mer ✉ 66650

****Les Elmes**, Plage des Elmes, **t** 04 68 88 03 12, *www.hotel-des-elmes.com* (€€€–€€). Pleasant seaside rooms and an excellent restaurant, **La Littorine** (€€), with a superb new chef; half-board is excellent value. Also a training pool, hammam, and boats to hire.

****Solhotel**, N114, Cap d'Osne, **t** 04 68 98 34 34, *www.solhotel.fr* (€€–€). Simple little seafront hotel with balconies a short walk from the centre, with Wi-fi and parking.

Cerbère ✉ 66290

****La Dorade**, Front de Mer, **t** 04 68 88 41 93, *www.hotel-ladorade.com* (€€). The choice spot in Cerbère, owned by a friendly family. It has a restaurant (€€). *Closed Oct–Easter.*

Getting around the Pyrenean Valleys

By Little Yellow Train

Le Petit Train Jaune, t 08 00 88 60 91, *www.trainstouristiques-ter.com* or *www.ter-sncf.com*, begins at Villefranche Vernet-les-Bains (reached by regular rail connections from Perpignan) and travels 62.5km up a tremendously scenic narrow-gauge track into the Cerdagne. Begun in 1910, it's one of the most unlikely railways in France – a political project, meant to bring new life into the impoverished mountain valleys, and so difficult to build through the Pyrenees, along France's highest railway bridges, that it was only completed in 1927. Recently restored for the centenary of its opening, it runs year-round, taking skiiers up in winter and visitors to see the scenery in summer in open carriages. The last station, three hours away, is Latour-de-Carol (*see* p.282), the only place in the world where three rail gauges meet: you can catch a train to Toulouse (French gauge) or Barcelona (Spanish gauge) or a bus to Andorra.

By Bus

It's possible to see muuch of the Conflent and Vallespir by bus from Perpignan's ***gare routière***: for routes and schedules, **t** 04 68 80 80 80, *www.cg66.fr/252-les-bus-departementaux.htm*.

Southern Roussillon and the Pyrenees

Pyrenean Valleys: The Conflent

Canigou is an immense magnolia that blooms in an offshoot of the Pyrenees; its bees are the fairies that surround it, and its butterflies the swans and the eagles...

from Jacint Verdageur's poem 'Canigó'

Two major valleys, the **Conflent** (the valley of the river Têt) and the **Vallespir** (of the river Tech), slope in parallel lines towards the Spanish border. Don't think that this butt end of the Pyrenees consists of mere foothills; in between these two valleys stands **Canigou** (9,134ft) jauntily wearing a Phrygian cap of snow until late spring, a mountain so steeply flanked and imposing that until the 18th century it was believed to be the highest peak in the range.

The *muntanya regalada* ('fortunate mountain') of the Catalans is one of the symbols of the nation (north and south), and the subject of one of national poet Jacint Verdageur's best-loved Catalan poems. Legends and apparitions abound. Fairies and 'ladies of the waters' are said to frequent its forested slopes, and King Pere of Aragon climbed it in 1285 and met a dragon near the top. Some say it even shelters the Holy Grail.

On 23 June, on the eve of the Festa Major or St John's day (*nit de Sant Joan*), a bonfire is lit on the summit, and Catalans from both sides of the frontier run down the mountain in a torch relay, bringing down the flame that will ignite some 30,000 bonfires across the region. In August, there's a massive marathon run up and down the summit; if you want to make the ascent yourself, *see* below.

World's Biggest Barrel

t *04 68 53 05 42, www.byrrh.com; tours July–Aug daily 10–11.45 and 2–6.45; May–June and Sept daily 9–11.45 and 2.30–5.45; April and Oct Mon–Fri 9–11.45 and 2.30–5.45; closed Nov–Mar; adm*

From Perpignan to Ille-sur-Têt

The fish-filled Têt, before passing through Perpignan, washes a wide plain packed full of vineyards and fat villages. The fattest, **Thuir**, puts up signs all over Roussillon inviting us over to see the **World's Biggest Barrel**, in the cellars of the famous *apéritif* Byrrh –

wine mixed with quinine and 10 different spices, invented here in 1886, and once so popular that, when a new station was required for all the trains shipping it out, Gustave Eiffel was summoned to build it (the station is no longer used since 1989, but is still an impressive sight). And the barrel? Dating from 1950, it can hold over a million litres, and an impressive sight it is, too.

Château de Castelnou
t 04 68 53 22 91, www.chateaudecastelnou.fr; open July–Aug daily 10–7; April–June and Sept daily 11–6; Oct–Dec and Feb–Mar daily 11–5; closed Jan; last ticket 1hr before closing; adm

After an *apéritif* or two, head 6km west for golden-hued **Castelnou**, a perfectly preserved medieval village on winding, pebble-paved lanes and steps under the spectacular 10th-century **château** built by the Viscounts of Vallespir. Restored after the roof caught fire in 1981, this six-storey castle, unlike most military castles in France, never graduated into a lordly residence, and the rooms are mostly empty today; the owners also make AOC Côtes du Roussillon and Rivesaltes, which you can purchase on site.

Chapelle de la Trinité
closed Tues

The narrow D48 wiggling west of Castelnou is unabashedly beautiful: if you have a couple of hours to spare, you can circle around to the Prieuré de Serrabonne (*see* opposite) by way of the D2 to **Caixas** and **Fourques**, then on to the D13 for **Llauro** and **Prunet-et-Belpuig**, where the ruins of the **Château de Belpuig** offer a superb view and the 11th-century **Chapelle de la Trinité**, with a extraordinary medieval door and some rather unusual modillions (inside, its greatest treasure is a superb 12th-century Romanesque Christ in Majesty – on the cross, yet clothed in a kingly robe – that has been recently restored; there's also a very early polychrome wooden Virgin and Child). In **Boule d'Amont**, just up the road, there's another charming Romanesque church, **St Saturnin**, from the same century, with a Baroque retable squeezed into a Visigothic arch and another Virgin and Child.

Musée de l'Agriculture Catalane
t 04 68 84 76 40; open summer Mon–Fri 10–12 and 2–7, Sat and Sun 2–9; winter Wed–Mon 2–6, closed Tues

A shorter alternative, but on even more dubious roads, is to take the D2 north to **St-Michel-de-Llotes**, a village encircled by five **dolmens**; it also has the **Musée de l'Agriculture Catalane** in a collection of stone barns, with tools and displays on farming and wine production from the early 1900s. Then turn back to Serrabonne by way of **Casefabre**, with its tremendous views.

Centre d'Art Sacré
t 04 68 84 83 96; open mid-June–Sept Mon–Fri 10–12 and 2–7, Sun 2–7; Oct–Nov and Feb–mid-June Wed–Mon 2–6, closed Tues; closed Dec and Jan; adm

At **Ille-sur-Têt**, an attractive old town at the gateway to the mountains, neglected art from the 11th to 19th centuries from churches all over Roussillon (including the fascinating 12th-century frescoes detached from the nearby chapel of Casenoves) has been assembled in a 13th-century hospice for the poor, now the **Centre d'Art Sacré**, with changing exhibitions. Outside the museum, it's fun to seek out some lighter-hearted secular works: on the Rue des Enamorats ('lovers' lane') there's a statue believed to mark the site of a brothel, and at the corner of Rues Malpas and Carmes there's a pink marble *caganer d'Ille*, a figure in the act of defecating. The Catalans are merrily obsessed with bottoms and poo, seeing it as a sign of their essential earthy character; in southern Catalonia you

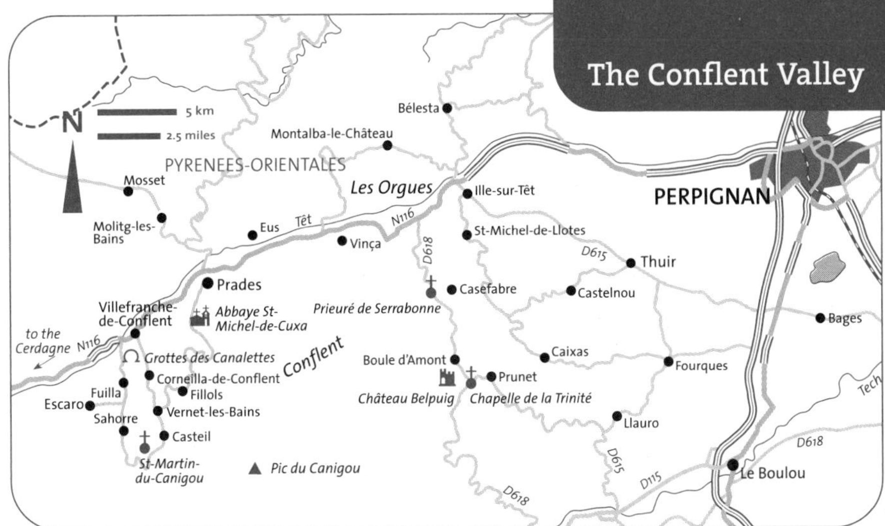

can buy *caganer* figures (either traditional models or squatting celebrities) to decorate your home and Christmas manger scene.

Northwest of Ille, the Chemin de Régleilles leads to some surprising landscapes: five-million-year-old 'fairy chimneys' and towers called the **Orgues**, that resemble eroded, dream-like buildings out of of Italo Calvino's *Invisible Cities,* with the forgotten ruin of a 12th-century tower and the Pyrenees forming a magnificent backdrop. The fortified church of **Régleilles** (from Ille, take the D2 over the river and after a kilometre turn right on to a little road) looks like a castle – a typical example of a monastic church, in an area without any castles, that grew into a fortress to protect the monks and the village. Ille in fact was located here before its population drifted to the present site.

Les Orgues
t 04 68 84 13 13; site open April–Aug daily 9.30–8; Sept daily 10–6.30; Oct daily 10–12.30 and 2–6; Nov–Jan daily 2–5; Feb and Mar daily 10–12.30 and 2–5.30; adm

Six kilometres north on the D21, in little **Bélesta**, the **Château-Musée** holds the treasure found in a 6,000-year-old Neolithic tomb in 1983 (explanations in French only) in its restored 12th-century castle looming up from a rock.

Château-Musée
t 04 68 84 55 55; open mid-June–mid-Sept Wed–Fri and Sun–Mon 2–7; mid-Sept–mid-June Wed–Fri and Sun–Mon 2–5.30; closed Tues and Sat; adm

Prieuré de Serrabonne

Prieuré de Serrabonne
t 04 68 84 09 30; open daily 10–6, closed major hols; adm

Seeing the finest medieval sculpture in Roussillon requires dedication: the most direct route to Serrabonne, 'the good mountain' (for others, *see* above) requires 13km of hairpin bends on a road where you dread oncoming traffic, starting from the D618 at Bouleternère, just west of Ille, and ending in a lofty, remote, barren spot on the slopes of a mountain called Roque Rouge, in the *commune* of Boule-d'Amont. Even once you finally arrive, the solemn, spare shape and dark schist of Serrabonne's church are not promising, making the surprise inside that much the greater, concentrated in a 12th-century single gallery of a cloister and in the capitals of the **tribune**, a kind of mini-interior cloister in rose-coloured marble from Canigou. Perfectly preserved in its isolated setting, the sculpture includes a fantastical bestiary, centaurs, a grimacing St Michael, reliefs of the four Evangelists and a fellow blasting on a trumpet. The style, by the school of sculptors that grew up at St-Michel-de-Cuxa, will become familiar if you spend time in the Conflent. Note the figure of the Virgin; a narrow window allows the sun's rays to illuminate it one day each year – the Feast of the Assumption on 15 August.

Prades and St-Michel-de-Cuxa

The love of one's country is a splendid thing. But why should love stop at the border?
Pau Casals

Prades festival
www.prades-festival-casals.com; late July–mid-Aug

Musée Pau Casals
t 04 68 05 41 02; open summer Mon–Sat 9–12 and 2–5; winter Tues 10–12 and 3–7, Wed 10–7, Fri 3–7 and Sat 10–1

Casa Perez
t 04 68 96 21 03, www.joyaux-catalans.fr; tours 15 June–15 Sept Tues–Sat at 10, 11, 2.30, 3.30. 4.30. 5.30; adm

St-Michel-de-Cuxa
t 04 68 96 15 35, www.cuxa.org; open May–Sept Mon–Sat 9.30–11.50 and 2–6; Oct–April Mon–Sat 9.30–11.50 and 2–5, Sun 2–5; adm

Prades is known around the world in connection with the chamber music festival founded in 1951 by cellist Pau (Pablo) Casals, but few people could place it on a map. Casals, in exile after the Spanish Civil War, spent much of the 1940s and '50s here, in the one safe corner of his beloved Catalonia. From the beginning, his **festival** attracted many of the world's greatest classical soloists, and it still does today. Otherwise, Prades is a typical stolid, slightly bohemian Catalan town with a rather worrying road system.

There are a couple of things to see, besides the festival. A small **Musée Pau Casals**, at 4 Rue Victor Hugo, has a section dedicated to the great man – photos, his piano and pipes, records, letters, and recordings. In the heart of Prades, the church of **St-Pierre** has a fine Romanesque bell-tower with a pyramid crown and, inside, an operatic Baroque retable in full 17th-century fig by Catalan chisel virtuoso Joseph Sunyer, along with an exhibition of church treasures. You can watch a film and see how the local garnets are made into opulent red and gold jewellery at **Casa Perez** at the Rond-Point du Canigou towards Perpignan.

Best of all, it's only a few kilometres from Prades through orchards to **St-Michel-de-Cuxa**, one of the most important monasteries of medieval Catalonia. Even in its reduced, semi-ruined state, the scale is impressive:; this was one of the great monastic centres from which medieval Europe was planned and built. Visigothic Catalonia had something of an artistic head start in the 9th century, along with the iron mines in the Pyrenees to provide the cash.

St-Michel de Cuxa was founded in 878 under the protection of the Counts of Cerdagne, after an earlier monastery, built in 840 on the banks of the Têt, flooded. The church, consecrated in 974, is a landmark on the road to the Romanesque style. One of its features is the more-than-semicircular 'Visigothic' arches in the nave, a style which never became too popular in Christian Europe, though the Muslims of Spain adopted it to create the architectural fantasies of Seville and Granada.

St-Michel's reputation spread across Europe; in 978, Doge Pietro Orseolo slipped out of Venice and retreated here incognito, living out his life piously like a hermit (he was canonized in 1731 – his relics are now in St-Pierre in Prades). Another who spent time here was Gerbert d'Aurillac (*c.* 946–1003), the future Pope Sylvester II, who as a young man showed so much promise that the Count of Barcelona sent him to learn mathematics in Spain, where he became fascinated with astronomy, Arabic numerals, and the whole sophisticated culture of al-Andalus; he would later re-introduce the abacus and armillary sphere to Europe.

In 1008, the famous scholar Oliba was made abbot and embarked on a major building plan, adding the abbey's massive yet elegant 130ft bell tower (originally there were two) and the unusual circular crypt, known as the **Chapelle de la Vierge de la Crèche**. This was originally located underneath a long-gone rotunda that held a prize relic: baby Jesus's swaddling clothes. The crypt, plain and rugged, is covered by toroid barrel vaulting, with a mushroom-like central column 23ft in circumference that is almost unique in medieval architecture. Antonio Gaudí used similar columns in Barcelona – a fascinating example of subliminal Catalan cultural continuity, especially as the crypt was only rediscovered in 1937, after Gaudí's death.

The French Revolution found St-Michel already in a state of serious decay. Looted and abandoned in the 19th century, one of the two bell-towers collapsed, and much of the best sculptural work went 'into exile' as the Catalans put it, carted off to the Cloisters Museum in New York. When restoration began, the rest of the cloister was found in a public bathhouse in Prades. The altar was found holding up a balcony in Vinça.

After years away from the public, Pau Casals performed his first public concert in exile in 1950 in the church – which had become so run-down that it didn't even have a roof. His interest was key in initiating its restoration, and today it remains a major venue for concerts during the festival.

In the **rebuilt cloister** (at 156 by 128ft, it was one of the biggest in region) are capitals sculpted out of the rose-tinted marble of Canigou: monsters from the medieval bestiary in the corners, intertwined with men on the four faces. There is an obsession with lions, almost Chinese in their stylization, biting and licking each other. One is said to represent the Sumerian hero Gilgamesh.

A small community of Benedictine monks from Montserrat, the centre of Catalan spiritualism, have occupied St-Michel since 1965 and make their own cheese, which you can buy in the abbey's shop. They also keep a beautiful iris garden, where every colour of iris imaginable bursts into bloom in May and early June.

North of Prades

From the Têt valley's main N116 , it's easy to spot the striking, pyramid-shaped village of **Eus**, 'one of the most beautiful villages in France', spilling down its granite hill northeast of Prades, in what it claims is the sunniest spot in France. On top, the 18th-century (but rarely open) church of St-Vincent stands amid the 11th-century ruins of a castle and a cactus garden and is rumoured to house elaborate 17th-century polychrome retables.

Heading up the Castellare valley, on the D14, **Molitg-les-Bains**, on a hill in the forest, has been a spa (specializing in skin disorders) since the Belle Epoque, with a suitably grand hotel with a lake, river and lovely gardens open to the public. The 12th-century village church St- Marie with its silo of a tower is another Casals festival venue.

Beyond Molitg, the road climbs up to the **Col de Jau**, a pass with stunning views, once the border between France and Spain, and a route to the Aude valley (*see* p.217). On the way, pause in the fortified village of **Mosset**, a little haven of artists and potters, where the landmark is the bell-tower of the church of St-Julien et Ste-Baselisse, with a dwarf 200-year-old pine tree growing out of the top. It also has a beautifully restored Romanesque chapel, the *capelletta*, and the round **Tour des Parfums**, the interactive 'Tower of Perfume' which offers a fun lesson in scents. Mosset is also proud to have the 'smallest ski station in the world', run by the *mairie*, with its blue and green pistes, chairlift and 6km cross-country course.

Tour des Parfums
t 04 68 05 38 32; open by request

Vernet-les-Bains and St-Martin-du-Canigou

I came here in search of nothing more than a little sunshine. But I found Canigou, whom I discovered to be a magician among mountains...nothing he could do or give birth to would now surprise me, whether I met Don Quixote himself riding in from the Spanish side...or saw (which each twilight seems quite possible) gnomes and kobolds swarming out of the mines and tunnels of his flanks.

Rudyard Kipling

The D27, the narrow road that snakes around the lower slopes of Canigou, is a pretty drive through the mountain forests. After St-Michel-de-Cuxa, it passes lively little **Fillols** before meeting **Vernet-les-Bains**, a bustling spa with most of the accommodation in the area and hot sulphuric waters that are good for your rheumatism and respiratory problems. Rudyard Kipling made his first of three visits in 1910, as so did so many fellow Brits that they built an Anglican church and erected the only monument in France to the 1904 Entente Cordiale between the UK and France; even Vernet's waterfall (a 90-minute trek) is known as the **Cascade des Anglais**, perhaps because *les Anglais* were the first to go trekking out to look at it for fun. Kipling even wrote a story called *Why Snow Falls at Vernet*, poking fun of his compatriates' habit of talking about the weather. The weather in fact was so fine that British residents started planting exotic trees, a practice Vernet has since adopted: today it's proud to be France's first official Village-Arboretum.

Parc Animalier
t 04 68 05 67 54, www.zoodecasteil.com; open mid-April–Oct daily 10–8; Feb–Mar daily 1–6; sometimes closed Mon and Tues; closed Nov–Jan; adm

St-Martin-du-Canigou
t 04 68 05 50 03, stmartinducanigou.org; open daily in summer; Oct–May Tues–Sun; guided tours only; adm

Jeep taxi
t 06 14 35 70 64

Three kilometres further up is **Casteil**, a wooded little resort with a family-run 20ha **Parc Animalier** on the mountain slopes, with deer, lions, bears, goats and more in a natural setting, visible along two discovery paths. Casteil is also the base for visiting the abbey of **St-Martin-du-Canigou** – a taxing though lovely 40-minute walk up or by way of **jeep taxi**). A monkish architect named Sclua designed this complex in 1009 for Oliba's brother, Guifré II, the Count of the Cerdagne and the Conflent. Sclua was a designer ahead of his time; his St Martin is a rustic acropolis, spectacularly sited with views around Canigou and surrounding peaks, and arranged as a series of courtyards and terraces on different levels. The church, with its immense, fortress-like bell tower, has two levels: an upper church dedicated to St-Martin and a lower crypt for a certain obscure subterranean Virgin Mary, Notre-Dame-sous-Terre. Some good white marble capitals can be seen in the cloister, heavily restored in the early 20th century, and medieval tombs, including Count Guifré's, survive in the upper church. But on the whole St-Martin, damaged by an earthquake in 1428, abandoned after the Revolution and restored between 1952 and 1971, retains relatively few of its former architectural glories. Since 1988, it has been reinhabited by women and men belonging to the community of the Béatitudes, who devote their lives to prayer.

Notre Dame
t 04 68 95 77 59; open June–Sept

To complete the tour of Romanesque Canigou, the village of **Corneilla-de-Conflent** was once the summer capital of the counts of Cerdagne, and has another 11th–12th-century church founded by Guifre II along the road to Vernet-les-Bains: **Notre Dame**, once part of a Benedictine priory, is full of fascinating sculpture, including a red marble tympanum of the Virgin and Child, in a mandala. An extraordinary window in the apse is decorated with five carved receeding arches, and there's a capital sculpted with winged dragons; inside are gaunt figures from a 15th-century polychrome Deposition and other statues, and a 14th-century Mozarabe walnut wardrobe.

Musée de la Mine
t 04 68 97 15 34; open July–Aug daily 2–6; June and Sept–Oct Sat and Sun only 2–6; organized 3½-hour walk of the mining sites departing at 9am from the museum from end June–Aug; adm

Side roads to the west, in the valley of the Rotja, can take you to several more churches, including rare 10th-century ones in the tiny villages of **Fuilla** and **Sahorre**. Canigou's iron, mined since 150 BC, is recalled in tiny **Escaro**'s **Musée de la Mine**, with trains, tools, old equipment and photos of the days when the mines employed 420 people and the village had three schools.

Climbing Canigou

If **Canigou**'s magnetism is working its juju, don't resist the call – but do make sure of the weather before setting out, to avoid getting caught in a late afternoon thunderstorm. The climbing season generally runs from May through September, when the mountain's 9,137 feet are free of snow. To do it entirely by foot takes 11 hours and means an overnight stay in one of the *refuges*, or you can drive up the forest road from Casteil as far as the **Refuge de Mariailles** (5,577ft) and make the 7–8hr climb there and back, by way of a 330ft scramble over the stone 'chimneys'.

Refuge de Mariailles
t 04 68 05 57 99; closed Jan

The easiest way, however, is to go by jeep as far as the **Chalet-Refuge des Cortalets** (7,053ft), the base for a fairly easy 3–4hr walk to and from the summit, requiring only a decent pair of walking shoes and a windcheater. Check the Vernet-les-Bains tourist website for other options, maps, jeep taxi services and contact numbers for Canigou's other *refuges* (to stay or eat at any, it's essential to book ahead).

Chalet-Refuge des Cortalets
t 04 68 96 36 19; open June–early Oct

Villefranche-de-Conflent

Some villages have their own ideas for welcoming visitors. This one casually points cannons down at you, by way of an invitation to drop in. Located where the Têt valley abruptly narrows, Villefranche has had a castle ever since the Counts of Cerdagne founded Villa Franca in 1092 – the 'franca' referring to tax and duty privileges meant to attract traders and workers. After the Treaty of the Pyrenees in 1654, Louis XIV hired his crack military engineer Sébastien Le Prestre de Vauban to refortify it to guard his new frontier. Vauban gave him a model Baroque fortress-town. Almost nothing has changed since, leaving a fascinating historical record, a sort of stage set of that era, although one filled with Roussillon's greatest concentration of tourist shops.

The town's 11th-century church of **St-Jacques** is its greatest medieval relic, with a rosy pink portal and capitals sculpted by the St Michel-de-Cuxa school. Inside there's another retable by Sunyer and, by the door, note the measures engraved in the stone, used by drapers who had market stalls in the square. Vauban incorporated the church and tower into his wall.

From 2 Rue St-Jean steps lead up Vauban's **ramparts** with their roofed walkway built through the walls – necessary because of the surrounding mountains. For those with sufficient puff and military curiosity, there's a steep climb up the remarkable 739 subterranean rock-hewn steps (at the end of Rue St-Pierre) to **Fort Liberia**, added by Vauban in 1681, on the one spot where an enemy could bring cannons to fire down on Villefranche. It was further fortified by Napoléon III and used as a prison, where you are invited to 'meet the villainous female poisoners' (don't be alarmed – they're made of wax). There were eight women sent here from Versailles accused of poisoning and witchcraft; one survived for 44 years chained to the wall.

Ramparts
t 04 68 96 22 96; open July–Aug daily 10–8; June and Sept daily 10–7; Mar–May and Oct daily 10.30–12.30 and 2–6; Feb, Nov daily 10.30–12.30 and 2–5; Dec daily 2–5 (and 10.30–12.30 during hols); closed Jan; audioguide; adm

Fort Liberia
t 04 68 96 34 01, www.fort-liberia.com; open June–Sept daily 9–8; Oct–May daily 10–6; adm; extra adm if you take the 4x4 shuttle up the hill

Le Petit Train Jaune

Cova Bastera
t 04 68 05 20 20, www.3grottes.com; open July–Aug 11–4; June and Sept 11.30–4.30; adm

Grotte des Canalettes
t 04 68 05 20 20, www.3grottes.com; hourly visits July–Aug 12–5.30; adm

Grotte des Grandes Canalettes
t 04 68 05 20 20, www.3grottes.com; open July–Aug daily 10–7.30; April–June daily 10–6; Sept–Oct daily 10-5.30 ; Nov–Mar Sat, Sun and hols only 11–5; adm; son-et-lumiere July and Aug at 7pm; adm

Besides offering trips into the Pyrenees on the remarkable **Petit Train Jaune** (*see* p.269), Villefranche has three caves all in easy walking distance, awaiting your inspection. Just across the N116 is the **Cova Bastera**, which was inhabited in prehistoric times, and later served as the headquarters of Catalan rebels in 1674; French troops made short work of them, but, to make sure it didn't happen again, Vauban fortified the entrance to the cave as well. The current owners have made it into 'An Encounter with History' with dioramas starting all the way back with dinosaurs.

Some of the Pyrenees' most peculiar stalactites await further up the road at the intimate **Grotte des Canalettes**, while the spectacular **Grotte des Grandes Canalettes**, discovered in the 1980s, has an extraordinary formation known as Angkor Wat, a splendid white chamber.

Market Days in the Conflent

Ille-sur-Têt: Wed and Fri; flea market on Sun.

Prades: Tues.

Activities in the Conflent

Summer and winter offer plenty of chances for dare devil sports for the entire family.

Cimes et Eaux, t 06 37 78 18 18, *www.escalade-canyoning-pyrenees.com*. Climbing, canyoning and *via ferrata*.

Exploration Pyrénéen, t 06 22 45 82 02, *www.ex-pyr.com*. Caving, canyoning, hiking and snow-shoeing; based in Villefranche-de-Conflent.

Kap oupa kap, t 06 88 48 06 45, *www.kapoupakap.fr*. Tubing, snow tubing, karting, jumping around like a kangaroo and winter sports.

Site d'Escale, t 06 07 31 88 25, *www.sitedescalade.com*. Rock climbing, canyoning, snow-shoeing.

Têt Aventure, Marquixanes (just east of Prades), **t** 04 68 05 72 12, *www.tet-aventure.co*. Forest acrobatic course (from age 3), rafting, tubing, canyoning, cross-country skiing and more.

Where to Stay and Eat in the Conflent

La Casa DaLie >>

Thuir ✉ 66500

La Casa DaLie, 21 Rue de la République, **t** 04 68 53 03 92, *www.casa-dalie.fr* (€€€). Young David and Julie locally source nearly all the ingredients of their excellent cuisine, with Catalan and exotic touches; they even make their own bread. Excellent-value lunch menus. *Closed Wed.*

Prades >>
10 Place de la République, t 04 68 05 41 02, www.prades-tourisme.fr; open Mon–Fri

Prades ✉ 66500

Les Loges du Jardin d'Aymeric, 7 Rue du Canigou, Clara (15 minutes south of Prades), **t** 04 68 96 08 72, *www.logesaymeric.com*. Pastel B&B rooms with a pool (€€) in a very peaceful setting, and sumptuous regional cooking (€€€) by chef Gilles Bascou. *Closed Sun, Mon, and Wed eve winter.*

Villa Lafabrègue >>

Villa Lafabrègue, 15 Av Louis Prat, **t** 04 68 96 29 90, *www.villafrench.com* (€€). Lovely B&B in a 19th-century Neo-Renaissance villa in a garden with a pool and views over Canigou, a short walk from the centre of Prades. Owners Kate and Nick Wilcock also offer hiking and other excursions, and can arrange airport pick-up and drop-off (Perpignan or Girona), breakfasts, picnics and transport to trail-heads. There are also two independent *gîtes*.

***Hostalrich**, 156 Av Général de Gaulle, **t** 04 68 96 05 38 (€). A big neon sign makes this easy to find; all rooms have TV and showers and some have

ⓘ **Ille-sur-Têt**
Square de la Poste, t 04 68 84 02 62, www.tourisme-ille.lescigales.org; open July–Aug Mon–Sat and Sun am; Sept–June Mon–Fri

ⓘ **Vernet-les-Bains >>**
2 Rue de la Chapelle, t 04 68 05 55 35, www.ot-vernet-les-bains.fr; open July–Aug Mon–Fri and Sat am; Sept–June Mon–Fri

★ **Château de Riell >**

ⓘ **Villefranche-de-Conflent >>**
32 bis Rue St-Jacques, t 04 68 96 22 96, www.villefranchedeconflent.com; open June–Sept daily; Oct–Dec and Feb–May daily pm; closed Jan

★ **Auberge St-Paul >>**

balconies. Avoid the restaurant if you can; the food is simple to the point of dullness. There's a wonderful chestnut-shaded garden as compensation.

La Meridienne, 20 Rue Marchands, **t** 04 68 05 98 31 (€€). A jolly warm welcome and some of the best food in town – try the mouthwatering scallops on a spit. *Closed Sun, Mon, and Wed eve in winter.*

Molitg-les-Bains ✉ 66500

****Château de Riell, **t** 04 68 05 04 40, *www.chateauderiell.com* (€€€€€–€€€). Molitg may have only 180 inhabitants, but it can claim Roussillon's top luxury hotel. The Relais & Châteaux Baroque folly from the turn of the last century is in a theatrically Baroque setting, perched on a rock with exquisite views of Canigou; it has elegant, luxurious Hollywood-style rooms in the château and maisonettes in the garden – and two pools, including one on top of the tower, perhaps the best place in the world to watch the Catalan bonfires go up on St John's eve. Lots of extras, and a restaurant (€€€) worthy of the décor. *Closed Nov–Mar; restaurant closed Mon–Fri lunch except summer.*

*****Grand Hôtel Thermal**, **t** 04 68 05 00 50, *www.grandhotelmolitg.com* (€€€). Less pricey, but also nifty, with marble spa rooms, a pool and marble terrace, glorious views and also a very good-value sunny yellow restaurant (€€€–€€), using healthy recipes by Michel Guérard. *Closed Jan–Mar.*

Mosset ✉ 66500

Mas Lluganas, just outside Mosset, **t** 04 68 05 00 37, *www.mas lluganas.com* (€). *Chambres d'hôtes*, plus meals (€€) based on its own produce of duck, guinea fowl, veal and *foie gras*. The same family also offers inexpensive *chambres d'hôtes* accommodation at **La Forge**, a peaceful retreat by the river. There is also a *gîte*. *Closed mid-Oct–Mar.*

Fillols ✉ 66820

Café de l'Union, Rue de l'Eglise, **t** 04 68 05 63 06 (€). A famous stop for *magret* and *morrels*, and live music on many summer evenings. *Closed Sun and Mon eves; ring ahead in winter.*

Vernet-les-Bains ✉ 66820

*****Le Mas Fleuri**, 25 Bd Clemenceau, **t** 04 68 05 51 94, *www.hotellemas fleuri.fr* (€€€–€€). At the top of the list, this century-old hotel is set in a pretty park, with a pool. *Closed mid-Oct–mid-April.*

****Princess**, Rue Lavandières, **t** 04 68 05 56 22, *www.hotel-princess.fr* (€€). A pleasant Logis de France with a better-than average restaurant (€€). *Closed Feb; restaurant closed Jan–mid-Mar and end of Nov.*

Bistrot Le Cortal, Rue du Château, **t** 04 68 05 55 79 , *www.bistrot-lecortal.fr* (€€). Lovely views from this renovated stable, featuring modern *bistrot* dishes or the chance to cook your own dishes on a hot chunk of lava (*pierrade*). *Closed Tues.*

Villefranche-de-Conflent ✉ 66500

Auberge St-Paul, Place de l'Eglise, **t** 04 68 96 30 95, *www.perso.orange.fr/auberge.stpaul* (€€€€–€€). Every season chef Patricia Gomez creates new wonders. *Closed Sun eve in summer, Sun eve, Mon and Tues in winter, and 3 weeks Jan, 1 week June and 1 week Nov.*

Au Grill La Senyera, 81 Rue St-Jean, **t** 04 68 96 17 65 (€€). Solid, traditional cuisine, simply prepared and delicious. *Closed Tues eve, Wed, Thurs eve and mid-Oct–mid-Nov.*

The Cerdagne

Long ago this spectacular, sun-drenched basin was a lake rimmed by lofty peaks. It's as close as we get into the Pyrenees, but at 3,940ft it's far enough for the real thing: mountain rhododendrons and blue gentians, hordes of skiers, herds of horses, and snow on

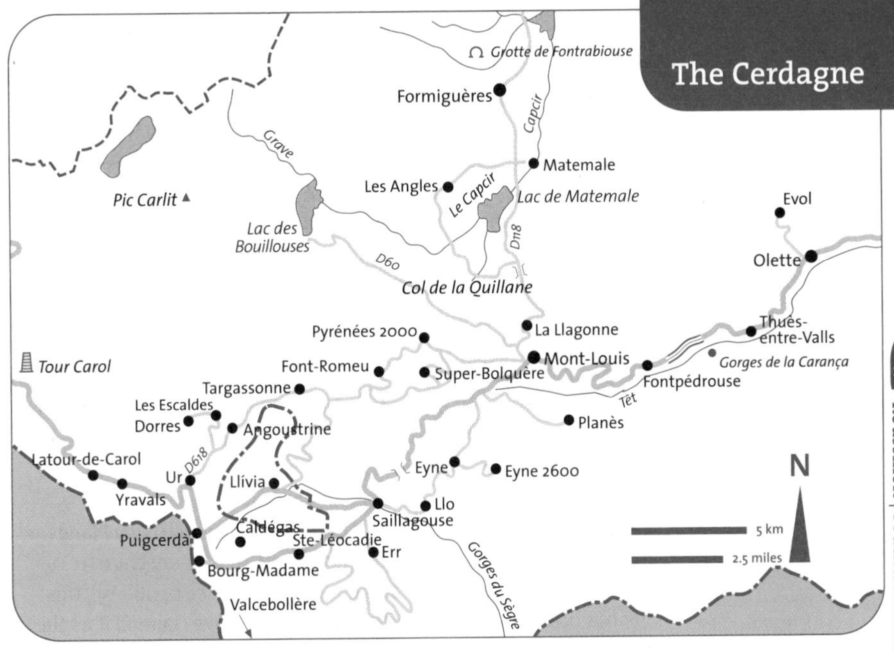

top until May or June. The Cerdagne (Cerdanya in Catalan) was an isolated and effectively independent county in the Middle Ages; from the 10th century its counts gradually extended their power, eventually becoming counts of Barcelona and kings of Aragon. In spite of this heritage, the Cerdagne was split between Spain and France in the 1659 Treaty of the Pyrenees. The completion of the Petit Train Jaune, or Little Yellow Train (*see* p.269) in 1911 brought the French Cerdagne into the modern world; skiing has made it rather opulent today. And besides skiing, you can see some good Romanesque churches, warm up at the world's largest solar furnace, visit the highest railway station in France – and circumnavigate Spain in less than an hour.

To Mont-Louis and the Capcir

After Villefranche-de-Conflet, the main N116 climbs dramatically into the mountains. There are a few possible stop-offs on the way, most of which have stations along the Petit Train Jaune as well: at **Olette**, you can turn off to explore nearly abandoned old mountain villages like **Nyer** and **Evol**.

A bit further up, at **Thuès-entre-Valls**, you can stretch your legs in the beautiful, vertiginous **Gorges de la Carança**, with its sheer cliff fitted out with gantries (allow four hours there and back, although you can also make this a two-day circular trek, returning on the Cami Ramader, with an overnight at the very basic *refuge* of **Ras de la Carança**). Afterwards, soak your weary bones in the delightful natural hot springs of **Fontpédrouse** at St-Thomas-les-

Ras de la Carança
t 04 68 83 15 19; open year-round

Fontpédrouse
t 04 68 97 03 13, www.fontpedrouse.pagesperso-orange.fr; open July–Aug daily 10–9; Jan–June and Sept–Oct daily 10–8; closed Nov; hammam closed Mon; adm

Bains, where even in a raging blizzard you can take a dip outside or in the Jacuzzi, visit the hammam or have a massage.

Climb, climb, climb, and at last you'll reach the gateway to the Cerdagne, **Mont-Louis**, named after Louis XIV, another work by Vauban and the highest fortress in France (5,250ft). Unlike Villefranche, tourist shops are few and far between; the army still resides here, to train commandos and look after the world's first **solar furnace**, built in 1953 by Félix Trombe and used, not for generating power, but for melting substances for scientific experiments; the huge mirror generates temperatures up to 6,000 degrees. It shares the small space inside the walls with some 200 residents. The tourist office offers **guided tours** of the village and of the Citadel to visit the commandos and the **Puits des Forçats**, the 17th-century wheel which lifted water from the wells dug into the rock.

Solar furnace
t 04 68 04 14 89, www.four-solaire.fr; guided tours only; documents available in English; open summer 10–6; spring and autumn 10–5; winter 10–4; closed first half Dec; adm

Guided tours
t 04 68 04 21 97; citadelle open July–Aug daily, other times Mon–Sat at 11 and 2; village tours July–Aug Mon–Thurs at 11.30 and 3.30; other times at Mon–Sat at 3.30; adm

A 7km detour up into the mountains will take you to tiny **Planès** and its equally tiny and unique triangular 11th-century church. Like the seven-sided model at Rieux-Minervois (*see* pp.188–9), this one has occasioned much speculation; some have claimed it as the centre of a network of ley lines.

The road to Planès is a dead end, but there are better choices from the big crossroads at Mont-Louis. To the north, the D118 leads to the isolated plateau of **Le Capcir**. It's a perfect place to get away from it all – after a road was built into the Capcir in the 19th century, almost the entire population deserted it, tired of scratching a living from land that would only support a few cows. They left behind beautiful pine forests and a score of little lakes. Skiing has brought the Capcir back to life since the 1960s.

On your way into Le Capcir, don't miss the church of St-Vincent in **La Llagonne**, 3km from Mont-Louis. Founded in 866 and remodelled several times since, the centuries have left it in peace, with a remarkable collection of medieval art, including an altarpiece and painted baldachin (12th- and 13th-centuries), and an excellent polychrome *Majestat*, or robed Christ on the Cross.

Further north, **Les Angles**, **Matemale** and **Formiguères** are the main ski centres. Les Angles has, as well as some 30 ski runs and a whole range of winter sports, a **Parc Animalier**, a partly free-range zoo with native fauna of the Pyrenees, both current and past residents, including bears, reindeer, wolves, bison and frisky mountain goats. A *télécabine* also runs in summer, affording some great views. **Formiguères** (not the ski station but the village, 4km away) is one of the prettiest and best-preserved villages in the region, hardly changed since the days when the kings of Majorca sojourned here to relieve their asthma. Further north, in the village of the same name, the **Grotte de Fontrabiouse** was discovered in 1958 while digging for alabaster; the hour-long tours take in the

Parc Animalier
t 04 68 04 17 20, www.les-angles.com; open summer daily 9–6; winter daily 9–5; closed mid-Nov–mid-Dec; adm

Grotte de Fontrabiouse
t 04 68 26 14 20; www.fontrabiouse.com; tours (with a break until 2.30 for lunch) July–Aug 10.15–6; April–June and Sept 10.30–5.30; Oct–Nov 2.30–4.30; Dec–Mar 10.30–4.30; adm

subterranean river and stalactites. The scenic D118 carries on north through the Gorges de St Georges to Axat in the Aude (*see* p.217).

This region is great for hiking. The best parts lie to the west, up the very narrow and winding D60 from Mont-Louis, on the slopes of the 9,584ft **Pic Carlit**, with the sources of both the Têt and the Aude in the Forêt de Barrès and the idyllic **Lac des Bouillouses**, a natural *site classé*; in July and August, a shuttle takes visitors from the Pla de Barrès car park up to the dam and the trailhead.

Font-Romeu and Around

The western road (D618) will take you through more pine forests to **Font-Romeu**; along with its new satellite towns, **Super-Bolquère** and **Pyrénées 2000**, this is one of the biggest ski resorts in France, linked by a shuttle bus to its station on the Petit Train Jaune. Font-Romeu grew up after 1910, around a now-closed *grand hôtel*. It prospers today partly from its excellent sports facilities, often used for training France's Olympic teams; it also has a golf course and casino. Stamped from the same mould as every other continental ski resort, it has plenty of fake Alpine chalets, innumerable pizzerias and snow machines to help out if the weather isn't co-operating. But no other resort has the world's largest **solar furnace**, 'stronger than 10,000 suns!', the successor to the one in Mont-Louis. With its curved mirror, covering an entire side of the nine-storey laboratory building, it reflects the Pyrenees beautifully while helping scientists work out all sorts of high-temperature puzzles; learn all about it at **Heliodyssée** at 7 Rue du Four Solaire. Above the town, the pilgrimage chapel of **Notre-Dame-de-Font-Romeu** has an exuberant altarpiece by Joseph Sunyer and a 12th-century statue of the Virgin.

Heliodyssée
t 04 68 30 77 86, www.foursolaire-fontromeu.fr; open July–Aug daily 9.30–7; Sept–June daily 10–12.30 and 2–6; adm

Another solar experiment can be seen at **Targassonne**, west of Font-Romeu on the D618; this big mirror was built to generate electricity, but hasn't quite worked as well as intended. The glaciers that reshaped the Capcir were busy here too, leaving a strange expanse of granite boulders called the **Chaos**. The Cerdagne is famous for its Romanesque churches and chapels, testimony to the mountain Catalans' prosperity and level of culture even in the very early Middle Ages. One of the best is **St-André**, at **Angoustrine**, west of Targassonne, with fragments of 13th-century frescoes representing the months of the year.

To the west, **Dorres** is a lofty granite *village perché* with another church, this one from the 12th century, with a strikingly primitive and much venerated 'black' Virgin inside, and a chance to soak in a granite hot tub at the **Bains de Dorres** with a rather sulphurous pong. Admission includes a **museum** on the local granite, which has been exploited since the cows came home – there's even a rather fetching granite dolmen in the next hamlet, **Brangoli**, and

Bains de Dorres
t 04 68 04 66 87, www.bains-de-dorres.com; open daily 8.45am–8pm; closed late Nov–early Dec; adm

granite columns from the ancient Romans baths higher up at **Escaldes**. For stupendous views from Canigou into Andorra, take the 45-minute walk up to the medieval Chapelle de Belloc.

The next village, **Ur**, apparently has nothing to do with its ancient Sumerian namesake; instead of a ziggurat it has another richly decorated Romanesque church, although it's usually locked.

The Vallée du Carol

From Ur you can make a northern detour into the Vallée du Carol, the western edge of Roussillon. **Latour-de-Carol** is a romantic name for another great border rail crossing most of us have blinked at in the dark, even if it is famous among trainspotters as the only place on earth where three different rail gauges come together at a single station (the Petit Train Jaune's narrow gauge, the regular SNCF train to Toulouse and the narrower Spanish RENFE line to Barcelona); there are also daily buses to Andorra. The name does not come from Charlemagne, as most people think, but the Carol river. Latour's church has more work by Joseph Sunyer. The best church in the area, however, is the **Chapelle St-Fructueux** in the minuscule holiday club village of **Yravals**, above Latour-de-Carol – with a wealth of medieval art inside, and a magnificent mid-14th-century altarpiece of *St Martha* by a Catalan named Ramon Destorrents, although again it's rarely open.

Further up this scenic valley, you'll pass the tower of the ruined 14th-century **castle** that gives Latour its name. The trees give out as the tortuous road climbs to the **Pass of Puymorens**. From here, if you have a sudden hankering for some tax-free Havanas, it's only 40km to the principality of **Andorra**.

Bourg-Madame, Llivia, Eyne and Llo

Espace d'Art Contemporain PuigMartí
t 04 68 30 11 60, www.bourgmadame.fr; open Mon–Fri 2–6

Eglise d'Hix and Eglise de Caldégas
to visit, ring ahead, t 04 68 30 11 60

Originally known as La Guingueta d'Hix and renamed **Bourg-Madame** in 1815 to honour the wife of the Duke of Angoulême, this village 'on the same latitude as Rome, but sunnier', as its brochure claims, is doing its bit to bring the Cerdagne into the 21st century with a new **Espace d'Art Contemporain PuigMartí** in Place de Catalogne, featuring works by local artist Josep PuigMartí, sculptor Lorenzo Quinn and other surprises. Its outer hamlets offer more traditional Catalan Romanesque churches. The **Eglise d'Hix**, an impressive 12th-century edifice with finely sculpted capitals, was built when the kings of Aragon were frequent visitors and contains a majestic Romanesque Virgin with a little kingly Christ child on her lap; and the **Eglise de Caldégas** contains six Baroque retables and 13th-century frescoes, including a hunting scene with falcons.

Bourg-Madame is also the crossing point for Spain; just across the border lies **Puigcerdà**, with a 14th-century church and a crack ice hockey squad. Alternatively, the N116 leads northeast from here back to Mont-Louis, completing your circumnavigation of Spain – or at least the tiny Spanish enclave of **Llivia**, marooned by accident by the Treaty of 1659. The treaty stipulated that Spain must give up the 33 *villages* of the Cerdagne,forgetting that Llivia had the proud and legal status of a *ville*; it had been a Roman *municipium*, the capital of the Cerdagne in ancient times. Llivia's historic centre is clustered around a 16th-century fortified church, Nostra Senyora dels Angels, housing a superb 13th-century sculpture of Christ (you may have to ask the sacristan to see it). Opposite, in the **Musée Municipal**, the unlikely attraction is the pharmacy Esteva, documented in 1594 and closed in 1942; it's one of the most beautiful, oldest and best-preserved in Europe.

Musée Municipal
t +34 972 896 011; open Tues–Sat 10–1 and 3–7, Sun 10–2; closed Mon

Further east along the N116, in **Ste-Léocadie** (home of the highest vineyard in Europe), the **Musée de Cerdagne** occupies a 17th-century farm (with plans to relocate to a more permanent building) and is dedicated to oral histories and photos of rural life, and the pre-ski trades of the great plateau – shepherding and farming.

Musée de Cerdagne
Cal Mateu, t 04 68 04 08 05, www.museedecerdagne.com; open July–Aug Wed–Mon 11–7; Sept–mid-Nov and mid-Dec–June Wed–Mon 10–12 and 2–6; closed Tues and mid-Nov–mid-Dec; call before visiting

A by-road leads up to Eyne and the beautiful **Réserve Naturelle d'Eyne**, which offers guided tours in summer. Come in May, when it's late enough to avoid the skiers from the resort called Eyne 2600 but just in time for a spectacular display of wild flowers and medicinal herbs in the Vallée d'Eyne. Here too is **Llo**, a name that linguists says is Basque, evidence that the Basques lived here in remote times. It has another Romanesque church with a lovely sculptured portal, the narrow **Gorges du Sègre** for hiking and yet more hot springs to enjoy afterwards at **Les Bains de Llo**, with indoor and outdoor pools.

Réserve Naturelle d'Eyne
t 04 68 04 77 07

Les Bains de Llo
t 04 68 04 74 55, lesbainsdello.free.fr; open daily 10–7.30, closed early June and mid-Nov–mid Dec; adm; you can hire or buy a cheap bathing suit; children welcome

The market town of **Saillagouse**, back towards Mont-Louis on the N116, completes the circuit of the Cerdagne. It has playful statues in its square and the famous shop and museum of **Bernard Bonzom**, purveyors of the Cerdagne's best *confits*, *charcuterie* and other goodies, including 1,500 hams drying in the barn; there's a film and demonstrations about *charcuterie* and more.

Musée Bernard Bonzom
t 04 68 30 14 27, www.confit-canard-charcuterie-artisanale-pyrenees.bernard-bonzom.com; museum open July–Aug Tues–Sun 10–12 and 3–7.30

Market Days in the Cerdagne

Puigcerdà: Sun am, the best market in the area.

Activities in the Cerdagne

Ozone3, Font Romeu, **t** 04 68 30 36 09, *www.ozone3.fr*. Cross-country skiing, dog-sledding, hot-air balloons, hot water canyoning, diving under ice, and much more.

Transpyr66, **t** 06 11 87 85 12, *www.transpyr66.com*. Snow-shoeing, botanical and other walks based in Saillagouse, Font-Romeu and Latour-de-Carol.

Where to Stay and Eat in the Cerdagne

Olette ✉ 66360

La Fontaine, Place de la Victoire, **t** 04 68 97 03 67, *www.atasteofcatalonia.co.uk* (€€). Nice five-room B&B on the village square in a large house run

Auberge des Ecureuils >>

Mont-Louis >
*3 Rue Lieutenant Pruneta, **t** 04 68 04 21 97, www.mont-louis.net; open Mon–Sat, also Sun in July and Aug*

L'Atalaya >>

Font-Romeu >
*38 Av E. Brousse, **t** 04 68 30 68 30, www.font-romeu.fr; open daily*

Les Angles
*2 Av de l'Aude, **t** 04 68 04 32 76, www.les-angles.com; open daily*

Planes >>

Bourg-Madame
*Place Catalogne, **t** 04 68 04 64 01, www.bourgmadame.fr; open Mon–Sat*

since 2006 by an English couple. Guest lounge available and terraces for eating out on and relaxation. Evening meals (€€) for guests only.

Mont-Louis ✉ 66210

****Le Clos Cerdan, t** 04 68 04 23 29, *www.lecloscerdan.com* (€€). Get a room with a view at this grey stone hotel on a cliff overlooking the valley; modern but very comfortable, with a restaurant (€€). There are also apartments to rent and a spa with gym.

Lou Rouballou, Rue des Ecoles Laïques, **t** 04 68 04 23 26 , *www.mont-louis.net/rouballou.htm* (€€). Cosy B&B in the village, by the ramparts.

Font-Romeu ✉ 66120

****Le Romarin**, 7 Impasse Romarin, **t** 04 68 30 09 66, *www.hotel-romarin.com* (€€). Very charming owners, offering well-equipped rooms and a good restaurant by the fireplace (€€–€).

****L'Oustalet**, Av du Marechal Leclerc, **t** 04 68 30 11 32, *www.hotelloustalet.com* (€). Chalet-style hotel with some family rooms and great views, a pool and a restaurant (€€). *Closed April–mid-May.*

Angoustrine ✉ 66120

Cal Xandera, t 04 68 04 61 67, *www.calxandera.com* (€€–€). Completely different: a beautifully restored 18th-century farmhouse serving flavour-packed traditional mountain cuisine. Also five rustic-chic rooms (€) for 2–6 people. Jazz concerts in summer.

Valcebollère (east of Bourg-Madame) ✉ 66340

***Auberge des Ecureuils, **t** 04 68 04 52 03, *www.aubergeecureuils.com* (€€). Friendly mountain *auberge*, offering charming rooms and local produce (€€€–€€). There's a heated indoor pool, Moorish bath, sauna and fitness room. Lots of interesting packages – go snow-shoeing, horse-riding or walking along smugglers' paths, or hunt for and cook wild mushrooms. *Closed Nov–early Dec.*

Llo and Saillagouse ✉ 66800

***L'Atalaya, Llo, **t** 04 68 04 70 04, *www.atalaya66.com* (€€€€€). A rare example of a country inn unconcerned with the skiing business; tranquillity is assured in this setting, close to the wild flowers of the Vallée d'Eyne and infinitely far from anything else, with a pool and an excellent restaurant in summer (€€€). *Closed mid-Jan–mid-April and mid-Nov–mid-Dec.*

****Planotel**, Rue de la Poste, **t** 04 68 04 72 08, Saillagouse, *www.planotel.fr* (€€). Modern, with a heated pool and restaurant and run by the same family that runs Planes (*see* below). *Closed Oct–May except school hols.*

Planes, Place des Comtes de Cerdagne, Saillagouse, **t 04 68 04 72 08, *www.planotel.fr* (€€). Planes has been hosting guests since 1895; the dining room (€€€–€€), with its huge fireplace, is a great place to eat Catalan anchovies and red peppers. Guests can use the facilities at the Planotel. *Closed early Nov–mid-Dec.*

Pyrenean Valleys: The Vallespir

The wooded valley of the Tech, the southernmost valley of Roussillon, and of France, winds a lonesome trail around the southern slopes of Canigou. Known for its mineral waters since Roman times, it traditionally made its living from these and from ironworking. When the iron gave out, there was always smuggling.

Now that the EU has made smugglers superfluous, the Vallespir lives by tourism, with some euros on the side from cherries and cork oak – the *primeurs*, the first cherries in the French market each year, and the *grand cru* corks that have kept the best champagne bubbly for centuries.

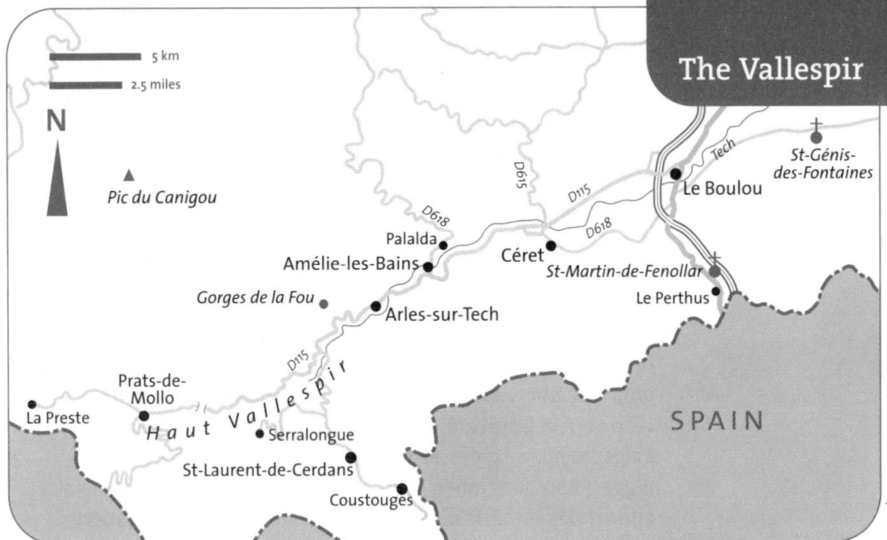

Le Boulou and St-Martin-de-Fenollar

From Perpignan, the quickest way into the Vallespir is by way of the A9, getting off at **Le Boulou**, a truck-stop known to every European big rig jockey. The ancient Roman teamsters knew it, too. Le Boulou has been fated by geography to be an eternal transit point, today jammed in summer with tourists heading up the N9 into Spain via Le Perthus. It also has a casino and spa, and a fine Romanesque **church** with a superb white marble tympanum sculpted by the Master of Cabestany, portraying the Resurrection of the Virgin. The cornice shows scenes of the Nativity, the Christ Child's first bath (also rarely depicted in art), the shepherds, Magi and flight into Egypt.

St-Martin-de-Fenollar
t 04 68 87 73 82; open July–Aug 10.30–12 and 3.30–7; Sept–June daily 2–5; adm

The A9 and N9 continue south into Spain, passing near Maureillas-las-Illas and its 9th-century church of **St-Martin-de-Fenollar**, with some of the most unusual and best-preserved 12th-century frescoes in the Midi, by the so-called Master of Fenollar. Nine-tenths of all early medieval painting is lost to us, and this is a rare example of the best of what is left: brilliant colours and a confident stylization, with an imagery untroubled by the dogma of later religious painting, as in the *Nativity*, where Mary lies not in a stable but in a comfortable bed under a chequered baldachin. The scene from the Apocalypse, of Christ in Majesty with the four symbols of the Evangelists and the 24 elders, was a favourite 12th-century theme on both sides of the Pyrenees. Picasso and Braque came and were suitably impressed.

Hannibal entered Gaul through **Le Perthus**, the last, or first stop in France. Archaeologists have uncovered, at Panisars, a monumental pedestal, identified as belonging to the **Trophée de Pompée**. Similar to La Turbie near the Italian border, this monument was erected by a victorious Pompey in 71 BC on the Gallo- Hispanic frontier. Part of the stone was used to build a priory in 1011 (the ruins are nearby); the rest was quarried by Vauban in the 17th century to build the **Fort de Bellegarde**, which has remained in such good nick that it was used as an internment camp for refugees from Spain in 1939.

Fort de Bellegarde
t 04 68 54 27 53; open May–Sept daily 10.30–6.30, guided tours at 11.30, 2.30 and 4; adm

Céret: the 'Mecca of Cubism'

Back in the valley of the Tech, the D115 streaks from Le Boulou to the heart of the optimal early cherry-growing region suspended between the Pyrenees and the sea. Amid the orchards in the hills around, Céret is a laid-back town under enormous plane trees, with perfect little café-lined squares (especially the **Plaça dels Nou Raigs**), medieval gates, **St-Pierre**, modestly famous for being the biggest Baroque church in Roussillon, a war memorial by Maillol and an elegant 14th-century bridge over the Tech. Céret takes its bullfighting seriously, with *ferias* in July and September, and it celebrates the *sardana*, the traditional Catalan dance in a ring, with a huge three-day festival in July.

Musée d'Art Moderne
t 04 68 87 27 76, www.musee-ceret.com; open May–mid-Sept daily 10–7; mid-Sept–June Wed–Mon 10–6, closed Tues; adm

Walking around Céret is the best preparation for its **Musée d'Art Moderne** on 8 Bd du Maréchal Joffre. The Fauves may have gone to Collioure, but Céret found its artistic destiny in the early 20th century with the Cubists, thanks to Picasso, Braque, Gris, Manolo, Matisse, Soutine, Kisling, Masson, Tzara, Lhote, Marquet and others who came to paint here, and whose paintings line these walls. Matisse donated 14 drawings from his first stay in Collioure, but perhaps best of all are the works donated by Picasso in 1953, among them 28 little plates painted in a five-day spurt of energy, all with variations on the *corrida* under a blasting sun. The museum has attracted just under a dozen art galleries to Céret.

Maison du Patrimoine
t 04 68 87 31 59, www.maisondupatrimoine-ceret.fr; open July–Aug daily 10–1 and 3–7; Sept–June Mon–Fri 10–12 and 2–5; adm

Musiques et Instruments du Monde en Catalogne
t 04 68 87 40 40, www.music-ceret.com

Although not quite as dazzling, the **Maison du Patrimoine Françoise Claustre** in the Tour Port d'Espagne (by the twin stone arches) houses well-arranged Neolithic, Classical and medieval finds from the Vallespir, as well as temporary exhibitions. At the time of writing, the Centre Internacional de Música Popular (CIMP) is about to open a new music museum, **Musiques et Instruments du Monde en Catalogne** at 14 Rue Pierre Rameil, housing traditional instruments from Catalonia and from around the world, along with items to put them in context.

Amélie-les-Bains and Arles-sur-Tech

Sulphurous waters, good for your rheumatism, have been the fortune of **Amélie-les-Bains** since ancient times; a Roman swimming pool with a vaulted roof has been uncovered, and the spa, rising on either side of the river Tech, still does a grandstand business. Named in 1849 after the wife of King Louis Philippe,

Amélie's pretty medieval ancestor, **Palalda**, is piled on a nearby hill, and offers a small **Musée de la Poste** for snail-mail nostalgia from the days of Louis XI to 1900, with a collection of stamps, and telephones; there's also a museum on how the locals lived in the past. A display on Charles Rennie Mackintosh (*see* p.264), who painted some of his landscapes here, is planned for Palalda as well.

Musée de la Poste
t 04 68 39 34 90; open May–Sept Tues–Fri 10–12 and 2–6.30, Mon and Sat 2–6.30, closed Sun; mid-Feb–April and Oct–mid-Dec Tues–Fri 10–12 and 2–5.30, Mon and Sat 2–5.30, closed Sun; closed mid-Dec–mid-Feb; adm

Just west is **Arles-sur-Tech**, the ancient capital of the Vallespir and last redoubt of the valley's medieval iron industry; the last working mine in Roussillon, up at Batère, closed down in the early 1990s. Arles is a curious old town built on a narrow maze of lanes and offers some even curiouser hagiography in its 11th- and 12th-century **Abbaye de Ste-Marie**, entered by way of the tourist office. This abbey was originally founded in the late 8th century in Amélie-les-Bains by Sunifred, brother of Wilfred the Hairy, but was later relocated here for safety. Its focus of devotion was an anonymous saint – an empty 4th-century sarcophagus known as *Sainte-Tombe* – until the dreaded *simiots* came to town, ape-like monsters that trampled the crops and violated the women. In despair, the abbot of Ste-Marie went to the pope asking for some holy relics. This was in 957, when demand for saints' bones was at its historic high, and the best the pope could offer was a pair of Persian martyrs named Abdon and Sennen. The abbot brought them back in a false-bottomed water-barrel, to fool the Venetians and Germans and any other relic thieves, and they dealt with the *simiots* as efficiently as if they had been the bones of St Peter himself. The story is portrayed in a 17th-century retable, in the chapel where Abdon and Sennen's relics are kept; back when times were more perilous, their bones were stored in cupboards that you can see high in the square pillars in the nave. Another telling feature that betrays the church's age is the fact that it is orientated towards the west – a mistake 'corrected' with a frescoed counter-apse chapel of St-Michel. The *Sainte-Tombe* itself, once a major pilgrimage attraction, is kept in a little enclosure outside the enclosed façade. It fills continually with perfectly pure water – some 500 to 600 litres a year, ceremoniously pumped every 30 July. Above it, on the wall, is the early 13th-century tomb stone of Guillaume de Gausselme.

Abbaye de Ste-Marie
t 04 68 83 90 66; open Mon–Sat 9–12 and 2–6; also open Sun pm April–Oct; adm

Two kilometres northwest along the D44 you can explore through the World's Narrowest Gorge, the **Gorges de la Fou**, a giant crack in the rock with sides towering 650ft, yet only a few feet wide at its narrowest point, with waterfalls and caves along the mile-long walkway (visitors are loaned hard hats). Legend made it the lair of witches, bogeymen and *Traboucayres*, an infamous band of Catalan robbers who pounced on passing diligences, whose story is told up in the hill village of **Montferrer** in the tiny **Musée de Montferrer**, which also has items dedicated to Napoleon and

Gorges de la Fou
t 04 68 39 16 21; open July–Sept daily 10–7; late May–mid-Nov daily 10–6; adm

Musée de Montferrer
ask at the Arles tourist office

Bear Frolics

There are some peculiar goings-on in winter in the upper Vallespir, starting with the ***Festa de l'Os*** (bear festival) in Prats-de-Mollo. Originally this took place on 2 February or Candlemas, a traditional Celtic cross-quarter day like Hallowe'en, although modern times have regulated it to the second Sunday of February half-term holidays.

The festival has suitably murky origins that go back to the days when there were more than a handful of bears in the Pyrenees. There may even be, deep in the Vallespir's DNA, Palaeolithic memories when humans and bears shared the same cave shelters, apparently in a friendly enough fashion, even though the now extinct cave bears were as big as grizzlies. Curious artefacts of *c.* 12,000 BC found in French shelters suggest odd human/ursine sexual fantasies. In historic times, hunting cultures such as the Ainu in Japan would capture bear cubs to be suckled by a human mother and reared like a sibling with her children in preparation for a bear festival in which, after many apologies, the bear would be ritually strangled and eaten.

In Prats-de-Mollo, a veneer of Christianity has allowed ancient rites to survive, notably the legend of a shepherd girl who was abducted by a lusty bear (the devil in disguise). The devil bear tried to have his evil way with her, but she prayed to Notre Dame-du-Coral (the chapel on the hill) who saved her honour for nine days, until the bear's howls of frustration reached a band of woodcutters, who rescued her.

While basically telling the same story, each town with a bear festival (Arles-sur-Tech and St-Laurent-de-Cerdans are the others) celebrates it on different days with slightly different versions of atavistic weirdness. In Prats-de-Mollo, young men are divided into 'bears' (covered in sheepskins, grease and soot) with long wooden sticks, and 'hunters' who have blanks in their guns and gourds filled with wine. The action starts with a chase and high jinks to music through the streets, as the bears try to smear everyone with their soot. Once all the bears are 'shot', they are chained up and brought to the main square to be 'shaved' with axes by flour-covered 'barbers' who use a *botifarra* (Catalan black pudding) for soap. Afterwards bears, hunters and barbers do a mad dance until a gunshot rings out and the bears drop down 'dead'.

Carnival in Prats-de-Mollo also preserves odd old customs that would immediately be cancelled if Health and Safety ever got wind of them. There's the Ball de la Posta dance, in which female dancers have to choose between kissing a painted image of the Virgin or the devil, before getting a playful smack on the bottom. In the evening, masked dancers cover themselves with flour and dance the *Tio-tio*, each dancer bearing a rolled paper 'log' on their back and each holding a lighted candle, with the idea of setting the 'log' of the dancer in front on fire! Fortunately, a referee with a broom is in charge of putting out the flames if they actually succeed.

Charles de Gaulle. A pair of watchtowers mark **Corsavy,** even higher up; it's nicknamed 'the balcony of Canigou' and is especially proud of its recently beautifully restored 1158 Chapelle de Sant Martí.

A detour south of the valley, on the D3, will uncover **St-Laurent-de-Cerdans**, famous for making espadrilles, and **Coustouges**, which has a lovely early 12th-century fortified church with a slate roof and two carved portals, one inside the other. Continuing up the valley, just south of the D115, the hilltop village of **Serralongue** has a church dating from 1018, with a fine portal and one of the only surviving examples of a Catalan *conjurador*; this is a small, square pavilion with a slate roof and statues of the four Evangelists facing the four cardinal directions. When a storm threatened, the priest would go up to the *conjurador* and perform certain rites facing the direction of the storm to avert its wrath.

Some towns just ask for it. As if having a name like **Prats-de-Mollo** weren't enough, this tiny spa advertises itself as the

'European Capital of Urinary Infections'. Prats-de-Mollo's other claim to fame is a European record for rainfall: 33 inches in 16 hours on 15 October 1940. The baths are really at **La-Preste**, 8km up in the mountains. Prats-de-Mollo itself is an attractive old village, with remains of its walls, and Fort Lagarde, a fortress refurbished by Vauban, together with other medieval buildings that recall the days when it was a textile centre, specializing in Catalan bonnets. Don't miss the whale bone stuck in the church wall.

This is as far as we go; the Spanish border is 14km away.

★ La Fontaine >>

ⓘ Arles-sur-Tech >>
*by Ste-Marie, **t** 04 68 39 11 99, www. tourisme-haut-vallespir.com; open Mon–Sat; summer also Sun pm*

ⓘ Céret >
*Av G. Clemenceau, **t** 04 68 87 00 53, www. ot-ceret.fr; open Mon–Sat*

★ Maison d'Hôtes L'Andreu >>

★ Le Mas Trilles >

ⓘ Prats-de-Mollo-la-Preste
*Place du Foiral, **t** 04 68 39 70 83, www.pratsde mollolapreste.com; open Mon–Sat; July–Aug also Sun*

ⓘ Amélie-les-Bains
*22 Av du Vallespir, **t** 04 68 39 01 98; www. amelie-les-bains.com; open Mon–Sat*

Market Days in the Vallespir

Céret: Sat.

Arles-sur-Tech: Wed.

Prats-de-Mollo: Wed and Fri.

Where to Stay and Eat in the Vallespir

Céret ✉ 66400

****__La Terrasse au Soleil__, Route Fontfrède, **t** 04 68 87 01 94, *www. terrasse-au-soleil.com* (€€€€€–€€). A restored, modernized *mas* on a hill above Céret, with a view, a heated pool and tennis court. Its restaurant, **Cerisaie** (€€€), is good, and there is also a cheaper *brasserie* (summer only) and a spa. *Closed Dec–Feb.*

***__Le Mas Trilles__, Pont de Reynès, **t** 04 68 87 38 37, *www.le-mas-trilles.com*, (€€€€–€€). A tastefully renovated *mas* with 10 rooms (most with private terrace, and big enough to sleep four) a heated pool and a charming garden overlooking a trout stream. No restaurant, just snacks, but there are two very near by. *Closed Oct–Easter.*

__Les Arcades__, 1 Place Picasso, **t 04 68 87 12 30, *www.hotel-arcades-ceret.com* (€). Artistically decorated (some of the artists who stayed left works behind), this hotel has rooms, some with air conditioning, some with balconies overlooking the market square; others have kitchenettes for longer stays.

*__Vidal__, 4 Place Soutine, **t** 04 68 87 00 85, *www.ceret.com* (€). In a charming, if quirky and sometimes noisy, listed building, with a colourful restaurant, **Bisbe**, with good food and a charming terrace (€€). *Open all year.*

La Fontaine, 10 Place des Neuf Jets, **t** 04 68 87 23 47 (€). Tiny restaurant in a pretty square, with delightful owners, and good-value, simple menus.

Arles-sur-Tech ✉ 66150

__Les Glycines__, Rue Jeu de Paume, **t 04 68 39 10 09, *www.logishotels.com* (€). Named for the ancient wisteria that shades the garden terrace, Les Glycines has modernized rooms and a restaurant (€€). *Closed Nov–Jan.*

Corsavy ✉ 66150

Maison d'Hôtes L'Andreu, 5 minutes from the village, **t** 04 68 37 57 22, *www.landreu.com* (€€). Stay amid the lush woodlands north of Arles in an artfully rehabilitated 19th-century hunting lodge; there's also a *gîte* in the former meat-drying barn. There's a pool , home cinema, Wi-fi and the choice of French or English breakfast.

Chez Françoise, **t** 04 68 39 12 04 (€€–€). Part village *épicerie*, part excellent restaurant, serving tasty Catalan specialities on a shady terrace.

Prats-de-Mollo-La-Preste ✉ 66230

__La Val du Tech__, 100m from the spa, **t 04 68 39 71 12, *www.hotel-levaldu tech.com* (€€–€). Patronized by walkers and spa clients, and you can choose between a modern and rustic room, and have fresh spa water brought to your room in the morning. There's a good restaurant (€€) and they'll make a picnic if you want to go exploring.

__Costabonne__, Place du Foiral, **t 04 68 39 70 24, *www.hotel-le-costabonne. com* (€). Simple en suite rooms and bar terrace in the centre of action during the bear festival; also a restaurant (€) serving Catalan dishes.

Language

A working knowledge of French will make your holiday more enjoyable, but is not essential in big cities, where you can always find someone working in a travel office, bank, shop, hotel or restaurant who speaks at least rudimentary English. Venturing into the less-travelled hinterlands may well require an effort to recall your school French; a small travel phrase book and English–French dictionary can come in handy.

Even if your French is brilliant, the soupy southern twang may throw you. Any word with a nasal *in* or *en* becomes something like *aing* (*vaing* for *vin*). The last vowel on many words that are silent in the north get to express themselves in the south (*encore* sounds something like *engcora*).

What remains the same as anywhere else in France is the level of politeness expected: use *monsieur*, *madame* or *mademoiselle* when speaking to everyone (and *garçon* in restaurants only if you add '*s'il vous plaît*'), from your first *bonjour* to your last *au revoir*.

See pp.55–58 for menu vocabulary.

Pronunciation

Vowels

a, à, â between *a* in 'bat' and 'part'
***é, er, ez* at end of word** as *a* in 'plate' but a bit shorter
***e* at end of word** not pronounced
***e* at end of syllable or in one-syllable word** pronounced weakly, like *er* in 'mother'
i as *ee* in 'bee'
o as *o* in 'pot'
ô as *o* in 'go'
u, û between *oo* in 'boot' and *ee* in 'bee'

Vowel Combinations

ai as *a* in 'plate'
aî as *e* in 'bet'
ail as *i* in 'kite'
au, eau as *o* in 'go'
ei as *e* in 'bet'
eu, œu as *er* in 'mother'
oi between *wa* in 'swam' and *u* in 'swum'
oy in middle of words as 'why'; otherwise as 'oi', above
ui as *wee* in 'twee'

Nasal Vowels

Vowels followed by an ***n*** or an ***m*** have a nasal sound.

an, en as *o* in 'pot' + nasal sound
ain, ein, in as *a* in 'bat' + nasal sound
on as *aw* in 'paw' + nasal sound
un as *u* in 'nut' + nasal sound

Consonants

Many French consonants are pronounced as in English, but there are some exceptions:

c* followed by *e, i* or *y* and *ç as *s* in 'sit'
c* followed by *a, o* or *u as *c* in 'cat'
g* followed by *e, i* or *y as *s* in 'pleasure'
gn as *ni* in 'opinion'
j as *s* in 'pleasure'
ll as *y* in 'yes'
qu as *k* in 'kite'
***s* between vowels** as *z* in 'zebra'
***s* otherwise** as *s* in 'sit'
***w* except in English words** as *v* in 'vest'
***x* at end of word** as *s* in 'sit'
***x* otherwise** as *x* in 'six'

Stress

The stress usually falls on the last syllable except when the word ends with an unaccented ***e***.

Vocabulary

The nouns in the list below are marked as either masculine *(m)* or feminine *(f)*.

If masculine, 'the' is *le*, or *l'* if the word begins with a vowel; and 'a' is *un*. 'Some' or 'any' is *du*. For example, *'A quelle heure part le train pour Montpellier?/Je voudrais un oreiller/du savon.'*

If feminine, 'the' is *la*, or *l'* if the word begins with a vowel; and 'a' is *une*. 'Some' or 'any' is *'de la'*. For example, *'Je cherche la sortie/une pharmacie/Je voudrais de l'aspirine.'*

If plural, 'the' is *les*, and 'some' or 'any' is *des*. For example, *'Où sont les toilettes/Est-ce que vous avez des cartes postales?'*

General

hello *bonjour*
good evening *bonsoir*
good night *bonne nuit*
goodbye *au revoir*
please *s'il vous plaît*
thank you (very much) *merci (beaucoup)*
yes *oui*
no *non*
good *bon (bonne)*
bad *mauvais*
excuse me *pardon, excusez-moi*
Can you help me? *Pourriez-vous m'aider?*

My name is... *Je m'appelle...*
What is your name? *Comment t'appelles-tu?* (informal), *Comment vous appelez-vous?* (formal)
How are you? *Comment allez-vous?*
Fine *Ça va bien*
I don't understand *Je ne comprends pas*
I don't know *Je ne sais pas*
Speak more slowly *Pourriez-vous parler plus lentement?*
How do you say ... in French? *Comment dit-on ... en français?*
Help! *Au secours!*

Where is (the railway station)? *Où se trouve (la gare)?*
Is it far? *C'est loin?*
left *à gauche*
right *à droite*
straight on *tout droit*

entrance *entrée (f)*
exit *sortie (f)*
open *ouvert(e)*
closed *fermé(e)*
WC *toilettes (fpl)*
men *hommes*
ladies *dames* or *femmes*

doctor *médecin (m)*
hospital *hôpital (m)*
emergency room/A&E *salle des urgences (f)*
police station *commissariat de police (m)*
tourist information office *office de tourisme (m)*
How much is it? *C'est combien?*
Do you have...? *Est-ce que vous avez...?*
It's too expensive *C'est trop cher*
bank *banque (f)*
money *argent (m)*
change *monnaie (f)*
credit card *carte de crédit (f)*
traveller's cheque *chèque de voyage (m)*
post office *la poste*
stamp *timbre (m)*
postcard *carte postale (f)*
public phone *cabine téléphonique (f)*
shop *magasin (m)*
central food market *halles (fpl)*
tobacconist *tabac (m)*
pharmacy *pharmacie (f)*
aspirin *aspirine (f)*
condoms *préservatifs (mpl)*
insect repellent *anti-insecte (m)*
sun cream *crème solaire (f)*
tampons *tampons hygiéniques (mpl)*

Transport

airport *aéroport (m)*
aeroplane *avion (m)*
go on foot *aller à pied*
bicycle *bicyclette (f) / vélo (m)*
mountain bike *vélo tout terrain, VTT (m)*
bus *autobus (m)*
bus stop *arrêt d'autobus (m)*
coach station *gare routière (f)*
railway station *gare (f)*
train *train (m)*
platform *quai (m) / voie (f)*
date-stamp machine *composteur (m)*
timetable *horaire (m)*
left-luggage locker *consigne automatique (f)*

car *voiture (f)*
taxi *taxi (m)*
underground/subway *métro (m)*
ticket office *guichet (m)*
ticket *billet (m)*
single to... *un aller* (or *aller simple*) *pour...*
return/round trip to... *un aller et retour pour...*
What time does the ... leave? *A quelle heure part...?*
delayed *en retard*
on time *à l'heure*

Accommodation

single room *chambre pour une personne (f)*
twin room *chambre à deux lits (f)*
double room *chambre pour deux personnes (f) / chambre double (f)*
bed *lit (m)*
blanket *couverture (f)*
cot (child's bed) *lit d'enfant (m)*
pillow *oreiller (m)*
soap *savon (m)*
towel *serviette (f)*
booking *réservation (f)*
I would like to book a room *Je voudrais réserver une chambre*

Months

January *janvier*
February *février*
March *mars*
April *avril*
May *mai*
June *juin*
July *juillet*
August *août*
September *septembre*
October *octobre*
November *novembre*
December *décembre*

Days

Monday *lundi*
Tuesday *mardi*
Wednesday *mercredi*
Thursday *jeudi*
Friday *vendredi*
Saturday *samedi*
Sunday *dimanche*

Time

What time is it? *Quelle heure est-il?*
month *mois (m)*
week *semaine (f)*
day *jour (m) / journée (f)*
morning *matin (m)*
afternoon *après-midi (m or f)*
evening *soir (m)*
night *nuit (f)*
today *aujourd'hui*
yesterday *hier*
tomorrow *demain*
day before yesterday *avant-hier*
day after tomorrow *après-demain*

Numbers

one *un*
two *deux*
three *trois*
four *quatre*
five *cinq*
six *six*
seven *sept*
eight *huit*
nine *neuf*
ten *dix*
eleven *onze*
twelve *douze*
thirteen *treize*
fourteen *quatorze*
fifteen *quinze*
sixteen *seize*
seventeen *dix-sept*
eighteen *dix-huit*
nineteen *dix-neuf*
twenty *vingt*
twenty-one *vingt et un*
twenty-two *vingt-deux*
thirty *trente*
forty *quarante*
fifty *cinquante*
sixty *soixante*
seventy *soixante-dix*
seventy-one *soixante et onze*
eighty *quatre-vingts*
eighty-one *quatre-vingt-un*
ninety *quatre-vingt-dix*
hundred *cent*
two hundred *deux cents*
thousand *mille*

Glossary

abbaye abbey
ambulatory a passage behind the choir of a church, often with radiating chapels
anse cove
arrondissement a city district
auberge inn
aven natural well
bastide taller, more elaborate version of a *mas*, with balconies, wrought-ironwork, reliefs, etc; also a medieval new town, fortified and laid out in a grid
beffroi tower with a town's bell
borie dry-stone shepherd's hut with a corbelled roof
buffet d'eau in French gardens, a fountain built into a wall with water falling through levels of urns or basins
cabane simple weekend or holiday retreat, usually near the sea; a *cabane de gardian* is a thatched cowboy's abode in the Camargue
calanque narrow coastal creek, like a miniature fjord
capitelle the name for *borie* in Languedoc
cardo the main north–south street in a Roman *castrum* or town
caryatid column or pillar carved in the figure of a woman
castrum rectangular Roman army camp, which often grew into a permanent settlement
causse rocky, arid limestone plateau, north of Hérault and in the lower Languedoc
cave (wine) cellar
château mansion, manor house or castle
château fort castle
chemin path
chevet eastern end of a church, including the apse
cirque round natural depression created by erosion at the loop of a river
cloître cloister
clue rocky cleft or transverse valley
col mountain pass
commune in the Middle Ages, the government of a free town or city; today, the smallest unit of local government, encompassing a town or village
côte coast; on wine labels, *côtes*, *coteaux* and *costières* mean 'hills' or 'slopes'
cours wide main street, like an elongated main square
couvent convent or monastery
crèche Christmas crib with *santons*
donjon castle keep
écluse canal lock
église church
étang lagoon or swamp
Félibre member of the movement to bring back the use of the Provençal language
ferrade cattle branding
gardian a cowboy of the Camargue
gare train station (SNCF)
gare routière coach station
garrigues irregular limestone hills pitted with caves, especially those north of Nîmes and Montpellier
gisant sculpted prone effigy on a tomb
gîte shelter
gîte d'étape basic shelter for walkers
grande randonnée (GR) long-distance hiking path
grau a narrowing, of a canyon or a river
halles covered market
hôtel particulier originally the town residence of the nobility; by the 18th century the word became more generally used for any large, private residence
hôtel de ville city hall
lavoir communal fountain, usually covered, for the washing of clothes
mairie town hall
manade a *gardian*'s farm in the Camargue
maquis Mediterranean scrub. Also used as a term for the French Resistance during the Second World War

marché market
mas a farmhouse and its outbuildings
mascaron ornamental mask, usually one carved on the keystone of an arch
modillon stone projecting from the cornice of a church, carved with a face or animal figure
motte hammock, or a raised area in a swamp
oppidum pre-Roman fortified settlement
Parlement French juridical body, with members appointed by the king; by the late *ancien régime*, *parlements* exercised a great deal of influence over political affairs
pays region or village
pont bridge
porte gateway
predella small paintings beneath the main subject of a retable
presqu'île peninsula
puy hill
restanques vine or olive terraces
retable carved or painted altarpiece, often consisting of a number of scenes or sculpted ensembles
rez-de-chaussée (RC) ground floor (US first floor)
santon figure in a Christmas nativity scene, usually made of terracotta and dressed in 18th-century Provençal costume
source spring
tour tower
transi on a tomb, a relief of the decomposing cadaver
tympanum sculpted semicircular panel over a church door
vieille ville historic, old quarter of town
village perché hilltop village

Further Reading

Barber, Malcolm, *The Cathars: Dualist Heretics in Languedoc in the High Middle Ages* (Medieval World Series, Longman, 2000). A solid history, and good for debunking occultist theories.

Baring-Gould, Sabine, *Perpetua: A Tale of Nimes in A.D. 213* (BiblioBazaar, 2009). An evocation of Roman life in Nîmes – an out-of-print title recently brought out by BiblioBazaar along with a number of other intriguing old books about France.

Bonner, Anthony, *Songs of the Troubadours* (Allen & Unwin, 1973). An introduction to the life and times of the troubadours, with translations of best-known verses.

Bromwich, James, *The Roman Remains of Southern France: A Guide Book* (Routledge, 1996). A special guide to what the Romans left behind in Languedoc-Roussillon and Provence.

Cheyette, Frederic L., *Ermengard of Narbonne and the World of the Troubadours* (Cornell University Press, 2004). The life and times of one of the most powerful women in medieval Languedoc.

Cross, John, *Walking in the Languedoc: 32 Routes in Haut-Languedoc* (Cicerone, 2007). Walks north of Béziers, mostly in the Parc Naturel du Haut-Languedoc and the Espinouse.

Davis, Natalie Zemon, *The Return of Martin Guerre* (Harvard, 1983). In the tradition of Ladurie's 'microhistory', the true story (earlier made into a film with Gérard Dépardieu) of a lost son who reappears in a 16th-century Languedoc village – but turns out to be an impostor.

de Sède, Gérard, *The Accursed Treasure of Rennes-le-Château* (DEK English translation by Bill Kersey, 2001). This is the novel that started all the fuss when it was published in 1967 as *L'Or de Rennes*.

Gaunt, Simon (ed) and Sarah Kay, *The Troubadours: An Introduction* (Cambridge University Press, 1999). A collection of scholarly essays about the troubadours and their songs.

Gorley, Peter John, *Gorley's Guide: The Wines of Languedoc-Roussillon* (Hamilton John, 2002). Hard to find but an excellent account of the wines and personalities of the region, with itineraries and maps.

Holt, Mack P., *The French Wars of Religion, 1562–1629* (Cambridge University Press, 2005). Excellent account of the conflict that tore Languedoc apart.

Kiessler, Bernd Wilfred, *The Canal Du Midi: A Cruiser's Guide* (Adlard Coles Nautical, 2009). Practical guide for barging holidays.

Ladurie, Emmanuel Le Roy, *Montaillou: Cathars and Catholics in a French Village 1294–1324* (Vintage, 2002). This is a newer edition of Ladurie's classic work of French 'microhistory': a fascinating and rigorous account of everything about life and work in a village of the Ariège in 1300, taken from copious local records. Montaillou was the last surviving community of Cathars. Ladurie expanded his work in *The Peasants of Languedoc* (University of Illinois, 1977) and *Love, Death and Money in the Pays d'Oc* (Scholar, 1982).

Lugand, Jacques, Robert St-Jean and Jean Nougaret, *Languedoc Roman* (Zodiaque, 1987). The best of Languedoc's Romanesque architecture, with plans, lots of photos and an English translation.

Lyons, Declan, *Cycling the Canal du Midi: across Southern France from Toulouse to Sète* (Cicerone, 2009). Practical guide on how to do it.

Mattingly, Alan, *Walking in the Cathar Region: Cathar Castles of South-west France* (Cicerone Press, 2005). Excellent walking guide to the Cathar castles.

Moon, Patrick, *Virgile's Vineyard: A Year in the Languedoc Wine Country* (John Murray, 2004). The expat-recounts-the-glories-of-rural-France genre comes to Languedoc, in a tale centred on wine-making.

Mosse, Kate, *Labyrinth* (Orion, 2006). Adventure set in medieval Carcassonne.

Murrills, Angela, *Hot Sun, Cool Shadow: Savouring the Food, History and Mystery of the Languedoc* (Allison & Busby, 2005). Murrills fell in love with the region and wrote this evocative, beautifully illustrated account.

O'Brian, Patrick, *The Catalans* (WW Norton, 2007). First published in 1953, an early novel by O'Brian set on the Catalan coast in pre-tourist times.

Oldenbourg, Zoe, *Massacre at Montségur, A History of the Albigensian Crusade* (Phoenix, 2001). Very readable history. The same author also wrote a historical novel on the era, *Destiny of Fire* (Carroll and Graf, 1999).

O'Shea, Stephen, *The Perfect Heresy: The Life and Death of the Cathars* (Profile, 2001). One of the best of a recent crop of histories about Languedoc's heretics. His new tome, *The Friar of Carcassonne: Revolt and Inquisition in the Last Days of the Cathars* (Profile, 2011) covers the life of the great Franciscan orator Bernard Délicieux, who fought against the forces of repression.

Patterson, Linda M., *The World of the Troubadours: Medieval Occitan Society, c.1100–c.1300* (Cambridge University Press, 1995). The major work in the field, covering all aspects of Occitan culture.

Stevenson, Robert Louis, *Travels with a Donkey in the Cévennes* (John Beaufoy Publishing, 2010). Recent reprint of the travel classic.

Strang, Paul, *Languedoc-Roussillon: The Wine and Wine Makers* (Mitchell Beazley, 2002). A complete, lavishly illustrated guide to the region and its recent wine revolution.

Sumpton, Jonathon, *The Albigensian Crusade* (Faber and Faber, 1999). Excellent historical account of the war that changed Languedoc forever.

Whitfield, Sarah, *Fauvism* (Thames and Hudson, 1991). A good introduction to the movement that changed art history.

Wright, Rupert, *Notes from the Languedoc* (Ebury Press, 2005). A *Times* journalist's affectionate and insightful account of Languedoc today, as well as its history and culture.

Zaretsky, Robert, *Nîmes At War* (Pennsylvania State University Press, 2004). A look at how the Protestant, Catholic, and Jewish inhabitants of Nîmes and the Gard coped during the Second World War.

Index

Main page references are in **bold**. Page references to maps are in *italics*.

3rd edition published 2012

Cadogan Guides is an imprint of
New Holland Publishers (UK) Ltd
London • Cape Town • Sydney • Auckland

New Holland Publishers (UK) Ltd
Garfield House
86–88 Edgware Road
London W2 2EA

80 McKenzie Street
Cape Town 8001
South Africa

Unit 1, 66 Gibbes Street
Chatswood, NSW 2067
Australia

218 Lake Road
Northcote
Auckland
New Zealand

Cadogan@nhpub.co.uk
www.cadoganguides.com
t 44 (0)20 7724 7773

Front cover photograph: Vineyards and Carcassonne © Jon Arnold Images Ltd / Alamy
Back cover photograph: © Pont du Gard © Bruce Winslade
Photo essay photographs © Dana Facaros, except © Bruce Winslade pp.1, 3, 6 (both), 14 (middle), 15 (top), and © Philippe Barbour pp.4, 5, 7, 8, 9, 10, 15 (bottom).
Maps © Cadogan Guides, drawn by Maidenhead Cartographic Services Ltd
Publisher: Guy Hobbs
Cover design: Jason Hopper
Photo essay design: Sarah Gardner
Editor: Dominique Shead
Proofreading: Linda McQueen
Indexing: Isobel McLean

Printed in India by Replika Press Pvt Ltd
A catalogue record for this book is available from the British Library

ISBN: 978 1 86011 436 6

The author and publishers have made every effort to ensure the accuracy of the information in this book at the time of going to press. However, they cannot accept any responsibility for any loss, injury or inconvenience resulting from the use of information contained in this guide.

Please help us to keep this guide up to date. We have done our best to ensure that the information in this guide is correct at the time of going to press. But laws and regulations are constantly changing, and standards and prices fluctuate. We would be delighted to receive any comments. Authors of the best letters will receive a copy of the Cadogan Guide of their choice.

Languedoc-Roussillon touring atlas

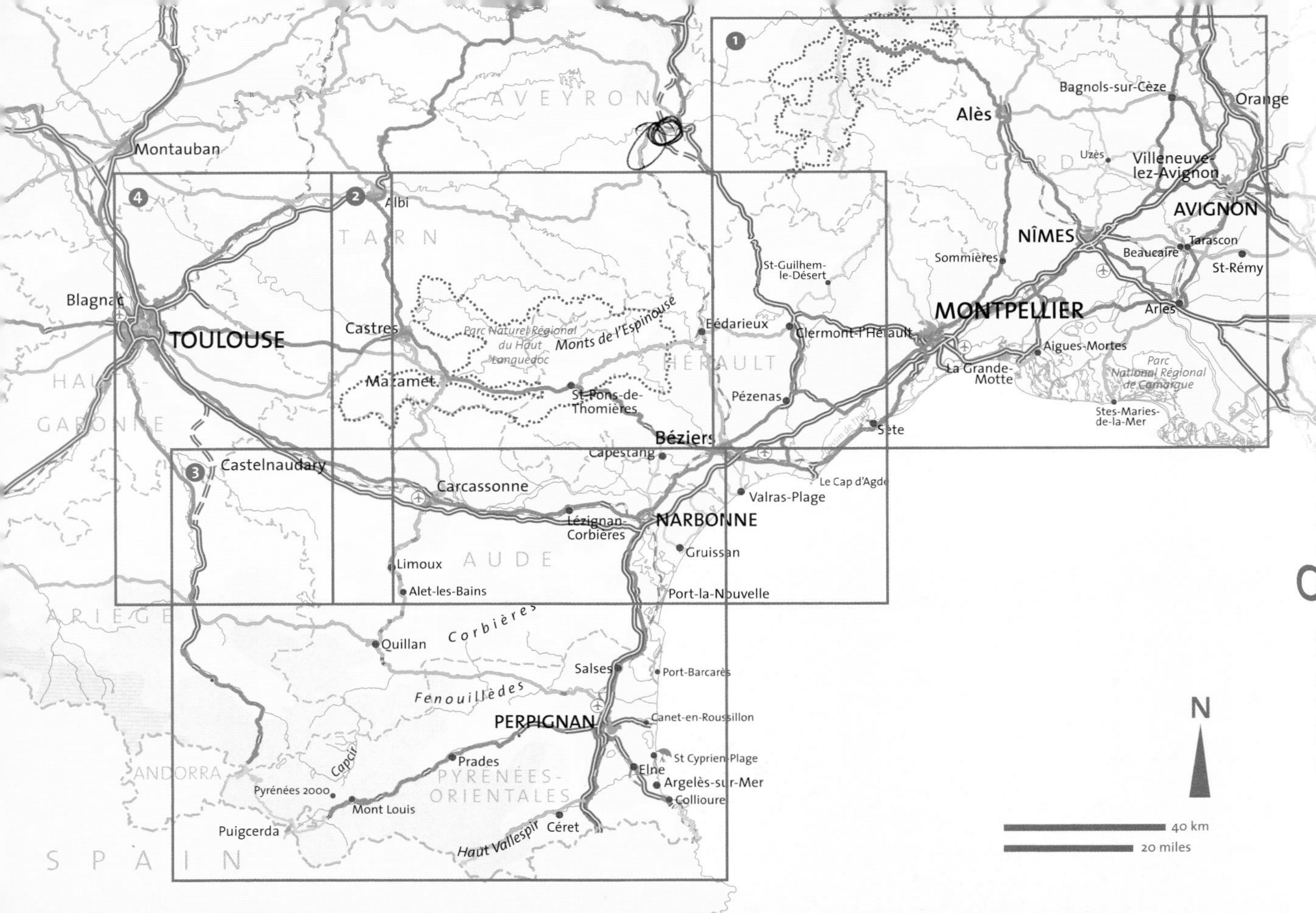

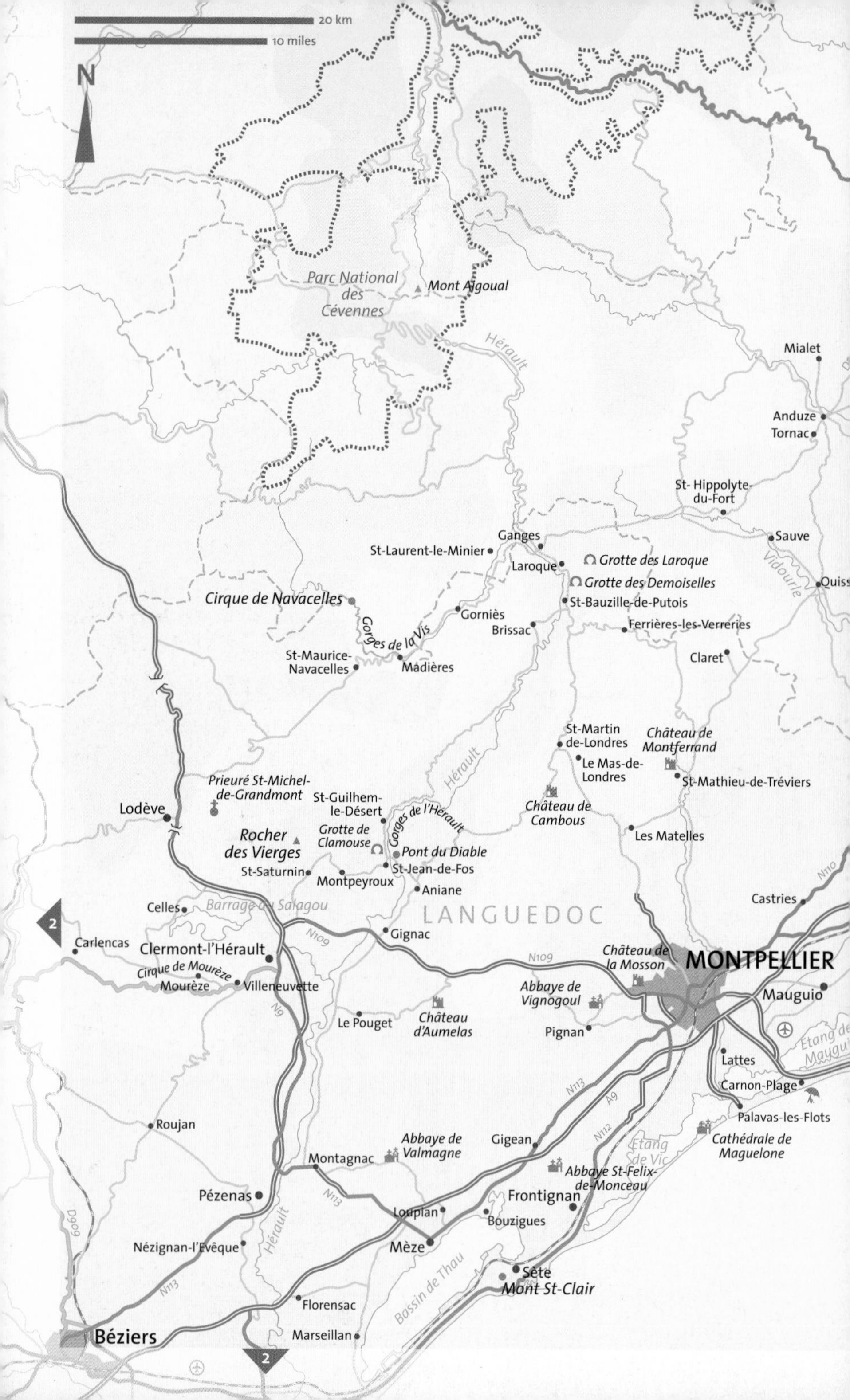

20 km
10 miles
N
Parc National des Cévennes
Mont Aigoual
Hérault
Mialet
Anduze
Tornac
St- Hippolyte-du-Fort
Sauve
Vidourle
Quiss
Ganges
St-Laurent-le-Minier
Laroque
Grotte des Laroque
Grotte des Demoiselles
St-Bauzille-de-Putois
Cirque de Navacelles
Gorges de la Vis
Gorniès
Brissac
Ferrières-les-Verreries
St-Maurice-Navacelles
Madières
Claret
St-Martin de-Londres
Château de Montferrand
Le Mas-de-Londres
St-Mathieu-de-Tréviers
Château de Cambous
Prieuré St-Michel-de-Grandmont
St-Guilhem-le-Désert
Gorges de l'Hérault
Lodève
Grotte de Clamouse
Rocher des Vierges
Pont du Diable
Les Matelles
St-Saturnin
Montpeyroux
St-Jean-de-Fos
Aniane
Celles
Barrage du Salagou
LANGUEDOC
Castries
N110
2
Carlencas
Clermont-l'Hérault
Gignac
N109
Château de la Mosson
MONTPELLIER
Cirque de Mourèze
Mourèze
Villeneuvette
Abbaye de Vignogoul
Mauguio
N9
Le Pouget
Château d'Aumelas
Pignan
Etang de Mauguio
Lattes
N113
A9
Carnon-Plage
Palavas-les-Flots
Roujan
Gigean
N112
Etang de Vic
Cathédrale de Maguelone
Montagnac
Abbaye de Valmagne
Abbaye St-Felix-de-Monceau
Pézenas
Frontignan
Loupian
Bouzigues
D909
Nézignan-l'Evêque
Mèze
Sète
Mont St-Clair
Bassin de Thau
Florensac
Béziers
Marseillan

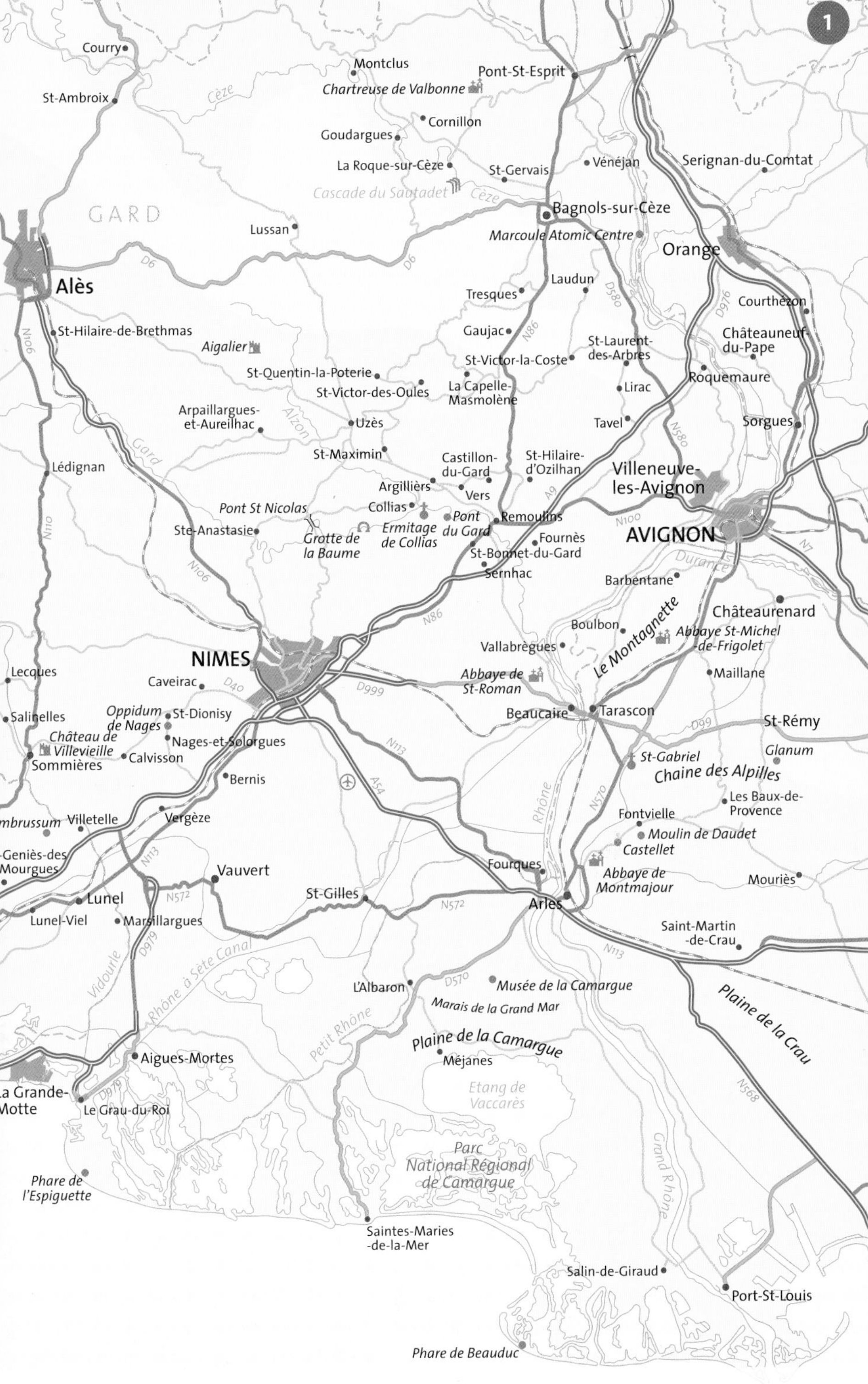
1
Courry
Montclus
Pont-St-Esprit
Chartreuse de Valbonne
St-Ambroix
Cèze
Cornillon
Goudargues
La Roque-sur-Cèze
St-Gervais
Vénéjan
Serignan-du-Comtat
Cascade du Sautadet
Cèze
GARD
Bagnols-sur-Cèze
Lussan
Marcoule Atomic Centre
Orange
D6
D6
Alès
Laudun
Tresques
D580
D976
Courthézon
N106
St-Hilaire-de-Brethmas
Gaujac
N86
Châteauneuf-du-Pape
Aigalier
St-Laurent-des-Arbres
St-Victor-la-Coste
St-Quentin-la-Poterie
Roquemaure
St-Victor-des-Oules
La Capelle-Masmolène
Lirac
Arpaillargues-et-Aureilhac
Alzon
Uzès
Tavel
Sorgues
N580
Gard
St-Maximin
Castillon-du-Gard
St-Hilaire-d'Ozilhan
Lédignan
Villeneuve-les-Avignon
Argilliers
Vers
A9
Pont St Nicolas
Collias
Pont du Gard
Remoulins
N100
AVIGNON
N110
Ste-Anastasie
Grotte de la Baume
Ermitage de Collias
Fournès
St-Bonnet-du-Gard
N7
N106
Sernhac
Durance
Barbentane
Châteaurenard
N86
Le Montagnette
Boulbon
Abbaye St-Michel-de-Frigolet
Vallabrègues
NIMES
Lecques
Caveirac
D40
Abbaye de St-Roman
D999
Maillane
Salinelles
Oppidum de Nages
St-Dionisy
Beaucaire
Tarascon
St-Rémy
D99
Château de Villevieille
Nages-et-Solorgues
Sommières
Calvisson
N113
St-Gabriel
Glanum
Chaine des Alpilles
Bernis
A54
Rhône
N570
Les Baux-de-Provence
mbrussum
Villetelle
Vergèze
Fontvielle
Moulin de Daudet
-Geniès-des Mourgues
N113
Castellet
Vauvert
Fourques
Abbaye de Montmajour
Mouriès
Lunel
N572
St-Gilles
N572
Arles
Lunel-Viel
Marsillargues
Saint-Martin-de-Crau
D979
N113
Vidourle
Rhône à Sète Canal
L'Albaron
D570
Musée de la Camargue
Marais de la Grand Mar
Plaine de la Crau
Petit Rhône
Plaine de la Camargue
Aigues-Mortes
Méjanes
La Grande-Motte
D979
Le Grau-du-Roi
Etang de Vaccarès
N568
Grand Rhône
Parc National Régional de Camargue
Phare de l'Espiguette
Saintes-Maries-de-la-Mer
Salin-de-Giraud
Port-St-Louis
Phare de Beauduc

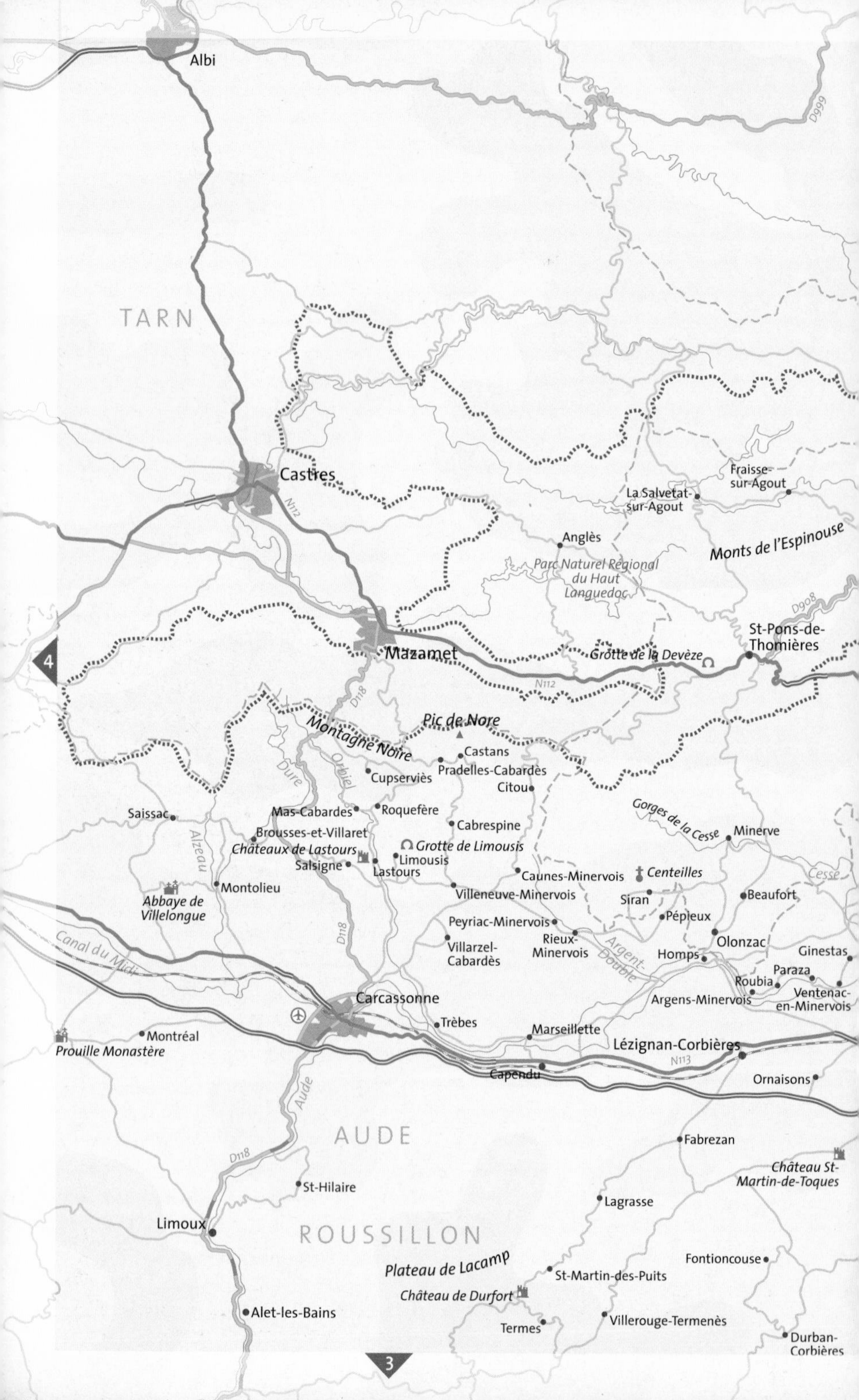
Albi
D999
TARN
Castres
N112
La Salvetat-sur-Agout
Fraisse-sur-Agout
Anglès
Monts de l'Espinouse
Parc Naturel Régional du Haut Languedoc
D908
St-Pons-de-Thomières
4
Mazamet
Grotte de la Devèze
N112
D118
Pic de Nore
Montagne Noire
Castans
Pradelles-Cabardès
Citou
Cupserviès
Orbiel
Dure
Saissac
Mas-Cabardès
Roquefère
Cabrespine
Gorges de la Cesse
Minerve
Brousses-et-Villaret
Châteaux de Lastours
Grotte de Limousis
Limousis
Alzeau
Salsigne
Lastours
Caunes-Minervois
Centeilles
Cesse
Montolieu
Villeneuve-Minervois
Siran
Beaufort
Abbaye de Villelongue
Pépieux
Peyriac-Minervois
D118
Canal du Midi
Rieux-Minervois
Olonzac
Villarzel-Cabardès
Argent-Double
Homps
Ginestas
Paraza
Roubia
Ventenac-en-Minervois
Argens-Minervois
Carcassonne
Trèbes
Montréal
Prouille Monastère
Marseillette
Lézignan-Corbières
N113
Capendu
Ornaisons
Aude
AUDE
Fabrezan
Château St-Martin-de-Toques
D118
St-Hilaire
Lagrasse
Limoux
ROUSSILLON
Fontioncouse
Plateau de Lacamp
St-Martin-des-Puits
Château de Durfort
Alet-les-Bains
Termes
Villerouge-Termenès
Durban-Corbières
3

1
2
St-Laurent-le-Minier
Cirque de Navacelles
Gorges de la Vis
Gorniès
St-Maurice-Navacelles
Madières
LANGUEDOC
Hérault
Prieuré St-Michel-de-Grandmont
St-Guilhem-le-Désert
Gorges de l'Hérault
Lodève
Rocher des Vierges
Grotte de Clamouse
Pont du Diable
St-Jean-de-Fos
Gorges de l'Orb
Lunas
St-Saturnin
Montpeyroux
Aniane
Agout
St-Gervais-sur-Mare
Dio
Celles
Sommet de l'Espinouse
Boussagues
Barrage du Salagou
Gignac
N109
Carlencas
Clermont-l'Hérault
Gorges d'Héric
Villemagne
Bédarieux
Cirque de Mourèze
Villeneuvette
Mourèze
Lamalou-les-Bains
Hérépian
N9
D909
Le Pouget
Château d'Aumelas
Olargues
Orb
Faugères
Jaur
HERAULT
Roujan
Roquebrun
Autignac
Abbaye de Valmagne
Montagnac
N113
N112
Pézenas
Murviel-lès-Béziers
Loupian
Bouzigues
Nézignan-l'Evêque
Mèze
St-Chinian
Abbaye de Fontcaude
Sète
Mont St-Clair
Bassin de Thau
Florensac
Bize-Minervois
Marseillan
Quarante
Béziers
Capestang
Colombiers
Argeliers
Poilhes
Oppidum d'Ensérune
Agde
Marseillan-Plage
Ouveillan
Nissan-lez-Enserune
Le Cap d'Agde
Le Somail
A9
Fort Brescou
Valras-Plage
Aude
Oppidum de Montlaures
Etang de Pissevaches
NARBONNE
Gouffre de l'Œil Doux
St-Pierre-des-Clars
St-Pierre-sur-Mer
Montagne de la Clape
Narbonne-Plage
Abbaye de Fontfroide
Notre-Dame des Auzils
Bages
Gruissan
N
Etang de Bages et de Sigean
Etang de l'Ayrolle
Peyriac-de-Mer
Réserve Africaine
Sigean
Port-la-Nouvelle
20 km
10 miles
3

3
4
2
Belflou
Mas-Saintes-Puelles
Castelnaudary
Montolieu
Salsigne
Abbaye de Villelongue
Canal du Midi
D118
Fanjeaux
Prouille Monastère
Montréal
Carcassonne
Aude
D118
St-Hilaire
Limoux
ARIEGE
Chalabre
Alet-les-Bains
Lavelanet
D117
Puivert
Arques
Espéraza
Couiza
Château Blanchef
Rennes-le-Château
Rennes-les-Bains
D117
D118
Quillan
Bugarach
D117
Pic de Bugarach
Lapradelle
Caudiès-de-Fenouillèdes
Axat
Puilaurens
Notre Dame de Laval
Gorges de St-Georges
Fenouillet
Aude
Grottes de l'Aguzou
Gincla
Quérigut
Col de Jau
PYRENEES
Mosset
Molitg-les-Bains
Formiguères
Capcir
Grave
ANDORRA
Matemale
Les Angles
Villefrance-de-Conflent
N116
Pic Carlit
Lac de Bouillouses
Lac de Matemale
Grottes des Canalettes
Evol
Corneilla-de-Conflent
Col de la Quillane
Olette
Fuilla
Vernet-les-Bains
Pyrénées 2000
La Llagonne
Thuès-entre-Valls
Escaro
Casteil
Sahorre
Tour Carol
Mont Louis
Font-Romeu
Gorges de la Carança
St-Martin-du-Canigou
Targassonne
Super Bolquère
Fontpédrouse
Les Escaldes
Angoustrine
Dorres
Planès
Cerdagne
Eyne
Yravel
Llívia
Eyne 2600
Latour-de-Carol
Llo
Caldégas
Saillagouse
N
Puigcerdà
Bourg-Madame
Err
Gorges du Segre
Ur
La Preste
20 km
10 miles
SPAIN

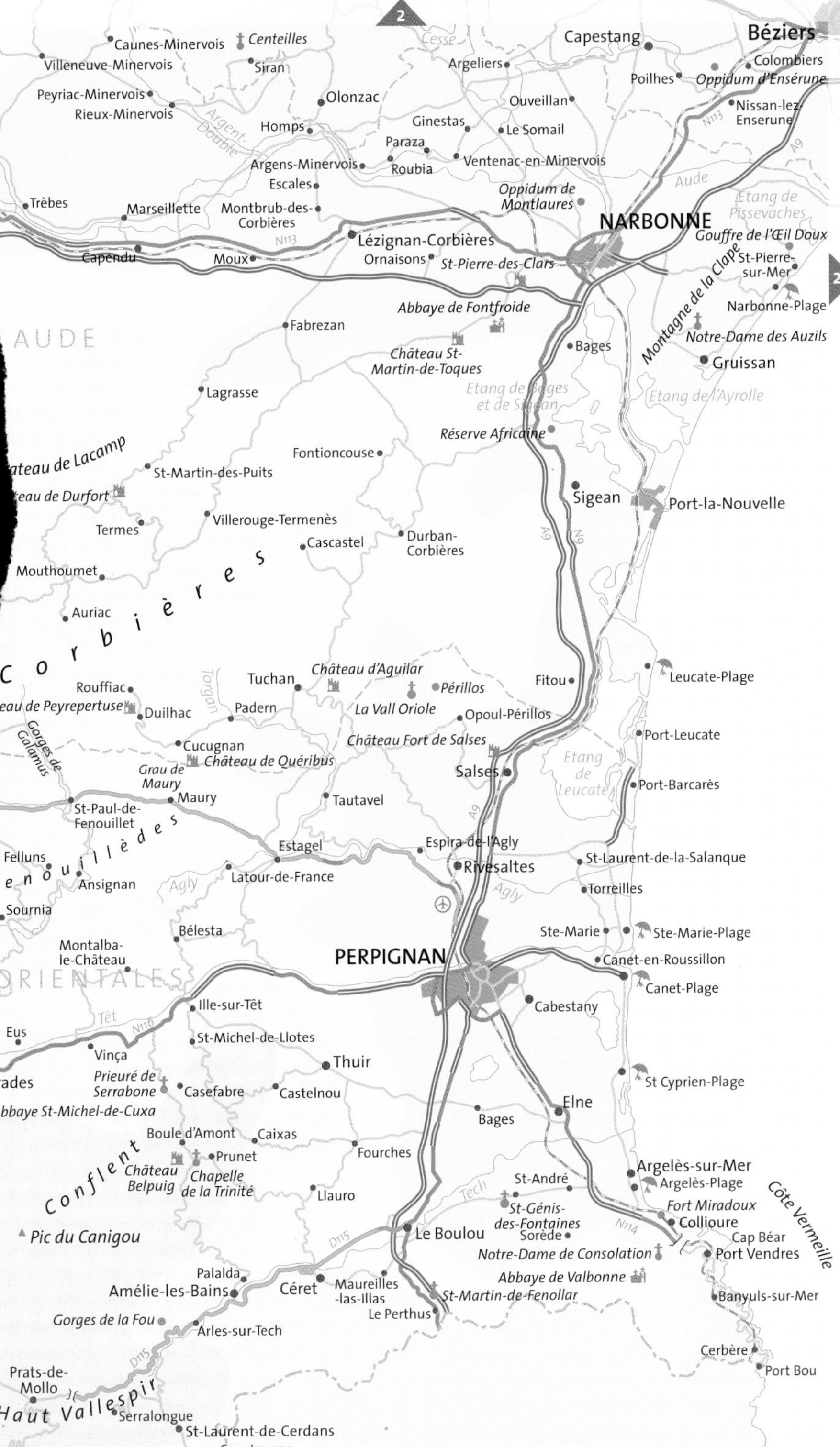

2
Caunes-Minervois
Centeilles
Cesse
Capestang
Béziers
Villeneuve-Minervois
Siran
Argeliers
Colombiers
Poilhes
Oppidum d'Ensérune
Peyriac-Minervois
Rieux-Minervois
Olonzac
Ouveillan
Nissan-lez-Enserune
N113
Argent-Double
Homps
Ginestas
Le Somail
Paraza
A9
Argens-Minervois
Roubia
Ventenac-en-Minervois
Escales
Aude
Etang de Pissevaches
Oppidum de Montlaures
Trèbes
Marseillette
Montbrub-des-Corbières
NARBONNE
Gouffre de l'Œil Doux
N113
Lézignan-Corbières
Capendu
Moux
Ornaisons
St-Pierre-des-Clars
St-Pierre-sur-Mer
2
Montagne de la Clape
Narbonne-Plage
Abbaye de Fontfroide
Fabrezan
AUDE
Notre-Dame des Auzils
Château St-Martin-de-Toques
Bages
Gruissan
Lagrasse
Etang de Bages et de Sigean
Etang de l'Ayrolle
Réserve Africaine
Château de Lacamp
Fontioncouse
St-Martin-des-Puits
Château de Durfort
Sigean
Port-la-Nouvelle
Villerouge-Termenès
Termes
A9
N9
Durban-Corbières
Cascastel
Mouthoumet
Corbières
Auriac
Leucate-Plage
Château d'Aguilar
Périllos
Fitou
Torgan
Tuchan
Rouffiac
Château de Peyrepertuse
Duilhac
Padern
La Vall Oriole
Opoul-Périllos
Port-Leucate
Gorges de Galamus
Cucugnan
Château Fort de Salses
Château de Quéribus
Etang de Leucate
Grau de Maury
Salses
Port-Barcarès
Maury
Tautavel
St-Paul-de-Fenouillet
A9
Fenouillèdes
Estagel
Espira-de-l'Agly
Felluns
St-Laurent-de-la-Salanque
Latour-de-France
Rivesaltes
Ansignan
Agly
Agly
Torreilles
Sournia
Bélesta
Ste-Marie
Ste-Marie-Plage
Montalba-le-Château
PERPIGNAN
Canet-en-Roussillon
ORIENTALES
Canet-Plage
Ille-sur-Têt
Têt
N116
Cabestany
Eus
St-Michel-de-Llotes
Vinça
Thuir
Prades
Prieuré de Serrabone
St Cyprien-Plage
Casefabre
Castelnou
Abbaye St-Michel-de-Cuxa
Elne
Bages
Boule d'Amont
Caixas
Prunet
Fourches
Conflent
Château Belpuig
Chapelle de la Trinité
Argelès-sur-Mer
St-André
Argelès-Plage
Côte Vermeille
Llauro
Tech
St-Génis-des-Fontaines
Fort Miradoux
Collioure
Pic du Canigou
D115
Le Boulou
Sorède
N114
Cap Béar
Notre-Dame de Consolation
Port Vendres
Palalda
Abbaye de Valbonne
Amélie-les-Bains
Céret
Maureilles-las-Illas
St-Martin-de-Fenollar
Banyuls-sur-Mer
Le Perthus
Gorges de la Fou
Arles-sur-Tech
D115
Cerbère
Port Bou
Prats-de-Mollo
Haut Vallespir
Serralongue
St-Laurent-de-Cerdans
Coustouges

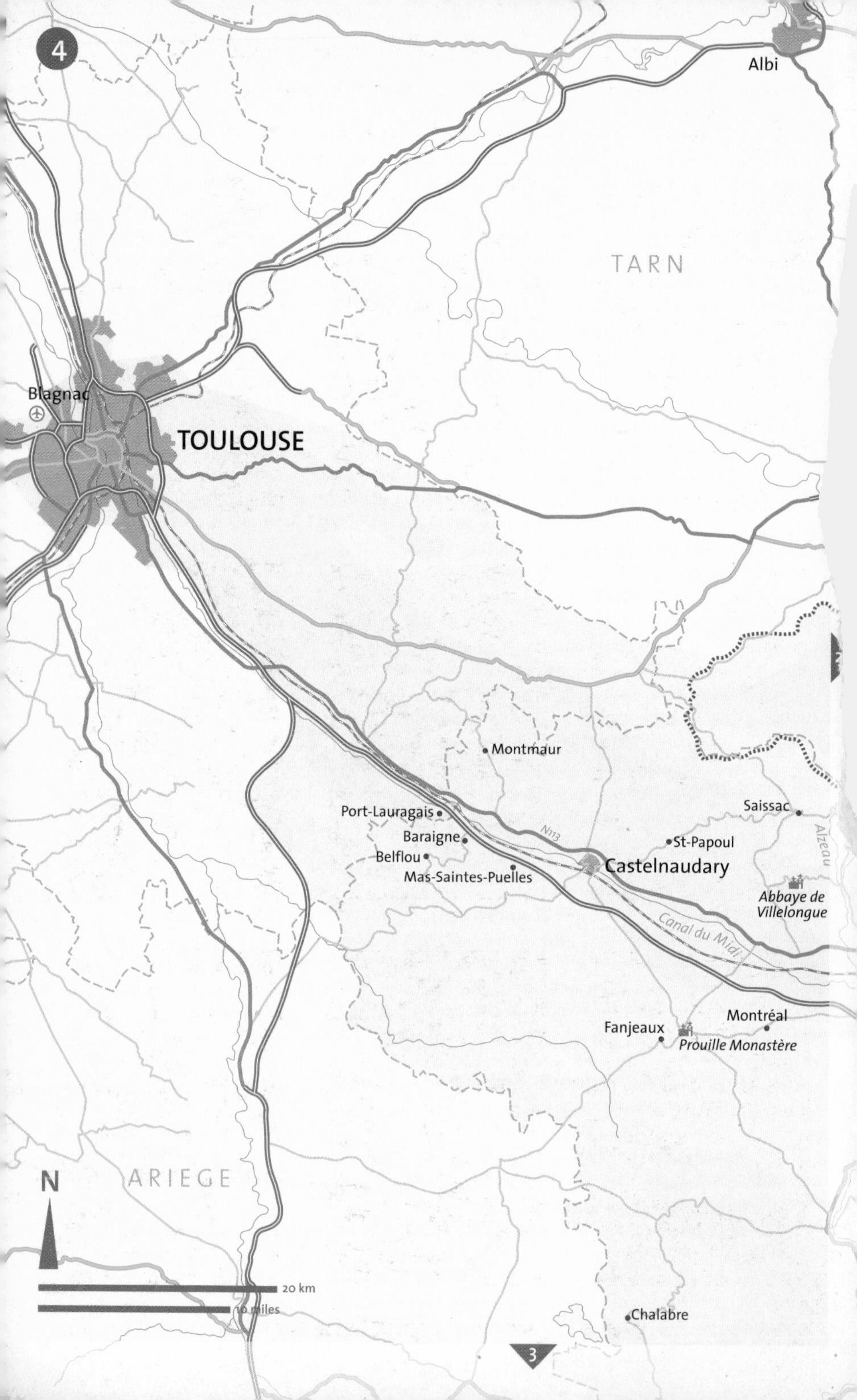
4
Albi
TARN
Blagnac
TOULOUSE
Montmaur
Port-Lauragais
Baraigne
Belflou
Mas-Saintes-Puelles
N113
Castelnaudary
St-Papoul
Saissac
Alzeau
Abbaye de
Villelongue
Canal du Midi
Montréal
Fanjeaux
Prouille Monastère
ARIEGE
N
20 km
10 miles
Chalabre
3